Dominican Fathers

The Rosary Magazine

Volume VII, July - December 1895

Dominican Fathers

The Rosary Magazine
Volume VII. July - December 1895

ISBN/EAN: 9783742800145

Manufactured in Europe, USA, Canada, Australia, Japa

Cover: Foto ©Thomas Meinert / pixelio.de

Manufactured and distributed by brebook publishing software
(www.brebook.com)

Dominican Fathers

The Rosary Magazine

THE ROSARY MAGAZINE

CONDUCTED BY

THE DOMINICAN FATHERS

VOL. VII.

July—December, 1895

NEW YORK:
THE ROSARY PUBLICATION CO.,
871 Lexington Avenue.

VOL. VII. JULY, 1895. **NO. 1.**

ZOLA AT LOURDES.

JOHN A. MOONEY.

I.

MILE ZOLA, not confining himself to the writing of indecent romances, has favored the world of art, and of the belles-lettres, with a number of essays that he is pleased to esteem critical. From one of these I quote the following passages: "Whoever writes poorly is very culpable; in literature this is the only crime that falls under my senses, I do not see where one can put morality when one pretends to put it elsewhere. A well-made phrase is a good action.... For me, the ignoble commences where talent ends." If, as Zola maintains, the only crime of which a writer can be guilty is the crime of writing poorly, then, to lie in good style must be virtuous; and a talent for lying ennobles the liar. And yet, elsewhere, the teacher of this most beautiful code of literary ethics claims that he and his disciples "are no other than savants, analysts, anatomists, whose works have the certitude, the solidity, and the practical application of works of science.' "I am acquainted," he adds, "with no school more moral, more austere." Fortunately for savants, not even the peculiar patent of nobility which Zola has laboriously acquired, compels them to acknowledge him as a brother. The science builded on the morality of the well-made phrase is not universally acknowledged as having that certitude, that solidity, that practical application, that austerity, which are attributed to the science builded on truthful fact. The science, whose sole moral principle should be: "the well-made phrase," would be a lie.

Still, there can be no doubt of Zola's deliberation when formulating his one ethical principle. In another of his essays, discussing the limits of the imagination in a "naturalistic" romance, he instructs his pupils in the proper method of manufacturing such a romance. I quote his words: "Take the real facts you have observed around you, classify them in logical order, *fill up the gaps by intuition*, obtain the marvellous result of giving life to human documents, a characteristic, complete life, adapted to an environment, and you will have exercised in a supreme order your faculties of imagination."

Fill up the gaps by intuition! Thus one may become a "scientist" of a supreme order. The space conceded to the lie is not too definite. Fill up the gaps with it! Lest I should leave a gap in my presentation of Zola's code of literary morals, I shall quote a few words of encouragement generously offered by him to those who may be hesitating to dishonor truth. "We experiment," writes the intuitive romancer, "that is to say that, for a long time to come, we must make use of the false in order to arrive at the true." An ennobling morality!

Having heard from Émile Zola's own sweet mouth, the method he has adopted in the making of romances, we can feel neither surprise, nor pain, when literary men and scientists accuse him of "unveracity." Even with a pair of sole-leather gloves on our hands, we would not dare to turn over the pages of all of his foul romances; but, in the interest of religion and of science, we shall test his truthfulness in the latest of his speculations, the tale of *Lourdes*. To the facts he pretends to have observed, we shall oppose the *real* facts. To his "living human documents," we shall oppose living human beings, whose testimony has the certainty, the solidity, the practical application of experience itself.

Our work has been made easy, thanks to Dr. Boissarie. How he has helped us will be apparent, through the following quotation from the *Medical Record*, (New York, Jan. 5th, 1895.) "An Exhibition of Miraculous 'Cures' has been taking place in Paris. Fifteen persons who declare that they were miraculously cured at Lourdes of terrible diseases presented themselves for inspection at a lecture given by Dr. Boissarie of the French Bureau des Constatations at Lourdes. Dr. Boissarie's object was to refute various statements made by M. Zola in his book on Lourdes, and in order to prove that the cures which take place at the scene of Bernadette's visions are truly miraculous he brought from various parts of France fifteen persons healed within the last two or three years at Lourdes of diseases which medical science had pronounced incurable....This procession of 'miraculés,' and the medical diagnoses and certificates which were read, produced an extraordinary impression. The audience was largely composed of doctors and medical students."

Dr. Boissarie's remarkable lecture was delivered on November 21st, 1894, in the hall of the Luxembourg Club. An authorized report of this lecture was recently published; and it is with this living document in hand that I purpose showing Zola's fidelity to his ennobling moral code. Fifteen hundred persons listened to Dr. Boissarie, heard his proofs, and saw his witnesses. Paris journals that could not be suspected of "clericalism," acknowledged that Zola's contempt for facts had been fully established. *La France Nouvelle* put the case plainly: "Writing his book *Lourdes*, M. Zola lost a fine chance to keep silent....It is evident that if he wished to paint Lourdes 'just as it is,' he succeeded in describing it 'just as it is not.'"

During forty years, extraordinary cures have been effected at Lourdes; cures of which no scientific explanation can be given. There can be no doubt as to the cures. All possibility of doubt is excluded, for the reason that every cure reported is tested, on the ground, by medical experts. Dr. Boissarie is the official examiner and annalist of the cures. The cures are tested in the " Bureau des Constatations," or "Verification Office." To this office all physicians are welcomed; and they are at liberty to examine those whose cure has been noted either at the fountain, or at the baths or the Grotto, or within the church, or on the roadway as the Most Blessed Sacrament is carried in procession.

During the National Pilgrimage which takes place annually, in August, the sick who desire to visit Lourdes and who are too poor to bear the expense, are transported from every part of France free of charge, and are housed and cared for, during their stay in Lourdes. The charges of the poor are borne by charitable subscribers to a special fund. In order to enjoy the privileges of this pilgrimage, however, the sick are required to produce a certificate of the physician who has treated them; and this certificate must specify the disease diagnosed by the physician, with such details concerning the progress of the disease, the duration of the treatment, and the actual condition of the patient, as should be required in a thorough medical record. Should one of these pilgrims claim to have been cured at Lourdes, the certificate of the physician who has had charge of the case is conclusive evidence as to the physical condition of his patient when setting out on the pilgrimage; and the medical examination made in the "Verification Office," immediately after the cure, is conclusive evidence as to the physical condition of the same person at the time of this examination. The details of the examination in the "Verification Office," are recorded; and the cure is noted, if cure there be. With the care such a document deserves, the certificate of the physician who had charge of the patient before the visit to Lourdes, is filed. Nor does the action of the "Verification Office." end here. Every effort is made to follow up the cures verified at Lourdes, so as to determine their permanency. The details of the cures verified by Dr. Boissarie and his assistants, are reported in the *Journal of the Grotto*, and in the *Annals of Lourdes.*

The documentary evidence of the cures at Lourdes, has, therefore, "the certitude, the solidity, and the practical application of a work of science." Zola knew this, and he is forced to acknowledge it. He was permitted to enter the "Verification Office;" and, though he remained there for a couple of hours only, he saw more than one cure verified in the presence of not less than twenty physicians. The *Annals of Lourdes,* and the *Journal of the Grotto* he read. Many of the characters, and of the incidents, of his romance were suggested by these periodicals. How he used the scientific documents Dr. Boissarie has cumulated, we shall see.

In his romance, Zola pretends that he is a passenger on one of the trains carrying the National pilgrims to Lourdes. Among many sufferers who are in the car with him, one especially attracts his attention; a woman to whom he gives the name: *La Grivotte*. " She was a tall woman who had passed her thirtieth year, ungainly, odd-looking, with a round, worn face, which her fuzzy hair and burning eyes made almost beautiful. She was a consumptive of the third degree....She was a mattress-maker; with one of her aunts, going from house to house, she had made mattresses at Bercy; and it was to the infected wool she carded in her youth, that she attributed her disease. During five years, she had gone from one hospital to another in Paris. And so she talked familiarly of the great physicians. The Sisters at the hospital of Lariboisière, seeing her passion for religious ceremonies, had completed her conversion and convinced her that the Virgin awaited her, at Lourdes, to cure her. You may be sure that I need a cure," she says; " they tell me that one lung is gone and that the other is not much better. Cavities, you know....At first I had trouble only between my shoulders, and I spat froth. Then I grew thin, a pitiable sight. Now I'm always in a sweat, I cough to break my heart, I can't spit any more, it's so tough....And as you see, I can't stand up, I don't eat....A choking fit stopped her, she grew livid."

After this realistic description, which seems to me to be tough rather than tender, Zola does not permit us wholly to forget *La Grivotte*. Twice, as the train pushes southward, he points her out. She is coughing, choking, suffocating. At the Lourdes station, the attendants carry her from the train to the hospital of Our Lady of Sorrows. By " intuition," Zola sees her in the hospital, seated on a mattress, her hands joined, begging that some one will bring her to the Grotto. "Was not this," asks the austere, scientific romancer, " the commencement of a miracle, this awakening of the will, this feverish desire of a cure, that raised her up? Swooning, inert " when she arrived, she is now sitting up, turning her black eyes this way and that, watching for the

happy moment when they would come for her; and her livid face
flushed with color, already she was being raised to life."

La Grivotte next appears in a procession of the sick, on her way
to the Grotto, "raising herself on her two hands." Reaching the
baths, she attracts our attention by her complaints. Weeping,
she exclaims: "They say that I'm a consumptive, and that they
cannot dip the consumptives in cold water.... This very morning
they put one in, I saw it. Then why not me? For a half hour
I've not ceased protesting that they are grieving the Blessed Virgin. I'm going to be cured, I feel it; I'm going to be cured."
Thereupon an attendant tried to quiet her, saying that they intended to consult the reverend Fathers about her case, and that,
if she acted sensibly, perhaps they would put her in the bath.

Not long after this scene, "a little blond monsieur, a writer of
some talent, an influential editor of one of the Parisian journals
most widely read," entered the "Verification Office," by the special permission of Doctor Boissarie. There he found from twenty-
five to thirty physicians verifying a puzzling cure. Suddenly, to
quote Zola's words: "The office was turned topsy-turvy. *La
Grivotte* had entered like a blizzard, with a dancing gait, crying
in a loud voice: I'm cured, I'm cured! And she related that, at
first, they did not wish to bathe her, and that she had to insist,
beg, sob, before they decided to do so, after having the formal
permission of Father Fourcade.... And just as she had said beforehand: "Within three minutes after they had plunged her,—
covered with perspiration, with her consumptive rattle,—into the
icy water, she felt her strength return, just as if her whole body
had been lashed with a whip. An exaltation, a flame agitated
her, stamping her feet, radiant, unable to remain in one place.

"I am cured, my good gentlemen.... I am cured."

Is it any wonder that one of Zola's fellow-idiots was "stupefied" at the sight of *La Grivotte;* or that, after seeing her, he put
questions to his powerful intellect? "Was this the girl whom he
had seen, the night before, prostrate on the car-seat, coughing and
spitting blood, her face cadaverous? He could not recognize
her, straight, lithe, her cheeks afire, her eyes sparkling, with a desire to live and a joy in living that buoyed her up."

At this point, Zola's scientific habits induced him to observe

the physicians present; and, according to his report, Doctor
Boissarie first read three medical certificates, all of which were of
the same tenor. *La Grivotte's* case was described as one of advanced consumption, which certain nervous symptoms complicated and rendered peculiar! After reading these certificates, the
Doctor examined *La Grivotte's* lungs, and then invited his medical guests to make a like examination. Doctor Boissarie " murmured that he heard nothing, or almost nothing; " while another
physician said very positively that: " he heard nothing at all, and
that the woman had never been a consumptive." Zola does not
report what the others said. There was much noisy talk in the
room; and certain " scientific " romancers can report fully, only
when the rest of the company is mute.

However, Zola does report that Doctor Boissarie dictated to
one of his assistants the result of the examination of *La Grivotte;*
as he also reports that: " the little blond monsieur, the influential
writer of Paris, went away disappointed because he had not seen
a true miracle." And yet his weak-minded friend, Peter, passed
out through the doorway with *La Grivotte,* and saw the crowd
gather around her and touch her, and heard them question her,
while she, " her cheeks all purple, her eyes flaming, could only
repeat, with a dancing air: I am cured....I am cured!"

After eleven o'clock of the same night, according to Zola's untruthful story, he saw *La Grivotte* again. She lay abed in the
hospital of our Lady of Sorrows. " In a fever of extraordinary
activity she raised herself up, in order to say to each new comer:
I'm cured, I'm cured. And then she related that she had devoured half a chicken, she who had not eaten anything for
months. Besides, for almost two hours she had followed on foot
the torchlight procession. Certainly she would have danced until morning, had the Blessed Virgin given a ball. I'm cured, oh!
cured, wholly cured." Once more, before *La Grivotte's* departure
from Lourdes, Zola observed her, and noted a fact whose scientific importance is inestimable: she was " devouring " a piece of
bread, calling out meantime: " I'm cured, cured, completely
cured! "

Now let us compare Dr. Boissarie's observations of *La Grivotte's*
case, with Zola's report. During the pilgrimage of 1892, about

which Zola romances, a consumptive, named Marie Lebranchu, was cured; and in the story entitled *Lourdes*, it is Marie Lebranchu that is represented under the fictitious name of *La Grivotte*. Selecting a consumptive cured in the icy water of the miraculous spring, Zola could have chosen any one of thirty whose cases have been reported in the *Annals of Lourdes*. Indeed, on the very day that *La Grivotte*, after an immersion of three minutes in the bath, proclaimed her cure, another consumptive, Irma Montreuil, was, if I may be pardoned a Zolaism, resuscitated.

The cure of Irma Montreuil was no less astonishing than *La Grivotte's;* and Irma's case was the more pathetic of the two. Thirty-three years old, the wife of a miner, she was the mother of seven children. On the way to Lourdes, so desperate was her condition that it was deemed advisable to give her Extreme Unction.

However, we must not keep Dr. Boissarie waiting. Here is the record of *La Grivotte* as entered by the estimable Doctor in the register of the Verification Office. " Marie Lebranchu, aged 35, Paris, Championnet street, 172, according to the certificate of Dr. Marquezy, physician of the hospital, is affected with pulmonary tuberculosis, with softening and cavities. Her father and mother died of consumption. Marie Lebranchu has been treated at the Hôtel-Dieu, under the charge of Professor Germain Sée. There, her expectorations were examined, and, in them, the bacilli characteristic of tuberculosis were found. For ten months past, she has been in the French-Netherlands' hospital, which is especially devoted to consumptives. She lay abed constantly, she vomited blood, she had lost forty-eight pounds' weight, and she filled her spittoon with pus. Besides, she retained no food: it was a case of consumption in the final stage."

Though more precise and briefer than Zola, Dr. Boissarie is no less scientific in his statement of *La Grivotte's* condition before she joined the pilgrimage to Lourdes. The Doctor gives details omitted by Zola, but, as a whole, the latter's report cannot be called misleading. The incident at the baths, where *La Grivotte* wept, sobbed, protested, because they would not bathe her, was touching; and Dr. Boissarie acknowledges its truth. " She was a real skeleton spitting blood. To put her in the water meant either a miracle or a death; and, between these alternatives, the attendants might well hesitate."

Here Dr. Boissarie reads from his register the following entry: " After her first immersion in the bath, on Saturday, August 20th, Marie Lebranchu came to the Verification Office. She was carefully examined, and, in her chest, neither rattle, nor bellows' sound, nor consolidation, nor the slightest trace of lesion of the lung was found. On the following morning, the 21st, she was re-examined. She does not cough or spit, and she eats with zest. Every day, up to her departure, the fact is verified that the cure is perfectly maintained."

The little blond monsieur, the influential writer of Paris, saw Marie Lebranchu (*La Grivotte*) in the Verification Office, cured. He knew her condition when she was on the train that brought her to Lourdes. He knew her condition when she presented herself at the baths and was denied admission, lest she should die in the icy water. If the influential writer was disappointed, he must have been very hard to please. Should he refuse to accept Marie Lebranchu's cure as miraculous, he ought to explain it scientifically; or else, reporting the facts, leave his readers to form a judgment. Can Zola explain this cure, scientifically? No! nor can any living savant, analyst, anatomist, medical professor or practitioner. Whoever refuses to call this cure a miracle, must acknowledge, at least, that he is face to face with the inexplicable.

Instead of confining himself to a truthful statement of facts, Zola tried to break their force. Describing the scene in the Verification Office, he reported that *La Grivotte's* physicians qualified her case as peculiar, because of certain complicating nervous symptoms. Reporting thus, the romancer had an eye on several " gaps " that he meant to fill, " intuitively " and imaginatively. Dr. Boissarie makes no mention of these peculiar nervous symptoms; and we may safely say there were none. What peculiar nervous symptoms could complicate the case of a consumptive like Marie Lebranchu? The peculiarity about her case was that, die she must, speedily, unless cured miraculously.

Zola is not the only one who has been silly enough to offer the fanciful theory of " suggestion " in explanation of this cure, and of all the other cures effected at Lourdes. Marie Lebranchu, (*La Grivotte*) may have been cured, he imagines, by a peculiar sort of "suggestion," — "auto-suggestion." The notion of one "suggesting" a cavity out of one's own lungs is uniquely scientific; nearly as scientific as would be the notion of my "suggesting" a cavity into the lung of one of my readers. Lest "auto-suggestion" may not completely explain Marie Lebranchu's cure the austere romancer begs us to consider "the inspiriting influences of the journey," though it was he that described the woman, "prostrate on the car-seat, coughing and spitting blood, her face cadaverous." And then, there is the "healing breath, the unknown force evolved from the multitude in the crisis of faith." How beautiful the phrase! What a profound knowledge of science is displayed by the savant! Have our American physicians duly considered the power of the "healing breath" of a crowd of pilgrims, especially in the case of consumptives, "of the third degree"? And do our physicians take due advantage of "the unknown force evolved from the multitude in the crisis of faith"?

"Ah! the things we don't know, the things we don't know!" are words Zola puts in the mouth of another of his idiots; an idiotic physician, who, believing in the supernatural, doubts miracles. Through this personage, the romancer lets the world know his opinion of medical men. "I understand very well," he says, "why this worthy Dr Boissarie coolly calls upon the doctors of the whole world to study his miracles. The more doctors there should be here, the less the truth would be established, amid the battle of diagnostics and of methods of treatment." This choice compliment from a "scientist" will be appreciated by the medical profession. And yet, notwithstanding Zola's contempt for medical men, I believe firmly, that twenty doctors might agree in diagnosing that a lung was free from cavities; and I am positive that, occasionally, Professor Germain Sée may have felt safe in diagnosing a cavity, especially if a little bit of the lung remained. Indeed many will join me in holding that even in "the crisis of faith,"—whatever that funny thing may be,—a youthful physician will discover a cavity with more ease than Zola fills a "gap." The ear, better than the most "naturalistic" imagination, or intuition, helps one to attain certitude.

After the romantic moralist had favored us with an important "human document" in the shape of a piece of bread that *La Grivotte* was devouring, he took good care not to see her again until after he had written one hundred and sixty-nine dreary, trashy pages, in which her name is not mentioned. As the pilgrims' train is starting from Lourdes, on the return to Paris, he kindly observes her once more. 'Her eyes are feverish,' and,—well-made phrase,—she is in a state of 'dancing excitement.' Just after the train passed Riscle, which is hardly fifty miles from Lourdes, Zola reports a change in her condition. She looked 'haggard, excited, her eyes restless, and her cheeks were marked with violet patches.' By the time they reached Morceux, fifty miles further on, 'she looked livid and tortured and thin; nay, more, in a sudden fit of agony, she stood up straight and grasped the partition. A moment later she fell into the arms of a Sister, and from her arms tumbled into the seat of the car. She coughed furiously. For five minutes her poor body shook as if it would fall to pieces. Then red streams flowed, she spat blood by the mouthful.' Leaving Bordeaux, which is about seventy miles beyond Morceux, *La Grivotte* 'was as motionless as if she had been felled by a blow: she breathed with difficulty, and the rattle was continuous.' When the train reached Poitiers, a distance of one hundred and fifty miles from Bordeaux, *La Grivotte* was 'shivering with an intense fever, and had a new attack of her horrible cough.'

Notwithstanding the poor woman's condition, Zola permitted her to live twenty-six pages longer. When she arrived at Paris, a charitable lady, who accompanied the pilgrimage for the pleasure of nursing the sick, kindly took *La Grivotte* out of Zola's romance, and thus did a better action than if she had written a well-made phrase. Had Zola's contract with his French and American journals bound him to write another hundred pages, he would have killed the consumptive cured at Lourdes, and would have thrown her body from the car window into some naturalistic "gap."

Now we shall compare Zola's fancies with the real facts. Marie Lebranchu, the original of *La Grivotte*, returned to Paris with the pilgrims. On the road she grew neither livid nor thin; nor did she shiver with fever, nor cough, nor spit the smallest

quantity of blood.   Dr. Boissarie testifies to the facts.   Zola
made the good lady who took *La Grivotte* out of his book, send
her to an hospital.   Marie Lebranchu went to an hospital, of her
own accord.   She was homeless.   For many months the hospital
had been her home, and naturally she returned there for shelter.
When the physician in charge saw her, he was astonished.   He
examined her lungs, and was more than ever astonished.   " Send
that young woman to my office," he said to the Sister, " I want to
examine her carefully."   The second examination was long and
minute.   After making it, the doctor's remark to the Sister was:
" I'll give no more certificates for Lourdes; that woman does
with her body what she wills."   Evidently the doctor was a kind
hearted man.   Had he been as ruthlessly " scientific " as Zola, he
would have "suggested " at least one cavity into one of her lungs.

These two examinations did not satisfy the hospital physician;
so he ordered that she should be sent to one of his confrères during the day.   Together they examined her,—a third examination.
When they had finished, the name of Marie Lebranchu (*La Grivotte*) was removed from the books of the hospital.   Eight days
later she went to Sens, where she remained a year.   On the 23d
of August of the following year, 1893, she returned to Lourdes,
on the National Pilgrimage.   Again she visited the Verification
Office.   Many physicians were present.   They examined her, and
found no lesion whatsoever in her lungs.   Her cure was complete,
and permanent.   In August, 1894, she presented herself at the
Orléans station, as the National Pilgrimage train was taking up
the passengers for Lourdes.   She came to see old companions
in suffering and to wish them relief.   The physician in charge
of the pilgrimage observed her, and reported her healthy, lively,
" with purple cheeks and a dancing air," as the modeller of well-
made phrases would say.   The physician does not represent her
devouring a piece of bread, or shouting: "I'm cured! I'm
cured!" but, even without these details, he adds to the proof that
Marie Lebranchu (*La Grivotte*) was cured, miraculously, and that
she stayed cured.

If Zola took no trunk to Lourdes except the one in which he
carries his morals, he paid nothing for freight or porters' fees.
The cure of Marie Lebranchu, he could not deny; it was and is

undeniable. Unwilling to accept the miracle, he tried to break its force; first by idiotic suggestions, and then by an attempt to kill Marie with a clumsy lie. Thus one acquires a "naturalistic" title of nobility.

Zola has many things to learn. Since writing *Lourdes* he has learned: that the person who lies, with the purpose of discrediting the Blessed Virgin Mary,—"the Mother of God and of men,"—will, in this world, suffer exposure at least. The deliberate falsehoods about Marie Lebranchu, (*La Grivotte*), by means of which Zola intended to deceive and mislead, will not have the effect he desired; but the exposure of his lies will centre the attention of a still larger number of thinking men and women, on the wonderful cures that take place at Lourdes; cures that human science cannot explain;—miraculous cures.

VESPERS IN NEW YORK.

CAROLINE D. SWAN.

THE yellow light is falling faint and sweet
  On the stone splendors of the city street,
  Each silent mart accepts its touch of Heaven
The rest divine of one day out of seven;
A softened world, athirst for dew outpoured,
Awaits Thy Benediction, gracious Lord!

On brick and marble, over reds and grays
And snowy tracery wrought in wondrous ways,
A mighty mist of strange, aerial gold
Tenderly falls, like love, to wrap and fold;
And hearts as hard awake with one accord
To seek Thy Benediction, blessed Lord!

Thou knowest how disaster haunts our days,
How tangled briars vex our darkening ways;
Seest our bitter struggles, hope-bereft,
When Patience seems the only angel left!
Oh, make this breath of violets our reward,
Come down to us in Benediction, Lord!

Thy Presence can reverse our ebb of tide:—
Lo! twilight burns, our sorrow-mists divide,
The last of Earth becomes a dawning light,
Life's afterglow on Heaven's mysterious height!
Comfort us now,—and then,—with one sweet word,
Thy pardoning Benediction, Jesu, Lord!

•

THE EIGHTH CENTENNIAL OF THE FIRST CRUSADE.

Rev. Reuben Parsons, D. D.

II.

HE first to receive the cross, the distinctive mark of the crusader, from the hands of Pope Urban, was Adhemar de Monteil, the bishop of Puy-en-Velay, whom the pontiff created his legate and spiritual chief of the expedition. After the Council of Clermont had terminated, the proclamation of the Holy War was continued throughout France by the bishops; and the Pope remained for eight months in the kingdom to encourage the work. The enthusiasm of the French soon communicated itself beyond the Alps, and nearly every family in feudal Europe gave one or more of its members to the holy cause. But in this First Crusade, not one of the kings of Europe took any part. Henry IV. of Germany still waged his sacrilegious war against the Holy See. Philip I. of France, excommunicated for simony, was prevented from imitating Henry only by indolence. Spain was engaged in her own constant crusade against the Moors, and her monarch did his duty by Christendom right well by giving occupation to one of the bravest races which had professed Islam. England was represented neither by her king, William Rufus, nor by any of her barons; the successor of the Conqueror simply watched the agitation on the continent, intent on seizing any occasion for the increase of his power, and destined to find in that agitation an opportunity to attach to his crown the French duchy of Normandy. But the abstention of the sovereigns was scarcely noticed, and it formed no obstacle to the action of the western feudataries. All difference of nationalities was lost in the grand unity of the Christian family, the head of which had summoned it to rescue the Sepulchre of the Crucified from defilement. Constantinople was to be the rendezvous for all the crusaders; and they marched in four divisions, each following a different route. The first army

THE CRUSADERS,

was composed of men from the eastern portion of the France of
our day; from Lorraine, Flanders, and Holland; and it was commanded by Godfrey de Bouillon, duke of Lower Lorraine. Godfrey was the second son of Eustache, Count of Boulogne, by St.
Ida, a daughter of Godfrey IV., Duke of Lower Lorraine; and although he received from Henry IV. the investiture of Lower Lorraine as a fief of the Holy Roman Empire, history always speaks
of him as De Bouillon, the town and chateau of that name (in
Belgian Luxembourg) having been the dowry of his holy mother.
The second army, recruited from the west and centre of France,
had for its principal leaders, Hugh de Vermandois, brother of the
French king; Stephen, Count of Blois; and Robert Courte-Heuse,
son of William the Conqueror. The third army, raised in the
south of France, was under the orders of Raymond, Count of
Toulouse. The fourth, composed chiefly of Normans of Italy,
was led by the able and crafty Prince of Tarento, Bohemond, a
son of Robert Guiscard. On the Feast of the Assumption, 1096,
Godfrey de Bouillon led his army out of Mayence, and began his
march across the German provinces of the Holy Roman Empire.
Henry IV. had closed his German territories to the preachers of
the Crusade; and when the army of Godfrey first appeared among
them, the Germans fancied that the French chivalry were bent
on some capricious and chimerical adventure. But the Teutons
soon caught the crusading fever; and there came to Godfrey so
many recruits, that he found himself at the head of 80,000 men
before he arrived at the Hungarian frontier. A bitter disappointment awaited the crusaders when they appeared before Constantinople. Alexis, who had so pathetically besought the aid
of Latin Christendom, had begun to doubt whether it were not
good policy to imitate his many predecessors in buying off the
enemies of the empire, rather than to be beholden for safety to
the detested Latins, who might even profit by the Crusade to de-
spoil him of his crown. He treated the leaders with every courtesy; but forbade their followers to enter his capital. Growing
arrogant when he perceived that the barons did not complain of
his chicanery, the Greek refused provisions to the men whose
aid he had invoked; but they did not wish to starve, and obtained by force the necessaries to sustain life. Then Alexis in-

sisted that the crusaders should promise to hand over to the
Greek Empire whatever conquests they might effect, or, at least,
retain them as fiefs of the emperor.   It required all the firmness
and persuasive abilities of Godfrey de Bouillon to prevent the
fiery westerns from declaring war on Byzantium, and from refusing the empty form of paying homage to its unworthy sovereign.   When this ceremony had been completed, Alexis hastened
to transport his unwelcome allies across the Bosphorus, promising to provision them well, and to join his own forces to their
army. As we do not intend to enter into the military details of this
expedition, it is well to note here that the Greek emperor furnished only 4,000 men for the Holy War; that when, after a bloody
siege of two months, the soldiers of the Cross were about to enter
into Nice, they found themselves defrauded of the fruit of their
bravery by the sight of the Greek standard floating over the towers
of the captured city—a consequence of a secret treaty made by
Alexis with the besieged; that when the crusaders, having reduced Antioch, were threatened with destruction by the immensely superior forces of Kerbogha, sultan of Mossoul (Nineveh),
Alexis gladly led back to Constantinople a reinforcing army of
40,000 men which he had destined to share the glory of what had
appeared a certainly predestined victory.

When the crusading army was reviewed in the plain of Nice,
it numbered 100,000 knights and other mounted soldiers, and
600,000 infantry.   When it arrived before Jerusalem, on June 7,
1099, it consisted of only 50,000 men, of whom one-third were incapable of bearing arms.   Terrific battles, famine, pests, and the
necessity of leaving garrisons in Antioch and Edessa, had caused
this sad diminution.   The city of Jerusalem, which Christendom
was about to wrench from the polluting grasp of Islam, was only
in name that city which had been the capital of Judea.   Divine
vengeance had overtaken it; and in less than ten years after it
had shed the blood of the Messiah, Titus had accomplished the
menaces of the prophets, and had razed it to the ground.   In the
early years of the second century, the emperor Adrian had rebuilt
it, but in order to efface the souvenirs of its history, the name of
Aelia Capitolina was given to the pagan city which Adrian substituted for that of David; the emperor's name being Aelius

Adrianus. The glories of Jerusalem had become so obscured,
that at the General Council of Nice its patriarch was termed,
" bishop of Aelia."   However, the great Constantine swept away

THE CRUSADERS BEHOLD JERUSALEM.

every trace of the long profanation of the places where Christianity had originated; and during three centuries our ancestors in the faith could give vent to their yearning affection and

sublime veneration for the soil which had been saturated with the blood of Jesus.   But in 636, the caliph Omar captured Jerusalem; and then, for more than four centuries, the Holy City was subject to many successive Arabian and Turkish dynasties.   Completely transfigured by its various pagan and barbarian masters, Jerusalem no longer occupied its primitive site on the summits of Sion and Moriah.   The city of Adrian did not include Mt. Sion; but it did include Golgotha, which was outside the walls at the time of the sacred Passion.   Thus God had willed that Golgotha, which cemented the New Alliance, should take the place of that Sion which was the personification of the traditions of the Old Law.   It was precisely in front of Calvary, in the Valley of Ephraim, that Godfrey de Bouillon, now the chief of the holy expedition, fixed his headquarters for the siege.   The Mussulman garrison numbered 40,000, all ready to die in order to preserve to Islam a city which the followers of the prophet also regarded as holy.   The walls were high, and the crusaders had no machines of war; but nothing could discourage the soldiers who were ever animated by the cry: "God wills it."   Again and again they rushed to the assault; and on July 15, they entered Jerusalem. The massacre which ensued was terrible; but we must remember the nature of war in those days, the horrors of an assault even in our day, and the fearful atrocities which the Islamites were then required to expiate.   But Godfrey de Bouillon acted like a true knight and a true Christian.   When he perceived that victory was assured, he immediately sheathed his glorious sword; and barefooted, in the dress of a simple pilgrim, he performed the Stations of the Cross.   Arrived at the Holy Sepulchre, he prostrated himself, face to earth, and thus remained in prayer for many. hours.   This noble example produced its effect upon the other barons: and doffing their ensanguined armor, they wended their way to Calvary.   Very soon the rank and file formed a similar procession; and like so many gentle anchorites, they raised their voices to Heaven, in detestation of their past sins, and in promises of future holiness.

On the ninth day after the conquest, the barons assembled for the election of a king of Jerusalem.   Having implored the assistance of the Holy Spirit, they devised an ingenious expedient, whereby it might be determined who was the most worthy of the new diadem.   A committee of prudent and experienced knights was appointed to examine, under oath, all the officers and servants

of each feudatary, as to whatever they knew concerning the merits
or defects of their lords.   The result of this investigation was the
elevation of Godfrey de Bouillon.   " His exalted nobility," says

THE TAKING OF JERUSALEM.

Foucher de Chartres, one of the committee, " his knightly valor
his genius and prudence, and especially the purity of his life, rec-

ommended him to the judges." We must here note that one of Godfrey's officers brought a quaint accusation against his master. With great gravity his steward declared that the duke had a very annoying habit of remaining in church, after divine service, in order to inquire from the clergy the meaning of all the pictures in the edifice. Very often, complained the poor man, this conduct of the duke caused much chagrin to his retainers, and to whatever guests he might have at the time; for on such occasions, the dinner, which was always ready at the proper hour, became thoroughly cold. This fault weighed little with the judges; and despite the humility of Godfrey, which led him to decline the office, he was conducted to the Holy Sepulchre, to receive the sacred unction. But no entreaty could prevail upon him to wear a crown where his Lord and God had been crowned with thorns; and he accepted the title, not of king of Jerusalem, but of Baron of the Holy Sepulchre.

The Holy War proclaimed by Pope Urban II. was legitimate in its object, useful in its effects, sublime in its means, and it commands the gratitude of posterity. The nation which contributed, more than all others combined, to its success, no longer obeys the sceptre of the heirs of Clovis; but that same nation is still ready to continue the *Gesta Dei per Francos.* The immense majority of Frenchmen still feel that their country will continue her divine mission. One of the noblest of them, one who had no passions in his heart save the love of God and the love of France, thus encourages his countrymen: "Lift up thy head, noble land! Have confidence in thy divine vocation! Thou hast not yet fulfilled thy divine mission; for shouldst thou disappear, thou wouldst leave a void which divine omnipotence alone could fill. If some days of forgetfulness have called down punishment upon thee, many centuries of devotion to Christ and His Church demand pardon for thee. Thou wilt resume thy glorious destiny, remaining in the world the soldier of Providence, the armed apostle of faith and of Christian civilization. Just as in the past, deliverance will be sought from thee by the weak and the oppressed of the universe. Thou wilt repeat those grand days of thy history, when all that was most venerable on earth was protected by the sword of Clovis, of Charlemagne, of Godfrey de Bouillon, of St. Louis, of Joan of Arc." [1]

---

[1] Mgr. Freppel, in a Discourse for the Benefit of Wounded Soldiers, Feb., 1889.

THE ANEMONES OF PALESTINE.

A LEGEND OF THE VISITATION OF OUR LADY.

MARY CONROY.

HEN from Gabriel's lips our Queen received
    The tidings strange to hear :
    That her aged cousin had conceived,
    And a holy son would rear;—

Over the rocky and barren waste,
    Her own glad news to share,
To the hills far-off she went in haste
    To visit her cousin there.

Three months she dwelt with Elizabeth,
    And toiled with loving will.
One day to the fount (the story saith)
    She went, her jar to fill.

Weary she was, and she sat awhile
    To rest her aching feet;
Near by, a flower like an angel's smile,
    Looked up, our Queen to greet.

Mary, to gather the blossom, bent,
    Then paused and softly said:
" Nay, let not thy beauteous life be spent,
    Thy bloom so quickly sped.

" Live thou to honor the gracious Hand
    Which made thee blossom there! "
Blushed then with rapture the flow'ret, and
    Blushing, became more fair.

Now unto this day in Palestine,
    Anemones, 'tis said,
(Which in snowy vesture elsewhere shine)
    Wear robes of rosy red.

THE LILY OF CHIMU.

A TALE OF THE INCAS.

Rev. A. H. de Viras, O. P.

Chapter XV.

Paraymi, proud and independent, could yet be basely humble and meanly servile when his vile interests required; but under the present circumstances another of his pet passions came into play,—a raging anger seized him and made him forget for a moment his great hazards—he would once and forever throw off the yoke the witch had put upon him; he would declare war against her, an eternal war.

But she, the canny creature, guessed it all, and as she wanted the herbalist for the accomplishment of her dark projects, she quickly prevented any word of his, by exclaiming in a tone of cold indifference which contrasted strongly with her excited howlings of the moment before:

" I do not oblige thee to be my ally,—who cares? I told thee once I do not want thee for anything,—I do not want anybody; but as true as thou art standing there, if I am not with thee, that means, if I am not for thee, remember, that notwithstanding the promise Gupanqui made yesterday, Mocllanta will marry Apa-muyu, and thou, falling down most shamefully from the high position thou hast built for thyself at this court, with so much struggling, thou wilt be reduced to the most degrading condition,—perhaps that of scullion at the court of Tupayachi."

As the fiery bull, its nostrils held fast by the iron pincers of its fearless daunter, roars, jumps, shakes its sides, but then bends, lies down, rolls its head in the dust, and vanquished and subdued, licks the feet of the one that has mastered it, so was Paraymi overcome by the powerful menace of the sorceress. From that moment it was evident, more than ever, that he was to be the tool of the desperate hag. The fear that she would leave him to contend alone with his rivals lulled the storm of anger that was rising in his breast, for he knew that, single-handed, he would never be able to overcome them;—no, the dark woman was an indispensable ally; it was best, it was necessary to serve her.

She eyed him keenly for a moment, and then resumed:

" Thou art complaining most bitterly about me; but what about thyself? How hast thou kept thy promises? Our compact is a compact of blood and mutual vengeance. I am the executioner of thy revenge, and thou art the instrument of mine. There is a difference, thou seest; without me thou canst not do any thing;— without thee I can do all, but it pleases me to employ thee as I employ my tiger-cat and my scorpions.... Where are the victims thou hast promised to my hatred? Where the prey thou hast offered to put into my hands? "

" Where are the wonders thou didst prophesy to me thou would work for the success of my snares? "

" Where are they? Odd question, indeed. Art thou blind, Paraymi? Look around thee. Is it not wonder enough for thee that a new Manco-Capac came forth at the temple from the image of the Sun, effected numberless prodigies, and among them, the greatest of all, that which thou seest before thy very eyes at present, that I should be transported from my solitary, desolate, wild cave to the splendors of this palace? Dost thou ask for more wondrous events? What, then? "

" I do not say that, but I really do not see how the apparition of Racuna-Capac and thy presence in this palace of thine enemy, although it is a marvellous thing of which I would never have dreamed,— I do not see how it favors in the least the execution of my plots,—the capture of Gupanqui and the carrying of Ollacpya off as a prisoner."

" Thou dost not see! Simpleton thou art! I pity thee, indeed. Where are thy eyes? Thou dost not see that since Racuna-Capac has put his foot in this palace, every thing is turned up side down, every thing is disorder and confusion here? Military discipline is a forgotten affair, the keeping of guard day and night is interrupted, vigilance relaxed, order done away with. Where a god appears, men disappear. Nobody commands, nobody obeys. It is not a rebellion of subjects against their chief, but worse than that,—an entire laxity in every shape and form. This citadel has become an open public square; every body enters—goes out—at any and every hour of the day and night. Didst thou thyself find any sentinel to hinder thee at the gate? Didst thou find any obstacle to thy penetrating, at this advanced hour, into this inmost apartment of the court of honor? Didst thou meet the soldiers, the bodyguard? Yes, and how? Watching, making the round trip as is their task? Rather thou didst come upon them dead drunk, lying here and there along the walls, in the court, many of them out about the city. Pious and holy worshippers of the gods! Surely they know how to honor befittingly the divinity, and to render it thanks for sending them a new Manco-Capac! Their gratitude is none of the secret kind,—it has for proof, barrels emptied of chica, and stomachs full of the same beverage!"

And the witch laughed like a whole gang of devils set loose from hell together.

" Possibly," she continued, " there is in this palace one man, but one only, who does not at this hour sleep the heavy sleep of drunkenness, and that man is the Curaca Gupanqui. He is intoxicated in another way,—with the fury of wounded pride. He, in the depths of his soul, curses me, and is actually rabid over my presence here. He is alone,—alone, thou hearest. Why should not this be the moment for doing what thou hast to do? Go to his apartment, with some wild story that thou canst invent,—he will admit thee, for thou knowest he has absolute confidence in thee; then when thou hast gotten him interested, suddenly draw his attention to some corner of the apartment, and when he turns to look there, quickly slip this over his head and face,"—and the sorceress held up before Paraymi a piece of closely-woven network fitted so as to be at once a gag to prevent utterance, and a blind to the eyes—" then bind him, hands and feet, and...."

" And——?"

" And I will know what to do with him. Thou wilt tell me when thy work is done."

The sorceress gave a peculiar whistle, and at this queer call, two monkeys, invisible till then, jumped out from the corner of the room where they had been hidden behind the tapestries.

" Thou seest," she sneered, " I have my bodyguard also, and they are more faithful and temperate than are those of the Curaca, no matter if a god should come from Heaven to earth. These devoted servants of mine will take good care of Gupanqui, and transfer him from this palace to one of another sort. Thou in the meantime wilt secure Ollacpya. I hope that will not give thee so much trouble, and thou wilt take her to my cave before daylight. But remember, she has to be delivered to me safe and sound, not injured in the least. Woe to thee if she suffers any wound or insult. If thou succeedest—and why shouldst thou not?—to-morrow at the rising of the Sun, thou shalt be proclaimed Curaca of Chimu by Racuna-Capac, thou wilt be Mocllanta's happy possessor, and thou wilt have, in the jail of this citadel, at thy disposal, Tupayachi and Apamuyu. A few moments of hard work,—hard I say—not so hard, after all, for a man of thy astute strength and muscle,—and then, power, glory, and fortune."

"Oh, oh!" exclaimed Paraymi, fascinated, crazed by the satanic eloquence of the hag, and intoxicated by the hopes of a satisfied vengeance and ambition. "Is it possible! thou dost not deceive me?"

"Do I deceive thee? Why would I deceive thee? No, no; as truly as I hate the Lily of Chimu, thou shalt be Curaca to-morrow if thou serve me, and if thou promise me to do what I shall ask thee afterwards as the first act of thy power."

"And what is that?" asked Paraymi, instinctively shrinking at this announcement of another request, perhaps another hard condition from the sorceress.

"Thou wilt deliver to me in the most secret way, the first night of the new moon, twelve maidens, virgins all, beautiful all, and each aged but fifteen years."

Even the black-hearted herbalist was horrified at this demand, and he shuddered as he asked:

"And what for, may I know?"

"I could answer thee that that is my own business, and refuse to satisfy thy curiosity, but never mind; I will tell thee my purpose. Know, then, that I learned years, years ago, when yet a child, from an old.... ah! ah! what was I saying? Oh, thou knowest I like to puzzle people; but thou art my ally, I say the truth to thee, I learned, from a discoverer of my magic art, that if an old woman, no matter how old she may be, and ugly, and disgusting, if she does but bathe herself at midnight, on the first of the new moon, in a warm bath of the freshly-shed blood of twelve tender virgins, she becomes instantaneously young and beautiful and lovable....that prodigy I want to effect for myself; I am tired of being old and ugly. I long for youth again, that I may again experience the keen zest of pleasure, may indulge in wilder orgies and more intoxicating revelries."

Paraymi was thoughtful:

"And would this same prodigy take effect for a man as for a woman?" he asked.

"It would, certainly," she replied; "but, then, instead of twelve maidens, twelve youths of the same qualifications would be required."

"By Supay!" thought the herbalist, "one day I will profit for myself of this marvellous craft."

"Dost thou promise, Curaca Paraymi?" articulated the hag, dwelling intentionally on these last two words.

Paraymi hesitated a moment, then a singular smile played about his lips as he answered decidedly:

"I do promise."

The sorceress interpreted that smile, and said very coldly:

"I scarcely think thou art such a fool as to imagine that when thou art in power thou canst forget or refuse to keep thy word, or attempt any thing against the witch of Huanchaco. I can tell thee this,—that at thy first daring to be ungrateful or to interfere with thy benefactress, thou shalt be a dead man, bodyguards or no bodyguards. Remember this well, Paraymi."

The herbalist bowed his head without replying. He was convinced that the hag had all the power of an enchantress, as well as her faculty of reading hearts.

"Now, get to work. Gupanqui first,—Ollacpya next. My monkeys follow thee, and will wait for thee at the door of the Curaca's apartment."

Paraymi's ambitious anticipations were at their climax, and nothing could make him waver; but an objection came to his mind, and he formulated it thus:

"Racuna-Capac, thou sayest, will proclaim me Curaca of Chimu to-morrow,—but will the people accept me as such? Will the Inca ratify so irregular an appointment?"

"As to the people, they are all stark mad over the new messenger of the gods; no one would dare to resist the least ot his orders. As to the Inca, we will arrange all this in good time also, through Racuna-Capac's ministration."

Paraymi could not help thinking to himself that if Racuna-Capac were a god, would he favor two such criminals as were himself and the sorceress; but, after all, this was about the least of his worries, and not being more of a theologian than to know that there were gods of good and gods of evil, he concluded that possibly Racuna-Capac belonged to this latter category, and that that would make the matter all right.

"Do not lose time," observed the sorceress; "every thing has to be done before dawn."

"Art thou sure I will not be molested?" asked Paraymi.

"Most sure. See, rather," and the witch drew aside the curtain of the entrance.

The scene without was, in some respects, one of strong contrast to the strife that was ensuing in the breasts of those two crime-smitten beings to whose base intriguing we have been auditors. Peaceful, smiling stars kept watch in the heavens, their soft rays the only lamp to guide him who might be wayfaring,—for the moon had not appeared, nor would she that night, among the lesser lights which therefore sparkled their brightest. Strange that heaven so often wears a countenance calm and undisturbed. though looking face to face upon an unjust, wrangling, and passion-tossed earth.

The massive walls of the fortress stared, in the dimness, still more than ever defiantly at any aggressor, did such happen to draw near them; and like sturdy sentinels, the four grim towers stood watching the further distance. But what were these material protections when the master,—Mind, lay about the court, deadened with the fumes of chica, instead of keeping guard at the portals; when the mumbling of intoxicated dreams took the place of the faithful watch-cry, "all's well!" The practised eye of the sorceress gave one sweeping search over the scene, and she said:

"See how the night favors us; it it just dark enough to conceal thy doings, and light enough to guide thee through them. Be quick now, my lord Curaca, no time to lose!"

" No time shall be lost," he repeated, and was about to step out into the open air to reach the Curaca's apartment,—for it will be remembered that the different rooms of the building did not communicate with one another, but all opened upon the court—when, with the suddenness of an apparition, a number of men were seen moving noiselessly along, stealing cautiously over the sleeping guards, here and there, and making for the very entrance to which Paraymi had been on the point of betaking himself.

The witch seized him by the arm. " Hold!" she said; " some treachery here."

" Dost thou not see who it is? That accursed Apamuyu! He has been crossing my path and my luck for the last twenty-four hours. If he were alone now, it should be the last of him."

It was indeed Apamuyu, who, knowing the distressed state of affairs at the court, and that Mocllanta was exposed to the common perils, had come with a bodyguard to avert the danger.

Paraymi and the witch took turns in cursing the intruders who caused this postponement of their schemes of blood and crime.

"After all," she said, " it will only be a day later; have patience, —vengeance is sweeter the longer it is delayed."

(*To be continued.*)

A TRUE devotion to the Blessed Virgin has always been looked upon as an assured sign of salvation; but a devotion with a bad intention does not protect one from the danger of damnation. It is therefore very important to distinguish the devotion which saves, from the devotion which may lose a soul forever. We have a true devotion if we honor Mary as the Mother of fair love, of the fear of God, of an enlightened knowledge, of a wise discernment of the practices agreeable to Him; and lastly as the Mother of holy hope, of a confidence as far removed from despair as from presumption. In other words, that our devotion to Mary may be true and profitable to our souls, it must animate, excite, and develop in us these four virtues: love, fear, knowledge, and confidence.

Love of Mary is so closely connected with love of God that one cannot exist without the other. The fear of displeasing Mary is the avoidance of sin, the object of honor to her as well as to God. The knowledge of Mary is the surest means of arriving at a great and profound knowledge of God. Confidence in Mary throws us, obedient and reassured, into the arms of God's mercy. Such are the marks of a good, solid, and saving devotion; if it is thus that we honor the Blessed Virgin, we may rest assured that our homage is pleasing to her, and may count on her powerful protection.

Rev. J. B. Petitalot, S. M.

THE PRECIOUS BLOOD.

HELEN GRACE SMITH.

THE Lamb was slain, the precious Lamb of God,
   And all the toilsome way, the way that He
   Had followed through the gloom to Calvary,
Was marked with blood-prints where His feet had trod.

Those tender feet His Mother's knee had pressed,
   Those feet that, weary, travelled night and day—
   Ah! they had bled, had bled along the way,
Those blessed feet that Mary had caressed.

And the dear hands.   Ah, Lord! we cannot bear
   To see Thy wounds, nor see the thorn-crowned Head.
   We know, ah, Love! we know that Thou hast bled,
The blood drops falling from Thy forehead fair.

We whom Thou hast redeemed, we love Thee, Lord,
   For this, the shedding of Thy blood.   We sing
   Thy grateful praises for an offering
Of love.   We sing the praises of Thy word.

We take Thy chalice in our trembling hand
   As Thou hast bidden, and we, eager, cry,
   "O Precious Blood of Him, our Love on high,
Give strength that we obey His wise command!"

" Give strength, for we are weak, and very low;
   Low by Thy Cross we gather, and we kneel
   There at Thy wounded feet that we may feel
How Thou hast loved us, and hast borne our woe.

" How Thou hast loved us.   God forgive, we pray!
   Forgive us through the Precious Blood of Him
   Whose Heart was pierced, and, though our eyes be dim,
Teach us to follow still the upward way."

OUR LADY OF CARMEL.*

VERY REV. PIUS R. MAYER, O. C. C.

OW many reminiscences does not the very name awaken! Like a spur of the famous Lebanon the promontory projects into the Mediterranean sea. Olives and laurel skirt its base, oak and pine crown its summit. Abundant waters diffuse themselves over its pasture grounds and fields, rendering it at once one of the most fertile spots and one of the most enchanting views. Hundreds of caves big and small pierce its limestone, affording shelter to the husbandman and his cattle, refuge to the fugitives, and homes to the recluse. Can we therefore wonder that Carmel in the Sacred Scriptures stands for the type of beauty and bountiful blessing, or its devastation as the figure of the divine chastisements? In Isaiah [1] the reign of the Messiah is compared to the beauty of Carmel, and in the Canticle of canticles [2] the bride herself, on account of the beauty of her head, is likened to Carmel.

Thus are the shape, environment, and fertility of the mountain in themselves reasons sufficient to arrest the gaze and rivet the attention of the beholder; but there are historical reasons to render the mountain sacred, surrounded by the halo of sanctity, and pointing it out as a fountain of grace. Even before the division of Solomon's kingdom, the inspired seers of old were wont to retire to Carmel for the purpose of communing with God. But when the Thesbite gathered the scattered sons or disciples of his predecessors, and founded on Mt. Carmel the first school of prophets, the fountain of Elias supplied not only the water for slaking the thirst of bodies, but a spiritual fountain sprang up, changing the desert of souls into a blooming garden, laden with the fruits of holiness, and diffusing its sprays of hope and patient desire over the downtrodden chosen people.

A large cave 60′ long and 45′ wide, was the cradle of this school. There the promise of a Redeemer, made in paradise, was elucidated; there the adepts were told that personal sanctity, intercessory

---

* Carmel, " The Woods of God, or the Garden of God."
[1] xxxv., 2.   [2] vii., 5.

prayer, and fervent desire might accelerate the fulfilment of the promise, and an anticipated " Rorate, cœli desuper," rose from the assembled prophets.

Hence we need not be surprised that God, in answer to so many aspirations, gave a sign. Elias sees rising out of the sea a little cloud shaped like a man's foot, and inspired by the Holy Ghost, he knows it to be not only a sign of the rain promised to Achaz, but a token of the immaculately conceived Virgin, who rises pure out of contaminated mankind, a pledge of the coming Redemption. The signal is given. Henceforth the sons of the prophets centre their aspirations in the future Mother of the Messiah, and as prophet succeeds prophet, as the prophecies become clearer and more pointed, as the time of fulfilment approaches, their hopes grow stronger, their longing more intense, their prayers more fervent.

Could it be otherwise, after Achaz had been told: " The Lord Himself shall give you a sign. Behold a virgin shall conceive and shall bring forth a Son, whose name shall be Emmanuel, that is, God with us"? Could they sigh for the coming Redeemer without yearning for His Mother? Could they pray that the second Adam would retrieve the lot of fallen mankind, without looking for the second Eve, who in an eminent sense was to be the mother of all the living?

Thus there is a nucleus of devotees of our Lady of Carmel anticipating her veneration, and this nucleus at the same time foreshadows, as far as possible in the Old Law, the highest flower of devotion—Religious Life. For these sons of the prophets formed a community under an acknowledged superior; they had their devotions in common, and the traditions of their school were as sedulously guarded and as conscientiously handed down as the constitutions of any Religious Order of the New Law. Why should this not be so? As everything else of the New Law found its figure and type in the Mosaic dispensation, so the prophetic school prefigures the perfect abandonment of man to God, which is the essence of Religious Life.

As the plenitude of time approached, God revealed the fact to some of these sons of the prophets, and by them the joyful tidings were communicated to St. Ann, the mother of the Blessed Vir-

gin. It would indeed be difficult to picture the transports of delight engendered by this news. What they had so long and
ardently prayed for, their own eyes should behold realized. Their
own gaze should fasten upon the morning dawn, heralding the
rising of the Sun of Justice. From this time the intercourse between Nazareth and Mt. Carmel was not only frequent and amiable, but it was the intercourse between a sovereign Lady and
her vassals. Deeply interested in the weal or woe of the favored
persons, the sons of the prophets never for a moment lost sight
of the fact that it was the Mother of the Redeemer of the world
and its co-redemptrix, they were privileged to see and to speak
to. And the more the extraordinary graces became patent, which
God showered upon this child, the more tender and reverential
their affection for her grew. They anticipated the Magnificat:
"Behold, from henceforth all generations shall call me blessed."

When the holy night saw the birth of the Saviour, and angelic
hosts announced the glad tidings to the shepherds in Bethlehem,
they spoke to Essenians, and these Essenians stood to the sons
of the prophets, the hermits of Mount Carmel, in the same relation
as a third Order does now to the first Order. Consequently the
inhabitants of Carmel were soon apprised of the occurrence, and
the " Glory to God in the highest, and on earth peace to men of
good will " resounded in the caves of Carmel.

The years pass; the hermits are witnesses of the hidden life in
Nazareth, of the public appearance of the Messiah, of the catastrophe of Golgotha. They fully understand the heroism of the
sorrowful Mother and the deep significance of the " Son, behold Thy
Mother." Tenderness, sympathy, gratitude, and love, all combine
to render Mary dearer and dearer to them, if such a thing were
possible. The sermon of St. Peter on Pentecost finds them attentive
listeners, and the waters of baptism, there and then received,
transform the hermits into a Christian community, the shadow
yields to light, the type finds its complement, and the Mother of
Jesus for them is no longer the Mother of a promised Redeemer;
she has become their own Mother, because in giving birth to redemption beneath the cross she bore also them as branches of the
true vine. This filial love finds expression in the erection of a
sanctuary on the heights of Carmel, dedicated to Mary in the year

38, during her lifetime. *It was the first church in the world, in her honor.*

Vicissitudes of life come. The persecution of the synagogue and the Roman empire thins their ranks, drives them for a time from their asylum on Carmel. Hundreds die for the faith, but their ranks close again, their numbers are replenished, and the tradition is kept alive, according to which their chief object of life is the veneration of the Blessed Virgin, our Lady of Carmel. Pilgrims visiting the sepulchre of our Lord are sure to visit also the hermits of Carmel, for as Jerusalem enlivens their faith and love for our Lord, so Carmel nourishes their devotion to Mary.

The conquest of the holy land by Arabs, and later by Turks, gave occasion to the Crusades. Some of the Crusaders remained in the holy land, joined the hermits on Mount Carmel, and owing to the difference of nationality, education and aspiration transformed the eremitical into a cenobitic life, electing St. Berthold their first Latin General, in 1156; but since the victories of the Crusaders were soon changed into defeats, and life in Palestine became impossible to the Religious of Mount Carmel through the persecution of the Mohammedans, they resolved to leave Palestine and settle in Europe.

The years from 1238 to 1244 saw the foundation of monasteries of the Carmelites on the Isles of Cyprus and Sicily, in England and France. Pope Innocent IV. in 1245, counted them among the mendicant Orders, and in 1247, approved the rule of the " Order of the Blessed Virgin of Mount Carmel."

No good work was ever successfully accomplished in this world without opposition, and the Carmelite Order experienced its full share of it. So much so in fact, that its very existence was for a time threatened. St. Simon Stock, then the General of the Order, in this extremity did not try to secure help from the mighty ones of the world, he addressed himself to her, praying for a token of her protection. Our Lady of Carmel did not remain deaf to his fervent appeals, she gave him and through him to the Catholic world the Brown Scapular of Mount Carmel.

At the same time she appeared to the Pope, commanding him to announce authentically her gift, and to be favorable to her Order. Like the sun breaking through the clouds and dispelling the gloom, this revelation changed matters for the Carmelites. Their enemies were silenced, their friends exulted, the devotees of Mary felt themselves bound to them by a mystic link. They hastened to enroll themselves under this new banner of their Queen, and to wear her livery in order to enjoy the privileges attached to it.   The membership of the Order increased so rapidly, that in a very short time its monasteries dotted all Europe, so that it was said a pilgrim might start on foot from Norway for Rome, and spend every night of his journey in a Carmelite monastery.

But since even the Church of God has its vicissitudes, sees its times of ebb and tide, mourns to-day over the defection of some of her children, rejoicing the next day over new accessions to her ranks, we are not surprised to see also this old and favored Order share in the drawbacks of the world.

The western schism inflicted upon it a deep wound, of which it never fully recovered. The great apostasy of the sixteenth century involved hundreds of its monasteries in the general ruin. Those that escaped for the time, fell victims to the thirty years' war, or later still, to the French Revolution, the Russian persecutions, the rapacity of Italy and Spain, and the hatred of France. Thus this strong tree was shorn of its principal limbs, and it bore the aspect of a trunk withered by lightning. Yet, as the Blessed Virgin assured St. Peter Thomas, the vitality of this trunk is indestructible, because it blossoms under the ægis of the scapular. Slowly it recovers from all the blows, and even pinching poverty can but retard its progress.

Wherever there is a Carmelite monastery, it forms the natural centre of the devotion to our Lady of Carmel, and especially the feast of the Scapular, the historical anniversary day of the first apparition of the Blessed Virgin to St. Simon Stock, is solemnized with all the pomp at command. The confessionals are thronged, the number of communicants is surprising, the churches hardly hold the people, flocking to the devotions of the Confraternity of the Scapular.

To see these manifestations of an ever increasing love of our Lady of Mount Carmel on the part of the faithful, we need not migrate to the Old World, we have the proofs in our very midst.

In 1864, two friars of Mount Carmel arrived on American soil, without patronage, without money, strangers to the English tongue. In thirty years they increased to nine monasteries, with a membership of about one hundred and twenty. Of every one of their churches it is true that it forms the natural centre of devotion to our Lady of Carmel.

Since our Holy Father, Pope Leo XIII., extended to the Carmelite churches the privileges of the Portiuncula, the circles are getting wider and wider, the interest taken by the people and clergy is intensified, and questions innumerable are asked by those who are not content with the general information of the people, but wish to know the exact tenor and extent of the obligations and favors of the scapular, the Sabbatine privilege, the Third Order of Mount Carmel, etc.

To satisfy these queries and to spread, as in duty bound, devotion to our Lady, the White Friars at Falls View, Ontario, have published since January, 1893, a monthly, *The Carmelite Review*, and the rapidly increasing number of subscribers, as well as the unsolicited encomiums of the press, prove that the venture was a timely one, and will prove successful. It does not, therefore, savor of arrogance if we recommend this periodical to all the clients of our Lady, the more so, as the annual subscription of one dollar places it within the reach of all.

Everything bad and reprehensible nowadays is ventilated in the press. Why should not also the good use the same channel, to reach the multitude, edify them, and thus stem the tide of corruption emanating from the secular press? Mary, with her Son, has been a stumbling-block for thousands, but also the redemption of thousands. Who will count the number of those who, by means of the scapular, were recalled from infidelity or indifference, who were rescued from the very jaws of hell on their death-bed? Who can count those who were defended in peril of soul and body by this scapular? No wonder then, that the scapular, like the rosary, has long surpassed the limits of a mere private devotion, but has become an important factor in the life of the Church. At least one hundred millions, about one-half of the members of the Church, wear the scapular to-day, and the number is constantly on the increase. The more willingly the people enroll themselves under the livery of the Blessed Virgin, the more powerful her intercession will be, and it will be found by every devout wearer of the scapular, that our Lady of Mount Carmel still holds herself bound by her promises, that the scapular still is what it always has been, " a sign of her confraternity, a safeguard in danger, a token of everlasting alliance," and that he that piously dies in this scapular will not suffer hell-fire.

BEADS FROM THE HOLY SEPULCHRE.

Ellen Downing.

My Lord! it was a tender thought of my sick-room and me,
Which brought this hallowed Rosary far over land and sea;
The pilgrim-bearer little knew for whom the beads were meant,—
From Thee and from Thy loving Heart the sacred gift was sent.

Thrice blest, upon Thy tomb it hung, and 'twas for this alone
Thou didst inspire a friendly hand to place it in mine own;
For soon as on my heart it lay, I fast began to prove
How every bead was teeming o'er with token-words of love.

It spoke of all Thy wanderings, it told of all Thy tears,
Thy shame and pain and agony, Thy weariness and fears;
It asked, with thrilling tenderness, if greater love could be
Than this which brought my Saviour down to the cold tomb for me.

And then my thoughts rushed onward, and questioned if it came
Because this faster beating heart and more exhausted frame
Are but of my own early grave a token and a sign
Which I could meet more tranquilly for this kind glance from Thine.

Oh! be it word of life or death, to Thee my soul I lift
In thanks for all the tenderness that breathes from out Thy gift;
And still, at every bead I pray for blessings on the hand
Which placed in mine the Rosary from the far, Holy Land.

THE CALENDOLI TYPE-SETTING MACHINE.

ONDERFUL as are the time, labor, and space-saving machines, which a visitor to our great American printing establishments may see automatically setting type, or moulding characters in stereotyped lines, after use distributing automatically either the type or the matrices, it must yet be acknowledged that here in inventive America there has been nothing achieved over olden methods, in the work of composition, that compares with the achievements effected in the line of presswork since the invention of printing. In olden times the hand-press turned off one hundred copies an hour; the great presses of to-day issue eight hundred a minute: a marvellous advance —the work of hundreds of hand-presses. A good compositor working in the old time method, setting up type letter by letter, places in position easily about three thousand letters an hour. An expert operator on the swiftest machine can do the work of four compositors: an advance, assuredly; but to what degree in comparison with that in presswork? It has remained for a Sicilian Dominican, Father Calendoli, to give to the art of printing a typesetting machine that eclipses all previously resulting from inventive and mechanical genius. We are pleased to present to our readers, a portrait of Father Calendoli, together with an illustrated description of his great work, constructed by the mechanician Bibant, under the direction of the Reverend inventor, and to which the French Government has justly given his name.

Like other type-setting machines, this possesses a keyboard bearing the alphabet. The letters of others are struck as are the keys of a typewriter, one after the other, each letter appearing but once on the board. The originality of the keyboard or " checkerboard " of Father Calendoli's instrument consists in: first, the repetition of the vowels and their position in relation to the consonants near which they appear in words; secondly, the number of times

each set, or " square," of the alphabet exists on the " checker-board." A glance at the illustration of the board will show that
each row of letters in the " squares " is repeated after the manner of the octaves of a piano-forte. As on the piano-forte chords may be formed by striking simultaneously ten notes with the ten fingers of both hands, so may a word of ten letters be formed by the simultaneous action of the ten

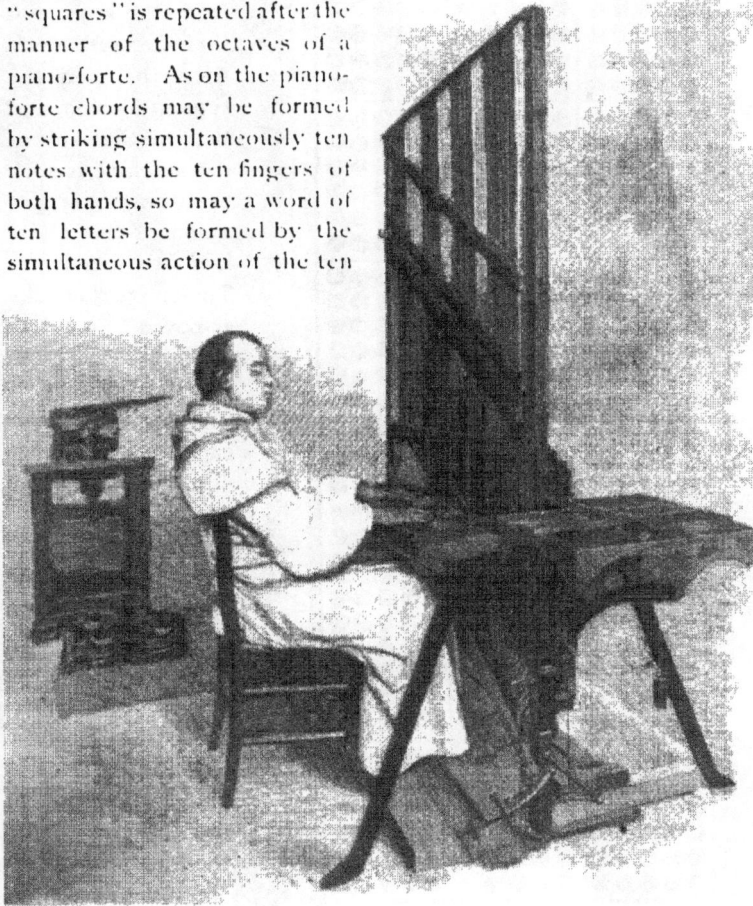

1.

ELECTRIC BATTERY.   REV. FR. CALENDOLI, O.P.   " CHECKER-BOARD. "   ALPHABET TUBES.   INCLINED WIRE AND GALLEYS.

fingers on the knobs of Father Calendoli's " checker-board."
More than this; owing to the position and repetition of the
vowels, and the closeness of the keys or knobs on the board, two

letters, it is claimed, may be struck at the same time by one fin-

2.—THE "CHECKER-BOARD."

ger. It is the up-lifting of the fingers from the keys, not their pressure upon them, that sets the type in motion, and the mechanism of the machine is such that the proper po-sition of the letters in words is secured. The entire " check-er-board " consists of eighteen squares, three of which to the right, contain capital letters, the diphthongs, a n d j, k, w, x, in small letters. F i f t e e n squares contain the small letters, · with the exception of j, k, w, and x, the po-sition of which has been given.

We here present an enlarged view of one of these squares, the fifteen of which are similar. It will be seen that the vowels a, e, i, o, appear in three different posi-tions; the u twice, besides a third time in conjunction with q. With a little practice the operator will easily learn which knob con-taining the vowel he needs can be touched most conveniently. So, too, will he acquire facility in placing his fingers simultaneously on the several letters contained in successive words of the copy.

In a line extending across the entire "checker-board," the punctuation marks (and a mark which we take to be the spacer), are placed, occurring each five times, while the sign & and the e, with its different accents, appear once.

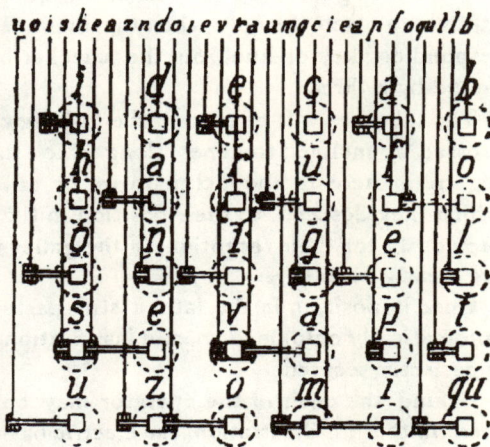

3.—A "SQUARE" ENLARGED.

The letters are marked upon little electric knobs, which act upon the corresponding character contained within the vertical tubes of the instrument.

The type is contained in the four series of metallic tubes adhering to one another, each containing about one hundred and fifty letters, there being about one hundred and thirty tubes in all. These form the harplike, horizontal part of the machine. The

type is not touched by the operator; it is manufactured and introduced into the tubes by a machine specially for the purpose, and is destroyed as soon as used.

We give here the letter S—very much enlarged from the type itself—to illustrate the form of the characters.

The type is much shorter than the ordinary; the little slug of lead is hollowed underneath the slope permitting the characters to run upon the inclined rail, into position in the galleys.

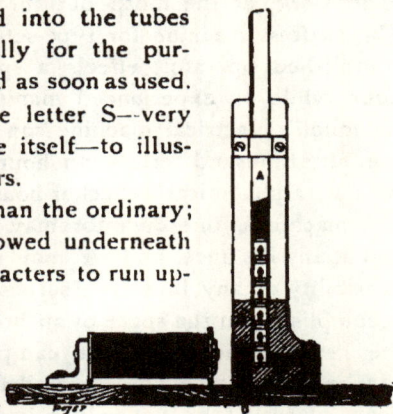

5.—A BOLT OPEN.

In figure 5 we see at A, one of the vertical tubes. At the foot of each tube there is a bolt C, which receives, when it is open, a letter, which falls into

the conductor D, when this same bolt is closed, as seen in figure
6. In both figures may be seen at E, the electro magnet which
attracts to itself the bolt when the finger is lifted from the corresponding key or knob on the checker-board, to which it is
bound by a thread.

The tubes, as will be seen in the full view of the machine, are
crossed by inclined trenches along which the letters glide, passing from there to the inclined wire or rail (see figure 7), over
which they descend, to their position in the lath or bar arranged
previously for their reception, in the galleys, which in this figure
are clearly visible.

Once in position in the lath, a stiff paste
automatically enfolds them, and justification
is perfectly secured.

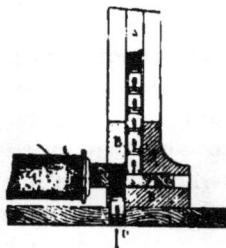

6.—A BOLT CLOSED.

Behind the chair of the operator may be
seen, in the full illustration, the electric battery furnishing the current, which is the only
and all-sufficient impelling power of the instrument.

And, now, let us sum up the advantages of
this machine.

1. An expert workman can set up, by the prevailing method of
hand work, at the most, but three thousand letters an hour.
The swiftest machine for type-setting, in the hands of an accomplished operator, effects a speed of fourteen thousand an
hour, while an experienced manipulator of the keys of Father
Calendoli's electrical machine can place in position, ready for
use, fifty thousand letters an hour. Add to this the fact that
with an alphabetical "checker-board" electrically bound to several machines, one operator may multiply galleys indefinitely,
and at any distance, and we may indeed question if there is a
possibility of any invention surpassing this in amount of work
accomplished in the space of an hour. Even as one who knows
the keys of the piano-forte can produce a chord as fast as it
can be named, so may one familiar with the alphabetical keyboard place in type, not only a letter, but words of ten letters,
even as rapidly as they may be pronounced.

2. Easy and correct justification, owing to the fact that each

letter is separate, glides into correct position, and is held there imbedded in a stiff paste.

3. Avoidance of the work of stereotyping plates; solidly supported on the laths, the characters may be placed directly on the presses. Changes may be easily effected by hand, by a very ingenious process. The type used may be that for the flat-bed press, or the cylindrical.

4. Avoidance of distribution; the type is not saved for future use; a great blending machine directly charges the tubes with a new set of type, the old being destroyed as soon as its service on the press is over.

5. Avoidance of material, boxes, font cases, etc., etc.

6. Lightness of weight; the species employed weighing six times less than that now in use.

Thus, in the closing days of the nineteenth century, science finds itself indebted to a friar for a most wonderful invention, as previous ages had been indebted to the much-maligned monks for many of the most valuable discoveries and inventions recorded in history.

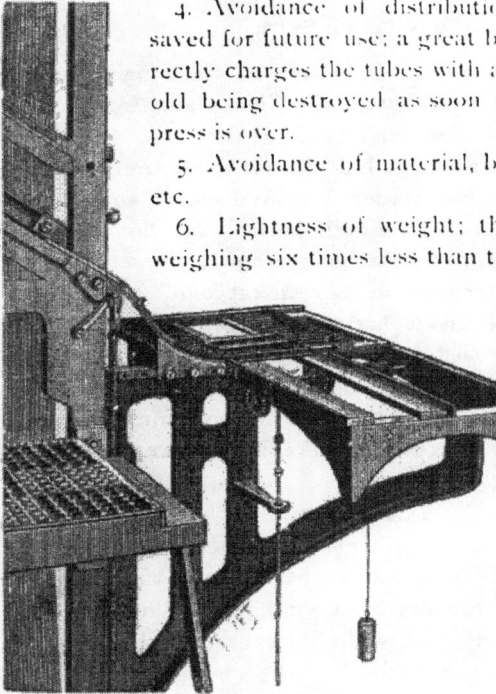

" CHECKER-BOARD."   INCLINED WIRE.   GALLEYS.

LOST A HUNDRED YEARS

John Talbot Smith.

WHEN a coal train left the track one day, and plunged into Lake Champlain, from a cliff fifty feet high, it found a depth of ten fathoms in which to hide its mangled timbers. The nearest station was Willsboro, and to this point the superintendent sent his wrecking train, with instructions not to hire any divers if the bodies of the five men lost in the accident could be found without such aid. But the divers had to be employed, and Captain René Forest was the first to offer his services, at fifty dollars a day with the use of his tug-boat thrown in.

"Couldn't think of it," said the superintendent, briefly; " figures too high ;" and other divers of inferior rank and lower prices were sent on.

"I'm pritty certain," said Captain Forest, "you'll hev to send for me at the last, secin' as I'm a man that knows old Champlain from end to end, hevin' been a pilot there sence I was a boy, an' Willsboro rocks bein' too much for strangers. Why, the water mus' be nigh on to forty feet, with holes here an' there, not to speak o' them measly quicksands."

It turned out that the strange divers could do nothing either in the matter of finding the bodies or of lifting up paying portions of the wreck. The superintendent had to accept the Captain on his own terms, which paid very well in the end, for he sent up four bodies in two days, pumped tons of coal to the surface, rescued three cars still undamaged, and promised greater things for the week. The superintendent was so pleased with this success that he ordered his deputy to discharge the Captain as soon as the body of the engineer was found, and let the cheaper divers

complete the job. In this way still more money would be saved
to the company. But the engineer's body was not found until the
very day the last load was sent up from the bottom, it having been
held fast by the wreckage of the engine; and the company had to
pay a first-class price for as fine a piece of diving work as had
been ever seen on Champlain.

"An' the best of it is," said Captain Forest to his Willsboro
friends, "that I've had two weeks to hum at the expense of the
company, an' I've found out where the old treasure-ship lies,
an' besides, I played the superintendent jes' as cute a trick as ever
was played on sich a mug as he is."

The loungers on the hotel veranda cried for an account of the
trick first, but Calvin Wool, who had his fortune to make, and was
anxious to do it in a hurry, asked a dozen questions in a breath
about the location of the treasure-ship, which for a hundred years
had troubled the dreams of the impecunious in the town.

"The day the superintendent came up to see how I was a-gittin'
along," said the Captain, ignoring Wool's request, "he gived or-

ders that I was to git the bounce jes' as soon as Tom Robbin's
body was found. He thought I didn't hear him, seein' as I was
on the bottom jes' then, a-lookin' for Tom ; but my helper heard
him, an' tipped me the wink nex' time I came up. Pritty mean
way to treat a man after a-comin' all the way from New York to
do the job nobody else could do—bounce him when the wust
part o' the work was done, an' let others take the money. I reckon I'm on to a thing or two, though. You all remember, boys,
that poor Tom wasn't found till the last day o' the job."

They all remembered except Calvin Wool.

"It went agin the grain to do it," said Forest, "for I knowed
Tom sence he was a little bit o' feller, brought up alongside of
him in the Point; but I knowed he wouldn't care, anyhow, an'
that kind o' eased my conscience. Why, boys, I found him ten
minutes after my helper had told me o' the order to gin' me the
bounce, an' I jes' up an' tied the body to the engine, an' kep' it
there till the last load went up. It didn't do Tom no harm, sence
he'd been in the water five days then, an' I know he'd like to see
the company git soaked so bad."

The crowd laughed, commended the Captain's shrewdness, and
acquitted him of all guilt in his treatment of the body. Then
Calvin Wool was allowed to repeat his questions about the treasure-ship.

"Well," said Captain Forest, leisurely, "I found the old ship,
or what's left of her, lyin' right off the cliff in a hundred foot o'
water, with a crevasse only ten foot away that mus' be nigh on to
five hundred, an' p'raps goes through to t'other side for all any
one knows. If she'd a sunk there I reckon I wouldn't a found
her so easy. But there she lies, as she's been a-lyin' a hundred
years, only now her hull is clean out o' sight with all the mud
that's been swept onto her. Some day I'm goin' to hev a try at
her, an' see if any o' the money said to hev gone down with her
is a-lyin' around."

Calvin Wool put the Captain in the witness box for a half hour,
and got all the information possible as to the history and present
location of the ship. It was known to the townspeople as the
Queen, and had been wrecked in Revolutionary days, while carrying a sum of money to Burgoyne's army. The amount was not

known, but tradition put it at a half million, and Calvin Wool promptly laughed at tradition, quoting history to show that ten or twelve thousand dollars lay in the ship's treasure-room at the bottom of the lake.

"That's enough to suit me," said Calvin, "an' I hereby announce that I'm going to get a share o' that money, while willin' to accept the help of anyone here present."

"You can hev my services at the start for fifty dollars a day." said Captain Forest.

"Taken," answered Calvin, promptly, "and I call the boys to witness the contract. I'll be ready to talk business Sunday, when I've looked over the ground a bit."

No one took the young man seriously, and Captain Forest forgot his contract in visiting his friends and relatives before returning to the city. It surprised him that the talk among his neighbors was forever turning upon the *Queen*, whose ribs lay in the mud just outside Willsboro bay. No subject had any charm compared with the ship, and the Captain got very tired telling all he had seen of it at the bottom of the lake. In twenty-four hours the town had gone raving mad on the subject of sunken treasures.

"You're a nice one," his son Raoul said, "to give away a fine chance to make a fortune in a week easier than ever man made it."

"And we might have had our share, too," said pretty Ida Greenwood, with a pout, "and been married all the sooner. Such a foolish man! It's just like your father, though," she added; "if he had only chosen some nicer person than Calvin Wool!"

"You're a-talkin' o' nonsense," said the Captain. "There is no fortune to be made in a week, an' I never said anythin' to Calvin Wool that he or any other sharper'll make any money out on."

A few minutes later, however, his son-in-law attacked him on the same point, and, as he had not the highest respect for the man who had married his daughter, irritable words were exchanged. The matter did not end there. The Curé of the parish, who had baptized and married him, and whose word was law for the Captain, took him aside one day, and protested against the excitement he had caused in the town.

4

THE CURÉ OF THE PARISH TOOK HIM ASIDE ONE DAY

" You are old enough to know, René," said he, " that these simple people cannot stand such visions of wealth as you have been
giving them since your arrival by your stories of the *Queen*, and
your talk of finding the treasure. They are now thinking of nothing but treasure, and may organize a company to hunt for it.
Have you also started that? " The Captain shook his head do-
lorously, and disclaimed all responsibility.

" It's the doin's o' that Calvin Wool, Monsieur le Curé. I have
not said a word sence the fust time I spoke on it in the hotel. I
don't believe there's no treasure there, an' w'en Wool asked me
to do the divin' for him at fifty dollars a day, w'en he was ready
to take up the job, I thought he was only foolin'.· S'elp me."

" Do what you can then," said the Curé, " to quiet the people.
They are all gamblers when the fever takes them, and this may
prove the costliest of freaks."

Captain Forest found it unnecessary to oblige Monsieur le Curé,
because Calvin Wool had so spread the disease that there was
now nothing to do but let it take its course. In secret a company
had been formed to hunt for the treasure, the stockholders of
which were three of the prominent townsmen: but everyone knew
that the hundred shares were actually held by ninety of the poor
workmen of the neighborhood, who had risked all their savings on
a romantic venture, Calvin Wool and his associates having no more
than two shares apiece. As treasurer and general manager the
clever Calvin had placed twelve thousand dollars in the bank to
his own credit, where before he had never a cént at all. But no one
knew, and no one would ever know, that he had admitted as
stockholders all who applied, and could be trusted to keep their
connection a secret. He notified Captain Forest that he would
hold him to his contract, and that work would begin at once,—news
which sent the Captain to Monsieur le Curé with humble explanations.

" I acquit you of all blame, René," said the Curé. " And perhaps it is as well that this delusion should be destroyed in this way.
But Calvin Wool is one who waits to make money like a highwayman; he will take it from the first that comes along. Be on
your guard; and if you can discover any crookedness in time
to save his victims, let me know. How does he propose to begin the work?"

"Well," said the Captain, with a dry laugh, "I don't know much about science, but he calls it the science way. He has a rod, what tells where gold is lyin', whether in the ground or in the water; an' his idee is to hold that over the wreck an' send me to look where the rod points. He believes in it, an' nothin' I could say amounted to shucks to change the mind o' the people about it. I'm a-gettin' fifty dollars a day for my share, an' you kin bet three weeks 'll make 'em tired o' me."

Monsieur le Curé took a great interest in the search for the treasure, and praised Calvin Wool for going about his work in so business-like a fashion. He was curious, too, about the use of the divining rod, and attended daily with a hundred of the villagers to see it in operation. It was a time of excitement for Willsboro village and the entire county. The population turned out in numbers to see a diver make his daily descent into depths that only the dead and the fishes had reached hitherto. If money had only been more plentiful in the mountains, Calvin Wool might have added fifty thousand to the sum in the bank. As it was, he was forced to invest his money in the banks of New York to prevent an exposure of his little game.

Captain Forest had enough to do to prevent his own family from giving their savings to Calvin. His son Raoul, and Etienne Calais, his son-in-law, had to receive a lecture from Monsieur le Curé before they would listen to his assertions of Calvin's crookedness; and they bore him a grudge for having spoken to the priest at all. As the Captain had foretold, the prominent stockholders grew tired the first week, of an expensive diver, murmured the second week, and revolted the third. He was dismissed, and his dismissal was followed by a sensation. Calvin Wool announced that he would do the diving himself, as he had foreseen the dismissal of Captain Forest, and had taken lessons in the art in secret: and in the presence of the Captain and the company he made a very creditable descent, and stayed down an hour.

"He has the courage of the devil," Forest said to his relatives. "An' I mus' say I saw nothin' wrong while I was with him. But that rod, bless your soul, they beant a-goin' to find a copper with it. The fust few days it pointed right over the wreck, but after that it went a-rovin' round, fust on one side, then on the other,

then back agin; one minute ten foot behind the stern, the next a
way ahead o' the bow, deep in the mud.   I didn't find nothin', an
I don't think they kin ever find anythin' in that way."   " Do ye
think, Dad," said Raoul, "that there's any treasure in the old
ship? I'm sure there is. What's your opinion about it?"

"W'en I come back next spring to see you an' Idy git married,
I'll tell ye," said the Captain.   " Meantime keep yer eyes on Cal.
Wool, an' ye'll learn a lot about it."

All summer and fall the search for the treasure was kept up, and
public interest did not fail with the passing days.   Calvin was an
enterprising genius, knew his audience as well as a theatre manager, and never allowed them to get weary.   In all weathers he
could be seen on the deck of his schooner, making scenic preparations to descend to the wreck of the *Queen*.   The divining
rod first did its little act of promenading the deck in the hands
of the diver, until it had located the place to be searched that
day.   Then the diving suit was put on with pomp, and the blue
waters closed over his head as if a being of the nether world had
returned to his home.   At proper intervals he brought up from
the mysterious bottom weird and ancient things, such as old coins,
a cutlass or two, bits of the wreck, and a small cannon.   The excitement in the town when these things were put on exhibition
was intense, and Calvin was besieged each time with petitions
for stock.   How many he granted will never be known, but small
as his heart was in other ways, in this it was too large to turn
away the importunate.

Winter came and the treasure remained in the hull of the *Queen;*
but Calvin kept the days picturesque by numerous meetings of
the known stockholders, who voted him thanks, accepted his
financial statement, and applauded the accounts of his adventures
on the bottom of the lake.   When Captain Forest visited Willsboro in March, just a month before the ice leaves the bosom of
Champlain, he congratulated Calvin Wool on the success of his
enterprise, and hoped he would find the treasure.   The financier
smiled, because he had already found all the treasure that would
ever be taken from the ribs of the sunken ship, and it lay in foreign banks, where never a diver could get.   If he had but seen
Captain René Forest that evening close the doors and the blinds

of Etienne Calais' parlor, and had heard the discourse of that costly diver to his son Raoul and his son-in-law Etienne, he might not have been so satisfied with himself.

" There's no use in beatin' around the bush," said the Captain. " I've come up to find the money that's buried in the *Queen,* an' I mus' hev the help o' my relations, o' course." Raoul bounded from his chair with a repressed shout, his father pushing him back again.

" Then you believe in the treasure? " said cautious Etienne.

" Yes; but not in Cal. Wool an' his fool's rod. I don't say nothin' agin the rod, mind, for he's fooled more money out o' Willsboro with it than he'll ever git out o' divin' 'roun' the *Queen.* But I've thought the thing over all winter in New York, an' I feel now there's money there. Here's the lay of it. W'en that ship went down, accordin' to all accounts she went down so sudden that her crew had jes' time to git to the boats, an' no more. O' course her officers knew she was a-goin' to sink a little sooner, an' had time to transfer the money to the magazine, an' lock it up so's it would keep safe, an' be easily found if the water wasn't too deep there."

" The magazine, you know, in them old timers is lined with lead an inch thick, an' that alone is wuth the trouble o' takin' up an' sellin' sometimes. Now if there wus any money in that boat, an' it went down with her, it's in the magazine, which is in the starn end, an' that's buried so deep in the mud that no kind o' divin' could ever tech it. But my idee kin tech it. The pipe on my tug kin pump every bit o' mud out o' the rotten hull in one day. The magazine is jes' as good to-day as ever it was; a crowbar will open it; the money is in small kegs inside, an' whether it's a thousand or a million, it won't take long to send it to the top."

(Conclusion next month.)

<hr />

MARY, Queen of Virgins :
　Thus we love to call
Her who is through Jesus,
　Mother of us all.

To this Queen of Virgins
　Lilies of the field,
As she walked the meadows,
　Did sweet homage yield.

But a sweeter homage
　Than the lilies even,
Can a Christian maiden
　Yield the Queen of Heaven

Mary, Queen of Virgins,
　Aid us by thy prayer ;
Lilies never needed,
　As we need thy care.
　　　　　—Eliza Allen Starr.

THE FRENCH DOMINICAN CONVENT, ROSARY HILL,
SHERMAN PARK, NEW YORK.

N the Harlem River Railroad, about thirty miles from New York, the traveller of to-day, alighting at the Unionville station, and securing his conveyance for the desired destination, is driven up a winding ascent for ten minutes, till the summit of Rosary Hill is reached. Standing upon the portico of the humble guest house, and gazing around while awaiting the brother porter, who will answer his summons, the visitor cannot repress an exclamation of surprise, of admiration, at the panorama of natural scenery that unfolds before him. Upon the beautiful vista, looks down, as though in benediction, our Lady of the Rosary, the exquisite statue of which arises from the circular mound that forms its natural pedestal.

It is with pleasure, therefore, that we present, in text and illustration, a brief history of the Province of Lyons, which has within the past year established its house of studies here, at Sherman Park, one of the beautiful and fast growing suburbs of New York City. In this congenial and health-giving spot nearly fifty sons of St. Dominic sing the Divine Office at given hours of the day and night, and prepare themselves for their future missionary work by the study of St. Thomas, and other branches of Sacred Science.

The Order of St. Dominic, founded by this great Spanish saint, was commenced in the South of France nearly seven centuries ago. During the lapse of time it has had days of glory and of trial, but it has always been a valiant champion and fearless defender of the Church of God. From its foundation till the French Revolution, the Order of St. Dominic in France rendered great services to the Catholic cause. The list of its illustrious men—doctors, apostles, martyrs—is long and full. One of

DOMINICAN CONVENT, ROSARY HILL, SHERMAN PARK, NEW YORK.

the four Dominicans who have occupied the See of St. Peter, was a Frenchman,—Innocent V. The Order in France has given to the Church many cardinals and bishops, many great writers and orators of fame. An interesting fact in Dominican annals may with propriety be here recorded.[1] The history of the Dominican Order in France is a glorious page, till the end of the last century, when, with the other Religious Orders, it was swept away by the French Revolution. At that time the Order numbered about one thousand members in France. They were either martyred or exiled, and all their churches and convents were sold by the Revolutionists, who applied the proceeds to profane purposes.

Towards 1840, half a century after the Revolution, nearly all the French Dominicans had died in different parts of the world, and the Order, in its French character, had become an object of past history. It was unknown except to students.

---

[1] The last Comte du Dauphiné, Humbert II., having lost his only son, and being a widower, was inspired with the noble design of renouncing his title and territories, and of consecrating himself to God in the religious state. The offer of his estates and honors was first made to King Robert of Sicily, but was not accepted. Among the nobles and prelates afterwards considered, the King of France was decided upon. The matter was laid before John, Duke of Normandy, eldest son of Philip of Valois, and consequently heir to the throne. The condition named by Humbert was that thenceforth the eldest son of the French king, the heir, should be known as *the Dauphin*. After the prudent and prolonged deliberation so important a matter demanded, with the full sanction of the reigning Pontiff, Clement VI.,—the compact was sealed. The abjuration of title and territories was made July 27, 1349. The next day Humbert took the Dominican Habit in the Convent of Lyons. He was thirty-seven years of age when he thus closed a worldly career marked throughout by true nobility and by valorous loyalty to an earthly sovereign. His solemn profession took place in July, 1350. In December of the same year he was ordained by Clement VI., at Avignon, where the Holy See was at that time established. He was ordained subdeacon, deacon, and priest, respectively, at the three Masses of Christmas, celebrated at midnight, daybreak, and noontide. Eight days afterwards he was consecrated by the Sovereign Pontiff patriarch, not only of Antioch, but of Alexandria. He became administrator of the diocese of Rheims, and later was named for the See of Paris, but did not live to fill this important post. He died a holy death in the midst of his religious brethren, in the fifth year of his religious profession.

But God was pleased at that time to raise up a man powerful in words and deeds, destined by His divine providence to be a second founder of the Order of St. Dominic in France. Henry Lacordaire, born in Burgundy in 1802, first became a lawyer. He

left the bar, where a bright and sure future was in store for him, to enter the Seminary of St. Sulpice. Ordained priest; he worked in the ministry in Paris for several years with great distinction. He inaugurated the famous lectures of Notre Dame, by which he revealed himself to the astounded capital as the first orator of his time.

When he had reached, as it seemed, the apex of his fame, he suddenly left France, went to Italy, and became a novice in the Order of St. Dominic. Sudden as seemed to all the taking of this step, it was in reality the result of a deep study of the wants of his own spiritual nature, and of those of his country. It was the result of long and fervent prayer to discern the will of God in his regard. After a year of probation he made his solemn profession on the 12th of April, 1840.

During his novitiate he wrote in his golden style the life of his spiritual father, St. Dominic, which with a pamphlet on the establishment of the Friars-Preachers in France, previously published, attracted the attention of the French people, and provoked the enthusiasm of a good many young men who came to offer themselves to him to be the foundation stones of the re-establishment of the apostolic Order of St. Dominic in modern France.

Amongst these first vocations was a young priest from Loraine, Father Jandel, who was destined to be placed, a few years later, by Pius IX., at the head of the entire Order of St. Dominic. For more than twenty years he labored unremittingly for the extension and regeneration of the Order throughout the world.

Another recruit was a young artist born in Alsace. He had gone to Rome to study the masterpieces of the Italian painters, and there he became acquainted with Father

FATHER JANDEL.

Lacordaire, and soon resolved to join his first companions. His name was Danzas. He was destined to be the next Provincial of the French province after Father Lacordaire, and to become the founder of the Lyonese Province.

These first French novices after the Revolution, eleven in number, began their novitiate in May, 1841, in two convents of Italy,—in that of Our Lady of the Oak, near Viterbo, and in the convent of Bosco, founded by the Dominican Pope, St. Pius V., in his native village, in Piedmont. For a few years they prepared themselves for their difficult mission in silence, prayer, and study. In the meantime Father Lacordaire had reappeared in the French

FATHER DANZAS.

capital and in the pulpit of Notre Dame, with his tonsured head and his friar's Habit. In his first lecture he spoke on " The Vocation of the French Nation," and so wonderful was his eloquence that it became a passport for his proscribed Habit. He thus won for himself and his Order, and we may say, for all the other Orders, the right to wear publicly the religious garb which had been so dear to the people in past centuries, but which had become obso-

CHALAIS.

lete and the object of the mockery and sneers of the new generation.

In 1844 the first convent was established in Nancy (Loraine). Soon after, another was founded in Paris. Novices came in great numbers, and Father Lacordaire bought, in the mountains of Delphinate, between Grenoble and Lyons, an old monastery which became his first novitiate. Its name is Chalais. Before the Revolution it was a dependency of the Grand Chartreuse, a kind of infirmary, where the old monks were sent to enjoy a little rest and a milder climate. Chalais, where the first generation of the new French Dominicans were educated, is a delightful spot, especially in summer. Those who have seen it cannot forget the majesty of its mountains, the mystery of its high woods, the charm of its deep solitude, and the beauty of its incomparable scenery.

In 1854 Father Lacordaire, who had governed the province of France since its restoration, asked to be relieved of the burden, and Father Antoninus Danzas was elected Provincial.

It was then that a certain number of the French Dominicans, at

the head of whom were the Master-General and the Provincial of
the French Province, desired to try to carry out a more perfect
observance of the rules and constitutions of the Order, than it had
been possible to practise up to this time, on account of the small
number of the brethren, the imperfect knowledge of the rules, and
various other reasons.

In order more easily to realize this project, a convent was
founded in the city of Lyons, to which were assigned only the religious who desired to carry out the observances of the Order as
they were practised in the golden ages of the past, *e. g.*, rising at
midnight for Matins, etc.

Even then in the mind of the Master-General the convent of
Lyons was destined to be the head of a new province, "a work," he
wrote, "that has been the dream of sixteen years of my life, and
the object of my best hope for the future of our Order."[1]

In the beginning the convent of Lyons was opposed, both in
France and Italy, but it was commenced with the purest and best
intentions by the supreme authority of the Order, and the Provincial of France, with the encouragement, first, of the Pope, and afterwards, with his most formal sanction and approbation.

This convent at Lyons, built first on a very modest plan, with
a temporary chapel, was formally opened on the eve of Christmas, 1856, with six priests, besides the Father Provincial and two
lay brothers.

In 1858 the convent was placed under the immediate jurisdiction of the Master-General. The members of the community being augmented by other Fathers of the Province of France, and by
the entrance of many novices, the Lyonese Fathers were soon
able to found another convent in Carpentras, in the South of
France. The Convent of Corbara, in Corsica, having been placed
at their disposal by the Master-General, they had secured the necessary conditions, in 1862, to be erected into a province, which
was called the province of the Immaculate Conception of the
Blessed Virgin, and its first chapter was held that year, in the
convent of Lyons.

This first convent and the first chapel were temporary, and so

[1] Circular Letter of Feb. 18th, 1857, to the Province of France.

CLOISTER OF THE DOMINICAN CONVENT OF LYONS.

poor that the Fathers spent in them some very uncomfortable
years.   But without delay they put their hands to the great work
of building a convent according to the traditions of the Order,
and when one sees the cloister of the convent of Lyons, one is
forcibly reminded of the beautiful description of Father Lacordaire, in his *Life of St. Dominic:*

" A cloister is a court surrounded by a portico; in the midst of
the court, according to ancient traditions, should be a well, symbol of the Living Water springing up to Eternal Life.   Beneath the
stones of the portico, or covered walk, were the tombs; funereal in-
scriptions were graven on the walls; and in the arched vaulting of
the portico were painted the acts of the saints belonging to the Order, or to the monastery.   This spot was sacred; the very monks
paced there in silence, their minds filled with the thought of death
or of their predecessors.   The sacristy, refectory, and large general rooms, were ranged around this solemn gallery, which communicated with the church by two doors, the one leading to the
choir, the other into the nave.   A flight of steps led to the upper
stories, constructed above the gallery and on the same plan.
Four windows, opening at the four corners of the corridors, supplied them with light, abundant light, and four lamps illumined
them at night.   Along these spacious and lofty corridors, the sole
luxury of which consisted in their cleanliness, the charmed eye
discerned a symmetrical line of doors on the right hand and on
the left.   In the intervening spaces were suspended a thousand
simple souvenirs of Heaven and earth, such as old pictures, maps,
plans of cities and ancient castles, and a table of the monasteries
of the Order.   At the sound of a clock every door gently opened,
hoary and serene-looking old men, men of precocious maturity,
young men in whom penance and youth had formed a kind of
beauty unknown to the world—every age of life, here appeared
wearing the same garb.   The cell of the Cenobites was poor, but
sufficiently large to contain a straw or horse-hair bed, a table and
two chairs.   A crucifix and a few religious pictures being the sole
ornaments.   From this tomb where he spent his mortal life, the
monk passed to that tomb which precedes immortality.   Even
there he was not separated from the living and departed brethren;
he was laid, in monastic garb, beneath the pavement of the choir;

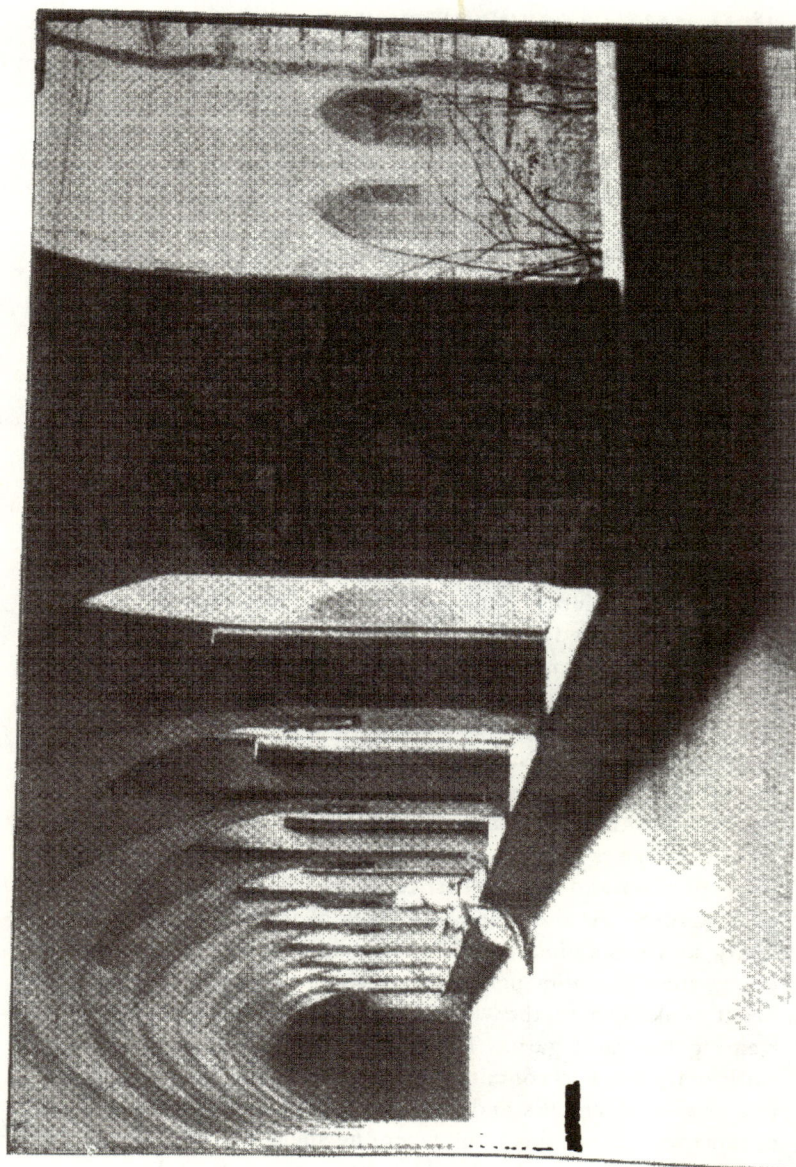

his dust mingled with that of his predecessors, whilst the praises
of the Lord, sung by his contemporaries and successors in the
choir, re-echoed around his tomb.   Amiable and holy dwellings!
Earth has witnessed the erection of several splendid palaces,
sublime sepulchres, temples all but divine; yet never have human skill and love created aught so perfect as the cloister."

The new church
at Lyons was built
according to the
purest traditions
of the Order. It
rose from the
ground under the
direction and plans
of Father Danzas
in the elegant ogi-
val style of the
thirteenth century.
It was solemnly
dedicated on the
16th of August,
1863, the feast of
St. Hyacinth. Its
harmonious pro-
portions, the im-
posing majesty
and elegance of its
architecture, the
beautiful tinted
windows in which

THE DOMINICAN CHURCH, LYONS.

an artist of perfect and exquisite taste, Father Danzas himself,
has painted with richest colors the principal mysteries of our
Lord and the Blessed Virgin, the history of St. Dominic, the
portraits of the Apostles, of the founders of Religious Orders,
and of many of the saints and blessed of the Order of St. Dominic,—all these things make it resemble a vision of Paradise.   It
is in this church that the present Master-General was elected
in September, 1891.

This noble church, in which the Divine Office had been chanted day and night for years, in which the beautiful ceremonies of the Order had attracted crowds of the pious faithful of Lyons, was desolated and profaned in 1880, with nearly all the other churches of the Religious in France.

PULPIT,—*Tubisch, Sculptor;* AND WINDOWS,—*Fr. Danzas, Painter.*

The Freemasons were then so completely masters of the Government of France that they thought it was a propitious time to free the country from the Religious Orders, and in consequence of certain decrees, all the doors of the convents of men, the doors also of their churches, were broken open by the police, aided by the worst characters liberated from the jails for the occasion. Accompanied by soldiers armed with guns and bayonets, and gendarmes with their drawn sabres, the authorities entered the cells of the Religious, and expelled from their homes the peaceful inhabitants of the convents, leaving only a few as guardians. They sealed also the doors of the churches, and even the doors of the tabernacles, and for years the people were forbidden to visit these places of prayer.

At that time the students of the province of Lyons were in the convent of Carpentras, near Avignon. They were brutally expelled with their professors on the 30th of October, 1880. The intention and the wish of the Freemason government were to discourage them, and render the pursuit of their vocation impossible; but they were frustrated in their design,—not one abandoned his vocation. It seems, on the contrary, that this unjust persecution made them more resolute and generous.

MOST REV. ANDREW FRÜHWIRTH, O. P.
(Present Master-General of the Dominicans.)

They gathered around their superiors and professors, and emigrated to Switzerland. A large hotel had been rented for them in the village of Sierre, Canton of Valais, in the beautiful valley of the Rhone, near its source. There they prosecuted their studies, and continued to pray for their country and their enemies. But in 1883 the Protestant Federal Government of Switzerland, at the instigation, no doubt of Freemasonry, signified to the French Dominican exiles that they could no longer enjoy the hospitality of the Republic. Switzerland accords a liberal hospitality to the worst Socialists and Revolutionists of the whole world, to the Nihilists of Russia, the Communists of Paris and London; but some poor Dominican students were, of course, more dangerous!

Consequently, in the summer of 1883 they shook the dust of this Republic from their feet, and started for another foreign country.

DOMINICAN CONVENT, RIJCKHOLT, HOLLAND.

A convent had been prepared for them in the little village of Rijckholt, in Holland, not far from the Belgian frontier, and there the province of Lyons had her single novitiate and convent of studies for eleven years. The intention of the persecutors in throwing the Religious on all the roads of exile was to diminish the number of vocations, and so extinguish, little by little, the Orders.   But, as Father Lacordaire has put it: " *the monks are immortal as the oaks.*"   Before this persecution the province had few vocations.   Once the novitiate opened in a land of exile the vocations became plentiful; young Frenchmen did not hesitate to cross the frontier to increase the number of those proscribed friars so terrible to their enemies by their life of penance and prayer.

Thus it became possible for the province to develop her mission in the English Antilles, where more than twenty of her children are now laboring, where almost as many have died, obscure, but devoted pioneers of the truest civilization.

However, in France, persecution against the Church and the Religious Orders, which are her advance guards, was going on systematically and shrewdly.   The men in power, slaves of the lodges, received orders from them to direct more powerful batteries against clericalism, and by all means to shatter it.   In 1889 a law was passed in both Houses of France, by which all young clerics were obliged to serve in the army.   The intention of the Legislators was less to increase the French army, already well-nigh innumerable, than to dry up the sources of clerical life by exposing the young aspirants to the priesthood to the corruption of the barracks.   Thus, they said, vocations for Religious Orders would become almost impossible, and those for the secular clergy would be greatly diminished.

This military law caused great embarrassment and anxiety amongst the Religious Orders.   However, there was an article of the law providing that all Frenchmen out of Europe, before the age of twenty, would be dispensed from military service in time of peace, if they had a regular position as students or merchants, etc., on condition that their names would be inscribed at the French consulate of the nearest town, and that they would appear before the French Consul once a year, till the age of thirty.

The law left a chance of saving the novices from the barracks in time of peace.   The province of Lyons resolved to seize it, and seek a refuge for its novitiate outside of Europe.   From 1890 to 1894 the novices were sent to the convent of Jerusalem, built a few years before by Father Matthew Lecomte, a son of the Lyonese province, on the very spot where St. Stephen had been stoned.

In the meantime, Father Laboré, the Provincial of Lyons, sought another spot, one of milder climate, and offering the possibility of bringing together all the students of his province.

HIS GRACE, ARCHBISHOP CORRIGAN.

In the Spring of 1892, Father Laboré, returning from his visitation of the mission in the West Indies, passed through New York. At that moment he conceived the possibility of placing his future Dominicans somewhere in the environments of this great city, where he received a kind welcome from the American Dominican Fathers. He was invited to do so by His Grace, Archbishop Corrigan, and encouraged by other good friends.

Father Laboré visited many places in the neighborhood of New York, and was especially charmed by one of them. Deciding upon it, he resolved to accept a proposal of the Sherman Park company, and to take as his future convent of studies, the Hotel Tecumseh, built the year before on a hill, near Pleasantville, commanding one of the most beautiful views in the vicinity of New York. It stands in the centre of the land owned by the Sherman Park company, where a new town is springing up, at a distance of scarcely forty minutes by rail from the great metropolis. The place chosen is indeed a delightful spot.

Like the Palisades of the Hudson are the wooded heights in the far distance, while but two miles away nestles beautiful Pleasantville amongst trees, surrounded by an undulating crown of hills, beneath which expands the emerald valley with its silvery stream.

This is one view; that in an opposite direction is not less inviting. The two green sides of the hills stretch far into the distance, the interior of their valley studded with clusters of trees, from the midst of which rise, like flowers in an expansive garden, the red and white houses of White Plains.

DOMINICAN CONVENT,—WINTER VIEW.

The Hotel Tecumseh, as it stood at the time of the purchase, was unfortunately not large enough to harbor the numerous spiritual family the Lyonese Provincial intended to transfer to its shelter. He was obliged to build an addition to the dwelling, together with a chapel, so that to-day the institution is double its original size. The work of building was commenced at the end of May, last year, and when the community arrived from Europe in September, the work was sufficiently advanced to allow the chanting of the Divine Office, and the observance of all the other religious duties. Matins was said for the first time at midnight on the feast of St. Michael, secondary patron of the new convent.

SIDE VIEW OF CHAPEL FOR THE LAITY.   CHAPEL FOR THE RELIGIOUS.   REAR VIEW OF DOMINICAN CONVENT, SHERMAN PARK.

The church and convent were solemnly dedicated by His Grace, Archbishop Corrigan, on October 30, 1894, the fourteenth anniversary of the violent expulsion of the community from Carpentras. The meaning of the Introit of the Mass said on these two days, at an interval of fourteen years, was striking, indeed: *Multæ tribulationes justorum, et de his omnibus liberavit eos Dominus—*"the tribulations of the servants of God are many, and from all the Lord has set them free;"—*Dominus costodit omnia*

THE CHAPEL FOR THE LAITY.

ossa eorum, unum ex his non conteretur"—"the Lord keeps all their bones, and not even one will be broken."

Therefore, with full heart and soul did the community chant the following words: "*Benedicam Dominum in omni tempore: semper laus ejus in ore meo*"—" I will bless the Lord at all times: His praise shall be always in my mouth."

WHERE shall an Infant God be sought
  But at a Virgin's breast ?
Can we adore the Son, and not
  Believe the Mother blest?

Where shall we fondly hail the bud
  But on the parent stem ?
How can we look to Jesus' Blood
  And Mary's tears contemn?
    —Sister Mary Alphonsus, O. P.

A PAGE OF CHURCH HISTORY IN NEW YORK.

ST. JOHN'S, UTICA.

Very Rev. J. S. M. Lynch, D. D., LL. D.

Part IV.

THE wife of Col. Dodge, whose conversion was mentioned in the previous paper, was baptized by Father Quarter in the first church after it had been removed across the street, where it is still standing.[1] The ceremony took place on the Feast of St. Ignatius of Loyola, July 31, 1836. The new convert took the name of Edah[2] Ignatius, choosing for the patron of her baptism the illustrious Founder of the Society of Jesus, on whose festival she had the happiness of being received into the church. Her sponsors were Captain J. H. Dwight—a convert himself,—who formerly lived in Schenectady, and had been received into the church in Albany; and Mary A. Manahan, afterwards Mrs. Owen O'Neill, the mother of Father Ambrose O'Neill, a priest of our parish, of whom we are justly proud, and of whom we are constantly reminded as his picture looks down upon us from the beautiful memorial window in the right transept of our church.

The eldest daughter of Mrs. Dodge—Diane de Roberts—then ten years of age, was baptized with her mother. Her sponsors were John C. Devereux, the father of Catholicity in Utica, and his highly esteemed wife—a convert herself,—whose delight it was in her home on Main street, to provide a place for the celebration of Holy Mass, long before the erection of a Catholic church in Utica. This young girl became afterwards the wife of Francis Xavier Manahan, the brother of the illustrious and well-known writer, Doctor Ambrose Manahan.

She died in Utica, March 5, 1856, at the age of thirty years. The following obituary notice was published at the time:

"Died; in Utica, March 5th, Mrs. Diane de Roberts, wife of Francis Manahan, and daughter of David F. Dodge, of Pompey Hill.

---

[1] Bishop Hughes was evidently mistaken in stating that Colonel Dodge and wife were baptized on Christmas day.

[2] She was usually called "Ada."

"In the life and death of this singularly gifted, lovely, and pious lady, her sorrowing friends have many reasons for consolation and for holy hope.

"At the age of ten years, having been instructed in the tenets of the Catholic Church, she, with a thorough apprehension of its divine truths, was received with her parents into its communion, and from that happy day till the day of her death, she strictly, lovingly, devoutly, 'kept the faith.'

"Living in the midst of Protestants, she was necessarily much in their society, but never swerving for an instant—never for an instant moved by the arguments or jests of her less favored companions. She always maintained her principles, observed always the practices of devotion, bravely and nobly defended the truth, whenever and by whomsŏever it was attacked in her presence, and compelled respect from those who would have derided her. And the influence of her example, as well as the force of her arguments, brought forth fruit. More than one have reason to name the beloved Diane with benediction,—more than one to thank God for the faithfulness and the unobtrusive, yet untiring zeal of His youthful servant,—her 'spotless life,' her earnest faith, her deep devotion, her abounding charity!

"Who shall say yet what fruits are reserved for them? Endowed with talents of a high order, she was never so happy as when employing them in the service of religion. Her brilliant wit, ready and tenacious memory and extraordinary reasoning powers, never so shone forth as when elucidating its truths, or meeting the assertions of its opposers. Her poems, informed with that intense love of the beautiful which seemed to overflow her soul, were most eloquent when their theme was divine; her exquisite painting, most perfect when it adorned the sacred vestments of the altar.

"In all the relations she sustained—as friend, sister, daughter, wife—she was most lovely, most beloved. Her warmth of heart, her playful spirit, the perfect simplicity of her character, her constancy and devotedness, with a thousand endearing qualities, will ever live in the remembrance of those who had the happiness to know her well. Yet all earthly love was subordinate with her to that whose source and end is God. Only in Him and through Him were her affections cherished.

"And her death was worthy of such a life. Lying at the feet of Jesus, as she herself expressed it, she was so blessed as to feel that His eyes were ever compassionately, ever lovingly, bent upon her. Her calmness and serenity, her more than patience in suffering, the devotion and sweetness with which she received the last sacraments, were each a proof of the living presence of her Lord."

Mr. and Mrs. John McCarthy, of Syracuse, were intimately acquainted with this daughter of Colonel Dodge. They have in their possession a poem written by her when only fifteen years of age. It is of a very high order of merit. The writer evidently had a foreboding of an early death.

Through the kindness of Mr. and Mrs. McCarthy I am able to reproduce entire this youthful effort of the gifted convert:

SONG OF THE WEARY ONE.

(Written for the " Freeman's Journal.")

I'm weary of this prison house, this frail abode of clay,
I would I had the eagle's wings, that I might fly away—
I long to dwell forever in the mansions of the blest,
Where the wicked cease from troubling, and the weary are at rest.

I would be with departed ones, whose forms, arrayed in light,
Come in my hours of loneliness to bless my mental sight;
They whisper of their happiness in that bright land above,
And thitherward they beckon me, those long-lost forms of love!

Though youth and health are on me, I've seen enough of earth,—
I long to go where angels tune the harps of sacred mirth;
For the gaiety of mortals bringeth sorrow to my heart,
And maketh discord to my ear—oh, when shall I depart?

I've always trod what earthly poets call a "flow'ry way,"
But in its dang'rous windings I would never wish to stray—
For the roses quickly wither, and disclose the thorns beneath,
And the smiling road but leads us on to everlasting death.

I have longed to quit this tenement, but why, my soul, oh why?
And art thou perfectly prepared—quite ready, then, to die?
Is death the portal *always* to the mansion of the blest,
And the passage *only* to that place of everlasting rest?

The Saviour trod the winepress of His Heavenly Father's wrath,
And watered with His precious blood, the sure, but narrow, path,
And canst thou hope the guerdon of His followers to gain,
Not having taken up thy cross, and trod His course of pain?

Repine not, but wait patiently until the Bridegroom come,
And see thy lamp be lighted when He calls His chosen home!
Watch, fight, and, praying, conquer in the might of Jesus' power,
And prove thyself, that thou, prepared, mayst meet Him in that hour.

D. D.

Colonel Dodge had been previously baptized in the year 1835, in the church of St. John the Baptist, in the village of Salina, now a part of Syracuse, by Rev. J. O'Donnell, at that time pastor. There is no record of his baptism in the church register, which does not open until June 18, 1836. His sponsors were Thomas

McCarthy, one of the fathers of Catholicity in our Episcopal city, and Eliza Lynch, wife of James Lynch, the other patriarch of Syracuse, both of whom were intimate friends of the Dodge family.   Robert McCarthy, of Syracuse, who is still living, was present at the ceremony, and remembers distinctly the reading of the Profession of Faith by the fervent neophyte.

Another daughter of Colonel Dodge became a Sister of Charity, and was for more than twenty years Treasurer of Mt. St. Vincent's Academy on the Hudson.   She was known in religion as Sister Marie, and died only a year ago.

The peddler—the hero in this romantic story—was Francis Murphy.   He lived in Syracuse for more than forty years.   He was one of the founders of St. Lucy's church, Syracuse, the parish of the Very Rev. Father Kennedy, the Vicar-General of our diocese.   He died in the year 1888.   His daughter became a Sister of Charity, and is at present at St. Columba's school, Chicago, known in religion as Sister Raymond.

By a happy coincidence, the youngest daughter of old St. John's—St. Agnes' church,—founded by the lamented Father Toomy, whose name is last on the memorial tablet—is now presided over by Father Michael O'Reilly, who, for twenty years in Pompey, cultivated the good seed sowed there by the Irish peddler, and the present pastor, Father John V. Simmons, was transferred from this very parish to Pompey, where he is now carrying on the good work of his zealous predecessor.

LAST DAYS OF THE FIRST CHURCH.

The old church was removed across the street in the summer of 1835, and the corner-stone of the second church was laid January 14, 1836, by Bishop Dubois, when Andrew Jackson was President of the United States, William L. Marcy, Governor of the State of New York, and John G. Osborn, Mayor of Utica, and so closes the history of the first church.

Such were the zealous priests that spoke the word of God to our Fathers in the faith in that little church of long ago. Shorn of its beauty, completely altered as it stands across the street, no longer the house of God, but devoted to commercial uses, it preaches to us yet its great lesson of apostolic work well done. We thank God that· it still remains to link the old with ·the new, so that the past may not be forgotten. Through the kindness of Mrs. Francis Kernan, who with jealous care has preserved a pencil sketch made by the drawing teacher of her girlhood days, I have been able to secure a handsome engraving of this sanctuary of religion, and we may now see exactly how it looked when it stood upon this hallowed ground.* The church was completed in 1820, and Milbert, a French traveler, wrote of it: "On an isolated elevation rises a new church. It is elegantly built of wood, in Gothic style. I attended the ceremony of its dedication, which was performed by the Catholic bishop of New York, August 19th, 1821." The *Catholic Almanac* of 1822 has the following:

"In Utica a large and beautiful church has lately been erected and consecrated, which reflects great honor on the Catholics residing there. Their number is not great; neither are they generally wealthy; their zeal, however, *for the house of God and the place where His glory dwelleth*, has enabled them to surmount every obstacle to the exercise of their piety. From the multitude flocking annually to this flourishing village, no doubt can be entertained but this will shortly become one of the most numerous and respectable congregations in the diocese."

The *Utica Directory* of 1828 thus describes it:

"The chapel is a beautiful structure at the corner of Bleecker and John streets; is of wood, 45 by 60 feet, with a cupola, and was erected in 1820. The society acknowledges with pleasure liberal assistance from Protestants generally."

As I look upon that little picture, and read these descriptions of that dear little church, methinks a vision comes upon me, and scenes, one after another, float across my imagination. I see the bold Genoese navigator, spurred on by that holy monk, braving unknown seas and planting the cross of Christ in the virgin soil of this New World. I see heroic missionaries—Franciscans, Dominicans, Jesuits—falling in his wake and dotting every portion of this continent with the sign of redemption. I go backwards in the past two hundred years, and stand on this very spot. I see the Oneidas and the Mohawks, and all the brave Iroquois, roaming through this vast wilderness. I see these children of the forest putting on their

---

* See cut in June issue.

war-paint and seizing their tomahawks and their battle-axes. I hear their savage yells as they rush into deadly conflict. And lo! the scene changes. I see the Black Gowns coming up the majestic St. Lawrence in their little canoes, and entering into our inland lakes and following the Indian trails, and soon the hymns of Mary resound over the sparkling waters, and under the broad canopy of heaven I behold these children of nature bending low before their rude altar and worshipping the God of the Eucharist; and St. Peter's in the beautiful valley of the martyrs below us, and St. Mary's of Ganentaa, on the shores of the lake which surrounds our episcopal city, bind in a common faith the Oneidas with the Mohawks and the Onondagas. Again the scene changes. Advancing civilization of a type hostile to our holy religion destroys these vestiges of faith, and a pall covers with its darkening shadow the church of the martyr Jogues and the Lily of the Mohawk. But the blood of the martyrs is again the seed of the Church. She rises once more as from the catacombs, and even as of old the children of St. Patrick planted anew the Church of Christ in every country of Europe where barbaric invasion had almost wiped out its very existence, so now, again, these twelve Irish missionaries, like the apostles of old, looked out from the isle of saints towards the setting sun at this vast field of missionary labor, stretching from the frigid snows of the north to the sunny plains of the south; bathing the shores of the Atlantic on the one side and looking out from the Golden Gate of the Pacific on the other, to the vast empires of the East. And so they came, burning with holy zeal—apostles of Christ —to revive once more the Church of Columbus in the land of Columbia. And when, in the living present, we look around us and see the fifteen hundred churches, the two thousand priests, and the two millions of Catholics scattered over the diocese where at its formation but a single priest ministered, must we not bless the memory of those consecrated servants of God who began this noble work?

BISHOPS AND PRIESTS OF THE SECOND CHURCH.

DECEMBER 25, 1836—DECEMBER 25, 1869.

Before beginning the history of the second church, I would call attention to a coincidence which should not pass unnoticed.

Whilst we were celebrating the praises of the first church in Central and Western New York, on that very day old St. Peter's church of New York, the first Catholic church in the State—the cradle of Catholicity—was celebrating, with solemn pomp and ceremony, the 108th anniversary of its foundation.

It may not be amiss to give a brief sketch of this ancient church, which was the mother of our own.

St. Peter's church stands not only as the first church of the Catholic denomination erected on Manhattan island, but one whose history reveals a most remarkable and vivid description of the rise and progress of the Church of Rome in America.

On November 23, 1783, New York city was evacuated by the last of the British troops, and allowed to enjoy the freedom hard-earned, after a seven years' war. It was then by no means a large town.

On June 11, 1785, the little Catholic community, without priest, altar, or edifice, organized without venturing to consult the recognized ecclesiastical authorities of the Church of Rome, and incorporated St. Peter's church under the general act of the Legislature on April 6, 1784. St. Jean de Crevecœur, Consul-General of France; Jose Roiz Silva, John Stewart and Henry Duffin were named as first witnesses. An Irish Capuchin Father, the Rev. Charles Whelan, who had as a chaplain in De Grasse's fleet seen the overthrow of Cornwalis, and subsequently been taken prisoner, came to New York in 1784 with letters from Lafayette. The Rev. John Carroll, the Prefect Apostolic of Catholics in the United States, gave the Rev. Charles Whelan faculties to perform church rites under the Rev. Father Farmer.

Shortly after the demise of Father Farmer the trustees of St. Peter's purchased of Trinity church corporation a plot of ground on the corner of Barclay and Church streets. The corner-stone for the proposed new edifice was laid on November 4, 1785, by the Spanish Minister. The church was completed in 1786.

The Rev. Andrew Nugent succeeded the Rev. Father Whelan, but the former priest had not long been presiding over the destinies of St. Peter's when his strong and decisive sentiments and feelings expressed and demonstrated so forcibly among the congregation caused his appearance before the Grand Jury for being guilty of inspiring riot. The Rev. Father Nugent was removed, and Rev. William O'Brien, a Dominican Father, was then installed as pastor of St. Peter's, and under the guidance of this priest the prosperity of the new church became the more promising.

BISHOPS.

Even as three bishops of the diocese blessed with their presence the infancy of our parish, so three blessed our childhood days—three ruled over our second church—Bishop Dubois, whose

life I have already sketched; the great Bishop Hughes, and the first
Prince of the Church in the United States—Cardinal McCloskey.

BISHOP HUGHES.

It is needless to say that Bishop Hughes was one of the most
remarkable men that the American Catholic Church has ever

BISHOP HUGHES.

produced.   He lived in the days of giants—of the Clays and the
Websters and the Calhouns,—and yet he shone above them all.

Bishop Hughes was born in the County Tyrone, Ireland, on the
Feast of St. John the Baptist, June 24, 1797.   He was educated
at Mt. St. Mary's, Emmitsburg, under Bishop Dubois.   After his

ordination he was for several years pastor of St. John's church, Philadelphia. He was consecrated Coadjutor Bishop of New York by Bishop Dubois, January 7, 1838.

The aged bishop's health had been gradually failing, and in about a fortnight after the consecration of his coadjutor, he was attacked with partial paralysis, from which he never fully recovered. Bishop Hughes assumed the management of the affairs of the diocese in August, 1839, and then began a most eventful era in the Catholic Church of America.

The life of the great Bishop was cast in stormy times, but he never quailed before the tempest. Like a general in the midst of battle, he seemed to be everywhere, encouraging the timid by his presence, and dealing telling blows upon the advancing hosts of the enemy. Facile with pen, at home on the rostrum as in the pulpit, he was a very champion of God's Church, silencing the tongue of slander by his masterful logic, disarming prejudice and bigotry, and vindicating her claims before the world. A mere mention of a few of the acts of his administration will give a faint idea of his busy life.

With one fell blow he destroyed the system of secular incorporation of lay trustees which circumstances had compelled Archbishop Carroll to tolerate, but which had produced havoc in many parts of this Catholic fold. He visited Europe in 1839, was presented to King Louis Philippe in Paris, induced the Ladies of the Sacred Heart to found an academy in New York, spent three months in Rome, laying before the head of the Church the condition and wants of his vast diocese, returned by way of Ireland, and was introduced to the great Daniel O'Connell. He held a diocesan synod for the first time since the See of New York was created, and framed wise regulations for the clergy. He founded a theological seminary at Rose Hill, Fordham. He introduced into New York the sons of Blessed Jean Baptist De La Salle—the well-known Brothers of the Christian Schools, who have been such an ornament to the diocese ever since. He reorganized the Sisters of Charity under the rule and dress of Mother Seton, and placed them under diocesan management. He brought over a colony of Sisters of Mercy to take charge of hospitals and asylums, and to carry on their numberless works of charity among

the poor. n called to orner-stone of the magnificent cathedral
of New Yoı · .   1858, and we glory in the fact that of the
six suffragan bis....rd that surrounded him on that great occasion, there were four whose names are on our memorial tablet.
When the Civil War broke out, his voice was raised for the starry
flag that protects us all alike, and its thunder tones rang out, kindling the fire of patriotism in every Catholic breast. When France
was hesitating on which side to lend her influence, the Government
appealed to our great Catholic Archbishop, and his powerful
plea with Napoleon III. saved, perhaps, our Union from destruction. One of the last great works of his life was the purchase, at
less than one-third of its cost, of a fine building on Ida Hill,
at Troy, erected by the Methodists for a University, and with its
grounds occupying some thirty-seven acres. His intention was to
provide a seminary, not only for the diocese, but for the
whole province, embracing New England and New Jersey, as
well as New York. He did not live to see the seminary actually
established, but it is flourishing in our days, after a quarter of a
century's noble work.

Such was the life of Bishop Hughes. He died with a smile
upon his lips. He had fought the good fight; he had won the
crown. He had seen four dioceses carved out of his own, and
even a greater progress in the spirit and devotedness of Catholics
to their religion. Truly might his illustrious successor, in that
eloquent eulogy which he pronounced at his obsequies, say that
if ever there was a man raised up by God to do a special work,
that man was John Hughes.

CARDINAL MC CLOSKEY.

After the storm came the calm, and the meek, gentle, amiable
Bishop McCloskey gathered in the fruits of the labors of his
fearless predecessor, and raised high the spiritual edifice upon
the solid foundations which had been laid.

  Bishop McCloskey was born in Brooklyn, in 1810. As a boy
he was one of that little band of Catholics that were obliged to
cross the East River, in the early part of the century, to hear Mass
in New York. His first pastor, Father Farnan, was also the first
pastor of our parish. He began, in Mt. St. Mary's, Emmittsburg,

that great career in which he was to she   lustre on t ·
American Church.   He first came into \·   ⸱ as Preside·
of St. John's College, Fordham, the theological seminary of the
diocese.   He was afterwards Rector of St. Joseph's Church, New
York City.   He was consecrated Coadjutor Bishop of New York,

CARDINAL MCCLOSKEY.

by Archbishop Hughes, March 10, 1844.   He became Bishop of
Albany a few years later, and was duly installed by Bishop
Hughes, September 19, 1847.

How well he governed that new diocese of Albany for the next
seventeen years, how it grew and developed and strengthened
under his fostering care, and how deeply he was interested in the
efforts of his people, is best asserted by the universal regret at his

leaving, when called to preside over the great See of New York, May 6, 1864.

It seems but yesterday that I stood in that surging crowd that filled every nook and corner of the vast cathedral, and heard the sighs and the sobs on every side as in the rich tones of his sweet, melodious voice, he bade his beloved people a last farewell, discoursing on that beautiful text of St. John: " Of them whom Thou hast given me, I have not lost any one."

For twenty-one years this great bishop ruled over the archdiocese of New York. Under his gentle and prudent sway, like a garden this Church of New York blossomed. Churches and schools, academies and colleges, hospitals and asylums, sprung up, and the Catholic population multiplied until the numbers were almost incredible.

Well, indeed, had he earned the high honor which, for the first time, was bestowed upon our Church in this country; proudly do we name him as the first American Cardinal.

He died October 10, 1885, his successor in the See of New York pontificating at his Requiem, and his successor in the college of Cardinals pronouncing his panegyric.

Fortunate witness of his obsequies, never shall I forget the solemnity and the impressiveness of that scene—the burial in the New World, for the first time, of a Prince of Holy Church, which took place in that cathedral, the pride of our country, and whose completion was the crowning work of his life.

PASTORS.

REV. WALTER J. QUARTER.

DECEMBER 25, 1836—NOVEMBER 1, 1839. DIED DECEMBER 15, 1863.

As the second church rises in our parish, a new period also opens in the history of our advancing civilization.

Many recently went down to the depot to see the Dewitt Clinton, with its original pioneer train of three coaches, which made its first regular trip between Albany and Schenectady, August 9, 1831. In the very year in which our second church was completed, (1836), cars began running on the Utica and Schenectady Railroad. No wonder that they were watched with curious interest when we recall the fact that ten years previously there was not a railroad in America.[1]

Did it strike you, that whilst this miniature train looked like a

FATHER QUARTER.

toy in comparison with the train of palatial railway coaches that was on exhibition beside it, yet it meant, in those days, simply a revolution in the mode of traveling; it was the death-knell of the stage-coach and the packet-boat, and was destined to have a remarkable influence on the spread of the Church in these parts.

The opening of the Erie Canal planted the church in this vicinity; the iron horse penetrating the wilderness, and opening up the avenues of civilization, scattered the blessings of the true religion in the remotest parts of our State.

Father Quarter had the happiness of ministering for nearly three years in the church which, at so much sacrifice, he had erected. A link between the old and the new in the history of our parish, he had also the pleasure of welcoming to Utica, during his administration, the old and the new Bishop of the diocese.

Bishop Hughes made his first visit to our parish, and saw, for the first time, our second church, in the summer of 1839.

It was on this visitation of the diocese that he consoled the little flock of converts in Pompey, now numbering sixteen, by saying Mass for them in the private chapel of Colonel Dodge.

Father Quarter had now labored more than six years in Utica — a much longer period of time than any of his predecessors. He

---

[1] Exhibits returning from the World's Columbian Exposition in Chicago.

had opened with wonderful success the second brilliant period in the history of our parish—our childhood days.

It was during these first years of our second church that Queen Victoria, in 1837, ascended the throne of England, and began that long reign which still bids fair to last for many years to come. Martin Van Buren was President of the United States during this portion of Father Quarter's pastorate, and William H. Seward was elected Governor towards its close. It was also during this period, in 1838, that the first regular passages of the Atlantic were made by steamships. And just as his remarkable pastorate was coming to an end, the first train of cars ran between Utica and Syracuse, June 27, 1839, and there was great rejoicing along the whole line. The road ran most of the way through a dense forest—the tracks were laid upon piles without filling between, so that the train seemed to run in the air. And so with a new era dawning upon Utica, and the world, Father Quarter brought to a close his labors amongst us.

He was transferred to St. Mary's Church, New York City. In 1842 he became pastor of St. Peter's Church, Jersey City, which place had at that time a mere skeleton of a church, which Father Quarter finished. He found the Catholics in strife and parties; but in two years he made St. Peter's congregation one of the most pious and prosperous in the United States. Even the Protestants of Jersey City revere his memory to this day.

St. Peter's Church is now in charge of the Jesuit Fathers, and is in a most prosperous condition. There is a large college connected with the church.

On the 28th of November, 1843, Chicago was erected into a diocese comprising the whole State of Illinois—that hallowed ground sanctified by the footsteps of Father Marquette nearly two hundred years before. Father William Quarter, brother of our Father Walter, who had often preached in Utica during his brother's pastorate, was selected as the first Bishop of this important See. Father Walter accompanied his brother to Chicago, and was appointed Vicar-General of the new diocese. In his new field of labor, his zeal increased with the magnitude of the work, and soon the wilderness blossomed like the rose. Churches, hospitals, schools, Religious Orders and Confraternities, a Seminary, a University, collegians, seminarists, professors, all sprung up rapidly, and worked in perfect harmony. The Bishop confided most of the care to Father Walter, and he labored in good earnest until the diocese of Chicago became the centre of Catholic Faith in the West.

The prosperity of the West was in harmony with that of religion. The Bishop found Chicago a village of shanties, and left it a city of palaces. Later days witnessed the erection of a white marble palatial residence, on the Lake front, for the Bishop. But in those days the poverty of the Bishop was so great that we are told that the treasurer often reported the funds as low as six cents. The Bishop was obliged to appeal to his friends in New York. He collected in that city, $2,000, and Father Walter collected $1,600.

It is related that the two brothers possessed about $1,300 when they went to Chicago, and all of it was spent on lots for future churches and convents, and in the erection of churches, schools, and asylums, and in every way forwarding Catholicity.

The value of the property secured and paid for by Bishop Quarter and his brother has been estimated at millions by persons qualified to judge of such matters.

Upon the death of Bishop Quarter, April 10, 1848, Father Walter Quarter became the administrator of the diocese, which responsible position he held until the appointment of Bishop Vandevelde, in 1848, as the second bishop of Chicago.

Father Quarter left Chicago in 1851, and returned to New York. He was for a short time assistant priest at St. Brigid's church, in that city. He was then appointed pastor of St. Lawrence's church, Yorkville.

The old St. Lawrence church on 84th street, near Fifth avenue, now giving way for a more imposing structure, the Academy of the Sisters of Charity, the Catholic schools which he established in this parish, are monuments of his zeal.

This venerable priest crowned with labor and zeal for the glory of God, peacefully expired at the Rectory in Yorkville, at five o'clock, A. M., December 15th, 1863.

Impressive services were held in our second church on the occasion of his " Month's Mind," which took place January 19th,

1864. Solemn High Mass was celebrated by his nephew, Rev. Patrick J. McGlynn, then pastor of Potsdam, N. Y., who had previously been attached to this very church, erected by his revered uncle. There were some twenty priests present in the sanctuary. After the Mass, Father Daly, whose privilege it was to bring to a happy end the glorious work of the second church built by the brilliant priest whose memory they were honoring, preached an eloquent and appropriate discourse on the life and virtues of the deceased priest, who had occupied such a space, not only in the history of the church of this city, where he erected the very church where his " Month's Mind " was being celebrated, but also in every other city where he was called to labor. He spoke of the many priests, many of them now living, who, through the instrumentality of Father Walter, had become zealous laborers in this vineyard, and faithful ministers at the altar. Father Quarter seemed to have inspired them in early youth by his own good and holy example, with a love, a respect, and veneration for the priesthood and the altar, of which he himself was such a worthy minister.

The history of Father Quarter was the history of the young Church of America. He saw it almost in its infancy, struggling against fanaticism, hatred, and persecution, and by his great zeal, his indomitable energy, and his silent charities, he not only won the respect and the love of his own people, but also of those who were opposed to him in matters of faith. Hence his great success in reclaiming sinners, in building churches, schools, and convents, not only in the diocese of New York and Albany, but in the far West, where he labored incessantly with his brother, the first bishop of Chicago.

Wherever he was called to labor, churches and religious institutions seemed to spring up as if by magic; he was the guiding spirit that infused energy into all around him. Every place where he had been stationed during his long life and faithful ministry may be seen monuments of his zeal and labors for the glory of God and the salvation of souls.

Such a life, so full of sacrifices, so unselfish, so exemplary, so everything that we are apt to admire in the lovely character of the faithful priest of God, must command the respect and vener-

ation of every one. But he has gone to his great reward. Peace
to his ashes, honor to his memory!

Who shall say that the true priest of God is soon forgotten,
when so beautiful a tribute is paid to a pastor nearly a quarter of
a century after he had left us?

Father Quarter needs no monument to perpetuate his memory
in this parish. He stands a striking character between the old
and the new. His name is enshrined in the memory of old parishioners, and the story of his zeal and piety will be handed down
to generations yet unborn.

CHILDREN OF THE ROSARY.

On Independence Day.

Hurrah, hurrah, for the dear old flag,
    That waves so glad and free !
Hurrah, hurrah for the stars and stripes,
    For the grand old colors three !
Hurrah for the patriots brave and bold
    Who rang out "LIBERTY !"
Hurrah for the "UNION" of "BLUE AND GREY"
"From the centre to the sea !"
Hurrah for the motto : "IN GOD WE TRUST,"--
And praise and bless—'tis meet and just !

NAN'S TREASURE.

E. A. LEMAN.

N a wretched New York hovel not far from the North River, lived an old woman named Poll Craigen, who bore an evil reputation, and had often been in the hands of the law.

With her lived a girl of thirteen, who believed herself to be the old woman's grandchild.

She went by the name of Nan Craigen, although she knew little of her parents, for the old woman would tell her nothing.

Nan spent most of her time around the steamship wharves, where she was quite a favorite with the numerous boatmen and longshoremen.   She was generally barefoot.

Being under the evil influence of the old woman, Nan thought nothing of being dishonest, and would commit a theft whenever the chance offered itself.

But she was in many ways good at heart.   She was incapable of stealing from anyone poor, although Granny Craigen had tried to make her a thief under all conditions.   At one time she suffered a cruel beating at the hands of the woman rather than rob an old blind beggar of some pennies that were lying exposed before him in his tin cup.

One summer afternoon, when Nan was loitering around the pier of the French line of steamers, she was suddenly attracted to a string of red beads lying near the wheel of a large truck.   Quickly making her way among some horses, she succeeded in gaining possession of them.

"Somebody has dropped them, I reckon," she said to herself, as she examined them.   "Some passenger, I s'pose.   They're dandies."

It cannot be said that Nan felt the spirit of theft while she held the beads, for no thought of that kind came to her.   I cannot say what she would have done had she at the time discovered the loser—whether she would have given them up, or have dishonestly retained them. As the case was, she was innocent of anything wrong.

"They're kinder broken. Guess I'll mend 'em, and make 'em do fer my neck."

Nan seated herself on the stringpiece of the dock, and proceeded to arrange the beads for a necklace. They were broken in several places, the parts being tied together instead of linked.

"What you got there, Nan?" cried the captain of a tugboat alongside the wharf.

"Somebody's julery, I guess. Kin yer tell rubies, Tom?"

"I ought to be able."

"Then look at them. Kin I come aboard?"

"Certainly."

Nan sprang aboard the boat, which was called *Judge Richmond,* and displayed her treasure to the captain.

"Why, those ain't rubies, Nan," laughed he. "They're nothing but common red glass."

"Sure, Tom?"

"Sure as anything. They're funny lookin' things, anyhow. Every ten beads you come to, there's a big one besides."

"They'll look good on my neck, just the same," said Nan. "Have yer got a bit of a string?'

"Yes, in my pocket. Here."

Nan improved the beads somewhat in appearance, and then encircled them about her throat.

"There, Tom. Don't I look fine? When yer up on Fifth Avenue, drop in an' see me."

"You're a great girl, Nan," laughed the captain.

"You bet. I'm goin' home now to Granny Craigen."

Nan took her way to the hovel, and found the old woman seated on a rickety chair, with a pan in her lap, paring some half-decayed vegetables she had obtained from a neighboring grocer's barrel.

"It's time you're back, young lady." said she, sharply, as Nan came in. "Where have you been spending your time, I'd like to know?"

"Round the river."

"The river sees too much of you, I'm thinking. You ought to be at work. Do you know your absence this afternoon has been the means of a serious loss to me?"

"How so?"

" An accident happened outside the soap factory, and a fine crowd gathered. If you had been here, you could have helped me work their pockets."

Nan said nothing. Somehow, she was glad she had been absent to escape such a task.

" What's that on your neck?" asked the old woman, gruffly.

" I found 'em round the pier."

" Come here till I see them."

Nan approached closely, and submitted her neck to a clear view. A fierce scowl overspread Granny Craigen's face.

" Do you know what you've got on you, girl?" she exclaimed bitterly.

" Beads, I reckon. Red ones."

" That miserable thing is a rosary."

" What is that?"

" A string of beads for hypocrites to pray on. Take them off."

" Yer won't take 'em from me, I hope," said Nan, clutching them eagerly. " They look so nice and red on my neck."

" Did you hear what I said? Take them off! The sight of them fills me with hate."

" But they are so pretty! "

The old woman sprang from her chair, and tearing the beads from Nan's neck, flung them to the floor.

" That's where they belong," she said, spitefully. " And they'll end up in a worse place yet."

Nan looked wistfully at her lost treasure, the gleaming red beads appealing to the fondness of her girlish heart. In after years the picture remained vivid in her memory.

That evening Granny Craigen went out, taking the beads with her. Nan watched her closely through a broken window, and saw her cast them into a pail of refuse resting on the curbstone.

" She has thrown 'em away," moaned Nan. " I wonder if I could git 'em again without bein' caught? I'm goin' to try. A rosary! Wonder if it means anything like roses? Guess not, for roses ain't made out of glass. For hyp'crites to pray on! I think I know what that means. What kind do real good people use? Blue ones, I s'pose. If ever I pray on 'em, guess I'll use the hyp'crite kind till I get the others."

It was growing dark. Nan crept cautiously out to the pavement. Looking up and down the street, she made sure that Granny Craigen was not in sight. Then plunging her hand down deep into the waste, she found the beads, and drew them out.

"I bet they won't be seen on my neck again when Granny's 'round," she told herself, cleaning them. "They're the only julery I got, and I'm goin' to be careful of 'em."

The next day Nan became acquainted with the little daughter of a canal boat captain, whose boat was lying at a wharf near the Battery. The little girl's name was Teresa Gale. She lived aboard the boat with her father and mother.

Nan happened to be strolling about the pier when she met Teresa; and a short while after, she was invited aboard the boat, by the child's mother, to have a glass of milk and a sandwich. In the midst of their conversation Nan showed her beads, and told how she had found them. She also asked many questions concerning them, which were ably answered by Teresa and her mother, who were Catholics.

"Somehow, I'd like to pray on 'em myself," said Nan.

"Then do it."

"But it would'nt work with the way I live."

"Why not?"

"I've got to steal if I want to live with Granny Craigen. Since I've found these beads, I begin to hate all I've done, and would like to give up the bad."

"Then why don't you, Nan? Is Granny Craigen really your grandmother?"

"She says she is. But Jim Bradley, who lives next door, says Granny Craigen's a fake. Whether she's my grandmother or not, she ain't a prize."

"She is not fit for you to live with, at any rate."

"I think I'll try and give her the slip."

"If you were dressed well, Nan, and were to become more refined, you would make quite a pretty girl, and a good one, too, with the aid of your beads."

"That's what I'd like to be. I've been a terror, so far."

"Oh, no, you haven't. You've only been under evil influences," said Mrs. Gale. "If Captain Gale, Teresa's papa, would be willing, I'd let you live here on the boat with us. How would you like that?"

"That would be immense."

"I'll ask him about it, and Teresa will help me. He is very kind, and generally lets us do anything we like. Besides, you would be quite useful to us in many little ways."

John Gale readily gave his consent, and Nan, to her delight, took up her home on the *Sally Ann.*

The beads having had no crucifix when Nan found them, kind Mrs. Gale affixed one, and the sight of the cross and its Victim caused Nan to think.

Under the instruction of Teresa's mother, and with the loving companionship of Teresa herself, Nan grew into a beautiful character. She cherished a constant affection for the red beads, and often prayed on them for the unknown who had dropped them on the pier.

SEVEN.

Sister Mary Alphonsus, O. S.

The clock strikes seven ! Oh, think awhile
    What sevenfold grief is here,
And, would you bask in Mary's smile,
    Be kind to Mary's tear.

Mourn for the heart that pined so long,
    The eyes that wept so much ;
And, if unmoved at Jesus' wrong,
    Let Mary's sorrow touch.

'Tis said the hearts so stern and cold
    That doomed the Son to die,
Were strangely softened to behold
    The Mother standing by

THE SOCIAL CLUB.

Henry Coyle.

N Holliston, one of the pleasant towns of New England, there lived a retired merchant named James Stevens, and his wife. They had two children,—Charles, about thirteen, and Alice, eleven years old. They were the companions and friends of their parents, who loved to have them with them, to read to them, talk and walk with them.

Possessed of a modest fortune, the Stevens family lived comfortably; every advantage within reach for their instruction was lavished upon the children, and they spared no pains, thought, nor expense, to provide for them healthful and agreeable amusements.

In order that they might not acquire selfish and disagreeable habits of thought and action, the parents, among other plans for social entertainment, set apart one evening in the week during the winter, on which occasion they invited a number of young people, the children of neighbors, to spend a few pleasant hours with them.

The cottage was surrounded with trees; from their eastern windows they saw hills which, in the summer mornings, were covered with silvery mist, and in the evening glowed like burnished gold where the western sun touched them with his rays. A river ran winding among the hills, and between the house and the river lay green fields.

In the summer time the little garden contained almost every flower common in our country, and Mr. and Mrs. Stevens were enthusiastic botanists. It was often said in the town that what they did not know about trees and flowers " wasn't worth knowing." This taste they tried to cultivate in their children, and in winter there was a large room entirely devoted to the plants which were brought in from the garden.

Another large apartment was called the club-room; a great open fireplace occupied one side of the chamber, and there were materials and instruments for every sort of game.   During the winter the club met at seven o'clock; a half hour was then devoted to some game, and the rest of the evening they listened to an instructive talk or story from Mr. Stevens, who was president of the club.

THE FIRST EVENING.

The first Wednesday evening in November, the Stevens family were preparing for their guests.   Charles was arranging the chairs, but was soon interrupted by the sound of merry laughter and voices outside.   Before the bell rang he was at the door, and in less than ten minutes all the members of the social club had arrived.

The first exercise on the programme for the evening was their game.   The members decided upon " Blind Man's Bluff."   When the half hour was up, Mr. and Mrs. Stevens entered the room; the latter rang a bell to call the meeting to order.   The members took their seats in a circle before the fireplace, with the president in the centre; and then Willie Conners, the secretary, called the roll.

" What game did you play this evening? " asked the president.

" Blind Man's Bluff."

" A very ancient game; it was invented by the Greeks; the Italians call it the ' Blind Cat.'   Gustavus, the great king of Sweden, often took pleasure in playing this game with the officers of his army.   There is another way of playing this game, which is new to you, I think.   No one runs but the blind man, who is forbidden to make use of his hands except to hold a stick or a handkerchief, of which some one of the company seizes one end, after another player has spoken; but it is not generally the one whose voice is heard who is holding the stick or handkerchief."

" We must play that some evening," said Charles.

" Our first talk will be on the study of botany," said Mr. Stevens.
" The garden, the field, the forest, and indeed all nature is full of entertainment and instruction to the person who studies the habits and varieties of plants, trees, insects, birds, and animals.   What shall be our first subject? "

No one answered, and after a few moments' silence, Mrs. Stevens suggested a tree.

7

" Very well, then," said Mr. Stevens; " let us imagine that the trunk and branches are transparent. We see in the centre of the trunk and every branch a slender column of pith. What is pith?"

" Pith is the soft and spongy substance in the centre of the stems of plants and trees," answered the secretary.

" Around this pith," continued Mr. Stevens, " there is a circle of heart-wood; next comes new wood, which is called alburnum. This wood abounds with veins for the passage of the sap, which we observe is passing up, on the principle of capillary attraction, till a portion of it reaches the extremity of every leaf."

Just then the president happened to look toward the right, and observed George Roach holding his hand to his face.

" What's the matter, George? Got a toothache?"

" No, sir," he replied; " but that last nut was too hard for my teeth to crack."

" What nut?"

" Oh, er—cap—capi—something or other; a regular jaw-break-er!" answered George, who was still in the primary school.

" Oh, I see," said the president, with a smile; " capillary attrac-tion was too much for you. Who can tell me what it means?"

" Capillary attraction," answered Mrs. Stevens, " is the power which causes water to be sucked up by sugar, sponges, and other like substances."

" The leaves are furnished with small pores for evaporation and exhalation; through these pores a part of the sap escapes; if our eyes were microscopic, we should see a tiny thread of gas con-stantly resting over every leaf; the sap returns again to the root, but not in the channel in which it ascended. How did it ascend?"

" Through the new wood," said Alice.

" Right, but its homeward passage is through the bark. As it proceeds it is constantly robbed by little suckers along the sides, secreting from it the various substances which they require to form the oils, resins, and gums."

" I should think there would be very little sap left by the time it reaches the roots," observed George.

" This does not matter, for the extremity of each fibre in a root is furnished with a little sponge, with which it sucks up the juices from the earth. Let us turn again to the leaves. We have no-ticed a mass of vapor rising from the upper surface of each, and we may also see a volume of gas pressing into the pores on the under surface of the leaf; this is carbonic acid gas."

" Is that like the gas that gives us light?" asked little Mary Williams.

" Oh, no," replied Mr. Stevens; "carbonic acid gas is much heavier, and would extinguish our gas. It is death to breathe it, and it is this gas which causes the explosions in mines. What favorite beverage is composed of this gas?"

" Soda-water," replied Mrs. Stevens, as no one else answered.

" Yes; this gas is very heavy, and rests close to the earth; for this reason the lower surface of the leaf is adapted to absorb it. Part of the carbon goes to form the substance of the leaf, and part evaporates during the night through the pores on the upper surface of the leaf. Why should plants never be allowed in our sleeping rooms?"

" Because the carbon, which is poisonous, evaporates during the night," answered Willie.

" Yes; through the day every leaf is busy throwing off oxygen, a kind of gas, which it is constantly receiving from the sap, but in the night this order is reversed—they absorb oxygen, and throw off carbon. Every autumn we see the leaves wither and fall; why do they fall?"

" Because they are worn out with their summer work, and die of old age," Charles suggested.

" No, you are wrong; they die of starvation. Who can tell me what silex is?"

" Sand, stone, and other hard substances," replied John Wilson, who was about to enter the High School.

" Well, every soil contains more or less of this silex; this earth will not dissolve in liquid, and it rises with the sap in small particles; these accumulate at the base of the stalk, obstruct the progress of the sap, and thus deprive the leaf of its necessary nourishment."

" A quarter to ten," interrupted Mrs. Stevens.

" Why, so it is," said the president; " I now make a motion to adjourn the meeting to next Wednesday evening."

" Second the motion," said George, and the members, headed by the president and Mrs. Stevens, filed into the dining-room, where some light refreshments were served. Promptly at ten o'clock the last guest took his departure, and the Stevens family, after their usual devotions, retired for the night.

Plump and rosy, bright and sweet,
Why, 'twas made to love and kiss.

Now and Then.

Apples ripe and rosy red,
  Bushel basket brimming o'er,
Kit and Ben with careful tread
  Carry to the farm house door.
Apples—they were made to eat—
  But an apple, just like this,
Plump and rosy, bright and sweet,
  Why, 'twas made to love and kiss.

Darling baby, happy, fair!
  Shall you ever be as now,
Shielded with a loving care?
  Morn and eve we, prayerful, bow,
Fearful we that grief may fall.
  Faith our question answers: "Yes,
One there is who guides through all;
  God will ever shield and bless!"

AN ANGEL TEACHER.

SECOND ROSARY MYSTERY.

And now, Elizabeth to greet,
She treads Judea's hills;
Her soul doth magnify the Lord,
Her heart with rapture thrills.
    —*Mary A. Mannix.*

HE Visitation, dear Angel! tell me how to meditate upon that," pleaded the child who so loved the Angels, as her head bent over her folded hands which fondly held her beads.

In a moment the beautiful thought came in the Angel Guardian's whisper, and ever after the child could see this lovely picture in her young mind when she said the Our Father, the ten Hail Marys, and the Glory be to the Father, of the Second Joyful Mystery, the Visitation:—

Dear Little Child :- The second mystery of the Rosary is called the Visitation, because the Blessed Virgin, our dear Lady, went to visit her cousin St. Elizabeth, to bring to her a great blessing in the name of God. You know, dear child, what is meant by a visit. Friends call on one another, and are pleased to welcome those who come to see them. This is what is meant by a visit.

But the visit of the Blessed Virgin to St. Elizabeth was a holy and heavenly visit, because she went in God's name, and to carry graces and blessings to St. John the Baptist, the son of St. Elizabeth. This holy child was to grow up and become the great speaker for our Saviour before the people. Therefore, he was blessed by our dear Lord through the words of His holy Mother. And our Lady said to St. Elizabeth that ever afterwards all nations would call her Blessed. Therefore, dear little child, you speak of your Mother in Heaven as the Blessed Virgin.

Think of these things while you say the decade of the second joyful mystery, and ask that you may be blessed by having our Lord come to your heart, and remain with you by His loving grace. Pray also that you may make good visits to friends, to the sick and the poor, who are so happy when any one comes to them to help them. If you do this, dear little child, God will bless you, and you will be God's dear messenger to bring blessings to others.

Puzzles.

ANSWERS TO MAY PUZZLES.

I. Rome,—t-ome; c-ome; d-ome; s-ome; h-ome.
II. Waterloo; Marblehead; Palestine; Flint; La Salle; Defiance.

The following have won the prize, giving correct answers to all the questions in May ROSARY MAGAZINE:

Henry Firth, John A. Judge, Bessie Edel, Julia Casey, Margaret Wallace, Harrietta R. Riston, Maggie Griffin, Mary A. O'Reilly, Ida E. Grossman, Thomas Bierne, Grace H Maleady, Eddie Wilson, J W. Connolly, Alice Mannix, Mary Cavanaugh, Rosa Cavanaugh, John K. Monahan, Minnie E. Crosby, Mamie Manning, C. Louise Parsons.

Special mention is here made of the answers given by Henry Firth, in which not only the names of places were mentioned, but their situation.

The following solved all but one question:

E. Morgan Murphy, Mary A. O'Neill, Mary Louise McSwyny, Katie G. Mulligan, Helen V. Branley, John J. Cummings, Harold Hirst, Kathryn P. Cassion, Sarah R. McCullagh, James Aloysius Murphy, Mary A. Griffin, Richard Carey, Joseph O. Barrett, Eleanor McKernan, Edward Dooley, Mae Handley, Mary Oates, Della J. O'Dea.

The following solved a less number; all gave proof of careful study:

Agnes K. Prendergast, Mary Ravenscroft, Maggie E. Kane, Agnes Smith, B. Barnes, Marie Flesher, Stasia Somers, Michael S. Ripple, Lizzie F. Reilly, Joseph J. Flynn, Katie Smith, George J. Lawrence, Daniel William.

PUZZLES FOR JULY.

HIDDEN PLACES, ANIMALS, INSECTS, FISHES, VEGETABLES, AND PARTS OF THE BODY.

(Following each other in many places will be found letters spelling some of the above.)

1. The electro you want is here.

2. Whenever I escape, let me assure you of my fidelity.

3. Disturb, O stony heart, his rest! Rather let him sleep in peace.

4. He was pushed into the wheel; miraculously was he saved.

5. This gem O use always. It will be a never-failing souvenir.

A prize will be given to everyone solving the above puzzles.

CONDITIONS FOR BECOMING SOLDIERS IN THE ANGELIC WARFARE.

1. Send your full names to be enrolled.

2. Wear around the waist under the clothing, the little white linen girdle that must be blessed by a Dominican priest, or by a priest who has permission from the Dominicans.

3. Strive in every way to be pure in soul and body.

4. If you cannot buy the girdles in your neighborhood AQUINAS will buy them for you. When you write enclose ten cents to cover the expense of the girdle, leaflet, and postage. You may send stamps. But let no child hold back from becoming a Soldier in the Angelic Warfare on account of poverty. To those who cannot pay we shall send all free.

5. Address your letters to AQUINAS, ROSARY OFFICE, 871 LEXINGTON AVENUE, NEW YORK CITY.

EDITORIAL

The month of July, sacred by the spirit and piety of the Church, to the Precious Blood of our Blessed Redeemer, appeals tenderly and pleadingly to the clients of our Lady, especially in the sorrowful mysteries of the Beads. Dear Rosarians, be mindful of those sacred drops that ran so freely and generously down, in bitterest pain and sorrow, that we might be saved. Count them we cannot, but sadly and lovingly we can dwell on their spilling while we take into our sinful hearts some understanding of their preciousness, since one drop alone could have washed the guilt of the human race away. From the day of circumcision our memory can reach out to Gethsemane's dark hour, when the full flood came of that blessed Tide that finally rose to the mountain top whence a world's sins were swept away, in the outpoured Blood of our Blessed Redeemer. Following in the sorrowful way, we may accompany our suffering Lord while agony of soul, and scourge and thorn and heavy cross, and great, sharp nails make unnumbered issues for that saving stream that rushes forth with a holy gladness because sinners will be saved. And for very impatience of its eager love, and that its joy in sorrow might be full in its giving, when no more would remain, the sure courier of the soldier's lance found the heart fountain, and drained it dry of that most sweet and precious reserve that came forth as a last and solemn witness that Love could do no more. May the dear, blessed, sacred drops of our loving Lord's redeeming Blood, fall upon us, upon our up-turned, pleading faces, and upon our bowed, guilty heads. And may our Blessed Queen of the Rosary teach us, as she only can teach, the value of that precious and absolving shower wherewith our sins have been washed away. This is the study of the sorrowful mysteries of the Beads. May their fullest grace be the gift of every Rosarian.

With a fairly wide experience, and with many peculiar opportunities of observation, we have met few Catholic laymen willing to draw their check in behalf of the propaganda of Catholic literature in Catholic homes; but we have met hundreds whose purse is yearly open, and widely, for the campaign fund of their political party. "Spread the light" of Democracy, Republicanism; make popular the doctrine of free silver or of a gold standard, or of bi-metallism; advocate free trade or a high tariff. But let the Faith stand or fall; let school and Church yield little fruit because home is not prepared; let the present generation live indifferent to their precious gifts, and careless of the generation to come; let our brethren, our fellow-citizens, sit in darkness and in the shadow of death—nevertheless, not a dollar for the campaign fund of this vital cause of the Church! Such, we might say, describes the attitude and disposition of many Catholics to-day. Is it not sad? Good reader, how do you stand? What are you doing? Are you even interested? Are you active as means and circumstances permit? Be up and doing, for it is a most worthy cause, and help is needed "all along the line."

The second joyful mystery of the Rosary commemorates the visit of our Lady to St. Elizabeth. On this happy occasion John the Baptist was sanctified by the grace of our Lord, through the word of our Lady, who proclaimed, in her canticle of glory to God, that henceforth all generations would call her blessed. To fulfil this prophecy is our glad privilege, and in no way more lovingly than in the counting of her Beads. May our Lady visit all our Rosarians on this her beautiful feast of the Visitation, in graces and blessings needed. And may our Rosarians feel the inspiration of holy charity, after the example of our Blessed Mother, in the visits they may make to friends and acquaintances. This is a practical lesson of the second joyful mystery of the Beads.

Willingly and hopefully we appeal to the charity of our readers in behalf of the Japanese missions, and especially for the leper settlement near Kumamoto. Father J. M. Corre, the missionary apostolic who is stationed at Kumamoto, has sent out a piteous statement telling of the sufferings of the unhappy victims of leprosy's dread scourge. We may not give the details. Our readers are sufficiently familiar with this disease to know something of its ravages. Father Corre wishes to build a hospital for these poor victims, and therefore, he turns to the charity of Catholics in this country, from whom he hopes to receive material aid. We do not often present appeals to our friends, nor do we make THE ROSARY MAGAZINE a bureau for indiscriminate collections; but we know how deserving is this cause. Therefore, we commend it earnestly and tenderly to our readers, and we hope that many will respond. Offerings may be sent directly to Father Corre, or to the Father Treasurer, St. John's Seminary, Brighton, Boston, Mass.

We cannot rejoice because new aspirants for literary honors are making their salutatory acknowledgments, in the name of religion, to a long-suffering public, North, East, South, and West. Previously and plainly we have declared that mere number is not what we need; nor are we improving because "organs" are multiplying. With grim satisfaction we mentally record the demise of some that die, not too young, though charity for their mourning friends withholds a public expression of our rejoicing in the shape of an obituary notice.

Frequently, during the past year, we have been invited to exchange with some sheet that springs forth absolutely without promise of any good. We cheerfully give away many copies of THE ROSARY MAGAZINE, where charity calls, but exchanging with mushroom productions is equivalent to encouraging what ought never to exist. Intruding themselves on clergy and people, such sheets ought to be gently, if not promptly, suppressed, by refusing to them any recognition. Left to themselves they generally find an early, if not honored, grave. Henceforth; in justice to our friends and to the cause of

genuine literature, we shall abstain from noticing a certain class of hybrid publications that are a stumbling-block in the way of progress.

In the newspaper and magazine of today, a valuable, if not essential, adjunct is the advertising section. This department has ceased to be a mere catalogue of articles and prices; it has a literature and illustrations peculiarly its own, the skill and finish of which give just meaning to "art in advertising." While the main purpose of the advertiser has not changed, his methods have undergone a complete transformation. In his effort to come into business relationship with the purchasing public, the man who has aught to introduce or to sell, adopts every lawful (and sometimes, unlawful) means to present his case in the most attractive way. Thus an immense and constantly developing industry, with literary and artistic accompaniments, has come into existence, and apparently it is prepared to stay. In these circumstances our position as Catholics needs to be emphasized. Far be it from us to interject religion into mere business; but we raise the question advisedly, and because the matter has been practically determined for us. A large amount of money is spent by our people in business, for which, largely through our own fault, we receive no recognition in the way of advertising. Different explanations may be given of this fact. Our notion is that many of our people are not aware of the value of advertising; its importance is not appreciated. To some it is a meaningless thing; the presence of the advertising pages is regarded as an intrusion which they ignorantly resent. Of course, such individuals are few. The bulk of our people, however, while they do not take such a stupid view, can receive with profit, some instructions on this point. While no question of religion should ever be allowed to enter into mere buying and selling, the claims of religious periodicals must not be ignored as mediums through which the merchant or tradesman may address the people of any particular denomination. In this view of the case two difficulties confront Catholics. We are charged with the crime of poverty, and where that does not hold, many say that we are not a reading class. The second difficulty arises from the multitude of petty sheets and magazinettes serving neither literature nor devotion, and adding no credit to the Catholic name, but notwithstanding, vigorously claiming a share of the advertising of our leading business men. Considering the views held by some of these, and knowing how they are beset by paltry sheets clamoring for recognition that they do not deserve, we are not surprised at the position taken by such advertisers. When, however, on just and truthful grounds a reputable Catholic publication is accepted, and receives a share of the enormous advertising business of the country, disappointment is, at times, loudly expressed. It is not that Catholics do not spend money, not that they do not observe the advertisements, not that they are not influenced by them, but it is because, in many instances, they fail to show their interest in the deserving Catholic magazine or paper, they neglect to make their purchases known to the sellers as a result of advertising in a Catholic periodical. With many non-Catholic publications the case is different. The disunion that marks them in doctrine has a counterpoise in their united front in certain lines of Church work. The various denominations have their respective organs to which they give a somewhat steady support. We are one in Faith, but manifold in works. And so far as papers and magazines are concerned, every man with sufficient intelligence to form a judgment is convinced that quality is sacrificed to quantity, and mere numbers, though they be only dwarfed sicklings, are considered signs of a healthy growth. This condition honest men openly denounce. And though we know " it hurts "—the weaklings, that ought to be hurt,—we shall continue to warn our people against them. As a practical conclusion to this brief article, we ask our readers to consult the advertising department of THE ROSARY MAGAZINE. We are careful in its preparation, though we bow neither to prudery nor fanaticism. We can, therefore, commend to our readers the various business announcements that appear in our pages; and we ask our friends to remember that the financial benefit of revenue derived from such sources, is devoted to the welfare of THE ROSARY MAGAZINE, and, therefore, to the interests and advantage of our readers.

QUESTIONS AND ANSWERS.

SUBSCRIBER.—*May I offer the Beads for the intentions of the League of the Sacred Heart, or for any other intentions?* Certainly; the offering of your prayers in the Beads is of your own choice. We here, however, take occasion to commend to all our readers the special intentions that are published monthly. We trust that they are remembered by our Rosarians.

PHILADELPHIA.—*Can the Dominican indulgences be attached to the seven decade beads, such as worn by Franciscan Sisters?* No; beads must be of five, ten, or fifteen decades, in order to have the Dominican blessing given to them. This is explicitly stated in the faculties granted by the Master-General of the Dominicans.

REVEREND.—*Have I, by my ordinary faculties, the power to bless Rosary rings?* The wearing of gold or silver rings, with ten little balls or knobs cut in them, was at one time the practice of some pious people. By a decree of the Sacred Congregation of Indulgences, June 20, 1836, it was forbidden to bless such rings with the Rosary blessing. Our answer to a Philadelphia subscriber, taken in connection with the citation of this decree of the Congregation, disposes of all beads or pious ornaments made in the form of a decade, or ring, as not suitable for receiving the Rosary blessing.

BOOKS.

From Longmans, Green & Co., London and New York, we have received A MEMOIR OF MOTHER FRANCES RAPHAEL, O. S. D. (Augusta Theodosia Drane), by Father Bertrand Wilberforce, O. P. The " literary world " may not welcome this volume. We shall not be surprised if it be passed over in silence by many who keep abreast of much of the transitory trash that finds ready sale in the shops; but we feel safe in saying that this is not an ordinary volume, for it is the story of an extraordinary life. The name of the author of " Christian Schools and Scholars " will live in true English literature when the sifting process of time will have relegated to oblivion much that lives and lies to-day as successful books. In THE ROS-

ARY MAGAZINE for September and October, 1894, we gave a brief sketch of Mother Drane's life, with a complete list of her various published works. Father Wilberforce's Memoir is thorough, and he assures us that he has, so far as possible, allowed Mother Drane to speak in her own words. The addition by the compiler, of some of her spiritual notes and letters, increases the value of this most interesting biography. Readers of all classes will find in the study of Mother Drane's life a source of spiritual and intellectual delight. With great satisfaction we introduce this work to our friends.

From Benziger Brothers, New York, we have received ON THE ROAD TO ROME, by William Richards. This is the story, pleasantly told, of the conversion of Mr. Richards and his brother. The reading of such a book by Catholics will broaden their view as to the difficulties of Protestantism, while their sympathies must deepen for those who are " on the road to Rome." The appearance of the lecture at the present time is in line with our Holy Father's appeal for union. We trust that many non-Catholics will read this volume, which is a dainty piece of book-making very creditable to the publishers.

From the Pilot Publishing Company, Boston, we have received A LADY AND HER LETTERS, by Katherine E. Conway. To all our young girl readers we recommend this pretty little book. We advise them to read it, because it is worthy. They will receive from it much solid and useful information for their guidance in life, on points where many err. It is a practical book, and they advised well who counselled its compilation.

From John Murphy & Co., Baltimore, we have received LOYALTY TO CHURCH AND STATE, by His Excellency, Francis Archbishop Satolli, Apostolic Delegate. This collection of speeches and addresses delivered by Monsignor Satolli has been edited by Father Slattery of Epiphany College. His Eminence, Cardinal Gibbons, has written the preface. It was a happy thought that suggested this publication. Many will be glad to have in compact and convenient form the various utterances of the Apostolic Delegate on the many interesting subjects he has discussed since coming to the United States. The publishers have made a

good book, and we commend it to all our readers.

We have received from D. & J. Sadlier, New York, a copy of a new edition of THE ORPHAN SISTERS, by Mary I. Hoffman. This novel is up to the high moral standard displayed by Miss Hoffman in "Agnes Hilton," "Alice Murray," and her many other writings. There is, besides, a true Catholic spirit, a depth of thought upon theological subjects, and the indication of a breadth of reading shown by the author, very satisfactory to find in these times of the "latter-day" novel. There are touches of pathos throughout the book, just sufficient to harmonize with the happy termination of the difficulties which beset the earlier years of the heroines of the title. Miss Hoffman is to be sincerely congratulated upon the wholesomeness of her writings, and may rest under that assurance, which must always be consoling to the writer, particularly of fiction, that those who read the "Orphan Sisters" will, outside of mere entertainment, be morally benefited.

We have received from Benziger Brothers, New York, the first volume of OUTLINES OF DOGMATIC THEOLOGY, by Father Sylvester Joseph Hunter, of the English Province of the Society of Jesus. Two volumes are to follow this one, the set, when complete, to cover the matter embraced in a three years' Seminary course. The work is intended to introduce the laity into the Province of theology, from which hitherto many have been barred, owing to the fact that theological works have always been written in the Latin language. Educated laymen should not fail to secure a copy of this work. Its exposition of the dogmas of theology is so clear and orderly that a careful reading will doubtless bring to them an accurate and comprehensive knowledge of matters which hitherto have been perhaps too vague and shadowy. They will also find the Appendix, containing as it does an explanation of the scholastic method of carrying on disputations, very instructive and interesting. In the preface, the author touches upon an idea, which cannot be too strongly emphasized, namely, the necessity of clear exposition in controversy. Too often is this neglected. If disputants carefully define their positions and join issues squarely, there will be less beating of the air, and a speedier adjustment of differences.

MAGAZINES.

The *Revue Thomiste* for May comes with its usual number of interesting and instructive articles. Scriptural scholars will read with pleasure, and with profit, Father Brosse's article on the "Site of Eden; or, Where was the Garden of Paradise Situated?"

To those who delight in theological discussions, we recommend Father Guillermin's patient criticism of his "former companion in arms," now the Abbé Gayraud. The subject of the discussion —the relation of God's action to His own foreknowledge, and to the free will of man—is an old one. M. Gayraud tried to throw new light on it by giving a new interpretation of certain texts from the writings of St. Thomas Aquinas. Those who try to be too subtle are sometimes lost in the nothingness of their own distinctions. God's causality—the decree or determination to do something in time—is not the *reason why* God is a subject capable of knowing; but it is the *reason why* He knows, before they occur, those things which He has determined to cause in time: and they will occur just as He has decreed that they shall take place, *e. g.*, by the free act of man. This is the traditional interpretation of St. Thomas' words, and the Abbé Gayraud cannot change it.

Amongst the questions treated in other able articles, we note the following: the distinction between man and brutes; socialism; the problem of knowledge, as it is discussed in English and American Reviews.

Form is the name of a neat little monthly recently launched by Dempsey and Carroll, the art stationers of Union Square, New York. *Form's* scope will be peculiarly social, but its work promises to be highly artistic, as well as literary. As an authority on social etiquette, *Form* opens its columns to all questions sent to it, and correct answers will be given. We are assured by the publishers that *Form* will be conducted on strictly high class lines, and that nothing objectionable in any manner will be admitted to its pages. As a guide to etiquette in its many pleasant phases, we commend to our readers *Form*.

In the quarterly *Scottish Review* for April there is a fine paper on that modern abomination, "the woman question," the appropriate heading of which is "The Malcontent Woman." It is a sweeping article, and yet reverent and tender for true women, while unsparing of the modern termigants who disgrace their sex.

The Messenger of the Sacred Heart for June might be called a Eucharistic number. We mention especially the interesting and richly illustrated articles: "Corpus Christi in Quito;" "A Sanctuary of Reparation;" and "A Eucharistic Art Museum," the last being an account of the splendid collection of vessels, emblems, etc., in honor of the Blessed Sacrament, gathered at Paray-le-Monial.

In *The Forum* for June, Justin McCarthy gives his estimate of Joseph Chamberlain. The study is just, and because it is just it is practically an exposé of the true character of this distinguished political Judas. Mr. McCarthy presents all the good points, but the former Radical of Birmingham can take little comfort from this public discussion of his character. "The Only Cure for Slums" renews the great tenement-house question. It is a good article, and earnestly suggests the English method, adopted in 1890. The recent tenement-house commission in New York offered some salutary advice in favor of the improvement of the home conditions of the poor, from which we hope for practical results. Other articles in the June *Forum* that we wish to mention, are, "Why the American Voice is Bad;" "The Great Libraries of the United States;" "The Free Silver Argument," with answer: "The Grotesque Fallacies of Free Silver;" and several papers on educational questions.

The Catholic Reading Circle Review, for May and June, contains full particulars of the Plattsburg and Madison Summer Schools, the programmes of both being given in detail. The former will open its fourth session on July 6th, and close on August 19th. The Madison School will open on July 14th, and close on August 4th. We hope that both Schools will be generously encouraged, and that all our readers who can visit one or the other will endeavor to attend. In the May number of Mr. Mosher's

Review, we find an interesting report of the meeting recently held under the direction of Archbishop Janssens of New Orleans, for the inauguration of a Winter School in the South, on the lines of the Catholic Summer Schools of the North. Father Mullany of Syracuse was active in the movement, and made many valuable suggestions. It is good to see this zealous work growing, and so we shall look for still further particulars and tidings of the success of the Winter School of the South.

The current (April) number of *The American Catholic Quarterly* is of particular interest to the general reader, because of a clear, convincing paper on "Maryland or Rhode Island—Lord Baltimore or Roger Williams—which was First?" Doctor Richard H. Clarke answers this question satisfactorily; he proves that the first great work in behalf of freedom of conscience as recognized by government, belongs to Lord Baltimore and the Catholics. Full credit is given to Roger Williams, to whom honor is assuredly due, but Lord Baltimore preceded him. Doctor Clarke's article is a valuable bit of history. "Italy's Reconciliation with the Holy See;" "Indifferentism;" "Indian Bibliographies;" "The Correlation of Order and Jurisdiction;" and Father Freeman's always agreeable "scientific chronicle" (the present number on petroleum) are other features of this issue of the *Quarterly*. We are glad to learn that a reduction in the subscription price of this periodical is seriously considered.

The library question is at present receiving earnest and generous treatment. In *Blackwood's Edinburgh Magazine* for June, we find an account of the famous Cottonian Library. In *The Nineteenth Century* for June, there is a pleasant and instructive paper on "The Gentle Art of Book Lending," from which we make, with satisfaction, one extract: "A Society for the Prevention of Cruelty to Books would find me a ready supporter, and I am far from convinced as to the immorality of rescuing, by theft, a treasure from the clutches of a brutal owner, if by so doing I could give it a good and comfortable home." In *The Century* for June, the artistic aspects and the ideals and working conditions of the New Public Library in Boston, are freely discussed, while on another line, a writer in *The New England Magazine* for May,

C. Howard Walker gives a minute, interesting, and discriminating account of this library. The description of the architectural points and beauties is particularly attractive because of its clearness, and the absence of technical terms, the bugbear of the uninitiated. The building was planned by Messrs. McKin, Mead, and White, who at the outset had a difficult task, from the fact that piles had already been driven for the foundation of a building of a different plan, and because the ground was treacherous. "After these difficulties were overcome," writes Mr. Walker, "the problem of choice of architectural style had next to be decided. * * * The first conception of the front was suggested by the design of the Bibliothèque Ste. Geneviève in Paris; but the two buildings have only this in common, that the chief motive in each is that of a noble arcade in the second story, and that tablets containing the names of writers, painters, architects, and others, appear in corresponding positions in each." The description of the inside harmonizes in magnificence with that of the outside. The grand stairway, vestibules, galleries, delivery room, waiting room, are worthy of the cause in which they are built. Of Bates Hall, of which so much is spoken and written, Mr. Walker says: "The hall is cool, in color gray, and, without rich contrast, with the single exception of two doorways, which in consequence seem imported, and not indigenous, or part of the design, excepting in form. Perhaps this was intentional. The ceiling, noble as it is, would gain much by richer color, and by gold—and with the wall panels filled with decorative painting, such color of the ceiling will be necessary." In the waiting room is to be placed Edwin Abbey's famous frieze of the legend of the Holy Grail, of which a portion was exhibited at the Chicago Exposition. "When this frieze is placed," says Mr. Walker, "Boston will possess a room which can be compared favorably with many of the rooms abroad which form meccas for the students of art." The capacity of the library is 2,000,000 volumes, and the methods for cataloguing these, supplying them to applicants and returning them to their places, are the most rapid and improved. To quote Mr. Walker again: "The library is worthy of its purpose. It is as great an object lesson in dignified monumental architecture as were the finest buildings at the World's Fair, and it is a permanent object lesson. It is one of the few examples in this country, which, as years go by, will prove to the people that to obtain the best at some great expenditure is worth the cost, and it is to be hoped that it is the first of a number of equally notable buildings."

"The Execution of Mary E. Surratt," by Charles S. O'Neill, is the title of a paper in *Donahoe's Magazine* for June that will bring light to the minds of many on the unhappy ending of a woman who died innocent of the crime with which she was charged. At least the testimony against her would not convict her to-day, and men who have carefully studied her case do not hesitate to speak of her "judicial murder."

Students of Irish political history will find in *The Fortnightly Review* for May a thoughtful and suggestive article on "The Future of Irish Politics." It will bear careful reading.

To all who have "caught the Napoleonic fever," as evidenced by the magazine notoriety which the great soldier has achieved, we commend "The Dream of Bonaparte—A Napoleonic Study," by the Reverend William Poland, S. J., in the June number of *The Catholic Reading Circle Review.*

The opening paper of the June *Century* is "The Comédie Française at Orange," by Thomas A. Janvier. It is an interesting sketch of the theatre at Orange, which was founded by the Romans, during the time of Marcus Aurelius, but "abandoned by them when the Northern barbarians overran the land." This grand theatre seems now, after repeated attempts, "destined to arise reanimate from its ruins." Last August, under the patronage of the government, "Œdipus" and "Antigone" were presented. The illustrations of the article, which are very fine, are after the drawings of Louis Loeb. Mr. William M. Sloane's fine life of Napoleon continues on its career.

"Life and Work in the Powder Mills," by Cleveland Moffett, is a pleasantly written sketch in the June number of *McClure's Magazine*, of the great Delaware mills of the du Ponts. The paper is a most interesting one, being a history of the work, lives, and in some instances tragic deaths, of this truly wonderful family, the du Ponts. "Napoleon's Relations with the United States" is a supplementary paper to his life, by Ida M. Tarbell. "Before Grant Won His Stars," is a sketchy paper about the early life of "the silent man," by E. J. Edwards, which, by the way, goes to show that Grant's noted taciturnity was rather a matter of policy and prudence than natural inclination.

In *Scribner's* for June, Mr. Robert Grant discusses the use of time, in continuation of his series on the art of living. Readers naturally look for help to writers "with a purpose." In this case we question the value of the assistance they will receive. Mr. Grant defines the best modern living as "a happy compromise in the aims and actions of the individual between self-interest and altruism. If one seeks to illustrate this definition by example, it is desirable, in the first place, to eliminate the individuals in the community whose use of time is so completely out of keeping with this doctrine, that it is not worth while to consider them." Among these he reckons, "murderers, forgers, criminals of all kinds, drunkards, mere pleasure seekers, idle gentlemen," and "on the same theory we must exclude monks, deliberate celibates, nuns, and all fanatical or eccentric persons whose conduct of life, however serviceable in itself as a leaven, or an exception, could not be generally imitated without disaster to society." It is always taking an unfair advantage to use a single quotation for the condemnation of a whole book or article; so to avoid this injustice, it is well to state that we do not believe that it is Mr. Grant's intention to put nuns and priests upon a plane with murderers and forgers, though the quotation might lead one to think this. They are obviously, however, upon the list with "fanatical and eccentric persons." To contest this point with him would be like trying to prove that blue was blue to a man who was colorblind. It is simply impossible for Mr. Grant to enter into, or realize the motive in the lives of Religious. To transpose one of his own sayings to suit the purpose, it is evident that he is so "in the thick of modern life," that he needs "more time in which to think," and so cultivate his "spiritual nature," which part of his mentality is evidently in a blunted condition. In regard to the general tone and style of Mr. Grant's paper, it is strictly colorless and neutral. This is Mr. Grant's strong point. He is nothing if not neutral; for this reason we acquit him of understandingly making an assertion which necessitated positiveness of thought, though we deplore the narrowness which appears upon its face.

Beginning with Philip G. Hubert's paper, "The Wheel of To-day," the bicycle in all its phases—athletic, social, and hygienic—is discussed in several papers by different writers well posted and enthusiastic upon the subject.

"Chicago Before the Fire, After the Fire, and To-day," by Melville E. Stone, is a graphic account of what Mr. Stone calls, "the most romantic and dramatic history of modern times."

A writer in *The Nineteenth Century* for May exposes the infamous dealings of Russia with Georgia. The outraged treaties between these countries are set forth, to the shame and disgrace of the Northern Bear.

A delightful paper in the same number is "A May-Queen Festival, with Letters from Mr. Ruskin." We also mention "The Ancient English Office of the Easter Sepulchre;" and "Women in French Prisons," articles of much interest. The paper on Joan of Arc would have more value if it had less bitterness. The writer would profit by reading "Joan of Arc Before the Bar of the Church," as published in THE ROSARY MAGAZINE for April and May.

In *The American Magazine of Civics* for June, "Woman's Part in Political Sins" is a sharp arraignment, by a woman, of the noisy and annoying political women. It is refreshing to read a true woman's word in protest against the false position into which her indiscreet sisters would thrust her. "The Coffee-House as a Rival of the Saloon" is an encouraging account of successful work on behalf of temperance.

St. Luke's Magazine for May concludes the account of the horrible death of Luther to which we referred in our May- number. No man reading these articles can reasonably deny that the unhappy end of the Reformer came by suicide. This young magazine is doing creditable work for Catholic literature.

The Chautauquan for June publishes a sketch of *The Sun's* great editor, Mr. Charles A. Dana. Commending the scholarly work of *The Sun* and its fidelity to the best newspaper standards, the writer in *The Chautauquan* lashes the sensationalism of modern journalism as encouraged and abetted by some New York papers. The following extract needs no comment further than the expression of our hearty agreement:

"This era of *opera bouffe* journalism reached its full efflorescence in the Sunday newspaper, which is now an iridescent dream of Bedlam and chaos. The first and most obvious result of this masterful endeavor to fit the newspaper to every order of imbecility was the disappearance of all form or system in the makeup of the sheets. Confusion rampaged on every page. Advertisements grew to the proportion of posters and imitated their audacity. They found their way into the reading page and cut the most interesting bit of news through the middle. The reader was asked, in deference to the advertiser of soap or liverpads, to go wandering through the n azes of the other pages for the conclusion. Sunday journalism in this stream of inflammatory and disjunctive commonplace began to swell like a drowned dog. The people on the Sabbath were presented with oceans of ink and forests of cuts. They bought their Sunday paper in bulk—forty, fifty pages, and of course they did not read it. To do that would be well-nigh a physical and wholly an intellectual impossibility. What they did do was to hunt with exasperation and wonder, through the jumble of advertisements, sensations, and fakes, for what they wanted, and then throw the paper down. To suppose for one moment that this catchpenny order of journalism was influential, educational, or anything in fact, but a cheapjohn system of entertainment for weak minds, would be doing great injustice to the Alfred Jingle who invented it."

"The Tale of the Turquoise Skull" is the title of a highly exciting and lurid story, in which a Dominican Friar appears, in the June number of *The Pall Mall Magazine*. The sketches of Italian art are continued, the Visitation of our Lady, and St. Mary Magdalene being the subjects of the present paper.

Those who are interested in the study of faces will find in the May number of *Blackwood's Edinburgh Magazine*, an article discussing the question, under the heading, "Trades and Faces." It is well written, suggestive, but the medical doctor who is the author, manifests a dislike for the clergy which becomes viciously pronounced when he refers to the Irish priesthood. These serious blemishes mar an otherwise agreeable paper.

The Review of Reviews for June contains a full, illustrated article on "The Chicago Newspapers and their Makers," a character sketch of the leading journalists and daily journals of the inland metropolis. The other matter of *The Review* is, as usual, timely and varied.

The Atlantic Monthly for June gives "Some Reminiscences of Christina Rosetti;" "A Pilgrimage to the Great Buddhist Sanctuary of North China," in which honorable mention is made of the Catholic missions seen on the way; and "Vocal Culture in Its Relation to Literary Culture." The other articles are after the manner of *The Atlantic*.

"Here and There in Catholicism," is the fifth paper of a series by Henry Austin Adams, which appears in the May number of *The Catholic World.* Cuba is the point chosen by Mr. Adams for special mention, and we find it of peculiar interest, partly because of the late notoriety given to Cuba through the press, partly because of the quaintness and picturesqueness of the subject, and much because of Mr. Adams' agreeable manner of treating it. He describes, graphically, the natural beauties of Santiago de Cuba, the archiepiscopal see, which is of a great age, as Columbus stopped here on one of his late voyages, and "the house in which he slept still stands." The mingled population is thus described: "Chinese are here in large numbers, married to Spanish women, whose fathers were pure French. The thrifty Catalan is there, plying his trade with wily Scotchmen from Auld Reekie, and broad-faced Dutchmen with unpronounceable names, and Yankees, and Mexicans, and Cubans!" In regard to the religious aspect of matters, Mr. Adams writes: "At Santiago the student of ecclesiastical affairs will find enough to fill his mind with interest and speculation. The city is sufficiently supplied with churches, the grand cathedral, with its two graceful towers, superb old chancel, and air of indescribable devotion, being the fruitful mother of a dozen of them. * * * To our utilitarian, aggressive, missionary minds, the dreamy and devotional surroundings need practicality and more of what we style "applied Christianity." * * * Yet there is not the less of beauty and its own sweet mysticism in the "Manana Chicho!"—To-morrow, my dear!—of that contemplative, poetic people, whose nervous tension has been relaxed by centuries of siestas in a land where "it is always afternoon."

Another paper of travels is 'Glimpses of Italy," from the pen of E. C. Foster. The old subject is ever new and beautiful; one never wearies of the constant sunshine and flowers of Naples,—the bronzes of Florence, the paintings of Tuscany, the architecture of Turin, the combined glories of all the other cities centred in Rome. "The Genius of Leonardo da Vinci," by Mr. John J. Shea, is a sketch of the great Master's life, but more particularly a critical analysis of his most famous painting, "The Last Supper."

The Sun, New York, June 2, published an article entitled: "Told in the Priest's House; the Tragedy of the Convent." The heading caught our eye, and we be-

gan to read, pleased at first because of the style and the life-like reality of the picture, interested then as the scene unfolded, and finally deeply affected as the sad end came. This article, written by a physician, is a novelette "with a purpose," and though we do not feel that the story should be the regular channel of conveying moral and economic lessons, we are satisfied that the author of this sketch made a happy choice, and effected a still happier execution. He aimed to show the terrible havoc made by consumption as a disease among nuns, and we believe that he is right. Tenderly and reverently he wrote, and our own experience seconds his statements. Many precious lives have been lost to the service of Religion and humanity through the indifference to ordinary laws of health that has marked the management of certain communities. The article in *The Sun* can, in no manner, be distorted into an attack on rules or observances of religious orders. It is, however, a just denunciation of their abuses, the remedy of which will be found, we hope, by the authorities of the Church. The sad story on many a convent cemetery cross that we have read, speaks eloquently and bitterly of the needless waste of young lives that had so generously been offered for the glory of God in the service of their fellow-men. We earnestly commend this article, and we unite with a priest correspondent of *The Sun* writing later in approval of it, and we hope that a copy of this excellent sketch may be laid on the table of every Bishop in the country. The essentials of the religious life are sufficiently onerous without adding to them useless infringement on the imperative laws of nature.

The Seminary for June contains the third of Mr. John A. Mooney's admirable papers on Zola. Again we counsel our friends to read them, while we announce with great pleasure the opening article of Mr. Mooney's series in this issue of THE ROSARY MAGAZINE. We are justified in expecting solid and lasting results from these fine essays of Mr. Mooney. We trust that our friends will zealously make known such good things, in honor of our Blessed Lady, in defence of whose shrine at Lourdes Mr. Mooney has prepared his series.

In the June *Seminary* there is a goodly share of other agreeable matter—"The Goldsmith's Art in the Past and Present" being especially worthy of mention.

THE VIRGIN OF THE GOLDFINCH.

(After Fra Bartolomeo).

The Rosary

VOL. VII.   AUGUST, 1895.   NO. 2.

ZOLA AT LOURDES.

JOHN A. MOONEY.

II.

ZOLA, I have said, might well have chosen Irma Montreuil, instead of La Grivotte, as a character in the romance of *Lourdes*, had his purpose been to impress a reader by means of descriptions truthfully realistic. On the same day with La Grivotte, Irma was cured. For three years she had suffered with consumption; and, during the seven months preceding her visit to Lourdes, she had been confined to bed. Her physician wrote to Dr. Boissarie that she was rapidly sinking, and that death was close at hand. Reaching Lourdes, she presented herself at the Verification Office. There Dr. Boissarie met her. Describing Irma's condition, Dr. Boissarie's language is realistic enough to satisfy the most austere of experimental romancers.

"She entered our office," says the Doctor, "supported by a Sister who continually moistened her mouth with a feather soaked in a solution of boric acid; her mouth was filled with froth, a sort of whitish cream that completely lined the surface. This froth is the final symptom. In April"—more than four months before her visit to Lourdes,—"a running sore had opened, and from this sore pus freely flowed....At the baths, they refused to immerse her; she insisted, by signs she implored; they placed her in the water, once, twice, thrice. A violent shock disturbed her whole body, her chest was riven by it, and hot flames rushed through the running sore....Suddenly, instantaneously, like a flash, all pain, all suffering ceased....She stepped out of the bath and went to kneel at the Grotto. Soon after, we saw her once more in the Medical Office, still accompanied by the Sister carrying in her hand the feather and the bottle that had been used while moisten- . ing Irma's mouth. Doctors Seauze, Rousseau, Descornières ex- amined her most carefully. No longer was there a trace of a lesion of the lungs, there was no froth, the running sore had been cicatrized instantaneously; in its place was a whitish, solid groove. A resurrection! tubercles, running sore, froth, interior lesions and visible lesions, all had disappeared in a second."

Irma Montreuil did not have a relapse on the way home. On the 21st of November, 1894, she was in Paris, on the platform with Dr. Boissarie, ready to be questioned by any one of the fifteen hundred present. Her cure was not only instantaneous, it was also permanent. As she received Extreme Unction on the train that brought her to Lourdes, even Zola, with all his audacity, might have hesitated to suggest that she was favorably affected by the "inspiriting influence of the journey." About those un- realities, "the healing breath, the unknown force evolved from the multitude in the crisis of faith," Irma was as ignorant as Zola. But one thing she did know: after a few short moments in the icy water of Lourdes, every symptom of her deathly disease had disappeared.

Beside Irma Montreuil, on the platform with Dr. Boissarie, sat Marie Le Bourlier. Marie was cured of consumption on the same day with Irma Montreuil and La Grivotte. Her father died of consumption. During ten months, Marie had not been out of her room. On the journey to Lourdes, a blister—the eighteenth she had worn—inspirited her. How feeble she was, a single fact will tell: the attendants supported her suffering body on a sheet, while dipping her into the bath. At the third dip Marie was cured; so cured that, on the same day, she nursed and bathed and carried the sick as valiantly as any of those who had never worn a blister over their lungs. Two years and nigh three months had passed, when, on November 21st, 1894, Marie Le Bourlier presented herself before Dr. Boissarie's Parisian audience. As poor as La Grivotte, working no less hard for a pittance as mean, Marie's restoration to health is as worthy of note as La Grivotte's. Instantaneously she was cured; and her cure was permanent.

A moral, scientific writer, setting down simply and truthfully all the facts of the pilgrimage Zola selected as a subject for his ignoble caricature of *Lourdes*, would not only perform a good action, but would also help many to arrive at the true, by means of the truth; Zola seeks the false, and attains it by the winding road of the falsifier. To the proofs I have already adduced, showing his loyalty to his own lying principles, I shall now add others drawn from the same pure, translucent source.

Élise Rouquet is the name Zola confers on "a thin young woman" who rode in the same car with La Grivotte, during the journey of the National Pilgrimage to Lourdes, in August, 1892. Of Zola's narrative, I shall here present the first literal translation printed in the English language. Besides the version with which Americans were favored, another has appeared bearing the name of a resident of England, who learned several years ago, from an experience with English courts, that, in an English version of Zola's books, economy of language is not criminal; while verbal correctness may compel the law to interfere with the personal liberty of a translator. The English version of *Lourdes* is more humane than the American version; though the American equals, if it does not surpass, the English version, in infidelity to the text.

M. Ferdinand Brunetière, whose words I have elsewhere quoted, qualifies Zola as an ignoramus, with a miserable style, who knows neither the sense, the place, the usage of any French word, nor of a word of any other language. How precisely M. Brunetière defines the literary incapacity of the moralist who boasts that he can conceive but one crime—that of writing poorly,—a bold translation of his lingo can alone establish. Illiterate, the English and American versions of *Lourdes* are; but not literally illiterate enough to convey an accurate notion of the meanness of

Zola's style, or of his "serene" ignorance. Trained critics, and writers claiming authority as scientists, have not hesitated to call him obscene, brutal, unveracious, criminal, and even insane. Scribbling, such a person could not help becoming notorious; and his notoriety may have led the inexperienced to assume that Zola was gifted with originality.   And he is; but it is a peculiar originality;—the glorious originality of his unique ignorance.   To dim this glory by softening his language, by ordering his phrases and sentences, by correcting his grammar, by substituting right for wrong words, would be to do Zola an injustice.   What this lover of "the well-made phrase" most despises, that he most deserves, —veracity.

Thus premising, I begin my translation of the tale of Élise Rouquet, as it is told in the pages of *Lourdes.*   When Zola introduces the poor girl, she says that she is hungry.   Her face is enveloped in a black kerchief, or scarf.   A charitable lady offers to cut Élise's bread into little bits.   While the kind lady is cutting the bread, Zola tells us that Élise is a native of Picardy, who had to leave her home and settle in Paris.   There she resided with a sister that treated her harshly.   At none of the hospitals could the afflicted Élise obtain admission.   She was most devout, and for months had felt an ardent desire to visit Lourdes.

"Are the bits small enough? Can you get them into your mouth?" asked the charitable lady.   "Under the black kerchief, a hoarse voice growled: Yes, yes, Madam."

"The kerchief fell down.   It was a case of lupus which had invaded the nose and mouth, then little by little it grew, a slow ulceration spreading ceaselessly under the scabs, destroying the mucous membrane.   The head elongated like a dog's snout, with her coarse hair and her two big round eyes, she was frightful to look upon.   The cartilages of the nose were almost wholly eaten way, the mouth drawn backward and to the left, by the swelling of the upper lip, resembled an oblique slit, foul and formless.   A sweat of blood, mixed with pus, flowed from the enormous livid wound."

Seeing Élise Rouquet carefully slip the little bits of bread into the "bleeding hole that served her as a mouth," Zola reports that her fellow-passengers turned pale.   "And the same thought arose in all those souls filled with hope. Ah! Holy Virgin, powerful Virgin, what a miracle if such a disease should be cured! "

At Poitiers, about two hundred and ten miles from Paris, the train halted, and many of the pilgrims dismounted, seeking a breath of fresh air. Élise Rouquet, who had replaced her kerchief, was among the crowd; but it was cold water, rather than fresh air, that she sought. "Devoured by a desire for cold water, she was looking for a fountain;" and she found one. A certain Madame Maze, a pilgrim, " going to the fountain to wash her hands, came upon Élise Rouquet as she was drinking. Madame Maze recoiled at the sight of the monster, of that dog's head with the gnawed snout who held forth the oblique cut of her wound, the tongue hanging out and lapping. All those around shivered and hesitated to fill their bottles, jugs, and cans, at the fountain where she had drunk."

After the departure of the train from Poitiers, Zola neglects Élise. Once we hear of her,—eating a bunch of grapes, with her face uncovered. When Zola notices her again, she is leaving the train, at Lourdes, in the company of a Sister, who, having wrapped up Élise's face, carefully, is about to take her to the Hospital of Our Lady of Sorrows. It was early morning, and before visiting the Grotto, the baths, or the church, the thoughtful Sisters wished the pilgrims to lie abed for an hour or two. Zola, peeping into the hospital, saw Élise Rouquet opening her basket, " to take out of it a clean kerchief, much annoyed at having no mirror."

Up to this point, Zola's recital of Élise Rouquet's doings, sayings, and appearance, is as near truthful as could be expected from one whose trade it is to distort and exaggerate facts, when not engaged in making gaps and filling them with lies. Élise Rouquet is a real person, who visited Lourdes with the National Pilgrimage of August, 1892. The " romancer," from motives of delicacy, substituted Élise for Marie, and Rouquet for Lemarchand. Marie Lemarchand is the true name of the distressed woman, whose " dog's snout " Zola inhumanly pictures, as if hate and contempt, rather than sympathy or pity, moved him. Marie Lemarchand's disease was lupus, a true tuberculosis or consumption; a disease differing from consumption of the lungs in this respect only: that it is the skin, and the underlying membranes,

tissues, cartilages, and even the bones, which are destroyed by
the bacillus to whose activity all diseases of a tuberculous character are attributed.   Zola's description centres the attention of
the reader on Marie Lemarchand's face.   His purpose is not, as
one might assume, to be audaciously truthful; but to conceal and
deceive.   Besides the lupus of the face, Marie, as Dr. Boissarie
relates, was also suffering from consumption of the lungs, and, in
addition, from a lupus on one leg.   A plain statement of the
facts of her case is more impressive than Zola's disgustingly realistic description of her mouth, nose, and tongue.   The condition
of her tuberculous lung was more worthy of note than the " bleeding hole " in her face.   Zola's exaggerations are not always imaginative; generally, they are studied, lying tricks.

At present, I shall not set the medical testimony concerning
Marie Lemarchand's case against Zola's narrative; but I shall
confine myself to warning my readers that, when the romancer
told us Élise Rouquet was " much annoyed at having no mirror,"
it was he, and not Marie Lemarchand, who had a use for the
mirror.   While we were looking, sympathetically, at the afflicted
girl's face, he was secretly digging one of his artistic gaps; a gap
so long and wide that only an idiot of idiots could think of filling
it with a mirror.   Thus warning my readers, I return to the elegant text of Zola's *Lourdes.*

The pilgrims were anxious to make a first visit to the shrine of
our Lady.   Finally, at a quarter to eight o'clock in the morning,
they were told to make ready.   It is to Élise Rouquet that Zola pays
most attention, while the women are dressing.   " Élise Rouquet
had ended by discovering a pocket mirror, between the hands of
one of her neighbors, an enormous woman, dropsical, very coquettish about her person; she had let herself borrow it, she had
placed it upright against her bolster; and, absorbed, with an infinite care, she tied the kerchief elegantly around her head, to
conceal her monster's face, with the bleeding wound."

Élise's infinite care must have ended; for, shortly after the incident of the coquettish, dropsical woman's mirror—an incident
narrated with an illiteracy truly Zolan,—the girl with the lupus
presented herself at the miraculous spring.   A long, low stone
wall faced her.   The crowd was so great that " though there were

twelve taps that flowed into the narrow basin, lines had to be formed." A particular friend of Zola's, whose name—Peter,— and whose occupation—that of a Zolan stock-idiot—I have mentioned in a preceding article, was standing near the spring, and became especially interested in Élise Rouquet, who, " deeming it useless to go to the baths for the frightful sore by which her face was eaten, had contented herself, since morning, with washing herself at the spring, every hour. She knelt down, removed the kerchief, applied for a long time to the sore a handkerchief which she soaked, like a sponge, and, around her, the crowd rushed in such a fever, that they no longer remarked her monster's face, washed and even drank at the same spout at which she soaked her handkerchief."

Peter and Zola visited the Verification Office, later in the day. While they were there: " Élise Rouquet appeared, with her monster's face, which she exposed, taking off her kerchief. Since morning she washed herself with cloths, at the fountain, and it seemed indeed to her, she said, that her sore, so inflamed, commenced to dry and grow pale. It was true, Peter acknowledged, much surprised, that the appearance of the sore was less horrible. .... Dr. Bonamy (Boissarie) advised Élise Rouquet to continue the lotions, and to return every day for examination. Then, he repeated, with his prudent, affable air: At any rate, gentlemen, there is a beginning, without doubt."

On the night of the same day, about 11.30 P. M., Peter, to whom Zola grants many rare liberties, entered the woman's dormitory at the hospital; and there he " perceived the head of Élise Rouquet, sound asleep, without the kerchief, with her monster's face in the air, whose horrible sore, however, continued to grow paler." Three-quarters of an hour later, at 12.15 A. M., Sunday morning, we have an additional bulletin: " Élise Rouquet alone, stretched on her back, slept peaceably, displaying her frightful sore drying by degrees."

It is more than probable that Élise went to Mass on Sunday, even though the coquettish, dropsical woman refused to let her mirror go out of her hands; but we hear nothing of the thin young woman with the lupus until after nightfall. Then Peter saw her among the thirty thousand pilgrims that marched in

procession, carrying lighted candles.   She passed, says Zola, " like
an apparition of a damned soul,* with her face bare and red."

On the following morning, a young physician, Dr. Ferrand, visited the hospital.   The case of Élise Rouquet impressed him.
" It was now becoming certain that the lupus, the sore of which
was eating her face, was improved.   She continued the lotions at the
miraculous fountain, and had just come from the Verification Office, where Dr. Bonamy (Boissarie) had triumphed.   Surprised,
Ferrand advanced, examined the sore, already paled, somewhat
dried, which was far from being cured, but in which was beginning a whole concealed labor of cure.   And the case appeared
so strange to him, that he promised himself to take some notes
of it for one of his former teachers at the medical school, who
was studying the nervous origin of certain diseases of the skin,
determined by a disturbance of nutrition."

" You have felt no prickings? he asked.   No sir, no.   I wash
myself and say my beads with my whole soul, that's all! "

The physician went on his way; and, a few minutes later, " Élise
Rouquet, paying attention to no one, had taken her mirror, was
absorbed in the contemplation of her face, which she thought she
saw grow beautiful visibly, since the sore dried."

On Monday, the last day of the National Pilgrimage, Peter paid
a farewell visit to the Verification Office.   As fortune would have
it, Élise Rouquet was in the Office; and Dr. Boissarie, if we
should believe Zola, was examining her lupus.   For the third
time " she came to verify the increasing cicatrization of her sore.
Gentlemen, exclaimed the Doctor, have you ever seen a lupus
improve after this fashion, so rapidly?....I know indeed that a
new work has appeared on faith healing, in which it is said that
certain sores may be of nervous origin.   But there is not the least
proof in the case of lupus, and I challenge a commission of physicians to assemble and agree in explaining, by the ordinary ways,
the cure of this young lady?   He stopped, he turned to Father
Dargelès: Father, have you carefully noted that the suppuration
has completely disappeared, and that the skin is resuming its
natural color? "

---

* The official English translation puts it thus: " like a damned apparition."

Here ends Zola's tale of Élise Rouquet's doings and sayings while on the road to Lourdes and while at Lourdes. When the incident of the mirror was introduced, I warned my readers to look out for the gap which the naturalistic artist meant to fill with lies. Exaggerating certain features of the case of the woman with the lupus, Zola had purposely concealed other features no less remarkable. However, neither exaggeration nor concealment could break the force of Élise Rouquet's experience at Lourdes. Of the weakness of his method Zola was conscious. Hence the gap and the lies. Every incident related by Zola since first he mentioned the mirror, is a lie. The story of the visit to the spring, and of Élise's washing her diseased face every hour, is a lie in every detail. The story of her first visit to the Verification Office and of Dr. Boissarie's action and speech, is a lie. The story of her appearance, as she slept in the dormitory, is a lie. The story of her looking "like a damned soul," during the candle-light procession, is not only a shocking story, but also a shocking lie. The story of Dr. Ferrand's interview with her, in the Hospital of Our Lady of Sorrows, is, in every particular, a lie. The story of her final visit to the Verification Office is, from beginning to end, a lie.

To substantiate my charges, I shall now appeal to the medical testimony in the case. Marie Lemarchand, to whom Zola gave the name: Élise Rouquet, arrived at Lourdes on the 20th of August, 1892. Dr. Boissarie has reported her condition: lupus of the cheek, the lips and a portion of the mouth; tuberculosis of the lungs, and a lupus on one leg. Dr. La Nëele, of Caen, her physician, informed Dr. Boissarie that he considered her as "absolutely incurable."

And yet on the day after her arrival at Lourdes, Marie Lemarchand (Élise Rouquet) was cured in the icy water of the baths. The cure was instantaneous and absolute.

In proof of her miraculous cure, I quote the following passages from Dr. Boissarie's address delivered in Paris, at the Luxembourg Club, on the 21st of last November. "Dr. d'Hombres, who was a witness of the cure of this young woman, has recorded all the details in a written deposition. 'I remember very well,' he says, 'to have seen Marie Lemarchand in front of the baths, awaiting her turn to take a bath. I was struck by her appearance, especially repulsive. The two cheeks, the lower part of the nose, the upper lip, were covered with an ulcer of a tuberculous nature, and secreting a most abundant pus. The cloths which covered this face were all stained with pus. Coming out of the bath, I went immediately to the hospital, beside this woman. I recognized her very well, though the appearance of her face was entirely changed. Instead of the hideous sore that I had just seen, I found a surface still red, indeed, but dry, and as if covered with a newly-formed epidermis. The cloths that had served as a dressing, before her entrance into the bath, were beside her, and all spotted with pus. This poor, infirm woman had also, before the bath, a sore of the same nature on one leg, and this sore, like that of the face, had been dried in the bath. I confess to you in all sincerity,' adds Dr. d'Hombres, ' that I was deeply impressed by this so sudden change, determined by a simple immersion in cold water, it being conceded, as you know, that lupus is an affection most rebellious to every kind of medication.' "

Dr. Boissarie was in the Verification Office when Marie Lemarchand (Élise Rouquet) entered, accompanied by Dr. d'Hombres. " Our office," says Dr. Boissarie, " was crowded, at the moment, with physicians, littérateurs and journalists. The skin of Marie Lemarchand's face was red and shining; her newly-formed epidermis showed a recent cicatrice. Her complexion was not yet that of the lily and the rose. But, from the first instant every trace of suppuration, of a sore, had entirely disappeared." To these testimonies Dr. Boissarie adds that of Dr. Nëele : " The physician of Caen was not deceived as to the character of this cure. Seeing his patient return perfectly cured, he wrote to us: ' I am still much moved at having been able to touch with my finger this absolutely supernatural cure. Marie Lemarchand had besides an advanced tuberculosis, of which I had no doubt whatsoever, and of which I no longer find a trace.' "

M. Brunetière credits Zola with a talent to which he lays no claim. He does not write romances, M. Brunetière asserts; but he does write Vaudevilles,—plotless farces, in which all the characters are extravagant caricatures. The more nonsensical and vulgar the action and language, the more consummate is the art of the Vaudevilliste. He ridicules truth, perverts it. In mankind and in life, he observes only the mean and the insignificant. Without a hand mirror, the Vaudevilliste could not write; and in his mirror, he sees neither the poor, nor the suffering, nor good souls, nor gentle and sane folk, but only a world of senseless mannikins. The talent of the writer of Vaudevilles appears on every page of *Lourdes*. As La Grivotte was caricatured, so is Marie Lemarchand. Vulgarity, extravagance, cheap ridicule, perversion of the truth,—with these contemptible weapons Zola would annihilate Heaven and undo God's wonderful works.

Though Élise Rouquet (Marie Lemarchand) was miraculously cured of lupus of the face, lupus of the leg, and consumption of the lungs, on the first day after her arrival at Lourdes, Zola, ridiculing and perverting the truth, caricatures her to the end of his Vaudeville. Having seated her in the train that is to carry her back to Paris, he farcically informs us that she " had bought a pocket-mirror, a large, round mirror, in which she did not tire of looking at herself, finding herself pretty, establishing from minute to minute the progress of her cure, with a coquetry that made her purse her lips, attempt smiles, now that her monster's face was becoming human again." At night, he watches her making an elaborate toilette, " with the face always in her mirror ....tying around the head the black kerchief which had served to conceal her sore, looking if she was pretty thus, with her lip unswollen. And once more Peter was astonished at that sore in the way of healing, if not healed, at that monster's face that one could now look upon without horror. The sea of incertitudes recommenced. Was it not even a true lupus? was it only a kind of unknown ulcer, of hysterical origin? Or indeed must it be admitted that certain lupuses badly studied, proceeding from malnutrition of the skin, could be improved by a great moral shock? It was a miracle, unless it should reappear, in three weeks, in three months, or in three years, like the consumption of La Grivotte."

Thrice, after this Vaudevillistic scene, Zola caricatures Élise Rouquet (Marie Lemarchand). The first time, he represents her praying to Bernadette Soubirous ' to intercede for the completion of her cure.' The second time, she is examining " her nose, mouth, cheeks, admiring herself, drinking herself in (*se buvant*), finding that she was becoming decidedly very pretty"; and the last time, as the train nears Paris, she is taking "a final glance at her mirror."

"Ah! Holy Virgin, powerful Virgin, what a miracle if such a disease should be cured!" These words, Zola says, expressed the thought of every passenger aboard the car with Marie Lemarchand (Élise Rouquet), when, letting the bandage fall from her face, she slipped the little bits of bread into "the bleeding hole that served her as a mouth." The fatal disease whose ravages Zola described, again and again, so vulgarly, so heartlessly, was cured, on the instant, in the icy bath at Lourdes; and, in the same instant, Marie Lemarchand's consumption of the lungs was cured; and besides, a lupus sore that had eaten into her leg. Reading the scientific evidence of this triple cure, every intelligent believer in the supernatural must exclaim: "Ah! Holy Virgin, powerful Virgin, what a miracle!"

Even the Vaudevillistic idiot, Peter, was willing to admit that if Marie were cured with Zola's lotions and rags, "it was a miracle, unless it reappeared in three weeks, in three months, or in three years, like the consumption of La Grivotte." The consumption of La Grivotte, you will remember, did not reappear. Zola tried to lie the joyful mattress-maker into a relapse; but, thanks to the merciful God, and to the holy, powerful Virgin, he failed.

Besides the intelligent believers, and the Vaudevillistic idiots, there are the doubters more or less intelligent. What will, what can they say, in explanation of Marie Lemarchand's extraordinary, cure? Will they fall back on Zola's "healing breath," his "auto-suggestion," his "unknown force evolved in the crisis of faith;" or will they prefer to put their trust in "moral shock" as a curative agent in hopeless cases of lupus, complicated with consumption of the lungs? And should "the sea of incertitudes recommence," will they seek certitude on one of those floating islands recently discovered by Dr. Zola, and charmingly named by him: "Nervous Lupus," "Hysterical Lupus," and "Unknown Ulcer"?

The doubters have their choice. However, I am convinced that many who have doubted, in good faith, will be cured of their doubts concerning the miracles at the shrine of our Lady of

Lourdes, through the "moral shock" they will experience as they count up the lies, and measure the audacious ignorance, the brutality and the buffoonery, paraded on every page of the Vaudeville of Zola's *Lourdes*. As in the cure of La Grivotte, of Irma Montréuil, of Marie Le Bourlier, so also in the cure of Marie Lemarchand, intelligent, unprejudiced men and women must admit that, unless the absolutely miraculous character of this cure be acknowledged, it is otherwise inexplicable.

THE MASTER-TOUCH.

MARY THERESE WEST.

THE rose responds to the nightingale,
    In her sweet, familiar way,
And tender snowdrops, fair and pale,
    Peep forth at the robin's lay.
The clear streams image the starry skies,
To the thrilling voice echo's note replies,
Soft zephyrs toy with the swaying bough,
There's naught unresponsive, my heart, but thou.

Hast seen the smile of the sunbeams melt
  • All the winter's frost away?
Hast watched the ocean when it felt
    The strength of the moon's bright ray?
Hast heard the earth praying rain from Heaven,
Till refreshing showers once again are given?
For deep responds unto deeps that call,
And prayer is answered when blessings fall.

Yet there are chords in the human heart
    That in golden silence wait
For a master-touch to bid them start,
    And with melody vibrate,—
Like ships becalmed far out at sea,
Waiting for winds to set them free,—
Unmoved they lie, and impassive, till
Some power unseen bids them swell and thrill
Into inspired melody,
Breathing of God and infinity,
Praising the One Who had made them such,
Quick to respond to His master-touch.

OUR LADY'S ASSUMPTION.

ELIZA ALLEN STARR.

HERE is a rustle of ripe grain on the far stretches of sunny meadows, on the rounded slopes of fertile hills; a sound of reapers, too, before the dew has dried on the fields; only, at noon, there is a hush, and under some spreading oak or hickory, perchance elm, the harvesters are resting in the shade, their dinner brought to them from a home nestled among its own trees. There is a flutter, too, among the meadow-larks, overtaken by the reapers before their younglings are fully fledged, while high among the branches of the friendly maples, mother-birds are coaxing their broods to try their wings. It is the time of the first fruitage, of the first harvest. The sunshine is growing every day more intense, the shadows deeper, while the shrill monotone of the August crickets in the grass, tells us that we have come to the height of the year's beauty, to the limit of the bliss in existence for bird, and bee, and butterfly. Thenceforth there will be a chill in the night air, a sensible shortening of the day, a check in the growth of branch and foliage, while the vine shows a purple tinge under its broad leaves,—the phase of glorious perfection, yet casting the first shadows of decline; the sun no longer at its zenith, but nearing the resplendent west. Like the season, also, our mystery leads us to the very height of the ecclesiastical year—the Feast of our Lady's Assumption standing, like some lovely chapel that crowns a summit overlooking mountain and plain, river and valley, perchance some inland sea.

Of the glories of this festival of our Lady's Assumption, history, and the annals of the fairest cities in the world, are full. Cathedrals, like that of Siena in Tuscany, dating back to so early a time as to have been built on the site of pagan temples, have claimed as a title, "The Assumption," the master builders of these sublime monuments of architectural genius, finding, in the Mystery itself, a never-failing source of inspiration.

The earliest representation of the Assumption, according to present researches, was found by Father Mullooly, O. P., in the subterranean church of San Clemente, Rome, and dates no later

(*After Fra Angelico.*)

than to the ninth century, perhaps to the eighth. In this fresco, to be seen only by the light of tapers on a wall hidden for nearly a thousand years from the eye of man, our Lady, sustained by four angels, is rising into the air above her tomb, her arms extended in an ecstasy as she looks upward to her Son, who has come to take

2

her to Himself in an aureole of glory. Standing on the earth
around her empty tomb, are the twelve apostles, with every demonstration of awe, of joyful surprise, of devout acclamation. To
one side, at the edge of the picture, stands St. Vitus with a round
nimbus, who is from the sixth century; and on the other side, the
figure of a pontiff with a square nimbus, because still living when
the picture was made; while below the picture runs the following
inscription like a border: " That this picture may outshine the
rest in beauty, behold, the priest, Leo, studied to compose it."
" If this be," as Father Mullooly says, " Leo III., it was painted
before the year 795; if Leo IV., before the year 847; " but in either
case, we have a picture painted not only under pontifical permission, but by pontifical suggestion, and therefore embodying an
authorized ecclesiastical treatment which would confirm the belief of Christians in the Assumption of the Blessed Virgin Mary,
so early as the eighth or ninth century.

Another picture, although departing from the San Clemente
Assumption in its arrangement, is one which has a strong hold
on our affection. It is in the chapel of the magistrates of Siena,
within the Palazzo Pubblico, where the Signory of Siena held
counsel with the Holy Spirit before counselling with each other.
On the walls of this chapel are painted: the gathering of the
apostles around the Blessed Virgin at the time of her death, the
carrying of her body to the tomb, and– its Assumption! Above
her bed of death, our Lord is seen in a *mandorla* or almond-
shaped glory, receiving her soul into His arms as one would receive an infant; as Mary, indeed, is seen in several noted mosaics
(as in the lower section of that in Santa Maria Maggiore) which
represent her death. But, this Assumption is unlike any other,
we believe, in the world.

All around stand the sharp peaks of the Valley of Jehoshaphat
in gloomy grandeur, over which steals the first dawn of a summer day. In the foreground is the tomb in which our Lady is
couched; but, skimming low through the air, comes our Lord surrounded by rosy seraphs, His arms outstretched towards His
Mother, who is half rising, as if she heard Him say: " Mother, it
is time to rise!" and she holds out her hands to meet His, as if answering, with the old, sweet alacrity of Nazareth: " Yes, my Son!"

and the rosy seraphs place their wings under her, to raise her from her couch into the air, and thus accompany her Son to His celestial home. The picture touches one, if attentively considered, as few things do even in the art of that beautiful period when the imaginations of people and of artists seem so familiar with the ways of our Lady and of her Son; for one cannot help feeling, when looking upon it, how often He must have come to her in the hush of the early morning, with the same sweet words on His lips, to win from her the same response. This picture is by Taddeo Bartoli of Siena, as are its companions.

In the Campo Santo of Pisa, above the principal door, Simone Memmi—also of Siena, and in the same century as Taddeo Bartoli, viz., the fourteenth, only in the earlier part of it—painted an Assumption with every expression of jubilation. She is borne to Heaven by a choir of angels, singing, playing their instruments of music with the gestures of a not-to-be-told happiness; nor does this jar upon the solemnity of the precincts of a burying-place as the Campo Santo really is. Simone Memmi himself, and all those for whom he painted, believed, implicitly, that these bodies would rise, and, united to the soul, would be received into Heaven. They saw no difficulty in believing that our Lord, after having eaten with His disciples, walked with them to Mount Olivet, where He parted from their midst, and rose into the air until a bright cloud received Him out of their sight, carrying with Him to the right hand of His Father, the flesh which He had received from His Mother, the Blessed Virgin Mary. Neither did it seem strange to Simone, or those for whom he painted, that having thus glorified His own humanity, He should rescue from the corruption of the grave that flesh from which His own had been formed; and this, together with His own Ascension, made the Assumption of His Mother only another assurance of His intentions towards our bodies at the day of the general resurrection. It was the intention, also, of the pious Simone, to lift the heart of every mourning Pisan from the darkness of the vaults of their pathetic Campo Santo, to the brightness of Heaven itself, where our bodies, as immortal as our souls, will rejoice in a glorified reunion with them, in the very presence of the Redeemer with His five wounds shining like five suns, His humanity resplendent as never upon earth, even on Mount Thabor, while at His side will stand the Virgin Mother from whose immaculate flesh He took His own.

Never have such words been penned of these frail, dying bodies of ours, as are scattered through the sacred Canon of the Mass itself, setting before us a hope full of immortality, and which inspired the artists of the ages of faith to depict, not only the Ascension of our Lord, but the Assumption of His Blessed Mother.

Nor was it to brush and color, or stuccoed wall alone, that piety committed her ecstatic conceptions of the glory of Mary's entrance into Heaven. On one of those four portals opening into that temple which deserves, for its beauty, the name given to it— *Santa Maria del Fiore*, or Saint Mary of the Flower, in Florence,— Jacopo della Quercia set forth the claims of the Assumption to the devotion of Christendom. In choosing this subject, Jacopo della Quercia considered not only its charming possibilities as to composition and forms, but the devotion of the Florentines to this mystery in the career of our Lady. It was not by mere chance that they celebrated this festival with such splendor, the very splendor being an outcome of the sentiments and affections of the people. Therefore, when della Quercia was called to carry out the magnificent decorations of side posts and lintel, of pilaster and capital, of the door opening towards the church of the Annunziata, by Nicolo di Piero of Arezzo, by giving a group in sculpture to the face of the pointed arch, he knew that he should take with him the heart of Florence by setting high, in the midst of mosaic and sculpture, this delightful mystery of the Assumption. Our Lady is represented ascending, surrounded by the *mandorla*, or almond-shaped glory, which is sustained by angels, while others are singing, and others still making melody on those musical instruments which suggest strains of joy, the movements of these celestial choristers full of grace, and their upward flight as easy as that of larks which " fly towards Heaven's gate and sing as they soar."

Still, it is in the person of the Blessed Virgin herself that della Quercia finds the inspiration for all his accessories. The slender figure, mantled from head to foot, every fold of the drapery majestic in its line, yet so pliant that a breeze might stir it; the face, so delicate in its oval, so benignant in its expression, not lifted to

Heaven, but turned towards her children on earth,—a certain elegance which we see afterwards in Raphael, in the pose; the action
determined by one of those graceful legends which give a picturesque charm even to exalted subjects,—make this composition in
marble one of the most serenely gracious ever conceived of our
Lady.   If we compare the pictures or compositions of a devout
period, when art seemed a natural outgrowth of the sentiments of
the age, not pledged to dramatized representations, we shall bye-
and-bye come to discern and to understand this quality of benignity, for which we always discover a reason.   In the present instance, it is called forth by the legend, to which we have alluded,
of St. Thomas and the girdle.   The imagination of those poetic
ages was not without logical consistency, and we always find St.
Thomas a little less ready to believe than any of the Apostles. Therefore, when these sorrowing sons of a heavenly Mother visited her
tomb to find, instead of the venerated body of the Virgin, only
lilies and roses, and immediately divined that her Son and Lord
had taken this precious body to Himself, Thomas doubted.
Then it was that the benignity of this Virgin Mother was truly
shown; for as Thomas raised his eyes to Heaven, she appeared to
him in all her beauty, and as if pitying the doubting mind of one
ready to bear witness to her Son by his death, and, to assure him
of the truth and the reality of the vision, dropped into his hand
her girdle.   It is this act of gentlest benignity to an Apostle who
was to be a martyr for Christ, which gives such a charm to the
Assumption of Jacopo della Quercia, on the door so admired by
the Florentines, and called by them, *Porta della Mandorla*, or,
" Portal of the Mandorla."

How few of the hundreds that every year pause in Florence, os-
tensibly to study its art, do more than follow the guide-book
along the niches that beautify the originally plain exterior of *Or
San Michele;* while still fewer are those who do more than glance
at the medallions by Andrea Orcagna on the celebrated shrine
which is an epitome of Florentine social and religious life.
Eight medallions give the principal events in the life of our Lady;
but the space at the back of the picture, for which the shrine was
designed (the whole being quite detached from the wall, like the
ancient altars), is covered by one large relief in powerful sculp-

ture, representing the death of the Virgin, and, above this, her glorious Assumption. The same almond-shaped aureole contains her ascending form, surrounded by angels bearing her upward and singing her triumphs, while one suppliant figure makes a link between her and the world she is leaving. The magnificence of this sculpture is unsurpassed by any relief, we believe, in existence, and was completed in the year 1359. The medallions are enclosed in a border of cockle-shells; but this large relief is set between the pillars of the Gothic canopy, and the round arch above is elegantly finished with drops, throwing it into a recess.

Two celebrated paintings still remain to be cited as proofs of the powerful inspiration which this mystery has given to art in later ages. The first in time is that beatific Assumption, by Perugino, which still makes the glory of the *Belle Arti* of Florence. We say beatific, because of the profound peace which characterizes its rapture. The stillness of noontide in midsummer pervades the picture. We have angels accompanying their hymns and canticles with stringed instruments; the Virgin Mother's mandorla is bordered with cherubs' heads; the whole borne upward by two blissful angels, graceful as willows, who only touch the mandorla as acolytes touch the vestment of the celebrant at the elevation. Above is the Eternal Son bearing the world on His palm; angels' heads surround Him; angels run, with hands folded adoringly, at His side. Below is the Virgin Mother, seated on clouds, the tips of the beautiful hands touching each other in ecstasy, the eyes lifted in transport to those of her Son and Creator bending so tenderly towards her—but all is peace, fulfilment. Heaven and the beatific vision are already hers! To the carrying out, too, of this unutterable fulness, this hush of transport, are the four personages called, "The Four Ambrosial Saints," who stand on the earth, not so much gazing on this vision as meditating upon it. Movement, intense life, melody, are in the picture; but each and all as harmonious, as noiseless, as the spheres moving through . the infinite spaces of our universe. *

---

* These Ambrosial Saints, so-called because they seem to have been translated from earth, and to have fed on the ambrosia of Heaven, could claim another article to bring out, fully, their stories, and their special fitness to the place given them by Perugino. It is one of the sad lapses in art studies, that few, comparatively, of those who visit foreign galleries and churches are as well-read in the stories of the saints as in the lives of pagan emperors.

The last we shall mention is Titian's Assumption, the most generally known of all; as a conception, however, in perfect contrast to the Assumption by Perugino. Time was when we turned away from Titian's as noisy; for we could hear the cries of joy, the exclamations of delight, from the angels circling around that radiantly buoyant figure, ascending with raised hands to meet her Beloved in the glory above; could hear the cries of the astonished Apostles on earth, and almost hear the whisper of the angel at the ear of the Son, pointing to the Mother below. But the moment our eyes lighted on the Assumption on the wall of the subterranean San Clemente, criticism died from our heart. For, strange to say, although the Assumption of San Clemente had been hidden for ages before Titian lived, as it was hidden for ages after his death, his conception follows, more literally than any other, that of "the priest Leo," who had "studied to compose" one in honor of this mystery so profoundly rooted in the belief of Christendom. It was not, then, a mere following of an outward type by Titian, but a genuine expression of the same exultation of soul with which "the priest Leo," of the eighth or ninth century, had conceived this event. And this exultation of soul, whence does it come, if not from realizing that the Assumption corresponds to our own expectations, even more closely than the Ascension of our Lord can possibly do? He arose of His own will, by His own omnipotence. Mary is carried to Heaven by angels at the will of her Son; and thus it comes that her hope is ours also; and the realization of her hope, the realization of our own; the creatureship of the Immaculate Virgin forming a link of blessedness between the humanity of the Eternal Son and our humanity, subject as it is to sin, and to death, and to corruption, but to which His Incarnation has opened possibilities which we should fear to contemplate, but for their authorization even in the missal we use for Mass every day of our lives. Where, indeed, is that people so blessed as we? Where are lives enriched like ours with an immortality for body as well as soul? Draw us, ineffable Mother, that as thy immaculate heart dwelt in Heaven with thy Son from the moment of His Ascension, so ours may follow thee in thy rapturous, most consoling Assumption!

THE MEETING OF ST. DOMINIC AND ST. FRANCIS.

O. F. W.

WAS night, and in Rome's great Basilica,
No worshippers were left save one alone:
One pilgrim still before the shrine entranced,
Breathed ardent pleadings to the Eternal Throne.

His garb was that of Austin
  Canon's white;
His prayer: "O Lord, to sin-
  ful men show ruth! "
A starry radiance crowned his
  brow serene,
For he was Dominic, the son
  of truth.

And lo! as his great heart, like
  Jacob once,
Wrestled with God, in words
  of earnest prayer,
He saw before him his Re-
  deemer stand,
Who in His hand three venge-
  ful arrows bare.

With upraised arm, He was about to hurl
  The pointed shafts on man's polluted race,
When kneeling suppliant at His sacred Feet
  His Mother asked for pardon and for grace.

" Oh, spare Thy people, Thy redeemèd spare!
  Speed not Thine arrows barbed with dread intent!
For these Thy servants, save! " and as she spake,
  She pointed to two figures prostrate bent.

What forms flashed then on Dominic's keen gaze?
  The first, white-robed, his own reflection shows.
The other, clothed in Poverty's dark garb,
  In whose wan face seraphic ardor glows.

With softened eyes the Saviour saw them kneel;
  And from His hand the harmless darts fell prone:
" My Mother, for thy servants' sake I spare!"...
  The vision passed, the pilgrim was alone!

Next morn to Mary's shrine he wends his way,
  But when he reached the threshold, paused amazed,
For there, spellbound in depths of speechless prayer,
  Upon the beggar of his dream he gazed!

And Francis, for Assisi's saint it was,
  Turned and arose, warned by prophetic grace,
And looked on Dominic, till their mutual love
  Surged up, and locked their hearts in fast embrace.

No rivalry within those noble breasts,
  That fellow-toiler in their work should share;
One only word sprang to the lips of each:
  " Together we will fight, that God may spare! "...

And still, that kiss is ringing thro' the world,
  For ever, riven by the memory sweet,
As brethren, while the ages roll, the sons
  Of Francis and of Dominic shall meet.

LET us say boldly with St. Bernard, that we have need of a mediator with the Mediator Himself, and that it is the divine Mary who is the most capable of filling that charitable office. It is by her that Jesus Christ came, and it is by her that we must go to Him. If we fear to go directly to Jesus Christ our God, whether because of His infinite greatness, or because of our vileness, or because of our sins, let us boldly implore the aid and intercession of Mary our Mother. She is good, she is tender, she has nothing in her austere or repulsive, nothing too sublime and too brilliant. In seeing her, we see our pure nature. She is not the sun, who, by the vivacity of his rays, blinds us because of our weakness; but she is fair and gentle as the moon, which receives the light of the sun, and tempers it to render it more suitable to our capacity. She is so charitable that she repels none of those who ask her intercession, no matter how great sinners they have been; for, as the saints say, never has it been heard since the world was the world, that any one has confidently and perseveringly had recourse to our Blessed Lady, and yet has been repelled.

—*Blessed Louis Mary Grignon de Montfort, O. P.*

HELEN TOWNSEND'S CHOICE. .

E. M. HUBBARD.

SUMMER day among the hills is nearing its close. Half an hour ago the sun went down behind the cliff that overhangs the winding road, and in the shade the tired oxen, not yet released from the yoke, are drawing deep draughts of the sweet, cool air. There is a sharp sound of tinkling cow-bells behind the cliff. The cows are running down the sloping pasture, and will soon come in sight, and watch, with expectant eyes, for the letting down of the bars.

Beyond the shaded road the sunlight lies in patches upon the meadow, where the bumble-bees that must have been flower-cradled in the oppressive heat and stillness of noon, are now lading themselves with honey from the clover. How sweet the clover smells, and how the sunbeams are caught in the net of lily-pads that well-nigh cover the surface of that small crescent-shaped pond lying in the bosom of the green meadow!

The murmur of a stream we can distinctly hear. There it flows, beyond that winding fringe of trees, and the low, rumbling sound heard at intervals tells one that beyond the bend in the road, the river is spanned by a bridge,—covered, undoubtedly, and weather-stained. A grassy plain skirts the farther bank of the stream, whence in a broad sweep, a hill, clad in green and crowned with trees, rises grandly to meet the sky.

Near the roadside, upon a mound sheltered by a clump of sturdy oaks, are to be seen a group of three persons. Two—a young man, with clear grey eyes, and a lady, every feature of whose pale, fair face indicates repose and peace—are engaged in sketching, pausing occasionally to reply to the words of a young girl, who has closed her sketch-book, and is glancing restlessly about her. " Look!" she suddenly exclaims, pointing toward the edge of the pond below them, where a crane, startled at the moment of alighting, had gathered poise, and was taking to rapid wings again. Three pairs of eyes watched its flight until, lost among the trees, it reappeared, became a speck, and vanished.

" I like this place," broke out the young girl, " because it contains and suggests things so unlike! The sight of that bird makes me half expect to hear the crackling of twigs on yonder bank, and to see a deer come out to feed upon the lily-pads. That's the wilderness for you. Let Farmer Goodman, with his full ox-cart and the field of wheat behind us, stand for the pastoral life, and those cars "—pointing to a distant train whose winding, snake-like movement followed the river's course,—" what do they not remind us of at home? "

" We shall leave you to separate fact from fancy, my dear cousin," returned the young man, smilingly; " still I think that it would be better perhaps for the people here if you could carry further the primitive life, and have the direction of the city suggested to you —well, by the migration of birds, if we stay long enough to see it."

" I know what Cousin Harold is thinking of, Helen," said the young girl with that liberty of construction which is not easily pardoned except in the youthful and charming; " he has not forgotten Mrs. Armstrong's hospitality, when we accepted an invitation to tea at her house. Sandwiches and tea were served in the parlor from which daylight had been shut out, and which was lighted by ill-smelling lamps. The poor woman had evidently mixed some vague ideas of matinees and ' five-o'clock teas.' We were almost stifled, for not a breath of the delicious air stirring outside could come through the closed blinds and closely-drawn curtains. The efforts of the company to appear at ease, and our hostess's complacency, were perfectly amusing. You should sketch the picture, cousin,—but no, that would not do; you would leave yourself out, and the effect would be as unsatisfactory as watching the play of Hamlet, with Hamlet himself behind the scenes. My camera would have done better."

" I am afraid that the picture would not have been a true one then," said Helen, laying her hand half-repressingly upon her companion's, and closing her book; " your mischief-loving face would be missing."

" Oh, you think I have been talking too much about my neighbors," said Dora, puting her arm around Helen's neck. "You dear Saint Helena!"

" I think," said Helen, gently, "that we must not make this one poor, foolish act a standard by which to measure our neighbors here. What greater simplicity can we find than in Mr. Goodman's family, and how perfectly adapted their ways are to their surroundings!"

" Yes," said the young artist heartily; " let us do homage to the man that perceives the relation of things in his own sphere, and I claim as brother him who does his work simply because he believes that it is for him to do, although he may have no fine words to set forth his creed. I like the Adam Bedes, who ' hate to see a man's arms drop down before the clock's fairly struck, just as if he'd never a bit of pride and delight in his work,' and have a pitying admiration for those whose persistent efforts, beset by cruel limitations, are set forth in the melancholy humor of Caleb Plumer when he desired to put as much nature in the bark of a toy-dog as Old Tackleton's price would allow him. Yes," continued the speaker, " the old pagan was right: ' Blessed is he who recognizes the relation of things.' Those who are seeking it form the great fraternity, and 'tis all one, whether we speak of the scientist in search of natural laws, of the woman of wisdom guiding her household by the laws of love and duty, of the artist endeavoring to express the relations of the beautiful, or of the honest workman doing his work for his work's sake."

These words, spoken with feeling and enthusiasm, fell upon Helen's ears as a strain of music in which the sustaining notes are wanting. The artist perceiving her hesitation, said quietly: " By the way, I saw a beautiful sight on Sunday, when I was taking my usual stroll in the village. It was a procession that was escorting the bishop from the priest's house to the church. Green arches had been placed at intervals, and before the bishop walked the children of the parish, the girls dressed in white, and carrying flowers. The whole scene was very simple and unaffected. I have seen something like it in some of the villages of Quebec."

A quick flush that mounted to Helen's temples passed as sud-

denly away, leaving her cheek paler than before. "Yes," replied
she, simply, "I knew that the bishop had come."

"Well, good people," cried Dora, "do you see old Dick coming
over the hill?"

This announcement was the signal for the gathering together
of chairs, books, and umbrellas for the boy to take home in his
wagon, and while Dora was assisting, she had time for this mental
soliloquy: "I wonder if my pretty story about Helen is to be
spoiled? Poor child! And I am sorry for Harold, too—only
men always think that they can carry everything before them,"
this sage young lady went on; "perhaps it will be a good lesson,"
not very clear as to whether her cousin was expected to suffer
magnanimously, for the shortcomings of the sterner sex in general, or for his own presumption in particular.

And now they pass around the bend in the road, and reach the
bridge whence the sounds not unlike the distant mutterings of
thunder have proceeded. "Oh, these myth makers!" exclaimed
the artist, leaning against a rail, looking down into the chasm
where the stream flowed deep and swift; and then listening to the
mingled sounds of the rustling leaves, the flutter of wings, the
twitter of birds, and the chirping of insects coming from the cliff
that rose with its mysterious recesses of gloom before them.
"How easily we can imagine Diana resting from the chase under
that oak, and the goddess of the lake—for nothing less than goddess can she be, with all that golden mist proclaiming her presence—floating in the air above the lilies, with her golden hair
around her, and her dark eyes cast down; dryads venturing out in the
twilight to sport upon the meadows; and see how this rough and
boisterous river-god is wooing, with too harsh caresses, that gentle
hamadryad," pointing to a willow whose graceful boughs touching
the surface of the stream, were swaying to and fro.

Dora quickly seized the fancy, and half in sport, half in earnest,
she peopled the way to the farm-house with these old creations
of a race that had looked into the eyes of Nature, and found them,
by turns, fateful and terrible, gentle and loving.

After reaching the village inn, and taking supper in the long,
bare dining-room, the artist sat down in a secluded part of the
veranda, lighted a cigar, and gave himself up to the review of cer-

tain episodes of the day, with their relation to his own hopes. "'Tis but a question of loving," he murmured once. Presently a half-frown, habitual to him when in perplexity or deep thought, was furrowed upon his forehead. Stages rolled up and departed unnoticed, and the inn had settled down to its nightly silence before he bethought himself of the lateness of the hour, by seeing in the dim starlight, a familiar figure lingering about the steps.

"Halloo, John! Is that you? What time is it?"

"It is nigh upon twelve, sir."

"Waiting to lock up? Have I kept you waiting?" and the old hostler heard the clinking of coin. Even in this retired place there was the degeneracy of service on the constant look-out for gain.

"There ain't nothin' mean about Mr. Campbell, there ain't," the old man muttered as he shuffled away, rattling the coins in his hands.

It was on account of his lavish generosity that Campbell, when a dashing young Sophomore at college, was dubbed by his boon companions, Prince Harold. His popularity was undoubtedly increased by the fact that he was a capital "pitcher" and a "prime one" at the oars; for even at the time of which I write, a fine muscular development was a factor not to be overlooked in forecasting the rank that a college man would be likely to hold among his fellows.

The title given to him on an occasion of reckless enjoyment was approved in the higher classes from a tacit acknowledgment of his natural leadership; and as certain sterling qualities had more than one opportunity for being strikingly displayed, even the cynical did not grudge him the name. When he called upon the President, upon leaving his Alma Mater, and the last words of the venerable old man were: "Go, sir; *go, prince*, and become every inch a king," never before had the young man felt a stronger thrill of honest pride, or a firmer determination to wield his good sword well.

But not as his friends desired, who looked with disappointment upon his choice of an artist life. Two years after his graduation he is hard at work in Paris. There is no struggle with poverty to record, for Campbell was rich, careless enough of his wealth, after the simple wants of a student's life were supplied, being even inclined at this time to depreciate its use, as those are apt to do who have aims in another direction than that of accumulating money, and yet have never felt these aims thwarted through want of it.

It would be agreeable to declare that our hero was above the pettiness of human vanity. It was not so, and when he saw other men carrying off prizes that he had hoped for, he indulged for a time—let us pardon him—in that mental swagger that comes in moments of disappointment like his, to many a soul of honest purpose. "Confound these Frenchmen and their knavish tricks!" he exclaimed, showing by an odd association of ideas, his Anglican tendencies, and his opinion that the royalty of justice had been attacked in the case in hand, by subtlety truly Jacobite. Bye-and-bye he learned to think less of himself in comparison with others, grew more humble as he came to realize more the greatness of his art, did simpler work in a painstaking way, and so came to see a little deeper into nature, "into the relation of things." After several years, his pictures began to be talked of a little, and then fair things began to be predicted of him.

It was at the house of his aunt, Mrs. Aitken, after his return to America, that Campbell first saw Helen Townsend, and heard her story rehearsed by the sympathetic Dora. How the experiences of human life, ever repeated, are ever new through their varying relations to the individual soul as the aspect of the sky is ever changing according to the position of mist and sun! And as the first inquiries for a given day may be,—where lies the mist? How goes the wind? Does the cloud lie in the valley, or is it riding on high in a depth of blue? So is it not the great question in the day of our life: How fares thy spirit, brother? How fares thy spirit, sister?—Toward thy knowledge and thy ignorance, toward the health and sickness of thy body, toward thy work and thy play, toward friends and toward strangers, toward all the blessing and trials that go to make up the sum of thy earthly existence?

(Conclusion in September.)

JOAN OF ARC.

Margaret E. Jordan.

Speed the glad day when on thy virgin brow
    May shine Heaven's laurel wreath of sanctity;
When not "sweet Maid" we'll breathe in prayer as now—
    But from all hearts shall rise exultingly
To loving lips, a glorious "Saint Joan,"
To ring and echo throughout earth's great span.

O thou who freed thy land in per-
        il's hour,
    And to the throne did rightful
        sovereign bring!
Behold, to-day doth reign a van-
        dal power!
    Behold, the throne is wrested
        from the King!
The throne is wrested from the King
        of Love—
A Godless standard waves Christ's
        Cross above!

O Maid of might on battlefield of
        France!
    Saint yet to be—God grant! on
        altar shrine!
Thy martyr-palm more powerful is
        than lance
    Of earthly combat, in the strife divine,—
Lift thou for France thy pleading, prayerful hands!
Legions await thy virginal commands!

Legions angelic! and wilt thou besiege
    How many a citadel of human hearts
Till in their depths is Christ proclaimed the Liege—
    Till faith and hope and love—thy battle darts—
Have vanquished Godlessness, thy country's foe.
And laid beneath Christ's Cross its standard low!

ST. PHILIP BENIZI.

VERY REV. C. H. McKENNA, O. P.

N the 15th of August, 1233, Philip Benizi was born. The son of an excellent Florentine family, his birth was hailed with joy by all who knew his parents. They had been married for years without offspring, and Philip was regarded, like Samuel, as an answer to their prayers. His biographers tell us that the boy was born at the hour when the Confraternity of the Laudesi were chanting the praises of Mary, and at the very time when Mary was communicating to the Seven Sainted Founders the secrets of Heaven.

Albaverde, like the mother of St. Dominic, had a premonition of her son's future sanctity. If Blessed Joanna saw her child under the figure of a whelp, with lighted torch, running hither and thither, setting the world on fire, Albaverde saw Philip as a brilliant flame, illumining the world by its brightness. Our Blessed Mother must have smiled on the new-born boy, for his mission was to propagate devotion to her sorrows. Philip was destined not only to give form and stability to her new Order of Servants, but to him was given, more than to any other man since the days of the disciple of love, to lift the veil that hides her sorrowing heart, and gaze down into that fathomless sea of woe which engulfed her soul on the heights of Calvary.

Philip was one of the Florentine infants, who, long before the dawn of reason, proclaimed the sanctity of the Seven Founders, and gave the name to their future Order; for, when yet but a few months old, he begged his mother, in clear, unmistakable words, to give relief to the Servants of Mary. Like the manger of Bethlehem, Philip's cradle was his first pulpit, whence he commenced to preach to a sensual world the doctrine of prayer and of penance, and to point out by his example the narrow path that leads to Heaven. For, long before the period when reason asserts its sway over the mind of children, Philip began on fast days of

3

the Church to deny himself his food, and as soon as he was
able to crawl out of his little bed, he would be found by his nurse
either prostrate on the floor, or kneeling apparently absorbed in
prayer.

For a time his good mother and his nurse did all they could to
make their charge take his food on fast days, thinking, says his
biographer, his was only a childish freak; but they were finally
forced to desist, and let him have his own way, or rather, leave
him to follow the attractions of grace.

To a sensual age like our own, how strange all this must appear! Our children must be indulged, pampered, kept as hot-
house plants; yet they wilt and die by the thousands. Our young
people must seek every remedy for bodily ills, every preventive
against diseases, every means of prolonging life; yet the ceme-
teries are filled with their graves, whilst many of God's saints,
who ever treated their bodies as their enemies, have lived to a
round old age.

Witness the life of Anthony of the desert, of Paul the first hermit, of Basil, Jerome, and so many others. Who to-day has a
brighter intellect, or works harder than our illustrious Pontiff;
yet who has lived more abstemiously? The same was also true of
England's late Cardinals.

But apart from the life of the body, which abstinence and fasting help to prolong, the saints knew no other path to Heaven.
It was the lesson taught by the Master. For if in one place He
tells us that we must renounce all to be His disciple, in another He declares that we must deny ourselves and take up our
Cross daily and follow Him. He said, "The grain must rot and
die before it can bring forth fruit," and His Holy Spirit already
began to speak to the heart of Philip, though yet a child, teaching him to commence the life of an apostle by self-denial, prayer,
and fasting. The venerable ascetic Benedictine, Father Baker,
says: " Our duty in our present state, the whole employment of
our lives, should be to co-operate with divine grace; endeavoring constantly to conquer self-love, pride, sensuality, and other
vices of our fallen nature. And by the practise of the opposite
virtues, we should daily aspire to unlimited holiness, even to
that perfect union with God enjoyed by Adam before his fall."

" Self-love and all affection for creatures must be utterly extinguished in us," he says, "except in as far as we love creatures in God,
and for Him; and that they help us to aspire to God." [1]   To this
union with God all are called, for all are called to be perfect, and
to this God's Spirit urges all men.   But, like the seed that fell
among thorns, the divine voice is stifled in most men by the cares
of the world, and by the demands of sensuality.   The flesh will
brook no contradiction.   It must be satisfied, even to the ruin of
soul and body.

Like most of God's saints, Philip was given a holy mother,
which, says the Curè of Ars, is one of the greatest blessings that
can be given to a child.   Albaverde and her devout husband
were delighted with the early manifestations of piety in their boy,
and, knowing the necessity of surrounding his youth with every
safeguard of virtue, they sought for him a learned religious tutor.
Alas, that in our days parents are so indifferent with regard to the
environments of their children!   They permit, nay, they force
their little ones to associate with the offspring of the degraded,
the vile, the adulterous, unmindful that a " bad tree cannot bring
forth good fruit."   These parents seem satisfied with the teachings
of institutions to which God never promises His Spirit.   To His
Church alone He gave power to teach the nations those principles of faith and of morality without which conscience is
blinded by passion; and men and nations hasten to their ruin.

Philip's tutor left nothing undone to advance his pupil in virtue and learning.   Before the age of ten, he daily recited the
Litany of the Saints, the Seven Penitential Psalms, the Office of
the Dead, and the Little Office of our Blessed Lady, practices
which he maintained during his laborious life.   It was edifying,
said one of his biographers, to see the little boy assist with his
good mother at the services of the Church, and to notice with
what recollection he was present at Mass, and how eagerly he
drank in the instructions and sermons of the preacher.   He was
scarcely twelve when he was sufficiently advanced in his studies
to enter the University, and his father concluded to send him to
Paris.

Paris had then the most famous University of the world.   Its

[1] Holy Wisdom, p. 33.

University was also one of the most dangerous places to the morality of youth. Why, it may be asked, did James Benizi expose his
boy to the dangers of the University, where so many immoral young
men from all parts of Europe were congregated? One reason is
given, that he dreaded least his son should enter some Religious Order, whilst he desired for Philip some honorable position in society.
The father was proud of the wonderful talents manifested by the
boy, which were surely destined to lead to a brilliant future.

At that time Florence was filled with religious enthusiasm.
The world was ringing with the fame, both of the Sons of St.
Dominic and of St. Francis. Their respective novitiates were
crowded with men of all ages, desirous of serving God in the
more perfect way. In Florence itself the fame of the seven holy
founders was daily increasing, and many of her best young men
were knocking for admittance at the gates of Monte Senario.

Whether James Benizi dreaded that his gifted son might seek
admission into one of the Religious Orders, or whether he simply
sought his higher education, we know not; he certainly spared
nothing for the advancement of his boy's temporal interests, and
we have reason to believe that he strongly hoped our Blessed
Mother, whom his son so ardently loved, would preserve him from
the corruptions of the University.

Nor was the father disappointed in his boy. Philip continued
in Paris the same life of prayer and of mortification, which he had
pursued in his father's house. Nay, he redoubled his austerities,
and gave more of his nights to prayer, lest the enemy of his virtue should gain any entrance into his virgin heart.

The University of Paris was then chiefly noted for its faculty
of Theology. The Dominicans came to Paris in 1217, and the
Franciscans one year later. Among the latter, Alexander Hales
had taught with wonderful fame, "leaving his mantle to one of
his Order greater than himself," the Seraphic St. Bonaventure.
Among the Dominicans, Albert the Great was then at the zenith
of his glory. So vast was the number of young men who flocked
to hear him that no building could contain them. His chair was
placed in an open square which to-day is known as Place Maubert, or place of Master Albert. Among the pupils of Albert was
one of his own brethren, the great Aquinas, "great as the master
himself, nay, greater, one whom to have trained honors the teacher more than all his works." It is impossible to describe the ef-

fect of such men's teachings on the brilliant religious mind of Philip.

James Benizi did not leave his son to finish his studies in Paris, but sent him to the University of Padua, which in law and medicine excelled even Paris, and there, when " he had hardly completed his twentieth year, he passed the customary examinations in philosophy and medicine so brilliantly, that his degrees were conferred amidst unanimous applause."[1] Philip returned to his proud parents, and commenced the practice of medicine. In a short time the city was full of admiration of the skilful young physician, so retiring, so humble; at the same time, so charitable, and so attentive to the poor. Philip was now courted by the best society in Florence, but he shunned its enchanting snares, frequented the churches and the sacraments more than ever, and hungered for that peace and solitude which the world cannot give or understand.

One of the shrines, in which Philip delighted to pray, was the Annunziata, which was amongst the most devotional places in Florence. Here, pilgrims came from all parts of Europe to pray, and to gaze on its miraculous picture of the Annunciation. This chapel was built by the new Order of Servites; and, in gratitude for the wonderful vision which they received on the Feast of the Annunciation, they determined to have a picture of our Lady as represented in that Mystery. A large space was reserved behind the altar for the frescoe, and one Bartholomew, then famous as a painter, was selected for the work. The artist, a devout man, prepared himself for his work, as was his custom, by confession and communion, and commenced by first painting the Angel Gabriel, then the neck, hands, and body of our Lady, but hesitated to paint her face. It may be he had a vision of the Immaculate One which overpowered him. Again and again he made the attempt to finish his picture, but to no purpose. Bartholomew slept, and on awaking, behold! a wondrous face had been given to his Madonna. The news spread with lightning speed. The whole city was moved. Artists came from afar to gaze on the miraculous painting, so beautiful, so heavenly. Michael Angelo, the great painter, was asked by the Duke of Tuscany his opinion of the painting. He said: " If any one were to tell me this was painted by human hands, I should say that it was untrue, and I know something of my business."

[1] Life, p. 22.

It was on the 25th of March, 1252, when the miraculous painting appeared, and, immediately, wonderful miracles began to be performed in favor of those who came to pray before it. No wonder Philip loved to visit this miraculous image! A short time previously, whilst his heart burned with love for God, and with an ardent desire to leave the world and all its goods, and consecrate himself forever to his Master's service, he heard a voice as if coming from the crucifix to his heart, saying: " Go, Philip, to the high hill; ascend to the spot where the Servants of My Mother dwell, and thou wilt do what is pleasing to My Father." [1]

Philip's heart seemed to melt within him. His name was uttered with such sweetness! His tears flowed in abundance. Here was another proof of the love of Jesus for the Servants of Mary, and for those who love to honor her sorrows. Though this should have sufficed to point out his vocation to Philip, he wanted a clearer evidence of the will of Heaven. For this purpose he sought the aid of the Annunziata, and poured out prayers and tears before the miraculous Madonna. Suddenly his soul was stilled. A wondrous vision opened before him. He saw the world like a frightful desert, full of yawning abysses. Hissing serpents and savage beasts appeared on every side ready to destroy him. Paralyzed with fear and terror, he raised his eyes to the Madonna, when he heard a sweet voice calling him by name. In a clear blue sky he saw a magnificent chariot surrounded by angels, and seated in the chariot on an ivory throne hung with black drapery, our Immaculate Mother, brighter than ten thousand suns, with a crown of stars on her head, and clad in a long, flowing black mantle. Then he heard the words: " Draw near, and join thyself to the chariot." At the same time our Lady beckoned him to approach, and showed him the Servite Habit. Philip was roused from his ecstasy by a brother of the convent telling him it was time to close the church. That night Philip spent in prayer in his own room. The vision was repeated. He could no longer doubt. He hastened in the morning to beg admittance among the Servites, imploring, with tears in his eyes, to be admitted as a lay brother, a servant of the Servants of Mary. Philip was received with joy, sent to Monte Senario, and there by vigorous penances and long vigils he prepared himself for that wondrous life of labor in spreading his Order, and in inflaming the hearts of men with love and pity for our Mother of Sorrows.

[1] Life, p. 35.

THE MESSAGE OF THE ANGELUS.

WALTER LECKY.

A T eve, with coming gray,
Ere darkness leads the way,
I heard an old bell say,—
  "Angelus Domini nuntiavit Mariæ."

A peasant heard the tale
Borne by a passing gale,
And sang in lower scale,—
  "Et concepit de Spiritu Sancto."

A shepherd on the height
Bid sleepy day " good night,"
And prayed with all his might,
  Ave Maria.

The bell then sweeter spoke,
A woman's voice awoke,
And through the air it broke,—
  "Fiat mihi secundum verbum tuum "

The shepherd-peasant made
A bow, and softer prayed,
Invoking Virgin's aid,
  Ave Maria.

Then louder sang the bell,
As if to break a spell,
And make this poor world well,
  "Et verbum caro factum est."

A monk within his cell
Dropt on his knees to tell
The message of the bell,
  "Et habitavit in nobis."

When ceased the changing note,
The scribe in Heaven wrote,
" From these be sin remote,"
  Gloria in Excelsis Domino.

THE LILY OF CHIMU.

A TALE OF THE INCAS.

REV. A. H. DE VIRAS, O. P.

CHAPTER XVI.

FROM the moment that Racuna-Capac had taken possession of the Inca's apartments at the Citadel, he had not again shown himself to the people of Chimu; but their religious enthusiasm, far from suffering any diminution by the withdrawal of his presence, only grew more and more intense, until it reached the verge of a delirium, of a devotional craze, the limits of which not even the wisest heads were able to foresee.

It is always and everywhere thus with fanaticism and superstition; the credulous masses may be irresistibly drawn to build visible and palpable idols of stone or wood, or even of mud; but no god has better chances to inspire fear and admiration, to satisfy an instinctive need of servile worship, to excite religious passions, to cause the burning fever of a gross and absurd mysticism, than has an unseen god, a god hidden from the populace.

The visible object of adoration soon reveals its imperfections, its defects, the imposture that gave it existence; the very fact of its being exposed to view day after day and night after night is sufficient to divest it of its apparently supernatural character, and to deaden faith in the hearts of its most fervent adorers,—just as the very fact of constantly associating with the object of ardent passion is the death of love, of sensual love be it understood, in the heart of the libertine.

But the invisible idol, the idol that shows itself for an instant, and that by a wonderful lightning-like apparition, and then buries itself in the darkness of impenetrable mystery, concealing itself ever behind the massive iron gates of a temple inaccessible to the common crowd, or in the sombre vaults of a subterraneous crypt, or within the never-opened shrine of a perpetually veiled sanctuary, pronouncing therefrom its oracles, and ruling the bodies and the souls of its votaries, such a god, indeed, may fig-

ure as almighty; and provided it never permits any one to penetrate into the secrecy of its essence, its existence and its personality, its worship will never end.   So, too, will never end the passion of the ardent youth who contemplates from afar the beautiful maiden of his dreams, to whom he never whispers the sweet
words of love, whose rosy lips his never touch,   whose possession
is to him a fond fancy, but never a thing of hope, and less of
reality.

History is not wanting in its examples of such a faith and such
a love.

Racuna-Capac had then placed himself in the most fortunate
of conditions for a god by obstinately refusing to appear again in
public, notwithstanding the repeated demands and ever-growing
desires of the people, and when I say the people I speak not only
of the lower and meaner classes, but also of the higher ranks—the
priests, the officers, the civil authorities,—with possibly no more
than two exceptions, Tupayachi and Gupanqui,—Tupayachi, because he was not convinced of the divine character of Racuna-
Capac; Gupanqui because he feared that his own prestige with
the people would be eclipsed by that of the new Manco.

But Racuna-Capac was not acting thus by way of calculation,
indeed.   No; since the moment when Ollacpya and her hand-
maids had been appointed to attend and serve him, the unfortunate young man seemed to have lost that self-confidence in his
divinity which the sorceress of Huanchaco had instilled into him
by a training the most horrible in its nature.   The hypnotic influence under which he was held by the infernal practices of the
witch was gradually giving way to an influence new and altogether different, though unintended.   In Ollacpya's presence Racuna-
Capac was not the same man; he was incapable of giving any
order, of answering any question, of acting his part in any scene
of the dreadful drama for which he had been prepared.   The sorceress being present, the fascination exercised over him by that
infamous creature regained its empire, and he forgot other surroundings; but she, in her wiliness, did not often come near, lest
even the slightest suspicion might be aroused.

The morning after the interview related in the preceding
chapter, between herself and her accomplice, and the failure of

their diabolical plotting against the Curaca and his daughter, a superior officer entered the apartment of Racuna-Capac to receive his orders; the witch, with her own intent, entered also.

Ollacpya was absent; she had gone to take a little repose, for, with Mocllanta, she had watched the night through over the restless and troubled sleep of this son of the deity.

To the officer's inquiry he replied: " My mission here is ended. To-morrow I take my departure for Cuzco. It is the will of the Sun. Let the Curaca order fifty guards as my escort. Two litters shall be prepared; one for my use, decorated with gold and precious stuffs; the other almost as magnificent, shall be made ready for this favorite and confident of the divinity. It is the will of the Sun. Obey, mortal, or fear my vengeance! "

The officer bowed profoundly, and retired toward the entrance, with backward steps, through respect for the new Manco.

The witch remained, and with an imperative gesture, she beckoned away the female attendants who stood around. Then approaching the poor victim of her black arts, and fixing her eyes upon his with an expression meant to terrify, she said:

" Listen, son of the gods. The Curaca Gupanqui, the High-priest Tupayachi, and Ollacpya, the proud, execrable maiden who is now thy slave, must form part of thy cortege, and must follow thee on foot. This is the will of the Sun. Thou must take them with thee, and if they resist or disobey, death will be the penalty. Thou must condemn them and deliver them over to the vengeance of the people, of the faithful worshippers of the gods. The Sun will designate another High-priest and Curaca!"

" Condemn to death the Curaca and the High-priest! " shrieked out Racuna-Capac in accents of furious anger—"condemn to death the Curaca and the High-priest if they disobey the orders of the Sun! "

" Condemn to death Ollacpya! " added the hag, imperatively.

Racuna-Capac shuddered, hesitated, but then repeated:

" To death, the Curaca; to death, the High-priest."

The sorceress stretched her skinny hand over his head, and vented her atrocious rage by spitting into his face; then she exclaimed:

" Now wilt thou endure such torture as thou hast never yet endured, for thy disobedience! "

For a moment the eyes of Racuna-Capac were lighted up with
the flashes of free will rebellious against enslavement; he looked
defiance at the witch and her menaces—a look she had never before seen him wear.

But a terrible voice, that same voice he had heard so many
times before in the depth of the cavern as a prelude to cruel
torments, howled from above:

" Let this miserable one be punished!   Let him suffer scourg-
ings, harrowings, for opposing my sacred will!"

The wretched youth, overcome by terror, fell upon his knees,
and raising his hands imploringly, cried out:

" Mercy! O Father Sun! have mercy on me!   Pardon! pardon
me!"

" Then death to Ollacpya!" roared out the pitiless, horrible
voice above:

" Death....to....Ollacpya," moaned he, so feebly as scarcely
to be heard, and as if the mental torture he had experienced in
uttering the words had been more atrocious than all the corporal
torments to which he had ever submitted, and with which he was
again threatened.   He cried out in anguish, then fell fainting on
the stony floor, striking his head against the pedestal of a massive golden perfume-burner.   From a gash cut on the forehead
just near the temple, the blood gushed forth and ran streaming
down his pallid face, and reddening the silken garments that
graced his form.

The witch saw and was anxious, not in the interests of the poor
wretch lying at her feet, but for the consequences such an accident could have over her own future; muttering a blasphemy,
she started quickly towards her apartment to procure medicines,
cordials, and balms, which she had there.

Passing through the court, she found the female attendants waiting.   She gave them orders not to disturb the god during her absence; but they had heard his cry of distress.   They looked at
the sorceress with diffidence, and one of the guards remonstrated
that he had not to receive commands from her.   Others were of
the same opinion, and despite her curses and menaces, advanced
a few steps, about to open the thick curtain that closed the entrance to Racuna-Capac's apartment.

The witch turned her face towards the room, dissimulating her rage under a smile of contempt, and in a loud voice demanded:

" Racuna-Capac, son of the gods, these temarious and sacrilegious ones listen not to the commands of thy servant; deign thyself to speak to them."

She no sooner ceased, when, in grave, angry, and menacing tones, she was answered from behind the tapestry—tones that none would have refused to recognize as those of Racuna-Capac:

" Leave them to consummate their sacrilege; thou beloved friend of the Sun; leave them to learn what is my vengeance; but woe to whomsoever puts his foot into this, my sanctuary of rest, before he shall be called."

The effect produced by these words was magic: the listeners amazed and wonder-stricken, drew back, and stood like statues of marble, some even betaking themselves to flight at the risk of punishment for abandoning the post assigned them as guards.

The sorceress was triumphant, sure that no one would now attempt to break the defense; once more her marvellous faculty as ventriloquist had served her well.

She hastened onward to prepare her drugs, and while thus engaged, and alone, soliloquized:

" Ah, I suspected it all. I thought that hated girl would try her seductive arts on him, and see now, she almost succeeded. But never mind, he is yet in my hands; I have lost nothing of my power of fascinating him; but she, miserable girl, is lost forever. I have her now; this evening will finish the work,—we shall have fine times, indeed. I shall see that he accomplishes my plot to the last tittle. Either she and her accursed father obey his orders, or they disobey. In the first case, Paraymi can easily take them on the journey, and deliver them up to me for my vengeance; in the second it will be better still—for if they disobey, Racuna-Capac will condemn them to death in the name of the gods,—the populace will lay hands on the Curaca, and put an end to him; but it shall be my sole delight, drop by drop, to take the life of Ollacpya. I will bathe my hands and my face in her blood. I will rend her breast, and extract her heart,—that heart which in itself I abhor more then herself. I will feed upon it, still trembling, palpitating; oh, will it not be something delicious to taste the living heart of the Lily of Chimu! But no, no; that would not be enough for me; I must invent a fate more horrible still, a long drawn-out torment, a torment eternal, if possible. Ah, pretty Lily of Chimu! another night and thou wilt know what it means to be hated by the daughter of Supay! "

And now, having finished the work of carefully concocting her drugs, she went to join her victim. When she had reached the entrance of Racuna-Capac's room, she was surprised to find there a group of sentinels with Apamuyu as commander.

As she approached, the young warrior cried out to her:

" Backward, witch! we have word from Racuna-Capac to permit no one, be he who he may, to come near him at present."

" I know this," angrily retorted the sorceress; " but this restriction concerns not me. On the contrary, he himself required that I attend him all the day long."

" What sayest thou? Dost thou dare to lie so audaciously in my very face! Backward, I repeat; backward, or—"

The sorceress stood stupefied. What could have happened? How, in so short a time, had this body of men gathered here when she believed that she had cut off all communication with Racuna-Capac only a few moments before? She tried to insist, and even to force her way in spite of Apamuyu's remonstrances, but the energetic attitude of the young officer and sentinels gave her to understand that it was useless. She was too far from the apartment to employ the fraud of ventriloquism; besides, she knew that Apamuyu had too much good sense to be caught by trickery. She therefore concluded it were better not to expose herself to a more signal defeat, but to curb her wrath till time should enable her to exercise it still more direfully. And so she went away, venting her fury in multiplied curses upon those who had crossed her path.

That which was an inexplicable mystery to the hag, was in reality a very simple fact.

The distressed cry of Racuna-Capac for help had been heard by several of Ollacypa's attendants. They, unlike the soldiers, delayed not to discuss with the witch. They not even waited for any explanation, nor stood perplexed by the fraud of ventriloquism, but went at once to rouse their sleeping mistress.

To listen to them, to leap from her hammock, to call Mocllanta and fly with her to the apartment of Racuna-Capac, was for Ollacpya but the work of a moment.

Had she in that moment tried to analyze her sentiments, and to explain to herself why she was so alarmed, why so fearful, so interested, she would perhaps have discovered in that alarm, in that interest and that fear, something of a character totally different from worship, and from mere consciousness of her responsibility as the appointed attendant of so important a personage.

She had been sent by the Curaca to wait upon Racuna-Capac, to serve him almost as a slave,--but was it in obedience to this paternal commission that she was now acting, or to the impulses of her own heart?

Any one who had watched her just at this instant would have been tempted to accept this last interpretation.

When she had reached the threshold of Racuna-Capac's room, the guards undertook with all respect, to make her understand that the messenger of the gods had, a few seconds before, forbidden with menaces all approach to his presence. Ollacpya seemed to pay not the least attention, as if it were a thing well-known that such commands were not for her, and quickly passing on, she raised the tapestry lightly, and entered the room.

No one dared to follow her, not even Mocllanta.

Ollacpya uttered not a word to express the downhearted grief that seized upon her at the sight she saw. Dissolved in tears, she threw herself down beside the apparently lifeless youth, took in her arms his pale, senseless, and blood-stained head, and then called upon him in words of touching importunity to look at her and speak to her.

"Oh, it cannot be," she said, "that I came too late! Why did I leave him for an instant alone? I might have died in his stead had I been faithful to my post. I went to take my rest while he was in danger. No, no; I will not believe that he is lost to me forever!"

And bending low, she whispered into his ear as if to communicate a lost and lingering confidence, speaking as would a mother to a beloved and only angel child before yielding it up to the casket and the grave.

" I knew it, I knew thou wast not a god! Thou didst not come from Heaven,—no; thou art the victim of a monstrous and ravenous ambition. Forgive, oh, forgive me if I, I alone have surmised something of the dreadful secret of thy wretched past! I never sought to penetrate it; but these two sorrowful nights that I have watched by thy bedside, held there and drawn to thee by a mysterious attraction incomprehensible even to myself,—the wanderings of thy feverish dreams—ah, what things they have revealed to me! . . . . . And when I had hoped that I was happily destined by the gods—no, no, by the God, the one only and true God whom the white woman showed to me, whom Tupayachi declared to me —when this God had destined me to deliver thee from the abyss of crime and misery into which perverse ones had plunged thee, I know not how or why,—she, that evil-hearted woman, has killed thee! Yes, I am sure it is she! Who else could have————"

Suddenly the young girl stopped. Her tears were stayed, the blood flushed her cheeks and brow, and she drew back shuddering, letting fall from her arms the head of the wounded youth. He whom she had thought dead reopened his eyes, and first stared at her with unconscious terror, and then, with an ardent tenderness and supplicating tone, he murmured:

" O mother, dear mother, save me! Do not abandon me again! Send away, far away from me, that woman! "

At these last words the whole body of the unfortunate youth shook with convulsions, his eyes glared in indescribable horror, while drops of cold sweat stood out on his pale face. He stretched out his arms, and closed them around Ollacpya in a violent grasp-like embrace—so tightly that she almost shrieked from pain,—but like the sudden rebound of the steel spring, when broken or distended by over-effort, he loosened his hold, drooped his head, and again closed his eyes.

For one moment Ollacpya hesitated, then resolved with herself. And sure now that the Sorceress of Huanchaco had been the cause of Racuna-Capac's sad condition, fearing too that this miserable woman might attempt to renew her malicious work, she repressed her emotion, and with an exterior of calmness and self-composure she left the apartment.

Precisely at the moment the sentinels on watch were being

relieved by others, their officer was substituted by Apamuyu.

" God is with us," she thought; and addressing herself to the young chief, she said:

" The messenger of Heaven forbids any one, even the Sorceress of Huanchaco, to approach his apartment."

" So we were told," retorted the other officer, whose time of guard had expired, " but it seems that thou makest no difficulty of disregarding that command."

" The Lily of Chimu is above all laws, human or divine," gallantly replied Apamuyu, while disposing his sentinels around.

A universal applause went up from all the soldiers, who knew Ollacpya, as did everyone in the city of Chimu, and loved her—almost adored her—for her beauty, her good-heart, and her noble soul.

She seemed not to have heard the words uttered in her praise, and retired behind the tapestry confident that as long as Apamuyu should be there, that is for a fifth part of the day, no danger could either threaten her nor Racuna-Capac.

(*To be Continued.*)

A NORTHERN STORM.

J. K. FORAN.

As the sun went down, through the purple haze,
    On horizon's rim, he was blood-like red;
" What a glorious eve! " was my simple phrase;
    " And an awful night," the Indian said.
Yet the air was calm, and the sky was bright,—
    Could it be that the dusky guide was right?

An hour: and the folds of the darkness swept
    Over mirror lake, over mountain high,
While his lonely watch by the loon was kept,
    And the echoes answer'd his ghoul-like cry.
The forest murmur'd, and the very air
    Was as weird and strange as if ghosts were there.

Still another hour: as we paus'd to hear,
  Like distant thunder came a rumbling sound:
The partridge flutter'd in its sudden fear,
  And the hare leap'd past with a zig-zag bound.
For a time it ceas'd, while its giant form
  The pine-tree braced for the coming storm.

Then the hissing gusts that hurriedly sped—
  As they sounded their warning notes on high,—
Like heralds of war through the forest fled,
  And shriek'd to the woods as they gallopp'd by.
Defiant the elm, and proudly the ash
  Prepared their limbs for the coming crash.

The van of the storm was upon their heels;
  Down the mountain side its battalions rush'd.
As when broken rank in the onset reels,
  And the trampled dead are in hundreds crush'd,
Came the first wild charge of that fearful fight;
  And the trees bent low to the tempest's might.

A flying-column made a sweep in flank,
  Deploying its force on the rolling lake,
While the waves leap'd up o'er the steepest bank,
  As if by assault the woods they would take.
On the hills, in their stalworth, steady lines,
  With the giant blast fought the stately pines.

How the thunder boom'd!   How the lightnings flash'd!
  As when avalanche down St. Gothard shoots,
Through grove and thicket had the monster crash'd,
  And upwrench'd the pines by their very roots.
Just one dreadful hour of destructive wrath,
  While the Boreal scythe mow'd its level path.

How the scudding clouds rolled near and far,
  Till a rent was slit by the wind's keen knife,—
Then above, in the blue, shone a silent star,
  That calmly smiled on the wreck and strife.
My God! in all truth, 'twas "an awful night:"
  I had found that the dusky guide was right.

THE ROSARY.

THE CATHOLIC CLUB AND ITS LIBRARY.

EDWARD J. McGUIRE.

None of the finest of the new club houses of the city, looking out upon Central Park, a royal close for a front door-yard, is a series of lofty, extensive rooms filled with rare and valuable books, in number more than twenty thousand. The house is the home of nearly a thousand men. They form a society, which they endeavor to have represent adequately, the Catholic laity of the Archdiocese of New York. Fostered by the protection and patronage of the Apostolic Delegate, and their own beloved Archbishop, they work in a noble sphere for a great end, the gathering together of the Catholic manhood of New York in a centre of truth and enlightenment, and of intellectual and moral progress. Blessed materially with an abundance of means, excellently equipped with financial resources, the Catholic Club of New York rejoices in its youth and strength, and goes on prosperously in its high mission.

In November, 1866, the first effort to form a permanent social organization among the educated Catholic young men of New York was made. It ended in failure. The idea which underlay it, however, was not to be defeated.

There had been established on the feast of the Immaculate Conception, December 8th, 1863, in the College of Saint Francis Xavier, the Xavier Alumni Sodality, whose object was the encouragement of virtue and Christian piety among the educated Catholic young men of the city, and the promotion of Catholic interests by their united efforts, and which sought at the same time, by reviving collegiate friendships, to provide for its members congenial associations.

In February, 1871, the Council of the Xavier Alumni Sodality took up the work of forming a social organization, upon the basis of the Sodality, to be called the Xavier Union. The President of the Sodality was then Professor Charles G. Herbermann, of the

College of the City of New York. The work of the new society was vigorously taken up, under the leadership of Mr. Joseph

Thoron, a merchant of large acquaintance and of unbounded enthusiasm and zeal. He was the chairman of the committee which framed its constitution and by-laws, and was chosen its first president. He is justly called its founder, and is to-day still vigorously at work, foremost among the friends and laborers for the society. The powerful interest, patronage, and zeal of the Jesuit Fathers fostered

vigorously the infant organization. The Reverend Patrick F.

Dealy, S. J., was the moderator of the Sodality at the foundation of the Xavier Union, and became its director.*   He filled this important office for seventeen years, beloved and venerated by all its members.   The Union began with a capital of $1,250, raised by subscription, and occupied part of one of the houses owned by the College at 59 West 15th Street. In May, 1873, it was incorporated by act of the Legislature.   In March, 1876, it had grown sufficiently prosperous to purchase a home of its own at No. 20 West 27th Street.

On January 1st, 1888, the name of the Xavier Union was changed to the Catholic Club of the City of New York.   It remained in 27th Street until March, 1892, when its present palatial home, at No. 120 West 59th Street, having been completed at a cost of over $350,000, it established itself there with its collections of books and accumulated treasures of twenty-one years.

PROFESSOR CHAS. G. HERBERMANN.

The great work of erecting and furnishing its club house was principally borne by Mr. Charles V. Fornes, its president for five years, of whom Chief Justice Joseph F. Daly, its present president, has eloquently said that he found the Catholic Club housed in the respectable home of the burgher, and left it established in the palace of a prince.   To him the Club owes constant gratitude.

From the very beginning of the Xavier Union the idea of a

* We regret that it was not in our power to procure a photograph of. Father Dealy, S. J.   The illustrations of the Club building, which we have selected from the many contained in the Album of the club, represent, respectively: Front view of the building, facing Central Park, general view of the library, the east wing of library, a hall connecting with the ball-room. showing portrait of Pius IX., and the main hall.

vast library had been a most important one in the minds of its founders.   Its first home was opened on May 8th, 1871.   Its first library circular was issued in the November of that year.   It sought even then to establish a standard Catholic library of reference, and to promote among Catholic young gentlemen an intelligent interest in the important religious, scientific, and esthetic questions of the day.

The library in 1872 already contained 5,000 volumes.   At this time the Club began the custom of lectures under its auspices, which has been continued to the present.   Among the titles of its first lectures are "Darwinism," by Rev. Louis Jouin, S. J., "Positivism," by Rev. Philip Doucet, S. J.;

MR. JOSEPH THORON.

Bishop Lynch, of Charleston, Wendell Philipps, Daniel Dougherty, Rev. Augustine F. Hewit, C. S. P., Rev. Joseph Shea, S. J., General John Newton, and Dr. Isaac N. Hayes, the arctic explorer, were among the earlier lecturers.   On January 1st, 1875, there were 6,000 volumes in the library, of which but 81 had been purchased from the funds, the others being donations or purchases from subscriptions to the library fund, which up to that time had reached $2,700.

On January 1st, 1878, the library had grown to 8,100 volumes. In March, 1886, was made the great gift of the "Lake Library," which gives the Catholic Club library its unique value and interest. This was the gift of the generous friends of the Club in the name of Father Dealy, its director, and at his solicitation.

The history of the Rev. Henry S. Lake, the son of a wealthy

merchant of the city, from his pampered youth of dilettantism through the period of his religious zeal and enthusiasm to his end in obscurity and sorrow on the Pacific coast, is sad beyond expression. During his residence at the University of Louvain, he spent four happy years in an enthusiastic search for valuable and rare theological and philosophical works, and became known throughout Europe as a generous and intelligent collector. He scoured the book stalls and auction rooms of the continent for whatever was rarest in this field of knowledge, and expense never stood in the way. The complaint was made that he had greatly raised the prices of the dealers, by his ardor for the possession of treasures in both mediæval and modern ecclesiastical literature. On his return to New York, he brought his books with him, but they remained in their cases, stored in his father's lofts, undisturbed until his death. On the death of his father, which followed soon after, they were put up at auction, and an elaborate and useful catalogue of the sale was printed at large expense. At the last moment, however, the friends of the Catholic Club purchased them, and the most valuable private collection of books in this field in America was saved from dispersal.

MR. CHARLES V. FORNES.

To quote from a description published at the time: " In canon law, mediæval controversies, the writings of the school men, history, and sacred antiquities, the collection is almost without a rival. Some of the earliest specimens of the art of printing,—incunabula, black-letter prints, gross tomes bound in solid oak, are to be found here. Among the rarer works are those of Justus

Lipsius, Gronovius, Hospinianus, St. Bernadin, and Petrus de
Aquila.   An old black-letter of John of Lubeck, printed at Cologne in 1477, eleven years after the first book ever printed there,

is among the rarities, as also an old folio of the decretals of Innocent IV., bearing the date, Venice, 1481."
    It contains also the best modern edition of St. Thomas Aqui-
nas, printed at Parma, from 1852 to 1873, in twenty-five volumes

quarto. The largest single set of books is Migne's " Patrology of the Greek and Latin Fathers," which embraces all the writings extant of all the Fathers of the Church from the time of the Apostles to the close of the 12th century. There are 324 volumes in the set. The stereotype plates were destroyed by fire in Paris after only a limited number were printed, and as a consequence, the value of the edition is very great.

One of the most valuable works is the Acta Sanctorium of Johannes Bollandus, S. J., commonly known as the Bollandist Lives of the Saints, which has been more than two hundred and fifty years in course of production, and is still unfinished. The Club's copy is in fifty-one volumes, folio, contains most valuable portraits and plates, and reaches to October 16th. It will probably take one hundred years more to complete the work. The destruction of almost the whole edition of two of the volumes for October during the French Revolution, stopped the work for seventy years. It contains exhaustive lives of the saints for each day of the year, as far as completed. It is a treasury of interesting and important facts.

The library at the present time contains, in round numbers, 21,000 volumes.

The rooms of the library occupy the entire third floor of the club house, and are four in number. The east room is occupied by the works in Fiction, English Literature, Drama, French, Spanish, and German Literature, Latin and Greek classics, Art, Music, and Literary Biography. It is used also as the reading room, with electric reading lamps, comfortable chairs, and a long table covered with magazines and current periodicals. The centre room contains the General History section, with departments of English, French, and general European History, and a separate department for works on the History of the United States, which is very complete, and includes some of the rarest and most curious volumes on the subject. The west room is the largest. On its walls, rising to the height of fifteen feet, are arranged two tiers of cases; the highest surrounded by a gallery. Here are the works on Travels, Geography, Oriental Countries, Ireland and Gaelic Literature, of which there is a rare and valuable collection; Encyclopædias, Dictionaries, Reference and Hand-books, Gazet-

teers, and the books which give the Library its character, and
greatest value: those relating to Catholic Philosophy, Theology,
History, Hagiography and Archaeology. In the section relating to
Catholicism in the United States, a special effort has been made to

make as complete a collection as possible of contemporary books,
pamphlets, circulars, and reports, to serve the purpose of
the future historian of the Church in America.   The Lake Library, after its curious wanderings and history, here finds its proper home, where its unrivalled treasures are respected and cared

for, and are open for use and reference, awaiting the coming
of Catholic men of letters. On the upper tiers are the
Patristic Writings, including the Migne Collection above men-

tioned, of which there are but a few other copies in the United
States. In the ante-room are ranged the cases containing the
special literary treasures of the Club, including rare copies and
editions, ranging from specimens of block printing, incunabula,

and black-letter, to the most gorgeous and costly works of the modern European and American press.

Here are Klauber's Paraphrase of the Litany of Our Lady of Loretto, with numerous exquisite symbolical engravings, Augsburg, 1738; Pia Desideria of Father Hugo, with most delicate plates, Antwerp, 1676; Pope Adrian VI., Questiones, Paris, 1511; Terence, published by the great printer, Robert Stephani, at Paris, in 1529, an exceedingly beautiful volume; Tibullus Catullus and Propertius, Venice, 1487, and more curious still, the great black-letter volume and incunabula, printed from engraved blocks in the method which preceded the invention of movable types; the Sermons of St. Vincent Ferrer, printed at Cologne in 1487, with the initial letters inserted by hand in colors, and containing the manuscript notes of some old student. Here also are the Sentences of Peter Lombard, Venice, 1477. The beautiful work of the presses of Plantin, the Aldi, the Elzevirs, is represented by valuable specimens. An old manuscript missal of the fifteenth century, written on vellum finer than paper, and illuminated richly in gold and colors, stands beside the incunabula missal of some old monk in its black-letter ugliness, bound in its shiny white pig-skin covers, which are secured by linen tapes instead of clasps. It would take a volume to describe adequately, all the rarities. Among modern works of great value, are the History of the Vatican Council, in eight folio volumes, bound in red Turkey morocco; the large edition of Racinet's History of Costume; Roma Subterranea of De Rossi, the Italian Government's publication regarding Pompeii, with plates; and the Abbotsford edition of the Waverly novels, besides numerous rare and costly collections of richly illustrated works on the fine arts and architecture.

By reason of the manner of its growth, almost wholly by donations and subscriptions, the library is miscellaneous. But though it may lack completeness, it is a charming place in which to roam at will. There are no restrictions whatever on the use of the general library. One wanders freely from room to room and case to case, picking out an odd volume here and there; reading a while in one department, and moving to another for a taste of something else curious and interesting. There is complete freedom of choice, and when a book is found which tempts to further study, it can be taken away with only the simple formality of signing a receipt blank. The books are classified by cases, their subdivisions by shelves, all fittingly placarded and labelled. This method forms a simple subject catalogue. The work of cataloguing, however, is being cared for rapidly. A finding list is in press, and the work on the card catalogue advances. It is a very long and tedious task, which, it is hoped, to have finished within this year.

Especially to one accustomed to the restrictions of the public library, who sees the books rising shelf upon shelf behind barriers and gratings, this range through a large library is very delightful. It is almost an education in literature; it creates a broadening of ideas. The handling of the books, dipping into them here and there, the examination of the quaint old broadsides, tall copies, little hand-books and closet companions, that belonged to men of centuries ago, has a surpassing charm. The getting acquainted with books that one has known only by reputation, the insight into the wide extent of the intellectual activity of the men of the older age, evidenced by their ponderous tomes whose very size almost affrights the modern man, has a good influence. An afternoon or evening spent in this way, is like the conversation of a learned company ; it makes one modest ; it makes one feel spurred on to some effort beyond the grind and sordidness of this age of material things.

If a knowledge of the early struggles and difficulties of our Catholic fathers and grandfathers, in the United States, is sought, here are the documents from which history will be written. Instead of hearing what some one says was done, here one can have the witnesses themselves speak to him.

If one cares to be a student, and to go deeply into the study of any great questions of morals or religion, his materials lie about him in profusion.

One question is often asked by visitors to the library,—Why should a club give so much of its space, money, and time, to a library? The answer can be found in the earliest records of the organization. It was established as a means by which to aid in the attainment of one of the greatest aims of the society. To quote an early document, " It is to be remembered that it is

the ' Catholic,' much more than the social character of this association, which has secured its success in the past, and which will give it value and permanence in the future.   The social bonds of union are comparatively unsubstantial and transient. The union of Catholics for the higher objects contemplated by this organization is strong, active, and enduring." It is founded to elevate its members, to keep alive the fires of faith and virtue in them, to progress in moral growth, and to advance intellectually, and, to use a favorite phrase of Matthew Arnold, " To make reason and the will of God prevail."

The use of the library is not confined solely to members.   It is open for reference and study, but not for circulation, to any of the Catholic clergy of the city, upon application.   Cards of admission for limited periods are issued by the Library Committee to gentlemen desiring to consult the library upon request of members.   It is hoped, however, that in the future it may be possible to open the library as a reference library to all who wish to consult it.   Upon the completion of the card catalogue this can be arranged.   The formation of a library endowment fund will then be undertaken to provide the library with the best of the current literature, especially on topics of American Catholic interest.   It is beyond the means of the Club at present.   One of its cherished ideals, however, is to have within its walls an arsenal of truth in an essentially Catholic library, complete and well-arranged.

HON. JOSEPH F. DALY.

Every Friday evening, from October to June, Chapters meet in the library for the discussion of various topics.   The principal work of the present year has been in the field of History, in relation, especially, to the growth of the rights of the people in England and France.   Papers are prepared for each evening.   These are followed by a discussion.   This work gives a great impetus to the use of the library, and has led to much serious thought and effort.   It gives promise of permanency.

If the blessings of Providence are given as abundantly to the Club in the future as in the past, the work it will do in the coming years, for the advancement of Catholic thought and literature, will be, it is hoped, most worthy of its great mission.   It will be a crown and a glory for the Jesuit Fathers who nursed it in its infancy, and an imperishable monument to the earnest, intelligent, pure, and high-minded Catholic men who gave to its foundation and its building-up, so much zeal, labor, and unflagging patience, and guided it along the paths that lead to the upper world, of peace and purity and joy.

The president of the Club is Hon. Joseph F. Daly, Chief Justice of the Court of Common Pleas, who is an exemplar of the character of a cultured Catholic gentleman.   Its director, the Reverend Matthew A. Taylor, fills his office admirably, and is constant in his fidelity to the highest ideals of the Club.   Its vice-president is the Club founder, Mr. Joseph Thoron, who is "the Grand Old Man" to all the Catholic Club, and to whom every one cries out, *ad multos annos!*

REV. M. A. TAYLOR.

MARY is my ark of mercy
  In God's covenant with man;
Hers the only spotless vesture
  Ever since man's sin began.

Mary is the shrine of Jesus,
  For my Lord is ever there;
There my prayer is heard in glory,
  Never need I there despair.

Mary is my refuge-city,
  Where no harm nor wrong comes nigh;
When the water-flood sweeps o'er me,
  She the rainbow in the sky.

Yes, I lean upon her wholly,
  On my Lord to lean the more,
Leaving all to His kind forethought,
  Body, soul, and earthly store.

When I cry to God, my Father,
  From my depth of sinful woe,
Safe beneath my Mother's shelter
  To His goodness can I go.

When I dread the wrath of Jesus,
  Who with her is never wroth,
Then I whisper: See, Thy Mother
  Is the Mother of us both!

LOST A HUNDRED YEARS

John Talbot Smith.

(*Conclusion.*)

AOUL bounded from his chair in profound excitement, as his father outlined his plan of action. He tried to shout his joy.

" Be ye a boy or a man?" said the Captain severely. "This is a man's job we hev on hand, an' we can't afford no monkey shines. The man that goes crazy over riches afore he's got 'em, isn't far off from a lunatic asylum."

Raoul apologized, and subsided, and the Captain resumed:

" We've got to look out for Cal. Wool, an' we've got to look out for the Willsboro folks, for they think that money's theirs now by all rights, an' they won't stand' no meddlin'. My plan is simple. Jes' as soon as navigation begins, I'll fetch my tug into the lake, an' anchor far enough off to hinder people we know a-seein' of it. Fust night I git there you two come aboard early, an' about twelve o'clock we drop anchor near the *Queen,* an' begin work. At four o'clock we go back to my hidin'-place till the next night, an' so on till the job's finished. I want you two because if any consid'able money's found, 'twouldn't do for me to be alone with strangers, an' my plan is to share an' share alike with ye both. What d'ye say?"

The two young men said many things, of course, and during the stay of the Captain in the town their conferences were many, too many and too feverish to suit the calm, hard-headed old fellow with his cautious ways and restrained feelings. Raoul was for a time out of his wits, though sensible enough in his father's presence. He could not conceal his exultation of spirits from his neighbors, and in the company of his future wife, Ida, his mind gave way altogether. Money was the theme of his wild talk, oceans of money, with the odor of deep waters upon it. He would buy lands and houses and jewels and pleasures for himself and his friends. They would travel the world together, and see its wondrous sights from palace cars and gorgeous yachts. He promised Monsieur le Curé that he would build him a new church that summer, and, when the old priest made inquiry into the mad promise, Ida Greenwood told him the strange words and doings of her lover for a week past. She had quarreled with him, and he did not seem to mind, saying that he would now marry a princess, and break her heart.

"And why did you quarrel?" said the Curé.

"He declared that he would never marry me; yes, he even swore it," Ida said tearfully, "until the treasure in the *Queen* was found. I answered that I would not wait so long for any man. And then he repeated his oath with the addition about the princess.

"He is crazy for the time," said Monsieur le Curé. "I think that can be cured, and I shall see about it."

He visited the Captain at the house of Etienne Calais, and said to him severely, "René, you are here to seek that deplorable treasure, and great mischief is sure to come of it. What, have you lived so long and seen the use men make of riches left to them by their fathers, not to know that money acquired suddenly by the poor is almost sure to work their ruin? Here now is this fine boy of ours, Raoul, that I trained myself, gone clean out of his mind by your schemes to get the treasure."

The brown face of the Captain turned white.

"Raoul," he murmured; "impossible!"

"I do not mean that he is yet fit for the asylum, René; but it will not be long. Is he here now? Bring him in, then, and let me show you the wreck you are making."

Raoul came in quietly enough, because his father's eyes were upon him; but the fever in his face was evident, and the effort to restrain his excitement was not to be hidden.

"I have become a partner in your scheme, Raoul," said Monsieur le Curé, "and I too am to have a share in the money. What do you say to that?"

5

" It means luck," cried Raoul excitedly; and now that the treas-ure was his theme, the young man forgot his caution, and rattled away at pleasure.

" But why did you quarrel with Ida," said the priest, " and leave the poor girl in grief because one day you are to be rich? "

" It was but a joke," stammered Raoul. " I could never leave Ida."

" Then go and tell her so now," said the Captain, " and remem-ber what I said about them that goes crazy over riches afore they gits 'em."

The old men looked at each other after he went out, and sighed.

" Do you think he is really in danger? " said the Captain.

" Where are your eyes, my friend? But ,tell me, what do you intend to do that this boy should take it so seriously, and perhaps I may advise what ought to be done? Raoul is not to be sacri-ficed for a hundred treasures."

" I would throw a million to the fishes first! " cried the Captain in anguish, " but I thought I was actin' all right; " and he told his story from first to last, and his hope of securing the lead if nothing else could be found, the rich lead of the magazine. " Better that you had let it alone," said the Curé; " and if you find money in quantity, the chances are that it will bring more sorrow than joy. But since you have begun so sensibly, I cannot bid you stop for a scruple. I shall do what I can to save this poor boy from mischief. To give up now would certainly do him harm, and if he is not restrained in time, disappointment will surely complete his ruin. René, age has not taught you good sense. You have money and health and joy, and you are not content. If you should get more money, and pay for it with your son's reason or life, would there be any further happiness in this world for you? "

" None, my father," answered the Captain, with head lowered to hide his tears. Etienne Calais, his son-in-law, agreed with the Curé that Raoul needed treatment, and gave his opinion that the young man was too great a fool in ordinary circumstances to undergo the strain of a search for the treasure. He was thinking how large his share would be if Raoul went into an asylum. The ten days that the Captain spent in the town were days of bitterness, and already trouble was crossing his pathway like a deadly vapor from the rotten ship at the bottom of the lake.

Under the Curé's sharp remonstrances and loving care Raoul got back his mental balance, and devoted himself once more to his ordinary work and his Ida; and when the time came for him and Etienne to steal away to his father's boat, which lay at anchor

behind a convenient point, he had sufficient nerve to carry himself through the ordeal like a man. It was a bright, chill night in early April when the treasure hunters crept to position over the wreck of the *Queen.* The ice had left the lake early that year, but navigation had not opened, and their boat was alone on the water. Two of his trustiest men attended the Captain, utterly ignorant of the object in view, except that a lump of valuable lead was to be fished up secretly. At midnight they were anchored with all lights out, and the diver was at the bottom guiding the big pump in its work of clearing the rotten hull of the ship from its grave in the mud of a hundred years. The throb of the engine seemed to Raoul like the throb of his own heart. Etienne and he had nothing to do but keep a lookout for strangers, and avoid talk with the men, lest an unguarded word should betray their secret. Of what was going on in the depths of Lake Champlain no one could speak, and the diver's attendant, with his hand on the single line, whose other end was in the strong and masterful grasp of Captain René, alone might guess at what part of the famous wreck he was working.

The diver was surprised at his success the first night. The powerful pump cleared a space around the stern timbers in three hours; a few strokes of his axe sent the rotten wood into splinters, and with his hands he could feel the lead lining of the magazine, now stripped of its covering, but as solid as when it first sank in the lake. It was a prize in itself, and would relieve Raoul's disappointment mightily if no treasure were found. Working in profound darkness, and forced to use the utmost caution, it was a long time before he reached the door of the magazine, and with the iron handle of his axe, smashed it open. It was safe to enter, for the great weight of metal kept the leaden room immovable. There seemed to be a variety of things within, but Captain Forest felt only for a small keg, and when he had found it, and hugged it a moment to his bosom with joy, he replied to a signal from above that he was ready to ascend. It was time. Four o'clock had sounded, and daylight was threatening.

No one saw the keg as he mounted the deck and took off his armor, because it hung to the ladder, and was not removed until the Captain could take it secretly to the cabin, and examine it alone. He had indeed found the lost treasure! The little keg held ten thousand dollars in English gold, and poor René was a made man! He kept his secret, saying only to his sons that the treasure was there, and leaving the keg carelessly in a corner of the cabin. The second night would complete the work, if nothing happened. And the second night he put on his armor like a knight going to battle, and smiled at the stars through the glass of his helmet as he stood on the deck. It might be his last look at them, and in the midnight they looked very beautiful; but if he ever saw them again, it would be as a rich man, probably, and destined to shine in his own small skies. The men moved about in silence; the lights were put out, the word was given, and he had stepped to the ship's side when a note of alarm came from the lookout. Not a hundred yards away was a strange vessel that had crept upon them in the darkness. The Captain's

mind was like light in solving dark problems. He gave two orders: " Keep quiet; let no one aboard," and sank to the bottom
of the lake to begin work furiously. He knew that Calvin Wool
had discovered him, had tracked him, perhaps seen the keg
opened, and was here to do battle for his share. But if he had
cheated the others, Captain René would show him that he was
not to be cheated.

He felt every corner of the magazine, and fished out ten kegs
of various sizes, which he carried to the surface at once, and gave
in charge of his sons. There was nothing left but the lead. It
had to be cut in convenient pieces, and attached to ropes to be
hoisted to the deck. As he hacked away at it, wondering what
Calvin Wool would venture to do, he became suddenly conscious
that someone was approaching him in the terrible darkness,—was
near him,—actually at his side. At the next moment his body came
in contact with the armored body of his rival. It was the purest
accident that the meeting should have occurred, but in an instant
the two men had seized each other by the arms, Wool in rage and
hate, Captain René in honest defence. As their helmets touched,
the Captain cried out:

" You're no match for me here! It may mean death to both,—
a fight! Wait till we get ashore. Don't be a fool! "

Calvin was astounded to hear this voice in the depths of the lake,
for he had not learned that divers can talk with their helmets together in almost any depth of water. He did not recognize the
Captain, did not know with whom he was dealing, being filled
with a blind rage against these marauders upon what he considered his property. He yelled back:

" Who are you? What right have you here? "

" The same right as yourself, and never mind who I am," was
the reply.

" You are a thief ! " shouted Calvin. " This is my property.
You must leave it to me! "

" Haint teched nothin' but the led o' the magazine," said the
Captain, an' I'll give ye half if ye prove ownership."

" The magazine! The magazine! Did you find the magazine?
Then you have found more,—you have found gold, and you have
robbed me, the owner! "

"Oh, not half as much as you robbed the Willsboro people,"
the Captain broke in. "An' now I'm done with ye, an' all I want
ye to do is to git out, an' lemme finish the work here. If ye want
money, make it. There's none in this place."

He had no desire to take a human life, even as mean as Calvin
Wool's, and at the first grasp he flung him from him, and moved
away suddenly towards that crevasse in the lake bottom, which
he had discovered on his first visit to the *Queen*. A slight movement of the water around him told that Calvin had rushed past
him in the direction of the fatal pit. He waited a few minutes
with his hands outstretched to feel the next movement of the
water, indicating Calvin's approach, but it never came. Then
as calmly as ever he returned to his task, and saw the last piece
of lead sent up before he left the wreck of the *Queen* for the last
time. Such a heart of steel had Captain René! It was six o'clock
when he stepped out of his armor, and the dawn was lighting up
the mountains, but the tug was miles down the lake at sunrise,
and few would ever know the share he had in securing the sunk-
en treasure. His men told him a story of turmoil and horror on
the strange vessel around five o'clock: how two men cried
out that a diver was perishing at the bottom of the lake, for his
air-pipe and signal line had parted; how they called for help to
the tug, and had not received so much as an answer, for as Captain René's assistant said, if it's a diver, he's dead, and if it's a
trick, why that's dead too; and so they soon ceased shouting and
took to cursing, as they sailed away. "It was the crevasse," said
the Captain to himself; and he could almost see the fatal step,
the sudden sinking into the vast depth, the bursting of the air-
pipe, the hands thrown up in agony, and the convulsed face
pressed against the glass of the helmet, as Calvin Wool and his
mean ambition sank into the awful gulf, forever.

The kegs contained a pretty sum for three poor men to share,
something like two hundred thousand; and the best of this good
fortune was that no one dreamed it had fallen to the Captain and
his sons. The two men who returned to Willsboro with the story
of a mishap to Calvin Wool, a strange ship, and a broken pipe as
a witness, were treated as conspirators with Calvin to cover his
escape to Europe with the funds of the unhappy stockholders;

and to this day the tradition of the swindle, which left Willsboro many thousands poorer than it ought to be, so prevails that it has wiped out the popularity of the *Queen* and its supposed treasure.

Only Monsieur le Curé knew the secret of the gradual but marked rise of the Captain and his sons to solid positions in the world. It was by his advice that this prudence was observed, and thereby the treasure hunters not only escaped the suspicion of their neighbors, but avoided the dangers attending the sudden accession of riches.

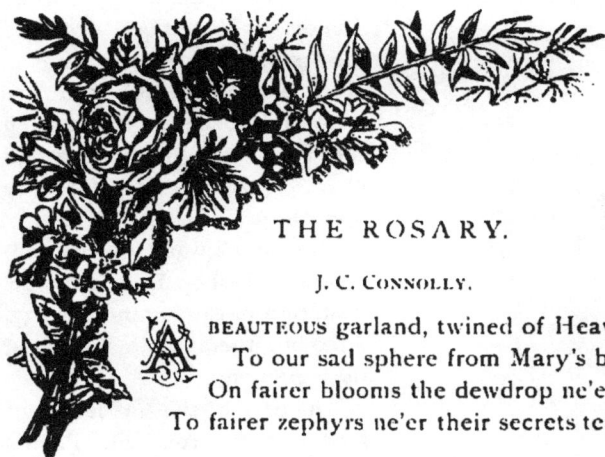

THE ROSARY.

J. C. CONNOLLY.

A BEAUTEOUS garland, twined of Heaven's roses,
 To our sad sphere from Mary's bowers fell;
On fairer blooms the dewdrop ne'er reposes,
 To fairer zephyrs ne'er their secrets tell.

The crimson heart-hued roses tell the story
 Of griefs that ruthless rent her tender heart;
The white and gold tell of the joy and glory
 That bade her heart with gladdest pulses start.

But wherefore fell this garland to earth's bowers?
 Why met the heavenly and the base terrene? —
That we might have a worthy wreath of flowers
 To crown earth's fairest own—now Heaven's Queen.

A PAGE OF CHURCH HISTORY IN NEW YORK.

T. JOHN'S, UTICA.

VERY REV. J. S. M. LYNCH, D. D., LL. D.   .

PART V.

FATHER QUARTER'S ASSISTANT PRIESTS.

REV. WILLIAM BEACHAM.

DECEMBER 23D, 1836—JULY 22D, 1837. DIED MARCH 10TH, 1876.

FATHER BEACHAM was born in Drummond, Queens County, Ireland, in 1806. He commenced his theological studies at Carlow College for the diocese of Kildare. He was ordained by Bishop Dubois in November, 1836, and his first priestly ministry was in Utica, under Father Quarter. He had the honor of celebrating the first Mass in our second church, which was formally opened on Christmas, in 1836.

The church was probably dedicated by Bishop Dubois on his visitation in the summer of 1837, although there is no record of the ceremony.

Through the influence of Father Quarter St. Peter's Church, Rome, was dedicated by Bishop Dubois, July 19th, 1837, and Father Beacham was appointed its first pastor. He found but five Catholic families in the village. His field extended as far West as Buffalo, as far North as the St. Lawrence, and as far South as Binghamton. He labored on this arduous mission for over forty years. With the exception of the venerable Father Havermans, of Troy, who is now sixty-four years a priest, Father Beacham was, at the

REV. WILLIAM BEACHAM.

time of his death, the oldest priest in the State of New York. His name is held in veneration to this day in the city of Rome, where he labored so long and faithfully, and his zeal for God's glory is inherited by his worthy nephew, Rev. Patrick H. Beacham, pastor of Baldwinsville, N. Y., one of the most esteemed priests of our diocese.

REV. JOHN LEWIS WARIATH.

JUNE 6TH, 1837—AUGUST 31ST, 1837.   DIED——

There is very little recorded of Father Wariath. All we know is, that he was appointed assistant pastor for the Germans, June 6th, 1837, and he appears to have been with Father Quarter until August 31st, 1837. The Germans were not organized into a parish until four years later, during the pastorate of Father Martin. Thus far, all my efforts have been fruitless to find the time and place of Father Wariath's death. Forgotten by men, we trust that his works are not unknown to God, and have followed him into eternity.

REV. PATRICK McCLOSKEY.

JUNE 27TH, 1838—JANUARY 13TH, 1839.   DIED SEPTEMBER 28TH, 1861.

We have no record of the early life of Father Patrick McCloskey. He was probably ordained in Ireland, and came to America in his priestly youth. He assisted Father Quarter from June, 1838, to January, 1839. He was afterwards appointed pastor of Schenectady, and subsequently became the pastor of St. John's Church, Albany, which was formally a Dutch Reformed church. Here he remained until his death. He was a remarkable man in many ways—thrillingly magnetic in his preaching, winning in his manners, and burning with holy zeal for the salvation of souls. He died September 28th, 1861. As a boy I attended his funeral, and seldom or ever did I witness such a remarkable tribute paid to the memory of any priest or bishop as I saw on that occasion, which is still fresh in my memory.

RT. REV. DAVID W. BACON, D. D.

JANUARY 13TH, 1839—OCTOBER 24TH, 1839.   DIED NOVEMBER 5TH, 1874.

Father Bacon was born in the city of New York, September 15, 1815, and after a preliminary course in the academy of Mr. James

Shea, completed his studies in Montreal College, and Mount St. Mary's, Emmittsburg.   He was ordained, December 13th, 1838, by Archbishop Eccleston, of Baltimore, one of the most distinguished members of the American Hierarchy.   He came to Father Quarter in the first days of his priestly fervor, and even during the few months of his ministry, he left an impression upon the parish which still remains.   After leaving Utica, he became pastor of Ogdensburg, now the seat of an Episcopal See.   Returning soon to New York, he was assigned to B r o o k l y n, where he completed the church which our first pastor, Father Farnam, had started under such unhappy auspices.

This church of the Assumption soon g r e w t o large proportions, and he began the erection of another church—St. Mary's, Star of the Sea.   In the midst of his labors, at the close of the year 1854, he received the bulls appointing him Bishop of Portland, Maine.   He was consecrated the first bishop of this new diocese, April 22d, 1855, by A r c h b i s h o p Hughes, the sermon being delivered by Bishop, afterwards Cardinal, McCloskey.   His is the second name on our honored roll of priests to receive the mitre.

RT. REV. DAVID W. BACON, D. D.

The States assigned for his episcopal labor were not a very encouraging field.   New Hampshire, by her constitution, excluded Catholics from the Legislature and all high offices.   Maine was the very hotbed of Knownothingism at that time.   The church at Manchester, N. H., where now resides, so peacefully, the first alumnus of Troy Seminary to receive the mitre, was destroyed by a

mob. The church at Bath was set on fire, and entirely consum-
ed. Father Bapst, a Jesuit, was seized, in Ellsworth, by a mob,
coated with tar and feathers, and injured so severely that he never
recovered from the fiendish outrage. Attempting to lay the corner-stone of a new church in Bath, Bishop Bacon was driven away
by a mob. Such was the field into which our kind and gentle
Father Bacon, as he was known here, was sent. And to crown his
trials and sufferings, when the anti-Catholic agitation had ceased,
and Christian sentiments began to prevail, the city of Portland
was laid in ruins by a conflagration on the 4th of July, 1866. Of
the cathedral property nothing was left. In a few hours the chapel, the episcopal residence, the houses, and the academy of the
Sisters, with nearly all that they contained, had been consum-
ed. Nothing daunted, Bishop Bacon assembled his flock in a
shed on the Grand Trunk wharf, and set to work with energy to
rebuild his temporary chapel, which he dedicated on Christmas of
that year. Bishop Bacon, after a life of labor in the Lord's vineyard, leaving behind him the memory of his pious and zealous
works, closed his eyes where he first saw the light—in his native
city of New York. His remains were taken to Portland, and
buried in the vault of the present Cathedral.

REV. FRANCIS FERRALL.

OCTOBER 25TH, 1839—DECEMBER 4TH, 1840. DIED DECEMBER 4TH, 1840.

Born in Ireland, in the year 1812, Father Ferrall emigrated to
America at an early age. After completing his studies, he was
ordained to the holy priesthood by the illustrious Bishop England, the first Bishop of Charleston. He labored for a short time
among the hard missions of the South. Coming North, he became affiliated to the diocese of New York. He built a church
in Belleville, N. J., which was dedicated by Bishop Dubois in
December, 1838. He was afterwards assigned to duty in the episcopal city. He was appointed pastor of our church, October
25th, 1839, by Bishop Hughes, who had taken charge of the administration of the diocese only two weeks previous. Father
Ferrall was therefore the first pastor of this parish to receive his
appointment from Bishop Hughes. His ministry was brief
amongst us, but the impression which he made was lasting.

It was during the pastorate of Father Ferrall that the first election for mayor took place, and the city manifested its sense of obligation to one of its old pioneers, by electing John C. Devereux, one of the founders of our parish, as the first incumbent of that office elected directly by the people.

After two weeks' sickness, Father Ferrall peacefully passed away in the home of Capt. Dwight, on Charlotte Street, where he boarded. His remains were carried from his residence to the church on a hand-bier, on the day of his funeral. He was buried in a private cemetery in the yard of St. John's Asylum, adjoining the church. On his tombstone were inscribed these words:

I. H. S.

This tomb has been erected by the congregation of St. John's Church, Utica, in memory of Rev. Francis Ferrall, who was born at Maydon, County Longford, Ireland, and died in this city, December 4th, 1840, aged 28 years.

"Abounding in zeal for the salvation of his people, he fell an early victim, lamented by all. His talents, his piety, and amiable disposition endeared him to his flock, who will long cherish the recollection of his virtuous life, his holy, his edifying death."

The following obituary notice is taken from the *Utica Gazette* of December 8th, 1840, and shows the esteem in which he was held by his people, and the sorrow caused by his death.

Died—On Friday, the fourth of December, inst., at his residence in this city, after an illness of about two months, the Rev. Francis Ferrall, aged twenty-nine years.

Thus, ere the meridian of life, has the deceased been taken from the field of his earthly labors, where his talents and his virtues gave promise of so great usefulness, and where his loss will be most severely felt. This dispensation, coming from a Providence that orders wisely the affairs of men, should be bowed to without a murmur; yet it has filled with deep and sincere sorrow a circle of acquaintances, by whom the deceased was warmly esteemed, and a congregation among whose members he had discharged the duties of the ministry with the most unwearied solicitude for their spiritual welfare. At an early age he left Ireland, his native country, and after due course of preparation was ordained a clergyman of the Roman Catholic Church by the Bishop of South Carolina; subsequently he spent several years in the duties of his avocation at Newark, New Jersey, and in the city of New York. In October, 1830, he was assigned to the pastoral charge of the Catholic congregation in this city, the duties of which station he performed, up to the time of his illness, in the most exemplary and satisfactory manner. Simple and unassuming in his manners, cheerful in temper, social in his character, possessing natural abilities of a superior order, and a mind cultivated and enlarged by study and reflection, he commanded the respect and esteem of those who differed from him in creed, while his sincere piety, exemplary life, and untiring exertions for the welfare of those under his charge, secured to him their love and admiration. With an eloquent tongue he portrayed the misery and deformity of vice and the beauty of virtue, and with an active zeal he labored to prevent the dominion of the one and ensure the blessings of the other, by giving to the youth of his congregation a sound and virtuous education. But the eloquent tongue is now mute; the hand that was ever active in discharging the offices of charity and philanthropy, is cold in death; the kind and solicitous pastor, who but a short time since walked among us, exemplifying by his practice the beauties of those divine precepts which he taught, has passed to another and, we trust, a happier world. Deeply do his acquaintances and the members of his congregation in this city regret his loss; long will they cherish his memory.

Utica, December 7th, 1840.[1]

It was during the pastorate of Father Ferrall that Francis Kernan, a young man of twenty-three, removed to Utica, and soon after entered upon the practice of law. Marrying, a few years later, a daughter of Nicholas Devereux, one of the founders of our parish, he seemed to take his place as a leader and wise counsellor in church affairs—a position which he never relinquished until the day of his death. For half a century he shed lustre on this city of his adoption. Rising to the heights of power in state and nation, he wielded a magnetic influence over men, born of that purity of life which forbade the very suspicion of insincerity. Whether we look upon him as a lawyer, a statesman, a citizen, or a Catholic, we feel proud that Utica can boast of such a son.

It is a curious fact, that although our parish had been in existence for twenty-one years, and though eighteen priests had pre-

---

[1] The following lines, whose author's initials only—N. L. M. A.—are given, appeared in a local paper at the time, and will be of interest to those who still remember this good young priest—the first on the roll of our deceased priests who never officiated in our first church:

LINES ON THE DEATH OF THE REV. MR. FERRALL.

Why weep, ye mourners, that he dies,
  And sleeps in death, at rest?
His soul has sought its kindred skies.
  He's now among the blest;
The journey of his life is done,
  And if his day was brief,
The heavenly crown that he has won
  Should now assuage your grief.

The world hath nothing to bestow
  That could entice his heart,
To wish to linger here below
  Or grieve him to depart;
For early did he turn aside
  From all its vain parade,
To wed the Church, the only bride
  Whose charms will never fade.

Had he been like those whose years
  On folly's call attend,
To whom the rest of life appears
  To be without an end:
Whom fleeting pleasures e'er beguile.
  Till guilt has flushed the brow,
He had not died with that sweet smile
  Which lights his features now.

His " Miserere " he has read—
  His " canticle " is o'er,
The tapers on the altar shed
  For him their light nt no more; [woe,
For he's released from his anguished
  From pains and sorrows here,
And dwells where none shall ever
  The misery of a tear.   [know
              —*N. L. M. A.*

ceded him in ministering to the Catholics of Utica, Father Ferrall was the first to die in Utica, and the first whose remains were destined to stay with us.

At a subsequent period it became necessary to close the cemetery in the asylum yard. A beautiful portion of St. Agnes' cemetery was then reserved for the burial of priests, and on the sixth of October, 1886, the remains of Father Ferrall, after quietly resting for forty-six years, were transferred to our beautiful cemetery, and the church which had erected the first monument over his grave provided another, with an appropriate inscription, to mark the grave of this saintly pastor.

FATHER FERRALL'S ASSISTANT PRIESTS.

RT. REV. JOHN LOUGHLIN, D. D.

NOVEMBER 1ST, 1840—JANUARY 3D, 1841.   DIED DECEMBER 19TH, 1891.

Father Ferrall was obliged to give up all active work about the

RT. REV. JOHN LOUGHLIN, D. D.

middle of October. Father Beacham came from Rome a few times to assist him in his parochial duties, and on November 1st Father John Loughlin became assistant priest. He is the first on our roll of priests who had the honor of being elevated to the episcopacy. John L o u g h l i n was born in C o u n t y Down, Ireland, December 20th, 1817. At the age of six years he came to the United States with his parents, and settled in Albany, N. Y. He studied first in the Albany Academy, under the famous Latinist, Dr. Bullion, afterwards in Chambly, near Montreal. He completed his studies in Mt. St. Mary's, Emmittsburg, and was or-

dained to the holy priesthood, October 18th, 1840. He assisted
Father Ferrall in the last few months of his pastorate, and was
with him in his last moments.   He was then called to New York,
and became assistant priest at St. Patrick's Cathedral.   His co-
laborers in old St. Patrick's were Fathers McCloskey and Bayley,
afterwards Cardinal and Archbishop respectively.   He soon became rector of the Cathedral, and on the eve of his departure for
Rome, in 1850, Bishop Hughes appointed him Vicar-General of
the diocese, and administrator during his absence.   He was selected as the first Bishop of Brooklyn, by Pius IX. of blessed
memory, and was consecrated October 30th, 1853, by Cajetan
Bedini, Pronuncio of His Holiness, in the church where he had so
successfully officiated for years.   For thirty-eight years he ruled
over that important diocese whose episcopal city is deservedly
called the "City of Churches."   He saw the Catholic population
increase from 15,000 to over 300,000, and that island—the garden
of the state,—dotted with churches, colleges, schools, asylums,
hospitals, and all kinds of charitable institutions.   It was my
pleasure to be present at the celebration of the golden jubilee of
his priesthood, October 18th, 1890, and to witness the extraordinary manifestations of regard in which he was held by all classes
of citizens.   He expired peacefully, after a life of zealous labors,
in his episcopal city, December 19th, 1891.

REV. THOMAS MARTIN, O. P.

JANUARY 10TH, 1841—MAY 11TH, 1845.   DIED MAY 10TH 1859.

Father Martin was born in Ireland in 1794.   He partially completed his studies in his native country, and came to America shortly after reaching the years of manhood.   Like the first two Bishops of New York, Father Martin belonged to the illustrious Dominican Order.   He entered the Order of St. Dominic in St. Rose's
Convent, in Kentucky, and was ordained, in 1824, by Bishop Fenwick of Cincinnati.

It may be interesting to note the beginnings of his apostolic
work in the United States.   The See of Bardstown, Ky., was
erected at the same time as that of New York, in 1808.   The
whole State of Ohio was placed under the jurisdiction of the
new Bishop.   Dr. Flaget, like our own Bishop Concanen, was

reluctantly compelled to defer, for several years, setting out for the See committed to his charge.

He entered the State of Ohio for the first time, October 7, 1811, accompanied by Rev. Stephen T. Badin, who had the honor of being the first priest ordained in the United States. He received Holy Orders from the hands of Bishop Carroll, in Baltimore, May 25, 1793.

The missionaries stopped at the log hut of a settler who proved to be a Catholic. When he heard that his guests were from Kentucky, he exclaimed: " From Kentucky! They say there are churches and priests there. Wife! we must go thither; it is thirteen years since we saw either a church or a priest, and my poor children—!"

Here Bishop Flaget, deeply moved, interrupted him:

" No, my children, stay where you are; I am your Bishop. I will endeavor to send you a priest at least once a year to console you."

The astonished man could hardly believe the reality of what was told him.

It was to carry out the promise then made that Bishop Flaget called upon the Dominican Fathers of Kentucky, to take charge of the missions in Ohio. Father Fenwick, at that time Provincial of the Order, and who was destined to become the first Bishop in Ohio, took the lead in this great work. Associated with him was his nephew, Father Young, and Father Martin. A log church in honor of St. Joseph was built; a two-story log house, near it, became the first Dominican Convent. From this as a centre Father Martin and his associates, in the year 1825, extended their ministry in all directions. Father Martin built a neat frame church, dedicated to St. Mary, at Lancaster, where he attended every month a congregation of twenty families. He labored for twelve years in these difficult missions, which included a range of country now sufficient for several dioceses. In 1836, he visited Rome on business of his Order. Upon his return, at the desire of his Provincial, he offered himself as a missionary in the diocese of New York.

Bishop Dubois assigned him to duty, in 1840, as pastor of Newport and Schuyler, in our vicinity. Upon the death of Father Ferrall he became the pastor of our parish, January 10, 1841.

Father Martin, with the true spirit of an apostle, labored with great zeal while amongst us.   He is described as " one of the most distinguished priests of the older generation."   He organized the first Temperance Society in Utica, and was noted for his zealous efforts in suppressing the frightful evils of drunkenness.   And so well did he plant the good seed of Catholic total abstinence, that in after years, the enormous number of 1,500 men were banded together under the banner of Father Mathew, and the first church remodelled and altered, where they used to meet, was known as Father Mathew Hall.

Father Martin boarded, while in Utica, at Mrs. Ann Farnon's, who lived at that time in Bleecker Street, between Burnet and Charlotte Streets.   Mrs. Farnon was one of the historic characters in our parish.   She was received into the Church, in Boston, as an adult, by Father Cheverus, who was consecrated the first Bishop of Boston in 1810, and afterwards became Cardinal Archbishop of Bordeaux.   Mrs. Farnon came to Utica in 1820.   Her husband, John Farnon, taught school in that old building in John Street known as Richard's carpenter shop.   He also performed the duties of sexton of St. John's Church for many years.   Mrs. Farnon died March 23, 1887.   Her exact age was not known, but it was thought that she was about 105 years old.

As the little cemetery in Steuben Street was now wholly inadequate for the size of the parish, Father Martin purchased, June 3, 1844, in the name of the church, five acres of land for burial purposes.   This ground forms a portion of the present St. Agnes' cemetery.   Amongst other acts of his pastorate, Father Martin made an earnest protest against the intolerance of the State government which forced the employees of the State Lunatic Asylum to attend Protestant worship.

He is remembered especially for his extraordinary charity towards the poor.   He was constantly inquiring for the needy and the destitute.   Mary Savage and Rose Shaughnessy acted as his almoners in the distribution of the money which he appropriated for the wants of the deserving poor.

After leaving Utica, Father Martin labored in New York City, where he became pastor of St. Brigid's Church, where he remained until 1853.   He was transferred to old St. Peter's, in New

York City. Here he did some notable work. When the ship fever, as it was called, raged throughout New York, St. Peter's parish was one of the most afflicted parts of the city. The streets towards the Battery swarmed with emigrants, in and around boarding houses, in cellars and in garrets, and in outbuildings.

Here Father Martin showed his sacerdotal zeal. Day and night he labored till fever seized on his own frame, and he was confined to his bed. One happened to be at his bedside who at the time found his feet bleeding from the wear of his shoes in his indefatigable and ceaseless visits to the suffering poor. Father Martin was prematurely an old man. The hard missionary years of his earlier life were the cause of it. Of his labors temporarily in other parishes, at Rondout, at St. Brigid's, at Holy Cross Church, in Forty-second Street, and finally at St. James', it is unnecessary to speak. Wherever he went he was edifying in his words; in his conduct he was always a priest. In a world where the good and edifying are not too many, he shone in the light of an earnest and a consistent life. His often expressed desire—that he might die in a convent of his Order, with his Dominican brethren, to whom he was so faithfully attached, about him—was not gratified. Was it not better, as it happened, that he should die as he had lived, at the post of duty, and in the field where he had helped so many thousands to live and to die Christianly !

Shortly after Father Martin began his pastorate, William Henry Harrison, of Ohio, the grandfather of the distinguished citizen who has so recently occupied the Presidential chair, was inaugurated the ninth President of the United States. He had been just a month in office when he died. By the terms of the Constitution, Vice-President John Tyler succeeded him in the office of President, and remained at the head of the Government during the whole period of Father Martin's administration.

It is difficult for us to realize that it was during this period, in 1844, that the first telegraphic message in the history of the world was sent, flashing the news from Baltimore to Washington that James K. Polk had been nominated to succeed Tyler in the office of President.

ASSISTANT PRIEST TO FATHER MARTIN.

REV. GEORGE McCLOSKEY.

OCTOBER 12TH, 1844—JUNE 1ST, 1845.   DIED AUGUST 3D, 1890.

For over three years, Father Martin labored alone in this parish.   In the fall of 1844, Father McCloskey was sent to assist him.

Father George McCloskey studied at the Theological Seminary at Fordham, and was ordained by Cardinal McCloskey, August 15th, 1844.   He was sent here to Utica shortly after his ordination, and remained here until June 1st, 1845.   He was then appointed assistant priest at St. Patrick's Cathedral.

In 1846, he assisted, at Nativity Church, Father Kein, the founder and first pastor of St. Brigid's, New York, and took turns with him in celebrating Mass in the Fourth Street Chapel, which was the beginning of St. Brigid's Church.

REV. GEORGE MC CLOSKEY.

His brother, Rev. William McCloskey, was consecrated Bishop of Louisville, Ky., May 24th, 1868.   Father George McCloskey then became affiliated to the diocese of Louisville.   He was appointed Vice-President of the Theological Seminary of the diocese, and afterwards Vicar General of the diocese, and President of the Seminary.   He retained this position until his death, which occurred at Louisville, August 3d, 1890.

REV. JOSEPH STOKES.

MAY 11TH, 1845—FEBRUARY 15TH, 1851.   DIED JULY 16TH, 1854.

Unfortunately we have no record of the early years of Father

Stokes.   It is probable that he was ordained in Ireland.   He took charge of the parish upon the departure of Father Martin, and labored for six years with unflagging zeal in building up the parish.   His failing health made it impossible for him to carry out all his projects for the spiritual improvement of the parish.   But he laid the foundation deep and well for his saintly successor to build high and strong the spiritual edifice.   But in spite of his infirmities, Father Stokes accomplished one thing for which alone he would be entitled to our everlasting gratitude.   The parish had now been in existence upwards of thirty years, and yet there was no parochial residence for the clergy.   A suitable rectory is rightly considered one of the necessary adjuncts of every well regulated parish.   We can imagine the inconveniences, both for the priests and people, for lack of this accommodation during that long period of time.   From the beginning the priests were obliged to board here and there at different houses in the parish.   The difficulty in the way from the first was that there was no convenient site that could be obtained.   The lots donated for the first church, covered only half the block on Bleecker Street, and had a frontage of only ninety feet on John Street.   All the lots in the rear of the church, extending to Burnet Street, had come into the possession of Rev. Eleazar S. Barrows, a retired Presbyterian minister, noted for his extreme antipathy to the Catholic Church.   He erected upon the ground a residence for himself.   The house was almost a counterpart of Dr. Wolcott's house on Bleecker Street.   There are a great many in the congregation who can recall it, with its quaint green blinds, and the wing in the rear.   It was about forty feet from Burnet Street, and unlike the present rectory, there was a space between it and the church.

Upon the death of Mr. Barrows, Father Stokes managed to purchase from his heirs the house and all the adjoining lots, thus securing a much-needed rectory, and making the church property run through from street to street, with a frontage of ninety feet on John Street, and one hundred and twenty feet on Burnet Street. This property was purchased June 10th, 1850, for $5,000; but Father Stokes never had the happiness of residing in the new rectory, as he was obliged to give up his charge in the following winter.

Father Stokes was remarkable for his sweet and kindly disposition. He won all hearts, and the older members of the congregation love to hear his name mentioned to-day, and to recall the memory of his many deeds of charity. He retired from the active work of the ministry after leaving Utica, in the winter of 1851, and died at Saratoga, July 16th, 1854.

It was during the pastorate of Father Stokes that the telegraph first came into use. The year previous to his coming, May 24th, 1844, the first message sent by telegraph was transmitted. It read: "What God hath wrought," and was sent by Miss Annie G. Ellsworth, daughter of the Commissioner of Patents, over a wire from Baltimore to Washington. The next year a line to operate in Central New York was organized, with headquarters in Utica. Three of our own citizens—Theodore S. Foster, John Butterfield, and Hiram Greenman, stage-coach pioneers,—conceived the idea of starting a line in this State. A line was completed from Utica to Albany, January 31st, 1846. Syracuse was the third point in the State to be reached by telegraph, before either New York or Buffalo. The working of two independent sections of line, in opposite directions, by the same main battery, was also first done between Albany and Syracuse, by a Grove battery of thirty-eight cups, grounded at Utica, the circuits being respectively fifty-three and ninety-seven miles.

Theodore S. Foster of Utica, brought the newspaper editors into co-operation, and the New York State Associated Press was inaugurated. The first daily reports to the press were sent January 1st, 1847. Brief bulletins of the battles in the Mexican War of 1848, were sent to the press, and were a great news feature. The election results in November, 1847, were for the first time transmitted by the electric wire. The inaugural address of President Zachary Taylor was the first important public document sent throughout the country by telegraph. In the beginning it was thought necessary to have a metallic circuit, so two copper wires were used. In 1846 it was accidentally discovered that the earth could be used as a part of the circuit. In 1847 it was learned by accident that iron wire could be used instead of copper. Thus it will be seen that it was the happy privilege of Father Stokes, during his otherwise uneventful pastorate, to see the beginning of this wonderful invention which has revolutionized the world, and Utica proudly boasts of the honor of having introduced it into the Empire State.

The pastorate of Father Stokes was coincident with an eventful period, both in the history of the world, and of the Church. It may not be uninteresting to recall the contemporaneous events of that time.

In 1845, Ex-President Jackson died. The illustrious Silas Wright was elected Governor of the State of New York. Sir John Franklin sailed on a voyage to the North Pole. In 1846 Pius IX. of blessed memory began his long and glorious reign, protracted unto our time until he saw the days of Peter. The Sixth Council of Baltimore solemnly chose the Blessed Virgin conceived without sin, as the Patroness of the United States. It was also during this year that the Mexican War began. In 1847 occurred the death of Daniel O'Connell, the liberator of Ireland. In the same year postage-stamps were first used in the United States. In 1848, the Pope was obliged to flee from Rome; the third French Revolution took place, and Louis Napoleon became the President of the new Republic. In this year also, gold was discovered in California, and several Uticans caught the fever, and left for the far West. In 1849, Wm. H. Seward, Jefferson Davis, and Charles Sumner entered the United States Senate. Pius IX. returned to Rome, and his authority was re-established. In 1850, New York was made an Archiepiscopal See, and in 1851 took place the famous *coup d'état* of Napoleon III., and the French Republic was again supplanted by the Empire.

ASSISTANT PRIESTS UNDER FATHER STOKES.

The parish had now grown to such large proportions that the labor was too much for a single priest. Besides, the health of Father Stokes was so very poor that he stood in constant need of active coadjutors.

During his pastorate he had no less than ten different Assistant priests. One of them is still alive—one of the five priests attached to the parish, still living, who celebrated Mass in the second church. The nine others are dead. You will see their names on the memorial tablet.

Father McCloskey, who had been assistant priest under Father Martin, remained with Father Stokes for three weeks.

REV. JOHN McMENOMY.

JULY 13th, 1845 –SEPTEMBER 1st, 1845.   DIED JULY 13th, 1892.

Father McMenomy was assistant priest from July 13 to September 1, 1845. After leaving Utica he went to Albany. A few years later he became pastor of Little Falls. He was subsequently transferred to Syracuse, and built St. John's Church, the present cathedral of the diocese. He was afterwards the pastor of St. Peter's Church, Saratoga, where he remained until his death, which occurred July 13, 1892.

If I might be pardoned for remarking a coincidence which is somewhat personal, I would say that twice I was attached to the church which Father McMenomy built in Syracuse— once when I went there in June, 1870, a few days after my ordination to the holy priesthood, to assist the venerable Father Guerdet; and the second time, in May, 1887, when, upon the erection of the new diocese of Syracuse, I went there as rector of the new cathedral.

REV. JOHN MCMENOMY.

REV. WILLIAM HOWARD.

SEPTEMBER 20TH, 1845—OCTOBER 6TH, 1845.   DIED FEBRUARY 25TH, 1888.

Father Howard was assistant priest for only a few weeks. He was afterwards pastor of St. Mary's Church, Constableville, and St. Mary's Church, Hudson, in which latter place he remained for several years. Later he was appointed pastor of the Church of the Annunciation, Ilion, which parish then included Herkimer and Frankfort. A few years later, failing health compelled him to

REV. WILLIAM HOWARD.

resign his charge, and he retired to Herkimer, where he lived quietly until his death, which occurred in that village, February 25, 1888. Father Howard was a real missionary priest. In all, he built ten different churches in various parts of the country.

REV. DANIEL CULL.

OCTOBER 12TH, 1845 - - JUNE 13TH, 1847. DIED MARCH 2D, 1873.

Little is known of Father Cull, who assisted Father Stokes for nearly two years. He retired from active duty many years before his death, and lived quietly in Saratoga, where his death occurred, March 2d, 1873.

REV. JOHN CORRY.

NOVEMBER 24TH, 1847- APRIL 2D, 1848. DIED JUNE 27TH, 1863.

Father Corry remained here only a few months. After leaving Utica, he labored zealously in the holy ministry in various places. He had the reputation of being a very successful church builder. He erected St. John's Church, Greenbush. This

REV. DANIEL CULL.

church was burned down a few years ago, but has since been replaced by a magnificent structure, built by Very Rev. Dean Duffy, the present zealous pastor.

REV. HIPPOLYTE C. DE LUYNES, S. J.

AUGUST 1ST, 1848 — SEPTEMBER 15TH, 1848.   DIED JANUARY 20TH, 1878.

During the Summer of 1848, Father Stokes went to Europe for the benefit of his health. Two Fathers of the Society of Jesus took charge of the parish during his absence.

One of them was Father De Luynes. Many will be surprised to learn that Father De Luynes was an Irishman, born in Paris, whose good old Irish name of Devlin, or something of the kind, was gallicized into De Luynes. Father De Luynes is still remembered by old parishioners for his kind and agreeable manner during his short stay among us.

After leaving Utica, he labored for over thirty years in that illustrious Order, which was so dear to him. He died at St. Francis Xavier's College, New York, January 20, 1878.

REV. THOMAS OUELLET, S. J.

AUGUST 13TH, 1848 — SEPTEMBER 3D, 1848.

I am speaking only of the dead priests, and I ought not perhaps to allude to the living. And yet I may be permitted a word in regard to the co-laborer of Father De Luynes in the Summer of 1848, in our second church.

Two years ago, when preparing the list of the dead priests of the parish, I had amongst the rest, the name of Father Ouellet (Wellett) of the Society of Jesus. Upon making inquiries touching the place and time of his death, I was very much surprised to learn that he was still alive, and laboring among the Indians in Canada.

As the result of my researches, I received a letter from him at that time, from Garden City, in the diocese of Peterboro, Canada. The following extract from this letter may prove interesting, at least to those who still remember this devoted priest of long ago:

"I am indeed the priest who was in Utica in 1848, attached for a few weeks to St. John's Church to help Father De Luynes replace Father Stokes, then travelling in Europe for his health. I am living yet, though old ; and after such a long time, I keep yet pleasant recollections of Utica and its good people, who edified me during my short stay among them. I am now a poor Indian missionary. During the late American war I was chaplain of the 69th Regiment, N. Y. S. V., Irish Brigade. I have been in many battles, particularly Fredericksburg, Antietam, the Wilderness, Cold Harbor, Spottsylvania and Petersburg, and then I have attended many wounded soldiers. Wherefore, I think I have done something for the Catholics of the United States and the happiness of the people under the Union. I think they cannot look upon me as a stranger, even though I am laboring among the poor Indians in Canada."

There are twenty-four priests alive who were at one time or another attached to this parish. Father Ouellet is by far the oldest of them all. It is a striking coincidence that he was born in 1819, the very year in which St. John's Church was organized as a parish. It may be interesting, therefore, to read an extract from another of the good old man's letters which I received from him a short time ago:

"I had to leave my Indian mission," he writes, " to come to this place for treatment and rest.

"This is our House of Studies for Philosophy and Theology, and, for the future, if it is God's will, and my health permits, I shall be one of those who take care of our young students. At present, apart from other infirmities, I am troubled with rheumatic pains, which nail me to my chair or bed, scarcely able to stir myself one way or the other. Still, there is nothing dangerous in it.

"I am happy to see your zeal for the departed bishops and priests respectively connected with St. John's Church, in which I took so much interest forty-five years ago. I wish I could help you in the good work.

"But sickness and want of recollection make it impossible to add anything to what I told you previously.

"Good Father Stokes! How he loved Utica, and what interest in the spiritual welfare of his parishioners he took himself as long as his health permitted!

"And when sickness compelled him to leave them, how solicitous he was in procuring priests to continue the good work, so that they might not suffer from the want of proper administration in his absence!

"It is then I had, with good Father De Luynes, the good fortune of doing something for St. John's Church and its dear people.

"Don't put my name yet on your tablet containing the names of deceased bishops and priests, but very likely I shall soon have to go there. And then, if you kindly do so, you will confer a great favor on me, as it will procure me many fervent prayers."

Surely I may say that, I need make no apology for this digression. I am speaking of the dead. Do not the words of the good old priest of your fathers sound like a voice from the tomb? [1]

ASSISTANT PRIESTS.

REV. PATRICK CARAHER.

OCTOBER 15TH, 1848—JANUARY 20TH, 1850. DIED OCTOBER 23D, 1890.

Father Stokes returned from Europe about the first of September, 1848, and the two Jesuit Fathers left the parish where in a

[1] Father Ouellet died at the Immaculate Conception College, near Montreal, November 26, 1894.

short time they had made so many friends.   Father Caraher was then sent as assistant priest to Father Stokes.   He had previously labored w i t h great zeal on the mission in the State of Maine.

St. Patrick's parish was founded in December, 1849, and he became the first pastor.   He held that position until a few years before his death, when he resigned his parish, and lived quietly at the church rectory. He often used to speak of the year and a half that he spent so happily in this parish as assistant priest under Father Stokes.

REV. PATRICK CARAHER.

REV. MICHAEL J. KELLY.

JULY 1ST, 1850—SEPTEMBER 1ST, 1850.   DIED JULY 11TH, 1886.

Father Kelly was here only two months.   He became, afterwards, pastor of St. Paul's Church, Oswego, New York.   His mental faculties becoming impaired, he was obliged to retire from active duty.   He was for more than twenty years under the care of the Sisters of Charity, at Mount Hope, New York, where he died July 11th, 1886.

REV. MICHAEL E. CLARKE.

OCTOBER 28TH, 1850—JUNE 15TH, 1851.   DIED MARCH 19TH, 1872.

F a t h e r Clarke succeeded Father Kelly as assistant priest, and remained here about nine

REV. MICHAEL E. CLARKE.

months. He subsequently labored in many places. We find him, in 1863, pastor of St. Mary's Church, Amsterdam.

He was appointed pastor of St. John's C h u r c h, Schenectady, in 1866. He died in that city o n t h e Feast of St. Joseph, March 19, 1872.

He is remembered as a very holy priest. Many very wonderful cures were attributed to him.

REV. WM. C. COGHLAN.

NOVEMBER 12TH, 1850—MAY 1ST, 1854. DIED JULY 7TH, 1862.

Father Coghlan became assistant priest to Father Stokes in the fall of 1850, with a view to look after the spiritual needs of Clin-

REV. WM. C. COGHLAN.

ton, where the Catholics were beginning to grow in numbers. He became pastor of Clinton, May 1, 1854, and built St. Mary's Church, in that village. He died in Clinton, July 7th, 1862.

SING, sing, ye Angel bands,
　All beautiful and bright;
For higher still and higher,
　Through fields of starry light.
Mary, your Queen, ascends,
　Like the sweet moon at night.

A fairer flower than she
　On earth hath never been;
And, save the throne of God,
　Your heavens have never seen
A wonder half so bright
　As your ascending Queen!

O happy angels, look!
　How beautiful she is!
See! Jesus bears her up,
　Her hand is locked in His;
Oh, who can tell the height
　Of that fair Mother's bliss?

And shall I lose thee then,
　Lose my sweet right to thee?
Ah! no—the Angels' Queen
　Man's Mother still will be,
And thou, upon thy throne
　Wilt keep thy love for me.
　　　　　— *Father Faber.*

CHILDREN OF THE ROSARY.

EIGHT.

Sister Mary Alphonsus, O. S.

The clock strikes eight—her strokes recall
    Eight states ' which Christ hath blessed,
Now, search my soul, among them all
    Where mayest thou find rest.

Ah! Lord! how sad if I should prove
    My thoughts so far from Thee,
That many a mild award of love
    Found thankless heart in me!

Teach me to think as Thou hast thought,
    To see as Thou dost see,
Nor ever turn away from aught
    Which hath been blessed by Thee.

' The Eight Beatitudes.

FLORAL INVALIDS.

HENRY COYLE.

HAT game shall we play this evening?" enquired Willie Conners, the secretary.

"Let us play 'The Blacksmith,' suggested Alice; "the room is not quite warm yet, and it is a lively game."

When the members were seated in a circle, one said to his neighbor on the right, "Cyclop, can you forge well?" to which the other answered, "As well as you, at least," and the first member said, "Well, then, forge with one hand." Then the two players struck with their hands doubled up, on their knee, and each one of them in turn asked their right hand neighbor the same question, and everybody was forging with one hand.

The game went on: "Cyclop, can you forge well?" "As well as you, at least." "Well, forge with both hands." The whole circle went on to say and do the same thing. The cyclop who stopped had to pay a forfeit; the smiths were obliged to keep time in their motions. Then they forged with both hands and one foot; again, with both hands and feet; and finally with hands, feet, and head.

The joyous blacksmiths were all in motion, and they worked so violently that they were hardly able to laugh. No one stopped, but when it was necessary to forge with the head, hands, and feet, the game became difficult. Soon shouts of laughter announced that the blacksmiths had ceased forging.

Alice had failed to keep up with the members in the game, and paid her forfeit with the following charade:

> "But for my first, no one had now been here;
> In four and twenty hours, my second flies;
> My whole returns with each revolving year,
> And when my second's gone, it also dies."

This was answered by George, just as it was about to be given up. The answer was "Birth-day."

The meeting was called to order by Mrs. Stevens, and the secretary called the roll. The president, who had been detained in the parlor by a visitor, now entered, and took his usual place.

"This evening we shall resume our study of botany," he said. "We shall notice the diseases of plants."

"Do plants have diseases?" asked George, with surprise.

"Yes; as certainly as you or I. Plants are also subject to deformity."

"How dreadful!" exclaimed Alice.

"Deformity in plants is not always ugly; it is sometimes highly ornamental. To the gardener's eye, a double flower is a beautiful thing; but to the botanist it is a monster. In what flowers is this kind of deformity frequently seen?"

"I saw a double pink in Boston, last summer," said Mary White.

"And I have seen double roses, hollyhocks, and marigolds," said Mrs. Stevens; "what is the cause?"

"When the anthers are supplied with too much nourishment, they perish, and——"

"But what are anthers?" this from one of the younger members.

"Anthers are frail tendrils, which are in that part of the flower from which the bees obtain their pollen. When the anthers wither, the stamina (look this word up in the dictionary) gradually expand till they attain the size and color of the rest of the petals. Another deformity is the changing of stems into leaves; sometimes the leaflets, from lack of proper nourishment, grow into tendrils. Thorns are originally the young shoots of branches, but the sap not being sufficient for their full development, they are forced to stop and take the form of thorns."

"It is curious," remarked Mrs. Stevens, "that lack of nourishment should in one plant produce soft, delicate tendrils, and in another make hard, sharp thorns."

"Yes; and if the plants are removed from a poor to a rich soil, the tendrils and thorns no longer grow on the plant. The leaves are to plants what the tongue, the breath, and digestion are to us. When a plant is thirsty, its leaves droop; when it is cold, they curl themselves up like kittens, as if to keep warm."

"How strange!" exclaimed Alice.

"Yes; and when the plant is sick, its leaves grow pale, just as our faces do when we are ill. Disease is sometimes caused by improper light, heat, air, or soil. When there is too much light or heat, oxygen is thrown off, and the carbon is deposited so rapidly that the sap cannot support the strain."

"How would it do to keep the plant well watered?" said Mrs. Stevens.

"Yes, that might prove a remedy; but the result in the case of a tree would be a rich foliage, and very little fruit."

"What causes the leaves to fall from our house-plants in winter?" asked Mrs. Stevens.

"They fall because the temperature of the room being too cold, the sap does not evaporate as fast as the roots absorb it, and the consequence is, dropsy. Another strange thing about plants is, that they must exercise in order to keep in good health."

"Exercise!" repeated some of the members, incredulously.

"Yes, plants exercise; if they did not, they would not flourish. Wind is to plants a substitute for the power of locomotion, and when the leaves are shaken by the breeze, it quickens the circulation of the sap. Plants have a great aversion to a smoky atmosphere; can you tell me why?"

"Perhaps it makes them cough," this from George, with a twinkle in his roguish eye.

"Or makes their eyes water," suggested another.

"No; it is because the small particles of carbon, of which smoke is composed, clog the pores of the leaves," said Mr. Stevens.

"But I thought carbon was the natural food of plants?" said the secretary.

"It is; but for plants to receive carbon through the pores of their leaves would be like an animal receiving its food through the pores of the skin. The plants admit carbon only through the tiny sponges at the end of their roots. Some diseases are the result of external injuries, such as loss of leaves or bark. It is a serious loss for a plant to be deprived of its leaves—those beautiful little workshops where nature carries on her operations."

"When the plant is pruned too closely of its leaves, what is the result?"

"The sap accumulates in the stem, and forces out new leaves. Again, there are diseases caused by insects; they bite into the plant, and deposit their eggs. The young, as soon as they are hatched, eat their way out. There are certain diseases caused by parasites. What is a parasite?"

" The dictionary defines the word as a plant growing on another," replied the secretary.

" Yes; such as mosses, lichens, and fungi. Do you all know
what fungi is? "

Some of the younger members shook their heads, and even a
few of the older ones looked doubtful.

" Mushrooms and toadstools are fungi.   There are no less than
three hundred and forty different kinds; forty of these attack
plants on the outside, and three hundred on the inside. Have
you ever seen an ear of corn, which, on being opened, appeared
to be filled with a fine, black dust? "

" Yes; and I have often wondered what was the cause," replied
Charles.

" It is caused by an internal fungus.   The most common reason
of death among plants is the failure of strength in consequence
of bringing too many seeds to maturity.   This may be remedied
by preventing the seeds from growing, and thus economize the
strength of the plant."

" Is it true, Mr. President, that each blossom of the oak tree
has six seeds? " questioned a member.

" Yes; but it brings only one to maturity, so that the labor of
transporting the sap is very little, when compared with a fruit
tree.   Some trees and plants are stronger than others, and so resist more successfully the attacks of disease."

" Do plants and trees die of old age? In a warm climate, I mean? "

" I think not; for this reason: They have the power of supplying themselves every year with a new layer of wood for the ascent of the sap, and a new layer of bark for its descent. By
means of the sap, branches and leaves may be multiplied; there
seems to be no reason why the process should not go on to the
end of the world."

" Quarter to ten, Mr. President."

" What, already? It has been decided that the meetings for
the next two months be suspended, and that the members attend,
instead, the course of lectures to be given by distinguished
scholars at the Town Hall.   All in favor say aye."

" Aye," said the members in chorus.

" I now move that the meeting be adjourned until the first
Wednesday after the close of the lecture course."

" Second the motion," said George, and after the usual refreshments the members retired.

"Fetch It."

Oh, the jolliest times have we,
Playing in the lovely sea.

" Fetch it,
fetch it,
Prince! "
I say,
Throwing
far the
s t i c k
away.
Dear old
fellow!
he swims
out,
Catches it,
and turns
about,

Brings it proudly back to me,
Oh, the jolliest times have we!

Prince, he saved my life: One day
In the woods I lost my way;
Prince, he found me, and, you know,
Ever since I've loved him so!

Sometimes we are, oh, so gay—

Sometimes not a word we say.

I just look at him, and he

With his big eyes looks at me.

Though he doesn't know one letter,

No one says " I love you " better!

But a frolic in the sea—

That's what Prince likes best, with me!

*   *   *   *   *

Life it is a changing sea—

Ended soon will playdays be.

Older will the girlie grow,

And the doggie staid and slow.

Still will doggie cling—true friend !

Till the dear brute life doth end.

Beats a heart in doggie's breast—

In dumb ways its love expressed.

Kindly word with loving pat—

How each dog-heart beats at that !

Kicks or cuffs, words harshly spoken—

Doggie's heart is well-nigh broken !

Children ! kind to dumb beasts be—

God gave them to you and me !

CHERRY LEAF.

A FABLE.

EDWIN ANGELOE.

HERE once lived, at an old country homestead, a very black pig of the name,
Cherry Leaf.

She was a plump, chubby creature,
nine months old, and had the reputation
of being very handsome.

Cherry Leaf was glad that she was
black, for she hated everything of a
conventional order; and she was well
aware of her charms, often conceitedly wondering why she was
not the idolized favorite of some fashionable household instead of
being only the pet of a plain home in the country.

Had she not been the inky, shapely pig that she was, she had
long ago met her doom at the cold, sharp blade of the butcher's
knife, a fate that had befallen her parents, brothers, and sisters—
poor, fat animals of no refinement or attractions whatever.

Cherry Leaf knew well what she had escaped, but she didn't
care. She was continually unhappy, longing ardently for things
beyond her, and vainly placing herself above her surroundings,
till at length she came to look upon herself as a pig of great importance.

One afternoon, when Cherry Leaf went out for a walk, she observed an old gray goat and a homeless-looking brown dog in
close conversation.

As she drew near she soon learned that they were discussing
the fame of a certain animal known as Tony Redpath's Educated
Pig.

" His success has been undeserved," said the goat, somewhat
jealously. " I don't see what the people saw in a vulgar pig that
they should take him to their hearts. Think of him going to appear in London."

"It does seem queer," said the brown dog, a meek look in his eyes. "But I feel glad for the pig's sake."

"I should think you would be very much 'cut' about it," said the goat—"you who have no home. I'm sure a dog is above a pig any day in the week."

"I've had a hard time of it, I admit," returned the dog. "But, all the same, I like to see another reach success, even though I never do get there myself. I belong to a very common breed, or I'd have had a good home long ago—with a blue ribbon about my neck, I dare say."

"You ought to find a home even now," said the goat. "It would be good if you could get into a plain, poor family."

"I haven't given up hope yet. Some day I'll meet somebody who will take a fancy to me. You see, if I had an education like the pig's, I might find it easy."

"Education! What does the pig's education amount to?" sneered the goat.

"They say he has much talent, and is very clever."

"I don't believe he knows any more than myself. He's skilfully advertised—that's all."

The brown dog felt sure now, that the goat was speaking from jealousy, so he determined to say no more.

At that moment Cherry Leaf approached them, and said:

"I beg pardon, but were you not discussing a pig just now?"

"Yes," said the others.

"I think I heard you say he was educated?"

"Yes."

"Tell me all about him, please, for I am very much interested."

"I don't know much about him, except what I've heard from my friend, the goat. He can tell you more than I know," said the dog.

"Yes, I know all about Tony Redpath's Educated Pig," put in the goat, with an air. "I used to live very near him before I was sold to my present owner."

At another time Cherry Leaf would not have stopped to talk with either the dog or the goat, for she was usually very proud and haughty; but now that she had caught a few words about an animal of fame, and a pig at that, she was ready to listen to information about him from any source.

The goat briefly told all he knew concerning the Educated Pig, making sure to give him a " dig " at every opportunity.

" Have you ever seen him perform? " asked Cherry Leaf.

" No, and I don't want to. I wouldn't make so little of myself as to lend my presence to one of his entertainments."

" How can the Redpath home be reached? " inquired the black pig, after a thoughtful pause.

" Why, do you intend to go there? "

Cherry Leaf answered evasively, for she did not wish the goat to know just what was going on in her mind.

Full directions were given her, the goat regarding her curiously.

After learning all she could, Cherry Leaf thanked both animals, and bade them a formal " good-afternoon."

She returned home, and for the rest of the day gave herself up to wild, ecstatic dreams wherein she was a dazzling " star," under the management of Master Tony Redpath, with the whole world flocking to see her, and her name and beauty the subject of every tongue.

The following day Cherry Leaf stealthily left the homestead, saying to herself, as she slyly crept out through the gate: " I shall never come back to this sleepy place. I am too good for these surroundings."

She made the best of her way to the town of Plympton, where dwelt the much-talked-about Educated Pig.

As she drew near Tony Redpath's home she saw a well-fed looking cat sitting outside, on the garden railing.

" I beg to ask is this the home of Master Tony Redpath? " said Cherry Leaf, in a sedate tone.

" Yes," answered the cat, bluntly. " Who are you? "

" Does the Educated Pig reside here? " asked Cherry Leaf, heedless of the other question.

" Yes," said the cat, a cloud coming over his face, as if the famous animal were a distasteful subject to him.

" I should like to see him very much."

" You can't, unless you are a newspaper reporter."

" I am a belle."

" A dinner bell? "

" How very ignorant you are! A belle—a handsome young lady."

" You had better go back where you came from, for I'm sure the Educated Pig doesn't wish to be disturbed by visitors."

" You might at least do me the favor of asking him if he will grant me an interview."

" No, I won't," snapped the cat. " If you must know the truth, the Educated Pig and I are not on speaking terms. I never notice him—the vulgar thing!"

" I think he is delightful."

" What do you know about him? Have you ever seen him?"

" No; but I have heard of him. He is educated and famous. I adore notoriety."

" I wouldn't be seen walking with the Educated Pig."

"Don't worry about that, Toby—you'll never get the invitation," chimed in a jolly little chicken that just then ran up.

" You mind your own business, Crab Apple, and go back to your coop. Nobody asked you to interfere."

" Well, you're always backbiting the Educated Pig, and I like to pull you down a peg whenever I hear you doing it."

Then Crab Apple turned to Cherry Leaf, saying, " How do you do? "

She simply bowed. Then she said:

" Perhaps you, sir, will take a message to the Educated Pig? "

" I will, with pleasure."

" You are very kind. I have no card with me, but you may tell him that Miss Cherry Leaf, of Brandywine, would be charmed to have an interview with him."

" Miss Brandy Leaf, of Cherrywine? "

" No, no; Miss Cherry Leaf, of Brandywine."

Crab Apple scampered off, while Toby the cat sneered and walked away.

The black pig looked very demure as she awaited the chicken's return.

(*Conclusion next month.*)

THE ASSUMPTION.

Words by MARCELLA A. FITZGERALD.

Music by LOUISA MORRISON.

1ST Sop. *Allegro moderato. f*

2D Sop.

1. Heav'n's gates stand wide, O bright and fair, 'Mid dazz-ling ra-diance
2. Her fond de-sire through wea-ry years, Her fer-vent prayer has
3. "Hail, Queen of Heaven," the an-gels sing; Hail, Queen of Heaven, thy

ALTO.

pour-ing down; The an-gel hosts en-rap-tured bear Our La-dy
an-swer won; Haste from the shadowy vale of tears To end-less
chil-dren pray; Win for us from our Lord and King Un-ion with

to her throne and crown, Our La-dy to her throne and crown.
un-ion with thy Son, To end-less un-ion with thy Son....
Him for aye, for aye, Un-ion with Him for aye, for aye....

Chorus.

List-en, O Moth-er, while we pray, We show thee all our cares and needs,

pray,...   needs,

f

As plead-ing for thy aid we say The A-ves on thy bless-ed beads;

rit.

As plead-ing for thy aid we say The A-ves on thy bless-ed beads.

AN ANGEL TEACHER.

THIRD ROSARY MYSTERY.

Beneath the stable's humble roof
We hail the Saviour's birth,
While Angels glory sing to God,
And peace to men on earth.
                    —*Mary A. Mannix.*

HE child knelt, silent, for a few happy moments, her lips pressed to the beads her hands lovingly held. She felt that this was a mystery very, very dear to the Angels when so many of them had sung of it to the poor shepherds on that blessed Christmas night. Soon she spoke softly: "Tell me how to meditate about it, dear Angel; maybe you were one who sang the beautiful hymn to the shepherds the night the dear Jesus was born."

Until she meets that loving Angel in Heaven, the child will never forget his lesson of meditation on the Third Joyful Mystery, the Nativity of our Lord.

Dear Little Child:—The third joyful mystery is called the Nativity of our Lord in Bethlehem. A long time ago, nineteen hundred years ago, our Lord came down from Heaven, and as an infant, was born in a poor stable, in the little town of Bethlehem. The people of this place did not know the Blessed Virgin or St. Joseph, and no one gave them any welcome to a home. But they found shelter in the cave where animals rested, and there our dear, good Lord was born, a little babe, for you and for all people in the world. You wonder why He did this. Yes, dear child, it is much to be wondered at, for it is a strange and beautiful thing, and this is what it means: Our Lord came down from Heaven to become Man, that He might live with men, speak to them as they speak to one another, and teach them how to be good. And after all these blessings, He wished to die for them, because they had offended His Heavenly Father, by their sins, and because they could not feel enough sorrow for their bad deeds, till our Blessed Lord taught them, and till He gave up His own life to show them how much displeased God had been because man committed sin.

Look, then, dear little child, on your Blessed Infant Lord, and as you say this decade, think how good, and gentle, and loving, and tender, and humble, and poor He is, your sweet little Lord, and tell Him how much you wish to love Him and to be like Him. The Blessed Virgin, Queen of the Holy Rosary, will help you to obtain this great blessing.

Puzzles.

ANSWERS TO PUZZLES IN JUNE ROSARY MAGAZINE.

Colorado—(Color-ado).   Delaware—(Dell-aware).
Massachusetts—(Massa-chew-setts).   Nebraska—(Knee-brass-car).
          Kentucky—(Ken-tuck-key)

COLUMN PUZZLE.

```
              V E I N
              E A S E
              R A W
VERMONT.      M A Y      NEW YORK.
              O H I O
              N E A R
              T I C K
```

Correct answers to the June puzzles were received from the following:

Frank J. Cahill, Lillian Mulvey, Katie G. Mulligan, John A. Hoban, Ida E. Grossmann, Nellie Everard, Mary T. Collis, John Joseph Cummings, Rosie T. Coyle, Bertrand A. Jockum, Florence A. Lyons.

The following solved all but one, correctly:

Mary E. Ives, Mary McCabe, Catherine Gillooly, Joseph O. Barrett, George Ellers, C. G. J. Crimmins, Mat. P. Geisser, Mary Lonergan, Minnie Devlin, Alice V. Curran, John J. Donohue, H. Richter.

The last list of solvers gave *Illinois* (Illy-noise), instead of Colorado, and many gave *talk* for *tick*. These answers were so nearly correct that we shall give them a prize.

PUZZLES FOR AUGUST.

Fill the blanks with a kind of animal that will make complete the sense of the sentence.

1. I saw a man —— the grass.
2. I saw a lady —— a letter.
3. I saw a monkey —— his owner's ways.
4. I saw a thief —— a rich man's footsteps.
5. I saw a noble soul —— with many an insult.
6. I saw a villain —— a hole in a ship.

A RIDDLE.

I'm the queerest little fellow
  That ever you did see;
I live always in the city,
  And in society.

You can dance, I'm sure, without me,
  But without me cannot sing;
I'm absent in the Summer,
  But always here in Spring.

I'm never here in Autumn;
  Though then I'm never missed;
You'll greet me in the Winter—
  So keep me on your list.

You cannot die without me—
  Without me cannot live,
My Name? To the first right solver
  A present I will give.

                              --*J. H. F.*

Those who send an answer to the riddle will please state the time they received the Magazine, and the time they solved the puzzle. In this way we can judge fairly for those who live in distant places.

A picture of our Lady of the Rosary will be given to all who solve the " blank " puzzles. Answers will appear in October.

Address answers to puzzles, applications for Angelic Warfare girdles, and Rosary Cards for the Poor, to AQUINAS. OFFICE OF THE ROSARY MAGAZINE, 871 Lexington Avenue, New York.

EDITORIAL

The beautiful feast of our Lady's Assumption is the special glory of this month. The natural consequence, in God's gracious design, of our Blessed Mother's Immaculate Conception, we hail her lifting up, after the Ascension of her Divine Son, as the fitting crown of the "great things" He hath done for her. The constant tradition of the Church, enriched by her poetry and art, has ever been a fountain of tenderest devotion to our Blessed Queen in the glory of her Assumption. And our Lady has not been unmindful of her clients. Graces and blessings have been showered down from Heaven, realizing for many a devout worshipper, the beautiful legends of the ascending Lady, from whose mantle flowers fell in sweetest fragrance on the desolate earth. In the spirit of this lovely feast, we ask our Rosarians to look above, in rejoicing and thanksgiving, because of our Mother's honor and triumph, and in pleading that we who still linger in this vale of tears may one day be lifted up to the heavenly land where Mary reigns as Queen. The special graces of the mystery of the Assumption are light and courage and hope: light to see this world's fleeting vanities; courage to overcome its temptations; and hope, to make us yearn for our Father's House. Our Blessed Mother will gladly assist us to merit these favors if we offer to her our tender devotion and our loving service. Our glorious Queen rejoices for every opportunity we give to her whereby she may more fully help us to the knowledge and love and imitation of her Divine Son. This is her powerful work in the Rosary. May it be plentifully shared by all the clients of our Lady, Queen of the Holy Rosary!

We now publish the second of Mr. Mooney's incisive, thorough, convincing papers on Zola at Lourdes. Written for Truth, and for the glory of our Lady,

these articles are a tribute of Catholic zeal and devotion, lovingly laid on our Blessed Mother's altar by a gifted champion of the Catholic cause. Our confidence is that much good will result from the publication of these searching, critical essays. By these papers, and those in *The Seminary* from the same master-hand, the infamy of Zola is laid bare, Lourdes' glory is enhanced, and the honor of our Blessed Lady, most powerful Virgin and Comfortress of the afflicted, is even more solidly established than if this realistic romancer had never published his vile book.

The feast of our Holy Father St. Dominic, Founder of the Order of Preachers, and divinely-appointed institutor of the Rosary, ought to be a day of great devotion for all the lovers of our Lady's Beads. Celebrated on the fourth of this month, it makes, after the Assumption of our Blessed Mother, the most notable Rosary event in August. In the broad Rosary sense, all the clients of our Lady, all who love her Beads, are children of St. Dominic. May he bless us on his feast! May he obtain for us a true and ardent devotion to our Blessed Mother, Queen of the Holy Rosary!

The sketch of Church history by Father Lynch, is welcomed by our readers, even beyond the borders of New York state. Our great regret is that we have not been able to present the portraits of all the priests whose good works have been recalled in these pages. Every available effort was made by Father Lynch and by ourselves, but in many cases no record of any photograph could be found.

We remind our readers of the monthly calendar of feasts, with list of indulgences and days of special devotion. During the present month we honor our Lady of the Snow, under which title the great basilica of St. Mary Major was dedicated in Rome. We also commemorate St. Hyacinth, the illustrious missionary, and St. Rose of Lima, the first of the New World's children to achieve the glory of canonization by the Church.

The article on the Catholic Club of New York, with special reference to its splendid library, we earnestly commend to our readers' careful consideration. The generous and truly Catholic spirit animating this Club in its zeal for Catholic interests, and in its desire that deserving Catholics may have the benefit of its fine collection of books, merits a public acknowledgment and a fuller recognition, in a practical way, than it has hitherto received. The apathy of which we have often spoken, which is one of the great hindrances in the way of earnest advocates of the spread of Catholic literature, confronts the Catholic Club at its own doors. Gladly would the members welcome to the privileges of its library, students and readers, but few seek admission. We trust that the present article may produce good results, in the

practical way desired. THE ROSARY MAGAZINE feels a justifiable pride in its efforts for a better understanding of the great libraries of New York. The present article is the seventh which we have published, beginning with Mr. John A. Mooney's paper, in November, 1894, which one of the librarians of the Astor Library pronounced "the best ever written on the subject," and of which the librarian of Columbia College wrote that he earnestly desired that Mr. Mooney might perform a like service in favor of the Columbia Library. We have, in preparation, other papers that will appear in due season, dealing with the libraries of other cities.

There seems to be a slackening of interest in the matter of "questions and answers." As frequently announced, we shall be pleased to answer all questions pertaining to the Rosary, the Confraternity and its indulgences. Our subscribers may feel at liberty to propose any doubts for solution, and in every case the matter will receive prompt attention. We suggest to correspondents to use some title instead of their own name.

BOOKS.

From the Catholic Truth Society, 18 West Square, London, we have received SAVONAROLA AND THE REFORMATION, by the Very Reverend Father John Procter, Provincial of the Dominicans in England. The occasion which called forth this little volume was the series of lectures recently delivered by Dean Farrar on the leaders of the Reformation, during which, "with unwarranted and unwarrantable assurance, he instanced Savonarola as one of them." The Dean qualified his statements by calling Savonarola a harbinger rather than a leader of the Reformation. We know that it is one of the popular fallacies that Savonarola's name is necessarily associated with Luther's in the latter's great rebellion. The English Provincial, as a Catholic priest, a Dominican Father, and a lover of truth, resented the aspersion of a true reformer's name, and his splendid protest issued by the Catholic Truth Society is a work of undoubted value. He considers the question from every view point, clearly, impartially. He quotes largely, judiciously, convincingly. Without ceasing to be the calm historian, he yet proves himself an eloquent and a successful advocate. We are glad that the Dean of Canterbury has stirred up this matter.

We owe him an indirect debt for Father Procter's fine essay, in which are gathered together, in a very agreeable form, all the facts illustrating the holy life and martyr death of the great Prior of San Marco. Speaking of his devotion to our Blessed Lady, Father Procter quotes the following beautiful hymn written by Savonarola, and which we are glad to reproduce:

O Star of Galilee,
Shining o'er this earth's dark sea,
Shed thy glorious light on me,
    Maria Stella Maris. *

Queen of Clemency and Love,
Be my Advocate above,
And, through Christ, all sin remove,
    Maria Stella Maris.

When the Angel called thee blessed,
And with transports filled thy breast,
'Twas thy Lord became thy Guest,
    Maria Stella Maris.

Earth's purest creature thou,
In the heavens exulting now,
With a halo round thy brow,
    Maria Stella Maris.

Beauty beams in every trace
Of the Virgin Mother's face,
Full of glory and of grace,
    Maria Stella Maris.

A Beacon to the just,
To the sinner Hope and Trust,
Joy of the angel host,
    Maria Stella Maris.

* Mary, Star of the Sea.

Ever glorified, thy throne
Is where thy Blessed Son
Doth reign : through Him alone,
  Maria Stella Maris.

All pestilence shall cease,
And sin and strife decrease,
And the kingdom come of peace,
  Maria Stella Maris.

From the Catholic Book Exchange, New York, we have received, PLAIN FACTS FOR FAIR MINDS, by the Paulist Father, the Reverend George M. Searle, Professor of Mathematics and Astronomy in the Catholic University, Washington. We consider this an excellent book. It is timely, in a happy sense of the word. Coming so close after our Holy Father's earnest words, this appeal to candor and common sense covers the ground of much ignorance and misunderstanding. It is a book for the people, and we earnestly wish it many readers. Within a range of 360 pages the author discusses the most practical questions, from Bible Protestantism to the good and the bad in the Church. Moreover, the publishers have issued a cheap, yet a well-made book, and they deserve the blessing of practical encouragement in their energetic work for the mission of the printed word.

From B. Herder, St. Louis, we have received THE VENERABLE MOTHER FRANCES SCHERVIER, Foundress of the Congregation of the Sisters of the Poor of St. Francis, a Sketch of her Life and Character, by the Very Reverend Ignatius Jeiler, O. S. F. The general sameness that marks the lives of saints renders it unnecessary to particularize our notice of this book. We find it a work of interest, of edification, and therefore, of value, apart from its historical merits as a portion of Church chronicles. The devoted children of Mother Frances Schervier are well known in this country. The admirers of the daughter will be pleased to learn something of the mother. Mr. Herder has made a solid volume, well-printed, well-bound.

From the Art and Book Company, London, through Benziger Brothers, New York, we have received GIULIO WATTS-RUSSELL, PONTIFICAL ZOUAVE. This is the story of a brave young life rendered heroically back to God, and in martyr spirit, for His Church. We commend it warmly, especially to young men and boys. It is a romantic sketch, the reading of which ought to inspire youth to greater earnestness and greater devotion to the Church.

From the same house we have received ELEMENTS OF RELIGIOUS LIFE, by Father William Humphrey, S. J. When we state that this is practically the larger work published eleven years ago by Father Humphrey in three volumes, entitled " The Religious State," we feel that further commendation is not necessary. That work was a digest of Suarez's " De Statu Religionis," the substance of which, in shorter form and at lower price, is given in the present volume. Assuredly it is a valuable book.

From Benziger Brothers, New York, we have received DIVINE LOVE AND THE LOVE OF GOD'S MOST BLESSED MOTHER, by the Right Reverend F. J. Weld. This is a devout and learned work, written by a man versed in the spiritual life. The style is not the easiest or the smoothest, nor is the arrangement always the best, at least so far as the printer's part is concerned. The dialogue, in passages, is somewhat confusing, because of want of due distinction on the author's part, in his sentences. And the compositors rendered little assistance, by distinction of type. However, these are only trivial defects. The book has beauty and tenderness as well as solidity and depth. We welcome it, therefore, and we applaud the author's generosity in sending it on its mission, not only for the direct good it will accomplish, but that the proceeds of the sale may be devoted to charity. The Fathers of St. Joseph's, Mill Hill, London, have acted as publishers, and in issuing such a book, well put together, and numbering nearly 600 pages, substantially bound, for three shillings, or seventy-five cents of our money, they have proved themselves lovers of good reading at a price available even for the poor. Therefore, we pray God to bless them, and to make their worthy enterprise successful.

From the Angel Guardian Press, Boston, we have received THE LIFE OF ST. ANTHONY OF PADUA, by the Reverend Ubaldus da Rieti, O. S. F. The recent celebration of the seventh centenary in honor of St. Anthony, has given a great impetus to devotion to this great and popular saint. The object of the compiler of the present sketch was not to offer a new or learned treatise. Rather, he intended to give to the many American clients of St. Anthony an opportunity of reading his life in a cheap and convenient form. The Brothers who conduct the Home of the Angel Guardian, in Boston, have done good work as the publishers of this volume, and therefore we commend their LIFE OF ST. ANTHONY to all our readers.

From H. L. Kilner & Co., Philadelphia, we have received THE SEALED PACKET, by Marion J. Brunowe. Though "a story for girls," we believe that boys will find pleasant reading in this well-sustained and well-developed tale. Miss Brunowe writes agreeably, and with a high-minded purpose. The encouragement of work done in such a manner is a sincere pleasure to a Catholic editor.

From Murphy & McCarthy, Baltimore, we have received HISTORY OF RELIGIOUS ORDERS, by the Reverend Charles Warren Currier. Though this is a large volume, numbering almost 700 pages, the author realized how inadequate it would be for a complete record of the work of religious Orders. His sub-title is, therefore, appropriate as well as explanatory. Father Currier designates the volume "a compendious and popular sketch of the rise and progress of the principal monastic, canonical, military, mendicant, and clerical orders and congregations of the Eastern and Western Churches, together with a brief history of the Catholic Church in relation to religious Orders." The author attempted a considerable task, even within this limited scope of "a compendious sketch;" but he has labored earnestly, taking as his chief guide the famous work of Hélyot. Father Currier has also availed himself of other material, and his own efforts have been diligent, in direct communication with different religious institutes. As he did not write for scholars, it is no reflection on his work to say that it is not satisfying to the student wishing to drink deep. For the general body of the faithful desiring to know the general practical features of the religious life, this sketch is available and valuable. The illustrations, showing the various habits of different Orders, will be found interesting and instructive, though they are not of a high artistic character, nor do they always convey a clear notion of their subject. The price of the volume is not given, but we trust that the publishers, who deserve encouragement for their enterprise, have placed it at a figure within the reach of those for whom the author specially wrote.

MAGAZINES.

The Outlook, July 13, devotes an editorial to "Zola's tremendously powerful book *Lourdes*," during which the writer remarks: "It is hard for any one to believe, after reading his book, that Lourdes, as a centre of pilgrimage, shows much but a skilfully devised plan for profiting by the superstitions of ignorant people. .... There is too much that is great and good in the Roman Church to warrant resort to such appeals to superstition as prompt these pilgrimages." *The Outlook* probably intended to be kind, compassionating our ignorance and superstition. We desire, therefore, to meet *The Outlook* in a friendly way, and we counsel the editor to read Mr. Mooney's papers in THE ROSARY MAGAZINE, the first of which appeared in the July number. After that we shall be pleased to hear a revised opinion of Zola's "tremendously powerful" work.

Littell's Living Age, now in its fifty-second year, continues on its way with old-time vigor. Each weekly issue of sixty-four octavo pages culled from the leading English magazines makes a generous and agreeable allowance for its readers. In number 2662, July 13, we find the following beautiful lines credited to *Cornhill Magazine*, under the heading: " At a Dominican Priory " :

In the old Priory garden the friars pace to and fro,
Long, level shafts of sunlight fall on each robe of snow.
No sound comes thither wand'ring of the world's jar and fret ;
With tears of Heaven only these garden beds are wet.
Here peach and golden nectarine mellow upon the wall,
And in the ancient orchard the red-cheeked apples fall.
And here are Mary's lilies, like virgins white and pure ;
And waving laurel branches for those who shall endure.
Like outpour'd blood of martyrs the crimson roses glow;
And sweet as little maidens the purple violets blow.
The cross-mark'd flowers of passion hang o'er the victor's palm,
And here is sad rosemary, and here is healing balm.
The bells of Benediction ring from the ivied tower ;
Slow creeping on the dial the shadow tells the hour.
Within the dusky chapel, the lilies in his hand,
The Patron of the Order stands, fair, and calm, and grand.
And calm as his, though living, is each grave monkish face :
Of mellow age no bright'ning, of youthful fire no trace.
No ecstasy of passion, nor mystery of pain :
No furrow plough'd—creaseless—by the heart's burning rain.
Nor bitter sweet of loving, nor agony of life ;
Nor trace of hopeless longing for respite from its strife.
Dim eyes, or bright, look sadly, unlit by joy or ruth ;
From under hoar-white tresses, or soft, dark locks of youth.
Can warmth of summer noontides, or sound of wind-blown trees,
Or subtile scent of violets borne on the jocund breeze,

Or silver hush of moonbeams flooding the mystic night,
Stir in these hearts no rapture, nor fill these eyes with light?

Calm—cold—to outward seeming as souls from star-lit lands,
They teach the clinging children, they clasp the wedded hands.

Does never aching longing in priestly hearts have birth
For earthly love and pleasure, for worldly joy and mirth?

We know not—none may tell us of spiritual jars;
Of struggling souls all vainly beating against the bars.

The long, slow years glide over as fall the rosary beads;
The weeks are told by aves, the months are marked by creeds.

Sun after sun arises, and sun sets after sun;
The daily prayers are uttered, the daily work is done.

With reverent hands they offer the daily sacrifice;
They stay the erring footsteps, they close the dying eyes,

Till comes unbroken slumber beneath the dewy sod;
And passing from the altar, they see the face of God.

In other recent issues of *Littell's Living Age* we find a number of biographical papers, which, though quite distinct in purpose, form, when taken as a whole, a series of articles bearing upon that horribly fascinating period of French history: the Revolution. The first paper of this character is "The Great Citoyenne, Madame Roland," by M. Dale. The introduction to this sketch gives a glimpse of the most prominent of the women of the Revolution. A later paper is "The Conciergerie," that famous prison so closely connected with the French Tribunal and its many victims. In another number, "A Heroine of France," by the late Mrs. Andrew Crosse, is a sketch of Madame Lescures, also of Revolutionary fame. There is no history so pleasant as that told by biography. The personal element makes an impression upon the interest and memory delightful and lasting.

In reading *Littell's Living Age*, one must admire the general tact and discrimination displayed in the selection of the articles; they are usually free from any touch or tone which might create either religious or national friction. As all the papers are from English periodicals, the task is doubtless, at times, a delicate one.

In both the June and July numbers of *Harper's Magazine*, Mr. Julian Ralph contributes a Chinese paper. The first is, "House-Boating in China," and the second is, "In The Garden of China," with illustrations by C. D. Weldon. The articles are in Mr. Ralph's own pleasant sketchy style, and though not dependent upon each other, the second forms a sequence to the first, and both are agreeable in these times of Chino-Japanese difficulties.

"The First Impressions of Literary New York" is rather pleasant, because of the subject, and in spite of Mr. W. D. Howells' unenviable style.

"Americans in Paris," and "The Grand Prix and Other Prizes," are companion articles by Richard Harding Davis, and appear respectively in the June and July numbers.

"Orisons," by Louise Imogen Guiney, and "All-Souls' Day," by Rosamond Marriott Watson, are poetical contributions of much beauty and value.

The Annals of Our Lady of the Sacred Heart, published by the missionaries of the Sacred Heart, Watertown, New York, is an edifying and an interesting little periodical whose good work we watch with much pleasure. In the same spirit we remind our readers of its merits.

Under the catching heading, "Beautiful and Brave Was He," a writer in the July *Atlantic Monthly* pleads winningly in favor of the shrike, and proves by interesting experiences that the so-called "butcher bird" is "not so bad a fellow" as popular tradition represents him. In the same number, John Fiske sketches the Elizabethan sea-kings; Percival Lowell discusses the canals of Mars; and Mr. Hill continues his very pleasant talks about autographs.

The Popular Science Monthly for July concludes Professor Sully's discussion of "Fear" in his studies of childhood. "The Armadillo and Its Oddities" is full of instructive points on this peculiar animal. "A Medical Study of the Jury System," by Dr. Crothers, is a good paper. It will confirm the opinion already held by many intelligent men, that "the methods of selecting jurors are literally open doors for the defeat of the very purposes of justice." The *Monthly* contains its usual supply of matter in its own special line.

One of the best exposures of the fraud and crime of so-called Italian unity that has recently been published, appears in *The Fortnightly Review* for June, under the fitting title: "Italian Disunion." The writer makes his paper specially strong by marshalling those most convincing things, "facts and figures," which so utterly condemn the Freemason crew who robbed the Pope, and whose infamous work now totters to its fall.

The American Architect, in its issue of June 15, devotes considerable space to the Catholic Club of New York. Illustrations of the plans, the building, and special rooms are well executed. *The Architect* praises the "institution," as it justly terms the Catholic Club, because of its fine appointments and splendid equipment.

In the July number of *The Ladies' Home Journal* the editor speaks plainly and boldly on a subject that requires plain and bold speaking. Mr. Bok discusses "The Blot on our American Life," under which he scores disrespect to parents and the aged, indiscriminate criticism of our neighbors, ruthless and malicious misinterpretation of motives, and abuse of the President and others occupying places of public honor and trust. Mr. Bok justly condemns as a "most unfortunate element in our American life," the license of what is called our "free press." To this he ascribes much of the prevailing spirit of disrespect so characteristic of many of our people. He holds, also, to strict ancient fathers and mothers who at their own table, around their own fireside, give pernicious example and encouragement to their children by their habit of uncharitable conversation, disrespectful criticism of those in authority, and general disregard of their neighbors' God-given right to be judged by Him alone. Mr. Bok's article is truly Christian, and we commend it as a manly denunciation of a growing abuse.

Lippincott's for July is a very agreeable number. The "new woman" is considered in two articles—one telling how women were viewed by men in the fourteenth century, the other holding out hope for her final and glorious evolution from duck-hood to swan-hood, now temporarily presented in the guise of goose-hood. "The Great Market of Paris;" "The Tea Ceremony of Japan;" and "The Railroad Invasion of Asia" are instructive papers. "McGheoghan's Lapse" is a touching little story. The couplets, quatrains, and general verse of *Lippincott's* are usually excellent.

The Peterson Magazine for July continues the historical sketch of George Washington, "the citizen, the soldier, the statesman, the patriot," begun in the June number. These articles are freely illustrated. "The New York Street Boy in Art," with pictures after the artist, J. G. Brown, is an interesting view of an always interesting subject.

Twelve of the leading English reviews are represented by sixteen articles in the July number of *The Eclectic Magazine*. The busy reader will find in *The Eclectic* many of the good things that appear in the foreign periodicals.

Among other pleasant contributions in *The Irish Monthly* for July, we find a delightful sketch of Bernard Overberg, the German apostle of Christian education in the last century.

The North American Review for June and July contains the Nordau discussion—the June number opening the attack on the author of "Degeneration," the July number containing his answer. Senator Lodge's paper in the June *Review*, "England, Venezuela and the Monroe Doctrine" is a manly, American protest against English greed and rapine. "The Personal History of the Second Empire" is carried down to the account of the Carbonaria and Napoleon III. Four articles on silver in the June and July numbers of *The North American* give readers the opposing views, while Mr. Harvey "stands by his guns," in a defence of his "Coin's Financial School," which appears in the July *Review*. Other articles noteworthy, are, "Wild Traits in Tame Animals,"—the third of a series,—and "The Disposal of a City's Waste."

"Confessions of a Literary Hack," in the July *Forum*, is a well-written paper, and contains some good advice to the aspiring youth who long to help the overworked editor "at current rates." In the same number of *The Forum*, the Income Tax decision is discussed, *pro* and *con*, by ex-Senator Edmunds and Assistant Attorney-General Whitney; Frederic Harrison states his estimate of "Charles Kingsley's Place in Literature;" ex-Senator Ross gives his personal reminiscences of the impeachment of Andrew Johnson; Dr. Nordau presents his views for society's protection against degenerates, and especially warns his readers against immoral reading. "Coin's Financial School" is attacked in an article entitled "Coin's Food for the Gullible," by Professor Laughlin, of the University of Chicago. Three very interesting papers on a more intelligible subject than finance are given under the general heading of "Successful Efforts to Teach Art to the Masses," and discuss, respectively, 'Work of an Association in Western Towns,' 'Picture-Exhibitions in Lower New York,' and 'The Art Work done by Hull-House, Chicago.'

A MADONNA.

(After Carlo Maratti.)

The Rosary

Vol. VII.   SEPTEMBER, 1895.   No. 3.

ZOLA AT LOURDES.

JOHN A. MOONEY.

III.

A SELECTION of the epithets applied to Zola by critics who use words discreetly, I have already quoted. Many of these epithets were memorable: "obscene, brutal, lying, ignorant, criminal, insane." There is one epithet, however, which the critics hesitated to print frankly. This epithet has been supplied by Doctor Boissarie.

When he was addressing the audience that filled the hall of the Luxembourg Club, in November last, Marie Lemarchand, the girl who was miraculously cured of the lupus, sat on the platform near him. Stating her case, Dr. Boissarie read from Zola's nauseous book, the passages in which he portrayed, with such inhumanity, the poor woman who had suffered so grievously. Marie was unaware that, in order to sell his volume among the heartless, Zola had so heartlessly maltreated her. A simple, good-hearted girl, it is more than probable that she did not imagine there lived a male animal, wearing a man's clothes, who would, publicly, abuse a woman so brutally as the founder of the "naturalistic romance" abused her.

When Marie Lemarchand heard Zola's description of her woman's head and face,—the one called "a dog's head," and the other "a dog's snout;" and when she heard the lying story of the visit to the spring, and of her tongue protruding from "the bleeding hole that served her as a mouth," and "lapping" the water,— like a dog's tongue,—the tears rushed to her eyes.

Having finished the reading of Zola's "well-made phrases," Dr. Boissarie turned to Élise Rouquet (Marie Lemarchand) and asked her to stand up, so that the whole audience might see her. Marie stood up. No "dog's head with a dog's snout" faced the audience; no "bleeding hole" served this girl as a mouth. The assembly looked upon a pale young woman, plainly dressed in black, and fair to look upon. Dr. La Nëele—who had treated her consumptive lungs, and the double lupus that, visibly, ate her life away; and who had been compelled to acknowledge that medical science could no longer avail,—sat on the platform with Marie. To Paris he came, as a witness to her condition when she took the Pilgrims' train for Lourdes; and as a witness to her cure;—an absolute cure, verified scientifically.

Imagine yourself among those who faced the thrice-cured girl,—the girl cured of consumption and of a double lupus! Turning suddenly towards her, Dr. Boissarie perceives that Marie is weeping. The cause of her tears he surmises, suddenly. Cool as he is, he cannot hold back the tears that force themselves outside the lids of his unwilling eyes. Moved by a manly impulse, he says, manfully, what the man feels. Nature is artless; hence these words:

"Yes, M. Zola," exclaims Dr. Boissarie, "here is Marie Lemarchand. She is cured and sightly in looks, and there is in her something still more beautiful that you have not seen, have not discovered, have not even guessed at..... I mean her soul! You lingered over the description of her sores, you forget only one thing, that this poor girl labored, and how hard! to maintain her father and mother; that she is the oldest of five children and their sole support. What do I say? You did not even dream of look-

ing for this intrinsic beauty.   In a land that is a land of all the
courtesies, you preferred to coin money out of the face of this
twenty year old girl, and you never sent a single gold piece to her
who works a month to earn one! "

" Greedy "—is the epithet omitted by the critics.   To satisfy
his greed, Zola has cultivated the vice of obscenity, of lying, of
brutality, along with his own serene ignorance.   Out of the vices
of other criminals, as out of his own " moral rottenness," he has,
for twenty years, laboriously coined gold pieces.   The one science,
the one art he has mastered, is the science, the art of a greedy
coiner.   What wonder that he should, soullessly, add to his treasury now, by coining money out of the sores of stricken woman,
who, suffering, labor, as only Christians will, to keep the life in
helpless parents, brothers and sisters!   Having coined money out
of our most loving Redeemer, in a way that would have gladdened
the infamous Voltaire's heart, why, coining money out of Christ's
gracious Mother, " Help of the Afflicted," should the infamous
Zola sacrifice his greed on the altar of suffering humanity?   Oh!
ye women, and you, sons and daughters of women, what a heartless, greedy crowd must be that which barters with this obscene,
criminal, insane, lying, ignorant fellow, for a share in his ill-gotten gold!

Impulsively resenting the cowardly cruelty of Zola, Dr. Boissarie performed a good action.   Learning from him, the critics
should be encouraged to say frankly what, heretofore, they have
ventured merely to hint.   Those who, shut out from all temples
but one, offer in the market-place blasphemies, brutalities, lies, in
exchange for centimes, pennies, or cents, should be lashed out of
the society of men.   With their fellow-beasts, or fellow-madmen,
or fellow-criminals, they should be compelled to live, or herd.

It is impossible to read the account of the incident I have just
related,—on the authority of an eye-witness, Pierre L'Ermite,—
without being moved deeply.   Emotion shall not, however, hinder us from proceeding, coolly, with our literal exposure of the
ignorance and unveracity of Émile Zola; ignorance and unveracity nowhere more apparent than in the pages of his Vaudeville
of *Lourdes*.

Zola's animus against suffering womankind, and his greedy wits, explain his choice of a little girl, Clémentine Trouvé, as a subject for one of his caricatures. Clémentine experienced a wonderful cure at Lourdes during the National Pilgrimage of 1891. In his book, the unselfish romancer made her a present that cost no gold coin: the new name of Sophie Couteau, to wit. The details of her case, he found in the "Annals of Lourdes;" and he used these details as became him. Changing his method this time, he dug his favorite gap before bringing Clémentine to the shrine of our Lady.

As the train carrying the pilgrims of August, 1892, is leaving Poitiers, an employee of the road pushes a little girl of 14 into a compartment, saying to her: "There is a seat for one, hurry up." A Sister, and one of the charitable ladies who nursed the sick, recognized the new-comer. The Sister having saluted her as one "whom the Blessed Virgin had cured last year," Peter, the stock idiot, could not resist a desire to question her. "A child of that age, so candid in appearance, and who did not seem to be a liar, this interested him keenly "...... "What is your name, my child?"—"Sophie Couteau," she answers.—"You are not from Poitiers itself?"--"No, indeed......We are from Vivonne, about a mile away. My father and mother have a small property; and things would not go at all badly, if there were not eight children in the house. I am the fifth. Fortunately the four others begin to work."—"And you, my child, what do you do?"— "Me, oh! I am not much help. Since last year, since I returned cured, they have not left me quiet a day, because, you understand, they came to see me, they led me to the Bishop, and then into the convents, and then everywhere.....And, before that, I was sick a long time, and I could not walk without a stick, I cried at every step, my foot pained me so."—"Then it is of a disease of the foot that the Blessed Virgin cured you?" Sophie had not time to answer. Sister Hyacinthe, who was listening, interposed: "Of a caries of the bone of the left heel, dating from three years. The foot was swollen, deformed, and there were running sores giving issue to a continual suppuration."

Hearing the Sister's words, all the sick pilgrims were excited. Those who could, stood up so as to see the better. To every one of them, "the sudden arrival of this child, elected by Heaven, was like a divine consolation, the ray of hope from which they drew the force to go to the end of the journey." Having first embraced Sophie, the lady who had spoken to her when she entered the car now said to her: " Certainly our little friend will tell us....Is it not, my dear, that you will relate to us what the Blessed Virgin has done for you?—Oh! yes indeed, Madam....As much as you wish.—She had her smiling and modest air, with her eyes shining with intelligence. Immediately, she wished to commence, raising her right hand in the air, in a pretty gesture which commanded attention. Evidently, she had already acquired the habit of the public. But they did not see her from all the places of the car, and Sister Hyacinthe had an idea."

" Get up on the seat, Sophie, and speak a little loud, on account of the noise."—" This amused her, she had to find her seriousness again to commence."—" Then, like that, my foot was ruined, I could no longer only (*sic*) go to church, and it had to be always enveloped in linen, because things not very clean flowed from it. Monsieur Rivoire, the physician, who had made a cut, to see inside, said that he would be forced to take away a piece of the bone, which would have surely made me lame. And then, after having well prayed the Blessed Virgin, I went to dip my foot in the water, with such a good desire to cure, that I did not even take the time to remove the bandage. And then, everything remained in the water, my foot had no longer anything at all, when I took it out."

" A murmur arose and ran, made of surprise, of astonishment and of desire, at this fine prodigious story, so sweet to the desperate. But the little one had not finished. She took a time, then terminated, with a new gesture, the two arms a little spread out."—" At Vivonne, when M. Rivoire saw my foot again, he said: ' Whether it be the good God or the devil that has cured this child, it is all the same to me; but the truth is that she is cured.' This time, laughs broke out. She recited too much, having repeated her story so often, that she knew it by heart. The remark of the physician was of a sure effect, she laughed at it herself beforehand, certain that they were going to laugh. And she remained ingenuous and candid. Nevertheless she must have forgotten one detail, for Sister Hyacinthe, who had announced with a glance to the audience the doctor's remark, whispered her softly:—' Sophie, and your saying to madam the Countess, the directress of your hall?'--Ah! yes, I had not brought much linen, for my foot; and I said to her: The Blessed Virgin has been very good to cure me the first day, for to-morrow my provision would be exhausted."

In a Vaudeville, a topical song about Sophie's new little boots would be considered artistic just here; and, sure enough, Zola introduces an unrhymed lyric on those important " human documents." To the placid mind of the idiotic Peter, the boots are disturbing. Evidently the girl was cured. Still he is impelled to cross-examine her further; and he concludes that: " Decidedly she was not lying, he suspected in her only a slow deformation of the truth, an embellishment quite explicable, in her joy at having been relieved, and at having become a little person of importance. Who knew, now, if the pretended instantaneous cicatrization, complete, in a few seconds, had not taken days to produce itself? Where were the witnesses?"

The charitable lady who invited Sophie to relate what the Blessed Virgin had done for her, now began saying that she had ·charge of the little girl, in 1891; but Peter, interrupting her, asked: "' Did you see her foot, before and after the immersion?" " No, no," is the answer Zola lyingly puts in the lady's mouth; " I do not think that any one could have seen it, for it was enveloped in ·compresses. She herself has said to you that the compresses fell into the bath." Then turning to the child: " But she will show you her foot. Is it not so, Sophie? Take off your shoe."

" Already she was taking off her shoe and her stocking, with a promptness and an ease that showed the great habit of it she had acquired. And she stretched out her foot, very clean, very white, even very carefully attended to, with rosy well-cut nails, turning it with an air of satisfaction, in order that the priest ·(Peter) might examine it conveniently. There was, below the ankle, a long cicatrice whose whitish seam, very defined, testified to the gravity of the disease. Oh! Monsieur Abbé, (said the child,) take the heel, press it with all your might, I feel nothing any more!"

" Peter had a gesture, and one might think that the power of the Blessed Virgin transported him.... What unknown force had acted? Or rather what false diagnosis of the physician, what concurrence of errors and exaggerations had ended in this fine story?"

The profound ruminations of Peter were interrupted at this stage. All the pilgrims demanded that Sophie should lift her foot higher up. Of course the little girl was only too happy to show her well-cut, rosy toe-nails to the desperate company. Thus the analyst, savant, anatomist,—and Vaudevilliste,—"scientifically" tests the miraculous!

Clémentine Trouvé, caricatured by Zola, under the name of Sophie Couteau, was cured of a serious malady at Lourdes, in August, 1891. A dozen Vaudevilles could not alter the facts. They are proven. No one with pretensions to ordinary intelligence or to common honesty can refuse to acknowledge that this cure was extraordinary. There are but two sets of facts that can interest an austere scientist: those relating to her malady and those relating to her cure. And yet this ignorant scribbler, Zola, fills page after page with farcical descriptions of imaginary scenes, hoping thereby to distract the reader's mind from the facts that have a real importance.

The evidence establishing Clémentine's extraordinary cure is convincing. Zola knew this. His own narrative proves his knowledge. He cannot contest the facts or explain them away. Hence Peter, Zola's idiotic priest, must bear the brunt of Zola's personal malice: "She was not lying, he suspected only a slow deformation of the truth".... "Who knew if the pretended instantaneous cicatrization had not taken days to produce itself? Who were the witnesses?" Hence the false statement forced on the lady who had charge of Sophie before she entered the bath: a statement to the effect that no one could have known the condition of the little girl's heel because it was enveloped in compresses. Hence the ludicrous question Peter put to himself: "What unknown force had acted? Or rather what false diagnosis of the physician, what concurrence of errors and exaggerations had ended in this fine story?"

Indeed Sophie was not lying. Why should she lie? She would have lied, had she said she was not cured instantaneously;

and living witnesses would have convicted her. But Zola is lying; and the same living witnesses shall convict him. His deformation of the truth is not slow. There are few more rapid de-
formers. The concurrence of errors and exaggerations in his fine
prodigious story, is not fortuitous; it is the studied result of his
" naturalistic " method of making gaps and filling them with foolish lies.

Audaciously, Zola pretends to report the details of Sophie's
visit to the Verification Office in August, 1892, while he was present. " A little girl pushed the door, smiling and modest, with
her bright eyes shining with intelligence."—" Ah! cried the doctor joyously, behold our little friend Sophie. A remarkable cure,
gentlemen, which was effected at this time last year, and the results of which I ask your permission to show you " . . . . " The doctor now gave the most precise explanation. . . . a caries of the
bone of the left heel, a beginning of necrosis which necessitated
excision, a frightful sore, suppurating, healed in a minute, at the
first immersion in the bath."

Here Zola, who is pardonably vain of his beautiful talent, favors us with a repetition of the Vaudeville scene enacted on the
train. Sophie tells her story almost word for word as it was told
to the pilgrims; and, at the invitation of Dr. Boissarie, she repeats
Dr. Rivoire's polished remark about " the good God and the
devil," and also her own saying to the Countess. Then the physician asks her to remove her shoe. " Briskly the little foot appeared, very white, very clean, even cared for, with the cicatrice
below the ankle, a long cicatrice whose whitish seam testified to
the gravity of the disease. Several physicians approached,
looked silently. Others, who had doubtless made their conviction, did not disturb themselves." A Vaudeville physician, " with a
very polite air, asked why the Blessed Virgin, while she was at it,
had not made a wholly new foot, which would have cost her no
more. But Doctor Boissarie answered warmly that, if the Blessed
Virgin had left a cicatrice, it was assuredly in order that a mark,
a proof of the miracle, should exist. He entered into technical
details, demonstrated that a fragment of bone and of flesh must
have been instantaneously re-made, something that was inexplicable by natural ways."

" Mon Dieu! " interrupted the little blond monsieur, " there is
no necessity for so many particulars.   Only show me a finger cut
by a pen-knife, and which comes out of the water cicatrized: the
miracle will be just as great, I will bow down."

The little blond monsieur, we know.   He is the writer of Vaudevilles; and never serious except when he is piling up " fetid
filth."   The long, whitish cicatrice on Clémentine Trouvé's foot,
he saw; a cicatrice that established the character of the disease
of which the little girl was cured instantaneously, according to
the testimony of many reliable witnesses, in the icy water at
Lourdes.   Did he bow down?   No!   He waited for Dr. Boissarie
to knock him down, and stamp on him, like a proper scientific
and Christian gentleman.

From Dr. Boissarie's lips, I state the truth about Clémentine
Trouvé's (Sophie Couteau's) case and cure.   When this girl took
the train for Lourdes, on August 18th, 1891, she had been ill for
three years.   During this time she was under the care of Dr. Cibiel, of Rouillé.   He certified that her disease was " caries of the
bone, which had resisted treatment by cauterization and by injections."   The heel bone of Clémentine's rosy-nailed little foot
was rotting away.   The foot was swollen and deformed.   Through
several ulcers, pus flowed continuously.   Dr. Cibiel expressed an
opinion that: " her malady was amenable only to a radical operation or to a treatment of long duration."

Considering these facts, what shall one say of Zola's inane
gabble about a " false diagnosis? "   A running sore is at least as
visible as the scratch of a knife.   Into the sore a physician can
introduce a probe.   If there be a channel up to the bone, the
probe will reach the bone and determine its condition.   Where
pieces of bone are discharged through a wound, any one not a
complete ignoramus would diagnose a rotting bone.   In Clémentine Trouvé's case the diagnosis was quite simple.   The bone of
the heel had rotted away almost wholly.

Zola pretended that he was in search of some one who knew
the girl's foot was diseased when she placed it in the bath at
Lourdes.   " Show me something else! " said he, contemptuously,
to Dr. Boissarie who had not seen the foot until Clémentine entered the Verification Office, after her cure.   Dr. Cibiel knew

that, when his patient started for Lourdes, the caries of the heel-bone was a fact. All the girl's townspeople knew Clémentine's condition. It was notorious. As it happens, the townsfolk are largely Protestant; and therefore not "superstitious." Nor is Dr. Cibiel a "credulous" believer in miracles.

The testimony as to Clémentine's condition is without a break. On the train, during the first day of her journey, (August 18th,) the heel was dressed. The running sores were visible. A second dressing was applied on the following day, the 19th. Again, on the 20th, the bandages were removed. Instead of improving during the journey, the foot had grown worse; the suppuration had increased considerably. Among others a Countess who nursed her—the Countess de Roederer,—saw Clémentine's foot before it was placed in the bath. She will not say no, no! to Zola's or to Peter's interrogatories.

On the 21st of August, the little girl, with the shining eyes, immersed her rotting, ulcerated foot in the bath at Lourdes. Instantaneously it was made whole. The long, whitish, solid cicatrice was complete. Rotted bone, and rotted flesh, had been replaced by sound bone and healthy flesh.

In the Verification Office, the physicians established the cure. With her, the girl carried the bandages she wore when she immersed her foot in the icy water. These bandages were completely covered with pus. When Clémentine returned home, Dr. Cibiel verified the cure; and we may be certain that he did not use the clownish phrase attributed to him by the golden-tongued Zola.

And now let me ask the doubters: Will "auto-suggestion," or "moral shock," instantaneously heal rotting bones and suppurating ulcers? Or will one or the other of these mysterious remedial agents fill open wounds with new-made flesh, or replace bones that have been eaten away? Is there a sane physician who will suggest, seriously, that Clémentine Trouvé's rotted bone and rotting ulcers were cured by "the healing breath evolved in the crisis of faith?" Have we one American Zolaist whose mind can be so troubled by the long cicatrice which "testified to the gravity of the disease," that he will ask himself if the cicatrice was not "hysterical?" The attempt to ridicule away "living human " facts, proves idiocy, madness or malice. Clémentine's cure, like the cure of Marie Lebranchu, of Irma Montreuil, of Marie Le Bourlier, and of Marie Lemarchand, was a miraculous cure. Should some one object to my use of the word " miraculous," I challenge that one to explain the cure, humanly. " An unknown force!" Who controlled the " unknown force?" I'll answer for you: The Almighty God, through His Blessed Mother. Dodge as the doubter may, he is in face of the Supernatural.

Being neither a professional liar, nor a boastful writer of obscenities, nor a greedy blasphemer of Christ, nor a speculator in the sores of dying women, my words will not reach Zola's admirers. I should wish that all of them could read the documents verifying the cure of a woman he spared: Amélie Chagnon. Amélie was a pilgrim in 1891. She rode to Lourdes on the same train with Clémentine Trouvé. You have heard Zola announce his willingness to " bow down " before a cut from a penknife, provided the cut were cicatrized in cold water. Amélie Chagnon would gladly have changed her disease for a penknife scratch. Severe as her malady was, she was instantaneously cured in the cold water of Lourdes. The cicatrice is visible. Her physicians shall state the facts of her case to you. Their certificates were read to the audience in the hall of the Luxembourg Club; and I translate them here.

I the undersigned, Piérre Dupont, Doctor of Medicine at Poitiers (Vienne), certify that Mlle. Amélie Chagnon suffered: 1st. From an inflammation of the left knee, of a scrofulo-tuberculous nature, with enormous swelling of the joint, especially in the region of the subcrural sac, excessive sensibility to touch, a tendency to disjoint and a considerable development of fungous growths. 2d. From a caries of the second left metatarsal, with a running sore and bony suppuration. For several months I gave my services to this young woman. At first I employed blisters, then actual cautery, with long red hot metal points, and finally applied along the whole length of the member a fixed dressing, which I removed about a month and a half ago, without the least result.

The pains at the joints were always very severe, the swelling persisted, and the fungous growths seemed to have even increased.

The state of the foot was the same. I then decided, when the general state (of her health) should be bettered by diet and an appropriate medical treatment, to extract completely the second metatarsal, and then to make interstitial injections of chloride of zinc in the tissues of the knee.

When I informed this young girl of the necessity of her submitting to these various operations, she begged me to defer them, because she had the intention of going to Lourdes. Naturally I conformed to her wishes, and up to the moment of her departure she did not leave her bed; the suppuration of the foot persisted, and the condition of the knee was such as I have above described it.

On the eve of her departure, I saw her suffer so extremely that I felt a certain apprehension, and I asked myself how she could support the fatigue of the journey.

On her return, here are the exact verifications I have made: the running sore of about o^m, o2 had disappeared; the cicatrization was complete, clean, solid. No sensation to pressure on the different parts of the joint.

In testimony whereof, I have delivered the present report, which I certify to be conformable to the truth.

Poitiers, August 30th, 1891.   (Signed): DUPONT.

The certificate of the second physician reads as follows:

I the undersigned, Hyacinthe Joseph Gaillard, doctor of medicine of the Faculty of Paris, inhabiting the town of Parthenay, certify that Mlle. Amélie Chagnon, aged seventeen years, residing at Poitiers, to whom I gave my services for a caries of the bone of the left foot and a chronic inflammation of the knee, is completely cured, and that no trace remains of these two affections. The sore of the foot shows a solid cicatrice, and the knee has the same volume as the right (knee); the movements are free and normal in both articulations.

In testimony whereof I have delivered the present certificate to her, to serve and advantage whomsoever it may concern.

Parthenay, September 5, 1891.   (Signed): DR. GAILLARD.

Zola missed a "fine prodigious" opportunity to lie splendidly, when he left Amélie Chagnon out of his Vaudeville of *Lourdes.* He might have worried Peter into his senses over the diagnosis of Doctors Dupont and Gaillard; he might have made these gentlemen talk like his vulgar clowns. He might have drawn tears from this girl of seventeen, as she heard him coining money out of her rotting foot and swollen knee-joint.

Dismissing him, and referring to the cure of Amélie Chagnon, need I call my readers' attention to the fact that her cure is even more extraordinary than Sophie Couteau's. By natural means, a similar cure is absolutely impossible. Amélie Chagnon came to Paris, last November. She stood up before Dr. Boissarie's audience. All present were invited to question her. I have already said that Élise Rouquet was present, as well as Marie Le Bourlier and Irma Montreuil. Besides these, the Doctor introduced M. Schnetzer, cured of total blindness at Lourdes, while he was walking in the procession of the Most Blessed Sacrament. Dr. Charcot had treated him; so had Dr. Trousseau of the *Quinze-Vingts;* and the two specialists, Doctors Fisher and Bull. The diagnosis of the four physicians agreed: Double atrophy of the optic nerves, atrophy of the papillæ. " Can never read," said Dr. Bull.

Constance Piquet was present, cured of cancer of the breast; and Rose Vion, cured of atrophy of the left arm; and Jeanne Creton, several of whose rotting bones were renewed at Lourdes. Then there were Jeanne Gasteau, cured of Pott's disease of the spine, and of an abscess due to tuberculous congestion of the lungs; Élise Lesage, cured of rotting bones; Claire Merrien, cured of consumption; Charlotte Renauld, cured of atrophy of the lower portion of the right leg; and Mathilde Saugé, cured of disease of the hip. (*Coxalgia*).

These wonderful cures cannot be ridiculed away, or " romanced" away, or " Vaudevillized" away; or " auto-suggested" away; or " hystericked" away. No physician can explain them, humanly. Either they are miracles, or—what? As they are humanly inexplicable, we accept these proven facts as miraculous.

Zola has his coin,—thirty times thirty pieces; but nothing more. Out of his greedy and malicious act, good has come. When an ignoramus, such as he is, assumed the robes of a Doctor of Science, he made the " science" which is based on atheism and agnosticism as ridiculous as only he could make it. That Ferdinand Brunetière should proclaim the " bankruptcy" of this godless science, is not surprising, when Zola dare pretend to represent it. The good he has unwillingly effected is apparent. Discrediting the foolish and unscientific claims that the miracles at Lourdes are " hysterical" accidents, he has centred the attention of thinking men and women on these wonderful cures: cures that human science can neither effect nor explain. He has, besides, moved unprejudiced inquirers, everywhere, to publish the details of the cures at Lourdes, and thus to bring them to the notice of many who would not otherwise know of them. And, through his very malice, he has increased devotion to the Mother of God, to whom be ever increasing honor for her loving kindness to the afflicted in body, mind or soul.

Like the pilgrims who accompanied the girl with the lupus, hundreds of thousands, reading of the miraculous cures verified publicly by Dr. Boissarie, will exclaim again and again: " Ah! Holy Virgin, powerful Virgin, what miracles are done through thy gracious intercession! "

TREES OF GOLD.

REV. S. H. GLENDON, O. P.

He dreamt he walked in shady ways, 'mid trees of verdant hue,
Where grassy lawns, in morning rays, lay sparkling 'neath the dew;

And flowers bloomed, with perfume sweet, by zephyrs gently fanned,

While songsters gay those perfumes greet throughout that happy land;

And gurgling streams, with fishes bright, like purest crystal flowed,
Reflecting in their limpid light the songsters' green abode.

Yet slow he walked, and sad at heart, where all was joy serene,
For though he searched in every part, no gold could there be seen.

At length his eager eye perceives a forest vast and tall,
Where from the trees, like Autumn leaves, the golden pieces fall.

His visage beamed, his pace grew fast, his soul was all on fire,
To find within his grasp at last his life's one long desire!

*   *   *   *   *   *   *   *

But soon there came a fearful change: a dreadful tempest blew;
No music then, but noises strange,—no trees, no flowers, no dew;

A barren waste was what remained; the miser stood alone;-
The place was bleak where beauty reigned, the gold was worthless stone.

His brow grew dark, he foamed with rage, he tore till blood did flow,
And, like a tiger in his cage, went stamping to and fro.

At last he cried, in loud despair, " I'll seek a watery grave,
And to the ocean fast repair, to plunge beneath the wave!"

*   *   *   *   *   *   *   *

But, lo! an agèd man appeared, with faltering steps, and slow;
Upon his breast a flowing beard, his hair as white as snow;

A pleasing smile lit up his face, while kindness filled his eye,
And wisdom found a resting-place beneath his forehead high.

The miser felt a genial ray light up his dismal soul,
As gazing on those features gray, he thought of Heaven's goal.

His heart was touched, he told his tale, the old man soothed his
      fears,
And bade him manly face the gale, and dry those foolish tears.

" Forbear, my son, have courage bold; seek not the ocean wave,
But learn a lesson from that gold, and be no more its slave.

" All wealth and power here on earth, all glory and renown,
With all the world's vain joy and mirth, form but a fading crown.

" Like grass that fades 'neath scorching sun, or flowers that lose
      their bloom,
All earthly joys, though dearly won, but hasten to their doom.

" Have sorrow, then, for errors past, on earthly treasures frown,
And you shall find in Heaven at last a never-fading crown."

      *   *   *   *   *   *   *   *

The miser wakened from his dream, and sighed no more for gold,
But, longing for the goods supreme, his goods and chattels sold;

And calling 'round the needy poor, he gave them all his hoard,
And then from earthly cares secure, himself gave to the Lord.

A life of penance long he led, in conflict ever brave,
Until, his " *Nunc dimittis* " said, his soul to God he gave.

THIS figure of the dawn, under which Holy Scripture and the Church represent to us Mary at her birth, justifies itself by three properties common to the
aurora and to Mary. The dawn is a mother almost immediately after her birth,
for the sun follows very quickly. The dawn becomes a mother without losing
any of her purity or integrity. And lastly, what is still more wonderful, the
dawn is mother of a sun of whom she herself is the daughter, being at the same
time the daughter and mother of the sun : his mother, for he proceeds from her ;
his daughter, for it is the sun who produces that first morning light which we
call the dawn.

Behold Mary, the young Virgin, early in life a Mother ; Mary a Mother without ceasing to be a Virgin ; Mary the Mother of the Eternal Son who existed
before her, and fashioned her with His own hands. So St. Augustine confounds
Manicheism, by making Jesus Christ to say : " The one whom thou dost despise, O Manichean, is My Mother, made by My own hand."

O Virgin Mary, sweet aurora, may your light enlighten our pilgrimage, till
we contemplate the Sun of Justice in the great day of eternity !
                                        —*Rev. J. B. Petitalot. S. M.*
                              2

HELEN TOWNSEND'S CHOICE.

E. M. Hubbard.

(Conclusion.)

HE main facts of Helen's life are soon told. One of her earliest recollections was that of her mother's clasping her in her arms and calling her "poor darling." Then came the growing perceptions of her mother's sadness. She was eight years old when she heard her uncle say to her mother, roughly: "You have mismanaged your affairs; but I will educate the girl. And after that, you must look out for yourselves with what you have left." The remembrance of these words strengthened a temperament naturally grave, and helped to fill the quiet school-years at the convent with patient study. When Helen began her chosen work her natural love and aptitude for it were manifest; her mother's little income placed that dear one above the need of worry, and Helen's life grew serene in its noble purpose and unaffected piety.

She was a beautiful woman. Campbell used to watch her as she went to her daily work of teaching—work that Helen accepted humbly, as a gift from Heaven, while the thought of any obligation to toil on her part was as irritating to Campbell as a conception of St. Genevieve's keeping flocks in some celestial region would be. Her simplicity and goodness, indeed, he looked upon as belonging to her in common with all pure and noble natures, for Campbell accepted very readily the poet's lofty ideal of good women; and he was blessed with comforting recollections of a beautiful mother. Yet, my dear, learned young lady, you would have found this young artist without well-defined theories in regard to certain so-called important questions relating to your sex, and would have declared his doubts as to the good results of certain experiments toward its "advancement" very provoking.

And this man prates about the relation of things? Yes; and you will certainly agree that it was very absurd in Mr. Harold Campbell.

Months passed, and Campbell was still in New York, notwith-standing an earlier determination to leave the city in April, to make some sketches in the country. There were so many old acquaintances to renew, and then, too, he was painting a picture —a St. Catherine. What was more natural than to ask Helen to do him the favor to sit for it? " There shall be no portrait," he said, smilingly, in answer to Helen's look; " I merely wish to have you help me to catch some ideas that, I must confess, are rather fugitive."

The picture was nearly completed, and Campbell was making the last touches, with Dora and Mrs. Aitken looking on, when the talk about future plans became general, and Mrs. Aitken ex-pressed some anxiety as to her being able to find a satisfactory place for rest and quiet during the summer months.

"Give me the commission, Aunt," said Campbell eagerly: " when I am settled in A—— I will look about, and I shall be sure to find something to suit among the fine old farm-houses there."

Then there was a long discussion as to requirements and local-ity, and Dora finally said, laughingly:

" Now I am sure, Cousin Harold, that you will find the place very easily. An old farm-house, with a wide hall, and spacious rooms on each side, with fire-places; convenient to reach, yet se-cluded; well shaded, with wide piazzas, on one of which you will find a St. Bernard keeping guard. The owner of the house has so benignant a face that you will hesitate about asking the price of board, and wonder if you cannot charitably arrange, in order to prevent further embarrassment, to have the money placed regu-larly in a rose-jar that stands upon the table. There is a summer house for mamma to rest in, and a river or lake within walking distance to row on. And you, you, dear old Helen, how miserable you will be when you have nothing to do but to be happy!" end-ed Dora, with profusion.

Two weeks later Campbell welcomed his aunt and cousin to A——, whither Helen was to follow them in a few days. When Dora's first delight had spent itself in rapturous exclamations, and in her mother's room she was secretly thinking that, unless she could rely upon her cousin for a devoted escort, she would find it

rather dull, she espied, a little below the house, a boat on the river
" Ah, mamma! " she cried, " when Cousin Harold comes to-night
we will have a row."

" You must not demand too much of Harold's time, Dora," answered Mrs. Aitken languidly from her lounge. " Remember that
he has a great deal to do."

" Oh, for that matter," replied Dora, " when he has sketched
the kitchens and old stables, and the old women in their sun-bon-
nets, and the little cow-boys in their bare feet,—all of which he
seems to delight in, I shall sit for him in some of his other favorite subjects. I'll be Circe, and one of the sirens, and, by pulling a
long face, I might do, in proper costume, for one of the Fates.
I would try to be as ugly as Michael Angelo's that you like so
much. I asked Cousin Harold the other day if those things were
never going out of fashion, and he said, in that quick way of his,
' Never, as long as the world stands! ' Oh, do not fear that I will
not sacrifice myself in the service of art," Dora went on, rolling
up her eyes; " and when Helen comes she can be all the saints in
one. By-the-way, mamma,"—in a different tone---" have you ever
thought that Helen would care for Cousin Harold? She is so
strange; she never thinks that she is admired! You remember
about Tom Stuart? Everybody understood except Helen herself!
But Cousin Harold is different. Why, I should fall in love with
him myself except it would be of no use, and even if it were, I
should lose a most excellent cousin, and it is so easy to find a
husband! "

" Dora! " said Mrs. Aitken, roused to a point of decided re-
monstrance.

" Now, mamma, you know very well what I mean. Must I always speak as other people do? or, after every sentence, translate
with the introduction, ' which, being interpreted ' ? " cried Dora
with a pretty pout. " But the tea-bell will soon ring, and we are
not ready," and she made a hurried exit.

Mrs. Aitken looked fondly after her. This good lady had
always skipped the articles in the magazines upon Heredity and
Environment, and, being a plain Swedenborgian, had lacked the
opportunity, afforded to members of certain sects, of instruction
upon scientific subjects from the pulpit. She was content with

the simple reflection: "Girls are not what they used to be when I was young; but Dora is a *good* girl. She has her father's kind heart."

How happy to Helen were those first days among the hills, opened by the songs of birds and the odor of fresh roses that climbed to her chamber window! How pleasant to hear the various sounds of life and work upon the farm; and how delightful the noon-day, with its stillness like that of Sunday, while the horses were champing their mid-day meal, and the harvesters were resting near the old well-sweep, under the sweet-smelling locust trees! Those long, quiet walks in the woods, with aisles and arches and "dim religious light" of a Gothic cathedral, with fern and moss and creeping vines, and a thousand thousand blossoms forming a mosaic that seemed too beautiful to tread upon! Here Dora's voice was hushed, and Helen's heart sang a *Te Deum*. And the rows upon the river, when at sunset they would be borne along the flood of golden color, until it faded, and the shadows were lost in the black water!

Then the delicious sense of being sheltered by God-sent human care and love made the very hills and sky—so does Nature lend herself to our thought and feeling—seem worthy wall and roof to enclose peace and charity. The loving messages from her mother, the thoughtful solicitude of Mrs. Aitken, the demonstrative affection of Dora, seemed all too much to Helen. And Campbell? It would be unlike Helen to give any special meaning to the kind attentions of one who was kind and tender toward every weak creature. She had seen him in the wood lay aside his sketch to restore a lost birdling to the mother-nest, and, as he followed the cries of the parent bird, hunt with patience until he found the place, in the hollow of a tree, surrounded with bushes.

But when Helen herself loved, she knew, and in the first moments of surprised and pure delight no doubt arose in her mind; this unspoken love she could carry in simplicity to our Blessed Mother, whispering her happiness. But not for many days. Helen had welcomed the thought that Campbell's was a soul, if not in the faith, yet of it, mistaking Campbell's tolerance toward all beliefs, and his responsive sympathy to her spirit of simple obedience, for a promised beginning of active faith. But she was confronted by the counsels of the Church, and her very love now quickened her insight, and made a weapon to be turned against itself.

Yet the confusion in Helen's mind was not merely a conflict between love and duty. It was rather a desire, God-implanted, to wrench herself from an affection that fettered while it caressed. The poor child had gone in her trouble to the white-haired priest, whose gentle wisdom had won for him the respect of all the villagers. He listened to her with pitying attention, and his last words to her were : " Follow the voice of God ; His love is best;" and he blessed her as she went away.

One way, then, lay before her. If she could but be alone ! Yet why ? That the burden might be more easily borne ? Should she make an excuse to go away she foresaw Mrs. Aitken's anxious inquiries and Dora's look of pained surprise. So Helen stayed ; and, except that Dora found herself oftener alone with Campbell where Helen was formerly their companion, and that she noticed that her friend was kinder than ever—" if that could be "—to the little children about her, the old life seemed to go on unchanged. If, alone in her chamber,—but there, Reader, you and I have no right. We may be sure that peace came, and I think that angels smiled upon her as she slept.

It was the sudden recalling of her pain, her struggles, and her resolve that brought the blood to her cheeks when Campbell described the Bishop's reception, and, while he was far from understanding what had passed in Helen's mind, the lover's jealous eye caught an explanation, not altogether true, of Helen's reserve. The one brief moment, days before, when Helen's love shone confessed in her eyes was like the instant of the tremulous burst of a lily into bloom. Who, looking into its pure cup, would not stay his hand from calling it his ? And while the humility of the true lover might make Campbell doubt that this pure creature were really his own, he was as sure of his treasure as he would have been had she spoken in answer to words of his. Into the future his thoughts took rapid leaps, and he saw his own life and work grow strong because Helen inspired them. And Helen herself ? He smiled as he thought of the luxury that his wealth would bring her, in happy consciousness that her thoughts were untouched by any desire of worldly gain, and that she would go with him as quickly to a garret as to a palace,—God bless her ! So for a time Campbell was securely silent. Helen's gentle effort not to pain deceived him, and he accepted without question Dora's excuse for her absence on their customary rambles. Then he perceived that she was troubled about something, and was glad to think of the time when he could be the sharer of every thought. At last, as we have seen, he believed he held the clue, and as he passed over the winding road, intent upon obtaining that day a promise from Helen's lips, he smiled to think how soon this cloud of doubt would be dissipated. He could the less easily imagine the thoughts that filled Helen's soul because he was conscious of no desire to see her faith change. That would be to him like a desecrated shrine. Possessing a tolerence which comes not so much from wide sympathy as from lack of personal conviction, Campbell had not the slightest misgiving that the ideal marriage would not here be found. Without the aid of Milton's portrayal of Paradise many a man has reflected with complacency that the woman whom he has chosen will be guided by his calmer reason; and Campbell was not without a lurking belief that his greater experience would be of avail in giving to his Helen's conscience that perfect balance which a sensitive nature and an introspective habit he felt had disturbed.

"But I have been castle-building indeed," Campbell said to himself, as he came in sight of the tree-embowered house. Yet Prince Harold in his heart was very sure of entering the castle where his lady was, and carrying her away to the one so "lightly, beautifully built."

    •   •   •   •   •   •

Two days later Campbell was on his way to the city. Early in the morning he had called upon his aunt to tell her of his sudden departure.

"Dora will be disconsolate," said Mrs. Aitken, when she had recovered somewhat from her surprise. "It is too bad that she is out driving."

"And—Miss Townsend ?" stammered poor Campbell.

"She is in the summer-house ; I will send for her."

"No, thanks; I am going through the garden, and will stop to

say good-bye;" and the young man hurried away. He was filled
with remorse at the reproaches given when he was blind with
disappointment. Clearer vision showed to him something of the
beauty and the strength of Helen's renunciation. He longed, yet
feared, to see her. He had measured her self-sacrifice by what he
himself was suffering; she had measured it by the Great Sacrifice, and found it to be nothing.

As he approached he saw Helen reclining in an arm-chair as if
resting after great weariness. It was not until Campbell was quite
near her that she was aware of his presence. She arose slowly,
and turned her pale face toward his.

"Will Miss Townsend pardon me for my intrusion and for my
injustice- " Here Campbell broke off. "Oh, my love, my love!"
he cried, "God only knows how this may end! Pray for me!"

A moment more and he was gone. Helen sank into her seat;
her lips moved. "For Christ's sake," she murmured; "and yet,
dearest Mother," a quick blush mantling her pure cheeks, "and
yet, dearest Mother, for me!"

OUR LIFE ROSARY.

ELLEN DOWNING.

How oft mine eyes have dwelt upon the "Virgin and the Child,"
How oft my heart hath lingered in a resting-place so mild!
Of all the sacred images, the sweetest 'twas to me,
But, now—with what an altered soul its loveliness I see!

I think the Joyful Mysteries are closing in my life,
Because where'er I lift mine eyes, to nerve me for the strife,
'Tis on the mournful crucifix their gaze is wont to stay,
And though the *God* still meets me there, the *Child* has passed
    away.

But as the Joys are all but gone, the Sorrows, too, will fly,
And then the Glories will come forth, to brighten earth and sky;
Till in these crowning mysteries we'll see with glad surprise,
With regal front, no more to die, the ancient Joys arise.

THE ISLE OF ST. VINCENT.

Rev. Bertrand Cothonay, O. P.

I.

EARLY HISTORY.

HE history of the Caribs of St. Vincent, one of the Lesser Antilles, is full of interest. The Island, discovered by Columbus, January 22, 1498, was colonized toward the middle of the eighteenth century, some time after the colonization of the adjacent ones, Barbadoes, Grenada, and others. The Caribs, flying before the Europeans, took refuge in St. Vincent. Several times, in the beginning of the eighteenth century, colonists from the neighboring islands tried to settle in St. Vincent, but they met to the full the fate of falling into the hands of cannibals. It was not till the fire-arms of France and England were called into requisition that the natives hid themselves in the mountains. Yet, as late as the beginning of this century, England has paid a dear price for their subjugation.

In 1773, after several battles, in which the English lost many valiant soldiers, a treaty of peace was concluded between them and the Caribs. The English gave the Caribs all the mountainous portion of the Island, now Georgetown, Sandy Bay, and Buna, the latter promising to cease their incursions into the white man's territory. The compact was not kept on either side; the treaty became a dead-letter, and hostilities continued. The English were obliged to build forts, and to keep numerous troops on the Island to prevent a general massacre of the colonists. The Indians retired to their mountains, descending sometimes on one side, and sometimes on another, making great ravage. So nearly inaccessible were their mountains that it was well-nigh impossible to pursue them.

However, the English had decided to put an end to these disagreeable neighbors. New troops were sent to the Island; the Indians were hemmed in, and pursued, at last, to their remote intrenchments. The majority were taken prisoners; some were put to death, and others, with their wives and children, cast upon an island of the Grenadines, called Balisseau, a few miles from St. Vincent. Many of the unfortunates died in prison of starvation. Then the government resorted to a radical experiment: the survivors were placed on board a vessel, which landed them in a bay in Honduras, where their descendants now form a distinct race.

Even after this summary performance a few Caribs remained hidden in the mountains. Their descendants are there to-day.

In a house in Kingston I saw a large picture, representing the victory of the English and the final defeat of the natives in St. Vincent. On one side the Albion warriors, arrayed in red waistcoats, are ascending the summit of the mountain, from the top of which they plant the British flag, and hurl before them into a precipice the unfortunate Indians. At the foot of the mountain there is a large number of dead and wounded. On the opposite side of the picture is a large column, on which is inscribed the names of the soldiers who perished in this war.

At the foot of the column are two shackled Indian warriors,— one red, and the other black—representing the two Carib races of St. Vincent. The black Caribs resemble the negroes, but their hair is long, and not frizzled. Tradition says that a slave-ship was wrecked, in the sixteenth century, on the coast of St. Vincent. The natives killed the whites, and liberated the negroes, who mixed more or less amongst them; hence the origin of the black Caribs whom Europeans found on the Island.

The area of the Isle of St. Vincent is about one hundred and thirty-one square miles. A ridge of mountains in the middle culminates in the volcano Morne Garou, about five thousand feet high. The entire Island, at the time of my visit, was embraced in one parish, in charge of but one priest, a zealous and indefatigable Irishman, Father Farrelly, who made his headquarters at Kingston, the capital of the Island. St. Vincent belongs to the archdiocese of Trinidad; I was detailed, a few years ago, by His Grace, Archbishop Flood, to assist the venerable pastor in pre-

A CHRISTIAN CAPTAIN AND HIS FAMILY.

paring for Confirmation those of his scattered flock of whites, Indians, and Negroes who were to receive the Sacrament. The novelty and beauty of the tour so impressed me that in the brief intervals of missionary labor I sought to preserve these impressions in a few word-sketches, which but feebly reproduce the original.

ST. GEORGE, KINGSTON. --FORT CHARLOTTE.

We left Trinidad for a month's sojourn in the Isle of St. Vincent, in January, 1888; after a night's voyage we steamed into the port of St. George, the capital of the Island of Grenada, at six o'clock in the morning, and spent four hours in the town.

The port of St. George is spacious, deep, and well sheltered. The deck of the steamer commands a fine view of the fertile hills, which tower above the town in the form of an amphitheatre. This general aspect of the Antilles enchants every European on his arrival, but the monotony of perpetual summer is experienced by many.

Although the rain was descending in torrents, I went on shore to celebrate the Holy Sacrifice of the Mass. Whilst in St. George's I had barely time to inspect the church, which is kept in excellent order, and contains a marble altar and beautiful statues, sculptured in Marseilles. It seemed to me much too small, as the Catholics number from five to six thousand.

The steamer resumed her voyage at ten o'clock, and passed in view of the Grenadines, a cluster of picturesque little islands which extend between Grenada and St. Vincent. They constitute a Catholic parish, the presiding genius being the oldest priest in the diocese. Father Petreto, a Corsican, is venerated by all within a radius of fifty leagues. I was presented with a picture of the port of Bequia (Grenadines), which is one of the most beautiful scenes of nature that I have ever seen painted. At four o'clock St. Vincent appeared in the distance, its mountains very rugged.

At half-past five we entered the port of Kingston, capital of St. Vincent, which is situated upon a beautiful, semicircular bay. When the Indians held possession they called it Sauseguny. This little town, with its red roofs, which seems to bathe its

MEMORIAL MONUMENT OF THE WAR OF THE CARIBS IN 1776.

feet in the sea, gives a charming appearance to this landscape of cocoanut trees and verdure.

The bay, which is situated to the southeast, is deep, and is reputed to be large enough to contain a fleet. On the northern side of this bay there is a fort over six hundred feet in height, with the English flag flying from the summit. It is admirably situated for the defence of the town.

We reached Kingston at half-past six, just as the inhabitants were assembling for Vespers. After service, through the courtesy of Father Farrelly, the pastor whose parish embraces the entire Island, and in his company, I enjoyed a drive about two miles from the town. I admired the scenery, and the people whom we met admired me even more, my habit being a novel sight to them! However, I was not the first Dominican who had landed on the shores of St. Vincent. During the time that the Island was in possession of the French, I think that the Dominicans from Martinique had a misson there.

The town of Kingston is formed of three streets parallel to the shore, about a kilometre in length. They are intersected here and there by the alleys, which extend even up the hills, behind the town, and on the savannah.

There are four churches, representing four different forms of belief. The Presbyterian church, I was informed, had been closed for two years because no minister could be procured. The majority of the members joined the Wesleyan church, which is centrally located. Opposite we find the Anglican church, the largest of all, with its lofty tower, which does not bear the cross, but simply two sticks horizontally crossed to indicate the four cardinal points. At a stone's throw from this massive edifice, which was erected at a cost of 1,200,000 francs, we find the Catholic church, of much smaller dimensions, situated on a transverse street, in a corner of the town. One of the three rivers which traverse this town waters the walls of the sanctuary. This church, notwithstanding its poverty, became very dear to me, not only because it demonstrated truth in the midst of error, but because it was scrupulously clean, and visited frequently by devout worshippers. It contains a stone belfry, a little organ, a beautiful marble altar, and, although many adornments are lacking, it is well to be seen

A VIEW OF KINGSTON, CAPITAL OF THE ISLE OF SAINT VINCENT.

that the good priest has left no stone unturned to procure the means of embellishing "this temple of the living God."

The Catholics of the entire Isle of St. Vincent comprise only one-tenth of the population. They possess only six churches or chapels, whilst the Anglicans have twenty-six, and the Wesleyans nineteen. This deplorable state of affairs is to be attributed to the lack of Catholic priests. There is only one Catholic priest, whilst the Protestant ministers number over twenty. Under the French domination the people, with the exception of the Caribs, were entirely Catholic; but since 1784, the time when the English took permanent possession, it fell into the power of Protestants. I have not as yet been able to discover any facts concerning the religious history of this town previously to 1815, but I find a Baptismal register which commences at this date. The entries are in French, and signed with the name of *Joseph Antoine Rendon.* The number of Baptisms does not exceed one hundred a year.

One morning during my stay, while praying in the church, I experienced the shock of a severe earthquake. No loss of life was the result, however.

The view of Fort Charlotte, which I early visited, is incomparable.

On one side the ravished sight beholds the bay and town of Kingston, appearing in the midst of the most luxuriant vegetation, encircled as with a sash of verdure, by the hills which attain a prodigious height. On the summit of the loftiest, the Morne Saint Andrew, is seen a fort constructed by the English to defend the Island against the Indians. They had hoisted here a large number of cannons. From Fort Charlotte the Grenadines can be distinctly seen on a level with the horizon, to the southeast. From the leeward side a magnificent valley inclines gently towards the sea. I think that it is still designated by a French name, which the people pronounce without comprehension,—*the lost creek.*

In place of the brave soldiers who formerly defended the town I found only a few disabled and sick ones. The fort has been converted into a hospital, a sanitarium, an asylum for old men, and a lazaretto. I conversed with all of these unfortunate creatures, who appeared to be resigned to their fate. A poor

FORT CHARLOTTE.

scrofulous patient from Dominica commenced to talk to me in French, and expressed his joy at being able to make himself understood in the only language which he knew. Two policemen sufficed to guard the fort during these peaceful times. Their occupation is to raise the signal flag on the arrival of ships, to fire the cannon at eight o'clock, and to return the salutes of the vessels which visit St. Vincent.

The day of my trip was followed by torrents of rain, with a wind which reminded me of one of the terrible hurricanes which have so often devastated St. Vincent and the adjacent islands. At Trinidad we have often a *little breeze*, but never a wind such as sweeps around St. Vincent. Not being accustomed to it, I was awakened by the tumult many times during the night.

THE BREAD-FRUIT.

The traveller cannot but notice the extraordinary fertility of the Isle of St. Vincent. Although the low price of sugar has caused the abandonment or neglect of many plantations, yet there is a profusion of what are there called " provisions,"—fruit and vegetables, which constitute the food of the inhabitants, the variety of which is marvellous. Many of the various kinds seem to be of a superior quality to those found in the other islands. The bread-fruit, especially, is more luscious and abundant. These trees may be found in nearly every garden; more abundant are they in the ravines, where, no doubt, there were formerly houses. The straw or wooden huts have vanished, but the tree remains, nobly elevating its head, its branches laden with fruit, above the wild plants by which it is surrounded.

Truly, a gift from Divine Providence is this tree. Its wood is excellent for building purposes. While standing it affords the shade so necessary beneath the tropical sun. During ten months of the year it is laden with fruit, upon which alone many poor people subsist. The tree which shelters their home is the granary which provides them with daily bread. The skin has only to be removed from the bread-fruit when there is found almost a kilogramme of spongy substance, a little insipid to the taste at first, it is true, but so closely resembling home-made bread that it has thus derived its name. This food, seasoned and prepared by the Creoles, who alone are versed in the art, is palatable and strengthening.

This tree is not originally from the Antilles. It was imported from Otaïti. Its introduction is historical. In 1787, by request of the inhabitants of the Antilles, a war-ship—*The Bounty*, commanded by Lieutenant Bligh, who had made a tour of the world with Cook—was equipped to import foreign plants from Otaïti. A long plank, pierced with holes, and capable of holding thou-

THE BREAD FRUIT.

sands of flower-pots, was placed on deck. Provision for fifteen months was furnished the crew; a quantity of glassware articles was to be given in exchange for the plants. After a very perilous voyage Lieutenant Bligh finally arrived at Otaïti. A tent was pitched on the shore, in order to shelter the trees. About thirty pots were placed under it daily.

On April 4, 1789, *The Bounty* set sail on its return voyage, with innumerable roots of young plants in the pots and in boxes. When

thirteen days out a mutiny commenced, and Lieutenant Bligh,
with eighteen companions, was placed in a canoe by the mutineers
and abandoned to the mercy of the waves. The treacherous men,
however, evinced a certain degree of pity towards their unfortunate
victims, consenting to give them one hundred and fifty loaves of
bread, twenty-eight gallons of water, a small quantity of wine and
rum, some pieces of salt pork, a few cocoanuts, four cutlasses, a compass, and a sun-dial. The nearest civilized land was the Holland
colony of Timor, a distance of 3,500 miles. They reached it
after twenty-one days of ceaseless battling with the waves, and
with hunger and thirst. Only one of the number succumbed. The
colonists at Timor received them most kindly, and shortly afterwards they were in a position to return to England.

Some time later ten of the mutineers were discovered and paid
the penalty of their crime on the gallows. The others, with
Adams, set sail for the island of Pitcairn, where they concealed
themselves, after having burned *The Bounty.* There they formed
the beginning of a colony which England adopted.

Lieutenant Bligh was more fortunate in a second voyage, which
he made, later on, to Otaïti. He reached his destination safely,
and introduced the bread-fruit to the Isle of St. Vincent in 1793.

TO THE LEEWARD SIDE.

From Kingston to Freasure, on the leeward side, is a thrilling
voyage of twenty-five miles. An old descendant of the Caribs
and his three sons accompanied me on this voyage. Fortunately
they were quite familiar with the place, and proved to be veritable
sea-wolves. The sea was very rough, and lashed the shore with
a deafening noise. Sometimes we passed between rocks so closely together that there was barely room for the canoe. *One* false
stroke would have plunged us into the seething waves. Twice,
in the midst of the foam which whitened the rocks, our canoe
touched the sand-bank, and I resigned myself to what I deemed
the inevitable.

This canoe is simply the trunk of a tree, hollowed by the Caribs,
and they warned me to sit perfectly still, in the centre, as the slightest movement would capsize it. The difficulties and dangers of
the voyage prevented me from admiring the scenery, which varied

every instant. I was reminded forcibly of the mountains of Switzerland, only those of St. Vincent do not equal them in height, and,
unlike those of Switzerland, no snow is on their summits. All
this part of the Island is very rugged. Often the mountains descend perpendicularly to the sea. Sometimes between two hills
there is a narrow valley, containing a few wretched huts, but interspersed we find small plains and larger valleys, where pretty villages
have sprung up, such as Layou, Baroualie, Chateau-Bel-Air, and
others. A number of sugar plantations display here and there
lofty red chimneys. Everywhere the tourist finds civilization making inroads on a grand, savage nature. During the voyage the
Caribs related what tradition had taught them concerning the
history of the places, unknown to me, but which they named as
we passed. Finally we arrived at our haven, the hut of poor old
Charles Maquez, situated at the foot of the sulphur mine Souffrière,
a volcano, the last eruption of which took place in 1812.

(Conclusion in October.)

OUR LADY'S NAME.

MARY A. CONROY.

SPOTLESS One ! O Undefiled !
  Immaculate and fair,
    What joy to speak thy holy name,
    What joy thy name to bear !

Such peace as loving thee doth give,
  Worldlings can never know;
Thy name can soften every ill,
  Soothe every care and woe.

O Blessed One ! To God so dear,
  The honored Queen of Heaven,
The Angels' Mistress—priceless gift
  By God to mortals given.

O Lady, help us on our way,
  Our beacon-light still be,
Thou peerless Maiden, Virgin pure,
  Star shining o'er life's sea!

A DISTINGUISHED ORIENTALIST.

MONSIGNOR CHARLES DE HARLEZ.

Rev. J. A. Zahm, C. S. C.

HE subject of this present sketch shall be the distinguished Orientalist and professor, Monsignor Charles de. Harlez.[1] In many respects he is the most remarkable man of his time. He is *facile princeps* among the most eminent and successful philosophers of the century. He has eclipsed the glories of Bopp and Klaproth, and overshadowed the most brilliant achievements of Whitney and Max Müller. Considering the adverse circumstances under which he has labored during nearly the whole of his life, it seems impossible that he should have been able to effect even a tithe of what he has actually accomplished. And did we not have before us the splendid monument of his genius and untiring industry, the story of his triumphs would appear incredible. In his case, as in so many others, truth is stranger than fiction, and I know of no nobler or more inspiring model for the studious youth of our age than Mgr. Charles Joseph de Harlez, the prince of contemporary Orientalists.

Monsignor de Harlez was born in 1832, near Liege, Belgium, of a noble and illustrious family. After a brilliant course of studies in literature and philosophy he graduated in law, and at the early age of twenty-three was at once admitted to the bar of his native city. He soon discovered, however, that his vocation was for the priesthood, and accordingly, the year following, he entered the episcopal seminary of Liege. In 1858 he was ordained priest. His bishop had singled him out as one who would best serve the interests of the Church in the capacity of preacher and theologian, but God, who doth all things well, had ordained otherwise. Whilst in the seminary he contracted an affection of the throat,

---

[1] For preceding sketches see "The Forerunner and Rival of Pasteur," in THE ROSARY MAGAZINE, September, 1894, and "Some Lights of Science and the Church," in the issue of March, 1895.

which not only rendered impossible the ordinary exercise of the sacred ministry, but which also prevented him from ever leaving the narrow confines of the land of his birth.

In consequence of his shattered health he was relieved from all duty for three years. At the end of this period he was given the direction of the episcopal college, an office which he held for four years, when he was compelled to resign by reason of a new outbreak of his malady. He then devoted himself to the study of theology, and was eventually selected by his bishop as one of his special counsellors.

Some time afterwards, his health being somewhat improved, de Harlez, then a canon, was called by the Belgian hierarchy to assume charge of a normal institute, established at Louvain, for the superior education of priests destined to teach in the various seminaries of the country. Everything was under the direction of the accomplished canon, and the success which attended his efforts soon confirmed the wisdom of the choice which his superiors had made when they placed him at the head of this important institution. After holding the rectorship for five years, the health of the devoted ecclesiastic again gave way, and he was obliged to retire to private life.

MONSIGNOR CHARLES DE HARLEZ.

It was while rector of the normal institute for the clergy that de Harlez discovered what was, in the designs of Providence, to become his life-work. Then it was that he realized, as never before, the necessity incumbent on Catholics of putting themselves at the head of every intellectual movement if they would hope to achieve any success in their warfare against infidelity, rationalism, and irreligion. In his philological investigations, especially, he had brought home to him, time and again, the fact that his co-religionists had practically abandoned to their adversaries some of the most effective arms at the disposal of the defenders of the faith. He saw with regret that but few, if any, of the great philologists of the world were Catholics, and that the most important works on language˙ and the science of language were from the pens of non-Catholics, and often from those of the professed enemies of the Church. He beheld the ravages caused by false systems of philosophy, and the countless errors that had their origin in the defence of false theses, and in the dissemination of sham science. Through the apathy of those who should be the leaders in science, the enemies of religion had long palmed off on an unsuspecting world the gravest errors in the name of a science of which they were the only recognized masters, and had not unfrequently substituted fancy for fact, and falsehood for truth. In linguistics Catholics were not merely discredited; they had not even recognition in the world of science. As a consequence, they were forced on all occasions to assume the position of apologists, and to put themselves on the defensive when it behooved them to move forward as a solid phalanx against the forces of error.

Strongly convinced of the necessity which existed of changing this sad and abnormal condition of affairs, de Harlez in his solitude cast about to see in what way he could best serve the interests of the Church, and promote the glory of God. During his previous studies he had already had occasion to devote some attention to the languages and literatures of India and Persia. One day, while reading the first volume of the " History of the Church," by the Abbé Darras, he came across a pretended apologetic argument, based on " the excellent translation of the Avesta by Anquetil."

This passage, of slight or no import to the casual reader, decided the career of de Harlez. He had, in these few words, a confirmation of views which he had long entertained, and saw, almost with dismay, what incalculable injury may be done to the science of apologetics by one who is ignorant of the value or nature of the authorities he quotes and adduces in support of his thesis.

It was then that the zealous Churchman realized the necessity of giving to the world a new and accurate translation of the Aves-ta, this most interesting and important work of the ancient Orien-tal world. Since the time of Anquetil, numerous works on the Avesta had demonstrated his ignorance as a translator, and had contributed considerably towards giving the true meaning of this old and curious work. But no one hitherto had succeeded in giving a correct translation of it, and de Harlez then and there determined to undertake the task himself.

His first intention was to give a translation which should em-body the results obtained by preceding investigators. But he soon discovered that everything was yet but little more than con-jecture and uncertainty, and that it was imperative to make long and profound researches before it would be possible to arrive at the true meaning of a book of which the language was unknown, and of which the study had been undertaken without either gram-mar or dictionary, or any other means which could assure the true signification of the words employed. It was necessary to study thoroughly several languages of India and ancient Persia; to decipher old manuscripts; to undertake, in a word, a labor which, although but a preparation for his self-imposed task, was in itself enormous in magnitude, and beset with difficulties which would have discouraged at the outset any but the bravest and the most determined spirit.

The work of preparation was eventually complete, and in due season the long-projected translation of the Avesta was given to the world. It received at once the recognition to which its un-questioned merits entitled it. The savants of Europe pronounced it a marvel of accuracy and scholarship, while the Zoroastrians themselves were so pleased with it that they had it translated into their own language, the Jazerati, for the use of their community.

This version was preceded by an " Introduction on the Study of the Avesta and the Religion of Zoroaster," which even M. Rénan characterized as " a veritable encyclopædia." It is with-out doubt one of the most important and useful of the many works which the illustrious author has ever written.

To facilitate the study of the Avesta its translator prepared a manual on the language of this ancient production, embracing a grammar, anthology, and lexicon, which quickly passed through two editions. In addition to this he likewise published a similar manual for the study of Pehlevi—that mysterious language of the Persian Zoroastrians, who flourished in the time of the Parthians,— a language in which had been made a version of the Avesta which was frequently more obscure than the text itself.

Since the publication of our author's translation of the Avesta there have appeared numerous exegetical works on the grammar and lexicology of this old Zoroastrian book. But Mgr. de Harlez has domonstrated in an unanswerable manner that all the systems of interpretation which have differed from the one which he first proposed have been either entirely fantastical or completely contradicted by the facts on which they are made to repose.

So great was now the authority of Mgr. de Harlez in all questions of Avestic language and literature that the Zoroastrians of the distant East on two occasions selected him as the arbiter of their religious differences, and the interpreter of obscure points of ceremonial. Think of it! The disciples of Zoroaster, the wise men of the Orient, coming to an humble Belgian priest as to their highest living oracle, and acknowledging him as the most competent authority to settle questions which among themselves had given rise to long and serious controversy!

After the appearance of his various publications on the Avesta, a number of other works came from the pen of de Harlez with amazing rapidity. Book followed book, brochure succeeded brochure, all original, and that, too, on the most recondite subjects in a way which astonished the learned world, but which astonished still more those who knew their author to be a chronic invalid. He was accomplishing the work of a score of men, and yet he never knew what it was to enjoy a day of perfect health.

Besides writing books and brochures, he was a frequent contributor to many Catholic reviews. In these he refuted many of the errors which had long obtained currency, and showed the utter falsity of the arguments which it had been the vogue to urge against the Church of Christ in the name of philology and Oriental literature.

One of the principal works of de Harlez, dealing with the objections which had been urged against Christianity by students of the sacred literatures of the Orient, is entitled "The Bible in India, Vedism, Brahmanism, and Christianity."

This book was written to refute a work published by a certain French author who pretended that the entire Bible, the Gospels included, was derived from the religious codes of Buddhism and Brahmanism. In proof of his contention the audacious Frenchman not only distorted, but actually invented texts, and appealed to authorities that had no existence outside of his own fertile imagination. His book was greeted with loud acclaim by the infidel and rationalistic press of Europe, and it was confidently announced that a *coup de grace* had finally been dealt to the long-accepted belief of the divine inspiration of the Sacred Scriptures. It was at once translated into nearly all the languages of Europe and America. It found its way to Mexico, Brazil, and even to the island of Mauritius.

The success of this imposture was, however, but short-lived. The reply of the eminent Belgian savant exposed in a merciless fashion the fallacies and fabrications of his impudent opponent, and so effectually was the work done that the book, which was thought by a certain school of irreligious sciolists to have disproved the traditional view respecting the Bible, rapidly fell into oblivion, and is now practically unknown.

In his well-known work, "The Origin of Zoroastrianism," the learned author was no less successful in his refutation of numerous errors that had long been accepted as so many demonstrated truths. Against all opponents he proved beyond cavil that the religion of Zoroaster had been profoundly affected by that of the Jews, and that much which was supposed to be original in the former was actually borrowed from the latter. The validity of his proofs is now generally admitted, even by those who at one time were his most pronounced antagonists.

After having thoroughly explored all that his earlier fields of labor had to offer him, Mgr. de Harlez, Alexander-like, sighed for other worlds to conquer. Unwilling to devote his attention to lands which had already been sufficiently well cultivated by others, he sought for something which, at least from the Catholic point of view, was still unexplored. After consultation with friends, in whose judgment he had confidence, he concluded to select the extreme Orient as the site of his future labors. Accordingly, in 1884, he entered upon the study of the difficult languages of Tartary, Thibet, Mongolia, and especially that of Manchuria. He was soon master of these strange tongues, and it was not long after that he gave to the world translations, with commentaries, of the principal religions and historical works of old Manchuria.

Mgr. de Harlez next turned his attention to China—to that land which, above all others, is involved in obscurity and enveloped in mystery, and which for centuries past has been the despair of the most eminent of the world's scholars. As in his previous investigations, he preferred to devote his time to matters which had hitherto received little or no attention: to the philosophy, to the religion, and to the legislation of China, ancient and modern. His numerous works on these topics have, in the estimation of all competent judges, opened up new avenues of thought, and contributed materially to clear up numerous. problems with which sinologists had long grappled, but in vain. Among these problems he took up that relating to the primitive religion of the Chinese, and showed incontestably that it was a species of monotheism, and not a kind of paganism or ghost-worship, as had been so long contended by a certain school of evolutionary philosophers.

The list of the published works of Mgr. de Harlez—many of which are before me as I write these lines—fills several large, printed pages. But in addition to the books which he has written on Tartary and Thibet, China and Manchuria, and his grammars and dictionaries of the ancient languages of Persia and India; in addition to his countless articles in various reviews of Belgium, France, Germany, and England, and in addition to his duties as professor of Oriental languages in the University of Louvain, he has, since 1882, been editor of, and chief contributor to *Le Muséon*, a publication devoted to the furtherance of philological studies, and to the exploitation of the more important literary monuments of the ancient Oriental world.

When one remembers that Mgr. de Harlez learned all the languages of which he is master without the assistance of a teacher, that he achieved all his triumphs in spite of continued ill-health, that he acquired his profound and accurate knowledge of the languages, religions, and literatures of the peoples of Asia without leaving the confines of his own country, that for more than twenty years he has been virtually a prisoner in his own house, one stands astonished and bewildered before the variety and magnitude of his achievements.

"How in the name of all that is wonderful," I asked him, on the occasion of a recent visit to his summer home in Herent, a small village near Louvain; "how have you been able to accomplish so much in your condition of continued ill-health?" "My right hand yet serves me," he replied, and, touching his forehead, "I still have something left here. God has not wished me to devote my time to the sacred ministry, and I have accordingly, to the best of my ability, endeavored to promote His glory and further the interests of His Church in other and different ways. One can always accomplish great things for God if one has the will. He has been pleased to bless my humble efforts; may His Holy Name be praised!"

As professor in the University of Louvain, Mgr. de Harlez teaches Sanscrit, Brahmanic, and Vedic; Iranian, the language of ancient Persia; Avestic, Pehlevi, Chinese, and the languages of Tartary, Mongolia, Manchuria, and Thibet.

In recognition of his remarkable services in behalf of science and religion, the Holy Father, years ago, made him a prelate of the Papal household, and has otherwise testified his high admiration for the man who is unquestionably one of the most learned as well as one of the most brilliant champions of the Church which our century has produced.

Never shall I forget the warm grasp of his hand as we bade each other good-bye; "*Au revoir*," he said; "strive to do great things for Holy Church. *Mon cœur est avec vous*—'My heart is with you.'"

This sketch, and those of other issues, I am fully conscious of the fact, do but scanty justice to the distinguished scholars whose achievements they briefly and imperfectly recount. They, however, suggest fruitful reflections and teach important lessons. The career of Cardinal Gonzales shows us that it is possible, even amid the cares of the most distant and unpromising missionary lands, to produce works which may serve for the instruction and edification of the world. The life of Mgr. Meignan evinces the fact that not even the arduous and manifold duties connected with the administration of a large diocese are incompatible with the prosecution of serious literary pursuits and the preparation of volumes of marked excellence on the most difficult topics of sacred science.

The marvellous achievements of Mgr. de Harlez is the best possible proof that a weak constitution and delicate health do not necessarily preclude one from taking a conspicuous part in the world of intellect, and from accomplishing results of far-reaching importance. Such lessons are certainly, to say the least, most encouraging, and should spur on all who are interested in higher things—and who is not?—to renewed efforts in the cause of Religion and Science.

And yet, strange to say, our cyclopædias and biographical dictionaries have little or nothing to say of those to whom the Christian world, not to speak of the scientific world, is so much indebted. Even in the last edition of his *Dictionnaire des Contemporains*, issued but a few months ago, Vaperau, who makes loud professions of being accurate and thorough, does not so much as mention the names of Hamard or Vigouroux. Meignan, Gonzales, and de Harlez he dismisses with a few words, while he devotes much space to the enumeration and analysis of the vile productions of Zola.

Yes, by all means, let us have a good Catholic biographical dictionary, written by one who is competent to produce a work comporting with the great importance of the subjects to be treated. There will, I repeat it, be no lack of material. The field is vaster and richer by far than is ordinarily imagined, and the good which shall accrue to the Church and her children from the publication of such a work should alone be sufficient inducement, if none other were offered, for some one of our Catholic *littérateurs* to supply what has long been a want keenly felt by all who are interested in having exact information, and in knowing the truth, pure and undefiled, respecting those of the Church's children who have deserved so well both of science and the faith.

THE LILY OF CHIMU.

A TALE OF THE INCAS.

Rev. A. H. de Viras, O. P.

Chapter XVII.

Seeing that Racuna-Capac was neither dead nor seriously injured, but only faint from a deep and ugly wound, Ollacpya again became tranquil. To her a new era was opening. Wholly unacquainted until now with any emotions that disturbed the serenity of her beautiful soul, she seemed suddenly to grow conscious of a strange, ardent, and indescribable happiness, which she could not and, indeed, did not try to explain to herself.

Was this new-born sentiment in the all-chaste heart of the Lily of Chimu a sweet presage of a suddenly wrought and all-ruling love? And if so, what was the nature of this love? Was it a species of adoration spiritualized by faith in its aspiration, though oftentimes materialized by sense in its expression,—the love of the ecstatic who, firmly believing in the mystic union of a Heavenly with a human being, and considering herself called to such a divine espousal, sees him whom she thus worships and cherishes above all men, and even above all gods, near her and seeking her embrace? Or was it the mother-like love of one of those angels of earth, sublimely generous and heroic in their sacrifices,—who through promptings of god-like compassion give their tender years, their maturer hopes, their very lives, for the redemption of straying souls, for the consolation of grief-oppressed hearts, for the common cause of suffering humanity? Or again, was it simply the first awakening of a woman's love in all its strength and power and wonderful capacity?

Who knows?

All alone, as if perhaps she were jealous of the hand that should share her task of mercy,—maybe to prevent anyone seeing the sad spectacle of the worshipped idol of yesterday, fallen to-day, —a victim to the common lot of humanity,—all alone, she fashioned upon the floor with tapestries and cushions an improvised

couch, and, the fervor of an affectionate devotion lending energy
to her frail form, she succeeded in placing him upon it, and saw
him resting almost comfortably. Then kneeling again at his side,
she tenderly and gently bathed with cool, fresh water, his brow,
washed the blood from his face, combed his disordered and long,
floating curls,—and, again and again, timid and trembling with
emotion, she placed her delicately shaped hand over his heart to
assure herself that it was still beating, while eagerly and anxiously she watched for the moment when he should be fully restored
to consciousness.

Either because of the reviving freshness of the water as it laved
his feverish face, or because of the vital warmth of the maiden's
hand, Racuna-Capac at length opened his eyes, and as if awakening from a long and reinvigorating sleep, he smiled sweetly upon
his beautiful nurse, with the smile of a babe but half-roused from
its slumbers, and beholding through the mist of its dreams, the
golden and nacreous wings of its protecting genius extended over
its cradle.

How handsome he was as he lay gazing silently upon her!

Ollacpya's hand was just then resting upon his heart; he grasped
it, and held it in his own, pressing it warmly, but without violence;
nor did she oppose this mute mode of expression.

" O mother! dearest mother! beloved mother! thou art here, thou
art with me again, and now thou wilt never abandon me more....
Mother! mother! say thou wilt not........"

Ollacpya did not reply, but, with the other hand, she lovingly
smoothed the young man's forehead. She seemed not surprised at
the words he used; evidently it was not the first time she had
heard them, for during the two previous days and nights, in his
strange delirium, they had many times passed his lips.

"Say, mother, say to me thou wilt not!" insisted the youth,
while a painful expression of distress contracted his features, and
something like a bitter impatience gleamed from his eyes.

" No, no, never!" exclaimed the young girl, almost instinctively
trying to calm and to pacify him.

An expression of the deepest gratitude and of happiness transfigured his sad, pale face; but soon a dark cloud again passed over
it, and his peaceful smile had gone.

" Thou lovest me, mother; thou lovest me yet as thou didst long
ago when thou wast wont to put me to sleep on thy knee, my head
nestled upon thy heart, and thy soft, glossy locks sweeping my
face?.....thou lovest me the same? ....."

Ollacpya shuddered; a sob escaped her, and tears moistened
her soft cheek.

" Thou weepest—thou....oh, I understand,—there where thou
didst go after abandoning me, other children were given thee by
the gods, and thou forgettest thy poor little Zompa....oh, thou
dost not love me! "

These last words were uttered in such pitiful despair, such distress and desolation, that Ollacpya forgot for the moment that he
was not the child which he seemed to himself to be, in his sad
hallucination, nor she the lost and recovered mother he called
upon,—or, may be, yielding to the irresistible tenderness of her
own heart, she said in a low murmur:

" Yes, I do love thee."

The first " I love thee " that falls from a maiden's lips contains
within itself, as well for her who utters it as for him who hears, an
indefinable sense of completeness; what is there to add, what
to answer, what to do, but to repeat again and again the same
three blessed words,—or rather to meditate in blissful silence
on their deep, fathomless meaning, and in a pure and tender kiss
from the very lips that uttered them, to taste the full delight
of their sweetness?

Yet such was not what occurred between the Lily of Chimu
and the pseudo-son of the gods. Ollacpya's " I love thee," at
least for Racuna-Capac, was a fond illusion, and could mean but
the due and expected manifestation of a mother's tenderness; with
the young girl it meant perhaps only the expression of an ardent
and compassionate charity.

The youth lay with wide-open eyes, gazing, not on the visible
world about him, but back upon the scenes of a bitter past—the
scene of his martyr existence, sad and terrible even to memory,
and now moving in quick succession before him.

A faint smile flitted across his countenance as he suddenly exclaimed:

"Mother, those white-faced and white-robed men, ministers of the new religion so incomprehensible to thee, were good to thy little Zompa—good, kind, and loving....and I, too, loved them, mother,....after thou hadst gone so far away from me....but I never loved them so much as I did thee—no, never so much.... They did not use the thunder and lightning to kill men—rather they smiled sweetly upon us....they told me the secret of that other land where the orphan child meets again its mother to part with her no more....Oh, I must be there now since I am with thee; yes, still, though thou sayest thou lovest me, thou dost not love me as when we were in that other home of ours, long, long ago....or why, then, dost thou not near thy lips to mine; why dost thou not kiss my cheek, my brow, the curls of my hair, as thou wast wont to do?....O mother, mother, kiss once more thy poor little Zompa!''

In his delirium the youth put out his arms, and would have circled them around Ollacpya's neck had she permitted. Her heart went out to him in tenderest pity; but, troubled and fearful, she, in consonance with the promptings of her chaste and virginal soul, drew back from the embrace he would have given her. Then, perplexed, she wondered what was her duty towards the sufferer. Should she try to rouse him from this mysterious delirium to a consciousness of his actual condition? Should she convince him that she was not the fond mother he so fixedly imagined her to be, but that that mother, wherever she might at the time stay, must still love him as of old? That a mother's love, like all love sincere, lives on forever?....And shall we question the truthfulness of her idea of that Heaven-born emotion which has its origin in the bosom of a Father who is eternal? Love partakes of His eternity. Time and space may indeed throw between true hearts, chasms over which there is no crossing, over which not even the longed-for message may be able to wing its way, brightening the sorrow of each, at least, into a passing sunshine; the chilling blasts of suspicion, mistrust, misunderstanding, may cool the fire that was not lighted at the great Throne of Love; but love, genuine in its nature, grows the more, the more it may be put to the test. Happy the one thus loved, and happy the one capable of loving thus,--a higher atmosphere that not all are capable of breathing, for it means much suffering. As none have loved so much as the Man-God, so none have suffered so much.

It was evident to Ollacpya that her seeming indifference had inflicted upon the hallucinated victim great anguish and torture, which moved across his sad and tired face, then left him plunged in a heavy stupor, apparently lost to all intellectual activity—the distant look in his unclosed eyes soon again telling of the visions that were passing before them.

After a little, he resumed his broken monologue:

" Oh, how good to me they were, mother dear, those white-faced and white-robed men!....they told me of a delightful abode beyond the blue cloud-curtain of the sky....of a pale woman who is there, its beautiful Queen....so beautiful, so pure, so merciful ....she rejoices to be a mother to little children whose own mothers may have gone over the dark waters of death....I wonder....can it be that thou art that blessed woman, thou who art with me now, can it be that we are in that land of happiness? ....Surely thou art that lovely Queen—a mother of the little orphan Zompa, but not my true mother, and that is why thou dost not kiss me....Ah, no, no; it is not so; for I remember, she was white; and thou art dark like me....she was pale-faced....I can see her yet as they showed her picture to me....pale-faced, and holding in her arms a pale-faced Child....but thou, thou hast no other child than me....then thou art my mother."

Ollacpya started, trembled, and almost lost consciousness for a moment. " A pale-faced woman holding in her arms a pale-faced Child!" Did she hear the words aright, or was she, too, dreaming? she asked herself. Had the memory of her own sweet vision come to haunt her so constantly that she heard whispers of it everywhere? With an effort she roused herself, and now listened to the youth from more than sympathy, for he seemed to her the interpreter sent by the spirit of her vision to make known to her its mysterious meaning.

" But they told me that no one could go to the delightful land above the bright blue sky,—no one could be loved by the white Lady and the white Child, except those whose forehead had been washed in the name of their God....and I wanted them to wash my forehead; but Teutile took me away, and delivered me into the hands of that horrible woman who tormented and tortured

me.... and I could not go with the happy children to where the
pale-faced woman is Queen.... but I remember it all, mother:
how they used to take pure, limpid water from the stream, and
while they poured it on the forehead of the children, they pronounced at the same time a few words in an unknown tongue....
but I know what they signified, for they told me, when they were
instructing me, that he who poured the water must say: " I wash
thee in the name of the Father, and of the Son, and of the Holy
Spirit.".... Oh, woe to me! these words were never said over me by
the priests; my brow was never washed in the name of the Blessed
Three of the pale-faced men; I shall never see the beautiful white
woman, nor the white Child in the Heavenly land above.... but
I am with thee, mother, dear mother; I will not grieve; I am
happy!"

Ollacpya, motionless, almost breathless, listened to what the
youth had been uttering. Her soul was full of the deepest
emotion, and was ready to lose itself in a transport of blissful realization. But she first called reason to her aid; she reminded
herself that Racuna-Capac was in a state of delirious fever, and
that, ordinarily, what one says in such a condition is to be heard
with discretion. Yet, the white woman and the white Child—could
they be other than the very same of her own late dream, which
she found it impossible to put from her thoughts?—Could such a
coincidence between them and the sweet Lady and Babe she had
seen, as if with her eyes wide open, be merely fortuitous? And
what of that prescribed sacred rite of the religion of the pale-
faced men?—What of its nature as something absolutely necessary?
—What of the vivid impression, in its every detail, it had made
upon the memory of this youth? All these things seemed to her
too important to be ignored, even under the inexplicable surroundings in which they had come to her. Above all, the
words uttered during the sacred bathing of the forehead impressed
her greatly in their mysterious, sublime simplicity, though she
could not understand their significance.

Both remained silent,—he living over the past, she searching
into the future.

" Mother," he then wandered on, " love me as thou didst before
that dreadful day when thou wast taken from me..... I can-

not be happy unless thou dost love me as then......" and he
put his arm around Ollacpya's neck, collected all the energy
which yet remained in his all-but-exhausted body, and drew the
young girl towards him.

Ollacpya only gently resisted.

At last their lips meet in a long and blissful kiss of love,—the
first ever given or received by the Lily of Chimu.

Strange affection! he thinking her to be his mother, and she
not knowing exactly to which of the many emotions of her heart
she was yielding.　Their happiness was suddenly interrupted by
an infernal, sneering laugh which resounded behind them.

Ollacpya sprang to her feet, and turned quickly around.

It was the sorceress of Huanchaco, who stood looking upon
them with the eyes of a dragon flashing fire.

At her feet lay her two enormous monkeys.

CHAPTER XVIII.

Ollacpya made an attempt to call for help; but before she had
time to utter a word, at a sign given by the hag she was seized
by one of the monkeys, which, with almost human dexterity,
gagged her and bound her hand and foot, while the companion
monkey was pursuing a similar course with the ill-fated Racuna-
Capac.

"Aha!" exclaimed the witch, with an intonation of fiendish triumph, "thou didst think, foolish girl, that thy fond Apamuyu was
watching at the entrance, and that thou couldst therefore enjoy
thy love without being intruded upon.　A pity thou didst forget
he could not stay to guard thee the whole day long!　A pity for
thee, indeed, that he and his sentinels had just now—thou in thy
ecstacy of love—to give way and leave the post of guard to
others in their turn.　The delay has been a bitter one for me, but
I have borne it patiently, knowing that my hour of revenge would
come.　And now it is here, proud girl!　Thou hast made thyself
a stumbling-block to me these long years; all my ambitious
projects thou wouldst bring to nothing if thou couldst.　Well,
thou shalt find that my vengeance can equal thy temerity.　Both
thou and thy insensate lover shall die a terrible death, in

torments no one has yet experienced or conceived. I hate thee, and I hate every human being that lives; and when I have settled accounts with thee, I shall go elsewhere among mankind to continue my work of retaliation."

She paused in her infamous harangue, and approached Racuna-Capac. He was dead. The spirit of the unfortunate youth had departed from his long-tortured body, either from that tremor of sweetness born of the kiss from the lips of a mother lost but seemingly found again—an excess of bliss,—or from the reappearance, sudden and terrible, of her who had been for years his cruel tormentor—an excess of fear.

A horrible blasphemy launched itself forth from the mouth of the sorceress when she discovered that one of her victims had thwarted her. Almost rabid in her disappointment, she returned to the girl, who lay on the ground so tightly fettered as to be motionless. The witch contemplated her for a while with a satanic expression of hate; then from her bosom she took a large cocoanut, in which were imprisoned two of her black, cruel spiders, and opening the hole in the nut, she held it over the maiden's face while the venomous insects crawled forth, one after the other, and lodged themselves right over the eyes of their victim. There the fiendish woman confined them to do their deadly work, she covering each with half a walnut shell.

The spiders, having been deprived of food for four or five days past, shut up in that secure way, and finding under them the soft, tender skin of the girl, began their meal, impregnating her with their poison, biting into muscle and tissue, corroding her flesh, and slowly sucking the fresh, warm blood.

It was a martyrdom indescribable in its horror, and all the agony that she was enduring could be distinctly read upon Ollacpya's face.

The hag remained, looking on in silent enjoyment for some time, as if loath to leave this scene of more than savage slaughter; but bethinking herself of the difficulty of explaining the circumstances to any one who should find her standing there, jubilant over the death—and such a death—of the Curaca's daughter, she started hurriedly from the room, left the citadel and the city of Chimu before pursuers could be put upon her track.

Chapter XIX.

A few hours later, and Tupayachi knelt alone at the bedside of the Lily of Chimu.

She lay upon the same couch that in those past days had served for Racuna-Capac. Her poor face presented a pitiful spectacle,— two deep, black, blood-foamy holes where once her Heaven-lit eyes had beamed forth blessings for every one.

The High-priest held in his trembling hands hers already cold with the coldness of approaching death, while his cheeks were bathed in an uninterrupted stream of tears, and he listened to her faint voice as one listens for a last time to accents grown dear to the heart during a friendship that was faithful and true.

"Taita, Taita!" she murmured feebly, "he told me that none ever go to the land where the white woman and the white Child dwell, save those whose forehead has been washed with purest water by a priest, in the name of the Father, and of the Son, and of the Holy Spirit. O Taita! grant me that supreme happiness ....oh, I suffer........I suffer........but I forgive her.... See, there the white woman and the sweet, pale-faced Child, wait for me.....they call me,........Taita, I die! Taita........ Oh, thou who hast been so good to me, thou wilt not refuse..... my last prayer........soon....soon....I die!"

Tupayachi had till now resisted the desire of Ollacpya, repeated again and again, since the moment he had come to her in her desolation.

But at this last supplication of the dying girl, he rose, took from a sandal, silver-chased stand a gold cup containing water, and raising his eyes above, he solemnly exclaimed:

"O God! Thou only and eternal One whom I adore, if this strange rite which I am about to perform be agreeable to Thee, and can bring to the soul of Ollacpya rest and happiness in the glory of Thy blissful bosom, look mercifully upon me, Thy ministering servant, and upon Thy pure and dying child. If the mysterious words whose secret significance I do not understand are really intended by Thee to open the immaterial gates of Thy immaterial kingdom, I, with all reverence, do now pronounce them from my inmost heart."

Then he slowly poured the water from the cup, and with his right hand carefully spreading it on the brow and the head of the maiden, he said:

"Ollacpya, I wash thee in the name of the Father, and of the Son, and of the Holy Spirit."

The Lily of Chimu moved her lips in the effort to utter a word of thanks to her dear and venerated friend, but she could not,— that last message from her grateful heart was unheard, save by the recording angel. She smiled, it seemed to a vision of the other world, extended her arms upward as if to embrace the white Child of her sweet dreams, and her spotless soul passed away to the joyful realms of an eternal life.

*   *   *   *   *   *

The City of Chimu mourned the loss of its Lily, and nothing was left undone to hasten the search for the villainous sorceress, but she was not to be found, despite the detachment of soldiers sent out in every direction by the afflicted Curaca. Paraymi also disappeared.

Five days after the burial of the Lily of Chimu, Mocllanta, though still mourning, married her lover at the altar of the Moon. Tupayachi blessed their union, and Gupanqui, persuaded that by so doing he would rejoice the spirit of his departed daughter, assisted at the ceremony with all his court.

The solemnities over, the Curaca had but just crossed the entrance of the temple, and was about to mount into his litter, when two *chasquis*, coming from different directions, presented themselves before him.

One of them, approaching him, said:

"Our lord and master, Huayna-Capac, the glorious Inca, has been recalled by the Sun, his Father, from earth to Heaven."

And the other came quickly after, exclaiming:

"The pale-faced warriors, armed with thunder and lightning, have been seen on the seashore in the far north of the empire."

(*The end.*)

Babe of Anna! Little Maiden!
We with transports overladen,
Spirits full, hearts almost broken,
Joy which cannot be outspoken,
We thy birthday greet, the dawning
Of salvation's happy morning:

Infant Mary! Joy of earth!
We with all this world of mirth
Light-hearted and joy-laden,
Greet the morning of thy birth,
Little Maiden!

—*Father Faber.*

A PAGE OF CHURCH HISTORY IN NEW YORK.

ST. JOHN'S, UTICA.

Very Rev. J. S. M. Lynch, D. D., LL. D.

Part VI.

RT. REV. FRANCIS P. McFARLAND, D. D.

MARCH 1ST, 1851—MARCH 6TH, 1858.

FATHER MCFARLAND now opens the longest and one of the most important pastorates in the history of the parish up to this time.

Francis Patrick McFarland was born in Franklin, Pa., April 16, 1819, almost on the very day when this parish, destined to be sanctified by his zealous labors, was organized.

In the providence of God, new countries are evangelized by missionaries from other climes, but in the course of time, native vocations spring up to meet the wants of the new kingdom brought to Christ. And so, whilst we shall never forget the debt of gratitude which we owe to that band of Irish missionaries that planted the good seed, still we glory in the fact that Father McFarland was the first product of our own soil—our first American pastor. He received a careful training in an academy conducted by Mr. James Clarke, subsequently a distinguished Jesuit. After a course of divinity in Mt. St. Mary's, Emmettsburg, he was ordained by Archbishop Hughes in St. Patrick's Cathedral, New York, May 18, 1845. He was Professor for a time in St. John's College, Fordham. After spending a short time in New York, Father McFarland was sent to minister to the wants of the Catholics in Jefferson County, N. Y. He became pastor of St. Mary's Church, Watertown, and from there attended Brownsville and other dependent missions. He remained in this position for about five years, and was transferred on the 1st of March, 1851, by Bishop McCloskey, the Bishop of Albany, to the charge of this parish.

The Utica of Father O'Gorman, 32 years ago, with its 400 houses and 2,000 people, had now become a thriving city with ten times that population, and the church had kept pace with the growth of the town. I need not speak of Father McFarland's work amongst us during this important period in the history of our parish. His zealous labors so well remembered, crowned the glory of the second church. His work was lasting. He made an impression in the parish which remained long after the hallowed walls of that church which he loved so well, had been razed to the ground. His memory is still green in Utica, the blessing which he left upon our church is still with us, and long, long will his name be revered in the parish which had the happiness of being the witness of his saintly labors.

It was during Father McFarland's pastorate that the Brothers of the Christian Schools came to Utica. Our beautiful school building, in which we take so much pride, was built during his pastorate. Assumption Academy was opened September 1st, 1854, and its long line of graduates are found among our citizens in

RT. REV. FRANCIS P. MC FARLAND, D. D.

every profession and in every walk of life. Father McFarland purchased additional lots for burial purposes, to meet the increasing needs of the congregation.

It was also during his pastorate that the first mission was given in the parish. It took place in the month of October, 1857. It was a memorable mission, conducted by those renowned Redemptorists, Fathers Walworth, Hewitt, Deshon, and Baker.

Many of the older members of the congregation will remember this mission from a circumstance which impressed it upon their minds. The veil of the statue of the Blessed Virgin, which had been placed above the high altar, took fire, and the church was for a time threatened with destruction.

Father McFarland was the first pastor to reside in the old Barrows house, which was the new rectory, purchased by Father Stokes, and which stood nearly on the site of the present rectory. In the very midst of his labors, the bulls arrived from Rome naming him as the third Bishop of Hartford. He left Utica for his new field of labor, March 6th, 1858. A large number of the congregation accompanied him to the train, and manifested their regret at his departure. He was consecrated in St. Patrick's Cathedral, Providence, R. I., March 14th, 1858, by Archbishop Hughes. The sermon was preached by Bishop McCloskey, of Albany, afterwards the first American Cardinal.

Providence was then the seat of his diocese. He threw himself at once into his work, building churches, schools, convents, hospitals, and asylums. Sixteen years of episcopal labors were not without their fruits. The territory comprised within the limits of the diocese at the time of Bishop McFarland's consecration, has since been divided, and the State of Rhode Island has been formed into a new diocese, with Providence as the episcopal city. Bishop McFarland transferred the seat of the diocese to Hartford, and secured a very desirable site for a new Cathedral. He did not live to see it erected, but through the zeal and energy of his devoted successor, there stands upon that spot to-day a magnificent temple, second, perhaps, to none in the United States, and entirely free from debt.

The impress of Bishop McFarland's zeal and piety is indelibly stamped upon the diocese of Hartford. His task was not an easy one. He was hampered very much in his work by the "Knownothings," who actually at one time gained control of the State. One of their first acts was to pass a law disbanding all militia companies that were composed mainly of Catholics. But the Civil War breaking out soon after, the iniquitous statute was repealed in a single day, and Catholic blood and Catholic valor proved once again that patriotism is a virtue akin to religion.

Bishop McFarland continued to rule over the diocese of Hartford until his death, which occurred in the episcopal city, October 12th, 1874. His obsequies took place in the Cathedral on the 15th, the venerable Bishop Loughlin officiating. At least a dozen bishops and nearly a hundred priests, and large numbers of the laity witnessed the impressive ceremonies over our once beloved pastor. Bishop Hendricken, of Providence, in his funeral eulogy, made this remarkable statement. He said that Bishop McFarland was a man of extraordinary piety.

" I have known him," he added, " from the morning of his consecration, and I have never been able to detect in him a venial fault.

" The poorest members of his flock or diocese could approach him without fear, and would always be sure to receive at his hands the kindest of treatment. He was a learned scholar in the best sense of the term, and a most profound theologian. As a citizen he was a valuable one to both this city and State, and also to Rhode Island when he resided there. During the late war he was not wanting in patriotism, and in a proper method of showing it."

And to show that these sentiments were echoed in this community, and that the lapse of sixteen years had not dimmed the lustre of the glory in which his name was held in Utica, we here quote the editorial published in the Utica *Observer* at the time of his death:

" Francis Patrick McFarland, Bishop of Hartford, died in that city on Monday last, in the fifty-seventh year of his age. He was born in Franklin, Pa., and educated at St. Mary's College, Md. (Mt. St. Mary's).

" He was ordained to the priesthood in 1845. After laboring successfully in Watertown for some years, he came to Utica, where he assumed the charge of St. John's Church. Here he won the most commanding success.

" His eminent piety, his unflagging zeal, his liberal culture, and, above all, his broad and Catholic charity, gained him numberless friends outside the pale of his Church, as well as within.

" He was sparing of others; he never spared himself.

" He never knew what it was to be idle. In the homes of the poor, in the room of sickness, and by the bedside of the dying, he was a frequent and faithful visitor. He shaped his life to the strictest demands of duty, and found his pleasure in doing good. Under his care his parish grew and prospered. In 1858, the Bishopric of Hartford, which diocese included the States of Rhode Island and Connecticut, became vacant through the death of Bishop O'Reilly, who was lost at sea on the ill-fated Pacific.

" Father McFarland was called to be Bishop of Hartford.

" He carried from Utica the love of every man, woman, and child, Catholic or Protestant, who had known him during his residence here. He took up his ' residence in Providence at a time when the prejudice against his Church was exceedingly strong, and before the passions engendered by this hostility had cooled.   He was, we believe, the youngest Bishop in the Catholic Church.   He resided in Rhode Island until 1872.

" He died on Monday, the 12th inst., in Hartford, after fulfilling a mission which falls to the lot of few men, with a steadfast faithfulness unsurpassed."

Let me recall a few of the contemporaneous events which signalized the pastorate of Father McFarland.   In 1851 Jenny Lind sang in the Bleecker Street church, and a thousand people paid five dollars apiece to hear the famous Swedish songstress.

In 1852 the First Plenary Council of Baltimore, composed of all the Bishops of the United States, was convened.   It was during this year, also, that Utica was honored with the visit of two distinguished men.   Louis Kossuth, the Hungarian patriot, came in June, and General Winfield Scott, the hero of the Mexican War, came in the fall.   Both were received by our citizens in a most enthusiastic manner.   In 1853 Franklin Pierce became President of the United States, the World's Fair took place at the Crystal Palace in New York, and Horatio Seymour, of whom our city is so justly proud, was elected Governor of the State. Europe saw the beginning of the great Crimean War.   In 1854, Pius IX. solemnly defined the dogma of the Immaculate Conception.   And in the very last days of this glorious pastorate an event took place in France, which has since come to be one of the most remarkable occurrences of the nineteenth century: I mean the wonderful apparitions of the Blessed Virgin in the grotto of Lourdes—the first of which occurred February 11th, 1858.

FATHER MCFARLAND'S ASSISTANT PRIESTS.

Besides Father Coghlan, who had assisted Father Stokes, and remained with Father McFarland until he became pastor of Clinton, May 1st, 1854, four other priests assisted Father McFarland during his pastorate.

REV. JAMES SMITH.

MAY 1ST, 1854—APRIL 1ST, 1855.   DIED SEPTEMBER 15TH, 1881.

Father Smith assisted Father McFarland for nearly a year. He became afterwards pastor of Fulton, Oswego County, which position he held upwards of a quarter of a century, until his death, which occurred in that village, September 15th, 1881.

REV. DANIEL P. FALVEY.

APRIL 29TH, 1855—AUGUST 4TH, 1855.　DIED JUNE 12TH, 1866.

Father Falvey was here but a few months.　He became afterwards pastor of St. John's Church, Schenectady, making the third assistant priest of this parish who was appointed pastor of that church.　He held this position until his death, which occurred in Schenectady, June 12th, 1866.

REV. JOHN McDERMOTT.

SEPTEMBER 6TH, 1855—MARCH 9TH, 1856.　DIED JANUARY 18TH, 1860.

Father McDermott assisted Father McFarland for a short time.　He then became pastor of St. Patrick's Church, Oneida, and built the first church in that village, which has since been replaced by the handsome stone structure, erected by the Very Rev. James A. Kelley, the worthy Dean of this district of the diocese.　Shortly after the completion of the first church, Father McDermott went to Philadelphia, Pa., where he died January 18th, 1860.

REV. JOSEPH H. HERBST.

MARCH 31ST, 1856—MARCH 22D, 1858.　DIED FEBRUARY 17TH, 1885.

Father Herbst was assistant priest for two years.　His health broke down shortly after he left here, and he was obliged to retire from active duty.　He died in the Hospital of the Sisters of Charity, in Troy, N. Y., February 17th, 1885.

REV. THOMAS DALY.

APRIL 25TH, 1858—DECEMBER 25TH, 1869.

Just as our parish was beginning its long career, in the autumn of 1822, an Irishwoman, with a babe in her arms, bade farewell to her native land, and braving the storms of the ocean, sailed away for free America.　That infant was Father Daly, destined to occupy so large a space in the development of our parish.　He was born in the city of Dublin.　His family settled in New York City.　Hardly had reason dawned upon his youthful mind, than he began to aspire to the holy priesthood.　He had the great privilege of being an altar boy in St. Patrick's Cathedral, and listening to the eloquent words of the great Archbishop Hughes.

He was one of the first to enter St. John's College, Fordham, which was then presided over by Bishop, afterwards Cardinal, McCloskey, where he was graduated with high honors. Thus it will be seen that two of his youthful preceptors were two of the greatest Bishops that ruled our diocese, and whose names are associated with his own on our memorial tablet. He was ordained by Archbishop Hughes, on the 30th of May, 1847. He was first appointed assistant priest in St. Peter's Church, Saratoga. Subsequently h e w a s transferred t o St. Joseph's Church, Albany, where he assisted Father Conroy, afterwards Bishop of Albany. Later on, he was pastor of St. Bernard's Church, Cohoes, St. Patrick's Church, West T r o y, a n d S t. Peter's Church, Troy. Finally, in 1858, his Eminence, Cardinal McCloskey, who was then Bishop of Albany, recognizing his superior abilities, appointed him pastor of this important church.

REV. THOMAS DALY.

A new era seemed to dawn upon our beloved parish upon the transfer of Father McFarland to a broader sphere of usefulness, and the coming of Father Daly. Under his administration a wonderful development took place. The child was fast becoming a man. His pastorate is remarkable in many ways. I have said that there are three periods in the growth of our parish. Father Daly was pastor for almost one-third of the entire period of its existence. His first care, upon taking charge, was to complete and perfect the spiritual edifice whose foundations had been so broadly and solidly laid by his energetic predecessor.

A few months after his coming, the Society of the Children of Mary, a confraternity composed of young ladies, and whose object is to foster piety and special devotion to the Blessed Virgin, was organized under the direction of the Sisters of Charity, December 8th, 1858, the very year of the apparitions of Lourdes. This Sodality is still in existence, celebrating, December 8th, 1893, the thirty-fifth anniversary of its organization, and the good it has accomplished in this parish during that long period of time will be known only in Heaven.

For two years Father Daly devoted himself in a special manner to the promotion of spiritual affairs. One of his first cares was to provide a home for orphan boys, and under his direction the Brothers of the Christian Schools opened an orphan asylum for boys in a portion of the school building on the corner of John and Elizabeth Streets. This great work was inaugurated on the Feast of the Annunciation of the Blessed Virgin Mary, March 25th, 1862. But he soon found temporal concerns thrust upon his attention, and calling for the exercise of his zeal and energy. The second church, which seemed too large when built, was now becoming altogether inadequate for the increasing numbers of the congregation, and he saw that it would be necessary to take immediate measures for the erection of a more spacious edifice. And so it was his privilege to be the last of those honored pastors that guided our destinies during the period of the second church. And even as the great Father Quarter closed the list of the pastors of the first church, and opened that of the second, so it was given to the beloved Father Daly to close the list of the pastors of the second church, and to open that of the third.

Mass was said in the second church for the last time on Sunday, June 8th, 1868. On Monday morning the work of tearing down was begun. That good old church, loved so well, was soon levelled to the ground.

The corner-stone of this present church was laid by Father Daly, in the afternoon of June 27th, 1869, both the ending of the second church and the beginning of the third occurring in the month of the Sacred Heart. The sermon on the occasion was preached by Rev. Dr. Keating, then pastor of Newport. The papers and coins which had been placed in the corner-stone of the second church, were found to be in a good state of preservation, and were deposited, with the other articles, in the corner-stone of the present church.

For a few years the congregation were compelled to make use of the Court House and Sisters' School building as places of worship.   Many parishioners remember the inconveniences and the hardships of those days.   Many remember, too, the trials and difficulties of Father Daly in carrying to completion so gigantic a task.   Even with failing health he struggled on to do what seemed almost too much for his physical strength.   Many remember the touching appeal he made in August, 1869, for funds, that the church might be completed for Christmas of that year.   Many will recall the joy and heartiness with which they worked to decorate the new house of God for that great Festival of Holy Church—that memorable Christmas of 1869.

The old Barrows house, which had served for a rectory for nearly twenty years, was also torn down during this same year of 1869, and the present elegant and spacious residence for the clergy was constructed.   While this work was going on, Father Daly boarded for a few months, from April to July, 1869, with Mr. Leslie A. Warwick, on Genesee Street.   Much to the delight and consolation of that good Catholic family, their house became, for the time being, a little church, and baptisms and marriages and other ministrations blessed their quiet home.   A house was subsequently provided for Father Daly at 58 Mary Street, where he resided until the completion of the new rectory.

But besides these two great works which demanded so much of his attention, another task was imposed upon him.   The accommodations for the orphan boys at the school building were found to be totally inadequate, and besides, the Catholics of the city generally were beginning to appreciate more and more the opportunity presented by Assumption Academy for a sound Catholic education, as well as the highest form of commercial and scientific instruction.   It became necessary, therefore, in the summer of 1869, to make better provision for the orphan boys, and the large and commodious and beautiful building was erected on the corner of Rutger Street and Taylor Avenue.   The school building was henceforward devoted exclusively to educational purposes, and the orphan boys were transferred to the new asylum now known as " St. Vincent's Industrial School."

This last decade in the history of the second church, and the first in the long administration of Father Daly, was a period remarkable in many ways. While Father Daly was prudently and zealously looking after the material and spiritual growth of our parish, stirring events were taking place, both in our own country and in the world, and history was being made faster than the chronicler could record it. In 1858, the first Atlantic cable, imperfect as it was, conveyed congratulatory messages between Queen Victoria and President James Buchanan, and the world saw with amazement an unexpected revolution in telegraphy. In the same year was laid, by Archbishop Hughes, the corner-stone of the present St. Patrick's Cathedral of New York.

In 1861 Abraham Lincoln was inaugurated President, and then began those four years of fratricidal strife which deluged our land in blood, and wasted millions of treasures. In the midst of the Civil War in 1864, which he had so loyally supported, the great Archbishop Hughes surrendered his soul to God. In the next year, 1865, Lincoln was assassinated, General Lee surrendered to General Grant, and the cruel war was over, and the Northern and Southern armies disbanded. In 1866 the Atlantic cable was at last, after many experiments, a complete success, and the Old and the New World were united as in a common family. In the same year, 1866, was held the Second Plenary Council of Baltimore. In 1869, Ulysses S. Grant was inaugurated President, the Pacific Railroad was completed, the Suez Canal was opened, and across the water the great Œcumenical Council of the Vatican, the first general council since the Council of Trent, was opened auspiciously by the saintly Pius IX. of blessed memory, on the feast of the Immaculate Conception, the patronal feast of the United States.

Local happenings were not less interesting during the last decade of our second church. Roscoe Conkling, one of Utica's favorite sons, was Mayor of the city, in 1858 and 1859. President Lincoln passed through here, February 18, 1861, on his way to the inauguration ceremonies at Washington, and was tendered a reception. With the firing upon Fort Sumter a little later, the city became filled with martial enthusiasm, and a local paper stated at the time that Utica was doing more in proportion to population to fill the ranks of the army than any other city or town of the State. Father Daly's flock were not behind their fellow-citizens in their devotion to the flag. James McQuade, the son of Michael McQuade, one of the pioneers of the church in our city, was at that time a devout member of the parish. When the war broke out he was Captain of the Citizen's Corps. On the day following the firing on Fort Sumter, he offered his own services and those of his entire company, to the Government for two years. They became a part of the 14th Regiment, of which he was elected Colonel. For gallantry and bravery in the seven days' fighting, from June 27th to July 3d, 1865, and at Malvern Hill, he was promoted to the rank of Brigadier-General. The city showed its appreciation of its loyal son by electing him Mayor in 1866 and 1870.

Many other local events are still fresh in the memory of the people of St. John's. The opening of the street railroad to New Hartford and New York Mills, in 1863, was an event in the history of our city. Many have not yet forgotten that great freshet on that memorable St. Patrick's Day, just before the war closed, when the water was two feet deep on the corner of Whitesboro and Genesee Streets.

Still fresh in the memory of many are the happy scenes of those bright June days, when amid the pealing of bells and the booming of cannon, and the sweet strains of " Home, Sweet Home," their loved ones came back from the field of carnage, nevermore to return. Many remember the unprecedented celebration that year of the 4th of July—the fireworks on Chancellor Square, and the stirring speech of Francis Kernan. And many recall, a little later —in 1868—the band of enthusiastic citizens pulling the rope of the City Hall Bell, and ringing a joyous and protracted peal, when the news reached the city, that for the first time the honor of being a candidate for the highest office in the land had fallen upon a citizen of Utica, the almost idolized Horatio Seymour.

Truly, our second church, in the closing years of her existence, was a witness of events that will not soon be forgotten.

FATHER DALY'S ASSISTANT PRIESTS IN THE SECOND CHURCH.

REV. PATRICK J. McGLYNN.

JULY 15, 1858 - OCTOBER 1st, 1858.   DIED DECEMBER 13th, 1867.

The church of Father Quarter was just of age—it was celebrating its 21st birthday -when his own nephew, Father McGlynn, came to assist Father Daly.   He studied first in St. Mary's College, Chicago, and then successively in St. John's College, Fordham; St. Mary's Seminary, Baltimore; and St. Joseph's Seminary, Troy, N. Y., where he was ordained in June, 1858.   Utica was his first mission.   He remained but a few months, just long enough to claim the privilege of having been attached to the church. It seemed singularly appropriate that he should minister at the same altar, and labor, even for a while, in the church of his illustrious uncle. After leaving Utica he labored in the northern part of the State, in what is now the diocese of Ogdensburg.   He lived to see, of the three churches, only that which his uncle had built, as he died before the second church was torn down.   He became pastor of St. Mary's Church, Potsdam, in the summer of 1858, and he remained there until his death, which occurred in that village,

REV. PATRICK J. MC GLYNN.

December 13th, 1867.   His remains were transferred to Utica a couple of years later, and buried in St. Agnes' Cemetery. Father McGlynn is the second on our long list of priests whose remains rest in our own city of the dead.   It may not be generally known that Mr. Wm. J. McGlynn, who is now a member of St.

Agnes' Church, Utica, is a nephew of Father Quarter, and a brother of Father McGlynn.

REV. EUGENE CARROLL.

October 10th, 1858 December 1st, 1860. Died July 16th, 1882.

Father Carroll labored first for several years in the hard mission of Hunter, in the Catskill mountains. He was then transferred to Utica, where he assisted Father Daly for nearly two years. Subsequently he exercised the holy ministry in Albany, where he was Chaplain, for several years, of the Boys' Orphan Asylum. He was later appointed pastor of Constableville and Port Leyden. He labored in this mission until his death, which occurred at Port Leyden, July 16th, 1882.

REV. JOHN McDONALD.

September 15th, 1864.—August 26th, 1866. Died February 4th, 1879.

Father McDonald is the last name on our memorial tablet of the priests who assisted Father Daly in the second church. He was a nephew of the present distinguished Archbishop Walsh, of Toronto. He enjoyed the unique distinction of being the first student of St. Joseph's Provincial Seminary, Troy, N. Y., ordained to the holy priesthood—the leader of that army of seven hundred soldiers of the Lord that marched forth from that noble institution of learning, founded by the great Archbishop Hughes, and directed by that saint and scholar, the Very Rev. Dr. Vandenhende, the pres-

REV. JOHN MC DONALD.

ent Vicar-General of Ghent. assisted by a corps of devoted priests from Belgium, who are still successfully carrying on the great work. Father McDonald remained with Father Daly about two years. After laboring in various places, he was finally appointed pastor of St. Mary's Church, Potsdam, where Father McGlynn, his warm friend, had labored a few years previously. He, too, died in Potsdam, February 4th, 1879.

LIVING FRUITS OF THE SECOND CHURCH.

Before we close the book on whose pages are recorded the glories of the second church, it may not be amiss to cast a glance at the men and women whom that church inspired and prepared for a consecration of their lives to the service of God.

I have no record of the names of those holy men and women trained in that second church, who immolated themselves entirely upon the altar of religion, and gave themselves wholly and completely to the service of their Master. But they were not few. In different Religious Orders and Communities they buried themselves from the world, and one day they will all stand amongst the white-robed virgins that follow the Lamb whithersoever He goeth, and praise the name of the second church.

As regards the priests, there were eleven, as far as I have been able to learn, that were the product of the second church.

Three of them have gone to their reward. Father Patrick J. McGlynn, of whom I have but just spoken, Father Ambrose O'Neill, and Father Edward O'Connor—three noble priests of whom the parish may be justly proud. Let us breathe a prayer for the repose of their souls.

There are nine still alive, laboring faithfully in the Lord's vineyard.

Very Rev. Thomas M. A. Burke is now the Vicar-General of the diocese of Albany, and the Rector of St. Joseph's Church in that city.[1]

Rev. George Quin is a member of the illustrious Society of Jesus. He is at present attached to St. Joseph's Church, Troy.

Rev. John F. Lowery, LL.D., is rector of St. Agnes' Church, Cohoes.

---

[1] He was consecrated Bishop of Albany, July 1st, 1894.

THE SECOND CHURCH

Rev. Philip Grace, D.D., is pastor of the Church of Our Lady of the Isle, Newport, R. I.

Rev. Thomas P. Grace is pastor of St. Mary's Church, Providence, R. I.

Rev. John P. McIncrow is rector of St. Mary's Church, Amsterdam, N. Y.

Rev. John F. Mullaney is rector of St. John Baptist's Church, Syracuse, N. Y.

Rev. William O'Mahony is rector of St. Paul's Church, Troy.

Rev. Joseph S. Tiernan is rector of Camden, New York.

LAST DAYS OF OUR SECOND CHURCH.

And so closes the history of our second church. In the "Annals and Recollections of Oneida County," published in 1851, we find the following in relation to St. John's:

"This church was organized in 1819, and was the first Catholic church formed in Central and Western New York since the settlement of the country. Its first church edifice was of wood, and which, about ten or twelve years since, was removed across Bleecker Street, and the present large edifice erected in its place. The late John C. and Nicholas Devereux were the greatest benefactors of this church, having contributed over $12,000 towards building the brick house of worship. The church is the largest in the city, and on Sundays and other days, when open for service, is generally filled to overflowing. Many attend here from considerable distances in the surrounding country."

I have said that the second church represents the childhood of our parish. The babe had safely passed through the most precarious period of its existence. Carefully nursed by those twelve Irish missionaries, it had outlived the trials and perils of infancy, and now a child tenderly placed in the lap of Father Quarter to begin a new period of its life. it was growing, strengthening, developing; but it was still a child,—not yet a perfect man.

But, people of St. John's ! the second church is dear to you because of its associations with your own childhood days. You are gradually growing old; springtime and summer have come and gone, and for many of you the autumn of life is approaching; many will soon feel the winter's chilly blast. For some of you the sun of life is fast sinking in the West. Your bedimmed eye, your silvery locks, your furrowed brow, your halting gait, your waning strength, warn you that the sands of life are running out.

Ah, you have fought well the battle of life! You have seen the giant oak uprooted, and the young saplings cut down at your side; you have weathered many a storm. Soon the Reaper will come closer to you. And whilst you look forward to the end so near at hand, you love to look backward, too, to the beginning. Fond memory brings you back again to the happy days of childhood—those days of innocence and sweet content—" when prosperous was the ray that painted with gold the flowery mead that blossomed in your way." You live once more in that dear old church of long ago. Oh, Fancy! take thy brush, and picture that church of childhood's days!

You remember it, people of St. John's! better than I can describe it, because I never had the pleasure of seeing it. Not as large as the present church—it extended only as far as the galleries that have just been taken down, as far as where the rear columns now stand,—you recall the altar with its four Corinthian columns, and high above all, the words " Gloria in Excelsis Deo," with the picture of the Lamb upon the front. You remember the tabernacle with the plain gable top to it, inscribed with the word " Jesus," the little crucifix surmounting it, and the beautiful heart of gas jets behind it, and the candles and flowers on either side. You remember the beautiful picture of the Crucifixion behind the crucifix. On the right you recall that work of art, " The Ecce Homo," presented to the church through Mr. Nicholas Devereux, by a Mr. Olmsted, of New York. Under this picture, in confirmation days, you remember the Bishop's throne, with a picture half concealed behind it. On the north side, where we have brought back our Blessed Mother, you recall the niche and that dear little statue of Mary that we still preserve with such jealous care; you see it again, as in days of yore, with candles and flowers on either side, and the little pedestal which was scarcely an altar, and the pulpit, run on wheels, brought out to the middle when required. You remember the seats on either side, facing the centre as far back as the first pillar; you remember the cosy little chapel up stairs, where the present choir gallery is, and the little altar, and the confessionals on either side.

Once more you are within those hallowed walls. It is the day of your baptism. You are borne in the arms of your godmother to the regenerating Font, and the robe of innocence is placed upon your soul, and you go forth like an angel, pure and spotless. You come again, when reason has developed, to ratify what was done in your name. It is the day of your First Communion. Robed in spotless white, with beating heart and beaming eye you approach that little altar, and for the first time receive upon your lips the Bread of Angels. You come again to receive from the hands of the Bishop the strengthening sacrament of Confirmation that was to make you strong and perfect Christians, and soldiers of Jesus Christ. You come again to Mary's altar with your ribbon and medal and your badge, to consecrate yourselves forever to her service, and to choose her for your Queen. Years pass on, and you stand once more before that same altar. You are not alone, and the love knitting two hearts together is blessed and consecrated by religion, and made like unto the love of Christ for His Spouse, the Church. Sadness follows joy, and you come before that same altar to bid a last farewell to your loved ones, and the Requiem is chanted over their remains, and Holy Church bids you not mourn as those who have not hope.

O church of hallowed memories! church of your fathers! church of your childhood days! no wonder that old men wept when its walls were taken down. Gone is that sanctuary of religion; departed its glories. No, it is not gone, because its work endureth forever The holy Religious who within its hallowed walls heard the Master's voice, and left all to follow Him for that promised hundredfold and life everlasting. They are not gone. Some in Heaven are pleading before the Throne of God for old St. John's; some on earth, by their lives of devotedness and self-sacrifice, are bringing down blessings upon that church which inspired their holy vocation. And the priests of God--His own anointed ones—laboring in His vineyard, working for His glory, trained in that church of long ago, continue still its blessed work though the material temple has passed away. No, the graces and inspirations, the pious thoughts and holy desires, that rose like sweet incense in that old church, have not departed. No, ascending Heavenward, carried to the Throne of God, blessed and sanctified before the altar of the Lamb, they have been brought back by angel hands, like rich mosaics, to beautify, adorn, and enrich the walls of this third church,—the offspring of the first and the second.

O dear old church of long ago! Church from whose pulpit were heard the learned and profound teachings of a Dubois, whose walls resounded with the powerful, majestic, and soul-thrilling eloquence of the lion-hearted Hughes, and through whose aisles floated the soft, sweet music of the gentle Prince of the church, our first American Cardinal—the beloved Bishop McCloskey. O church of a Quarter, a Ferrall, a Martin, a Stokes, a McFarland, and a Daly! May thy memory remain ever green in the hearts of the children of St. John's; may they never forget the noble bishops and priests whose names are connected with that second church; may they emulate their virtues and walk in their footsteps, and when another generation will have passed away, and this present church, which we now think so grand, will have done its work, and a monumental temple of granite or marble may perchance rise upon its ruins, God grant that when its story—the story of the third church—shall be written, it may not prove unworthy of the glory of the second church built upon this hallowed spot!

—

OUR LADY'S NATIVITY.

WILLIAM D. KELLY.

WHEN the short sway of the Summer is over,
    And Autumn the sceptre of royalty wields ;
When purple grapes peep from under green cover,
    And asters and golden-rods glow in the fields ;
When sweetly as songs that the heart doth remember,
    Long after their singers have vanished from earth,
On leafy lyres whisper the winds of September,
    Returneth the day of our Lady's blest birth.

Then shows in the skies a more scintillant splendor,
    And nearer, far nearer, seems Heaven to our gaze ;
The world wears a beauty more winsome and tender
    Than falls to the lot of less fortunate days ;
And dreams of delights drawing near with December,
    When He who was born of her visits the earth,
Enrapture the soul in these days of September,
    And gladden the morn of our Lady's blest birth.

SOME LITTLE INDIAN LIVES.

O WE not live in the age of unobtrusive sanctities, in the age when the greatest things are
wrought by modest, united efforts, beating
like restless wavelets against the rocky shores
of sin and prejudice? Since my visit to
Auriesville, I had longed to see an Indian
Mission, and to gather some of the flowerets of
Catholic sanctity midst the gigantic growths
of missionary devotion. My mind had long pictured those
scenes of rural life where labor and religion, clasping hands,
uplift the heart and mind from earth to Heaven. At length,
I broke away from routine and mental drudgery, and boarding the train of the " Great Northern Railroad " at St. Paul,
Minnesota, I set my face steadily toward a blessed spot of
which I knew,— St. Peter's Mission, Montana. Two days of
travel brought me to Cascade, Montana. I reached this little
mountain village toward dusk one afternoon, when the blue
foot-hills of the Rockies were already touched by the twilight's
tenderest amethyst. Disdaining the stage-coach, I determined to
wait the morning here. It was in the early May. Spring had
broken in upon the Mission valley, and the babbling mountain
waters tossing and tumbling down from stupendous cañons and
wind-beaten buttes, just burst from their winter chains, and jubilant with recovered freedom, proclaimed joy to all the land. I
had taken an early start in the blushing dawn, and with a pedestrian's frenzy had determined to foot it over to old St. Peter's
Mission.

I confess to sentiments of deep emotion as I treaded the mountain paths which Father de Smet had trodden, and which, by the
help of my vivid imagination, I could still see marked with the
bloody traces of the Blackfeet and Flatheads.

The exhilarating morning breeze, the exquisite fragrance of the
hour, the delicate touches of gold and roseate purple that the
dawn was casting on the eternal snows of the Rockies, the lingering traceries of white in the clefts and the undulations of the rolling

A GROUP AT ST. PETER'S INDIAN MISSION, MONTANA.

land,—all this filled me with an unearthly sense of the beautiful,
and that buoyant joyousness and energy which are the peculiar
possession of the pedestrian.   Nor was I alone in my morning
orison to nature.   My sympathetic presence seemed to be an event
of no little importance in the " prairie-dog towns " through which
I passed.   Seated on the summit of his little mound, the lord of the
manor, with tail erect, his restless little ears catching every fragment of morning rustle, each watch-dog seemed to invite me to
approach, but as soon as beguiled by his half cordial, half defiant
look, I approached, with a snapping bark and a pert wag of the
tail, he disappeared in the recesses of his little home.   Here and
there the retreating form of a hungry " coyote," the dim outline
of the graceful antelope against the sky, the lazy kine, the browsing sheep, and now and again the ominous warning of the rattle-
snake and the whirring of the owl, all told me that I was not
alone mid this magnificent panorama.   The wind for ages has
been at work, a mighty sculptor, in this region.   Traces of gigantic
erosion remain in adamant recorded, and I afterwards learned that
these upheavals are known as " buttes " in this section of our land;
and that each has received its peculiar name, in keeping with its
form.   " Fishback " pictures a shoal of leaping porpoises, and before
the crested " crown " I could have sat and dreamed, so loftily did
it seem to rise into the empyrean.   At length, breathless from the
exertion and the long hour's walk, I reached the top of a swelling
butte, from whence I could descry St. Peter's Mission, stretching
some two hundred feet below.

There it lay, in the early peace of the morning sunshine.   What
was my deep emotion to hear the chant of religious rite issuing
from the open window of a little log chapel!   Whilst I stopped to
listen and to sue for mercy, the door of the poor little church
swung back, and a long line of prayerful pilgrims began to mean-
der in and about the hills and fields.   It was the first of the Rogation days.   The sun stood high and glorious now, "tiptoe on the
misty-mountain top."   How long had it been since last I saw a
Rogation day procession!   It seemed to me that I stood no longer in the world of sin, but in a land of full, of simple faith.

First walked the Indian boys, two by two, led and directed by
their Jesuit prefects.   The symmetry of this line was somewhat

marred by the straggling devotion of the gay "metifs" and "trap-
peurs" and the semi-civilized "Courreur des Boys," who followed
with shambling gait in their gay-colored moccasins.

Next came the Indian girls, the Ursuline nuns, the Indian
women, and the officiating priest attended by two acolytes, "*A
peste, fame et bello,*"—and the hills seemed to take up the strain
and reverberate it even up to Heaven. "*Christus vincit, Christus
regnat, Christus imperat, Christus defendat nos, et omnia bona
nostra,*" I heard the priest chant alone, as he blessed the fields
and hills, and scattered holy water all about; and all seemed joyous in this land where Christ reigns and rules indeed. I followed
the long line reverently, first into the field that skirts the "Pom-
mel" and the "Saddle Back," and stretches East of the little chapel. Here upon our return I was rewarded with the most
satisfactory view of the Mission,—at my feet the little church:
all about the beautiful foot-hills of the Rockies, and due West,
"Amadeus Rock," with the Ursuline novitiate nestling at its foot.
At length the procession was ended. The boys went over to the
Jesuit College, and I followed the girls into the Convent, whither
my letters of introduction pointed. After a few moments' delay,
I was greeted by Mother Amadeus, foundress and general
Superioress of the Ursuline Missions. Here she stood, a woman of
most magnetic sanctity, whose labors and privations stood stamped
upon her face in those beautiful lines of the poet:

> "Her soul like a light within a vase,
> Touched every line with glory of her animated face."

After a hospitable patriarchal breakfast, I was conducted
through the establishment. The building, though in a wofully
unfinished condition, bespeaks great future usefulness and comfort as an Indian school. I stood amazed at its solidity and massive-
ness, but when I questioned as to whence the handsome stone was
quarried, "the Mother," as she was everywhere called, pointing to
the buttes within a stone's throw, answered: "This house is a
rock of the Rockies." Oh! I thought, that some more blessed
than myself with means and affluence, might case these windows
and doors, and thus lengthen these noble lives by lightening their
burdens. Upon nearing the classroom, "Watzinitha," when

called, stepped up to meet us, with the grace and lightness of the gazelle.   Half shy, half loving, this little Indian girl of some sixteen years, charmed me by her modest, maidenly way.   I determined then and there not to leave St. Peter's Mission till I had learned something of her little life, till I had unravelled to my readers the woof and web of some others of those mysterious little Indian lives as unknown and unnoticed as the mellow shades, the graceful slope of the lonely mountain side.

I followed Watzinitha then into the schoolroom, and the good Mother pointed out to me many of the child's companions.   Stalwart, healthy girls they seemed, with bright and laughing eyes, though some bore the blight of scrofula, a taint handed down to them, and not their own.

My guide showed me into the sewing-room, where twelve of the largest girls were running the sewing machines with faultless precision.   Next we went into the kitchen, where two middle-sized children assisted the novice in charge, whilst the little tots pealed the potatoes and washed the pots; into the laundry, bake-house and dairy, where at every turn I was greeted by starry-eyed, white-aproned Indian girls, who diligently worked under the direction of the presiding nun.   All this was comforting and beautiful to behold, and surprising, as was the children's proficiency in the classroom; and as in passing through the unfinished halls, and looking up at uncased windows, I noticed signs of suffering and poverty, I could but invoke a blessing upon the heart that had planned, the hands that had wrought, the marvel of self-sacrifice.

We people of the world think little of the Indian's individuality. Our sympathy, mayhap, is poured out upon them in the gross, as we see them called out upon a gala day to grace the pomp of our parades, or feed our craving for what is singular or curious.   Our hearts, perhaps, sometimes beat up with honest indignation as we read the rank injustice which a tribe or chief has suffered at the hands of money-making agents or ruthless traders.   But there is another view of the subject.   The Indian's life goes with ours toward making up the sum of humanity.   The Indian girl's heart, too, may be a delicate instrument "making sweetest music in the ear of Heaven," and may be mingling in the mighty and melodious unison of sanctities ascending from earth to Heaven.

This, our day, is the era of humble, unsuspected sanctities! This wretched world, this poor nineteeth century, is teeming with them; those saints, according to Cardinal Wiseman's definition, "souls that avoid venial sin," that fatten upon forgetfulness of self, that grow in athletic strength by the silent contemplation of the Blessed Sacrament, that " do what they do," that are all truthfulness and earnestness of simple purpose.   Such little lives did I single out from St. Peter's Mission records.

Watzinitha was born in the Gros-Ventre reservation some sixteen years ago.   Her father, " Agessannine," her mother, ". Eyaya, " were model Indians of their kind.

After long hours of silent pondering and consultation with the " Black Gown," they determined to give the girl a good and solid education.   She was to go to the Mission to learn all useful things, and bleeding though it left their hearts, the little sylph should be sent to the nuns.

Accordingly Agessannine and Eyaya conducted the child to the great " Black Robe " of their tribe, Rev. F. Eberschweiler, S. J., on the day that the big wagon was to leave the Milk River for the Mission beyond the Teton in the Blackfoot country.

Not many demonstrations did the Indian mother make as she placed the little trembling girl in the wagon, and saw her safely seated there between " Agessa," " Bushy Head's " girl, and " Atathan," the granddaughter of " Akipinaki."   But she saw that the kind " Black Gown " was there, and that there was much meat for the child to eat on the way, and that the horses were stout, and that the daughters of all the braves were there,—and she pulled the blanket tighter about the little one, and forced upon her arm one more bracelet, sent by the doting " Crow Chief," her grandfather, and looked into her liquid eyes, and said in her own maternal croning, not to be lonesome; that when the snows had come and gone, she would follow the wagon over to the Mission, bringing new furs and moccasins for the little one, and bright beads for her fawn-like neck.   And so, with this poetry of nature and the smiles of contented childhood, the mystery of parting was wrought once more, and when the heavy wagon wheels began to creak and turn, and the ponderous thing had rolled away, and a cloud of dust had received it into the unknown, the Indian woman threw herself upon the ground, and sobbed out the mighty yearnings of her untutored pagan heart. Ah! tell me, mothers of a fairer hue, are there no such accents in your love?

But the children in the mean time, in the cumbrous Mission wagon, were regaling themselves with the pemmican of berries and dried "bache fat" which their too fond parents had provided, and by furtive glances at one another, and a word now and again exchanged in their strange, inarticulate language, were beginning that life of union and mutual trust that they were to lead so many years together at the dear old Mission,—patent spell of childhood's friendships!

Here were three pagan girls—Watzinitha, Agessa, Atathan,—alike in age, in race,—alas! in degradation. Together they were to enter the pale of civilization; together they were to be regenerated in the saving waters of baptism; together would they make their First Communion ; together study, rejoice, suffer, and together at length would two of them be gathered into the garden where blow the " flowers of Jesus," " that loveth flowers —especially lilies."

Safely the little girls reached the Mission, where seven Ursuline nuns awaited them.

At this early date, their home was to be a little line of log cabins, 72 ft. x 20 ft., stretching East and West beneath the watchful stars, for the nuns had not then moved into their present home. St. Peter's Mission, Montana, had been opened as far back as 1858, by Fathers Hæcken, Imoda, and Brother Magri, S. J., but had been transferred to its present site at the foot of "Skull Butte " and " Bird Tail " by Father Imoda, S. J., and his still surviving companion, Brother Francis, S. J. Hither the Ursulines had been summoned in 1884, and here they had opened their novitiate and training school for the Indian Missions of Montana.

The coming of the wagon caused the most joyous excitement in the cabins—a species of holy emulation. With the truest joy depicted on their countenances, the nuns ran for their white aprons, brushes, combs, soap, towels. Each was ambitious to be the first to remove the blanket—to wash and comb the Indian girls. To whom should the honor belong? Lovingly they ceded this proud Christian joy to " the Mother." Thick and fast fell the tears when the Indian clothing was removed, when the tight bangles were taken from their scarred arms, and their ear-rings were laid aside, and these little red-skins had to taste the poison of soap and water, and their hair to feel the torturing comb!

But this sorrow vanished with its newness, and the three little Indian girls from the Gros-Ventre country, above all their companions, learned to love the Mission, and to be loved by those whose lives they began unconsciously to imitate.

Being of the same age and tribe, they were much alike in appearance. *Agessa*, with her father's deep-cut features and full head of hair, her modest droop of the eye, her gentle voice, her words all measured, seemed quite the saint of the band. She was always to be seen in the path of duty, and when spoken to by the nuns, would rise, cast down her lustrous eyes, and with a gentle sway of the head that reminded one of the turtle dove in the clefts of the rock, would coo out her gentle answer. Nor could you ever confuse Agessa, as a teacher can so many children, by repeating their answers, with the questioning rising inflection. Again and again the same words would Agessa repeat with an ever increasing but most timid assurance.

One day Agessa had been sick, and the nuns had brought her to the infirmary which, beside fifteen other different purposes, served also for the nuns' refectory and dormitory. The entrance to the cellar was from this little convent "living room," and one of the thoughtless girls descending for the precious store of potatoes, had left the candle behind her, close to the snow-white curtains. Agessa had gone to bed, and was alone in the room, when the smell of smoke and the blaze told the impending calamity. With all the self-possession of womanhood, Agessa jumped up noiselessly, and knocked at the door of the adjoining cabin, which was connected with the infirmary by a long, low porch, and where the nuns were taking recreation. "A little fire," she whispered as quietly as she might have said: "The sun is rising." Thus the prudent child saved the convent without spreading alarm in the schoolroom.

If guilty of any fault herself, or witness to any in her companions, Agessa would shed bitter tears, and thus often move them to a sense of right where their untutored hearts could scarce de-

tect a sense of wrong. One night poor " Bathay " had run away.
The nuns were in alarm; the "metifs" were on the lookout for
the poor wanderer, and as their mistress watched and waited that
night in anxious longing for the missing one of her flock she noticed Agessa saying the rosary until late in the night.

"What is the matter, Agessa?"

"I am praying for Bathay."

The next day poor Bathay came back. She was safe. She had
spent the night in the hay-stack.

One day Agessa had finished a pretty drawing—it was a crayon
of the Mission. Chief "Bushy Head," all bright with plumes
and elk-teeth, his ponies decked in gaudiest ribbons and precious
furs, had called at the Mission to see the darling of his heart, his
"Agessa," "Little Face." He was delighted with his girl's drawing, and standing with all possible dignity at a little distance,
and motioning with graceful gesture to the picture, "Mother,"
said he, to the Superioress, "let me take this 'little Mission'
to the camp and show it to my braves. My daughter 'Naninatz'
sold for 20 ponies, but 'Agessa' is worth at least 100, for she is
just like the white man's papoose." This was the measure of the
old pagan's love. But the words were Agessa's death-knell.
Again and again, and late into the night was she to be seen praying, with her arms extended in the form of a cross before the
statue of the Blessed Virgin which guarded the entrance to the
children's dormitory. How powerful were those simple, innocent
prayers the event showed, for Agessa was praying to die in her
maidenhood—a prayer heard all too soon. As soon as she felt
the grasp of scrofulous consumption upon her, she sent for her
brother, who was at the boys' school under the care of the Jesuit
Fathers. He was a Christian—a good, pious boy. For hours
these two children of the prairie would sit side by side, communing with each other without the aid of speech. Agessa was safe.
She was happy to die. One wish still was hers: to see her father
a Christian. She sent for him, and with the eloquence of love,
pleaded with the old chief the cause of his own immortal soul.
Now and again flashes of the supernal world, of which his child
seemed already a denizen, lighted up his darkened soul, and
"Bushy Head" would promise to be baptized, but the chains of

polygamy held him, and the promise vanished with the vision, like one of those celestial strains that lingers still awhile in hearts depraved to recall them to what might have been. Agessa lived on. She loved the Mother who had been so much to her; who had taught her the existence of God, the name of Jesus, the possibility and power of purity. Often would she press the Superior's hand to her heart, as though to fill its faintings with that life of sanctity and sacrifice which flooded her through the soft and soothing touch. At length the final struggle came. Upheld by one of her teachers, strengthened and soothed by the voice of the "Mother," assisted by the infirmarians, on the Feast of the Visitation, which was also the first Friday of the month, Agessa paused an instant at the portals of immortality. "Mother," she said, "do you not see our Lord? He is standing there. His dress is bright red. He bears a heavy cross!"

It was a quarter past twelve, and this first little life was ended: Agessa had passed beyond the reach of greed and love of gain, and had taken her rank at the great Court where sanctity is the one title to preferment. There was mourning at the Mission. The companion and friend of every one was gone, and the long-cherished hope of an apostolate among the Gros-Ventre was hushed in the majesty of death. Agessa's Indian name was descriptive, "Little Face." Her Christian name was no less so, "Agnes," which the Greeks read "chaste," the Latins, "lamb."

(*Conclusion in October.*)

HOPE's morning star, thus sparkling set
In Winter's frosty coronet !
Of all the shining host most fair,
To what shall we thy charms compare,
Save hers, who heralded the dawn
Of our redemption's promised morn?

The matin hour which calls to praise
Is lighted by thy beauteous rays;
And many a vestal's peaceful eye
Turns to the sapphire tinted sky,
To bid thee, radiant symbol, hail!
While flitting through the " cloisters pale."

Though mounting, swift, the chapel stair,
Her lips still move in happy prayer;
Though kneeling in her chapel stall,
Her heart doth still on Mary call,
For, "*Stella Matutina*," say
Those voiceless lips: *Ora pro me.*— E. A. Starr.

CHILDREN OF THE ROSARY.

St. Michael.

" Who is like unto God?"
     he cried,
   And legions flocked
     around him;
And he won the field from
     the demon Pride,
   And in riveless chains he
     bound him.
O glorious Prince of the
     Angel powers!
   Man's tireless interceder!
The strength of thy shield
     and lance be ours,
   In battle be thou our
     leader,
In peace be our defense,
     we crave,
Till Heaven itself crowns
     conflict brave.

✠ Sancte Michael O P N

SISTER RAYMUNDA'S STORY.

AQUINAS.

"LUCY! Lucy Colton!"

The girl turned at the low call in the familiar voice she knew and loved so well.

"O Sister, you *are* here with us again! Oh, I am so glad!"

The bright young face was lifted, and either cheek felt the pressure of Sister Raymunda's, as she greeted with a warm embrace, and "the nun's kiss," the young girl whom she so tenderly loved.

"I came early, Sister, to see if you were here,—you had not come yesterday. Oh, Sister! it seems as though I could 'offer up' anything but the trial of never seeing you again. The suspense has been terrible. Mamma says she has had no good of me during vacation any more than during school time, I am so wrapped up in you."

"Lucy!" In the voice, in the eyes that looked into the girl's, pleasure and reproach were mingled. Lucy was quick to catch both.

"You are pleased that I am so fond of you, but you fear I love you too much, Sister Raymunda?"

"No, child, I do not wish you to feel that—" a far-away look was upon the nun's face. "No, child," she repeated, "it is not *how much* we love, it is *the way* we love, that counts for or against our happiness here—and hereafter."

"You mean, Sister,—"

"I mean, Lucy, that perfection consists in doing the will of God, and that 'duty' is that Divine will expressed in one word. Do not let even the love of a nun pain a loving mother's heart. Do not let a companionship that brings you the sweetness of God, tempt you even in thought from a post that gives you God Himself. *He* awaits us, Lucy, where duty lies."

"Why do you say that, Sister? Sometimes it seems as though

you could read deep down into my very life. Mamma told me
only yesterday that it would be a good thing for me if you did
not come; that I was so wrapped up last year in my love for you
that to please you was the highest motive I had in doing anything."

There was a tremor in the girl's voice; the uplifted eyes were
moist with gathering tears.

"Sister," she continued, "I did not contradict mamma, but I
feel that, instead of its being so, it is, rather, only since I have
known you that I have had a higher motive than love for my teachers
and desire to please them in doing the best that I could. You
lifted me above that. You taught me to do my best for God—
no matter how little the work might be. Don't you remember
your first religious instruction in class, two years ago, now, Sister?
I do, oh, so well! It was on purity of intention—"

"Yes; and a serious faced young lady came to me shyly, afterwards, and asked for ' *some more instruction on doing things all for
God,*' " broke in Sister Raymunda, a half playful expression ban-
ishing for a moment the far-away look.

"And you did, Sister; and life has been so much—greater ever
since. It is no wonder I love you, Sister, and grieve for you
when you are gone, and watch so anxiously for your return that
I am good for nothing, and no help to anyone—not even my
mother." The concluding words came with a jerk and a look
upward at Sister Raymunda.

The uplifted eyes, so full of love, met not the expected loving
glance in response. A pain caught the ardent young heart. The
nun, loved with a love unmeasured, seemed, if the girl might
judge by the expression of her face, to have totally forgotten her.
Had she been listening at all to her outpouring of affection?

The girl might well question, for the nun's heart was in prayer
and in pain. "Now, at last, dear Lord, do I thank Thee, not
blindly as for long years, reading not Thy purpose in Thy painful
permission—"; but she withdrew herself forcibly from her retro-
spection.

"Come, Lucy," she said. She caught the girl's hand in one of
hers, and with the other parted the drapery of the little oratory of
St. Thomas Aquinas, for they were standing at the end of the

school corridor near it.   Lucy felt the hand clasping hers tremble.

" Sit down, child, I have a little story to tell you."

Lucy obeyed, caressing the large Rosary at the nun's side, and
wondering at her strange manner.

" Lucy, I once knew a young girl—none knew her better than
I, save God alone—whose home life was, in comparison with yours,
with many another, a worldly one.   It was a home full of tenderness, but God's name was seldom mentioned there.   In this young
girl's heart there were yearnings she did not understand, that
she never understood until the Sisters came to the city and opened
an academy there.   It was a school that from the first drew pupils
from the highest classes, and this young girl was sent there—because it was ' fashionable.'   It was her first meeting with Religious, the first realization of the existence of a life lived apart for
God, with God.   The yearnings of her heart had a meaning at
last.

" There was in that school a young nun, her teacher in music,
who became more to her than all others—more than I have ever
been, more than I could ever be to you, Lucy,—though in the
same way many times have I striven to help you.   This nun read
at once the aspirations of that ardent young nature in its unsatisfied longings for God and unworldly things, and by many a tender, helpful counsel did she strengthen them.   Not many words
of human affection did the girl speak, but every tendril of her
heart, reaching out to God, circled itself around the human
friend that was teaching her the things of God, till mother-love
lay buried beneath this love, home duty beneath the joy of this
presence, in which the young girl basked by day, of which she
dreamed by night, in which she wrapped herself up in longing
during times of separation.   The agony of suspense during vacation, not knowing whether or not the loved one would return,
was terrible to her.

" She was not blameless in this, for, oh, how often her angel
guardian would whisper to her of a mission at home ! how often
he would suggest, in the angels' way of beautiful thoughts, to repeat to the dear, worldly mother some of the good nun's helpful
words !   Had she opened her heart to the nun on this point,

surely she would have warned her of danger, and have counselled her aright. But the nun was young, and over zealous, perhaps, and her own life had been all spent in the convent,—she was an orphan, and at the age of sixteen had at once passed from the boarding school into the cloister. God, you see, had never led her by the way where await countless duties, little and great, to home and parents, brothers, sisters, friends. She measured the urgency of her pupil's call to God's special service by her own.

" There came a day, like the past days to you, Lucy, when suspense became unendurable—no, not that, God never gives a cross that is unendurable ; there came a day, I should have said, when *she would bear the cross of suspense no longer*, though but a week remained before the beginning of the school term. Her family was at its country home, and she had arranged a trip to the city 'to see if Sister was back for the coming term.'

" The morning dawned brightly ; the girl was in nervously high spirits, but her mother said suddenly, pleadingly :

" ' My daughter, will you stay with me to-day ? I don't know why I ask this, but I feel—'

" ' Mamma, dear, let me go,' she interrupted, half pleadingly, half pettishly. ' Ask me to give up anything but this! I must go! I feel as though I couldn't live without knowing if Sister is back!'

" Till to-day she can see her mother's sad, yearning look, as she met her child's refusal.

" ' Mamma,' the girl continued, ' Sister Colette has been more to me than any other human being. Much as you love me, mamma, and have done for me, it was Sister Colette who taught me to know God, and to love Him. I owe it to her to be there, the very first of her pupils to greet her, and this is the day set for her return, if she is coming at all. And there is something in my heart I must say to her.'

" ' Well, child, I shall never stand in the way of what you feel is your duty. God forgive me if I have failed in mine— your reproach is all too well merited. God grant there may be time for amends! But '—the mother pressed her hand to her heart as though in sudden pain ' if I am spared,' she added, ' you will teach me, and together we will know, love, and serve God. Give my greetings to the Sisters, and God bless you, my daughter!'

" At once came to the girl her guardian angel's warning whisper—*duty, which is duty ? to go or stay ?* and again,—*Sister Colette would bid you ' stay.'*

" The first great battle of her life was waging; a victory awaited her,—did she gain it?   Lest the counselling voice might speak too loudly for resistance, she hurriedly kissed the pleading mother, and hastened to the train.

" A half-hour more, and, weak from emotion and suspense, and with a violently beating heart, she heard the portress' gentle reply:

"' Yes, Sister is here.'

" A few moments more of anxious suspense, and her cup of joy was full.

" A heart to heart conversation with the cherished young nun, a presentation to the Mother Provincial then on her visitation, a few moments' earnest conversation with the calm, quiet, elder nun, whose matured judgment could decide so well for young hearts, and elated, the girl heard these words:

"' Child, I think you have a true call.   But you are very young yet—life holds for you many duties, perhaps.   You tell me your mother is, happily, still living.   The religious life is one of His counsels; but the love and service of a parent is one of God's commands.'

" The girl started—she had been trying to deaden the guardian angel's whisper—*duty —stay,*—and the nun's words woke them unto new life.   Had she been wrong?

"' But when spiritual direction has fully sanctioned your call,' the Mother Provincial continued, ' when you are free to leave the command for the counsel, child—our Sisters know you long and well, and I say freely, come to us,—our hearts and our convent doors are open then to receive you.   But remember always that God has His times, and means, and ways, and that His are the best.'

" There was a knock at the door, and the prioress of the house, calling the Mother Provincial out, held a swift, brief conversation with her.   Returning, the Mother laid her hand tenderly on the young girl's shoulder, saying, softly: ' A messenger calls you home at once; a carriage awaits you at the door—'

"A frightened look, a pain at the heart, an intuition, a swift re-calling of her mother's words,—'My mother!' the girl cried.

"'Has been taken ill—not seriously, God grant! child; but she calls for her daughter. Go in God's name, and may He ever guide you. Courage and hope and prayerful trust in Him will bring all things aright. And remember, child, that there is no better prep-aration for a future good religious life than a faithful doing of present duty, a loving acceptance of present pain and sacrifice.'

"They had reached the end of the garden walk. The young girl was borne swiftly homeward ; nor in her sudden grief and fear did it ever enter her mind that for the first time she had crossed the convent portals without a good-bye to her cherished nun.

"Lucy, the dear home-mother's first 'God bless you' was the last: Heart disease had done its deadly work; a loving glance of recognition was all that awaited her. Priest and doctor had been hastily summoned; a servant's hands had prepared all for the coming of the Divine Guest, and held the crucifix to the dying lips, while the child for whose presence the mother had pleaded as with a foreknowledge of what might be, was seeking God in ways and hours of her own choosing. And, Lucy, this sorrowful remembrance tempers every joy of her religious life to-day.

"Lucy, do you know why I have told you this story?"

Both arose; their eyes met. There was no need for words. Teacher and pupil knelt a moment at St. Thomas Aquinas' shrine, the gong sounded the hour for assembling in the classrooms—a new year of school life had begun. But no lesson of the year would bear for Lucy more precious fruit than this. And as her love for her dearest human friend grew more perfect, it grew, if that could be, more tender, more loyal, for she felt that a page of that dear friend's own life history had been given into her keeping. And on her heart seemed written these words: It is not *how much* we love, it is *the way* we love that counts for or against our happiness here—and hereafter.

Mother, by thy holy birth,
Bringing blessings unto earth,

Bless thy children, one and all,
Who to-day upon thee call ;

For thy blessing here below
Is a pledge of Heaven, I know.

With Robinson Crusoe.

Hides the sun 'neath dark'ning sky,
Summer storm winds murmur by,
On the beach rise wavelets high—
    What cares far-off laddie?

Power, none have they to beguile
His young spirit yet awhile
From a lonely sea-girt isle—
    Dream on, happy laddie!

Open page strange story tells,
And the youthful bosom swells—
With his famous hero dwells
    Our enraptured laddie!

   *   *   *   *   *

Boyhood days will pass, we know;
Still will fancy wandering go—
Hearts ne'er anchor here below—
    Do they, winsome laddie?

CHERRY LEAF.

A FABLE.

Edwin Angeloe.

(Conclusion.)

N a few moments Crab Apple came back.

"The Educated Pig will see you in about two minutes. He is busy, just now, eating a cucumber."

"Thank you, ever so much."

"That cat was very disagreeable," apologized the chicken. "He hates the Educated Pig, and is very jealous of him."

"I could see that. He reminded me of the goat I saw yesterday, who said he used to live near here."

"I guess you mean old Gray Billy. I never saw him, but I've heard of him. He went away from this neighborhood long before I came into life. He never had a good word for anybody, as a general thing, and was always boasting about himself. He was really of no use, and they were glad to trade him off for an old washtub."

"You don't seem to be jealous of anyone?" said Cherry Leaf.

"Why should I? I have no fame or education, but I'm very happy, just the same. Other folks' possessions never bother me, and I have a jolly good time all around."

"You are very sensible."

"So my mother says."

"And you have never in your lifetime been envious or jealous of anyone?"

"Never. I'd rather have the pip."

The Educated Pig greeted his visitor without the least formality, which was both a surprise and a disappointment to the black pig, for she expected to find him all dignity and pomp.

When Cherry Leaf heard the jolly little chicken address the other pig by the name of Barney, she was a little disgusted.

" Barney! " she exclaimed to herself. " What a plain, common name! Why doesn't he call himself Launcelot or Romeo? "

The Educated Pig was in an exceptionally happy mood, and he talked to Cherry Leaf very familiarly.

She was quite piqued when he made a mistake in her name, and said: "Hello, Cherry Pit!"

" Oh, do not call me that! " she cried; " it sounds so unrefined. My name is Cherry Leaf. I wish it were even Cherry Blossom. That has something poetic about it."

The Educated Pig grinned. " Is your name copyrighted? " he asked; but she didn't perceive what he meant.

" I have come," she began, "to see if you could help me to gain notoriety and the admiration of the people."

"What do you want notoriety and admiration for?"

" For the same reason that you sought them—for the delights that they give."

"To begin with, I never sought notoriety or admiration; and as far as the delights go, I wouldn't give a grain of corn for the whole business."

"Then why did you tempt fame and fortune?" inquired the Black Pig, who must have got the alliteration out of something she had read."

" I never tempted fame. It came to me. But I did go out for the dollars. My young master, Tony Redpath, had to support quite a family, so I had to work for all I was worth. Sometimes I used to wonder why the S. P. C. A. didn't object; " and here the Educated Pig gave a huge grin.

" Is it true that you are to face a London audience? "

" Yes. I am also threatened with Paris."

"Paris! Ah, how I envy you! "

" I wish London and Paris were not on the earth, for both cities mean hard work for me. I'll be glad when my professional days are over."

" I should think you were fairly dying to appear in those two capitals! "

" Well, I'm not. Sometimes I wish I had never been educated."

" And you don't care to be lionized by the people? "

" I do not. The people are of no importance, in my estimation."

"As for me, I thirst, I yearn, I burn for their plaudits. Oh, that I were in your place!"

"I wish somebody were in my place instead of myself."

"Do you think you could induce Master Tony Redpath to interest himself in me?"

"I once heard him say that he would never bother with any animal but *me*. Of course I don't know what your chances would be if I died, or became a hopeless invalid. Anyway, I wouldn't speak for you even if I thought I could influence him to take you. I have resolved never to help another to professional life— unless that person has to make his living by it."

"You are cruel."

"No, I'm not. A stage-struck person like you would be the very first I'd refuse to assist."

"Hear me," pleaded Cherry Leaf, dramatically. "I beg of you to ask Tony Redpath to let me accompany you to London and Paris. He would be pleased afterward, I'm sure, for the people would rave over my beauty."

"You can't tell whether they would or not. Maybe people wouldn't take to you at all. They fancied me because I'm ugly and funny looking. You're all dignity and polish. If you were crude, like me, perhaps there would be some chance for you. Take my advice, and go home."

Cherry Leaf's histrionic hopes were crushed.

She was inclined to believe the Educated Pig was artfully trying to keep her out of his field, so that he would not be in danger of having a rival, but upon studying him closely, she became convinced that he really spoke from sincere motives.

The black pig looked very sad as she prepared to depart.

"Will you give me an autographed photograph of yourself?" she asked.

"Do not ask for it," he replied. "You want it because I have made a name. Go home, Cherry Leaf, and try to think of me as a plain, unknown pig, without any education."

Tears came into Cherry Leaf's eyes.

"Do not cry. Some day you will thank me for this. It seems unfriendly now on my part, but some day you will see it differently. I will call Crab Apple, and he will show you out."

"No; I prefer to go out alone," said she, not wishing the chicken to see her in tears. "Good-bye!" she added, tremulously.

"Good-bye! Don't feel disheartened Go home, and you'll find it the place of true happiness."

Cherry Leaf came away.

"My beautiful dream is dead," she said, sorrowfully, as she took her way along the dusty road. "I shall never be happy again."

The Educated Pig's words kept ringing in her ears—"Go home, the place of true happiness."

"I cannot go home after leaving there in the manner I have. No, I am too proud for that; and the humiliation would kill me. I will never go back—never!"

She walked along in the depths of despair.

She soon reached the fallen trunk of a tree, projecting far out into a deep, muddy pond.

Climbing upon the trunk, she went recklessly out to the extreme end.

"One plunge will end my misery. I shall drown in this dark pool, and no one will know what became of me."

She leaned over, and looked into the forbidding water, with its green, slimy surface, when suddenly she saw something that made her utter a scream.

In those poisonous depths she saw herself, not dead, but living, with a thousand vile things creeping and crawling about her body, tormenting her with their sharp stings, and laughing at her suffering.

"There is no death for them that leap into this pool," they hissed, "and we love to torture them."

Cherry Leaf was terrified, and she fled from the scene.

She retraced her steps homeward, intending to follow the advice of the Educated Pig, but when she drew near the old familiar gate, her courage again failed, and her pride felt another twinge.

"I cannot go back!" she cried. "Oh, I cannot!"

She recovered a little, and managed to struggle into the garden, when again she weakened.

7

"Oh, I cannot! I cannot bear the humiliation after what I have done. They will all mock me. I will go away again, and become a homeless wanderer."

She was on the point of turning to go out again, when, overcome by exhaustion, she swayed, and sank senseless in a bed of violets and pansies.

And there the children of the homestead afterward found her, and took her in, and nursed her back to life and strength, telling her she had been a naughty pig to run away and give them such a scare.

Cherry Leaf was very grave and sad over her folly, and when she saw how kind they were, and what a truly beautiful home she had left, the words of the Educated Pig came back to her, and she was moved to tears.

THE END.

NINE.

Sister Mary Alphonsus, O. P.

The clock strikes Nine—Oh, joyous hour!
  Nine choirs of angels raise
Exulting hymns, with all their power,
  To their Creator's praise.

And while my earthly work I do,
  They teach my soul to share
In their unbroken worship, too,
  And never-ending prayer.

For prayer and praise are sweetly wrought
  Through every night and day,
In which God's will is simply sought,
  And self-will cast away.

AN ANGEL TEACHER

FOURTH ROSARY MYSTERY.

She bears him to the holy place,
He smiles in Simeon's arms,
And with prophetic words the sage
Her wistful soul alarms.

—Mary A. Mannix.

do not know how to think at all about this mystery, dear Angel; please teach me just what a child should know about so great a thing?"

Surely the angel's wings must have lovingly encircled the kneeling little one; surely an angel hand must have fallen in a caress, a blessing, on the bowed head. The beads passed through the child's fingers, and on her heart grew a beautiful picture, as the angel breathed his holy thought into the young soul; and this is the thought that ever after dwelt in her mind as she said the Fourth Joyful Mystery, the Presentation of the Child Jesus in the Temple:

Dear Little Child: The fourth mystery of the Rosary is called the Presentation of the Child Jesus in the Temple. You will better understand this when I tell you that the Temple was the great church of the people of God in olden times. It was in Jerusalem, and was a most beautiful building. All the people went there at different times to pray and to be blessed. After children were born they were carried to the Temple to be blessed by the priest, as little ones are now carried to the church to be christened.

Our Lord did not need this blessing, but He wished to show respect to the priest and to give good example. Therefore the Blessed Virgin presented Him, or offered Him, in the Temple, and thus it is called the Presentation.

And the good priest took the dear, holy Child in his arms, and embraced Him, praising God because he had the happiness of seeing his Infant Saviour. Then he told the Blessed Virgin that she would suffer many sorrows with her Divine Son.

Dear little child, you were once carried to the church, which is the house of God, and you were there blessed and baptized. Those who held you for the priest, promised that you would be good, and would keep God's commandments. You are now old enough to do this. Do you keep these promises? The Blessed Mother will help you, if you ask her, for the love of her dear, Divine Son, who became a little Child for your sake.

Think of these things while you say the decade of the Fourth Joyful Mystery, and beg your Infant Lord and His Blessed Mother to give you all the graces of the Beads.

A, E, I, O, U.

Margaret E. Jordan.

WE are just five little letters
 Of the great big alphabet;
 People always call us vowels,—
'Mongst the consonants we're set.

All of us but one are equal
 To a word, it will be found:
Tho' each word holds other letters,
 We alone could give the sound.

"Aye," "eye," "oh," "you," please just listen;
 Then us little vowels name:
A, I, O, U,— now please tell us,
 Are the sounds not just the same?

"People" couldn't do without us
 P - - pl -, how queer they look!
B - - k, nothing's left but covers
 If we're taken from a "book!"

P - n, —who could tell its meaning?
 But 'tis clear if you put in
Four of us in turn we'll make it
 "Pan," or "pun," or "pen," or "pin."

C - t,— who could tell, we wonder,
 What a person meant to say:
"Cot," or "cut," or "cat" three of us
 Make three words as plain as day.

B - t, what is it? You wonder,
 "Bat," or "but," or "bet," or "bit;"
All four words you'll have whenever
 Four of us take turns in it.

Reading, writing, speaking, people
 Always need our help, and yet
What are we but five small letters
 Of the great big Alphabet?

  * * * *

When five humble little vowels
 Are of such great use to man,
Little things must all have places
 In the great Eternal Plan.

With Other Young Folks.

Our Animal Friends, in its August issue, has a pretty article, by Stoddard Goodhue, on the goldfinch. There is a European bird and an American one; they differ somewhat in their color, but are alike in many other ways. The European bird is drab, with red about the head and bars of gold on the wings, while a full feathered American bird has a body of brilliant yellow, with black wings, tail, and crown. The European bird was brought to this country some years ago, and sometimes the two little fellows are heard singing together here in Central Park, New York. Mr. Goodhue says that even their call note is the same, they eat in the same way, and both fly with a long, undulating motion. Both of them make good cage birds, and very intelligent pets, and affectionate ones, too. Mr. Goodhue's little bird, he tells us, would perch on his shoulder as he wrote, and coax for seeds with his pretty "tweet"—which in bird language means "please," and if he thought he was neglected, he would give his owner's ear an occasional pinch.

He is not a rare bird at all, but is found both in the country, and in city gardens and parks. Some country folk call him "the wild canary," and others call him "the thistle bird" because he feeds on thistle seeds.

The little fellow does not wear his pretty feathered dress all the year; in the winter his costume is a plain, neat drab. And this is the dress of the mother-bird all the time, and of the young birdies during their first season.

Birds that live always in the foliage of tropical lands, and bright-colored birds who go away from the North to these lands in winter, usually wear their bright dress always. But the little goldfinch does not mind the weather; he stays North. Now, why does he change his plumage?

Mr. Goodhue says it is because he would be "so glaring a signal for the eye of the hawk or shrike when trees are bare." For the same reason, it would seem, the mother-bird who must sit so quietly and so long on the nest, is dressed in a plain color. She and her little nest would never be safe if her enemies, the hawk, shrike, and "bad boy," could see her pretty red and yellow plumage amongst the green leaves.

Is not this a beautiful mark of the providence of Him Who has said that not a sparrow shall fall unnoticed? Mr. Goodhue does not say so, but what is the highest mission of the study of nature? Is it not, boys and girls, to lift the heart to the Creator?

Miss Starr in her pretty book about flowers, and birds, and insects, says that "so perfect are the provisions of the Creator for the safety of His creatures, that they seldom need any care from man, unless actually in his service. But the moment man appropriates an animal he is obliged to care for its comfort." And the same is true of the birds.

The pretty goldie builds his nest much later than other birds, but when he does go to work he makes the daintiest of homes, where his mate, the drab mother-bird, will lay the precious eggs and hatch the wee goldies. And he is most devoted and tender all the while. Scarcely for an instant does he leave the nest, and when he must go for food, he lovingly coaxes his little bird-wife to come with him. He drives every intruder away fiercely, and when he would make her happy-hearted he sings to her a song, sweeter and more tender than those of other seasons. The article contains four dainty illustrations of the little goldfinches.

Birdies singing in the trees,
  Birdies chirping on the ground,
Birdies speeding on the wing,
  Birdies hopping all around.—

Do you ever doubt His care
  Who has made you bright and free?
Birdie's chirp and song say, "No;
  Never, never!" unto me.

Notes for the Children.

The interest in the Angelic Warfare continues, and the young people are working earnestly in this way for the precious girdles that have touched St. Thomas' own, the one given him by the angels, which he wore throughout his life, and which is still preserved in a Dominican Convent in Italy.

These girdles we give to all who work earnestly for the Angelic Warfare. One zealous captain, who has a company of thirteen, writes: " I do pray, and shall always pray, for the Angelic Warfare, and shall do what I can for it. I am very thankful for the girdle, which was entirely unexpected, and I know that I am entirely unworthy of anything so precious. I will send some more names as soon as I can. Ten of these girls in my band live away out in the country, and never heard of the Angelic Warfare before, and I only hope it may benefit them all as much as it has me, for I have many enemies to fight, and would never come out as well as I do if it were not for the Warfare. God bless it, and each soldier in it! I hope the number will grow larger each day."

A brave little fellow writes: " I thought I would like to be a soldier of the Angelic Warfare. I am in the hospital now. I had an operation on my leg. I send you the offering for the girdle and leaflet, but send them to my mother; she will take care of them for me. I am eleven years old."

A letter full of interest has come from that most zealous of Angelic Warfare companies, the soldiers in Villa Maria, Pa. The accounts of battles fought and won by the little folks give promise that life in the future will be lived in noblest ways.

Another touching missive reads thus: " I am a poor little girl twelve years old, living with my widowed mother and only brother ten years old. We both say a short prayer to our Mother in Heaven every night, that we may become soldiers, we are both preparing for Confirmation; please send us both girdles."

The good work of furnishing reading-matter to the poor and unfortunate goes on. One generous worker writes:

" I am very anxious to get one of those precious girdles, and I hope that you will have a great number of cards filled this year. I do not think it is right to leave it all to the children; grown people should help." And as a proof of the earnestness of her words she asks for five cards, which, by the way, have since come in, filled.

Another writes:

" I would like to have THE ROSARY MAGAZINE sent to my poor friend who lives all alone among Polish people. I told her I would send her some reading that I thought would please her." This card has come back filled.

From a wee one comes the request: " Please send me a ROSARY CARD, as I want to help Father O'Neil to send THE ROSARY MAGAZINE to the poor prisoners." In a few days the card came back, with the following dear little note, in the tot's own handwriting. " Please find enclosed $2.00 that I got for THE ROSARY MAGAZINE. I made a mistake in marking the beads on the card. Please send another; I will try to make them better.

" Many thanks for the girdle of St. Thomas Aquinas. I put it on my seventh birthday. I will try to be very good, and will pray for THE ROSARY, the Editor, and you. Yours was the first letter I ever got. When I can write well THE ROSARY will hear from me often." This little girl wishes THE ROSARY MAGAZINE to go to some poor prisoners. A few days more and another letter comes, with the card filled, and bringing a request for still another, which she is sure she can fill before it is time to go to school.

In two families a Rosary Card is kept pinned on the wall, and all the spare pennies go to "make its beads." This is a good example that might be followed in many a household.

Our young folks must not forget that September 16th brings to them the feast of dear little Imelda, who died of the intense happiness that filled her young heart when she received her first Holy Communion.

You all read her life, did you not? It appeared in THE ROSARY MAGAZINE last April, May, and June. Some time, we hope very soon, we shall have her lovely life in book form. She is the patroness of little first holy communicants.

Please send **The Rosary Magazine** *for one year*
to (*Here put name and address of poor person or institution.*)

(*Here put sender's name and address.*)

  If you wish to help send THE ROSARY MAGAZINE to the poor, please write
to AQUINAS for a Rosary Card.

Puzzles.

ANSWERS TO THE PUZZLES FOR JULY.

1. The electro you want is here.
2. Whenever I escape, let me assure you of my fidelity.
3. Disturb, O stony heart, his rest! Rather let him sleep in peace.
4. He was pushed into the wheel; miraculously he was saved.
5. This gem O use always. It will be a never-failing souvenir.

Heel, eel, Troy, ant, hen, Erie, ape, ass, Boston, heart, ear, rat, pea, wasp, asp, heel, eel, Elmira, mouse, seal, bean.

No solver sent a complete answer.

Una Ford, J. H. Flattery, and Mary A. Dougherty, found all but Erie. Ida E. Grossmann found all but heart. Answers from Marguerite Egan, Lily S. Garvy, May L. Carey, Annie A. D. Obenland, contained only three omissions. Answers with less solutions, yet showing careful work, were received from Vincent Ledwith, Mary Menahan, Nellie R. Gavin, Minnie C. Humphrey, May H. Daily, Molly McEnroe, Mamie Delaney, Henry Jochum, William Mitchell, Lily Maxwell, Annie Flynn, Joseph O. Barrett, Eleanor McKernan, and Mary Kelly.

PUZZLES FOR SEPTEMBER.

HIDDEN CATHOLIC AUTHORS.

Following each other in different places will be found letters spelling the last names of Catholic authors.

1. The book? It is a 16mo., on Eylie's table.
2. It was his first arrival since he began his career.
3. Mabel St. Ange? Lo! everyone knows her.
4. She is very coy; let her alone.
5. His name was Rob; Ru now everyone calls him.

A prize will be given to everyone solving the above puzzles.

CONDITIONS FOR BECOMING SOLDIERS IN THE ANGELIC WARFARE.

1. Send your full names to be enrolled.

2. Wear around the waist under the clothing, the little white linen girdle that must be blessed by a Dominican priest, or by a priest who has permission from the Dominicans.

3. Strive in every way to be pure in soul and body.

4. If you cannot buy the girdles in your neighborhood AQUINAS will buy them for you. When you write enclose ten cents to cover the expense of the girdle, leaflet, and postage. You may send stamps. But let no child hold back from becoming a Soldier in the Angelic Warfare on account of poverty. To those who cannot pay we shall send all free.

5. Address your letters to AQUINAS, ROSARY OFFICE. 871 LEXINGTON AVENUE. NEW YORK CITY.

The month of September is marked in special honor throughout the year as sacred to the nativity of our Blessed Lady. We greet her on this beautiful day as the Dawn soon to usher in the Sun of justice. Next in significance to the birth of Jesus Christ, as we contemplate the plan of God's wisdom and love in our redemption, is the birth of Mary. On this glad day, therefore, we hail our Blessed Mother and gracious Queen, with loving greetings from our hearts. Rejoicing in the honor that is hers, happy because of her exalted glory which is reflected on our poor humanity, we offer our devoted homage, our grateful love, our strong hope, in tenderest messages, in most earnest prayer. Let us also make, dear Rosarians, another offering, a testimony of affection, to our Queen. There is only one she desires, and not for herself, but that she may put upon it a gentle touch, a quickening breath, a merit not of earth. She craves our poor hearts, either in the freshness of innocence unspotted of this world, or in sorrow begotten of light that comes upon sin's darkness, when God's love is seen. She longs to possess those hearts, to make them the sure possession of her Divine Son. No offering will be more acceptable, no day more available, than the feast of her most holy birth who came, in God's loving design, to brighten and gladden our poor earth. Lift up your hearts, Rosarians, and lay them at the feet of Heaven's glorious Queen, who is also our most loving Mother.

The sessions of the Summer Schools, at Plattsburgh, N. Y., and Madison, Wisconsin, that closed in August, have left a record of successful work, with encouraging prospects for the coming season. Several of the Catholic weeklies published accounts of the various exercises while the sessions continued. Those not able to attend were thus furnished with a brief history of the two schools. THE ROSARY MAGAZINE expresses its hearty good wishes for the success of the Champlain and Madison schools, adding the hope that both will be practical, that their influence will penetrate Christian homes far beyond their immediate range.

The presence of Professor Maurice Francis Egan at Chatauqua was an evidence of good will and friendliness gratifying to all.

We close in this number Mr. John A. Mooney's fine series of articles on Zola at Lourdes. They have received the intelligent and appreciative recognition of many of our secular exchanges. We have looked in vain for any note of understanding on the part of many of our Catholic publications. As usual, we found the majority of them too heavily laden with boiler plate. They have no space for devotion, scholarship, or fine writing. Mr. Mooney uses a master pen, and never fails to adorn any subject that he touches. His articles in *The Seminary* and THE ROSARY MAGAZINE deserved a widespread and zealous recognition among Catholics. We deplore, because of the interests we serve, the apathy and indifference and "all-around" smallness of many of our Catholic weeklies. If they devoted one-tenth of the energy that they give to cheap gossip and cheaper flattery of men, to the broad interests of a cause they are supposed to serve, there might be a reason for their existence. We shall doubtless be charged, in this matter, with pique, a spirit of resentment because of supposed merits unnoticed. We anticipate the objection by cheerfully stating that the average notice of the average Catholic paper is so devoid of critical or discriminating spirit, that it is without value to any periodical or book desirous of something more than mere notice or stupid praise.

The feasts of the Holy Name, of the Blessed Virgin, of the Exaltation of the Cross, and of our Lady of Mercy, are days of special devotion for Rosarians. Consult the calendar. We also remind our readers that we are near to Rosary month. During October we hope that our friends will show their interest in our work in a practical way. If every one who reads these lines would secure even one new subscriber, how good it would be for literature and devotion!

During the recent General Chapter of the Dominican Order held at Avila, Spain, the Queen Regent revived an ancient custom that during recent years had been neglected. Formerly the Masters-General of the Franciscan and the Dominican Orders, by the very fact of their election, became grandees of Spain. On the occasion of the visit to Spain of our Most Reverend Master-General, the Queen Regent invested Father Frühwirth as a grandee. with all the usual ceremonies attendant on such an elevation. The investiture took place at the court, Madrid.

QUESTIONS AND ANSWERS.

ROSARIAN INQUIRER. -1. *Can the Confraternity of the Rosary be established in a place where a religious community and secular parishioners form one congregation under the same pastor?* It is forbidden to erect the Confraternity in the chapels of Religious; but in a parish church, no matter how small (no impediments otherwise existing), and independently of the fact that Religious attend the same church, the Confraternity may be regularly established.

2. *Can Religious teaching on missions in parishes, or otherwise engaged there by obedience, gain the indulgences of great Rosary Sunday (October), by visiting the parish church?* If the Confraternity is not established in a parish church, these indulgences cannot be gained there by Rosarians. Religious may gain such indulgences by visiting their own chapel, if they are regularly inscribed in the Confraternity. In the case mentioned, the parish church, if there be no other chapel for them, might be considered their regular chapel. This view being correct, they could gain the indulgences by such visits; but we speak subject to correction. So far as we know, no decision has been rendered on this rather practical question. We assure our worthy correspondent that we shall not allow the matter to drop.

3. *Can persons who are not Rosarians gain any higher indulgences by using beads blessed with the Dominican indulgences, than by using beads with other indulgences attached?* Yes; under certain conditions. We shall enter upon this question in a fuller way at another time.

4. *Kindly explain what is meant by a Rosary candle?* The Church grants to priests empowered to bless beads with the Dominican formula, the faculty to bless candles with a special blessing and indulgence in favor of members of the Confraternity. The regular wax candle is used. A plenary indulgence may be gained by Rosarians holding such a blessed candle at the hour of death.

NEWTOWN.—1. *Can any priest who receives his faculties from a Bishop, bless beads in the regular Dominican way?* No; he must have faculties from the Dominican Order.

2. *Does the power granted to priests in missionary parts, include the faculty to bless beads?* Yes; but not according to the Dominican method.

3. *How can a person gain Rosary indulgences who lives where the Confraternity is not established?!* Being properly enrolled and having beads properly blessed, say the fifteen mysteries within the week, and you will share in the good works of the Confraternity throughout the world, provided you remain in a state of grace. Private recitation of the Rosary, or with your family, will satisfy. For Communion, go to any church when it is not in your power to go to a regular Confraternity church.

4. *What book will tell me all about the Rosary?* The object of THE ROSARY MAGAZINE is to make known the literature of the Beads gradually, and in pleasant ways. If our friend wishes a manual giving concise explanations of the parts and mysteries of the Rosary, with a full list of indulgences, we would mention "The Crown of Mary," and "The Month of the Rosary," both by Dominican Fathers, and both for sale by the Rosary Publication Co.

BOOKS.

Part nine of THE BOOK OF THE FAIR finishes the twelfth chapter and the description of Machinery Hall. The opening of the thirteenth chapter, on Agriculture, is also given. The opinion that we have already expressed of this publication we cheerfully repeat. It is a splendid work, truly valuable. The text is clear, full, satisfactory. The illustrations are really artistic, and of undoubted value. The possession of this work, in its fulness will enrich any home. The Bancroft Company, Chicago, are the publishers.

We have received from the University of Notre Dame, Indiana, A BRIEF HISTORY OF THE UNIVERSITY OF NOTRE DAME DU LAC, INDIANA. This volume is more than a souvenir issue commemorating the recent golden jubilee; it is a history of a splendid institution whose foundations were laid more than fifty years ago by that venerable man, Father Sorin, whose name must ever be associated with the record of Catholicity's progress in education in these United States. The story is one of deep interest, and when we consider the far-reaching influences of the University of Notre Dame, we must add that it is also a story of undoubted value. Lovingly told and tenderly dedicated to the graduates who have entered on the battle of life after earnest preparation in the schools of Notre Dame, this volume should be welcomed, not only by the immediate friends of the Congregation of the Holy Cross, but by all lovers of Catholic education, by all who wish to read a beautiful chapter in the history of the Church of America. Most creditable is the work done in this compilation. Though the author modestly withholds his name, we greet him in congratulatory spirit. And we as cheerfully add that the publishers of the volume have done well, in paper, printing, illustrations and binding. The future historian of the Church in the United States will bless the makers of such books.

From Lord & Thomas, Chicago, we have received AMERICA'S MAGAZINES AND THEIR RELATION TO THE ADVERTISERS. This is a handsome brochure cleverly arranged, and full of "good points."

We have received from DODD'S ADVERTISING AGENCY, Boston, THE ADVERTISERS' NEWSPAPER MANUAL, for 1895. We notice this solid compilation because it is not a mere list of journals and magazines, though that would have value, but because it is another practical proof of the enormous and steady growth of advertising in this country. When agencies are willing to publish well-printed and well-bound volumes of four hundred pages devoted to the classification of various newspapers and magazines, whereby a bird's-eye-view can readily be obtained, of this great "fourth estate," it is assuredly of interest to all who wish " to keep up with the times." On this point we are glad to say that our people more generally realize the importance of the advertising department of a Catholic publication, as the matter has been presented to them in an intelligent way. They appreciate its influence for the publisher, as well as its usefulness to the reader.

We have received from St. Francis' College, Brooklyn, the thirty-sixth annual PROSPECTUS of this institution. It is not customary to comment on college catalogues, but we make an exception in favor of St. Francis', Brooklyn, which has been so creditably identified with the progress of Catholic education in Brooklyn almost since the establishment of a bishopric in that city. As Catholic affairs go in this country, this is a long period. And in the case of the Franciscan Brothers who direct St. Francis' College, it has been a period of earnest and devoted labor which has won the approval of the Catholics of Brooklyn in a hearty and affectionate manner. But the service of St. Francis' College has not been local. Its graduates are from all parts of the country, and in every honored calling they have won recognition and reward. The present PROSPECTUS not only tells of the good work of the past, but holds out the promise of still more energetic labor in the future. We notice that the address recently delivered to the graduates of the class of '95, by the Reverend Doctor Brann, on Christian Education, is published in the PROSPECTUS, on which we congratulate the Brothers for this happy thought. On the whole, the PROSPECTUS is pleasant reading. A copy will be sent to any enquiring friend.

From the Angel Guardian Press, Boston, we have received PORZIUNCULA; OR, A HISTORY OF ST. MARY OF THE ANGELS, AND ORIGIN OF THE ORDER OF ST. FRANCIS, translated from the Italian of Father Barnabas, by the Reverend Ubaldus da Rieti, O. S. F. Anything on St. Francis that approaches, in merit, to the subject, is always cordially received, for the " Poor Man of Assisi " is " a name to conjure with." This little book deserves a kind word and an approving recognition. It goes over old and familiar ground, but tenderly, reverently. Following its guidance will be pleasant and edifying. Therefore, we speak of it warmly, and we hope that many will turn to its pages for light and inspiration. We congratulate the worthy Brothers of the House of the Angel Guardian on their good work as publishers, and we trust that they will receive substantial encouragement to continue in their efforts to spread Catholic literature.

From the Charity Organization Society of the City of New York, through the courtesy of the Secretary, Mr. C. D. Kellogg, we have received NEW YORK CHARITIES DIRECTORY--a guide to the charitable and beneficent societies, institutions, and churches of the City of New York. This excellent compilation is true to its name. It embodies a large amount of valuable information that would otherwise be inaccessible to the general reader. We are glad to remind our readers of this Directory, a copy of which should be in every intelligent household. New York is considered a wicked city, but we doubt if elsewhere the world furnishes nobler examples of benevolence, philanthropy, charity. The poor we have always with us, and the people of New York remember the meaning of this word in a truly praiseworthy way.

MAGAZINES.

The Globe Quarterly Review, July, does not contain the usual amount of matter from the editor's pen, but there are notable articles. We think that his " William Penn and the Quakers " is the most valuable paper in the current *Globe.* Eugene Didier's " The Negro in Fact and Fiction," is a sweeping, sledgehammer, unmerciful arraignment of the black man who, according to Mr. Didier's mild terms, is " shiftless, shameless, brutal, deceitful, dishonest, untruthful, revengeful, ungrateful, immoral," as *naturally* given to lying as to stealing." Mr. Thorne supports his contributor to the extent of calling the negro " a loafer, a thief, and an immoral fungus upon the fair life of our southern lands for the last twenty years." Mr. Thorne does not, however, agree with Mr. Didier in accounting Emancipation the greatest robbery ever committed. Nor do we agree with him; nor do we think that the description so vehemently given of the negro is fully satisfactory in as much as it utterly fails to account for the white man's influence in partly making the negro in America what he is. Assuredly there is a heavy responsibility, but Mr. Didier shoots wide of the mark when he tells us of Lincoln's death as a divine punishment for emancipating the slaves.

The Notre Dame Scholastic has issued a special number commemorating the celebration of the golden jubilee of the University of Notre Dame. The story of this splendid affair deserves a permanent record, and the compilation by *The Scholastic* is, therefore, in line. The addresses delivered on the occasion, including those of Archbishop Ireland, Bishop Spalding, and Bishop Keane, are given in full. The University of Notre Dame has rounded out a half century of devotedness to the cause of Christian education, that has justly been crowned by the applause of admiring thousands even beyond the pale of its own graduates. And all has been accomplished under the special blessing of our Lady, whose honor has ever been dear to those gathered about the home of *The Ave Maria.* Our heartiest wishes go out to University and magazine that they may prosperously proceed on their noble work for many years to come.

The Chautauquan continues its series of papers on journalism in the different churches. The August number considers the Baptist denomination. The writer, a man of experience, and fair-minded and judicious in his treatment of the subject, makes some statements with regard to journalism among the Baptists that have a peculiar fitness for some Catholics. "The chief defect of Baptist journalism is the insane tendency to multiply newspapers beyond the needs of a region, and equally beyond any rational computation of its ability to support them. Benjamin Franklin once said that he had never known a family too poor to keep a dog, and if a family were very poor, they usually kept several. Some subtle principle of human nature, impelling men to act to the contrary of their real interests, must have directed the establishment of Baptist papers. *** Almost anybody can start a little paper; it requires a capital, whether of cash or brains, whose attenuation is known only to the initiated; and once started, a paper seems to have more than the nine lives popularly attributed to the cat. This is particularly true of those regions where the standard of culture is not high, and where, for that reason the people especially need papers of a high class. The trashy paper not better than nothing, but distinctly worse, since it keeps out something better flourishes in such communities, to the great loss of the denomination at large." These sentiments are so absolutely in harmony with what we have often expressed, that we take pleasure in quoting them. The Catholic cause is often hampered by elements that are not too plainly designated when we speak of them as incompetence, ignorant local pride, and utter disregard of higher interests than those of some petty bailiwick. The thinking man and the honest man see much to deplore in what is known as Catholic journalism in the United States.

The Forum for August opens with a solid article by Justice Brown of the United States Supreme Court, on "The Twentieth Century." Guided by the light of history, and holding the lamp of experience in his hand, the learned judge views the present condition of the country, and attempts a forecast of the next century. He writes clearly after having thought thoughtfully. He disposes of the absurd claims of those who demand an equal distribution of wealth, in the following undeniable statements: "Under our present social system, with all its faults, the civilized world is constantly growing richer, freer, more prosperous than ever before, the richer less ostentatious in the display of their wealth; the poorer better housed, better clad, and

better fed. Certainly the burden of proof is upon those who claim that this civilization is a failure. Nothing can demonstrate the soundness of their principles so well as a practical experiment in socialism upon a large scale. If a successful experiment of that kind could be offered to the world, they might have some title to claim that civilization should be reorganized upon that model. It must be confessed, however, that the efforts heretofore made in that direction, have rarely met the expectations of their founders." The unequal distribution of wealth is not only a consequence of unequal talent, but it is a stimulus to industry, and the occasion for multiplied industries and arts flourishing that would otherwise decay. While it must be admitted that the gulf between the very rich and the very poor is widening every day, causing a condition of restlessness and antagonism and bitterness on the part of many well-intentioned people, it must be borne in mind that there is much truth in Judge Brown's remarks, that "the average workingman of to-day lives better and possesses more of the comforts of life, than the average noble of six hundred years ago," and that "the sins of wealth, though many and grievous, have not generally been aimed directly at the oppression of the poor." We are pleased to find this distinguished jurist favorably considering the probability and the advantages of Governmental control of railroads, parcel express business, and the telegraph. It is a question that forces discussion, though a powerful opposition confronts it. While taking a hopeful view of the future, Judge Brown declares that "there are undoubtedly certain perils which menace the immediate future of the country, and even threaten the stability of its institutions. The most prominent of these are municipal misgovernment, corporate greed and the tyranny of labor." He discusses each point fully, and is just in assigning a measure of blame to rich and poor, ignorant and learned. He denounces the tendency of the trusts as well as the greed of the ordinary corporation, and suggests a complete overhauling of existing legislation on these heads. He speaks as a true friend of labor when he rebukes the tyranny of labor in misguided strikes, in unjust treatment of fellow-workmen. The concluding sentences of this valuable paper we quote: "So long as we can preserve the purity of our courts we need never despair of the Republic. Of justice it was eloquently said by Sidney Smith: 'Truth is its handmaid, freedom is its child, peace is its companion, safety walks in its steps, victory follows in its train: it is the brightest emanation from the Gospel, it is the attribute of God.' " Precisely. But we must add to the dangers threatening this country, the feeling entertained by many, the conviction held by some, that there are courts where justice does not preside, where there is one application of law for the rich, and another for the poor. And the daily press of New York, not to mention other places, has borne frequent and painful testimony to the ugly fact that the American goddess of justice is neither blindfolded nor furnished with evenly-balanced scales.

In the same number of *The Forum*, W. H. Mallock gives his views as to the alleged socialistic tendencies of an income-tax; Professor Schmidt writes sympathetically and entertainingly of the Goethe Archives in Weimar; an earnest appeal is made to housekeepers, that ought to have a wider circulation than that afforded by one publication; Dr. J. M. Rice pleads for a better equipment of school teachers for their work; Professor Cooke, of Yale, recounts the good results of the Chautauqua movement; while financial and economic questions are considered in three articles dealing with the Bond Syndicate, the drift of population to cities, and the deep-waterways problem. The literary recollections of Maurus Jókai reveal that Hungarian gentleman as a person to whom the *ego* is familiarly and affectionately known. He should have transferred the task of writing his panegyric to his friend and critic, Paul Gyulay.

In *The Westminster Review* for July, there is a notable article on "Education in Ireland, Catholic and Protestant," by H. A. Hinkson. This writer is an Irish Protestant. We mention this fact because *The Westminster* announces it in small capitals, and that it may be considered as sufficient evidence in exonerating Mr. Hinkson from any possible charge of partiality towards the Church. We have not space in which to allow this gentleman to present his own case. We cannot even make sufficient extracts to illustrate our point. We must, therefore, refer our readers to the paper itself, with the assurance that it is "well worth reading," and that Mr. Hinkson, Protestant though he is, proves the superiority of Catholic education in Ireland, over

that directed and controlled by Protestants.

In the same number of *The Westminster*, "Trial by Jury in England" is an instructive paper, while "The Waverly Novels After Sixty Years," by D. F. Hannigan, is an article that many may consider iconoclastic. We agree, however, with Mr. Hannigan in his estimate of Scott, and we believe he is right in his judgment, that in the twentieth century, the Wizard of the North will have few readers for most of his novels.

The Ladies' Home Journal for August contains a bit of practical advice from Ruth Ashmore that we advise our girls to read. It is entitled, "The Girl and Her Money." Like the suggestions generally made in the *Journal*, this article follows closely the line of common sense. The editor gives a brief sketch of "Tom Moore's First Sweetheart," a sad story of the brilliant actress, Mary Duff, who rejected Moore's offer of marriage, and after a varied theatrical career and abandonment of her Catholic faith for Methodism, found her last resting-place in a nameless grave in Greenwood Cemetery, Brooklyn.

The Review of Reviews for August numbers among its special features, " A Character Sketch of Theodore Roosevelt," who is now somewhat conspicuous because of his police work in New York; and "The Clearing of Mulberry Bond, the Story of the Rise and Fall of a Typical New York Slum." Both are interesting papers, especially the latter, which is by Jacob A. Riis, a leading authority in his special line of social and economic writing.

The Freeman's Journal, New York, July 27, did good service in publishing the full text of the Reverend Doctor Conaty's address on "The Roman Catholic Church in the Educational Movement of To-day," read at the Pan-American Congress, Toronto, July 23. In its issue of August 3, *The Freeman's Journal* gives the paper on "Roman Catholic Missions," read before this Congress, by the Very Reverend Dean Harris.

In *The Atlantic Monthly* for August, Mr. G. B. Hill continues his interesting talks over autographs, and Mr. Lowell discusses the oases of Mars. Two papers on political events, "How Judge Hoar Ceased to be Attorney Gener'," and

"President Polk's Diary," are valuable bits of history. In its other features *The Atlantic* runs its regular course.

The Popular Science Monthly for August continues "Pleasures of the Telescope," illustrated. Among other papers of this number we mention as of general interest, an illustrated contribution: "Apparatus for Extinguishing Fires: Development of American Industries since Columbus."

The third number (July) of *The Catholic University Bulletin* contains two articles that will appeal to the scholarly reader, who may not be interested in merely scholastic affairs: "The University of Paris," by the Reverend Doctor Bouquillon, and "German Schools in the Sixteenth Century," by the Reverend Doctor Shahan. In the former paper, the author takes as his guide the Dominican, Father Denifle, whose work on the universities of the Middle Ages he justly characterizes as truly monumental.

Among the miscellaneous questions, the story of the mediæval American Church is pleasantly recalled by the Reverend Doctor O'Gorman.

Percival Lowell contributes to the August number of *The New England Magazine* an article on "Mars: The Flagstaff Photographs," with twelve fine plates. In the same number, "The Story of the Boston Public Library" is told, in a pleasant way, with many pictures. "Machias in the Revolution, and Afterwards," is an interesting page of Maine history. In its remaining portions *The New England Magazine* follows its special line of New England life and description.

In the July number of *McClure's*, we have a fine article on "The Possibility of Life on Other Worlds," by Sir Robert Ball, Professor of Astronomy at the University of Cambridge, England; an account of the telegraphic systems of the world; one of Stanley J. Weyman's stories of adventure; Robert Louis Stevenson's address to the Samoan Chiefs, on the completion of a road to his country house at Vailima, which the Samoans built in gratitude to Stevenson; and a delightful sketch of Edward Kemeys, the great sculptor of frontier life and wild animals.

In the August number of *McClure's* Bishop Vincent and the Chautauqua work are entertainingly sketched in an illustrated article. The well-known war correspondent, Archibald Forbes, gives an insight into the character and methods of Moltke, the great German soldier. Some selections from the Pinkerton archives continue the strange record of criminals that makes weird reading. The story of the "yellow dog," by Bret Harte, is not improved by that would-be witty gentleman telling us how "Bones" died "in the odor of sanctity." The tendency to be smart, if not irreverent, is a bad strain in American humorists.

The opening paper of *Scribner's Magazine* for July, "Life at the Athletic Clubs," by Duncan Edwards, is necessarily an interesting one to the present generation, which is nothing if not athletic. Mr. Edwards deals comprehensively with his subject, and the article is illustrated by fine cuts of scenes from the various sports, and of prominent athletic clubhouses throughout the country.

The short sketch of Elbridge Kingsley, under the heading of "Wood Engravers," and "Posters, and Poster Designing in England," by M. H. Spielman, are attractive articles.

The August *Scribner's* is a fiction number, but those desiring heavier reading will find it in Mr. Theodore Roosevelt's "Six Years of Civil Service Reform."

The Monthly Illustrator for July takes a broad sweep in subjects and pictures. Japan, Norway, Cologne, and Costa Rica are included, with Indian bows and quivers and pottery. "The Artistic Value of Sea Weeds," beautifully illustrated, is a very interesting paper. The August number is not so agreeable, though it contains a generous allowance, barring one illustration of the realistic school. In general make-up *The Monthly Illustrator*, with occasional exceptions, is sustaining its good name as a magazine of art for the people.

The Century for July brings Sloan's Life of Napoleon down to the overflow of the Constitution. Brander Matthews gives pleasant "notes of a book-lover" while discussing "Books in Paper Covers." Fitzhugh Lee writes intelligently and instructively on "The Future of War: Military Operations Affected by the New Weapons." Senator Dawes sketches Vice-Presidents Breckenridge and Hamlin from personal recollections. Other papers that make part of this excellent number are: "American Rural Festivals;" "Picturing the Planets;" and

"A Japanese Life of General Grant," a curious and interesting translation from the Japanese.

The August number of *The Century* has much that is of interest and value. "The Battle of the Yalu," by Commander McGiffin, who participated in the engagement, and "Lessons from the Yalu Fight," by the distinguished writer on naval affairs, Captain Alfred T. Mahan, are given in a way agreeable even to the uninitiated. Sloan's "Life of Napoleon" still runs, with its wealth of illustrations. A sketch of Sonya Kovalevsky, the famous Russian woman who was professor of mathematics in the University of Stockholm; "Reminiscences of Literary Berkshire"; and "A Bit of Italian Merry Making," are in a lighter vein. Max Nordau answers his critics in an article that has considerable egotism, and some blunders (notably those touching the Crusades and the Beguins).

The American Magazine of Civics for August contains several papers of value in its chosen field. We mention a few: "Bimetallism and Currency"; "The Necessity of State Labor Tribunals"; "A cure for the Gerrymander"; "Populism Considered as an Honest Effort for the Securing of Better Conditions." Students will find this periodical a good medium in which to view various shades of opinion on political and economic questions. We do not announce it as an absolutely safe guide; rather, we counsel cautious reading.

Frank Leslie's Popular Monthly for August contains several interesting papers on Samoan life. "Three old Places" is a sketch of the American towns, Perth Amboy, Schoharie, and Setauket, the illustrations of which are many and good. The general reader will find "Caserta: The Italian Versailles," very pleasant reading.

In *The North American Review* for August, Sir Charles W. Dilke, M. P., discusses "The New Administration in England"; the Reverend Doctor Zahm, C. S. C., tells some good things about "Leo XIII. and the Social Question"; the Rabbi Mendes proposes as "The Solution of War," the restoration by the Powers, of the Hebrew people to their Palestine possessions, and the appointment of the newly organized nation as an international arbitrator. Quite an attractive theory, but we doubt if it will materialize. In the same number, the Assistant Secretary of the Navy, William McAdoo, considers "The Yacht as a Naval Auxiliary"; Sir Benjamin Richardson, M. D., tells "What to Avoid in Cycling"; and Her Majesty's Inspector of Prisons, Major Griffiths, supplements Lombroso's work by reflections and reminiscences bearing on "Female Criminals." But the opening paper of this number of the *The North American Review*, the one holding the place of honor, and entitled "The Menace of Romanism," is a piece of infamous drivel. We understand why both sides should be heard, but we fail to see any honorable motive inspiring the Editor of *The North American Review* to admit to his columns so ignorant and vicious a production as that emanating from the pen of the notorious Orangeman, Traynor, the president of the A. P. A. Such an effusion is not only an indecent exhibition of bigoted ignorance and malice, but it is an insult to the intelligence of every well-informed reader of *The North American Review*. The American public is tired of the Orange ruffianism known as the A. P. A., and no reputable periodical ought to admit to its pages the unscrupulous slanderers who are gathered around that un-American and anti-American standard.

The question of marriage and divorce is at present agitating the Church of England if we may judge from some of the English periodicals. *The Church Quarterly Review* for April devotes forty pages to an article on the subject. *The Contemporary Review* for July discusses "The High Church Doctrine of Marriage and Divorce in an article that called forth a reply from Canon Knox Little in the August number of the same review. To those who have the consolations of the true Church as their blessing, it is painful to witness the vagaries and the blind blundering of those whose "Church" goes back only to the unsavory record of a most scandalous divorce as its beginning. It is only the Catholic Church which has stood firm and consistent through all circumstances, on this vital question.

The Contemporary Review for the months of July and August, presents a variety of matter of much interest.

MADONNA OF THE COLONNA HOUSE.

(After Raphael).

The Rosary

| Vol. VII. | OCTOBER, 1895. | No. 4. |

Our Lady's Rosary.

ELEANOR C DONNELLY.

Illuminated missal of the blind!
  Nay, more, their sacred picture-gallery,
Revealing to the sightless (faith-enshrined),
    Visions of light and sorrowing majesty!
     Th' unlettered's school—the poor man's library
Are here. The chaplet of our Mother chaste
The sick and suff'ring bless, and, telling, taste
     Surcease from pain and sin's dread penalty!

Wreathe, then, around our Lady's virgin brow,
  O Angels of October, strong and sweet!
Her chain of roses. AVES, white as snow,
    Shall bind her temples—twine her holy feet;
Till ev'ry grain of her blest ROSARY
  A guiding star to Heaven and her shall be!

339

MAGNA CHARTA OF KING JOHN.

John J. Delany.

I.

MEMORABLE day indeed, in the history of the perennial struggle for human rights, is the 15th of June, in the year of our Lord, 1215, when, at Runnymede, after having been encamped for five days in full armor opposite the hostile tents of the king, the barons were witnesses of the fact that John had signed the Great Charter, which was to insure to them, to their posterity, and to the whole people of England, the beneficent and oft-sighed-for privileges, as they believed, of the Laws of Edward the Confessor. Never since, or before, did king surrender so much of what was commonly considered royal prerogative without having first broken both his sword and his strength in desperate endeavor to resist the demand. Never since or before, as truly may it be said, did a people groaning under such intolerable burdens, act so considerately in the very moment of the plenitude of their power with a despot already crushed in power and in spirit, or urge their demands with such clear-sightedness and moderation. And yet little, if any, credit is to be given either to King John for his prudence, or to the barons for their moderation and patriotism. But a short time before he signed the Magna Charta, John repeatedly asseverated with his usual blasphemous oath —" by God's feet " -that he never would by his own act give validity to that document which was to transform him from "a king into a slave." And the barons, who neither before nor after his coronation had borne any affection for John, whose title to the throne in the eyes of many of them was not at first indefeasible, and was only made so, suspicion whispered, by his having compassed the murder of his nephew, Arthur, were restive in their armor even while negotiations in reference to the Great Charter were pending, and frequently evinced a desire to fulfil, by more heroic means, the oath they had taken to restore

the ancient rights of Englishmen, or to die in the attempt.   The
credit for the seemliness and success which attended the whole
transaction is chiefly to be given to the two men who performed
the delicate and difficult function of mediators between the king
and the barons.   Calm in manner, inflexible in purpose, sagacious in
design, were William, Earl of Pembroke, and Stephen Langton,
Cardinal Archbishop of Canterbury, under whose leadership was
achieved this glorious and bloodless revolution.

Many causes extraneous of themselves aided the Archbishop
and the Earl in their undertaking.   John was crushed by the contemplation of his failures, by the realization of the strength of his
enemies, by the disappointment he had so frequently experienced
in so many of his recent projects, but more especially by the
fear of insecurity even in his own kingdom, which took possession
of him. . The barons, armed to the teeth, presented to his already
frightened fancy an aspect of pugnacious confidence.   He had
learned, too, that they had sworn to wrest from him the concession
of the rights embodied in the Charter, or to die in the attempt.
Some of these causes the Earl or the Archbishop had directly or
indirectly superinduced.   Shortly before, Langton had summoned the barons to assemble apparently for performing the observances of a religious retreat, but took advantage of the occasion to explain to them ancient laws of the kingdom, and to show
them what purported to be the Charter of a former king, which it
was said had been found in the long-forgotten archives of his
Cathedral, and having thus formulated the measures which they
most desired to secure, he administered to them a solemn oath
that each would be true to the other, and would, if need be,
fight to the death to re-establish the laws of the good King Edward.
The intrepidity of his spirit was displayed on his very entrance
into the primatial See of Canterbury, for before he would remove
from John the sentence of excommunication, he compelled him
to swear publicly upon his knees, that he would restore the reign
of justice among the whole people.   He was likewise capable of
availing himself of every argument drawn from abroad to harass
the king's mind.   He had not spent years on the Continent
without acquiring a thorough grasp of European politics, which
he knew far better than the king himself.   Had not men of

every clime sat at his feet drinking in his eloquence and erudition in the University of Paris? Did not scholarship everywhere on the Continent know and reverence his name? Could he not, by the sanctity of his own life, upbraid the king with the grossest licentiousness and debauchery? He was in himself a tower of strength to the cause, and while with all the burning eloquence of which he was the master, he argued with the king, at the same time he curbed the turbulent impatience of the barons with promises of certain success.

The king could not gainsay the truth of the Cardinal's statements, but the force of truth itself would never have swayed the judgment of this ruthless and arrogant monarch, had he not recognized the significance of its endorsement by so powerful a vassal, so rich and loyal a baron, and so ardent a patriot as William Marshall, Earl of Pembroke. The earl made the arguments of the Archbishop his own, and John thus saw, in the persons of the primate and Pembroke, both Church and State arrayed against him. He submitted with hypocrisy, and signed, when he could no longer avoid doing so, a treaty which he never meant to keep, but which is nevertheless the foundation of the British Constitution and the bulwark of English liberty.

The Magna Charta was intended, as one can see, at even a cursory examination of its provisions, to be purely remedial. Its very language implies, where it does not actually express, a purpose to correct abuses. The condition of the people of that epoch was not such as would permit them to indulge in any vague dreams of a theoretical existence. Such theorizing is only consistent with a higher civilization and social state than at that time was possible in England. The lower classes of the population were almost wholly Anglo-Saxon, while the upper and middle classes, with rare exceptions, were Norman. So long as the contest had been waging between the Anglo-Saxon for his hearth and home, and the Norman for a foothold in the country, whatever injustices or injuries were inflicted by one upon the other were regarded by both simply as the fortunes of war. But when the Norman ascendency became an undisputed fact, and the soil had been occupied for generations by those who had never seen and who cared little for Normandy, the Norman and the Saxon began to assimi-

late and take on more of a common national character.   Royal
aggression upon their rights and liberties was not sustained by
one class alone, but by all, high and low, whose positions were
subordinate to the tyrant.   No power restrained him.   The dearest rights which the husband and the father cherishes—the honor of
his wife and daughter—had been ruthlessly invaded by this lecher-
ous king.   Finally, the complaint of one class of the oppressed
found echo in the hearts of the other, and in one common suffering all classes discovered themselves kin.

By far the more numerous, and doubtless the more querulous,
were the Anglo-Saxons; for more than a century they constantly
yearned for the return to the usages and the laws of Edward the
Confessor.   No doubt the story of the peace and prosperity which
prevailed in the days of the good King Edward, ere the foot of
the Norman foeman had sullied the soil of England, had been
told, countless times, by many a winter's fire in the huts and hovels
of the poor, and sire had handed down to son the tradition of a
once exalted, peaceful, and happy Anglo-Saxon race.   The very
mention of these laws filled their minds with an idea of all that
was good for human kind, and it is not, therefore, strange when
the descendants of the Norman conquerors felt the iron piercing
their own souls, that they should condemn the system which made
it possible, and become possessed with that indefinite longing for
the condition for which the great mass of the vanquished yearned.
This yearning gradually assumed definite shape, and had its full
fruition in the Great Charter.

Beyond doubt, in this Charter many of the laws, ancient in the
kingdom, are reiterated.   In it, too, are many principles, fundamental to human liberty itself, and therefore, as applicable to the
polity of any other government as that of the Plantagenets, while
most of its provisions are specifically intended to correct grievances which were the natural outgrowth of the feudal system, and
which the progress of centuries has so refined as to render them
hardly intelligible or interesting now.

Hallam and many of the leading historians of recent times seem
to consider as doubtful the claim that Magna Charta was, to any
great extent, a re-adaptation of the laws of Edward the Confessor; but as this, and all similar doubts, owing to the meagreness

of the resources for historical proof of this period, must be based rather on strained analogy or pure conjecture than substantial testimony, it would seem to be safer to trust the general belief as expressed in the writings of chroniclers contemporary with the Charter, who tell us that the Norman conquerors, triumphant in war over the Anglo-Saxons, were compelled to adapt their condition and society to the jurisprudence of the latter before they could, with security, cultivate the arts of peace. This view would also seem more reasonable, if any credence is to be given to the popular traditions of the time, and these traditions are entitled to exceptional respect, for a people who, under such adverse circumstances, with all the professions, both lay and clerical, closed against them, and their masters speaking a foreign tongue, were able to preserve their ancient language with its idiom pure and its vocabulary little adulterated, are more worthy of belief in their traditions than any historian of six or seven centuries later in his analogical and abstract reasoning. This question, however, except in so far as it may bear upon the origin of the remedies for the abuses mentioned in the Magna Charta, is ot small moment in comparison with the importance of the Charter itself. No doubt the popular belief, right or wrong, had much to do with the unification of the various elements of which the England of that day was composed, and in this way contributed to the stability of the then forming national character, but the grievances were so many and so intolerable that only a faithful compliance with the provisions of such an instrument could give the people required redress.

With the Magna Charta begins the true development of the British Constitution and of the established recognition of what are now regarded as the inalienable rights of the people of England. The expression, established recognition, is used advisedly, because the Great Charter is really rather a reiteration of many rights more or less ancient, which had prevailed at different times, mostly, however, in the reign of King Edward, now in force, now revoked, ignored or disused, but perhaps not all of them in vogue at any one time. To-day a salutary law may have been announced by charter or otherwise; to-morrow either explicitly or implicitly revoked, according as might best suit the malice or

caprice of the king; rights may have been granted by one king
and violated by his successor, and so, while perhaps the main
body of the law comprising the Charter was recognized at one
time, the remainder had but a local, fitful, and disputed sway, enjoying undue force in one part of the kingdom, and being at the
same time a dead letter in another. The great value of this
Charter was enhanced by the fact that it was a codification of
these laws; that it was to be read in the churches twice each
year; that copies of it were to be deposited in all the Cathedrals
in the kingdom and in other places where records were preserved,
thus securing the diffusion of the information of its provisions
throughout the realm, and placing almost in the very hands of the
people the great testimonial of popular rights and the guaranty
of uniform justice to Englishmen of every rank, rich or poor.
Up to this time, the laws of Edward or Alfred or William, however salutary, might be consigned to oblivion or distorted by
their successors beyond recognition; but the publication and the
recording of the Magna Charta gave to it a vigor which, though
perhaps with the change of society it may not now be readily
perceptible, is permanent still. Could its effect ever be lost when
the power to enforce it was vested in a body of twenty-five barons, whose corporate existence was duly provided for in the Charter itself; when it provided that every subject should make oath
to aid in its enforcement, even to the extremity of distressing the
king, and when the king himself stipulated in it that he would
force that oath upon all unwilling subjects? Such an instrument
to be effective, required only the signature of the king, and the
royal power would be by it limited, and the right to enforce its
provisions would be claimed so long as a single patriot dared to
lift his voice or draw his sword for right and freedom.

Fifteen mysteries, on fifteen
   Decades of Blessèd beads,
The Rosary makes; he says it best
   Who best each mystery heeds.

Five joyful mysteries, like five
   Spring roses, snowy white,
Tell of the Holy Infancy
   Of Jesus with delight.

Five mysteries sorrowful, like five
   June roses, deep, and red,
Tell of our Saviour's sufferings,
   And how for us He bled.

Five mysteries glorious, like five
   Large roses, tint like gold,
The resurrection wonderful
   And bliss of Heaven unfold.
      —*Eliza Allen Starr.*

"CONSOLATRIX AFFLICTORUM."

D. J. Donahoe.

I sat in the silence of sorrow,
  Sat dumb in the dole of despair;
For the burden that weighed on my spirit
  Seemed more than a mortal could bear.
And my heart was bowed down on my bosom,
  And thought was more cruel than steel;
For death, with unmerciful torture,
  Had trod on my heart with his heel.

And the hours, with wings blacker than ravens,
  Flew slowly along through the day;
And the day followed slow to the darkness,
  And night to the dawn, cold and gray.
And still I sat motionless, dreamless,
  Nor knew how the hours went by;
Oh, woe for the silence of sorrow !
  For eyes that in weeping are dry !

Then suddenly burst from the darkness
  A glory as wondrous as morn;
And the veil of despair from my spirit
  Was suddenly rifted and torn.
And, lo! in the midst of the glory
  The Virgin appeared with her Child;
And her face wore a smile of compassion,
  So tender and loving and mild.

Then I saw a great multitude crying--
  The poor and the blind and the lame—
And the Virgin spake low to the Infant,
  And the stricken arose in His name:
Arose, and passed out of the darkness,—
  I saw them, with wonder-glad eyes;
And I heard them sing hymns and hosannas,
  That filled with sweet music the skies.

And raised unto hope by the vision,
  I knelt in the rapture of prayer;
And I cried to the Mother of Jesus,
  The wounds of my bosom laid bare.
Then morning rose fair on the mountains,
  The dew on the flowerets shone bright,
And the joy of serene consolation
  Uplifted my soul with delight.

SALUTATIONS.

AN OCTOBER DREAM.

J. W. S. NORRIS.

HE October moon rose beautifully, shedding its soft glow over prairie and meadow and the wandering, winding road.   All along the way in stately beauty, and oh, so pale and pure-looking, waked, or nodded and dreamed, the last of our lingering wild flowers.

Why could not we wake and dream with them?   The Chapel on the Hill seemed not so very far away where our Lady of the Tabernacle guarded, with legions of angels, Jesus, Lover of Souls.

Moonlight, meditation, the beautiful night, our urgent needs, and so many charms of nature to join in our salutations,—why should we not journey on?

For once the lowly shall be exalted, and the jewel weeds from beside their shady rill shall show their splendor on the broad breast of him who pontificates in our charming ceremonial.   The precious asters whose golden crowns seem in the sunshine fit to adorn some royal brow, now gleam like lovely silver stars chastely meet to circle the fair head of but one Fair Queen; the cardinal lobelia, sparkling with dew, becomes a gemmed sceptre, and the late goldenrod, paled to a silvery spray, waves its graceful benedictions as our prayerful procession passes.

Great bellflowers that seem now of the palest blue, swing pensively, nor disturb us in our meditative mood and way.   Even their color is suppressed, that beautiful blue of Heaven's skies, to honor, as it were, our Lady's spotless virginity.   The fringed gentian, too, our sweet little sister of the woods, as dear Saint Francis of Assisi would love to call the fragile darling, appears pale and beautiful, yet murmuring, doubt we not, as in sleep, its *Aves*, with virgin forehead veiled like a lily of the cloister.   We must wait till the morning sun beams o'er the meadow before its

·light slumber is broken by the hushed footsteps of the Bridegroom.

> " Then doth thy sweet and quiet eye
> Look through its fringes to the sky,
> Blue—blue—as if the sky let fall
> A flower from its cerulean wall."

Yes, all are, like ourselves, filled with the beauty of the October night, and seem to hasten us on our pilgrimage.

* * * * * * *

It is midnight now, and each dewy bell sounds, ever so silently, a prayer. The meadow is white with angels whose cloud-like wings wave hither and yon. Through these feathery clouds their sparkling eyes gleam like stars in the gloom, and their beautiful fingers drop tiny golden seeds, like electric sparks, into the hearts of our dear flowers, out of which other lovely blossoms, pure, silvery lily-buds, burst forth and bloom, some with the pearly purity of the moonlight, some with a starry shine, and some— eternal thanks be to our Heavenly Father ·with a golden radiance like the noonday sun. The constant heart's most fervent salutations are golden *Aves.*

Never ceasing in their wavy undulations, like the billows of the sea—though noiselessly—the lilies, pale, starlike, and golden, are wafted Heavenward—great sheaves in the arms of the angels, till the ascending and descending throng pulses like a vast white, feathery plume, almost motionless, on a pearl-hung stairway of stars.

The flowers seemed to sleep, and souls, purely passionate, bloomed about them. These, too, sent forth their lily-bells, and with a fragrance, we imagined, that must have haunted the bowers of the primeval Paradise.

Caught in the arms of the Holy Angels, flowers and blessed spirits soared Heavenward, and immediately a shower of ruby gold descended over the whole world. Our Lady of the Rosary had unlocked the Treasury of the Sacred Heart of Jesus! Oh, gracious prayers of the saints, and of suffering hearts! Oh, loving ministrations of the angels that turn the tears of woe into smiles of joy!

We had wound our way through wood and prairie, over hill and valley, to the lovely chain of lakes, so cold, so steel-like, so fascinating, reflecting here and there a solitary star, and there, when the moonlight melted into dawn, we heard the *Angelus* chime from the old rural church, and the legions of angels who had guarded the lonely sanctuary floated back to Heaven on the first sunbeam.

And there, glory be to God and our Dear Lady, nestling in a little damp hollow of the hillside, we found a cluster of pure white stars—angel-bloom! At once we exclaimed, when, behold! on the veined petals of each waxen star of this grass of Parnassus—so worthy of a poet's pious thought—were fifteen little beads of gold, the Fifteen Mysteries of the Holy Rosary!

We placed a spray of the Heavenly flowers at the Feet of the Immaculate with our sighs, and our pilgrimage was ended. *Deo Gratias! Ave Maria!*

MOTHER of God! when near thy Heart
  The unborn Saviour lay,
He taught it how to burn with love
  For sinners gone astray.
  O sinless Heart, all hail!
  God's dear delight, all hail!
Our home, our home is deep in thee,
Eternally, eternally.

Mother of God! He broke thy Heart
  That it might wider be,
That in the vastness of its love
  There might be room for me.'
  O sinless Heart, all hail!
  God's dear delight, all hail!
Our home, our home is deep in thee,
Eternally, eternally.

Mother of God! thy Heart and His
  Inseparably shine;
The Sacred Heart thou worshippest
  Is dutiful to thine.
  O sinless Heart, all hail!
  God's dear delight, all hail!
Our home, our home is deep in thee,
Eternally, eternally.
              —*Father Faber.*

THE ISLE OF ST. VINCENT.

Rev. Bertrand Cothonay, O. P.

II.

HOSPITALITY OF THE NATIVES.

WORD about my poor old friend, Charles Maquez, at whose house I spent the night. A good old man, at the time aged seventy, of a very melancholy disposition, yet a fervent Catholic. For thirty years he had lived at a distance of twenty-five miles from a church, and yet he remained as firm as the rocks of his mountains. Whenever in a position to visit Kingston he hears Mass, goes to confession, and Holy Communion, and returns home " contented." He is a Carib, not a full blood, but half negro; his wife appears to be a full blooded Carib. He has sons, thirty and forty years old, who are very fine types of Caribs, although of mixed blood.

All around the hut of the patriarch are clustered a number of similar ones, where his children live. This hut, covered with mountain herbs, is divided into two compartments, the dining-room and the bedroom, which was allotted to me, and specially prepared for my reception. A night of refreshing sleep followed the day of great fatigue.

Having with me my portable altar, the dining-room was easily converted into a chapel. It was decorated as much as possible for the sacred and unusual occasion. There I offered the Holy Sacrifice, gave communion to the good patriarch, his wife, niece, and an old Portuguese, and preached to my devout little congregation, encouraging them in their steadfastness in the Faith, amidst the many and great difficulties surrounding them. While elevating the Sacred Host It almost touched the roof of the hut. Rarely have I found greater consolation while saying Mass, so forcibly was the resemblance to the stable of Bethlehem impressed upon me.

TYPES OF CARIB INDIANS IN THE ISLE OF ST. VINCENT.

Here I would say that not only from this aged patriarch and his family, but from the natives in general throughout the Isle of St. Vincent, I received every demonstration of kindly attention. Practically was it evinced by gifts of eggs, fruits, and natural curiosities in quantities. Having expressed a desire for a chart and some views of the Island, I was immediately furnished with

HUT OF CHARLES MAQUEZ, WHERE THE HOLY SACRIFICE WAS OFFERED.

them. Several Protestants visited me at different stations of my tour, and expressed their delight at my visit.

THE VOLCANO.

Having long desired to see a crater, even if extinct, I resolved to visit this one now in reach, Morne Garou, commonly called La Soufrière. I found a mule which consented to carry me half way; when we came to a certain spot more rugged than any we had traversed, it was impossible to make the stubborn beast move. I had to continue on foot by a path barely distinguishable through the hard lava.

After a walk of three hours and a half we arrived at the ledge of the crater. The imposing spectacle of mountain slope and sea,

together with the sight of this crater, fully compensated me for
trouble and fatigue. Can I picture to you the novel scene?
Imagine on the summit of a mountain, a cupola, nearly round,
buried in the earth, two kilometres wide and two deep, and at the
bottom a sulphurous lake, and you will form some idea of the crater
of St. Vincent. The sides of this gigantic cauldron are of solid rock,
bearing the impression of the scorching of the flames. The lake
is accessible only from one side; the others are almost perpen-
dicular. I was told that a party of Americans, some years ago,
brought here a little canoe on the back of a mule, with a large

ON THE WAY TO THE VOLCANO.

quantity of rope to sound the depth of the lake, but they could
not reach the bottom. The lake seems to be on a level with the
sea. Around the cauldron are several chasms through which the
lava flows to the sea.

Ever since the last eruption several new passages can be distinctly seen, even through the cultivated fields. In one place the lava
fills a ravine. A sugar plantation was there at one time, and the
top of the chimney can yet be distinctly seen; all the buildings
and cane-fields are under the lava. This is the Pompeii of St.
Vincent's. All around the crater reigns the most supreme deso-

2

lation.   Here and there one encounters some stunted shrubs and
wild plants.

While contemplating this spectacle, one is really terrorized.   I
sat on the side of this crater, and very naturally my thoughts re-
verted to those three terrible days in April, 1812, during which
Caracas in Venezuela was destroyed, and ten thousand souls perished, when all the craters in the Antilles vomited forth simultaneously, and spread consternation and terror throughout their
vicinity.

Many old people here remember the disaster, and allude to it
in tones of terror.   The whole island appears to be of volcanic
formation.   All these islands of the archipelago of the Antilles,
which appear to be only the summits of a sinking continent, have
decided affinities, for at their base, some kilometres below the
sea, a fire is kindled, which from time to time causes them all to
tremble simultaneously.   Thus, when there is an earthquake in
these latitudes, it is generally felt in all these islands at the same
time.   When I visited the place the volcano had been extinct
during seventy-six years.

Very curious to relate, in the crater is found a species of bird
which is unknown elsewhere.   It is called the *invisible*, because no
one has ever seen it, although all those who pass in a path bordering on the volcano have heard it.   This assertion has been vouched
for by many persons.   An American publication, however, which
has just fallen into my hands, gives me more details concerning
this mysterious bird.   The anonymous author, an ornithologist,
who visited the Antilles some years ago, heard, as did I, the accounts of this *invisible bird*.   Wishing to capture it, he stationed
himself with his gun and some provisions, in a grotto formed by
the lava from the side of the volcano, resolving to remain there
until the mystery should be cleared up.   On his arrival he heard
the cry of a bird, unknown to him, ornithologist as he was.   He
gazed in all directions and could distinguish nothing.

The next day the same cry tantalized him, but he could discover no cause for it.   It was only on the third day, after prodigies
of patience, that he perceived one in a direction directly opposite
to the one from whence the cry emanated, which made him sus-
pect that the bird was a ventriloquist, a supposition which later

on, he says, transformed itself into a certainty. However, after
five days of patient expectation, whilst watching the bird, he
ended by touching it with a grain of lead. On taking possession of it he experienced a happiness which few men, he assures
us, have felt in the same degree.

  "Triumphing when this beautiful plumage touched my hand,"
he writes, "I had already forgotten the privations and hard labor,
of the price at which I had bought it. I had overcome all obstacles, and now I could fix my eyes on this mysterious bird, the
first, undoubtedly, which had been killed in the memory of man."

  Whilst making these reflections, my Yankee relates that he was
so much engrossed in admiration of his bird that he did not observe a frightful precipice until he rolled to the bottom of it with
his prey. If he had been superstitious he would have believed
the Coolie's assertion that the very sight of this bird brings misfortune. The Caribs, on the contrary, pretend that its voice is
that of the tutelary god of the volcano.

  Returning to Kingston, we visited all the principal places on
the coast. This was another voyage made on a tempestuous sea.

TO THE WINDWARD SIDE,--ESCAPE, GOMIÉ, MESOPOTAMIA.

  Escape lies about nine miles to the right of Kingston. I enjoyed its magnificent scenery, which really baffles description.
The road is good, and intersects the hills and little valleys not
far from the sea. My guide was a fine young man, half Spaniard
and half Portuguese, who initiated me in the history and customs
of the places we passed through; the majority of these names
are Indian, last relic left by the natives before their departure
from this island, the possession of which they disputed so long
with the Europeans. Here are some of them, the charming bay
of Colliaqua, from which flows a pretty river bearing the same
name; further on we encounter the river Bibishe; then the bay
Cubaimarou, Carapan, etc. I found the church of Escape in
process of construction,—the roof was not yet on. The last hur-
ricane which devastated Saint Vincent (they are of frequent occurrence in this island) swept away the church with its little presbytery. But this little chapel is built of solid masonry, and appears to be destined to defy the most violent tempests. Unfortunately, the poor pastor of Saint Vincent informed me that he

THE VILLAGE OF ESCAPE AND THE CHURCH OF ST. VINCENT.

had been obliged to suspend the work, his resources being exhausted. I encouraged him to hope for help from some unexpected and charitable quarter.

A glance at the map of the Isle of St. Vincent (see page 359), and my readers will be able to locate me when to the windward, that is to say, " to the wind of the island." I assure you that I heard this terrible wind which brought the sea to my feet, and caused it to foam against the shore. At Trinidad we are sheltered on all sides, and our sea is a peaceful lake, but at St. Vincent, specially at this side, it is always tempestuous. I spent the night at Escape, in a little plank hut, situated on the top of the hill, one hundred feet above the level of the sea, the hill being nearly perpenaicular with the sea.

The church not being finished, I said Mass in the little hut where I had spent the night, my congregation consisting of several negroes, and a few Portuguese, who for a long time had not been able to assist at the Holy Sacrifice.

At Gomié I found a little wooden chapel built on the summit of a very steep hill. There are but few Catholics here.

A short distance from Gomié I visited a curious boiling spring. The hole from which it rises like a water spout is about a foot in circumference. The water is very clear, very gaseous, slightly sulphurous. In Europe it would, in all probability, be worth a fortune. The physicians in the neighborhood say that it possesses very curative properties.

On leaving Gomié I descended towards a charming valley, where two limpid rivers flow parallel with each other. The Catholics have in this valley a little school, kept by a Portuguese, where I found forty children. This valley is called Mesopotamia. How delighted was I to find true " children of Abraham " in this valley so named!

On the windward side there is a species of small green lizard, which attracted my attention by its excessive familiarity, carried to the extent of jumping on my shoulder and eating from my plate. Curious little reptile! Instead of flying from the company of man, like so many others of its species, it seems to delight in his companionship. It stations itself at about two steps from the traveller, and regards him attentively for some time without mov-

ing. One of them afforded me a great deal of amusement. Clinging to a pane of glass, its fins serving the purpose of nails, it made
repeated efforts to bite a little grasshopper which was on the
other side. The poor little thing could not understand that the
glass was between itself and the insect. This useless struggle ended in another disappointment. One of its brothers was
on the other side of the glass, and seized the grasshopper without any trouble.

BELLEVUE.—GEORGETOWN. —DIAMOND ESTATE.

At Bellevue I found a little church, a school, and a presbytery·
The latter is a little further away from the sea than the one at Escape; it is about two hundred steps, yet the roaring of the sea is
heard as distinctly as though it were at the very door.

Many Portuguese are settled in this place, which owes its preservation of Catholicity to the generosity of a Scotchman, Mr.
Gerold, a convert from Protestantism, a man of great and practical faith, the proprietor of the Bellevue estate.   Upon his own
grounds, and at his own expense, he built church, presbytery, and
school.   During his lifetime he edified his laborers by his assidu-
ous observance of all the duties inculcated by our holy religion.
His life was prolific in charitable deeds, and his influence for
good was felt for miles around.   He died a few years ago, and his
memory is held in benediction amongst these poor people.   One
of his three sons became a member of the Society of Jesus; another
is an officer in the West Indian Army; the third is a lawyer, who
comes to St. Vincent occasionally to inspect the property.

Journeying on horseback from Bellevue to Georgetown, one
gets the full force of the sweeping wind, a sharp contrast to the rays
of the sun which beat upon the Bellevue chapel.   Between these
two points the landscape is magnificent, picturesque, imposing,
sublime!   Around Georgetown one is astonished at the aspect of
well-cultivated fields.   Georgetown contains two or three thousand inhabitants, about five hundred of whom are Catholics.   The
church is of stone, well built, and is another proof of the zeal of
Mr. Gerold, the generous benefactor of Bellevue.   The presbytery is two hundred feet from the shore, against which the enormous waves dash with a deafening tumult.

A family of Catholic Caribs came to see me from Sandy Bay,
ten miles away, where there are only three or four families of
Catholic Caribs; a few others dwell in scattered places, along the
coast from Curia to Fancy. Very few of them are of pure Carib
blood, negro blood being more or less intermingled.

Georgetown, on the windward side, is nearly opposite the hut of
Charles Maquez, which is on the leeward, and, like that settlement,
is situated at the foot of the sulphur lake, Soufrière. The lava
from the volcano seems to be diffused still more abundantly on
this side than on the leeward, and the sea which receives it in

such abundance, invariably returns it to the shore after having
intermixed great pebbles. The shore on all this side is formed
of a prodigious quantity of lava, and the houses are built of it.
The sand is as black as ink. Beyond Georgetown, to the interior,
lies the track formerly called Carib Country, being the country
allotted by the Government to the original owners of the soil.

Diamond estate is situated about a mile from the sea in the
midst of charming hills, half still covered with shrubs, and the
remainder cultivated with sugar-cane and arrowroot. At the warm
invitation of the manager, Mr. Da Silva, I there spent the day.
He is an old Portuguese, a fervent Catholic; he was happy to serve
the Mass, which I said in his house. A Christian of the old stock
is he, and his family interesting and worthy in every sense of the
word.

From the seashore I enjoyed, for nearly an hour, one of the
most beautiful spectacles possible to contemplate, even in the
West Indies, where nature everywhere blends sublimity and
beauty. Behind me a number of incomparable hills, a towering
amphitheatre, on a level with the high mountains in the interior
of the island, and before me the sea, the great Eastern sea, dashing against gigantic rocks, into a bay one mile in width. The sea
being very tempestuous here, has demolished the hills, heaped
the rocks together, and formed gigantic cliffs. However, with
all its strength it has not succeeded in sweeping away a little
island, a few kilometres wide, situated about a mile from the shore.
Further on, bordering on the horizon, appear the grenadines,
sparkling like brilliant gems under the burning rays of the sun.

Reluctantly I withdrew from this enchanting shore; this grand
spectacle so thrilled me that involuntarily I murmured:

"I love the bellowing waves which lash the giant cliff;" "Look through
nature up to nature's God."

Back again to the capital, Kingston. Protestants and Catholics
alike flocked to behold the sight so seldom seen on the island,—
the administration of the Sacrament of Confirmation. The Govern-
or and all the prominent citizens were present, and their attention
was edifying. The Protestants of St. Vincent have really a Catholic spirit, and a true appreciation of the Catholic ceremonial.

" I prefer indeed the Catholic Church," exclaimed one, " where everything speaks to the soul, and raises it to God." Nor is this the sentiment of one person alone among those outside the fold. But though the harvest is fast ripening in the Isle of St. Vincent and the adjacent isles, the laborers in that vineyard of the Lord are few.

SAINT LOUIS BERTRAND, O. P.

APOSTLE OF NEW GRANADA.

MARCELLA A. FITZGERALD.

HAIL! Saint of heavenly zeal, whose holy hand
  Reared Christ's dear Cross upon the pagan shore,
  Who for His sake the keenest sufferings bore
In the rude fastness of that savage land,
When mountains wild, and desert's burning sand
  Beheld the wandering tribes bowed down before
  Our Saviour and our King.   To Heaven's door
What countless voices rise in chorus grand,
  Earth's sweetest strains of fervent praise and prayer,
Upswelling from the scenes where once you wrought,
  Faith's blest Apostle! pleading for a share
In your heart's love,—pure heart with blessings fraught!
  Till safely led by your fraternal care,
  O Shepherd true! your sheep are homeward brought.

ST. BONAVENTURE tells us that all the angels in Heaven cry out incessantly to Mary : *Sancta, sancta, sancta Maria, Dei Genitrix et Virgo*—"Holy, holy, holy Mary, Mother of God and Virgin ! " and that they offer to her, millions and millions of times a day, the Angelical Salutation, *Ave Maria*, prostrating themselves before her, and begging her in her graciousness to honor them with some of her commands.

St. Michael, as St. Augustine says, although the prince of all the Heavenly Court, is the most zealous in honoring her, and causing her to be honored, while he waits always in expectation that he may have the honor to go at her bidding to render service to some one of her servants.

       — Blessed Louis Grignon de Montfort, O. P.

A TRUE STORY OF THE ROSARY.

F. H. M.

LMOST a century ago, there lived in Anne Arundel County, Maryland, a very lovely young Quakeress named Patience. It is not necessary to give her surname ; among the " Friends " any form of address save by that of the Christian name, was seldom, if ever used. So in our little sketch we shall speak of this young girl as she was spoken of by those who knew and loved her.

What a quaint, odd-sounding, and withal, pretty name—pretty because of its very oddity —Patience is to our modernized ears ! Unfortunately, though, it is a name which would be in many cases very unsuitable, but according to a tradition among the grandchildren of the Patience in question, she was most appropriately named, as the virtue of patience was one of her marked characteristics.

Indeed, we not only know her characteristics, but can readily bring before the mind's eye a vivid picture of the appearance and manner of this young Quaker girl. The effort is not by any means entirely one of the imagination, for often have we listened to word-pictures of her from the lips of one who so tenderly cherished her memory, that he never wearied of praising her graces of mind and person.

According to this devoted chronicler, besides her sweetness of disposition and brightness of mind, she was very beautiful, though she was, when he first remembered her, past girlhood.

We love to think of her, though, in her maidenhood, and study her character before the gaiety and bouyancy of a light-hearted girl were toned down to accord with the grey dress and wide brimmed bonnet, which partially concealed, only to enhance the charm of the fair face and innocent blue eyes.

These Quaker dames of long ago, had, however, their coquetries of dress, in spite of their demureness of manner. True, the drabs and greys and mauves were necessities as to color, but no church law controlled the quality of these sober-colored fabrics, so they could be as costly and elegant as the most fastidious feminine taste could desire.

We may fancy, then, our Patience, in rich silks, and brocades, and satins that stood alone, with a film of rare old lace about the delicately turned wrists and white throat, at which it was doubtless fastened by a cameo brooch, that in our day would be too large for any purpose, except to keep as an heirloom.

We can imagine, too, that as she stood before the small square, old-fashioned looking-glass, and put the finishing touches to the dark hair, piled like a turret upon the top of her head, and drawn over the dainty ears, as was the style of the day, that she experienced the same pleasure that any pretty girl feels when she sees the reflection of her sweet self. It may have been, too, (the most of us are fond of forbidden pleasures), that as she viewed her quiet-colored gown, she gave a little sigh of dissatisfaction, and longed for a bit of color with which to brighten its soberness.

That the girlish love for bright hues predominated, at least one time in her life, over the Quaker teaching in regard to " worldly colors," is certain, from her own account. She used to tell, how upon one occasion, when she was going to be present at a gathering of young people, she slipped into her pocket a piece of cherry-colored ribbon, which she made into a bow, and fastened in her hair, after arriving at what we would call " the party," though the term with us implies amusements,—dancing, and the music of the violin—which the sober friends would regard as most ungodly.

Trusting to good fortune and the silence of the younger Quakers, whose ideas in regard to dress were, in many cases, broader than those of their elders, Patience bloomed forth in her gay ribbon head-dress, and enjoyed it very much.

Unfortunately, however, her lucky star seemed to desert her; the story of the cherry-colored ribbon crept out, and the wearer of it fell into deep disgrace. For weeks after, the Aunts Deborah, and Hannah, and Rachel, assisted by many grave uncles and cousins, held up their hands in holy horror, and delivered long lectures to poor little Patience upon the wickedness of imitating the dress of the " worldly," and predicted all kinds of dire misfortunes as the result of her waywardness.

While all this may seem somewhat ridiculous from our standpoint, and when considering the triviality of the offence, there is nevertheless something very beautiful and attractive in the simplicity, the earnestness, the gravity, the repose of the Quaker and his belief.

There is a spirit of self-abnegation in their original rule, and a punctiliousness in its observance, which has in it one of the first elements of religion.   What a firm, unrelenting grip they seem to put upon the very foibles of human nature! what a fine discipline pervades their ranks!

The plain dress, the curbing of the natural disposition, which is necessary before they acquire the uniformly gentle deportment and repose of manner which mark them, the renunciation of pleasures which are in themselves harmless, all denote a willingness to bear mortification, which, no matter where found, claims admiration and respect, for who among us does not bow down in silent acknowledgment where we find the spirit ruling the flesh!

There is, occasionally, a mistaken tendency towards confounding the Quaker and the Puritan; it seems almost needless, though, to point out the direct antithesis between the doctrine of the Quakers and the numerous doctrines of " election " held by the Puritans.   The teaching of Quakerism is, that there is a direct revelation of the spirit of God to each particular soul; this light is universal, consequently the love and grace of God toward mankind is universal.   They do not recognize the necessity of a visible administration of the sacraments; with them all is inward and spiritual.   They accept Christianity as embodied in the Creed, but they hold that no form of religion is so good as a " patient waiting upon God in silence."

The only resemblance between these sects is that both denominations are strict and formal, but in the latter these qualities degenerated into fanaticism and intolerance, while the gentle Quaker only asked freedom to worship God as he pleased, cheerfully granting to others the same privilege.

They were, and probably still are, a clannish sect, and cut themselves off to a great extent from people of other religions, while
this same quality made them cling to their faith with a tenacity
born possibly of isolation.

They require a strict observance of rule by the members, and
what would seem, to an outside observer, "trifles light as air," assume in the eyes of the "Friend" a proportion which, taken
away from its background of religious discipline, seems almost
absurd.

Again, in turn, it can readily be understood that the strict adherence to form might sometimes become galling to the younger
and less disciplined of the Friends.

Be all this as it may, it is just possible that, when at about the
age of sixteen, the Patience of our story was guilty of an act of
open disobedience to church and parents, that the old cousins
and aunts and grey-beards may have shaken their heads solemnly, and felt a mild satisfaction in the fulfilment of their predic-
tions made at the time of the cherry-ribbon escapade. Indeed,
some of the more prophetic of the Friends—it is so easy to be
prophetic after events have taken place—may have indulged in
the usual but always consoling—" I told you so."

Of course this is a mere matter of surmise. All this happened
so many years ago that we cannot vouch for details, but we can
always vouch for human nature; consequently, we are safe in as-
suming that there was a very certain complacency mingled with
the possible regret of these soft-spoken, mild-mannered Quaker
folk, when their kinswoman defied the church law, and married
a first cousin.

The name of the young man was Jared H. He was a Quaker, too,
as his name indicates, and a man of sterling worth and fine ability,
but nevertheless a cousin. Whatever the law on the subject may
be now, it was, in those days, against the rule of the Quakers for
those so nearly related, to marry; consequently these two young
people, so the story has been handed down, by their disobedience
brought upon themselves the displeasure of family and friends.

There was the usual stir and talk that there is always upon such
occasions, but after the inevitable step had been taken, there was
nothing to be done but to accept the situation as philosophically

as possible; so the family made the best of the matter, and
strongly urged upon the young people the necessity of making
the one concession by which they might remain within the pale
of their church.

The condition offered them was a public expression of regret
for their marriage. As neither was willing to conform to the condition (and though it may be rather heterodox, we cannot help
applauding this evidence of their devotion and loyalty to each
other), they ceased to be regarded as belonging to the Society of
Friends, though they continued to wear the quiet garb, and use
the form of language peculiar to the sect, while they remained
staunch in their faith.

As the years slipped along, these two renegade Quakers were
singularly blessed with such things as bring earthly happiness—
a beautiful home, which had come to them by inheritance; honorable position for the husband; healthy and intelligent children;
and above all, a thorough congeniality and unity of purpose between husband and wife.

The only shadow which hung over this happy household was
the frail health of its mistress. While not a confirmed invalid,
being able to take upon herself many duties, she was nevertheless unquestionably delicate, and consequently a constant source
of anxiety to her husband and children, some of whom were now
grown.

Although naturally active, and accomplishing much in spite of
her constant indisposition, there was scarcely a day past of which
was not spent in needful rest, in order to guard, as prudently as
possible, her slim stock of strength.

One day in early springtime, feeling tired and ill, she lay
down for her accustomed rest upon a lounge in the family sitting-
room.

It was a lovely day; every window was thrown open, and into
the room came the sweet air laden with delicious odors from the
pink and white blossoms of the fruit trees. The birds were making merry in the glorious sunshine, and every now and then one
would send a shower of snowy petals to the ground, as moved by
some impulse, it flew swiftly away.

Back of the old-fashioned garden, with its wealth of thyme, phlox, hundred-.eaf roses and eglantine—the especial pride and delight of its mistress,—she could see the meadow in which the gentle cows were browsing; still beyond this, silhouetted against the soft, fleecy May-clouds, the line of spire-like Lombardy poplars, which outlined the limit of her husband's estate, and skirting the whole, the hazy, dark blue of the horizon which marked the course of the distant Patuxent river.

After enjoying all this loveliness till weariness overcame her, our invalid closed her eyes, and lay resting, though not asleep. In speaking afterwards of the events of this day, Mrs. H. made a particular point of the fact that she was not asleep.

"Suddenly," she says, "I heard a sound as of the rustling of silk. Opening my eyes to see what caused it, I beheld, to my amazement, a most beautiful woman standing just within the doorway. Her arms were extended, and in one hand she held a necklace of beads, on which hung a cross. Her dress was of white silk embroidered in gold, and upon her head was a crown of roses.

" Her face was so beautiful in feature and expression, and there was such an irresistible charm in her mere presence, that without any seeming act of volition, I found myself drawn nearer to her. I did not, as ordinarily I would have done, wonder how, or from whence this lovely stranger came, but only felt a peculiar peaceful satisfaction and joy in the knowledge that she was with me, and forgetful of physical ailment, I started rapidly towards her, when at that moment, without a word or sign, she vanished--simply melted from my sight."

Such is the account given by this Quaker lady, of an apparition of which, at the time, she had no understanding whatever; nor had she ever, within her recollection, seen a picture or statue of our Lady.

While this may seem incredible to us, we must bear in mind, not only that this happened nearly a hundred years ago, but consider how little intercourse there was between the Quakers and other religious sects.

Of course we readily recognize the above word-picture, but she who had witnessed the wonderful sight had not the faintest understanding of it. After the first impression of pleasure and wonder had passed away, Mrs. H. became greatly agitated, and started, hurriedly, from the room in order to see and speak with some one concerning what she had seen.

How often are God's instruments humble! At the door she was met by an aged negress, "Aunt" Mary Queen, a devout Catholic, who for years had been in service at the old "White Marsh" church, which is a landmark in the Catholic history of Maryland. The coming of the old woman was most unexpected; ordinarily, it was never more than once or twice a year that she had an opportunity to see "Miss Patience," to whom she was much attached; so her unusual coming upon this occasion was always regarded, both by herself and "Miss Patience," as by the especial direction of God.

The account of what she had seen was given with great excitement, nay, almost fright, by the refined lady to the humble serving-woman, interrupted by frequent ejaculations of praise and thanksgiving from the latter.

After the tale was told, this lowly friend explained, to the best of her ability, what she understood and believed the vision to be, and so full of zeal and faith were her words, that she succeeded in impressing her listener with a belief in the supernatural agency which had been exerted in her behalf.

So much indeed was she influenced by what she had seen, and what the good old woman said, that she promised to follow Aunt Mary's advice, which was to say nothing about the apparition to any one, and to see a priest at the earliest opportunity.

True to her promise, Mrs. H. went in a few days to consult the pastor of the "White Marsh," for so the old church was called for miles around, instead of by the name of the saint of its dedication. The name arose from the appearance of the bog that surrounded the church property, which was of a peculiar chalky whiteness.

The distance to the church was long, but this was a matter of small consideration to our newly-awakened soul, who longed for full enlightenment, and the peace and comfort which she felt it would bring.

"When I reached the White Marsh," Mrs. H. afterwards said to her son, "I was so frightened at what I was doing without Jared's knowledge, so excited at the idea of talking to a priest, when I had never even seen one, and so overwrought by the new and strange condition of my mind, that I could scarcely walk from the carriage to the house."

The manner of the good priest must have been reassuring, for she managed to pour out to him her wonderful story, "though," she said, "I did it so vehemently, so excitedly, that I've always wondered how he understood what I was talking about."

After listening kindly and attentively to the account given him, this new director promptly decided that God had seen fit to bless, in a special way, this favored soul. After talking with Father —— for some time, Mrs. H. became so convinced of the truth of his explanation regarding her "beautiful Lady," that she expressed a desire to read and learn of the Catholic faith, and so eager was this earnest neophyte, that the first instructions were given during this visit, and she carried away with her such books as her instructor deemed advisable.

The way to the faith now seemed to her plain and easy. The means taken for her conversion were so marked, so gratuitous, at least to her believing eyes, that it seemed only necessary to tell her husband and children of the favor bestowed upon her, in order to open their eyes as hers had been opened. When faith is real and living, it always seems easy to convey it to others, particularly to those we love, and who love us.

Alas for our zealous convert! In proportion as the spiritual life became clear and beautiful, the domestic life became dark and stormy. When Mr. H. saw that his wife was thoroughly interested in Catholicism, he was naturally, all the circumstances considered, much annoyed. Here, however, the matter rested; it was not until she declared her intention of entering the Church that his annoyance became anger, and he positively forbade her going again to a Catholic church, or holding any communication with its priests.

Imagine the trial that it was to this gentle lady, who up to this time had received only the most devoted love and consideration from her husband, to find that she must either incur his displeasure, or go in direct opposition to her conscience! Knowing that her first duty was to God, she disobeyed her husband's commands, and was baptized.

Now the opposition of Mr. H. began in earnest, opposition which amounted almost to persecution. In order to prevent his wife going to Mass, he sold her horses and carriage. The next Sunday she walked to church, a distance of ten miles. Failing by this means, every conceivable impediment was put in the path of her duty.

Of her eight children, all were now grown except two, aged respectively five and seven years. These two little boys she was obliged to take away from the older members of the family when teaching them their prayers and catechism, so strong and bitter was the animosity against her faith.

The elder of the two received the mother's teaching under compulsion, while the younger was docile and willing. A point is made of the different manner in which these two young hearts received the faith, because the beginning of their spiritual lives was an earnest of the end,—the elder of the two never accepted the teaching of the Church, while the younger died with all her rites.

But to return to their mother. During the time of severe trial to which she was subjected, she was unswerving in her devotion to her religion. Nor was this all; she was equally devoted to the interest and happiness of her husband and children in all that did not clash against her faith. Never was a single duty forgotten, never a single opportunity lost by which she might contribute to their comfort. In things small and great, she exercised a wisdom and tact, which could be nothing less than an answer to her unceasing prayers.

In spite of all this, Mr. H. could not reconcile himself to his wife's new faith, and in this opposition he had the sympathy and countenance of a large family connection. There are probably no people who regard with more respect and consideration the opinions of their relations than the Quakers, so their universal disapprobation was not the small cross to Mrs. H. that it may appear.

Among these relatives was a cousin, who must have been, judging by the light of after events, a very wise and just old Quaker. In deep grief and anxiety Mr. H. went for advice and guidance to this cousin, who besides being a relative, was a dear and valued friend.

After listening to the husband's story from beginning to end, and asking a question here and there, the old gentleman finally gave the advice which proves his wisdom. "Jared," said he, "I think the best thing for thee to do is to let Cousin Patience alone. If what she is doing is a mere whim, time will cure her, and opposition only makes her worse; but if," said he, solemnly, "the Spirit of the Lord is moving her, nobody can change her; so you see in any case the best thing is to wait, and see how it will all end."

From this moment Mr. H's open opposition ceased, though the dormant dislike of everything Catholic remained in his heart. God, however, sustained the wife when all earthly comfort seemed so far away.

Day by day her beautiful, resigned life, and unremitting devotion to our Lady in the Rosary, were producing their effect, although it could not yet be seen. In about a year after her baptism, her husband allowed her the means of getting comfortably to church, and wonderful as it may seem for one who had been so violently prejudiced, the bitterness of his feeling seemed to be gradually wearing away.

"I had not been a Catholic two years," said his wife, "when I saw him upon several occasions display the greatest anxiety when any incident occurred which threatened to make me late for Mass. Under no circumstances, though, would he accompany me; indeed, I never urged it, thinking it best to wait; the seed had scarcely been long enough planted."

In a very few years our heroine—surely a heroine in the true sense of the word—had the happiness of seeing her eldest daughter baptized, and, gradually, each one of her children with a single exception, followed in the footsteps of their mother.

The crowning joy and reward came, however, when the beloved husband, for whom his wife had shed so many tears and said so many prayers, joined the Church of which he ever after remained a devoted member.

So it was, that God not only loved and blessed her personally, but for her sake He blessed each member of the family with the faith so dear to the mother, with the exception of one son, for whom she never ceased to pray and hope.

An incident is connected with this miraculous conversion which carries with it a peculiar significance. Many years after Mrs. H. had become a Catholic, she was overlooking some much-prized books which had been in the family for generations. Present, was one of the Fathers from the White Marsh, a young Jesuit, indeed, it was for the purpose of allowing him to select from the books any that he might wish to read or study, that she was searching through these ancient volumes. From among them, the quick eye of the priest singled out a Bible of the old Douay edition, brown with age, but perfectly intact. On the fly-leaf, in typical English characters, was written, " Beulah Howell, St. Joseph's Parish," and under this, in the same hand-writing, a date prior by seventy years to Mrs. H's conversion.

The name Mrs. H. recognized as belonging to a far-back grandmother, but of her history, or how a Catholic bible came among her possessions, she knew nothing. Being much interested, she determined to trace out the story; so with the assistance of old letters, some written family history, and a little tradition, she discovered that " Beulah Howell " had been a young Catholic girl who renounced her faith to marry a Quaker, but had lived only a few years after her marriage. When dying, she had begged so piteously for a priest that this privilege was allowed her, and she had the happiness to receive the full rites of the Church.

The two little daughters she left were brought from Philadelphia, where their parents resided during the mother's life, back to Maryland, and reared Quakers, while the story of their mother's Catholicity was hushed up, as though it had been a crime.

But the voice of prayer cannot be hushed; it pierces all time and distance and conditions, till it reaches the Eternal Ear. Faith tells us that the impalpable hands of poor Beulah Howell, purified by Purgatorial fires, were raised in loving, passionate pleading to the throne of mercy for those descendants whom she had so wronged. True, she had sinned, but she had for an excuse, youth, swayed by that strongest of human passions, love.

Who can know how many bitter struggles this poor young Beulah had with her conscience before she gave up her religion for her Quaker lover! Who can know all the palliating circumstances of her sin,—her surroundings, the weakness of her heart, her longing for human love and protection, the dreariness and desolation of a life stretching out before her without these comforts!

Surely we cannot justify her, but looking into our own souls, and viewing clearly and honestly our own peculiar weakness, with a sufficient amount of temptation brought to bear upon it, we at least may repeat the words of the Master: "Who will cast the first stone?"

In His tender love we believe that God deals with us according to the strength or weakness of our natures. May we not believe that He considered the strength of Beulah Howell's temptation and the weakness of her nature, and that He indicated this by His giving her the grace of repentance?

Whatever may be the theology on the subject, this was the belief of the grateful Patience, who always attributed her own conversion to the intercession of this repentant, if erring grandmother, for whom she offered up many earnest prayers.

This Christian woman, after leading a life beautiful for its simple faith and loving charity, died at a good old age, in the full possession of every faculty.

The facts of this little sketch were given to the writer by a son of Mrs. H, who loved to dwell upon the conversion of his mother. The incident which led to it was regarded by her immediate family and many friends as a miracle, and the special graces she received were attributed to her unwavering devotion to the Rosary which she recited daily.

She to whom this signal favor was shown told the tale in all faith and simplicity; and in the same spirit that it was accepted then by her children, it is told to-day by her grandchildren, and accepted by their children.

The roses of summer are faded, quite gone,
    Not a lingering bud can we see ;
But the hedges of autumn are gay in the sun,
    They are blooming, sweet Lady, for thee.

The asters in pomp of variety stand
    Where the Golden Rod's sceptre appears,
While low in the meadow, " Our Lady's fringed eye "
    Is still lifted in beauty and tears.

The fairest and freshest from meadow and hedge,
    On thy altar, Blessed Mother, we lay,
For Mary is Queen of the Angels, and we
    Keep the feast of our angels to-day.

Oh, teach us, bright guardians, that song of delight
    Which was ancient when Eden was new,
And Mary will offer the praises we sing,
    In concert, dear Angels, with you.
                    —*Eliza Allen Starr.*

A PAGE OF CHURCH HISTORY IN NEW YORK.

ST. JOHN'S, UTICA.

Very Rev. J. S. M. Lynch, D. D., LL. D.

Part VII.

THIRD CHURCH.

December 25th, 1869 December 25th, 1893.

BISHOPS.

Thank God there are no names on our memorial tablet of
the bishops of the diocese during the period of the third church!
As there were three bishops who ruled the diocese during the life
of the first church, three who blessed with their presence the second church, so there have been also three placed by the Holy
Ghost to rule this portion of the church of God during the existence of this third church. We rejoice, however, that they are all
yet alive, in hale and vigorous health, and our prayer is that it
may be many, many years before the place on our tablet reserved
for their names will have to be filled.*

PASTORS.

REV. THOMAS DALY.

December 25th, 1869 October 11th, 1881. Died February 5th, 1885.

The life of Father Daly, up to the end of the second church,
has been sketched. After many trials and struggles in the erection of this third church, he had at last the great happiness of
celebrating Mass in this temple which was to be the crowning
work of his life.

The second church was opened on Christmas day, in the year
1836, by that grand old patriarch, Father Beacham; this, the third
church, was also opened on Christmas day, by Father Daly, in
1869. Just thirty-three years in the life of the second church,—the
years of our Blessed Lord Himself on earth. What a happy

---

* Rt. Rev. Francis McNeirny, the bishop of Albany, died a few weeks after these words were spoken January 2, 1894.

ST. JOHN'S, UTICA, NEW AND PRESENT CHURCH.

thought it was of these pastors of old to open the second and
the third churches on the beautiful Feast of the Nativity, thus
making the birthday of the Saviour the birthday also of these
temples dedicated to His glory!

Many will recall the very successful fair which was held in
this church immediately after that Christmas of 1869, at which
the large sum of $9,000 was realized.   After the fair, Father Daly
called for volunteers to assist in the plastering and stucco work.
His appeal met with a hearty response, the work went steadily on,
and after a few years the church was completed.

It was during this interval that Father Daly turned his attention
to another matter of no little importance.   It was the privilege of
Father Daly to complete the work of his predecessors, Father
Martin and Father McFarland, and secure a permanent and capa-
cious resting-place for the departed members of the parish.   In
1871 he purchased that narrow strip of land running along the
Gulf from South Street to Pleasant Street, and known as "the
farm."   About this time St. Agnes' Cemetery Association was
formed, and Father Daly was one of the original trustees.   The
five acres of land belonging to the church which had been purchased by Father Martin for burial purposes in 1844, and the additional lots purchased by Father McFarland, were conveyed to
this new corporation, and that portion of the "farm" bounded by
South, Third, Arthur Streets and the Gulf was sold by the church
to the trustees of St. Agnes' Cemetery Association.   Thenceforth-
ward the prosperity of St. Agnes' Cemetery Association was assured, and the Catholics of Utica rejoiced in a large and commodious burying-ground, conveniently located, and beautifully laid
out, and sufficiently large for their growing needs.

But the great day of Father Daly's life at last arrived.   Many
remember the joy which beamed on his countenance when at last
the work of his life was done, and he beheld, on that beautiful
Feast of the Guardian Angels, October 2, 1872, this splendid edifice dedicated to the Living God by Rt. Rev. John J. Conroy, the
Bishop of Albany, assisted by Rt. Rev. Francis McNeirny, the
coadjutor bishop.   I have said that the first church represents
the infancy of the parish, the second its childhood, the third
its perfect manhood: and is it not true?   But a short while ago

we celebrated the twenty-first anniversary of the dedication of this church. It had just reached its majority, its perfect manhood. Many will remember the touching words of Bishop Mc-Farland, the light of the second church, coming back so appropriately to preach the dedication sermon of the third. After congratulating the devoted and well-beloved pastor, Father Daly, and the people of St. John's Church upon the completion of the great work, he said:

INTERIOR OF ST. JOHN'S, UTICA, THIRD CHURCH.

"The elegant edifice in which we are now assembled is the third church which has stood on this site. The first church was built fifty-three years ago. The ground was donated by a respectable and liberal Protestant family; the church was built by faithful Catholics, whose names and memories are still cherished, and will always be revered by their associates. That church was occupied eighteen years, when, although very large in size, it had become altogether too small to accommodate the rapidly increasing congregation. The building was removed to the opposite corner of John and Bleecker streets, where, altogether greatly changed, it still remains. Later, another was built, which stood on this site for about thirty years. In that church the majority of the members of St. John's present congregation were baptized, and in later years received their first Communion and the other sacraments of the Church. Although held with sacred regard for the many affectionate memories which

·clustered around it and endeared it to every man, woman, and child, it was razed to its foundation. It was thought not to be what the congregation desired and required for its accommodation. About four years ago the work of building the present beautiful edifice was commenced, and now all rejoice at its completion. I am happy to rejoice with you, and glad in my heart to see so grand a building reared on this spot to the service of Almighty God. I trust that it will stand for many, very many years, and that it will be long before this congregation will be called to make other outlays and sacrifices such as they have so cheerfully done for this one. In conclusion, I pray that God may bless the deserving people of St. John's church; and that their patron saint, John, may intercede in their behalf, and obtain for them the choicest and greatest of blessings."

In the report of the sermon on that occasion we are told that it recalled to many minds the pleasant memories of years so richly laden with blessings when good Bishop McFarland was the pastor of this flock, which will always hold his memory dear.

Among the bishops present at the dedication was Bishop Loughlin, of Brooklyn, one of the former assistant priests in the second church.

Father Daly enjoyed the fruits of his labors for only a few years. Failing health obliged him to retire to the quiet retreat of Mount Hope, Md., where, under the tender care of the good Sisters of Charity, to whom he had been for so many years a father, he prepared for his final end. A few days before it came he felt a presentiment of his approaching death, and sending for the chaplain of the institution, he said to him: "Father, I often advised others to prepare for death. Now my time has come. I wish to make a general confession, and receive all the sacraments, and depart in peace."

And so died the pastor whose name will ever be connected with this third church. His funeral was one of the most impressive in the history of St. John's. The eulogy was pronounced by Rev. John Lowery, LL. D., of Cohoes, an intimate friend from boyhood of Father Daly, and whose deep personal sorrow lent touching pathos to his eloquent discourse. Beside his father and mother his remains were tenderly laid at rest in our own city of the dead. The funeral, according to the *Utica Observer*, " was one of the largest ever held in this city, and testified in a way as unmistakable as it was memorable to the regard in which the late pastor was held, not alone by his flock, but by the citizens of Utica in general. The grief of his parishioners told eloquently of their filial affection for him. It was more like the disruption by death of a happy family than the departure of an old friend. Many generations will come and go before the remembrance of the gentle, genial, and accomplished priest, who rests to-day in the cemetery which he provided for his beloved dead, will pass from the minds of the Catholics of Utica."

Through the zeal and energy of the lamented Father Cullen, a handsome monument was erected over his grave, a few years later, by the members of the parish.

Ah, people of St. John's! as you walk through our city of the dead, forget not to pause and kneel at his grave, and breathe a prayer for the repose of his soul. Strange it is that there is but one other on the list of our pastors whose dust we can claim as our own– the saintly Father Ferrall. All the others sleep in graves that are far away.

These last twelve years of Father Daly's pastorate, in the third church, were signalized by many important events. In 1870 the Pope was deprived of his temporal sovereignty, and ever since he has been a prisoner in his own palace. During that same year took place the Franco-Prussian War. In 1875 Archbishop McCloskey, of New York, became the first American Cardinal. In 1876 the centenary of American Independence was celebrated at Philadelphia by the Centennial Exposition, and that same year saw the invention of the telephone, which has now become almost a necessity in daily life. In 1878 Pius IX. of blessed memory passed away, and our present Holy Father, Leo XIII., was elevated to the pontifical throne.

Utica, during this cycle of years, showed signs of new life and increasing growth. When our new church was opened by Father Daly, in 1869, the population was 28,000. It was fully 35,000 when, at the end of a dozen years, he laid down his burden, and was increased to 40,000 before his death.

Our beloved parish kept pace with the steady growth of the city. In 1870, St. Mary's German Catholic Church was established within its limits, and in April, 1877, St. Francis de Sales' Church was cut off from the southern part, and Father Daly's assistant priest, Rev. L. G. O'Reilly, was appointed the first pastor of the new parish, and to-day, thanks to his zeal and energy, a handsome brick church is located in the very midst of the forest of early days.   But the old trunk, even after the lopping off of these branches, seemed to be more vigorous and full of life than ever. And so as Father Daly retired from the scene of his labors, after laboring for nearly a quarter of a century in the upbuilding of this parish, if he was not permitted to enjoy the fruits of his many sacrifices, he had the happiness at least of witnessing the dawn of an era of unexampled prosperity for his beloved parish.

FATHER DALY'S ASSISTANT PRIESTS IN THE THIRD CHURCH.

REV. PATRICK JOSEPH BIRMINGHAM.

NOVEMBER 1ST, 1872—JANUARY 1ST, 1873.   DIED AUGUST 24TH, 1883.

Father Birmingham was born in King's County, Ireland.   He

REV. PATRICK J. BIRMINGHAM.

was ordained in Maynooth Seminary, at the Pentecost ordination of 1872.   He assisted Father Daly for a couple of months towards the end of that same year. He was appointed assistant priest to Father Beacham of Rome, in January, 1873, where he remained until November, 1875.   He then became pastor of St. Mary's of the Assumption church, Cleveland, Oswego County, N. Y.   After laboring for four years in this difficult mission, he was appointed pastor of Florence, Oneida County, succeeding Rev. John Ludden, a cousin of our present bishop.

His labors in his new field were unremitting.   He was indefatigable in his efforts to reclaim sinners who had strayed away from the path of duty.   His repeated efforts to introduce into every home the devotion of the holy Rosary, and to have it practiced every day throughout the year, and the fact mentioned by the eloquent preacher at his funeral obsequies, that there was no mission in the diocese where the beautiful devotion of the Angelus was more thoroughly established and more generally practiced, testify to his deep devotion to the Mother of God.   His efforts to beautify his little church were most commendable.   He had scarcely finished the plastering and the frescoing which made it look so attractive, he had just laid out and improved the little cemetery which stood beside it, when he felt a premonition of his approaching end, and begging a Hail Mary from his parishioners, he hastened to place himself under the care of the spouses of Jesus Christ at St. Elizabeth's Hospital, Utica.   After five years of laborious work in this little parish, he calmly expired August 24, 1883, at the early age of 36 years.

He was the second of our priests to die in Utica; the first, Father Ferrall, having died in this city forty-three years previously.   His funeral took place from St. Mary's Church, Florence, and his remains are buried in the little graveyard close to the church where he so faithfully ministered.   He was a priest of a most delightful character, full of faith and piety, and won the affection of his people to a remarkable degree.   Of the five priests who labored with Father Daly in the present church, Father Birmingham is the only one who has been called to his reward.   The others, four in number, are still alive, actively engaged in the sacred ministry, and pastors beloved by their respective flocks.

REV. JAMES J. MORIARTY, LL. D.

MAY 18TH, 1887—DECEMBER 4TH, 1887.   DIED DECEMBER 4TH, 1887.

Father Moriarty was born in Dingle, County Kerry, Ireland, January 8th, 1843.   Like the pastor who precedes him on our roll of dead priests, he came to this country a babe in his mother's arms. When a lad of twelve he entered St. Francis Xavier's College, New York, from which he graduated with honor in 1861.   He finished his philosophical studies in St. John's College, Fordham.

He commenced his theological course at the Grand Seminary, Montreal, and when St. Joseph's Provincial Seminary, Troy, N. Y., was opened, he became one of its first students. When that great institution was solemnly dedicated, October 24th, 1864, Father Moriarty was chosen to deliver the address on the occasion on behalf of the professors and students. He was ordained to the holy priesthood by Bishop Conroy of Albany, November 11th, 1865. Shortly after, he was appointed pastor of St. Patrick's church, Chatham, N. Y., where he labored for about eighteen years. He had charge of several places, located within a radius of fifty-six miles. As a result of his earnest labors, the Church was freed from debt, a free parochial school was established, and new churches were built at New Lebanon, Philmont, and Stephentown. He became pastor of St. John the Evangelist church, Syracuse—now the cathedral of the diocese—December 13th, 1883. At the silver jubilee exercises of his Alma Mater, which were held in the Academy of Music, New York, Archbishop Corrigan presiding, June 22d, 1885, he delivered an eloquent address to the graduates, and was honored by receiving the degree of LL. D. from that noble institution of learning, St. Francis Xavier's College, New York.

The new diocese of Syracuse was established towards the end of the year 1886. Our beloved bishop was consecrated May 1, 1887. He selected St. John the Evangelist church as his cathedral. Father Moriarty was then transferred to this parish, May 18, 1887. Succeeding him myself in Syracuse, I am able to bear testimony to the place which he won, during his short pastorate, in the affections of that people. His elegant and powerful pulpit utterances, and his bold, outspoken stand on all questions which affected the interests of the community in which he lived, gained for him the esteem of all classes of citizens, while his kind and gentle manners, his heartfelt sympathy with the poor and the distressed, and his tender care for the sick and dying, endeared him in a special manner to his own flock. Keenly did they feel his going from amongst them. Many were witnesses, more than once, of the love which they bore for him in life and death. His labors in this church were of short duration. With a deep appreciation of the responsibility of the task imposed on him in presiding over the destinies of this important parish, he was already maturing projects for its advancement and well-being, when his light suddenly went out.

Besides attending to his various parochial duties, he found time, during his priestly life, to enrich the literary world with several valuable works, which, besides benefiting religion, were also the means of bringing many converts into the Church. Yes, for years to come, though dead, Father Moriarty will continue to speak to us, and "Stumbling Blocks Made Stepping Stones," "All for Love; or, from the Manger to the Cross," and the "Keys of the Kingdom; or, the Unfailing Promise" will keep his memory green, even when the granite pile which marks his grave will have crumbled into dust.

He died at his residence, corner Broad and Second streets, on Sunday morning, December 4th, 1887. It was forty-seven years since a pastor of this church had died in Utica. His funeral services took place from this church on the Tuesday following. The bishop of the diocese officiated, assisted by a large concourse of the clergy from various parts of the State. The eulogy was pronounced by his life-long friend, Rev. James H. McGean, pastor of old St. Peter's Church, in Barclay Street, New York.

Our own church, and the church in which he ministered in Syracuse, are both under the patronage of the "disciple whom Jesus loved," and with singular appropriateness his final obsequies took place in the Church of St. John the Evangelist, in New York. He was buried in Calvary Cemetery.

And so passed away our nineteenth pastor. His pastorate was the shortest of all in the history of the parish. And yet he was long enough with us to enable us to recognize those qualities of mind and heart that ennobled his passing presence, and will serve to keep alive the memory of his name.

REV. THOMAS F. CULLEN.

JANUARY 9, 1888—MAY 9, 1891. DIED MAY 9, 1891.

Father Cullen is the only priest amongst all those whose names are inscribed on our memorial tablet, who was born within the limits of the present diocese of Syracuse. Even as Father McFarland was the first pastor who was the product of American soil, so Father Cullen was the first to spring from our own State of New York. And, more than this, he was a native both of the diocese and of its episcopal city. Father Cullen was born in Syracuse, July 29, 1852. After acquiring an academic education in his native city, he entered the College of Our Lady of Angels, Suspension Bridge, where he was carefully prepared by the good Lazarist Fathers for the burden of the holy priesthood.

During his college days he edited the *Niagara Index*, and its columns gave evidence of that literary talent which was afterwards so conspicuously displayed in his sermons and instructions. He was ordained in St. Joseph's Provincial Seminary, Troy, N. Y., by Bishop McNeirny, of Albany. He is the only priest in our long roll of dead at whose ordination I had the pleasure of assisting, and upon whom, in union with the bishop and the clergy, I had the privilege of imposing my hands at that solemn moment when Holy Church teaches us that the Spirit of God comes down upon His chosen ones to bless them with the sublime dignity of the priesthood. Shortly after his ordination he was appointed assistant priest in St. Bernard's Church, Cohoes. He remained there five years, endearing himself by his zeal and piety to every member of the parish. He was appointed February 21, 1883, pastor of Norwich, N. Y. For five years more he bore the brunt of this hard mission, which then included Oxford. Through heavy rain storms, over rough roads, in the cold of winter and the heat of summer he travelled twenty miles, Sunday after Sunday, attending these two places. As a result of his unwearying labors Oxford has now a fine church and a settled pastor. The constant labors and successful work of Father Cullen, albeit so modest and unobtrusive in his ways, could not escape the vigilant eye of the shepherd of the diocese, and it was not long before the bishop felt that his zeal and piety fitted him for a broader sphere of usefulness. And so when a vacancy occurred in this parish by the death of Father Moriarty, Father Cullen was placed in charge. Protestants and Catholics alike in the village of Norwich, while they rejoiced at his well-deserved promotion, regretted exceedingly his departure from amongst them. There is no need to recount his labors in this parish. Coming in robust health and in the full vigor of manhood, thoroughly equipped for his task, burning with zeal for the salvation of souls, he threw himself into his work with an earnestness which gave promise of great results. I know from personal conversations with him, how his whole soul was wrapped up in the interests of our beloved parish. I know how he shrank from the burden at first, dreading the responsibility of the charge, but I know, too, once accepted, how complete was the sacrifice. Constantly conceiving and maturing plans for the spiritual welfare of his flock, his thought by day and by night was for the betterment of his people. It was during the pastorate of Father Cullen that this parish was designated by the bishop as one of the very few in the diocese whose pastor would be henceforth what is called, in the language of the Church, an immovable rector. As the parish was now in a condition to merit this marked distinction, and, as in the eyes of the bishop, Father Cullen possessed all the qualifications befitting the dignity, he was selected the first in the long line of our pastors to enjoy this high honor.

REV. THOMAS F. CULLEN.

But, alas! how fruitless were our forecasts, how illusive our dreams; the bright hopes that were built at his coming were soon to be dashed to pieces. He was to sow the seed, but not to reap the harvest. After presiding over the parish a little more than three years, he was stricken down, and after a brief sickness he peacefully expired in the Rectory—the first priest to die in the parochial residence since the formation of the parish, nearly seventy-five years before. His funeral was the most imposing that ever took place from our church. Many remember that great procession from the church to the station. There were the little orphan girls of St. John's Asylum and the good Sisters of Charity; there were the orphan boys of St. Vincent's Industrial School; there were the pupils of Assumption Academy, headed by a corps of the Brothers of the Christian Schools; there were the girls of St. John's School; there were the clergy in extraordinary numbers, and there was that immense concourse of his bereaved parishioners and that throng of citizens who shared with us a loss which affected the entire community. Three coaches were needed to accommodate the numbers of sympathizing people that accompanied the remains of the dead priest to Syracuse. He was buried in St. Agnes' cemetery, in that city; and so the city where he first saw the light, and which had loaned him to us while his soul quickened his mortal frame, took him back when that soul had fled, claiming for its own the body in which that soul had lived.

REV. JOHN J. TOOMY.

JANUARY 21st, 1883—JUNE 20th, 1887. DIED JUNE 13th, 1891.

We have come now to the last name in our roll of dead priests, the lamented Father Toomy. He is the only one of the entire number whose infant years were guarded, and whose vocation was encouraged and fostered, by a priest who himself is a child of old St. John's, the distinguished and beloved Father Lowery of Cohoes. He is also the only one of our deceased priests whose whole priestly life was acted under our eyes. From the very day of his ordination until his eyes closed in death he labored in our midst, either as assistant priest in this church, or as pastor of St. Agnes' Church, a parish carved out of St. John's.

Father Toomy was born in Cohoes, September 12, 1857. He began his studies in St. Bernard's School, in that city, under the good Sisters of St. Joseph, and pursued them afterwards at the Academy of the Brothers of the Christian Schools, in Troy. He made his classical studies in St. Mary's College, Montreal, under the Jesuit Fathers, and subsequently at the College of Our Lady of Angels, Suspension Bridge, N. Y. His theological studies were pursued in St. Joseph's Provincial Seminary, Troy. He was ordained by Bishop McNeirny on the vigil of Christmas in the year 1882, and celebrated his first Mass in the church of his baptism on the beautiful feast of the Nativity. He was immediately appointed assistant priest in this church, and began his labors here on the 21st of January, 1883.

Many will recall an incident which took place in the church on his very first Sunday. It was the solemn opening of the Forty Hours. One of the altar boys, in a moment of thoughtlessness, touched his lighted candle to the surplice of his companion, and in an instant two of the boys were in flames. The church was unusually crowded, and a panic was imminent; the congregation, terror-stricken, rose upon their feet, but the powerful voice of Father Toomy rang out from the sanctuary, and blended with the commanding tones of the lamented

REV. JOHN J. TOOMEY.

General McQuade from the choir. The people remained in their seats, and many lives were saved.

People of St. John's, you have not yet forgotten the zeal and piety of Father Toomy during the few short years of his ministry among you!

Indefatigable in the labors of his calling, tireless in his ministrations to the sick and dying, he was always cheerful and buoyant of spirit, and his smile was like sunshine as he passed along day by day. When old St. John's, the mother of so many children, gave birth to another, Father Toomy was chosen to preside over the destinies of her new-born child—her youngest daughter, St. Agnes. Jealous of her offspring, she would have it nursed by one who had rested upon her own bosom, been trained in her own household. For four years he labored in this new field.

Under the wise and careful administration of the present zealous
pastor, the beautiful church of St. Agnes, of which we are all so
proud, is now nearing completion.   The end has almost come,
but the beginnings are not yet forgotten.   The people of that
district will ever treasure in hallowed memory that young priest
who came amongst them in the flower of his youth, and brought
to his task so much devotion and self-sacrifice, and struggled on
against difficulties and trials and obstacles of every kind, in laying deep and solid the foundations of that new parish, the upbuilding of which had been confided to him as a sacred trust by
his bishop.   In the midst of his labors his physical strength gave
way, and the dream of his life was never to be realized.   He died
after a few days' sickness, June 13th, 1891.   His funeral took
place, from the basement of his new church, and most extraordinary were the demonstrations of grief on the sad occasion on the
part of his stricken parishioners.   His co-laborer in St. John's,
Father Ryan, of Camillus, delivered a touching eulogy at his
obsequies.   Accompanied by a large delegation of friends and
parishioners, his remains were carried from St. Agnes' Church
which he formed, to St. Agnes' Church where he was born, and
there, amid the sobs of another grief-stricken congregation, the
pastor of his childhood in eloquent words portrayed the virtues
of the devoted young priest whose dust had been brought back to
the parish which gave him the inspiration of his life.   He was
buried in the Catholic cemetery in the city of Cohoes.

His sweet and gentle disposition, his warm and generous heart,
his true and loyal friendship to those whom he loved, his solid,
though unostentatious piety, his zeal for the salvation of his people,
will not soon be forgotten, but will be treasured in sacred memory
that will bring him the return of fervent prayers in his behalf from
many a grateful soul.

Ah, people of St. John's! short-lived was the ministry of Father
Toomy, and yet dare we say that he did not live long enough to
accomplish the work which the Master sent him to do?   " For
venerable old age is not that of long time, nor counted by the
number of years, but a spotless life is old age."

The all-seeing eye of God searches the depths of our
hearts, and oftentimes the desires with which we are inflamed

are more precious in His sight even than our grandest actions.

A St. Teresa panting for martyrdom amidst the wilds of Africa,—a St. Francis Xavier closing his dying eyes on that kingdom which he thirsted to win to Christ, pleased God in desire, even though in the hidden designs of His providence those desires were never to be realized. And so may we not hope and fondly believe that Father Toomy has received a reward for the much that he wished to do, rather than for the little that he was permitted to do, for God?

Such is the history of our church as told in the lives of its dead priests,—its history written on its walls. The study of the names upon the list suggests another thought to my mind: How singularly they seem to preach to us devotion to that beloved Apostle under whose special patronage all these priests of God labored on this hallowed spot for the glory of their Master! And fittingly will that great event in the history of our church—the placing of this memorial tablet—be supplemented in a brief time by the blessing of a life-like statue of the beloved Apostle, which, raised aloft between our towers, will tell the world of what our great patron has done for us during the last three quarters of a century, and will be a silent prayer pleading for his powerful intercession in the ages that are yet to come.*

It often happens that when old churches are demolished and new ones are erected on the same spot, that their names are changed and new patron saints are selected. But we glory in the fact that the patron of our first church was St. John, the patron of our second was St. John, the patron of our third church is St. John; and the asylum under the shadow of our church, which for sixty years has done its blessed work for the little orphans, has always been under the patronage of St. John. Yes, the disciple whom Jesus loved watched over our infancy, guided us in our childhood, and still protects us in the full vigor of our manhood. It is a striking fact how the name of John appears on every page in the history of our parish. Every one of the bishops upon the

---

* The statue was blessed and erected on the Feast of St. John the Evangelist, December 27, 1893, a few weeks after the delivery of this lecture.

roll of the dead, who ruled the diocese from the foundation of the parish, rejoiced in the name of John.*

Each of the three churches built upon this spot was dedicated by a bishop whose name was John. Two bishops visited our first church: each was called John. Three bishops officiated in our second church: all three had the name of John. It was a bishop by the name of John that dedicated our first church; it was a bishop by the same name that dedicated our second church, and it was a bishop by the name of John that dedicated this third church. Every time the Sacrament of Confirmation was administered in the first church, in the second church, and in the third church, up to the time of its dedication, the name of the officiating prelate was John. The first name on our roll of priests, our first pastor, was Father John Farnan; the last name upon the long list is Father John Toomy. The first priest attached to our church to become bishop was Father John Loughlin. There is only one priest upon our roll who was trained up by a child of our parish, and his name, too, was John; and the good pastor himself,—the product of St. John's,—who led him into the sanctuary, was also blessed with the name of John. There were two who died while the tablet was being prepared, the last names placed upon it, and both had the name of John: Bishop John Loughlin and Father John McMenomy.

Oh, as we study the history of our parish, as we recall its rulers who have long since passed away, the picture of the great Apostle and Evangelist crosses our vision at every part, and we cannot but be inspired with a more earnest and fervent devotion to that great Saint who from the beginning was so wisely selected as the patron of our church.

And now my task is done. It has indeed been a labor of love. I have called the roll of the dead, and they have answered one

---

* It is a singular fact that, a few months after these words were spoken, Archbishop Corrigan presented a handsome marble altar to his Cathedral in memory of his predecessors. He dedicated this altar to St. John the Evangelist, to commemorate the fact that every one of his predecessors who occupied the See of New York bore the name of John. The altar was consecrated by Archbishop Corrigan, May 6, 1894, and may be seen in one of the beautiful little chapels on the epistle side of the Cathedral.

by one. I have raised them from the tomb. I have brought back the memory of their noble deeds, and they have lived before us as in days gone by.

Oh, may the characters chiselled upon the memorial tablet, recalling their names and indicating the anniversaries of their deaths, be a silent monitor to make all hearken to the injunction of the Apostle, to "remember your prelates who have spoken to you the word of God."

And now pardon my seeming egotism if, before closing, I beg to be allowed to take one more look at a few of those names which have for me an interest which is all my own. Some of them there are which recall to me memories that are sacred, days that will never be forgotten.

I look, and see the name of Bishop Loughlin. Attending in his boyhood days the very church of my own parish—that old, tumble-down structure that served the purpose before the purchase of the present St. John's of Albany—beginning his studies in the very school of my childhood, sitting on the same benches and reciting in the same class-rooms where, in after years, I followed him, I feel that there is a sort of kinship between us, and I hold the name of Bishop Loughlin in most affectionate remembrance.

I look again, and I see the name of Father Patrick McCloskey. He was the pastor of my boyhood days. It was he that prepared me for my First Communion, and his words of heavenly wisdom seem yet to ring in my ears.

I see the name of Cardinal McCloskey. It was from his hands that I first received the Bread of Life; it was he who anointed me with holy chrism in the Sacrament of Confirmation; and, later on, it was he that ordained me to sub-deaconship. It was in his hands that I placed my vow of perpetual chastity, by which I became forever bound to the service of Holy Church.

I look again, and I see the name of Bishop McFarland. It was he that led me into the sanctuary, and, cutting the hair from my head as a sign of the sacrifice, separated me forever from the laity, and placed me by clerical tonsure under the particular jurisdiction of the Church.

Again I look, and I see the name of Bishop Bacon. It was he that ordained me to the holy priesthood—that highest dignity upon earth; and as fancy paints for me the picture of that day of days in my life, so deeply imbedded in my memory, the form of dear Bishop Bacon comes up before me as he imposed his hands upon my head, and called the Holy Spirit upon me, blessing me in the office of the priesthood.

I look again, and I see the name of Father Cullen. He was my immediate predecessor. It was my melancholy privilege to pronounce the eulogy over his remains, and to speak words of hope and comfort to a sorrowing people; and then it was my lot to take up the plough that had fallen from his lifeless hands, and continue the good work which he had so happily begun, and gather the harvest sure to spring from the good seed which he had planted. With a deep appreciation of my unworthiness to walk in his footsteps, and a clear consciousness of my inability to do what he would have done had God spared him, there is mingled an affectionate reverence for his name born of that close relationship which must of necessity exist between the one who takes up the work which another has laid down.

Finally, I see the name of Father Toomy. Coming to me fresh from the anointing hand of the bishop, there sprung up between us an attachment which grew in strength until the very day of his death. In my long years of ministry he is the only priest who ever assisted me in my labors who has been called to his reward. He is the only priest upon our roll at whose bedside I stood in the last moments, closing his eyes in death. Oh, as long as life shall last I shall keep in prayerful memory the name of Father Toomy!

Ah, was I wrong in saying that this memorial tablet has for me a peculiar interest because of the names inscribed upon it? Need I say that I thank God that it has fallen to my lot to place it in our church? These good bishops and priests have passed away, but have I not special reason to keep them in memory, and to beg my people never to forget them in their prayers? In your keeping then, my people! I leave the dead priests of old St. John's. You have a roll of honored dead of which any parish might well be proud. It may be in Heaven they are guarding the interests of our beloved church; it may be in Purgatory they are crying for relief from their pains. Oh, hearken to the wail of woe which comes from the nether world from the consecrated sons of God! Oh, have pity on them, have pity on them, at least you, their friends, for the hand of the Lord hath touched them!

And that your supplications to the Throne of Grace may not end with your death, teach your children the sacred duty which rests upon them of praying always for the repose of the souls of those bishops and priests who spoke the word of God to your fathers in the faith.

(*The End.*)

"OUR LADY'S BEADS."

P. J. C.

I.

FT when the world seems bright and dear,
    And wily Satan with me pleads,
I've found sweet peace, relief from fear,
    By counting o'er " Our Lady's Beads."

II.

Bright precious gems to me they are,
    They know my secrets and my needs;
No earthly friends I'd trust so far
    As those mute stones, " Our Lady's Beads."

III.

A simple chaplet, old and stained,
    Yet oft for me it intercedes,
And oft rich blessings I've obtained
    Through telling o'er its sacred beads.

IV.

And when at length grim monster Death,
    Shall bid me follow where he leads,
May earthly sun upon me set
    While breathing forth " Our Lady's Beads."

TEN YEARS LATE.

JEROME TRANT.

> " It is growing dark !
> Yet one line more,
> And then my work for to-day is o'er."
> —*Longfellow.*

"STILL writing, or reading, or thinking, Hermit?" called out a bright young voice somewhere from the region of a still brighter garden. A pebble thrown up at a first-floor window succeeded better than some of the chance throws we see in life, for it hit the mark aimed at, the fact being announced by the unmistakable sound of broken glass, closely followed by one of human exasperation. A dry chuckle of gratified ambition greeted the latter, while a second and more consequential stone-message found its way into the opened citadel.

" That will do for this evening, if you don't mind; I am coming down," grumbled the besieged, very evidently accustomed to the practical and sustained warfare of attacking forces. The opening of a door, a quiet yet rapidly-descending tread, a pause in the hall, then the appearance of the vanquished in the person of a tall, well-knit figure, clad in a cool-looking, grey smoking-suit.

"Well, tease ! what do you want with me, now that you have succeeded in breaking up my afternoon's study ?" demanded the new-comer with pretended wrath, while his hands stretched forth to catch at a slim girlish figure which eluded his grasp skilfully, a mocking, yet sweet-toned laugh marking his defeat. A wild race round the diminutive flower-beds ended in victory for the smoking-suit, to the intense satisfaction of the owner, and corresponding disgust of the enemy. A dignified parley, drawing-up of treaty, and subsequent truce (very hollow, if past experience goes for anything) brought conflicting powers into peaceable and mutual subjection on a stone bench near the house, the reconciliation being cemented by a .... well, it is quite needless to specify what

some people call, cementing a peace. You and I would call it
old-fashioned, perhaps—before the world ; yet in our heart of
hearts we should approve and sigh—who knows ?—that our day
for that sort of thing is over. Were they then lovers, these
two, or—that most convenient of relationships—cousins ? No.
What then ? Guardian and ward ? *Nenni !* do not wander so far
afield in the realms of romance. Henry and Hilda Chudleigh
were plain, matter-of-fact brother and sister. Brother and sister !
In this giddy, novel-fed, and unhealthy-over-pressure generation,
we have well-nigh forgotten the hidden sweetness of such a bond.
Our *jeunesse dorée* seek their ideals in 'Ouidaesque' heroines,
spicy to their *blasé* palates, but bitter to their souls, (save the
mark ! do they believe in such a thing ?) our middle-aged men
plunge into the mysteries of " Bull" and " Bear," " striking oil,"
and railway-shares, and have no time for domestic ties, beyond
their well-dressed wives and dowered daughters,—and even these
in due season, while our " honorable old age " representatives devote their declining powers to whist and '63 port. Where then
shall we find a man simple and backward enough to confess, that
on and beyond, and above all this, lies a dewy land where the
pure flowers of God-implanted affection still bloom and die,
though unseen by worldly eyes?

It was said of old, in the sublimest book ever opened to the gaze
of man : " Seek, and ye shall find." Yea ! and we thank the Divine Speaker that diligent search can be and is rewarded, even in
such as our present one. Many are impure, but not all ; hosts
are worldly, but a chosen few are as the salt of the earth ; mul-
titudes are disappointing in their elderly egotism, but here and
there, as streaks of silver in an almost exhausted mine, we meet
with grey hairs before which our heads instinctively uncover.

Sir Henry Chudleigh, with, to the good, an honorable name
nine and twenty years of a studious life, a good constitution and
cheerful temper, a handsome presence (six feet in his socks) enhanced by the golden halo of £13,000 a year in Consols, not Irish
landed estates; and last, but by no means least, a winsome sister
some eleven years his junior, was not a man to quarrel with
Providence or his neighbors. Shall we add that the latter, particularly mothers with marriageable daughters and needy younger

sons, never dreamt of anything so unrighteous and imprudent on their side.

And of bonny, gleesome, and—truth compels us to throw it in —wilful Hilda have we nought to say ? Surely. If bright eyes grew brighter and fair cheeks flushed ever so faintly under the clear, yet somewhat grave and almost wistful glance of her tall, stalwart brother, many a manly heart beat a trifle quicker, many an honest pulse leaped more joyously as the dainty and imperious little beauty swept by at garden-party or crowded dance. More than one veteran in the lists had broken his lance and bent his knee at her shrine; had bent it, yes ! had offered his wreath of homage, but had never succeeded in getting more than a merry flash of the laughing brown eyes, with perchance a tinge of gentle irony thrown in to show she understood but hearkened not. She did not want to exchange her name or liberty just yet, no, not even for a high-sounding handle to the first, nor the most gilded of gold cages for the second. Had she not years of youth before her tripping footsteps ? Was her beauty to depart in an hour that she should be in a hurry to deck it with orange-blossoms ? Did she not worship, and was she not worshipped by her big, noble-hearted, large-minded brother, who, ever since Sir Stephen and Lady Chudleigh's death up the Alps, in the terrible avalanche of 1876, had guarded and fondled and watched over her saddened childhood and budding girlhood with the love of a mother and the tender gravity of a father folded into one ? He loved his books next to her ; she loved her violin next to him ; and so, amid the grave love of the one and the sensitive, elevating harmony of the other, brother and sister had strayed along life's brightest paths, knowing full well there were thorns beneath the rose-buds, yet seeking them not, and ignorant, as yet, of the sharpness of their point.

A maiden aunt of uncertain age and temper, but unquestionable dignity and sterling qualities, had consented, meddlesome people said, for a substantial consideration, to act as chaperon to her doubly-orphaned niece. For several years, therefore, she had continued to offer her protection to Hilda, and advice to her nephew. The first being desirable, was accepted ; the latter was neither the one nor the other. This did not prevent, however, a most cordial sentiment reigning among the trio, whether in London or Paris during the season, or in travelling during the rest of the year. Alternately worried and petted by the wayward Miss Chudleigh, poor Aunt Roxby (Roman Roxie, Hilda called her to intimates) had, on the whole, a by no means unexciting life.

"If only I knew what she intended to do next," groaned the afflicted lady to a friend; "but no, I can never depend upon dear Hilda. To-day we are quietly settled down in London, a month deep in engagements; to-morrow she may come and tell me that we are off to Norway, or Lapland, or the Sandwich Isles."

"But surely Sir Henry does not care for that kind of thing?" would be the listener's proffered consolation.

"Henry object to anything his sister fancied? You can have no idea of the way he spoils her. If only he would be a little firmer with her, we could have some peace. Ah!"

And Aunt Roxby would sigh despondently, as if she were not exceptionally proud of the deep affection existing between brother and sister.

"Poor, dear Roxie! she looks more like an injured Roman than ever," remarked Miss Chudleigh to her partner at one of the first dances of the London season.

"Why, what have you been doing to her now?"

"Nothing; I merely told her a few minutes ago that we shall leave this for France to-morrow."

"You are going away?"—this in a tone of deep despondency.

"Yes; why not? I am tired of all this nonsense."

"But you have only just dipped into it." The voice took, if possible, a still lower shade of despair.

Hilda laughed softly. "That is just it; having 'just dipped into it,' as you so accurately remark, I have adopted the plan I always follow with a stupid book."

"And that is?"

"I close it up, leave it down, put it out of sight. You seem disappointed!" There was a half-quizzical, half-interested intonation in the speaker's voice.

"Yes; no; that is, I mean to say——"

"Yes?"

"Well, would you think me very rude if I asked you where-

abouts in France you intend going ?   It is not a village, you
know, and so——"

"And so you could not find out my plans from your next-door
neighbors, you mean ? "

"Something of that kind."

"Well, we are going—— Sh—! there is old Mrs. Pintley looking this way, and trying to listen.   I do not want the entire nation
to awaken to-morrow with the knowledge of our destination. Ah!
poor Roxie has been pounced upon! What was I saying ? Oh,
yes. We intend going to Hâvre."

"To Hâvre ? "

"Certainly, to Hâvre-de-grâce in Normandy."

"Oh ! "

"Why ' oh ' ? "

"Because it strikes me that you will find just as many people
there as here, at this time of year."

"Well, and what of that ? "

"Oh, nothing. Only I thought you wished to get out of the
crush of fashion, and so on."

Miss Chudleigh looked at her partner severely.

"I see Henry over there. Mr. Dundas, will you take me to
him ? "   And taken she was, without another word of explanation
being asked or offered.   Just as the unconscious offender, however, was turning away with a subdued bow and air of general misery, the wilful little lady evidently repented of her harshness.

"Hâvre is a very good port for yachts, and not at all dull."
And with this enigmatical speech she turned away, smiling.

*   *   *   *   *   *

It is just a week after the above conversation that we have come
across the Chudleighs, being introduced to Sir Henry in a mock
bad temper, consequent on his sister's summary proceedings to
rouse him from his cherished studies. They had settled down
in one of the *pavillons*, attached to the Hôtel Frascati, so justly
renowned for its commanding position and excellent *cuisine*.
The much-tormented 'Aunt Roxby' had spent the entire day
within doors, writing to her English acquaintances on the deprav-
ity of the French nature in general, and the sinfulness of the

Hâvre Sunday in particular. Failing sympathy at home, she seeks it abroad. May her search be rewarded as it deserves!

Having succeeded in bringing her brother down to enjoy the evening breeze, Hilda appears to have satisfied all her ambitions, for she does not seek to break the silence which has settled down on them both. Her bonny little head resting on the grey coat, with eyes closed, and hands clasped loosely in her lap, she looks the embodiment of contented repose. Presently she glances up at the handsome face above her shoulder, and putting up two white fingers, gently strokes the glossy brown hair. The gesture calls forth an answering caress:

" Well, light of my eyes, of what are you thinking ? " And the speaker smiled as he noticed the wild-rose bloom which greeted his words.

" Of you, my Hermit; of myself, of Roman Roxie, and of—— oh! various things." She breaks off with a quasi-embarrassed laugh.

" H'm! And amid the ' various things,' am I to rank—?" He was not allowed to finish the query, for Hilda hastily rose to her feet, placing one slim hand over her tormentor's mouth, and pointing with the other to a dignified heap of clothes, " fearfully and wonderfully made," which was advancing along the verandah as fast as circumstances would permit, said circumstances being represented by a dog in-arms, and another tugging at the approaching figure's feet.

" Roman Roxie has finished abusing foreign morals on paper," and is coming to do some on sufferance!" remarked that lady's irreverent niece, with a malicious smile at the former's frantic efforts to keep her footing, in spite of the impediments her canine pets had cast in the way. Perseverance was rewarded, however, and landed Aunt Roxby safely at the foot of the hall steps. She had just caught sight of the two figures by the bench, and went towards them, her nephew springing up to pilot her, *sain et sauf.*

" I thought you were reading upstairs, Henry," she remarked languidly, settling down on a wicker chair which Hilda's good-nature had suddenly brought on the scene.

" So he was," replied the latter briskly; " but I persuaded him to come down."

" You forget to explain how," observed her brother, with an amused glance in the direction of the shattered casement. I only hope there are no robbers, or midnight assailants and Co. prowling about.

" Good gracious! Henry, what do you mean? " demanded his aunt, sitting up suddenly with a look of alarm, which, however, changed into one of discomfiture as a voice from the side of the garden exclaimed: " May I come in, good ladies and gentlemen? "

" I verily believe it is Mr. Dundas, and none of us are *en toilette*," groaned " Roman Roxie," glancing with dismay at her tea-gown. She managed luckily to escape unperceived, as Sir Henry went forward to open the little gate which communicated with the hôtel grounds, and welcomed the new-comer cheerily. Miss Chudleigh had at first made a movement to follow her aunt, but evidently thought it more prudent and— enjoyable, to stand her ground. She greeted the intruder with a faint smile, while a sudden accession of color (fortunately most discreetly shaded by the fast-descending twilight) could have betrayed to at least one of the three, that the guest was not unwelcome.

He was a fine specimen of English manhood, almost as tall as his host, and certainly, in a different style, quite as handsome. That he found some very powerful attraction in the latter's vicinity is proved by his presence at the French watering-place, when only eight days previously we saw him talking to Miss Chudleigh in a London ball-room. Whether that young lady, and not her brother, was the lamp to the moth, or not, remains to be seen later on.

After strolling around the tiny garden for a short space, Hilda discovered that it was five minutes past seven, and consequently time to dress for the dinner which had been ordered for the half-hour.

" You will join us, of course? " she said kindly, as she turned to re-enter the house; " Hermit is never so happy as when he can get hold of a congenial spirit to discuss the respective merits of Aristotle and Plato." The two gentlemen smiled as she disappeared.

" She is an indefatigable tease," observed Sir Henry, as he threw away his cigar preparatory to following his sister's exam-

ple. " Ta! ta! old man; don't mistake our table, number seven, by
the window in the *à la carte* room." His companion nodded
pleasantly, and turned away with a bright look and brisk step.

Twenty-five minutes later saw the *quartette* happily seated at a
pleasant bow-window overlooking the heaving waters of a sun-
set-tinted sea. Aunt Roxby, magnificently upholstered in old
gold and priceless lace, beams complacently at each of her companions in turn, and divides her attention most equitably between
the *potage bisque*, the two dogs sitting on the train of her gorgeous gown, and Reginald Dundas, whom, as a young man of undeniable prospects, she considers a most desirable addition to the
family party.

" And so you found London dull? " she is saying to the latter,
who seems to find some difficulty in deciding which is the most
attractive, the small hand of his *vis-a-vis*, or the dainty auburn-
crowned head. He evidently gives the points to the former, possibly because at that precise moment Miss Chudleigh turns her
gaze away from the sea, and fixes it on his face for a brief instant,
which prevents him from continuing his investigations.

" Dull? I should think so," was the fervent reply. " Besides, I
have a host of relations—aunts, cousins, and what not—over this
side of the Channel, and so I thought I could not do better than
run over to look them up."

" Hum! Yes; naturally. It is very refreshing to see youth sac-
rificing itself for its aunts and cousins!" and Aunt Roxby smiled
somewhat satirically, for she was by no means deficient in penetration, and had long ago come to the conclusion that Reginald
Dundas was never far distant from her handsome niece's prox-
imity. The dinner, like all things here below, soon came to a
close, and was followed by the taking of the usual *demie tasse*
and *liqueurs*, at a little table in the hôtel grounds, within ear-
shot of the band. Miss Chudleigh, who seemed in a curiously
abstracted mood, played absently with her tea-spoon while listening to a violin solo fairly well executed by one of the musicians.
A simply-made white gown of some soft, clinging material, drap-
ing itself into graceful folds, set off her delicate beauty to advantage, and went to make up a very fair picture of joyous girlhood.
Dangerously fair, her now-silent neighbor found it, if we are to

5

judge by the scarcely-veiled look of deep admiration with which
he regarded her.   Becoming doubtless conscious of his observation through that mysterious but silent sympathy which we sometimes note one nature to have with another, the young girl turned
towards him, and smiled."

"You will generally find us uninteresting, Mr. Dundas, whenever music is in the neighborhood; Hermit and I are mute as
long as a single note is to be heard. Ask Roxie;" and she laughed
lightly as that lady looked up, at the mention of her name, from
the engrossing task of persuading the fattest of the two pugs that
it had swallowed as many lumps of sugar as prudent regard for
its health demanded.

"You mute, my dear?" replied the wretched little animal's
owner, who had not caught the sense of her niece's observation;
"I do not recollect noticing any symptoms of——"

"Of a consummation so devoutly to be wished for!" interrupted the girl with a quizzical glance in her brother's direction,
and a little pat on Aunt Roxby's diamond-decked hand. The
latter seemed half inclined to rebuke the incorrigible speaker by
a show of extra dignity, but was unable to carry out her intention, as at that identical moment all her powers of generalship
and reproach were called into play by the improper haste with
which Ruby (pug number two) had endeavored to bolt two lumps
of sugar at once, the largest of which being a spoil plundered
from Bijou (pug number one). While the matter was being argued out between the three interested parties, Sir Henry rose,
saying he would fetch wraps for his aunt and sister, as the night
air threatened to become chilly. Mr. Dundas looked after the retreating figure appreciatively.

"He is a grand fellow morally and physically," he remarked
earnestly. "You are justly proud of your brother, Miss Chudleigh; I only wish Providence had meted out some one, built on
the same lines, to *our* family circle." Had he wished to say something inevitably calculated to advance him in his fair companion's good graces, nothing could have served his cause so well as
these simple words.

"I *am* proud of Hermit," she replied quickly, "and glad to
see you judge of him as I do. People who do not know him say he

is over-reserved and somewhat cold in manner, but that is a great
mistake; he is certainly not demonstrative in society, but a
warmer and nobler heart never beat in human breast." She ceased
abruptly, as if ashamed of the warmth into which the subject had
betrayed her usual cool self-possession. Her hearer thought, however, that he had never seen her in a more charming mood.

" You love him dearly? " he asked, as if anxious not to let the
matter drop.

" More than anyone in the wide world."

" He is a happy man, Miss Chudleigh," was the quick rejoinder,
while the speaker repressed a sigh and feeling of odd disappointment. Yet why should he have indulged in such a sentiment?
Did he expect a different answer; or, with the jealous hope of an,
as yet unavowed, lover, had he supposed that some exception
would have been made for him? Perhaps ; men in love are pro-
verbially exacting and impossible to deal with. Further conversation was put an end to by Sir Henry's return, and Aunt Roxby's
declaration that the night air was injurious to Ruby and Bijou's
constitutions. This meant a retreat home, whither the little party
turned their steps, escorted to the door by their disappointed
guest. He had hoped for a longer chat with the spirit of his day-
dreams, and returned to the hôtel, privately anathematizing
Roxie's precautions and solicitude for what he termed "those
horrid little beasts!"

*   *   *   *   *   *   *

Three weeks glided by smoothly in the pursuance of the usual
seaside devices for filling up the hours of life as commodiously
and agreeably as present civilization permits. Only a short span
of twenty-one days, yet fraught with experiences which, for at
least three of our acquaintances, would alter and color their after
pilgrimage through this land of rosy dreams and gray realities,
with that strange suddenness sometimes noticed in the lives of
men and women born with deep feelings, and destined for intense
suffering.

Aunt Roxby's recollections of that period may be summed up
briefly in an acquaintance's graphical language, as, "a Roman's
lament over the emptiness of (dog) friendship and the 'cussed-
ness' of mankind!" The two pugs of "greedy" memory had de-

serted their mistress for one who appeared endowed with more consideration for their insatiable appetite, and even went to the lengths of adding insult to injury by growling viciously whenever their late owner swept by during their hourly collation of chicken bones and veal *rissoles.* As for the views which the good lady entertained concerning the human race in general and the female portion thereof in particular, to say they were tinged with gloomy resentment and dignified condemnation is to express their real state but feebly. She was distinctly disappointed with her niece, horrified by her nephew, grieved by Reginald Dundas, and incensed against the latter's fifteenth cousin, a pretty girl of nineteen, who had known the Chudleighs for several seasons, and whom she had set her heart upon obtaining for Sir Henry's bride, whenever that gentleman could be brought to consider such a consummation as necessary for his happiness.

Hilda had often questioned her brother on this point, especially since the preceding year, when, from various slight links of evidence in favor of her suspicions, she had commenced to believe him thinking seriously about giving her a sister to love and cherish next to himself. Up to within a month of the visit to Hâvre, he had generally turned the subject aside with a grave and half-sad smile, but at last, perceiving that his unusual reticence wounded his adoring sister, he spoke frankly of all he hoped and feared.

Rose Dundas (a distant relation of Hilda's admirer) was the step-daughter of a widowed and worldly-minded woman whose one object in life seemed to be the finding of a titled and wealthy suitor, who would conveniently replace the husband whom (so people said) she had worried into an early and anxiously-desired grave. When step-mother and daughter met the Chudleighs, the former, from the first moment, decided that the handsome baronet united in his interesting person all the advantages so long and eagerly looked for. That he was her junior by several years, or that he might possibly be attracted towards her pretty step-daughter rather than her good-looking and frivolous self, never seemed to enter into her calculations. She liked him immensely; his rent-roll was substantial, his family restricted to a sister and an aunt whom she mentally determined to put aside as soon as her plans had succeeded; his manners and appearance were irreproachable, consequently, so she fondly flattered herself, naught remained but to bring him to the proposing point. This was easy to determine upon, but remarkably difficult of accomplishment. Of this fact she became disagreeably aware within a few months of their first meeting. Sir Henry might possibly be thinking of matrimony, but if so, his divinity appeared already selected, and she was not Mrs., but Miss Dundas. The empty-headed and narrow-minded *belle-mère* looked upon this arrangement as a personal slight, and, with all the jealous meanness of an ungenerous nature, determined that if *she* could prevent it, Rose Dundas would never be known as Lady Chudleigh. In accordance with this admirable resolution, she made arrangements for leaving London in the middle of the season, so as to prevent any further meetings between the Chudleighs and themselves. Although by no means a conceited man, Sir Henry could not close his eyes entirely to at least some of the various sentiments entertained by the silly widow in regard to himself. Courtesy, nobility of character, and real love for her unfortunate daughter, combined to keep him silent, both at home, which was no easy task on account of the loving intimacy existing between Hilda and himself, and even in Miss Dundas' presence, an effort hardly less painful than the first. Three times, during as many months, he had met the latter while travelling; three times he had been on the point of speaking to her of all which lay gathered up in his heart, when unexpected obstacles arose to close his lips ere the decisive words had been uttered. That Miss Dundas suffered from this continual frustration of her secret aspirations, was not to be detected by her unruffled face and manner whenever they met; and possibly, owing to this outward composure, her step-mother's original intention of avoiding Sir Henry and his party, became slightly modified. She did not, it is true, go up again for the next London season, but when they met abroad, instead of retiring from the place within forty-eight hours as heretofore, she remained on for a week, or even a fortnight, contenting herself with systematically frustrating any attempts at a "tête-à-tête" which she foresaw would be fatal to her policy.

Rose saw the game, but made no sign. Sir Henry saw it, too,

but his patience had worn to a gossamer thread, and with his mind made up to put an end to all uncertainty, told his sister as much of the case as an honorable wish to screen Mrs. Dundas permitted. He was not aware of the latter's presence at Hâvre until the morning after the little dinner of which we have already spoken. Sitting by the open window, an unheeded book lying at his elbow, he was listening to his sister's exquisite rendering of Beethoven's " Moonlight " sonata on her violin. She drew her bow gently over the quivering chords, glanced over at her listener's thoughtful and absorbed countenance, then quietly ceased. The sudden cessation of the melody attracted his attention, and called up a fond smile as the player's arm was gently placed around his neck.

" You are sad, my Hermit ? " she inquired softly, pressing her lips to the wide brow which showed a few lines non-existent a month before. He did not answer for a moment, then gently pressing her down on the low chair beside him, placed his hand on her head. There was something of a father's anxiety mingled with the brotherly caress which communicated itself to the girl's mind, and made her look up inquiringly: " Has anything disagreeable happened over Rose's affairs ? "

" No, darling, nothing; I have not written yet. Reginald told me last night that they were at the Grand Hôtel in Paris, a few days ago, so my letter shall be sent there. If they have left, it can be forwarded."

" Does Reg—— Mr. Dundas know of your intentions in that quarter ? " Sir Henry smiled at the slip over the Christian name. He made no remark, however, but after an instant's silence, asked somewhat irrelevantly: " At what time does Aunt take her *siesta ?* "

" Generally about two. Why? Any place on hand?"

" Oh! nothing in particular; only Dundas spoke of coming over towards three, and asked me to find out if the Roman shrouded herself in obscurity at that time!"

Hilda blushed very decidedly, then laughed as if intensely amused: " You must remain then to play propriety," she remarked demurely. Changing the subject then rapidly as if anxious to divert her brother's attention from the brilliant color which still persisted in holding its own, she asked him if he would accompany another sonata.

"Aunt detests the piano at this hour," he objected; "but if it pleases you, my queen, it shall be done."

For another hour the two alternately played and talked musical "shop," winding up by a beautiful romance of Schubert, which brought even "Roman Roxie" to the door communicating between her chamber and the little sitting-room.

"That's a pretty thing, my dear," she observed approvingly. "You ought to play it for Mr. Dundas." Then without waiting for a reply, she continued, turning to her nephew with a slightly humorous smile: "His cousin is here, Henry; I think you ought to go and look her and the dreadful widow up."

It must be stated that Aunt Roxby, with her terribly shrewd eyes, had made out a very fair impression of the true state of affairs, and of the "dreadful widow's" pretensions. Being quite certain, however, that the lady's hopes were doomed to a complete blight, she tolerated her society for her step-daughter's sake, inwardly resolved to give her a wide berth once the marriage took place. As for the last-named arrangement not becoming an accomplished fact, sooner or later, such a contingency had never even presented itself to her consideration; indeed, in her own mind she had already settled every detail connected with the ceremony, down to the color of the bridesmaid's ribbons.

Sir Henry looked somewhat surprised at his aunt's statement.

"How do you know they are here, my dear aunt?" he asked, wonderingly.

"Know they are here? Tut, boy!" (she forgot sometimes that the "boy" numbered nigh thirty years) "I saw them from my window while you were scraping away in here. Mrs. Dundas had on some excruciatingly youthful head-gear which made her look even more ridiculous than usual. She was mincing over the sands hanging on that martyred girl's arms."

As Sir Henry knew who the "martyred girl" was, he asked no more questions, but saying he would go over to the hôtel and find out if they were staying there, left the room more hastily than was his wont.

Aunt Roxby smiled one of her dry, ironic smiles, remarking that she hoped some people did not intend remaining fools always. As she vouchsafed no explanation to her laughing niece, beyond an emphatic nod in the direction Sir Henry had taken, we can fill up the pause for ourselves.

(Conclusion next month.)

SOME LITTLE INDIAN LIVES.

(Conclusion.)

RSULA ATATHAN was the second of our chosen band
—the second also to be called away into that land
from whose " bourne no traveller returneth." Her
name, " Ursula," the " little bear," recalling the valiant woman who centuries ago ran the gauntlet of
temptation, was not unsuited to the little Indian.
She too had early run the gauntlet of temptation,
had been exposed to learn life's hardest lesson.

She was ungainly in her appearance, shy,
full of merriment when frolicking about
with her favorite companions, whom she
loved to tease; she had a beautiful contral-
to voice; she was skilful with her brush and
needle; her darning was a marvel to behold.
She was singularly faithful to any charge
entrusted to her. She was true and truthful, conscientious in her performance of
duty, fond of prayer, most tenderly devoted to the Sacred Heart of Jesus and our
Lady of Sorrows. " I cannot be angry,"
she used to say, " when I look at the picture of the Sacred Heart!" Her fervor
at Holy Communion was of that strong,
earnest kind that made her conquer her
every repugnance, and even that burning
pride of ancestry, that often made her
exclaim:

" I am an Indian girl!—all Indian! I am
no half-breed!"

CAMP DRESS.

Her name, " Atathan," recorded the brief history of her mother's ignominy, and yet, by one of those miracles of uplifting
grace, this child lived and died another Teghakwita. Never was
she betrayed into any of those acts of levity so common to her

age, so almost unavoidable in her race.   There was something of
the sturdy oak in poor Atathan's nature.   She had been tenderly
nurtured by her grandfather, Akipinaki, who, fearing lest inherited blight might fall upon this pearl, had removed her, early, to the
Mission.   Conscious of her danger, Atathan loved St. Peter's Mission as we love the pure, untainted air, or the boundless freedom
of the lonely prairie.

But when she began to fail, Akipinaki determined to remove
her, and to try the potency of her native air—the freedom of un-
trammelled camp life.   He came, and with a majestic sweep of his
uplifted hand, and an easy grace which these children of nature
alone possess, he summoned " the Mother " and the nuns to council. It was rather a solemn scene. Akipinaki argued: " I am lonesome without my girl.   The falling snows will not find her if she
remain away from her camp.   I will protect her.   She is sick.   I
see her drooping like the elk that seeks the water.   Let me have
my girl."   And these reasons kept coming back, strengthened
now and again by a forcible: " I want my girl, my own little girl,"
and then, strangers to the old man's eyes, the big tears would
start up and course down the brown cheek thick with festive
paint.   Atathan, with the nuns, listened with downcast eyes to
the tilt of words.

The Mother, an undaunted heroine, was master of the situation.   Armed with the firmness of faith and true love, she repeated: " Helno et hampsto,—I stand firm like the mountains;
I do not change;" and then proceeding with the Christian Mother's
reasons: " Atathan does not wish to leave me.   She will be exposed to danger in the camp.   You know this, Akipinaki.   Atathan knows it.   Here she is safe.   I will take good care of the
girl, Akipinaki."

At length the old man arose, his athletic, majestic presence
forcing respect.   When all was silence, his brow knit like one
that struggles with an unknown, superior force, Akipinaki slowly
uttered these remarkable words:

" Mother, thou art a big chief.   Thou hast conquered Akipinaki.
None ever did this before.   As I journeyed here I had a dream!
I dreamed that all went well with me—that I had my girl, until I
came across an obstacle I could not conquer.   Mother, this ob-

stacle was thy will. I saw two roads: one was smooth and easy; the other was full of snow. Something pushed me into this road. The girl is thine. I am done."

Many of the nuns had been praying before the Blessed Sacrament with arms extended in the form of a cross while this tilt of words went on.

THE INDIAN GIRL'S FIRST LESSON.

The victory was won. Atathan breathed freely. No mere beholder could have guessed the emotion of that silent heart as the child sat motionless beside her grandfather, with her eyes fixed upon the ground like one that is helpless in the grasp of fate. But when the Indians had gone, she went to tell her joy to our Lord in the Blessed Sacrament. "I want to be like the Blessed Virgin," she was heard to whisper as she prayed with uplifted arms. And this prayer too was heard. Her little thread of life was almost spun.

Atathan's struggle with death at first was violent. At length poor nature yielded to the call, "Arise, the winter is past!" In order to soothe her last days, the Mother read to the child from Father Faber's "All for Jesus." She listened with wrapt attention, and was particularly impressed by those words of St. Paul of the Cross as quoted in the chapter, "Love Wounded by Sin." What! a God made man!—a God crucified!—a God dead! —a God under the Sacramental Species! Who? A God,—and the big tears roll down the Indian girl's face, to think of the blessed

Passion, and the nuns would gather about with their work to enjoy the spiritual feast.

One night the nun that watched by her bedside noticed that she was unusually restless. " I want my Seven Dolor Rosary," said the Indian girl, and winding it about her wrist, this child, whose very name meant degradation, whom religion had lifted from the lowest level to the highest possibilities of maidendood, began to pray with the fervor of an angel. Nothing in the spiritual world seemed now beyond her ken, and as the dawn broke, Sister saw that death was very near. " Atathan, would you like to receive the last sacraments? "

" Yes," she whispered.

And the nuns, with lighted tapers, grouped about her bedside, and listened to the solemn rite which gave this gentle child wholly to the Lord. At touch of the Holy Oil the little eyes that already saw the invisible were cleansed, if stain there could have been upon them; the sinless ears that had heard but the prayers of the nuns and the songs of the schoolroom, were still further purified.

How sweet are Thy perfumes, O Lord! How lovely are the mission flowers and the laden breezes of the hills! Atathan's taste and speech,—had they ever been at fault? Ah, child of gentle speech, we do forgive thee, as God hath done!

When the mysterious rite of purification was ended, Atathan called by name the children of her own tribe, and drawing the oldest, " Bathay," close to her side, she whispered her last greeting to her dear old grandfather, Akipinaki. When her mother's name was mentioned, inexpressible sadness darkened the poor child's face. She made an effort to speak, raised her eyes to a picture of our Lady of Sorrows that hung at her bedside, and soon this second little life was ended.

Of the three, Watzinitha alone remains. To meet her in the schoolroom, and to catch her shy and artless smile, you might almost think of some stray angel or wandering sunbeam. Full of grace and usefulness is this dear girl whom the hand of death seems to respect. I heard them call her "St. Agnes," and I marvelled at her sweet-toned voice in the schoolroom and in the choir.

Her loaves were the best moulded, the sweetest I tasted, in the bake-house, her work the neatest in the laundry and kitchen. I saw her at the sewing-machine, I saw her at the carving-bench, I watched her at her household work in the dormitory and refectory, and above all, my gaze was fastened upon her, all unconscious, as she looked with infinite trust up to the Blessed Sacrament.

> " O child! " I thought, " of many prayers,
> Life hath quicksand! Life hath snares!
> Care and age come unawares.
> Bear a lily in thy hand ;
> Gates of brass cannot withstand
> One touch of that magic wand,—
> A smile of God thou art,
> Sweet violet in the lap of primy nature."

Two episodes of this little life deserve to be recorded. In April, 1893, the " Mother" being called to Washington on business, travelled thither on a pass, accompanied by one of her nuns and Watzinitha. Which of the girls should be the Superior's travelling companion was left to the classroom vote, and unanimously the privilege was conferred upon Watzinitha, "the prefect of our sodality," they said; the best girl in the school; the one who has sent the prettiest work to the World's Fair in darning, carving, and embroidery. Watzinitha

AN INDIAN GIRL IN MISSION DRESS.

was accordingly made ready. In silent amazement the child

looked on.   Homesickness seized her when her beloved Mission
vanished from her view.   She had never seen the railroad cars,
had never seen a ship, a telegraph, a telephone.   Her sadness
grew to desolation soon, for every newcomer in the train questioned: " Mother, are you taking the little girl to Carlisle to
finish her education?" And Carlisle to the Indian girl is
" *Ohmeh*,"—" far away." It means separation from kindred,
the dread unknown.   It was only when the Mother promised
Watzinitha that she would not leave her, and that were she
a good girl she might visit her people before returning to
the Mission, that the smiles came back to her lips.   The cars
delighted her wondrously.   She gazed out upon the fleeting landscape in speechless wonder.   Nor did anything that had the
slightest touch of humor escape her eye.   She was seen furtively
taking notes, day by day, in her diary, and these were some of
the jottings I afterwards looked over.

" Of all the things I saw at the World's Fair, I liked the Indian
camp best, because it looked like home."

" Princess Eulalia has a glass dress.   I went to-day in a little boat
that runs by electricity, all around the World's Fair."

" We saw a large wheel that turns around and lifts you high up
in the air, and shows you all the city of Chicago."

" I saw many pictures to-day, but none that I liked of our Lord
and the Blessed Virgin," etc.

Not a river, not a city, not a lake, not a mountain that she passed,
but Watzinitha would note down its name.   Should Sister forget
to mention some new geographical point as they sped along, not
daring to importune, Watzinitha still would question with her
eyes.   Every day she was examined upon what she had learned
the day before.   If a name escaped her, she would pause and
study it over in her well-ordered memory.   Unlike other children,
Watzinitha never guessed or blundered.   She answered correctly,
or not at all.   Wonderful was the interest the little Indian girl
excited throughout the East; wonderful the kindness that greeted
her.   The child revelled in the wonders of the World's Fair,
whither she went accompanied by some friends and relatives of
the " Mother," and sang and played her simple ditties for all the
notabilities of the land.   His Eminence, Cardinal Gibbons, and

Monsignor Satolli, laid their hands in blessing upon her brow, the great and learned in the Church of God stooping graciously to that which therein is lowliest.

Hon. E. F. Dunne, of Florida, said in presenting the child to the Infanta, Princess Eulalia, that on this four hundredth anniversary he was repeating the work of Columbus, bringing the Indians of North America to the feet of their Catholic majesties, and the charmed Eulalia stooped and kissed the little princess of darker blood. And so little Watzinitha journeyed on—a marvel to all who saw what education and religion had done for the poor Indian girl. Nor were her guides ashamed of her gentle, modest ways, as they travelled on; nor in the halls of spacious academies, as she mingled with the daughters of wealth and fashion—the darling of the passing hour; nor when in communities, where they tarried, she followed the religious to the Holy Table, her rosary about her neck, her hands joined, her eyes cast down in prayerful recollection. Priests who saw her, who heard her confessions, singled her out amid all the other children, and inquired, "Who is the new-comer that prays and understands her religion so well?" Nor did Watzinitha lose her deep religious love of prayer. Wherever she went, she wore her rosary around her neck; even when, in the White House, she spoke with President Cleveland; and upon her return, she gladly greeted her humble Mission

WATZINITHA AS PRESENTED TO THE PRINCESS EULALIA.

home and dear companions. And they, in their turn, were glad to see Watzinitha, so dear still, and so unchanged, but grown more beautiful.

And rumors of her beauty, her long and wondrous journey, spread among her people, and the High Chief's son, "Ignaz," demanded her hand in marriage. The too-fond Indian mother, flattered in her secret vanity, favored the proposal, and so worked upon the Indian agent, Major Kelly, U. S. A., the eminent and highly cultured representative of the Government in the Gros-Ventre country, that he at length issued the order that Watzinitha should be delivered up into the hands of Ignaz, and should be stationed as assistant cook at the Agency school. The situation was alarming. Nothing could save the girl but her own free will, for the high-born Ignaz was an anointed warrior in his tribe, and the Agent's will was not to be resisted.

Watzinitha drooped, and seemed to fail. Her companions sought help for her in prayer. Earnest were these supplications. At length, one day, refreshed and strengthened by hope, Waztinitha got up from her sick bed, and, all unaided, penned in a clear and beautiful hand, the following letter to the Agent:

"*Your Honor:* I am not strong enough for the position you offer me. Nor am I as yet satisfied with my education. I want to continue my studies. I do not wish to get married. I absolutely refuse the hand of Ignaz, and the position you offer me."

The girl's own will had saved her.

Is there not much room for reflection in the above words of a poor Indian girl, so firm, and yet so modest? No flattered vanity, no foolish love of independence in that pure heart!

Close upon this letter to the Agent followed one to her mother, which elicited from that overfond and yet true heart the following reply, written by the "Black Gown," at its dictation.

"*My child:* I have your letter. I love you. Be at rest. Since you do not wish the hand of Ignaz, he shall not trouble you. I want only your good, and wished to have you near me. But you love St. Peter's Mission more than any other, and are happy there. Remain, then, where you are. I am well. Your sister greets you! I am done!"

So ended this simple romance. And the girl who, more than all the rest, had attracted my attention when first I entered the classrooms at St. Peter's Mission; still graces them in all her innocence and loveliness. Long years may she still continue there, the delight and consolation of the devoted nuns, who day by day, in silent, patient toil, work out the "Indian Question."

Have not our simple lines answered this oft-repeated question: Are not these girls well worth lifting up? And is not the silent, all-evangelical religious life at St. Peter's Mission, Montana, also worth a girl's loftiest aspirations? But further still.

The nuns have recently moved into a substantial, but unfinished house,—rough floors, uncased doors and windows. Plastering, through the charity of friends, is partially completed, where during the rough Montana winter they have seen it 15 degrees below zero in their kitchen. Some rooms the nuns have succeeded in finishing, but in their name and for their relief do we ask continual and increased assistance.

Surely are these self-forgetting women deserving of help.

> "Help the poor, ye rich, that Almighty God
> Who endows you all, to your sons give strength,
> To your daughters grace, that your vines produce
> Always luscious fruit, and that riper wheat
> Make your gran'ries bend, that you every day
> Better, holier be, and that you may see
> How the angels pass through your dreams at night."

And as these words of the poet, like sunbeams straying down from Heaven, albeit we know not when nor how, penetrate the Catholic households of America, may this blessing, too, of the poetic Indian race, follow them:

"Give, and may your men be ever brave, your women faithful, and may lilies bloom around your maidens' brows!"

O height incomprehensible! O grandeur immeasurable! O abyss impenetrable! Every day, from one end of the earth to the other, in the highest heights of the heavens, and in the profoundest depths of the abysses, everything preaches, everything publishes, the admirable Mary! The nine choirs of angels, men of all ages, conditions, and religions, good or bad, nay, even the devils themselves, willingly or unwillingly, are compelled, by the force of truth, to call her Blessed.

—Blessed Louis Grignon de Montfort, O. P.

OUR LADY'S ROSARY.

VERY REV. THOMAS ESSER, O.P., S. T. M.

THE sacred songs of the Old Testament have not been suffered to die away in the Church of the New Covenant. Far from it, they to this day constitute the chief portion of the Divine Office; so that in them the Church yet daily offers God the tribute of her praise and thanksgiving, the expression of her petitions and works of expia-

tion. It is the very spirit of God that breathes in them, and in the light of the Christ that came, their rich contents gain a clearness double that which they had already had in the twilight of promise and prophecy. "No song composed by man," as Cardinal Wiseman observes, "can therefore be so often repeated as these divine hymns. They remain ever fresh to the heart, as do the solemn melodies in which the Church sings them to the lips and ears. Both are therefore calculated to be used daily—yes, hourly—without losing their peculiar charm."[1]

---

[1] Cardinal Wiseman, Misc. Writings. (Germ. transl., Verm. Schriften [Köln, 1855], ii. 234). Additional light may here be thrown on what has already been said on the Rosary's adaptation to every condition of life. "All the elegiac

And what the learned divine, representing the Church, finds beautiful and ennobling in the Psalms, he, and the humblest laborer with him, may find again in the prayers of the Rosary. It has rightly been said that the Rosary is the laic's breviary. It is so in very truth. It can be chorally recited, as the Church recites the Psalms. But it is yet more,—for certainly the clergy should not leave this most excellent prayer to the laity alone. Let us therefore express ourselves otherwise. As the Psalter is a constant prayer of the Church to God, so is the Rosary her uninterrupted prayer to Mary; for Mary is the Queen of the Rosary. Rightly, therefore, do we call it the Marian Psalter, and rightly is the number of its angelical salutations made to correspond with that of the Psalms of the Royal Psalmist. And as the servants of the Church recite, in prayer, the entire Psalter of one hundred and fifty Psalms in the course of each week (in so far, namely, as the office is *de tempore*), so, likewise, should the members of the Rosary Confraternity, in the same length of time, recite at least one Marian Psalter of one hundred and fifty *Aves.*

In a foregoing paper[1] an intrinsic reason was assigned for the threefold division of the Marian Psalter into its joyful, sorrowful, and glorious parts,—namely, the clearly-defined distinction of the threefold train of thought included in the corresponding mysteries. But another ground for the division could be found in the like partition of the Psalter. Not alone that it was largely the custom, at prayer, in ancient monasteries, to recite the Psalter in three parts of fifty Psalms each,[2] but the very nature of its contents early gave rise to the threefold division, which

---

plaints that open tribulation has wrung from the souls of many generations, all that devout lyric inspiration has brought forth of the lofty, of the exultant, of the consoling, and of the heartfelt, of warning, of comfort, and of instruction —all is laid upon the lips of David, and sounds forth from his Psalter."—*Gorres-Mythengesch. 2 T., p. 473.*

[1] For preceding articles of this series see THE ROSARY MAGAZINE, October and December, 1894.

[2] Thus, for instance, St. Peter Damian, a Camaldulensian monk of the monastery of Fonte-Avellana, states that there the office of the dead, *cum novem lectionibus dicitur, tribus nimirum per quinquagenos Psalmos.* St. Pet. Dam., Opusc. 14 (Opp. ed. Constant. Cajetan. Paris, 1743; III., 162).

the expositors sought to adapt to the various conditions of the faithful, and to their standing in grace.[1]

At all events, it will readily be found that the three parts of the Marian Psalter may fitly be brought to bear upon the state of the innocent, of the penitent, and of the perfect. For it can hardly be otherwise than that the joyful part of the Rosary, with its innocent-breathing mysteries from the childhood of our Divine Lord and from the life of His spotless Mother, very specially comes home to innocent and childlike souls, and sweetly works upon them. So, too, the mysteries of the bitter passion of our Blessed Redeemer and the dolors of His sorrowful Mother must be grateful to those who walk in the path of penance, and never more so than when sorrow for their sins strikes deeply into their hearts. On the other hand, in the glorious mysteries our hearts break forth into joy, like that of Easter-tide, and in the as-

---

[1] Psalmi distinguntur in tres quinquagenas; et hæc distinctio comprehendit triplicem statum populi fidelis; scilicet statum *pænitentiæ*, et ad hunc ordinatur prima quinquagena, quæ finitur in "*Miserere mei Deus;*" qui est psalmus pœnitentiæ; secunda *justitiæ*, et hæc consistit in judicio et finitur in Ps. 100: *Misericordiam et judicium;* tertia *laudem gloriæ includit æternæ*, et ideo finitur; *Omnis spiritus laudet Dominum.—S. Thom. Aquin.* In prœm. in psalm.

Partitus est liber (psalmorum) in tres partes, id est in tres quinquagenas, secundum triplicem statum hominum. Omne enim genus hominum pascitur et docetur; in prima quinquagena, pascuntur incipientes pane hordeaceo; in secunda proficientes pane triticeo; in tertia profecti, sive pervenientes pane similagineo. Unde *Augustinus:* In triplicato autem quinquagenario, triplicis peccati remissio, id est cordis, oris, et operis, et ipsa Trinitatis unitas designatur, quæ totum hoc operatur. *Card. Hugo de S. Caro,* In prologo in postil. sup. psalter.

This tri-partition is also to be found in the oldest German translations of the Psalms (viz., of the XI. century). Cf. Mullenhoff–Scherer, Denkmaler deutscher Poesie und Prosa aus dem achten bis zwolften Jahrhundert. 2 Aufl. Berlin, 1873, p. 570.

St. Augustine says that the order of the Psalms, which appeared to him to contain a great mystery, had not yet become clear to him. Nevertheless, he rejects their division into five books (the close of each of which is indicated by the words *fiat, fiat*), while in the tri-partition of the one book according to its contents he finds something " right, and full worthy of consideration ":

" It seems to me to be not without purpose that the fiftieth Psalm treats of penance, the hundredth of mercy, and the one hundred and fiftieth of the praise of God in His saints. For in this wise we strive after the eternal and bless-

sured hope of our own glorification which they offer us we are
already admitted into the choirs of those who, made perfect, have
entered into the joy of the Lord. And through the Rosary prayers, we await the same joy from our Father who is in Heaven,
from God, of whose unity of essence and trinity of persons the
tri-partition of the Marian Psalter also puts us in mind.

In this parallel between the Marian Psalter and the Psalter of
David, the ten " Hail Marys " which enter into each decade, find
an exposition no less deep and significant. The Latin word,
Psalterium, means not only the collection or the Book of Psalms,
but also a stringed instrument, to whose music these sacred songs
were sung. This Psaltery, which may also be called a harp, had
ten strings. Hence David, in one of his sacred poems, exclaims:
" To Thee, O Lord, I will sing a new canticle; on the psaltery and
an instrument of ten strings I will sing praises to Thee." (Ps.

---

ed life, by first detesting our sins, then by leading a good life, in order, after our
detestation of evil and the consummation of a good life, to merit life eternal. In
the plan of His most hidden Justice and Goodness, God has also called those
whom He predestinated; 'and whom He called, them He also justified; and
whom He justified, them He also glorified.' Our predestination does not take
place in us, but secretly within Himself, in His foreknowledge. But the others
come to pass in us: vocation, justification, and glorification. We are called
to penance by preaching, for thus did the Lord begin His Gospel: ' Do penance, for the kingdom of Heaven is at hand.' We are justified by the call of
mercy and by the fear of judgment; therefore it is written: ' Save me, O God,
by Thy name, and judge me in Thy strength.' (Ps. liii. 3.) He does not fear
judgment who previously, by prayer, has obtained his salvation. Called, we
renounce the devil by penance, in order not to remain under his yoke. Justified, we are made whole by mercy, so that we fear not judgment. Glorified,
we enter into eternal life, where we praise God without end. .... Penance
afflicts with pain, justice calms, eternal life glorifies. The voice of penance
is: ' Have mercy on me, O God, according to Thy great mercy; and according to the multitude of Thy tender mercies blot out my iniquities.' (Ps. l. 1-
2.) It brings God the offering of an afflicted spirit and of a contrite and
humbled heart. The voice of the justice of Christ in His elect is: ' Mercy
and judgment I will sing to Thee, O Lord; I will sing and I will understand in
the unspotted way when Thou shalt come to me.' (Ps. c. 1.) For mercy helps
us to do justice, that we may come safe to judgment, by which all who have
wrought iniquity shall be scattered from out of the city of the Lord. The
voice of life eternal in the glorified is: ' Praise ye the Lord in His holy
places.' " (Ps. cl. 1.) –*St. Aug. Enarrat. in Ps. cl., n. 1-3.*

cxliii. 9.) And in another place: "Give praise to the Lord on the
harp; sing to Him with the psaltery, the instrument of ten strings."
(Ps. xxxii. 2.) In the holy Rosary, we respond to this exhortation
quite literally. For on it, the Marian Psaltery, we sing a new
canticle to the Queen of Heaven, we sing to her on a harp of
ten strings. And the Angelical Salutation ten times repeated in
each mystery, is the more appropriate because Mary's own canticle, the *Magnificat*, is made up of just ten verses, for which reason it has also been called a *Psalterium dechachordum*, a psaltery
of ten strings. How really beautiful is this conception, that every
first chord of this ten-stringed instrument of the Rosary is struck
with the Lord's Prayer, the "Our Father," and the last thrills joyously and dies out in the sweet tones of the "Glory be to the
Father, and to the Son, and to the Holy Ghost!" The last
sounds of the world's history will be those of the "Glory be to
the Father," and they shall not die away for all eternity.

The holy Fathers also find in the ten strings of the Psaltery
an allusion to the ten commandments, which, fulfilled, form the
most pleasing canticle of divine praise that can be offered to almighty God.[1] It will certainly not be without great profit to us
to remember this whenever we are at our beads; for the chief
fruit of our prayer should surely be a greater conformity of our
thoughts, deeds, and life to the sacred law of God. And if this
is actually wrought in us by the holy Rosary, as it certainly can
and ought to be, then its fifteen mysteries will be to us so many
steps or degrees, by which we ascend the holy Mount of God;
nay, more; not only will they, like the fifteen steps of the Temple
of Jerusalem, lead us up to the "Porch of the Lord," but also into the "Sanctuary" and into the inmost "Holy of Holies."

To some, however, there is a smack of superstition in the
circumstance that a determinate number of *Aves* is employed in
the Rosary. But such persons may readily be silenced, if it is
pointed out to them that, as there can be no measure without
number, so also no real order. For how could the Rosary be re-

[1] For instance, *S. Gregorius M., Moral.* lib. xxxv., cap. 16, n. 42: Denarius
numerus in Scriptura perfectus est, quia Lex in decem præceptis concluditur.
—*Id.* Homil. in *Ezech.* lib. ii. hom. 6, n. 5: Denarius numerus pro perfectione
semper accipitur, quia in decem præceptis Legis custodia continetur.

cited in common, like the Psalms, if it were not known how much
to pray?   Besides, for the reason that many members of the Rosary Confraternity bind themselves to one and the same devotion,
that devotion must needs be made up of a determinate number
of prayers.   But how could their devotion be one and the same,
if they did not all pray equally much?   If they agreed to pray a
greater or less number of *Aves* than 150, the question would again
present itself: "Why just so many?"   The question we have here
to deal with, proves then, at best, to be but one that betrays the
unreasonableness of the questioner, and, like many prattling inquiries of children, can hardly be answered.

Nevertheless, we will briefly consider the meaning, already referred to, of the numbers that occur in the Rosary. "The purport of number," says St. Augustine, "is not to be disregarded;
since many texts of sacred scripture show the careful reader of
what worth it is to be esteemed.   Nor is it said to no purpose in
the service of God; "Thou hast ordered all things in measure,
number, and weight." (Wisdom xi. 21.) [1]   These words refer
not only to the natural order, but also to the order of grace.   In
the Old Testament, as in the New, all the appointments and dis-
pensations of God in regard to the salvation of man came to pass
according to determinate numbers.   Whence, then, any unwil-
lingness to find these numbers occurring again in a prayer that
springs forth so naturally from the spirit of Christianity as the
holy Rosary?

After one hundred and fifty days, the waters of the deluge subsided, and we pray one hundred and fifty *Aves* in order, through
the mediation of the "Help of Christians," to avert both the
temporal and the everlasting judgments of God.

In the Old Law, every fiftieth year was a jubilee.   It was a
year of general release from all debts, for the discharge of prisoners, and for the liberation of slaves.   The Church of the New

---

[1] Ratio numeri contemnenda non est, quæ in multis sanctarum Scripturarum
locis quam magni æstimanda sit, elucet diligenter intuentibus.   Nec frustra in
laudibus Dei dictum est: *omnia in mensura, et numero, et pondere disposuiste.*
S. August. De Civitate Dei, lib. xi. cap. 30. On this subject, cf. Kreuser, a.
a. O. p. 519, etc. Id., Wiederum christlicher Kirchenban, Brixen, 1868, i. 5
and 6, etc. ; Bahr, Symbolik des Mosaischen Kultus, Heidelberg, 1837, i. 175, etc.

Testament, following this example, also instituted a jubilee every fiftieth year, in which, in consideration of special works of piety, plenary remission of the temporal punishment due to sin was solemnly granted to the faithful. Have we not, therefore, a right, after each fifty *Aves*, to hope for a rich participation in the atoning and blessed virtue of the Redemption—that sublime jubilee announced by the *Ave* of the angel? The tones of the " Hail Mary, full of grace," rang in the jubilee of Christendom with their solemn music. It was the same that set us free from the bondage of Satan.

On the fiftieth day after our Lord, by His resurrection, had finally triumphed over the powers of darkness, the Holy Ghost, a new Spirit, came down upon the Apostles and the Blessed Mother of Jesus. We wish fully to share in the Spirit of God's Sonship; so also do we desire to be set free from the rest of the servitude of Satan, from personal sins and guilt; therefore fifty times do we address Mary, who crushed our enemy's head. By means of conjoined mysteries, these fifty *Aves* are rounded into five decades, and with them we hope to vanquish our too powerful adversary, as David, going forth with a sling and five stones from a brook, met and prevailed over the Philistine. (I. Kings, xvii. 40, etc.) Futhermore, these five mysteries, devoutly meditated, provide us with spiritual nourishment and strength, like to the five loaves with which our Lord fed the multitude. (John vi. 7, etc.) It is not without significance, therefore, that we limit the meditations of an ordinary Rosary to five chief mysteries. We are wont, too, to reduce the many wounds that covered the dying Saviour, to five, which we consider as so many special tokens or instances of His love. And if we allot the usual Rosary five parts of *ten* " Hail Marys " each, it is sufficiently explained by this, that the number ten, complete in itself, is the most perfect of numbers. There is no new one above it. To go beyond it, we must needs return to the symbol of unity. Hence it is, too, that the simplest method of numbers is the so-called decimal system. Therefore did God demand a tithe, or a tenth part of all possessions as an offering to Himself, and its payment was the condition that insured the rightful ownership of the remainder.

In its numbers, then, the Rosary has a foundation and a superstructure, which, planned in strict accordance with the laws of architecture, give it the form of a grand minster, like the Gothic cathedrals of the Middle Ages.' As at the entrance of these noble structures, sculptured representations of the Fall, or of the Redemption, or of the Mother of God, or of a chosen group of saints, attract our attention and put us in mind of the whole work of the Redemption, and thereby of the meaning of the house of God, so do we first enter the temple of the Rosary through the beautiful and richly ornamented portal of the *Credo* (I believe in God, etc.), and through a vestibule, in which a view of the three Theological virtues fills us with devotion, and prepares us for an edifying impression of the interior structure. The five decades give us the effect of nave and fourfold aisle, with their lofty arches rising grandly above the springing of their graceful pillars, and raising up heart and soul to their highest summits. " Sursum Corda! " Approaching towards the altar, the two aisles on either side of the nave are merged into one, there forming but a triple interior;' and chapels are grouped about the choir, like an encircling wreath, and their pictured altars, than which no master-hand has produced more splendid, interiorly touch us with their richly-wrought charms.

Such are the mysteries which our meditative spirit considers as they unfold themselves to view, ever the same yet ever new. And the sunlight streams through the stained-glass windows, mellowed and grateful to the eye. More of heavenly brightness it cannot yet endure.

' Cf. Rippel-Himioben, Die Schonheit der Katholischen Kirche, (3 edit.) 1866, p. 200, etc., and a sermon by a Frisch, the skeleton outline of which may be found in Scherer, Bibliothek für Prediger, VI. 809, etc.

' Thus, for instance, in the Cathedral of Cologne, in the Marien-Kirche at Danzig, and in the minster of Ulm, the body of the church for the use of the laity consists of nave and four aisles. The eastern half of the structure, together with the choir, consists of nave and two aisles. They stand to each other in the symbolical relation of the Old to the New Testament. The former symbolizes the five books of Moses, the latter the mystery of the most blessed Trinity.

THE COLUMBIAN CATHOLIC SUMMER
SCHOOL.

HE countless and grateful readers of Dr. Maurice F. Egan's delightful " Sunday Evening Chats " will not be surprised to learn that among the many charming and fruitful ideas that have seen the light " over the tea-cups " in the ideal little home of "The Lilacs," near Notre Dame University, Indiana, none can more proudly lay claim to this " poet's corner " as its natal home than the great and successful project of the Columbian Catholic Summer School; for there was it born, and there it waxed strong, and thence was it sent out upon its lofty mission.

Rev. J. A. Zahm, C. S. C., Ph. D., of the above University, and Mr. H. J. Desmond, of the *Catholic Citizen,* Milwaukee, while spending a social hour with Professor Egan, the incomparable host of "The Lilacs," talked over the plan, decided to secure the co-operation of their friend, Hon. William J. Onahan, LL. D., of Chicago, the champion of every high Catholic movement in the

PROFESSOR EGAN.

West, and then to present the scheme for the consideration of a few able and influential leaders of the chief cities of the Northwest. Accordingly, two or three meetings were held in Chicago, a Board of Directors was appointed, Madison, Wisconsin, was chosen as a favorable site, a Committee on Studies, consisting of

Rt. Rev. S. G. Messmer, D. D., D. C. L., Rev. J. A. Zahm, C. S. C.,. Ph. D., Rev. J. F. X. Hoeffer, S. J., Maurice F. Egan, LL. D., and Condé B. Pallen, Ph. D., was selected, and the work of the Columbian Catholic Summer School was outlined; lecturers, the best talent of the territory, were secured; and the tiny mustard-seed planted in the fertile soil of a few noble minds upon that memorable evening at "The Lilacs" became, in less than one year, the delightful, far-spreading, and generous tree which sheltered so many beneath its bounteous shade during the three incomparable weeks of July, 1895.

Rt. Rev. S. G. Messmer, D. D., the learned and genial bishop of Green Bay, Wisconsin, as President of the School, set about with an earnest determination to make the undertaking a success. A true American spirit of enterprise, and a broad, sound Catholic tone, characterized the work of the School from the first. The Rt. Rev. Bishop's personality was visible throughout; for his example of untiring zeal and Christian courtesy and cordiality became contagious, and as one great family, with him as its revered father and head, the Columbian Catholic Summer School opened most auspiciously, and progressed in an orderly and systematic manner for the three weeks devoted to its course. Great credit and deep gratitude are due to the Rt. Rev. President and his able and generous co-laborers for the manner in which the work was carried on, and for the beautiful Christian spirit which they infused and maintained; for well might one exclaim, upon seeing the unity of faith and genuine fraternal charity that prevailed: "Behold how these Christians love one another!" Here one realized and saw exemplified the inexpressible charm of what Professor Egan defines as the only American aristocracy, viz., "the aristocracy of intellect and virtue." For the mission fulfilled by the Summer School was not only that of presenting the principles of science and ethics for the speculation and instruction of the cultivated mind, nor that of simply opening up new avenues of knowledge to the eager seeker after truth. All this was done in a scholarly and able way, conclusively proving, at the same time, that even in this sceptical age the Church of God, "ever ancient and ever new," is now, as she was in the glorious past, the true mother and nurse of science and art and literature—of every great and grand achievement of the human mind—all of which, when truest and most sublime, claim as their proudest privilege her inspiration and protection. Thus before and beyond this real intellectual profit was the revival of a deep, loyal, enthusiastic devotion to Holy Mother Church, a chivalrous pride in her gifted sons, both lay and cleric, the mutual understanding and cordial geniality of the members of the hierarchy, clergy, and laity,—the oneness of mind and heart, the bond of perfect sympathy which united the entire assembly, all glowing with the light and joy and charity of the Spirit of wisdom and

BISHOP MESSMER, D. D.

piety, recalling to the Catholic mind the days of the ages of faith, which, glorious as we know they were, could rarely boast a season more manifestly blest by God, and more thoroughly appreciated by godly and gifted men, than this unique assembly in Wisconsin's beautiful and favored capital.

The session opened on Sunday, July 14, with the celebration of Pontifical High Mass at St. Patrick's Church, Rt. Rev. S. G. Messmer celebrating, and Rt. Rev. F. S. Chatard, D. D., of Indianapolis, preaching the sermon. On Monday the attendance at the Fuller Opera House was most encouraging. The Rt. Rev. President tendered to all a hearty welcome, expressed his satisfaction in the lively interest and genuine good will manifested, and also his pleasure upon seeing in the audience so many religious—as some sixty or seventy were in attendance. These consisted of members of different Orders, among them being a large number of the Sisters of St. Dominic, whose mother-house is at St. Clara's Convent, Sinsinawa, Wisconsin. These Sisters conduct a most successful parochial school at St. Raphael's Church, Madison, and have a very promising academy at Edgewood Villa, about a mile and a half from the city. Among the other communities represented were: the Sisters of Mercy, from Independence and Cedar Rapids, Iowa; Sisters of Charity of the Blessed Virgin Mary, Dubuque; Sisters of the Congregation of Notre Dame, Chicago; Franciscans from La Crosse, and Benedictines from Eau Claire, Wisconsin, and Duluth, Minnesota. The Sisters were in attendance at all the daily exercises, and, through the courtesy of the gentlemen who gave the evening lectures, were favored with these papers also in the afternoon, at the Convent hall.

The first day of the Summer School was rendered happily memorable by the reading of the following highly appreciated letter, and the telegram of good-will from their fellow-workers in the Eastern field:

THE HOLY FATHER'S LETTER OF APPROVAL AND BENEDICTION, ADDRESSED TO HIS EMINENCE, CARDINAL GIBBONS.

The Holy Father, already informed of the good done in past years through religious conferences held in Summer Schools, has heard with much satisfaction that such a Summer School is to be held this year, in Madison, Wisconsin, from the 14th of July to the 4th of August. His Holiness does not entertain a doubt but the same interest will be shown in these lectures at Madison that has been accorded such conventions in the past, the importance of the matters to be treated and the ability of the lecturers to whom the subjects are intrusted being a guarantee of this. Desiring, however, to make known the interest which he also takes in the Summer School at Madison, and the hope he cherishes to see it bear good fruit in spreading religious truth, the august Pontiff wishes that Your Eminence express to the Rt. Rev. Bishop of Green Bay, and to all those who aid him, his fatherly satisfaction at the work they are doing, bestowing upon them also the Apostolic Benediction as a pledge of his paternal benevolence and of plentiful fruit. May Your Eminence be pleased to communicate these feelings of His Holiness towards the promotors of the Summer School of Madison, and permit me to profit by this occasion to express anew my sentiments of profound veneration with which I most humbly kiss your hand. Your Eminence's most humble and devoted servant,

M. CARD. RAMPOLLA.

TELEGRAM OF GREETING FROM THE PRESIDENT OF THE CATHOLIC SUMMER SCHOOL OF AMERICA.

The Catholic Summer School of America, in fourth session at Plattsburg, sends greeting to the Columbian Catholic Summer School, and wishes success to its efforts for Catholic higher education among the people.

THOMAS J. CONATY.

Reverend P. J. Danehy, D. D., St. Paul's Seminary, St. Paul, Minnesota, delivered the first lecture of the Columbian Catholic Summer School, and in his opening discourse sounded the key-note of the School's unparalleled success.   The effect was electric.   He had won at once the respect, confidence, and admiration of every auditor, proving himself to be a man of great natural gifts, profound

THE FULLER OPERA HOUSE, MADISON, WIS., IN WHICH THE SESSIONS OF THE
COLUMBIAN CATHOLIC SUMMER SCHOOL WERE HELD.

erudition, and magnetic personality.   His course of lectures on " The Sacred Scriptures" consisted of:

" The Origin and Development of the Canon;" "The In-spired Record of Revelation;" "The Genuine Text and Its Guar-anty;" "Rules of Biblical Interpretation;" "The Bible in the Family, the School, and the Pulpit."

These were presented in his own clear, masterly way, giving evidence of years of profound study, and of the grandeur and beauty of a gifted, keen, and deeply reverential mind.

"Science and Dogma" was treated in a course of five lectures by Reverend J. A. Zahm, C. S. C., Ph. D., of Notre Dame University, Indiana, his subjects being: "Some Modern Scientific Errors," "Agnosticism," "Evolution," "Origin and Nature of Life," "Design and Purpose in Nature."

Three lectures on the "Historical Development of Catholic Popular Education Before the Seventeenth Century" were given by Reverend Eugene Magevney, S. J., of Detroit, Michigan, under the following heads: "Christian Education in the First Centuries;" "The Monastic Institutions;" "Mediæval Schools and Scholars." The literary style of these lectures was remarkable for its finish and polish, and the treatment of the subjects under consideration was able and scholarly.

In addition to the above, Professor John G. Ewing, of Notre Dame, spoke ably on "Magna Charter and the Church," Miss Nellie Joyce, on "Physical Culture," tracing its course in development, decline, and resurrection from the days of the Greeks till the present. A masterly paper, "Christianity and Buddhism," prepared by Mgr. de Harlez, was read by Rev. D. O'Hearn, of St. John's Cathedral, Milwaukee; and a comprehensive paper on Joan of Arc was given by Professor J. W. Willstack, of Lafayette, Ind.

A public reception took place on Monday evening, during which Senator Vilas delivered an address of general welcome; Governor Upham spoke warmest words of greeting on behalf of the State; City Attorney John Alyward, on behalf of the city; Professor J. W. Sterns, on behalf of the State University; Rev. E. G. Updike, of the Congregational Church, Madison, on behalf of non-Catholics. Rt. Rev. Bishop Messmer and Hon. W. J. Onahan responded in their happiest vein. Thursday afternoon was spent amidst the beautiful scenery of Lake Monona.

An audience averaging six hundred persons attended the four daily sessions of the Summer School during its second week. The regular lecturers of this week were Rev. J. J. Conway, S.J., of St. Louis, on Ethics, and Dr. Egan, on Literature. "The Subject-matter of Ethics," "The Ethical Norm," "The Natural Law," "The Tribunal of Conscience," "The Doctrine of Right," were the subjects treated ably by Father Conway. " The Catholic Church and Literature," " Influences in Literature," " The Evolution of the Novel," " Romanticism and Realism in English Literature," " Hamlet," such were the subjects handled in Dr. Egan's delightful way.

" The Essentials of Criticism," and " The Qualities of a Critic," two papers read during the opening days of this second week, were the keenly discriminating work of Rev. Charles P. de Smedt, S. J., Director of the College of Bollandists writers in Paris. The papers were read by Father Danehy.

The course of this week comprised also the following subjects, all treated in a masterly way: " Aerial Navigation," by A. F. Zahm, associate professor of physics at the Catholic University, Washington, an authority upon questions of aerial transits; " The Spanish Inquisition," by Rev. J. F. Nugent, of Des Moines, Iowa; " The Missionary Explorers of the Northwest," by Judge Kelly, of St. Paul's; " Christian Science and Faith Cure," by Dr. Hart, of the Ohio Medical College; and " American Mound Builders and Cliff Dwellers," a paper prepared by Marquis Nadaillac, and read by Rev. D. O'Hearn.

The program presented by the Cardinal Gibbons Reading Circle, of Milwaukee, was a special feature of this week, while its greatest social feature was the evening reception tendered to His Grace, Archbishop Feehan, of Chicago.

The regular lecturers of the third week were Rt. Rev. S. G. Messmer, Dr. La Boule, and Hon. R. Graham Frost. " Man's Twofold Destiny," " The State and Its Power," " The Church and Her Mission," " Separation and War," " Union and Peace," such were the subjects that Bishop Messmer treated in his able way.

Father La Boule's instructive and entertaining course upon the " Eastern Schismatic Church " was presented in five divisions: " A Bird's-Eye View," " The Greek Schism," " The Russian Schism," " The Present Internal Condition," " Reunion with Rome."

Hon. R. Graham Frost, of St. Louis, Missouri, treated the subject of " Economic Questions" in five lectures, taking as the basis of his lectures our Holy Father Leo XIII.'s Encyclical on " Labor," and under the following heads: "The Foundation" (Value), "Wealth," "Hire," "Strife," and "Reconciliation," instructed his large and deeply-interested and attentive audience upon these ordinarily dry, abstract subjects in such a clever and original way that the hour, under his magic spell, sped unheeded, and the audience arose refreshed, enlightened, and eager for more.

This week's course also embraced "Savonarola," Condé B. Pallen's scholarly review of the life and times of this remarkable man; "Hypnotism," by Dr. J. K. Bauduy, and "Church Music," by Rev. Raphael Fuhr, O. S. F.

The final triumph of the closing week was the lecture upon "The Present Position of Catholics," delivered by a noble scion of a noble race, the son of a soldier and patriot, Reverend Thomas E. Sherman, S. J., of Frederick, Maryland. Suffice it to say of his success that he convinced every hearer by his earnest, clear, and indisputable statements of the grandeur and beauty of the truth he presented, and won for himself, by his truly charming manner, the admiration of his remarkably large and enthusiastic audience.

One of the most encouraging features of the Summer School was the lively interest manifested by the archbishops, bishops, and priests of the Western School territory. Their daily attendance at the lectures for the successive weeks was exceedingly gratifying to all interested in the welfare of the School. Among those who honored the School by their presence at some time during the session, and most of whom, by special request, expressed in short and happy addresses their interest in the undertaking, were:

Mt. Rev. P. A. Feehan, D. D., Chicago; Mt. Rev. John Ireland, D. D., St. Paul, Minn.; Rt. Rev. S. G. Messmer, D. D., Green Bay, Wis.; Rt. Rev. F. S. Chatard, D. D., Indianapolis, Ind.; Rt. Rev. John Shanley, D. D., Fargo, N. Dakota; Rt. Rev. J. B. Cotter, D. D., Winona, Minn.; Rt. Rev. James McGoldrick, D. D., Duluth, Minn.; Rt. Rev. James Schwebach, D. D., La Crosse, Wis.; Rt. Rev. Joseph Rademacher, D. D., Fort Wayne, Ind.; Rt. Rev. J. A. Watterson, D. D., Columbus, O.

Perhaps the greatest triumph of the three delightful weeks

was the lecture on "Patriotism," pronounced by veterans to be the grandest speech ever made under the flag, delivered by Archbishop Ireland, in Armory Hall, before five thousand eager and enthusiastic citizens. As the eloquent prelate concluded his powerful and soul-stirring discourse with the lines from the national hymn,

> " My country ! 'tis of thee,
> Sweet land of liberty,
> Of thee I sing,"

the orchestra took up the strain, the vast audience arose, and with one voice, as with one grateful and bursting heart, poured forth in song their love of God and fatherland in their country's glorious anthem.

A reception to His Grace, Archbishop Ireland, was one of the very enjoyable features of the closing week.

The Sunday services throughout the sessions took place in St. Patrick's and St. Raphael's churches. The preachers upon these occasions were : Bishop Chatard, Bishop Watterson, Bishop Messmer, Bishop Rademacher, and Rev. J. Denehy.

The musical talent of Madison added much to the religious and social features of the Summer School.

Financially, socially, intellectually, and numerically, the C. C. S. S. was in every sense a success. The register showed an attendance of at least twelve hundred pupils, and the treasury claims, after the defrayal of all expenses, nearly two thousand dollars.

One of the most touching sights of the assembly was the fervent faith of the members, manifested in a particular way by the hundreds who approached the Holy Table in honor of the Sacred Heart on the first Friday of August. Another striking feature of the School was the congregational singing of hymns and national songs before or after the different sessions. The hundreds who came from St. Louis, St. Paul, Dubuque, Chicago, Denver, Milwaukee, Cincinnati, and other cities, and who met as strangers and parted as friends, pronounced the same verdict: The C. C. S. S. has been a success beyond our fairest dreams. Madison, the beautiful and happy, must be the city of our choice. Enriched in mind, glad and grateful of heart, all returned to their homes with the Psalmist's song upon their lips: "Behold how good and how pleasant it is for brethren to dwell together in unity ! "

THE CHILDREN OF THE ROSARY.

ALTAR ANGELS.

CYRILLLE LAVIGNE.

ABOVE the altar, where the Monstrance shines
  At Benediction-time, when music peals,
  The sunlight streams in lovely rainbow'd lines
  About a niche where one sweet angel kneels.

His head is bowed, his lovely eyes downcast,
  His dimpled hands are crossed upon his breast;
So sweet his mien as from the heavens vast
  His fluttering wings are folding into rest.

About the altar-steps a Levite throng,
  Their surplice wings enfolded snow on snow;
Heads meekly bowed, and hearts that bear along
  The words of praise that like red roses glow.

Dear altar angel! in thy garments rich
  Whether they pray or play, or work or sleep,
Keep these young hearts within thy jewelled niche
  After the Benediction sweet, ah, sweetly keep.

THE PEARL ROSARY.

Mary Hancock Allen.

Chapter I.

A MODEL TEA-PARTY.

HE house next door was at last rented, and Agnes watched with interest the moving in of the furniture. The usual street urchins of all sizes and conditions in life were also interested, as could be seen by the way they swarmed in front of the vacant house, and discussed in their choice vocabulary the merits of the different articles of furniture that were scattered promiscuously on the sidewalk and in the yard.

It is needless to say that Agnes was apart from these miscellaneous onlookers. She viewed the scene from the spacious porch of her father's house.

She was giving a tea-party to her family of dolls; but after half-an-hour or so of pouring out sweetened luke-warm water into tiny cups that insisted upon tipping over every time they were touched, and drinking up each doll's portion (all that was not already spilled), picking up the dolls that took turns in falling off their chairs, and hearing only her own voice, it became insufferably dull, and she let her make-believe company do as they pleased, while she turned her attention towards the movers.

" That's a big house," she soliloquized. " I wonder who is moving into it? I hope there are some little girls—not boys." Here Miss Agnes turned up her nose. " Boys are such nuisances," she said, with an important air. " They are ten times worse than girls. They don't think so, because they don't know any better; but they are. My, what pretty chairs! Oh, look at those Elite Court children! I wonder how they happened to get over here? Oh, oh! " she exclaimed, becoming convulsed with laughter.

The crowd was growing hilarious, and got in the way of the men; the men dodged and stepped over half a dozen children at once in a way quite ludicrous, not to say alarming. It was useless to drive them away, as the men observed when, after having

with some difficulty cleared the place of these troublesome urchins, and congratulated themselves upon their good fortune,
they returned from carrying some immense piece of furniture upstairs to find them as thick as before.

"Well, that beats all," said the first man, opening his eyes with
surprise. "Look here, Bill, where did they all come from,
anyway?"

"I dunno," answered Bill, the younger, with a blank expression
on his face. "Seems as if they just growed!"

The large truck-wagon was nearly unloaded before anything
that looked as if it might belong to a child made its appearance.
When at last a boy's gun came to view, there was a shout of delight, and a chorus of voices, through which could be heard expressions like the following:

"Say, mister, what'll you take fer that?"

"Crackey! But that's a corker!"

A dilapidated looking type of the Lord Fontleroy style emphasized his approval by a succession of summersaults, which,
strange to say, did not soil or injure his suit, but seemed rather to
improve it.

Agnes viewed the gun with great disfavor, and when, a few moments after, a small trunk bearing the name of "Georgie Hewitt"
was taken from the wagon, she turned her head away in disgust,
and addressed her silent companions: "Never mind, dollies, dear,
if a horrid boy is going to live next door. We shan't let him
hurt us, shall we?"

Happening to look up just then, she espied her brother at the
gate.

"Halloo," he said, coming up the stairs. "Who's moving in
next door?"

"I don't know," answered Agnes, rather shortly, thinking of
her new grievance. "A lovely, sweet boy," she added, emphasiz-
ing the word "boy."

There was a marked sarcasm in her voice, which was not lost
upon her brother. He gave a long whistle. "Have you seen
him?" he asked.

"No, I haven't, and I don't want to. His name is Georgie
Hewitt." In spite of the curtness of her answer, she could not
resist giving this information.

"How do you know?"

"I shan't tell you," she replied, teasingly.

"Oh, pshaw! What's the matter with you?"

Upon receiving no reply, he looked around, and noticing the dolls and dishes, he inquired what she was doing.

"Having a tea-party," she answered, moving a little nearer the dolls' miniature table, on which the dishes were set, ready to protect them should her brother come too near.

"Well I should say you were," he said, eyeing the secluded corner curiously. "What's in that pitcher?"

"Tea," responded Agnes, promptly.

"Oh, I say, give me some;" and he drew nearer, knocked off a doll from one of the little red chairs, and appropriated it to himself.

"Now don't, Tom," said Agnes, with an injured air, as she picked up the doll and looked at it anxiously. "If you don't behave yourself you can't have any tea, or ever be invited to my tea-party again."

Tom looked very demure, although there was mischief in his eye, and said meekly: "Please, ma'am, may I have some tea?"

"Yes, hold your cup," said Agnes with dignity. "Clumsy thing!" she said, changing her tone; "how can I pour tea into your cup when you tip it over all the time? Now, you can drink up what spilled in the saucer!"

"All right," replied Tom, quaffing off with gusto the thimbleful of tea of Agnes's manufacture, and smacking his lips.

"Good, isn't it?" said Agnes, watching him. "Want some more?"

"Fine," answered Tom, who was equal to the occasion. "What kind of tea do you call it?"

"Oh, why, it is Ceylon tea, just brought from the World's Fair, you know," said Agnes, again filling up Tom's cup.

"Yes, that's what I thought from the flavor," and Tom exploded with laughter at this sally of his, in which Agnes joined.

After seven or eight cups, Tom grew weary, and said he guessed he had had enough; still he held out his cup, and thought he would try to see how many more he could drink.

Agnes found it a little monotonous pouring out the mixture so often, and as it seemed as if the pitcher never would become emptied, she gave the dolls each another cup, and made Tom drink them all. Tom made so much commotion in doing this, and his feet under the table interfered so much with the chairs, that Agnes remonstrated.

" Be careful, Tom, where you put your feet, or you'll tip over the table."

" Well, where on earth shall I put my feet? " asked Tom, feeling very awkward and big on his tiny chair.

" Put them under your chair. They're so big they take up all the room."

Tom tried this plan, but his feet caught in his chair, which tipped over, and landed him in an uncomfortable heap on the porch. He made a clutch at the table, but only succeeded in putting his hand into the pitcher of sweetened water. It tipped over, and he received some of the contents of it where he did not want it—on his neck, and down his back.

Agnes screamed, but managed to prevent the table from going over, and the dishes from being broken.

When she got over her fright, she vented her wrath upon her helpless brother, who was kicking vigorously beneath a heap of dolls and chairs, by thumping him upon his back.

At this interesting juncture, some one calling " Georgie " attracted her attention. She desisted from her thumping, and looked over at the newly-inhabited house. The movers and the crowd had departed long ago. Now she saw two stylishly-dressed ladies. They were evidently waiting for some one. Agnes forgot all about Tom in her curiosity to see the hateful boy.

A voice at her elbow startled her. It was her mother's.

"Agnes," she said, reprovingly, "what is the meaning of all this confusion? What have you and Tom been doing? Tom, get up immediately. I am ashamed of you both. Come into the house."

Tom got up with a very red face, and blurted out something, no one knew what. Agnes hung her head, and attempted no explanation.

She had just caught a glimpse of a figure, half hidden by a tree, in front of the house. The figure was that of a girl about Agnes' size, with laughing, dancing eyes. She was taking in the whole situation, and evidently seemed to enjoy it.

Again came the call, " Georgie," and as Agnes entered the house, she heard the girl say, " I'm coming," and saw her run and join the two ladies as they opened the door of their new residence.

Georgie was a girl.

(To be continued.)

AN ANGEL TEACHER.

FIFTH ROSARY MYSTERY.

Once more with sad solicitude
She seeks the sacred ground,
ut soon her tears are changed to joy,--
He who was lost is found.

—Mary A. Mannix.

EAR Angel, I could think, oh, so long, about our dear Blessed Mother and St. Joseph without the dear Child Jesus, and their joy when they found Him; but your lessons stay with me always, and are so beautiful and so true, I do not want to think my own thoughts at all, but to listen to yours, and to think of them ever afterward when I say the Fifth Joyful Mystery of the Rosary, the Finding of the Child Jesus in the Temple."

The child twined her beads around her hand, holding lovingly the "Our Father" of the last decade, and as her lips repeated that best of all prayers, and the Hail Marys, and Glory be to the Father, her mind and heart and soul drank in the angel's lesson —the sorrow and the gladness of the Fifth Joyful Mystery of the Rosary:

Dear Little Child:—The Finding of the Child Jesus Among the Doctors is the name of the fifth mystery of the Beads. When our Lord was a boy twelve years old, He went to the Temple of which I told you in the last mystery, with the Blessed Virgin and St. Joseph. It was on one of the three great feasts when the people went to Jerusalem to say special prayers.

After the ceremony, when they were going back to their home in Nazareth, it was found that the Holy Child was lost. He was not with St. Joseph, nor was He with the Blessed Virgin, though each thought He had been with the other.

Filled with sorrow, they went back the long journey to Jerusalem, and began to search for the lost Child. Wherever they supposed they would find Him they went, weeping, and with sad hearts. A whole day they thus spent, when at last they entered the Temple. Oh, blessed joy after all their sorrow! There they beheld the beloved Child sitting among the priests and doctors, who were questioning Him and listening to His wonderful answers. When He heard His Mother's voice, He told her that He had remained in the Temple to tell these wise men about His Heavenly Father.

But immediately He went with the Blessed Virgin and St. Joseph, to Nazareth, and there lived obediently with them.

When you think of these holy things, and while you say the decade, remember, dear little child, that if you are so unhappy as to lose your good Lord for a time, by committing sin, you will always find Him, as did the Blessed Virgin and St. Joseph, by going to the church. There our Lord is always present to receive lovingly all who come to Him.

TEN.

Sister Mary Alphonsus, O. S.

The clock strikes Ten—ten lepers sought
  Their cure in sore distress;
Yet, when the kindly cure was wrought,
  But ONE came back to bless:

The nine went hurrying on their track,
  Old friends once more to see,
The tenth, a stranger, turned him back—
  He had no friend but Thee.

Lord, to whose hands my life I owe,
  Still grant my soul to be
The pilgrim stranger here below
  For all sweet service free.

Puzzles.

ANSWERS TO THE PUZZLES FOR AUGUST.

BLANKS.

1. I saw a man **lie on** the grass. (**Lion**).
2. I saw a lady **seal** a letter.
3. I saw a monkey **ape** his owner's ways.
4. I saw a thief **dog** a rich man's footsteps.
5. I saw a noble soul **bear** with many an insult.
6. I saw a villain **bore** a hole in a ship. (**Boar**).

Riddle:
The
letter
i.

The special prize offered by the author of the riddle was awarded to Joseph O. Barrett, of New York, who solved it *two minutes after receiving the Magazine*. Special mention is made of Alice Mannix, of San Diego, Cal., who solved it immediately on reading it, but a day *after receiving the Magazine*; of Clara McKernan, of Dubuque, Iowa, who solved it in three minutes; of Madge McGuigan, of Auburn, R. I., who solved it in three or four minutes; of Catherine V. Dolan, of New York, who solved it in five minutes. Those who solved only the riddle, were: Katie O'Keefe, Madeline Becker, Emma Grossmann, Mary Higgins, Jennie Mallory, James Mitchell Barr, Matthew Walsh. Correct answers to the riddle, and also to all the blanks, were received from: Mary T. Collis, Helen M. Leary, Mamie G. Ryan, "Josephine." Edward Dooley, Grace H. Malcady, Minnie Devlin, Mrs. William T. McNamara, Helen O'Neill, Paul Kammerer, Lizzie Farley, Andrew Laurence, Mary Marsden, May H. Daley, Kate Seery, Alice Mannix, Loretto Shea, Mrs. John Howe Brown. The following sent correct answers to all the blanks, but did not answer the riddle: Margaret O'Hargan, Alicia P. Newmann, Julia Gleason, Katie Carroll, Rose Guinan, Annie A. Dominica Obenland, Josephine Foote, Henrietta Rose Riston, Francis Jos. O'Mahony, Agnes R. Langan, Lillie V. Donovan. The following answered the riddle correctly, but in the blanks gave as the solution of the first: "I saw a man *sow* the grass": Joseph O. Barrett, Regina Longhery, Laura O'Brien, Joseph F. A. O'Neill, John J. Cummings, Mary Lonergan, Winnefrid McGuchin. Mary Blake, Josie Flynn, and Maggie Woods, gave the same answers to the blank, but did not solve the riddle.

The above will receive the picture of our Lady of the Rosary.

EDITORIAL

Again, dear Rosarians, the month of our Blessed Lady offers to you its rich favors and blessings, while it also gives to you an opportunity for publicly and solemnly professing your loving devotion to the Queen of the Holy Rosary. Fathers and mothers! now is your season of benediction in the name of the Holy Family, around the family altar (and who so poor as not to have at least our Lady's picture with light and flower, be the setting never so humble?); bring your little ones, and ask, night after night, in the saying of the Beads, the special blessing of Jesus, Mary, and Joseph. Remember also the devotions in your parish church, where at Mass or at Benediction of the Blessed Sacrament, in union with the public recitation of the Rosary, you will learn again the lesson of coming to Jesus through Mary, and that the crown of true devotion to her is renewed love for Him. To young and old we appeal, and in our Blessed Mother's name we urge all our readers to make this October a time of devout and persevering prayer. Bearing in mind the oft-repeated cry of our Holy Father, be earnest in your daily and frequent recital of the Beads. Tell others of the Rosary, try to increase the number of those who call Mary blessed.

The twentieth of September, this year of grace, brought to the city of Rome a series of festivities, such as awakened in Christian hearts the world over, an indignant protest, as well as an outpouring of pleading prayer to God, and of loving sympathy towards His Vicar on earth. For these festivities were meant to commemorate the Silver Jubilee of a usurpation unparalleled in the history of the Church—that of a king professing the religion of Christ dethroning the representative of the King of kings, of a son despoiling the most loving of fathers of territory and of home.

With military display and festive games, United (?) Italy, under Humbert,

the son and successor of Victor Emmanuel the despoiler, greets the twenty-fifth anniversary of September 20, 1870, while the Christian world under Leo XIII., the successor of Pius IX., the despoiled, commemorates the day in penance and in prayer.

From that day in the early centuries, when a Christian sovereign for the first time wielded the sceptre of the Roman empire, and pagan persecution ending, the Vicar of Christ was free to come forth from the catacombs and govern the Church of God upon the martyr soil of Rome, the blessing of temporal domain has been his to possess, to govern with a fatherly hand, to hold intact while expending its revenue for the ever-increasing family of the faith; his to hold in trust for Pontiffs and people yet to come, leaving it, mayhap, for a painful exile of longer or shorter duration, but returning to the "Patrimony of St. Peter," his people's ruler and father. Yes, thus has it ever been, from the palmy days of Constantine to the lowering days of Victor Emmanuel, 1870; yet alas! one exception must we make, when for a brief time Napoleon I. held in his grasp the papal territory, proclaiming his infant son king of Rome.

Limited in extent was this papal territory, for the sovereign pontiffs in the possession thereof sought but the freedom indespensably necessary for the divine work of governing the Church, of upholding her just dignity, of ministering to her needs, ever increasing, as distant lands embraced the faith, or kindling the fire of persecution, swelled the ranks of martyrs, their blood becoming the seed of Christians as time went on.

A stretch of Italian ground, lying between Venetia on the North and the kingdom of Naples on the South, between the Adriatic on the East and the Mediterranean, Tuscany and Modena on the West, making an area of about 16,000 square miles, and containing a population of

3,000,000, such was the territory known familiarly as the States of the Church, in the days of 1859, before the despoliation was begun. In one year this territory was reduced to 4,500 square miles, with a population of 700,000. Annexed to the realm of Victor Emmanuel was all but this, of the lands of Christ's Church.

But even yet was the Vicar of Christ independent—a ruler among rulers, a subject of none. Rome, the see of Peter, the see to which the glorious St. Catherine of Siena, spiritual daughter of St. Dominic, the guide of Popes and kings, had, centuries before, brought back the Pontiffs after an exile of seventy years in Avignon, Rome remained, and its environments, remained beneath the beneficent sway of Pius IX., of saintly memory, and by the treaty of Porta Pia the Pope was still to be its ruler, and Florence was to be capital of United Italy. Alas! how doth history repeat itself! how is the Spouse of Christ, His Church, conformed to His likeness in her suffering!

Pilate would have freed Christ after scourging Him and crowning Him with infamy, but the rabble cries death unto Him, and weakly the ruler yields.

Victor Emmanuel would have paused midway, he would have left life to the temporal power of the Popes, but the freemasonry rabble cries death to the Papacy in its sovereignty, and the ruler in weakness yields.

On the 20th of September, 1870, the treaty of Porta Pia broken, the troops of Victor Emmanuel take possession of Rome, proclaiming the city of the Popes the capital of United Italy.

There is a mystery of the Rosary that is peculiarly one of joy, that has given to the world that wondrous canticle of divine praise and thanksgiving—the *Magnificat*. But to the Pontiff of the Rosary, telling his beads a prisoner in the Vatican, its *Aves*, ever recurring, must keep ever vivid the sorrow of his saintly predecessor upon the festival of the Visitation, 1871. As no city save that of the Popes would serve as Italy's capital, so no palace save theirs would serve as the home of Italy's kings. Nine months after his troops took possession of the city, Victor Emmanuel, making his official entry into Rome, July 2, 1871, took possession of the Quirinal, the palace of the Vicar of Christ, where amidst surroundings becoming the grandeur of his office of Head of the Church, his life had passed in the personal simplicity, austerity, and sanctity befitting the fisherman, Christ chosen.

And whence this territory so ruthlessly seized from a holy old man, crowned with the tiara of Christ's Vicar? By what right held the Popes of Rome this tract of country that United Italy looked so enviously upon,—a tract in area, at the time of its greatest extent, but one-half that of Ireland, scarcely a third that of the state of New York? Whence held they this power of human government to which a usurper so jealously denied them a right?

When the first Christian emperor restored the confiscated estates of the persecuted Christians, it is but legitimate to believe that he may have laid the foundation of the papal temporal power, though the "Edict of Donation," specifying rich grants made to Pope Sylvester I., has been proved a forgery. However, at the end of the sixth century, the Holy See was in undisputed possession of considerable temporal domain. The Eastern empire losing its power in Italy, the Popes were early looked upon by the people of Rome as their temporal as well as their spiritual guardians. To the Holy Father they turned in the eighth century, when the Lombard hordes bore down upon them. Pope Zachary drove back the invaders, and regained the captured cities. At a fresh invasion Pope Stephen II. called upon Pepin of France, who responded, conquered, and bestowed his conquests upon the Sovereign Pontiff. The temporal reign of the Popes thus nominally begun became a reality in the lifetime of Charlemagne, the son and successor of Pepin, who ratified his father's grants.

Early in the twelfth century, the Countess Matilda of Tuscany, Parma, Modena and Mantua, bestowed a rich grant of territory upon the Pope then reigning. Gregory VII. The German emperors contested the grant, until the vigorous reign of Innocent III., a hundred years after the donation, secured the rights of the Holy See. The States of the Church had remained a compact organization from that time, though the Pontiffs enjoyed by no means an untroubled temporal reign; but the patrimony was that of God's Church, bequeathed to it by its faithful children, and as such they guarded it, with more or less vigilance, its boundaries becoming more secure under Julius II. In 1596 and 1631 the additional territory of Ferrara and Urbino came by escheat to the Holy See. After the exile caused by Napoleon I., the Pope returned to a territory undiminished. But not the fifth decade of years has passed ere the Pontiff, whose days reached that of Peter's, calls to his children and the flower of many a land responds, and the blood of soldier and zouave sinks into the martyr soil of Italy in defence of the temporal and spiritual rights of God's Church so firmly bound together. Yet another decade, and the temporal patrimony of the Holy See exists no more. But the Papacy lives in the midst of destruction, governs the world while yet imprisoned, and a Christian empire of lowly, loving, loyal hearts, lays its voluntary offerings, in humble "Peter's Pence," at the feet of Christ's Vicar, and the Kingdom of Christ is extending in hearts and lands.

The sympathy of the Christian world was with Pius IX. in his just refusal of the stipend held out to him by the usurping government. Too often had evil been wrought for the Church in lands where her temporalities were under the administration of sovereigns who abused the confidence placed in their noble predecessors! Never in this should history repeat itself! and relying with unfaltering trust upon the Providence of Him whose Church he governed, Pius IX., despoiled of temporal resources, uttered bravely the *non possumus,*—" I cannot," which saved the Papacy from becoming a hireling of the State.

The Jubilee Carnival is over, and the Triduum of protestation against a quarter of a century of wrong! But still daily do the children of Holy Church protest against the spoliation of the Holy See, the confiscation of church property, the usurpation of Rome. Still, with the Vicar of Christ, do they wield the invincible arms of persevering prayer, and of unfaltering trust in Him who has promised that the "gates of hell shall never prevail." While trust keeps pleading hands uplifted unweariedly, the sympathy of our hearts with a suffering Church utters the plaint : "How long, O Lord! how long ?" Rosarians! the Triduum for the Church, the Pope, and Rome, is over, but we have entered upon a month of prayer, a month that recalls the saving of the territory of Christendom from Mohammedan hordes, by the potent uplifting to Heaven of Mary's Beads. Still do Christian hands hold this blessed weapon, and it is as powerful as of old for redressing the wrongs of the Spouse of Christ.

Daily, hourly, throughout the month of the Holy Rosary, will the *Aves* of Mary's Beads ascend, blending thanksgiving for the victory of Lepanto and appeal for redress of the breach of Porta Pia.

It is not without beautiful significance that the Church dedicates, in a devotional way, the month of October to the honor of the angels as well as to the honor of their glorious Queen. Though preëminently the Month of the Rosary by the special designation of our Holy Father, Leo XIII., October loses none of its peculiar characteristics as the Month of the Angels. The celebration of the feast of the Guardian Angels on the second of October fittingly opens this month to the devout commemoration, during its succeeding days, of those blessed spirits who have charge over us by God's command, and who ever watch, in loving care, for all our needs. Loyal subjects of our gracious Lady, they rejoice to do her bidding ; they find honor in fulfilling her commands. Standing between their earthly care and their Heavenly Queen, their solicitude for us is ever prompt to accept, as messengers for us, the favors bestowed upon us by our Blessed Mother. Hailing her in oft-repeated greetings of her precious *Ave Maria* during these October days, we hopefully count on special help through angel hands. Lovingly we ponder, in spirit, the dream of Jacob, and again we behold the vision of a mystic ladder reaching down from Heaven's court to our poor earth, a sacred pledge of divine love, a bond of union with Jesus through Mary. Its meaning is clear to us in our Rosary chain, and our multiplied "Hail Marys" are gathered up by waiting spirits, and soon the trooping angels coming and going make known, in special blessings, that ministers of grace are active in our behalf as messengers of our Queen who graciously hears our many cries. We counsel our Rosarians to cultivate a personal, tender devotion for their Guardian Angels. No day should pass without holy and familiar intercourse, in earnest prayer and loving thanksgiving, with those bright and glorious spirits whom Divine Mercy places by our side, who will, when necessary, "go before us and keep us in the way, bringing us finally to the haven prepared for us by God." Assuredly we should heed them, and obediently hear their voice.

We remind our readers of the great Rosary Sunday indulgences which may be gained in Confraternity churches, from the hour of first vespers (about 2 P. M.),

Saturday, October 5, till sunset on the Feast itself, October 6. A plenary indulgence may be gained, at *each* and *every* visit made to the altar of our Lady of the Rosary, during these hours. This indulgence is not limited to Dominican churches or to Rosarians, but may be gained by any of the faithful in any church where the Confraternity is established, and in the chapels and oratories of religious, by those who are living in such communities, and whose names are regularly inscribed in the Confraternity. Consult Calendar for particulars.

The present is the fifth October issue of our magazine, and we ask our readers to unite with us in thanksgiving to our Blessed Mother who has so graciously vouchsafed many blessings to our work during these years of building and trial.

We entreat our readers to make a special effort to be present at the Rosary devotions in their parish church. The Holy Father trusts to our fidelity and love, and we ought to give ready and glad heed to his call.

The special feasts of this month, following in solemnity the great Rosary festival, are those of the Maternity of our Blessed Lady, St. Francis Assisi, St. Louis Bertrand, the Archangel Raphael, the Apostles Simon and Jude, and the Evangelist St. Luke. Consult the Calendar.

Again we appeal to our friends, and ask their help in extending the influence of our work. No time is more suitable than Rosary month for generous cooperation in spreading THE ROSARY MAGAZINE. Good reader! speak to your acquaintances, tell your neighbors, write to your friends about THE ROSARY MAGAZINE. Every new subscriber means a new force for devotion, for virtue, for pure reading in the home. For ourselves we ask nothing except the consolation of our labors. We plead only for the cause, and in our Lady's name.

QUESTIONS AND ANSWERS.

DOMINICAN TERTIARY.—*Does the reception of the Dominican habit or profession in the Third Order of St. Dominic serve for enrollment in the Rosary Confraternity?* No. The privilege of being received to the Confraternity of the Rosary without the necessity of enrollment belongs only to those who have made at least simple profession in the Order, and who are living regularly or in community. This pertains to members of the First Order, and to nuns of the Second and Third Orders. Nor is it limited to those of the sisters who live under the jurisdiction of the Order. It is shared by all following the Dominican life in community, whether under the jurisdiction of the Ordinary temporarily or from the foundation of the monastery.

NERVOUS SUBSCRIBER.—1. *I am almost unavoidably subject to distractions. Sometimes I say one or two Hail Marys beyond the ten ; sometimes I forget to say the whole decade. Do I gain the Rosary indulgences?* We cannot enter into the merits of this question, as it involves the difficulty of distractions. We cannot say how far our subscriber is responsible. Nor can we determine, in any case, whether a person gains indulgences that are offered by the Church. We give, however, a general answer: It is maintained by competent authorities that a slight omission, through carelessness in the recitation of the Rosary, of one or two Hail Marys will not forfeit the indulgences, the person being otherwise well disposed and satisfying the essential conditions. The recitation of a greater number of Hail Marys than required by the decade must be considered as a mere excess in which, of course, the necessary number is included. While this might mean culpable distraction, nevertheless we judge that such a person fully satisfying the conditions as to the decade, may, therefore, gain the indulgences granted.

2. *Can I gain the Rosary indulgences as a member of the Confraternity by reciting the fifteen mysteries during the course of seven days apart from the routine of the week?* The obligation of reciting the fifteen mysteries during the week—from Sunday to Sunday—is of ancient custom in the Confraternity, of "immemorial use" as theologians put it. Having been approved by the Holy See, this custom has obtained the force of a law. On this we may quote Leo X., October 6, 1520; Clement VII., May 8, 1534; Paul III., November 3, 1534; Innocent XI., July 31, 1679; the Sacred Congregation of Indulgences, confirmed by Pius IX., January 22, 1858, and another decree of the same Congregation, September 18, 1862.

MAGAZINES.

The July number of *The American Catholic Quarterly Review* is, in some respects, the most interesting issue recently published. Bryan J. Clinch's paper on " The Russian State Church " will prove instructive to the general reader. " About the Utah Saints " reveals these worthies in an unenviable light. Doctor Parsons makes a fine character sketch of Gustavus Adolphus. Father Poland, S. J., discusses " Italy's Silver Jubilee " in a manner that lays bare the infamy of so-called Italian unity. Other articles of merit are " A Benedictine Restoration," a beautiful sketch of Dom Gueranger, and " Catholic Protectories and Reformatories." Articles of a scriptural or controversial character are " Pure *vs.* Diluted Catholicism," by the Very Reverend Doctor Hewitt, C. S. P.: "Old Testament Subjects in Early Christian Art," by Monsignor Seton; and " The Newly-Discovered Syriac Gospels," by Father Maas, S. J. Father Freeman's always interesting scientific chronicle discourses on " Precious Stones—Gems—Jewels."

Some tempests in tea-pots have recently been bubbling like baby geysers, and sending out cold steam on the tiresome subject of evolution. We here interject the suggestion that some of the evolutionary sky-scraping philosophers might try their trained hand at degeneracy—merely for a change. Among recent contributions that we have noted is one entitled " The Origin of Man and the Religious Sentiment," by A. Fogazzaro, in the July number of *The Contemporary Review.* This article is a translation of a lecture delivered by Fogazzaro, an Italian, before Her Majesty, the Queen of Italy, two years ago. If the translation does him justice, the lecturer or author of the article is evidently no scientist, and, notwithstanding his loud professions of Catholicity, dishonors the Catholic faith like a bird that would foul its own nest. He rather wishes to be considered a "spiritualist poet"; and certainly the whole performance is a painful effort of his imagination; but as a poet of any kind his flight is too much on the level of the mud-hen's, and his wings too bedraggled with earth-mould, to excite in us any higher sense than the ludicrous. His profound little bit of history of the "human mind " is a piece of the usual spaniel-like fawning bestowed by relig-

ious renegades on the small coterie of modern materialists and unpracticable theorizers who have obtruded their unwise notions in the name of science upon the common sense of the world for the past quarter of a century. Whilst professing to be in some sort a Catholic, the work of the author is a jumble of materialism and idealistic pantheism covered over with the sugar-coating of fine Christian terms, such as immortality, innocence, regeneration, love, God; and these terms he keeps tossing up with an irreverent familiarity which gives one the impression that his proper calling is that of word-juggler to Her Majesty.

He accuses the attitude of sober-minded Catholics in connection with evolution as one of " horror, outrage, and contempt," and claims "a universal consensus among scientific men in favor of the natural descent of all living species from one or a few primitive forms." On the contrary, the almost universal consensus of scientific men has dropped evolution as a dead issue. And it is principally Catholic science that defended the " passage " through which modern materialists and their camp followers, like Fogazzaro, strove to force their opinions against the outer defences of the Catholic faith. The pretended Catholic Fogazzaro is a religious traitor, striving to spread through the Catholic ranks the idea of surrender to modern infidel opinion. The article is a covert attack on the Catholic faith, a cowardly concession to materialists, and a dastardly attempt to impress even Catholic opinion into the ranks of evolutionism. Whatever concessions some accommodating Catholics may have made to the theory of evolution as regards the human body have not strengthened the cause of truth, either natural or revealed; and when these same Catholics and our thorough evolutionists can adduce a simple instance of derogation from the established scientific law and philosophical axiom proclaiming the everlasting fixity of species, then will it be time to give any further attention to a cause already examined, dismissed, and shelved.

The August number of *The Contemporary Review* lays bare the sad condition of Armenia under the Turks, in an admirable paper by E. J. Dillon. It is a shocking story. "The Crispi Dictatorship " is ruthlessly lashed by Ouida, who confirms the generally-known bad char-

THE ROSARY.

[Oct.

acter of the Italian Premier. The article has special value, coming from one who has little love for Pope or prelate.

Bishop Doane, of Albany, contributes the opening article to *The North American Review*, in giving some sensible, practical reasons " Why Women Do Not Want the Ballot."

" The Christian Endeavor Movement," by the Reverend F. E. Clarke, President of the Society of Christian Endeavor, purports to give the objects of this strange society. A careful reading fails to show much except indiscriminate mingling of young people beyond parental control, huge excursions the country over, a thinly-veiled plea for woman suffrage, and a vast amount of politics, especially of the anti-Tammany kind, despite the writer's statement that there is nothing political in the society.

" Evolution of the Cow-Puncher," in *Harper's Monthly* for September, is a clever article, exposing to view the very philosophy of Anglo-Saxon history and character. The author shows clearly and amusingly the fact that no one less than a genuine English lord can ever hope to become, under favorable circumstances and by very force of instinct—the toughest and wildest of cowboys! The thing is in him, and in *him only*, to the exclusion of all other nationalities and castes, just as the plant is in the seed!

" The Trilogy " is a pretty poem by Julian Hawthorne, illustrating the stability born of purity in human love, which purity, saving love from the combats of selfish passion and pride, carries it through the trials of life, and consecrates and transfigures it through immortal ages. The attribute of purity in human love, as the poem suggests, and as a matter of historical fact, is derived from the religion of Jesus Christ. There is something wrong, though, in the mechanism of the poem—too many feet in some verses, and in others an arrangement necessitating misplaced accents to preserve the rhythm. While granting that these verses are pretty, we consider the whole rather third-rate poetry.

Other contributions in the September *Harper's* deserving special mention are: "A Fifteenth Century Revival," an earnest plea for another Savonarola, by the Reverend Doctor Hobart; " Notes on Indian Art," richly illustrated; " Arabia: Islam and the Eastern Question," a vigorous protest against the continued atrocities of the Turks, in which the writer clearly shows that the religion of that highwayman and assassin, Mohammed, is the direct cause of the present unhappy condition of affairs in Turkey; " Three Gringos in Central America," a well-illustrated sketch of travel in Honduras, by Richard Harding Davis, who somewhat mars his paper by insinuating that the natives honor pictures of famous people—actresses, and other advertised characters—as representations of the Saints. That an ignorant peasant might confuse such illustrations we do not deny, but we feel satisfied that the confusion would not be greater than that of Mr. Davis in imagining the gay array of celebrities which he found on the walls of a Honduras cabin to be anything more than a display of native taste and liking for colors and pictures.

" The People We Pass; Petey Burke and His Pupil," by Julian Ralph, is a touching little story, redolent of New York East Side life, with a quaint flavor of humor, and an equally sad strain. It bears so close a resemblance to "Chimmie Fadden," that the reading of it means constant reminding of Townsend's hero, and a suspicion that Mr. Ralph was at least unconsciously affected by the record of " Sir Chames."

The illustrated sketch of Madame Henriette Ronner in *The Ladies' Home Journal* for September is the story of the only woman who has ever distinguished herself as a painter of cats. During the past few centuries there have been only three other artists who have gained fame in this line of work—Gottfried Mind, a Swiss; Hokusai, a Japanese, and Louis Eugene Lambert, a Frenchman. Madame Ronner (née Knip) was born in Amsterdam, Holland, and is still painting, though in her seventy-fifth year.

In the September number of *Godey's Magazine* we note one article deserving some consideration. It is entitled, " The Stage and *the Church*," by Beaumont Fletcher. The writer of this article quarrels with the Church for its alleged opposition to the stage, and to show the injustice of the Church's attitude, he tries to establish the claims of the stage to be regarded as a great moral teacher.

The article is misleading from its want of discrimination. His " church," and " churchmen," and " ecclesiastics," on whom he seeks to fix the mark of fanatical and wholesale opposition to the theatre, are certainly not the Catholic Church, nor Catholic Churchmen, nor

Catholic Ecclesiastics. In fact, the circle of this writer's ecclesiastical acquaintances seems to narrow down to the "good deacon that has cheated" (him) "many's the time, on 'change." With this kind of church and churchmen we leave him to get even.

Catholic sentiment is in accord with the writer, that the stage, when true to its mission, is indeed a great moral teacher; and we further state that the strictest and most learned Catholic Churchmen have ever maintained that the frequentation of the play, under proper conditions, is even the exercise of a moral virtue.

We are aware that among the writer's "churchmen" there appeared, and are yet to be found, religious fanatics who, from that feeling of unbalanced moral poise born of ignorance, fear to unbend the mind in any amusement lest they should be carried away into intemperate pleasure, and who for the same cause, if not from pure hypocrisy, frown upon the most innocent popular recreations.

But in Catholic Moral Theology one of the virtues enumerated as a part of the virtue of Temperance, is *Eutrapelia*, or *pleasantry in word and action;*—the virtue whereby we seek play or amusement in word and action as a rest for the body, and especially for the mind, in order that we may return with renewed activity to the sterner realities and duties of life. He who spurns all play, or frowns it down in others, is not a virtuous man.

If the stage will be true to its high mission, and by chaste wit and noble action paint the lofty moral which finds such swift response within the souls of men, it need not quarrel with Protestant Churchmen, and may expect nothing short of enthusiastic applause from Catholic sentiment.

The Atlantic Monthly for September gives a delightful paper by Agnes Repplier, headed, "Guides: A Protest." It is written in a light and pleasant vein, with a dash of humor that is gratifying to travellers who can look back and recall the days when they were "taken in" by a "guide."

In the same number of *The Atlantic,* John Fiske presents an excellent view of "John Smith in Virginia," and James Schouler tells, in concise but agreeable form, the story of "President Polk's Administration," including an insight into that national mortal sin, the war against Mexico. The literary papers are a discussion of "The Plot of the Odyssey."

and a sympathetic sketch of "Samuel Taylor Coleridge." "A Sailor's Wedding," by Bliss Carman, is a strong, weird poem of the storm and the sea.

We referred briefly in the September ROSARY MAGAZINE to Canon Little's paper on "Marriage and Divorce" in the August number of *The Contemporary.* The only merit of the article, though perhaps not intended by the author, is to put beyond a doubt the practical nonentity of the Anglican Church as a recognized established Church of England. In everything of moral import which should be supposed to constitute a Church—a witness and guardian of the doctrine and laws of Christ—it is opposed by the state which "at this moment permits and even encourages what is contrary to the law of the Church of England," as Canon Little admits. That Church derives its origin from a concession to the unjust divorce of King Henry VIII.; and the subsequent acts of the State regarding marriage, without consulting its already too accommodating creature, the Church of England, are, at least as regards that Church, in perfect logical right and legal order. But the dry, feeble whining of Church of England ministers—exemplified in this article—against the Divorce Act of 1857, affords a striking instance of the irony of fate; and while having no remedial effect on the mind of the nation, will serve, perhaps, to bring out yet more clearly the original mortal sin of Anglicanism.

The Review of Reviews for September contains a character sketch of Archbishop Croke, by William T. Stead, that reveals the distinguished prelate in a new light. It is written in an earnest and spirited vein, and is illustrated by portraits and views. This number of *The Review* presents also a symposium on industrial papers, covering electricity, wind as a motive power, Niagara Falls, and deep waterway transportation from the Great Lakes to the sea.

The Century for September is a good number. "Hunting Customs of the Omahas," a personal study of Indian life; "The National Military Park," giving a description, with maps, of the Chickamauga and Chattanooga battlefields; "Recollections of Henry Clay;" and "Aquatic Gardening," beautifully illustrated, will be found very agreeable and instructive. "The Life of Napoleon" continues its fine course, while some spicy recollections are also given of

"Life in the Tuileries Under the Second Empire."

The late Lord-lieutenant of Ireland, the Earl of Crewe, writes in a hopeful spirit of the future of Home Rule, in an article entitled "The Outlook for Ireland," which appears in the September *North American Review.* In the same number Max O'Rell tells a pointed story of "Petty Tyrants of America," in which he justly complains of the spirit in which Americans submit to many exactions and annoyances. Insolence on the part of those who are the paid servants of the public has become so general that favorable comment is made by the meek and long-suffering citizen who meets a civil and polite functionary. The supposed servants have become the masters, in a manner, but their petty tyranny ought to be resented and suppressed promptly and effectually. We quote, with satisfaction, the concluding paragraph of Max O'Rell's article: "If every official were educated up to the fact that he is paid by the State, that is to say, by the people, and that his duty is to administer to the welfare of the people; if every conductor of every railway company were made to understand that his first function is to attend to the comfort of passengers; if waiters, waitresses, porters, servants of all sorts, were told that a polite public has a right to expect from them politeness, courtesy, and good service, life in America would be a great deal happier." We may here add that obligations are mutual, and that too often unjust demands are made on those who serve; too often are they treated inconsiderately and rudely. We would also add to Max O'Rell's category of petty tyrannies, the often-discussed "tipping system," as it grows and spreads to-day. Reasonably interpreted, and as a recognition for special services, "tips" are cheerfully given; but even the most generous protest against the partial levying of salaries for porters, waiters, and other such servants by a system of "tips" that simply means a species of blackmail. This is an abuse; and it is growing offensively.

"Napoleon and the Regent Diamond" is the title of a very interesting paper in the September *Lippincott's* which will repay the careful reading of the studiously, as well as the curiously inclined. An instructive article on "Crabbing" appears in the same number, while the usual amount in lighter vein is supplied after the manner of *Lippincott's.* The

contribution, however, that is of greatest practical value, is "The Decadent Drama," by Edward Fuller. This writer tells us that the American public spends more for the stage annually than for books, and we think his opinion correct. He notes the increasing numbers of playhouses, but adds: "There is melancholy evidence on every hand that while the theatre is growing, the drama is decaying." Justly he says: "There are good plays and good actors still; but what proportion do they bear to the sickly, silly, nauseous, and vulgar stuff, and the coarse, crass, crude performers whose names are on all the play-bills in letters a foot long?" "The tendencies of the times are downward, and not upward. It is not a very long step to complete degradation." Mr. Fuller, who is even-tempered and calm in his discussion, ascribes the decay of the drama, (1) to too much "show," or mere "staging," "producing," instead of presenting a play; (2) to the triviality which makes the bulk of the theatrical fare offered to the public as of the frothiest kind; and (3) to the thoroughly vulgar, debasing, and immoral pieces that are brought upon the modern stage. He deplores the unhappy tendency, so frequently manifested, of ridiculing serious subjects, of making light of immorality, of fostering irreverence in youth, of begetting a familiarity with vice while preventing, through mock modesty, such a presentation, on judicious lines, of sin and sin's ways as would lead to a sense of shock rather than to a sense of laughter. Laughter and mere fun seem to be the highest purpose with many in going to the theatre. While granting the reasonableness and the desirability of such pastime, it should not be forgotten that the stage has a higher object, artistically and æsthetically and morally, and it is only in proportion to its fidelity to such lofty standards that it avails as a power for good. The "fun" part will take care of itself, and with a wide margin. What concerns serious people is the growing disregard of all other considerations on the part of many who patronize the stage. Anxious to see this great power for great good, as well as a source of legitimate recreation and amusement, we deplore the spirit that seems dominant in the theatre to-day, while we hope for such a regeneration as will lift the ban that is upon the drama, and that will enable the most delicate consciences to welcome as an auxiliary in the cause of virtue and truth, the influence of the stage.

CHRIST RAISING LAZARUS FROM THE DEAD.—(After Rubens.)

The Rosary

| VOL. VII. | NOVEMBER, 1895. | No. 5. |

MAGNA CHARTA OF KING JOHN.

JOHN J. DELANY.

II.

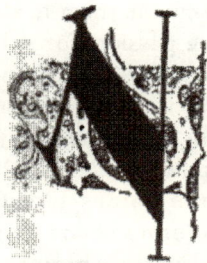

EARLY seven centuries have passed away since the execution of that Great Charter, and the British Constitution, conformably to the laws of social evolution, has been constantly broadening and extending in scope. The Plantagenets have been succeeded by the Tudors; the Tudors by the Stuarts, and the Stuarts by the Hanoverian Dynasty. The social and political condition of England, during all this time, has been more or less modified by the influence of continental politics, society, and commerce; wealth has been increasing with wonderful rapidity ever since the invention of the compass and the more important aids to navigation and the discovery of the New World; education, at one time the distinctive badge of a small section of the clergy, has, owing to the establishment of the printing press, exerted its civilizing influence on every class of the people; the demands of these ever-varying social conditions have necessitated legislation, confirmed usages into laws, given birth to new methods of jurisprudence, and very generally altered the superficial appearance of the British Constitution, and the lordly superstructure erected by the protracted labor of over six centuries may at first sight obscure its own foundation, but closer observation will reveal the fact that it rests upon the Charter of King John. Were it not for this Charter the now boasted liberties of England might never have been known to Englishmen, nor could that magnificent constitution rear its broad and lofty proportions until it has excited admiration to the whole world.

The distinctive feature of the Charter is the restriction which it places upon the power of the sovereign. The early Norman kings were almost absolute in their authority, and all the oppression which goaded the people into resistance against them was due to an excessive, uncompromising, and selfish abuse of this authority. Many of the kings before the time of John had granted Charters which promised certain immunities to their subjects, but they were mostly inspired by a desire to stimulate the people to supply them with money or men in order to enable them to attempt new conquests or to gratify an insatiable passion for soldierly display. Such Charters were accompanied by no guarantees which would insure their fulfilment in the interests of the public good, and as a result the people were still left to the mercy or wisdom of the king in the exercise of his power. Unlike all these Charters, Magna Charta provided that the barons should select twenty-five from among their number to form a council for the consideration of all complaints of abuse of the regal prerogative or of violation by the king of any of its provisions. They were to inquire into all such complaints, and if they found them to be real, were to appoint a Board of four barons to bring to the king's attention his infraction of the Charter, and demand of him proper reparation of the wrong. Should he refuse to comply within forty days, they were to call upon all the people of England to distress him in every way possible, "saving injury to his person or his queen, or to their children." This provision was most comprehensive in its purpose, and with the Great Charter, of which it formed so important a part, was recorded in all parts of the kingdom.

But the Charter did not stop at this limitation of the royal prerogative. It went further, and defined the rights of the people on which the king could make no invasion. This limitation on the executive authority stamped upon England, even at that period, the character of a Constitutional Monarchy.

Probably there can be no sadder commentary on the status of English society of the early days of the thirteenth century, than that section of the Charter which says: "We will sell to no man, we will not deny or delay to any man, justice and right." The social condition of the people, insupportable as it must have been by reason of royal oppression, became truly desperate when justice could be bought and sold, and the guilty escape, by undisguised bribery, the punishment due their offences. To this great abuse the Charter gave a decided check, as is evidenced by the guaranty just quoted. But it went further still, and provided for the establishment of a judicature which, though to our eyes it may now appear crude in form and narrow in scope, is still the prototype of that magnificent system which is now subdivided into the House of Lords, Court of Exchequer, Exchequer Chamber, Court of King's Bench, and the Court of Common Pleas. The judiciary in the reign of John, charged with the trial of all cases of importance, consisted of a court known as the Hall of the King, the Aula Regis, and followed his person whithersoever he went. The Charter, however, with the intention of rooting out the veniality, the uncertainty, the corruptibility attendant upon such a system, provided that the Court of Common Pleas should be held in Westminster, and in no place else; that Circuits of Judges should go through the various counties at frequent intervals during the year; that the Court's baron should have permanent and definite existence, and that appellate jurisdiction over all these Courts should be in the king's Hall alone. Changes in British society since that time have necessitated the modification of this judiciary, but if we follow its indications, history will show us that the present admirable system is but the development of the primitive judicature established by Magna Charta. Trial by jury, immemorial in usage under Anglo-Saxon as well as Norman rule, was by this Charter placed upon a permanent basis, and remains to this day the great safeguard of personal security to every British subject.

Under the primitive form of society which existed among the early Anglo-Saxons, natural justice was all that the people looked for, and the law itself was gradually developed by the application of this to the circumstances and conditions of society.

There was great suffering when a ruthless king trampled upon the rights of the people, and great peace and contentment when a wise and humane one administered the affairs of State. But as society advanced and its affairs became more intricate, positive legislation became more and more a necessity, and experience dictated the unwisdom of expecting proper legislation from the king or the select Council of Advisors with which he might surround himself. In the Charter of King John we discern the origin of an organized representative council vested with legislative power. As yet the times did not require the elaborate legislation which a later expansion demands; yet, in this Council of barons, to whom was delegated by the Charter the authority to restrain the king and to establish positive law for public welfare, we perceive the dawn of that institution which, as one branch of the present Legislature, is known as the House of Lords. And in so far as the provisions of this Charter were intended to apply, not only to the barons, but to the people at large, it contained the germ which, in the next reign, developed into a legislative assembly that, following the laws of social development, has blossomed into that admirable parliamentary body, the House of Commons.

The king was not divested by the Charter, of all the rights which constitute royal prerogative. As a matter of fact to this very day, by a fiction of the Constitution, he is supposed to possess absolute power ; but as he cannot act without ministers, and as all his ministers are responsible to Parliament for wrong-doing, and as the vote of Parliament is necessary to secure the payment of all bills, and the provision of all supplies, his absolutism is as unreal as the fiction which creates it. Yet, with the power left him by Magna Charta, he fills the paramount executive position, and is one of the trinity of powers which make up the King, Lords, and Commons, the constituent elements of the Legislature of England.

Thus much for the origin of the Constitution respecting the three great departments which Aristotle declared to be necessary for every form of civilized government,—the executive, the legislative, and the judicial. This constitution is the panoply which protects from assault the political structure of England.

We now advert to the influence of the Charter on the formation and development of the social condition of the people. If it be true that society is normal, when every right is protected and every public duty is performed, we have, from examination of the Charter, but one opinion, and that is that its effect must be salutary in the protection which it afforded to private rights and the injunction which it imposed upon the performance of public duty. Its effects were twofold in this respect. First on its own times, then on all times to come. It essayed to correct some of the most oppressive features of the feudal system. By feudal law all landed property was supposed to be derived from the Crown, and in consequence of this supposition great power was exercised over the persons and estates of tenants. Fines, known as reliefs, on the accession to an estate, were not fixed with any certainty, and were therefore frequently made so excessive as to amount to the value of the tenure itself. Marriages, too, could not be contracted without the consent of the lord and the payment of a fine. This system led to many abuses, which the Charter endeavored to abate. It limited reliefs to a certain sum, the waste committed by guardians in chivalry was restrained, the disparagement in matrimony of female wards forbidden, and widows secured from compulsory marriage. The franchises of the City of London, and of all towns and boroughs, were declared inviolable, the freedom of commerce was guaranteed to alien merchants, and the tyranny exercised in the neighborhood of the royal forests considerably checked.

Thus was the Charter effective in removing from the path of human progress some of the most extraordinary obstacles, and in softening some of the harshest features of the feudal system. But its chief effect cannot be confined to any time or condition, but has benevolently extended its influence over the whole people of the English-speaking world. Its essential clauses were those which afford protection to the liberty of the person and the property of freemen, giving them security from arbitrary punishment and spoliation. " No freeman shall be taken or imprisoned or disseized or outlawed or banished or in anywise destroyed but by judgment of his peers and the laws of the land." The great writ of Habeas Corpus was not yet originated, but who can doubt but the words just quoted establish the constitutional rights which the writ afterwards secured was only the means of protecting?

The potency of the Charter is often questioned because at times since its execution, its provisions have been violated with apparent impunity. But though no one asserts that it at once and completely corrected the existing evils, who can deny that it made a vast improvement on the condition of the people then, and has strengthened itself by its own operation since? Its publication taught the people their rights and inspired them with that courage which has spurred them many times since to take up arms in defence of their privileges against the aggressions of their king. It unified the people of England, and prepared them for that national character, the strength and internal solidity of which has since made them the wonder of the world. And lastly, it gave the most important and beneficent features of law universal sway in the kingdom.

Not only has this Great Charter poured out its exhaustless bounty of blessings upon the people of England, but it has been the origin of most of the rights and liberties of the people of America. It has shown itself capable of endless development, adapting itself to all the conditions and changes in modern civil society, and is calculated to furnish at all times and under all conditions a safe guide for the generations of men to come, in whose hands is to repose the destiny of their kindred and their kind, in the great future that is reserved for them. We glory in the achievements of ourselves and our times, of our fathers and their times, and in the magnificent superstructure which human brains and human blood and human treasure have been sacrificed to erect ; but let us pause and occasionally reflect how absolutely useless all this expenditure of brains and blood and treasure would have been if it were not for that great foundation which **Langton** and **Pembroke** laid when they wrung the Great Charter from the ruthless English king in 1215.

OH, turn to Jesus, Mother ! turn,
   And call Him by His tenderest names ;
Pray for the Holy Souls that burn
   This hour amid the cleansing flames.

In pains beyond all earthly pains,
   Favorites of Jesus ! there they lie,
Letting the fire wear out their stains,
   And worshipping God's purity.
          —*Father Faber.*

VISION OF BLESSED ALBERT.*

E. W. BROWNSON.

I.

ROM tender years, the Suabian youth implor'd
The Queen of Virgins, Mother of our Lord,
To robe his soul in virtue's fair attire,
Untouch'd till death by taint of gross desire;
And when, in riper age, at Pisa's school,
He still observ'd each point of virtue's rule
And laxer ways with constancy abhorr'd.
From Wisdom's Seat this precious light outpour'd
To know his Saviour's will achiev'd should be
When he a life of active piety,
Obedient to St. Dominic's rule had pass'd.
His fervent suit the habit won at last,—
But ah! the thankful novice fail'd to guess
What heavy cross should soon his joy repress.
Nor did he know what law all greatness rul'd,
Requiring heart and mind by sorrow school'd.
Or if he knew, ne'er deem'd the law concern'd
A mind whose grievous lack he well discern'd.
For though his artless manner held all grace,
And inward beauty dignified his face,
Yet scarce his hardest toil avail'd to force
A feeble stride in learning's painful course,
And he, whose mighty mind should yet explore
And overstep the bounds of human lore,

---

* The year 1221, signalized by the death of St. Dominic, gave to the Order
which he founded one of its most illustrious sons. This was the stupid Suabian novice, driven to despair during his novitiate, because he was too dull to
learn, but who, receiving the gift of profound intelligence from the Blessed Virgin, has been known to all succeeding ages by the title of Albert the Great.
His first lectures at Paris were delivered in the year 1248. No school in the
University was large enough to contain the crowds who flocked to hear him ;
so they and their master were forced to adjourn to the great square outside,—
since known as " Place Maubert," that is, " the place of Master Albert." In the
University of Cologne, he numbered among his disciples, Thomas Cantépratano,
Bl. Ambrose of Siena, Bl. James of Bavagno, Bl. Augustine of Hungary, and
greater than all—superior even to Albert,—St. Thomas Aquinas. He died in
his 87th year, A. D. 1280.

Must now the sting of ridicule endure
As one whose dullard brain was past all cure.
Not that his faithlessness deserv'd to lose.
The comfort which our Lady did refuse,
But that the anguish of this painful test
With higher qualities his soul should vest.

II.

So sore the strain of his distressful plight,
That unto Albert came the thought of flight;
Tho' long repuls'd with resolute disdain,
He now succumb'd the thought to entertain.
At silent night, his quiet cell he left,
Of the last vestige of soul-peace bereft.
No ruddy tint adorn'd his ashy face,
As with a frighten'd look and cautious pace,
Through dim-lit corridor and stairs' descent,
He crept like one on guilty errand bent,
Then gain'd the court-yard, where the moon's pale ray
About the holy Fountain sweetly lay.
With throbbing heart, from out the court he sped,
And at the convent-gate this farewell said,
(Tho' not without such falt'ring in his tone
As his should be, who, parting from his own,
And seizing buckler at his country's call
Breaks from his love, his little ones,—and all !):—
" Adieu! blest walls, whose shelter I had hop'd
To find a source of peaceful gladness op'd.
But not for me your fair retreat was meant,
Nor sweet the days within your shadow spent.
Then still in bounteous measure give to those
Who wake your favor, joys of true repose,
From whence I wander forth with bleeding heart,
Unwilling to remain, yet loath to part.
And Thou, O tender Lord! judge Thou not me
In my resolve with harsh severity;
For well I deem these walls Thou dost sustain
To bless with calm, not crush the heart with pain.

And they to whom no joyful waters flow
From fonts of cloister-life, not wisdom show
Their wretched time if they prolong in state
So little apt their souls with peace to mate."

III.

When thus he said, his eyes, bedimm'd with tears
He turn'd upon a world replete with fears..
But ere the hallowed spot he left behind,
He felt himself by secret force inclin'd
With backward step, within the open gate;
And turning, saw, as ancient annals state,
Our gracious Lady, clad in spotless white,
And circl'd by an orb of mellow light,
With sparkling gems and golden border grac'd,
An ample, azure sash begirt her waist,
And falling, met her richly sandall'd feet,—
A sight more graceful never eye did greet!
Well might its charm subdue his tortur'd heart,
And swift compel its anguish to depart!
Around that Mother's brow, the brighter glow
Was pure as purest light that stars bestow;
And all the sweetness of the first of May,
All vernal graces which endear that day,—
The fresh, green leaflets, and the robin's note,
Warm, balmy breezes o'er the fields that float,
All cheerful signs of earth's upwelling life,
And all the gladness in the woodland rife—
So much of tranquil love not these suggest
As in our Lady's smile was full express'd,
Or as her glance of tenderness bespoke,
Ere yet, with all the rapture they awoke,
These words like music from her lips did flow :
" Resigning counsel, whither wouldst thou go,
My erring son? If thou hast sorrow'd long,
The laughter's mark of all a sportive throng,
Nor ray of cheering light thy path hath cross'd—
Infer not hence thy Saviour's friendship lost.

For 'twas His wisest will this proof ordain'd
To show how frail, when not by Him sustain'd,
Thy reason's poor essay its charge to do.
The trial past, thy clear, unerring view
Shall now enable thee with ease to learn:
With ease truths deepest, subtlest, to discern.
But lest, forgetful of thy wisdom's source,
Thou pay deceitful praise to native force,
Thro' all thy days, this saving thought recall,—
Fair mem'ry's sway by sudden stroke shall fall
(When thy life's given span is nearly o'er),
And leave thee dispossess'd of all thy lore."

IV.

The Vision then withdrew from Albert's gaze.
No warmer heart e'er prompted grateful praise
Than bade the happy novice kneel and bless
Of this rich boon the gracious Authoress.
Not now his brethren deem him dull and slow:
Nay, rather admiration do they show
As more amazing proof each day they find
Of wondrous power lodg'd in Albert's mind.
And Albert grows to be their proudest boast,
Unequall'd 'mid a bright, unrivall'd host
Of men who join to saint the praise of sage,
Till he, the wisest, purest of that age
Fresh glory on his Master's name reflects.
From far and near, earth's chosen intellects
To Paris swarm, attracted by his fame;
And all alike their brilliant praise proclaim.
And him they so applaud—no narrow pride
Into his modest breast may ever glide,
While he oft ponders mem'ry's future wreck—
To vain, self-lauding thoughts a wholesome check.
In life's decline the fated hap arrives,
And of its brightest light the world deprives.
But sweetest pleasure fills great Albert's heart,
That so in lowliness he may depart
To Wisdom's fadeless realm, whose truth he sighs
To feast his soul withal—and calmly dies.

TEN YEARS LATE.

JEROME TRANT.

(Conclusion.)

HAT evening and many succeeding ones passed away pleasantly for the Chudleigh party, the addition of Miss Dundas, and even of her step-mother, for the former's sake, proving charming to all concerned. At the close of ten days Hilda's fate was decided, Reginald Dundas having proposed and been accepted.

"Be good to her, old man," said Sir Henry earnestly, when the young fellow came, full of joy, to tell him that he was "the happiest of men." "She is my dearest treasure, and worthy of a true man's love."

That evening the brother and sister had a long and serious conversation, through which ran a strain of melancholy, in spite of its subject, which was naturally the latter's engagement. Nestling in her usual seat, with her head leaning on the noble heart which loved her so well, she could not shake off a strange impression of coming grief, notwithstanding Sir Henry's gentle chiding at her expressed fears.

"I know it is foolish, my Hermit," she exclaimed, in reply to his reassuring words; "but I cannot divest myself of the idea that something painful is going to occur. What, I cannot tell; but it seems as if I were too happy—it will not last."

Her brother's face grew momentarily grave.

"You love Reginald, my darling, and trust him implicitly, do you not?"

"Oh, yes, with all my heart!" she replied quickly.

"And you will always live near your old Hermit?"

"Always."

"And you look forward to *my* marriage soon with feelings of pleasure?"

Hilda raised her head, and kissed the speaker fondly.

"You know I do. My happiness would not be complete if I were not sure of yours."

"Then why these fears, sweet one? Shake them off; think of Reginald, of Rose "—the earnest voice shook a little over the last name—"and tell me you feel at rest."

Hilda smiled, and appeared won away from her sad forebodings. That night, however, before falling asleep, the same painful impression returned with renewed force, and caused her fresh anxiety. She woke late and unrefreshed, and rung for breakfast to be brought up to her room. When the tray made its appearance, she found lying on her plate two notes and a tiny moss-rose. The latter was Sir Henry's daily morning greeting, but as a rule he pinned it at her throat with his own hands. To-day, however, her late rising had prevented the general routine being adhered to, and even was the cause of her not seeing him until lunch-hour. He explained in a little note that Mrs. Dundas had sent round to ask him if he could take herself and step-daughter out for a morning row, and naturally her request could not be set aside.

"I hope he will find some opportunity of speaking to Rose," was Miss Chudleigh's mental comment as she opened the second envelope with a half smile and tiny blush. Her first love-letter! Surely we shall not be so indiscreet as to look over her shoulder. Besides, which of us cannot tell, more or less, all that was therein contained!

Aunt Roxby came up to her niece's room just as the latter was putting the finishing touches to her toilet. Settling herself down on the comfortable lounge, she put up her glasses, and criticised the girl in her usual half cranky and wholly amusing manner, the same being interspersed with a running commentary on the foibles and appearances of her various acquaintances.

"White becomes you, Hilda, if only you did not insist on wearing that absurd *chiffon* lace collar; it reminds me of the ornament round Punch's dog's neck! .... Did you see that detestable Lord Brixton at dinner last night? Old sinner! he has one foot in the grave, and yet flirts like a young ape of twenty! .... Those shoes look rather tight, my dear. Don't be an idiot, or you will get corns from wearing them. .... I had a letter from Mrs. Glendon this morning. Her son has just made a fool of himself by——"

How young Glendon had made a fool of himself remained in Aunt Roxby's "inner consciousness," because at that identical moment a message from downstairs informed the two ladies that Mr. Dundas and lunch were waiting. During that quiet meal in the quasi-empty dining-room, Hilda chatted and enjoyed herself, having apparently forgotten the disagreeable misgivings of the previous night. Towards the end, and while the trio were still sipping their coffee, Sir Henry came in, accompanied by the two ladies with whom he had sailed over the main! A glance at her brother's pleased face convinced Hilda that he had not found the morning hang heavily on his hands. She was anxious to know what progress had been made, but until late in the afternoon no opportunity for a private chat occurred. At last, towards five o'clock, having despatched her *fiancé* into the town for some moss-roses which she wished to wear at the ball given by the municipality at the *Hôtel Ville* to all the "distinguished foreigners," residing at the Frascati and other hôtels, she led her brother into her own particular sanctum, whither she knew "Roxie" would not venture without being announced.

"Well, my Hermit, what news?" she demanded eagerly, drawing her chair, as usual, to his side. He smiled at her impatience. "News? Well, Gladstone is going to——Eh! What? Does it not interest you to know all he intends doing for the good of his country?" and the speaker laughed brightly at her threatening finger. "Well! well! I promise not to tease again. Listen, I have no news!"

"No news! What *do* you mean?" and Hilda sat up with evident dismay painted on lip and brow.

· "No news; that is to say, nothing definite in the way of an answer. I could not get more than two minutes alone with Miss Dundas." Then, in answer to his listener's indignant ejaculation, "but during those two minutes I contrived to tell her that I was hers, heart and soul."

"And she said?"

"Nothing, or almost nothing, for Mrs. Dundas came up to us; and she had only time to whisper that she would write me this evening. She said something about 'must let you know,' but I could not catch her exact words."

Hilda looked as she felt—disappointed; but not wishing to depress her brother, or cast down his evidently high spirits, she kept the feeling to herself, as far as words were concerned, and commenced speaking of all they would do when everything became satisfactorily settled.   Shortly before dinner, a message came from Mrs. Dundas not to expect her step-daughter or self, as the morning's outing had over-fatigued them, and might even possibly prevent their looking in at the ball.   Sir Henry was deeply disappointed, although he affected indifference when his aunt proceeded to give forth her opinion regarding Mrs. Dundas' weariness.   "Selfish old cat!" was "Roxie's" remark; "she thinks the game is lost, and so wants to prevent that poor girl from winning."

Her nephew pretended not to understand the allusion, but the irate lady's tongue was not to be so easily silenced.   Several times during dinner, and again at the *Hôtel de Ville*, she expatiated to Hilda and Reginald on the probable fate awaiting Mrs. Dundas in the next world.

"Don't tell me!" she exclaimed angrily to the former; "that woman is a spiteful hag, and will work her unfortunate step-daughter all the mischief she can.   Henry will not allow, of course, that she is anything but an eccentric lady with 'nerves!'   Pshaw! the woman's in love with him herself!" and with a snort of defiance, the angry speaker moved away with what Hilda called "her best Roman gait!"   The Chudleigh party returned home comparatively early.   Hilda was worried over her brother's trouble, for trouble it was, in spite of his repeated assurances that he knew all would turn out well, that everything would be settled to-morrow, and the rest.   However, he felt vaguely disquieted, and agreed privately with his aunt's opinion about Mrs. Dundas' readiness to be disagreeable.   He was not the man, however, to brood over evils, especially while they existed only in a possible future, so it was with a cheery, if somewhat involuntarily grave look in his deep gray eyes, that he bade his sister good-night.

The following morning he was up early, expecting every moment the promised letter.   Of course he commenced his watch for the messenger two or three hours too soon.   But when ten, eleven, and twelve o'clock passed without news, the feeling of expectation gave way to subdued restlessness. Reginald came to them at ten. " Had he heard how Mrs. Dundas was? No! Nor seen either of the ladies in the grounds? No! At a quarter past twelve, however, just as all had resolved on going over to in-quire the meaning of the unusual absence, a page-boy brought a highly-scented note, directed to Miss Chudleigh. She turned very pale as she read it, and passed it without a word to her brother, mak-ing a sign to Reginald to leave the room, together with her aunt. The latter, however, had not the faintest intention of remaining in ignorance of all that was going on.

" Well, Henry, don't be staring at that paper as if it were a death-warrant! What is it all about? " she asked peremptorily, masking her real emotion under a show of greater snappishness than usual.

Her nephew made a powerful effort to hide anything strange in his manner, and succeeded in speaking as calmly as usual. At least, a stranger would not have detected any difference in his tone. His sister, however, felt her heart wrung as he answered quietly: " Mrs. Dundas left Hâvre this morning for New York -accompanied, of course, by her step-daughter."

Aunt Roxby jumped up.

" For New York! Nonsense, Henry; you must have wrongly read that woman's dreadful scrawl! Give it to me! " and she pos-sessed herself of the fateful missive. " Pshaw! what a horrid odor of musk the creature has over her paper! H'm!—' Six A.M.: So sorry had to go. Unexpected news last night.' (What a lie!) —' Brother very ill at Baltimore.' (She never had a brother!)— ' Luckily, New York bound steamer starts at ten.' (Wish it would founder, only for the sake of other passengers!)—' Deeply regret' -' Poor Rose such a comfort to me.' (Poor martyr!)—' Shall write from America. Kindest regards. Renewed congratulations etc., etc. ' ——Well, of all the unparalleled specimens of brazen impudence!"—and Aunt Roxby dropped down into her chair again with a sniff of the direst disgust and contempt. She said no more, evidently out of compassion for her nephew's feel-ings. He glanced out at the sea, which was whitening rapidly under the influence of a strong north-easterly breeze, and saying he thought a walk would do him good, left the room without any of its dismayed occupants seeking to hinder his departure.

Not till late that evening did Hilda hear the anxiously-listen-ed-for step of her saddened brother. When he came into her room, she threw her arms around his neck, and kissed him fond-ly, but in silence. They understood each other so well, these two: no words were necessary to express what each felt. After keep-ing his head bowed lovingly against her soft hair for a few mo-ments, he drew himself up to his full height, as if protesting against the blow which had well-nigh felled his moral courage to the ground.

"She may write from New York," he said gently; "do not grieve for me, my darling. I am not despairing yet."

"My Hermit! my well-loved Hermit!"

The childish pet-name bestowed on him when she was a weeny fairy, and always kept up in spite of Aunt Roxby's dry sarcasms, sounded still more tender and affectionate than usual. A sus-picious moisture dimmed the strong man's sight for an instant, then—the moment of weakness passed: "All may be well yet, my own Hilda, do not get despondent; and now go to bed and get some rest, or 'somebody' will be-anxious to-morrow!" Even in the midst of his trouble he could remember others. Hilda smiled rather wanly, but did not make a move towards her dressing-room.

"And you," she whispered, "are *you* going to bed?"

"Immediately? No; I wish to write a letter."

"To her?"

"Yes!"

"But you do not know her American address."

"Oh! yes I do," replied Sir Henry, half-sighing; "Mrs. Dundas left one with the manager in case of any letters arriving for her."

Hilda saw that the best thing was to let her brother receive what consolation he could from the act of writing for any in-formation Mrs. Dundas would allow her step-daughter to give, so kissing him once again, she left him to his task. The following few days were very painful for the little party, so happy until now. Aunt Roxby's temper became strangely contradictory. At one moment she abused "that abominable widow," as she invariably now termed Mrs. Dundas; then her indignation was directed against that lady's step-daughter whom she stigmatized as "a poor, weakcharactered, back-boneless imbecile;" "as if she could not show some spirit and do something to let Henry know what that abominable widow was up to."

Hilda let the storm pass in silence, and at last, by her patient endurance of the ebb and flow of the troubled waters, reaped the general reward of the just here below, by overhearing her irascible relative tell Reginald that she was much disappointed in her niece, and grieved at his (Reginald's) tranquil composure.

" But what would you have her do, Miss Roxby, or any of us in fact?   After all, no settled arrangement...."

" Settled fiddle-stick! " retorted the incensed lady, interrupting the young fellow's speech abruptly: " If I were a man "—and she laid a withering emphasis on the *man*—" I would take the boat and follow that abominable widow at once, instead of allowing her to have it all her own way.   Not that I think the girl is worth all the trouble," she added, by way of a sarcastic rider.

Argument, reason, and common-sense explanations were out of the question under such circumstances; accordingly Aunt Roxby was triumphant all along the line, and had (that cherished trophy of the gentler sex) the last word!   When, however, at the end of three weeks, no news from the " Empire City " had crossed the ocean to explain what appeared unexplainable, and, in consequence, heavy lines of care gradually became permanent in her nephew's weary-eyed face, a change came o'er the spirit of Miss Roxby's dream; she spoke less often and more gently, and at last both astonished and touched him by the warmth and sympathy of her greeting a few days before their departure for Paris.

" Henry, my dear, you are a worthy son of your noble-souled parents," she exclaimed emphatically, laying her hand affectionately on his shoulder. " Your old aunt is proud of you;" and she wound up by letting him kiss her forehead, which concession, from a lady who openly declared she looked upon such demonstrations as indications of incipient idiocy, showed to what an extent her feelings had been touched by the fortitude and manliness before her eyes.

Three, four, seven months passed; still in Paris, and no message or sign of life from America came to let the Chudleighs know that anyone on that side of the Atlantic remembered Hâvre and

Hâvre memories. At the close of the seventh month, Sir Henry insisted upon his sister's marriage taking place in the following autumn. Reginald Dundas, in face of their sorrow, had been too delicate to press for an early date, but his natural desire to see all things settled was very apparent to all concerned.

"Be married next September, and leave you alone in your hour of sorrow? Oh! my Hermit, I cannot do it!" had been Hilda's reply when her brother first suggested the propriety of fixing the day. For several weeks she had invariably returned the same answer, when one day her objections were removed by a piece of information which Sir Henry had evidently been reserving for the very last moment. They were sitting together alone, in the latter's study (Aunt Roxby had insisted on an apartment being taken for a year in the *Champs Elysées*), where Hilda generally spent all her free hours. The open violin-case, and some sheets of manuscript music on the writing-table, showed that music, as ever, held undiminished sway over both.

"Play me one of Chopin's nocturnes, dear one," asked Sir Henry, half-dreamily; "his melodies speak to me in my present mood more soothingly than any others."

Hilda raised her bow and complied with the request without remark. At the end, and just as she was about to repeat the last few bars, which vibrated with peculiar sweetness, she found her hand suddenly imprisoned: her brother had risen from his seat and had come up beside her without her being aware of his presence, so quietly had the movement been made. Laying her instrument down at once, and clasping the detaining fingers lovingly, she gazed up anxiously in his face. Traces of some very deep emotion were visible in the large grey eyes bent so tenderly on hers, and sounded even in the voice as he said, slowly:

"Light of my eyes, you must have pity on poor Reginald, and consent to the arrangement of which I have spoken to you more than once. Nay! hear me out," he continued gently, as she made a negative gesture; "I wish to see you happily married before I...."

"Before you what?" interrupted Hilda, quickly, while an anxious look came into her attentive face.

"Before I leave the world," concluded her brother quietly, but growing a shade paler.

"Before you leave the world!" ejaculated his hearer faintly; "I do not understand, Hermit." Ah! yes! she did understand, only too well, only she would not allow the terrible truth to confront her without a struggle to turn it aside. Sir Henry meant to enter some monastery—her idolized brother intended to bury himself beneath the religious cowl. Oh! it was monstrous!—horrible!—not to be tolerated! She would not, no, she *would* not let him go. Aunt Roxby would forbid it, she would forbid, aye! Rose Dundas herself would forbid it, even if she (Hilda Chudleigh) had to seek the wide world through to find and bring her to her brother's side. What did she not say? What not urge, entreat, implore him by, to listen to the voice of reason,—to her, his darling sister's voice? All was in vain! She who had never seen her slightest wish disregarded, her lightest fancy set aside by him, now wept and pleaded all in vain—all in vain. When the storm of sobs which shook her slight frame, and his heart to its very core, had somewhat subsided, he drew her down beside him and talked long and earnestly over the motives which impelled him to act in such a serious manner, and with such unswerving resolution.

"My darling, I am not a man to love twice," he said sadly, yet firmly; "and I feel the necessity of devoting my life to soothing the sorrows and cares of those around me."

"But surely you could do that by remaining in the world, just as well; indeed, far better, than by shutting yourself up in a quasi-prison!" she exclaimed half impatiently. Her brother frowned for an instant, as if at some painful thought, then half-smiled:

"I am not going to imprison myself by any means; I shall be here, in Paris, in a monastery where active work is the rule, and where I shall be able to help others far, far more efficaciously than even in the world, as you suggest. Be reasonable, my queen, my sister, my all," and he kissed the tear-stained face again and again, until he saw that some kind of resignation appeared in the grief-shaded brown eyes. For more than an hour the two talked on, forgetting other mundane matters, until recalled thereto by an

imperative summons in Aunt Roxby's impatient tones, demanding
if they had forgotten that other people wanted their dinner, even
if *they* despised such helps to daily existence! Hastily escap-
ing to her room to remove the tell-tale traces of the afternoon's
upset, ere the lynx-eyes of her observant aunt could pass judgment, Hilda dressed rapidly, and entered the dining-room as the
dinner-gong sounded. Reginald, of course, completed the party
and exerted himself more than usual to keep the conversation-
al ball rolling, having instantly noted, with a fond lover's sagacity, the signs of recent trouble on his *fiancee's* slightly-flushed
face. After the dessert, Aunt Roxby rose, and asking her nephew
to give her his arm to the drawing-room, made a sign to the
others to remain where they were. Hilda instantly recounted
the stupefying intelligence, and was surprised to find it greeted
with calm.

"But you don't seem to understand, Reggie; he intends to enter a monastery,—to become a monk," and she said the last word
with an accent of despair which called up a smile on her betrothed's lips.

"Yes, dearest, I understand perfectly," he replied calmly; "but
I do not see anything so very dreadful in the contemplated step;
in fact, I was not at all surprised when he told me about it."

"He told you, and you never said a word to *me*. Oh, Reginald!"
and Hilda's voice expressed surprised sorrow.

Reginald colored slightly. "He asked me not to say anything
about it, as he wished to tell you himself; besides, I only knew it
this morning, so you need not be so angry;" and he went over to
where she sat, one white hand toying with a *marron glacé*, the
other lying on her lap.

Lovers' tiffs and the way they make them up are topics worn
threadbare, so leaving these two to settle affairs according to
the general rule, we shall turn our steps to where Sir Henry and
his aunt are having what she calls "a proper explanation."

She listens to his news in silence; indeed, were it not for the
occasional keen glances shot from her steady gray eyes (as gray,
and at times as gentle looking as his own), he would imagine that
she had not paid any attention to what he had recounted.

"And Rose Dundas, what of her?" she demanded suddenly,
going, as usual, straight to the main point.

Sir Henry winced for a moment, but recovering his self-possession almost immediately, said: "I have sought for news of her, and
waited long, without avail; Providence appears to have separated
us for some wise motive, unknown as yet to any one; why should
I fritter away my life in useless regrets? I feel drawn to devote
my life to God and His poor, and intend doing so, that is all."

"H'm! that's a great deal," remarked his aunt briefly; "and
how do you intend settling your fortune? You surely don't intend
to enrich the monks with it—though doubtless they hope you will
be fool enough to endow the monastery," she concluded satirically. Sir Henry shook his head.

"You are mistaken, aunt; the monks had the offer, not of my
entire fortune, but of a fair share of it, and they refused. I shall
give a certain sum to the house, shall insist, in fact, upon doing so,
but the bulk goes to Hilda, with, of course, an affectionate token
of my regard for you."

"Tut! tut! that will do," broke in his listener impatiently, taking off her glasses and rubbing them vigorously with her handkerchief. "Well, I suppose you have made up your mind?"

"Yes."

"And no argument will shake your determination?"

"None."

She looked at him fixedly, as though she would read his ruling
motive in taking such a step. He divined her thought, and said
impressively: "You distrust the suddenness of this determination; you fear, aunt, that I am but following an impulse that has
no deeper source of life than my shattered hopes, my blighted
human love. Ah, no; my vocation came to me in one blessed
moment of my darkened life, when my soul was crying out in
anguish: 'Lord, what wouldst Thou have me do?'. When I was
forcing lips and heart to repeat the *Aves* of these dear beads"
—and he drew his chaplet forth and held it caressingly—"*this*
revealed to me the life and the way. I go, God helping me, to the
Sons of St. Dominic, the Champions of this same dear Rosary."

"Well, my dear Henry, as I do not belong to that category of
human asses who will insist upon every other donkey braying in
their particular way, I have nothing to say, save: bray away as
you please, and....and God bless you!" The old lady used her

handkerchief again vigorously, but this time not on her glasses, and going over to where her nephew was standing, kissed him twice, as tenderly as Hilda herself. The latter coming in at that moment, all further conversation on the subject ceased, and the evening passed in cosy chat, as of yore.

*　　　*　　　*　　　*　　　*　　　*　　　*

Four months later, the Parisian chronicles of fashionable events recorded two incidents which became the talk of all Paris for exactly twenty-four hours, falling afterwards into that gulf of all sublunary interests,—Oblivion. The first, and most commented on, was the marriage at Sainte Clotilde of " Miss Chudleigh, only sister of Sir Henry Chudleigh, to Mr. Reginald Dundas, nephew and heir to the Right Honorable, the Earl of Glynn."

A short paragraph, almost unnoticed at the far end of the columns devoted to recording the bride's *corbeille*, beauty, and general deportment under the trying ordeal at church and *déjeûner*, informed the *beau monde* (or *bas-monde*, as you will!) that "the lovely bride's distinguished brother had retired from the marriage feast to put on the spotless garment worn by the Friars of the Order of St. Dominic." A few of the readers of the above statement puzzled for a moment over such an extraordinary taste, but the majority contented themselves with shrugging their shoulders and muttering *imbécile*. The fact of the speakers having frequently done justice to the *imbécile's* dinners, by no means deprived the expression of its zest and point. *Sic transit gloria mundi.*

*　　　*　　　*　　　*　　　*　　　*　　　*

Ten years have rolled away since those two events, recorded so briefly in the French newspapers, bearing in their train the usual sum total of joys and sorrows, hopes, and disappointments peculiar to the lot of mankind here below. To Aunt Roxby they have brought added dignity of deportment and acidity of speech, the latter being tempered —occasionally—to suit the youthful intelligence of her niece's two lovely children who are their fond parents' delight and pride. Lord Glynn (the uncle departed this life within three years of Reginald Dundas' marriage) and his beautiful wife are eagerly sought after by the *élite* of English and foreign society, charming all by the lavishness of their hospitality, and the uniform gracefulness of their unfailing courtesy towards high and low alike.

And Sir Henry Chudleigh!-- what of him? He still lives on his earnest, self-sacrificing, yet cheerful life, within the walls (and outside) of the monastery which he had selected as the place of his retreat. Known to rich and poor as "the good Father Bernard," he has moved along the road of Life, striving to imitate his Master as well as human frailty and man's weakness would permit, neither seeking nor shunning the world's comments or—of later years —praise. Had he felt the smart of the iron which can pierce through steel corselet and religious robe alike? Did he regret the hours torn from the world's grasp and devoted to assuaging the griefs of that world's victims? Was he anxious to hear the striking of that hour which, beginning on earth, would end—for him in another and a brighter land? These, and many other questions of a more frivolous nature, were occasionally asked by those who knew him best and least; but to all was an answer denied, unless the steady light of inner peace which shone in the deep gray eyes, or hovered constantly over unruffled lip and brow, could be taken as a gauge of the happiness of the calm-looking English friar. Often was Lady Glynn's well-appointed carriage seen outside one of the large Parisian churches, and no uncommon interest excited by a view of the brother and sister meeting face to face, the former clad in the picturesque white folds of his Order, the latter in all the gay trappings of youth and wealth. This the crowd saw; but what it did not see, even if it guessed thereat, was the unfailing sympathy and deep love which still existed, undiminished by circumstances or time, between the two who had grieved and sorrowed together ten years before.

*				*				*				*				*				*				*

One evening, as the tall figure of Father Bernard was about to leave the dimly-lit church, a female form, robed in deep mourning, approached hesitatingly, as if to detain him. Instantly thinking she might be seeking for some information regarding the hours of the services, he stopped and looked inquiringly. The stranger wished to know if he could hear her in the confessional.

"It is rather late for that now," rejoined the friar in a low tone, "unless the case is urgent. If not, it were better to return in the morning; the doors are open from six o'clock."

"I would rather speak to you now, Father: to-morrow may be too late."

The priest bent his head in acquiescence, privately noting the extreme weakness of the speaker's voice, and entered a large oak confessional in one of the side aisles.

Fully half an hour slipped through time's great minute-glass ere the sable-clad figure once more passed out into the deserted church. Long she knelt at the foot of the beautiful Lady's altar, with bowed head and clasped hands, but not so long as the motionless friar within the sanctuary, who seemed to have forgotten the flight of time in the intensity of his prayer. His penitent left the silent temple; but still he lingered on, until aroused by the entrance of a lay-brother, who came to call him to the evening meal.

In the quiet of his cell that night, sitting at the book-covered table, with eyes raised to a large crucifix on the wall, and hands folded over a letter seemingly stained with the yellow hue of age, Sir Henry Chudleigh—nay, Father Bernard, went over the records of the past. At first, the recollections which rushed through the flood-gates of memory, seemed bitter and hard to bear—witness the compressed lip and pallid hue of the pain-worked countenance; but, gradually, gentler and more soothing thoughts came to usher in anew the calm and peace which had found a home for so many years within the—at present—stormed-tossed breast.

Whence came the fragile pages which had awakened so powerful a tempest? Who was the crepe-covered stranger of that evening's meeting? Of whom did the agitated friar speak, when in the solitude of his cell, and with weary eyes fixed on his thorn-crowned Model, he breathed rather than said:

"And so she did write, although her message has come ten years late!"

Interesting queries, yea! but destined to remain forever unanswered in this world. None—no, not even his well-loved sister ever knew the reason of an added gravity in Father Bernard's manner, or the meaning of the deeper shade of peaceful rest which looked out from his pale, ascetic face. ... And so, Time moved on. The road of Life showed fewer mile-stones on ahead, and marked the fast approaching bourne by lengthening shadows across the traveller's way. The noble-hearted wayfarer felt that his task was well-nigh done, and gazed into the on-coming darkness with steady hope, knowing that the instant was at hand when the last line of his soul's history would be writ, not in sand, but on the Eternal Rock.

OUR LADY IN ART.

THE ASSUMPTION AND CORONATION.

MARY M. MELINE.

N the Acts we are told of the Descent of the Holy Ghost upon the Apostles, Mary, the Mother, and the other holy women. The Holy Spirit came to her as the Comforter in this public manner, but it was not the first time she had received this wonderful Third Person of the Trinity. He had already sanctified her, as we know, to fit her for her destiny. But it was meet that, as Queen of the Apostles, she should be with them when they received their baptism of fire. After this the Scriptures are silent as to the Mother, and Tradition comes with loving thought to give us the beautiful record of the last twelve years.

We know that St. John took charge of the bereft Mother after the Crucifixion, and consequently we may suppose that she dwelt with him in Mount Zion. But here, as during the eighteen hidden years at Nazareth, we have no revelation of her employment. Did she go about among the followers of her Son, strengthening their faith and comforting them in their human sorrow? Imagine our resplendent Lady entering our doors in the flesh, and bringing the solace of her pity to our sorrow-laden hearts! Or did she spend her hours in contemplation of those heavenly joys which were soon to be hers forever? We can only allow our imagination within certain bounds to picture to us this remnant of a life in which all of joy and all of sorrow had found fitting place.

Artists have taken up the story, and given us on canvas what we lack in words.

In the frescoes at Orvieto and in the bas-reliefs of Orcagna on the shrine in Or-San-Michele, at Florence, the angel floats downward with the palm encrusted with jewels which her Son sent her from Paradise in token that her long martyrdom was over. Fra Philippo Lippi gives us the angel kneeling and presenting a taper, which the Blessed One receives majestically. St. Peter stands behind. The taper marks this representation at once as indicative of our Lady's death, for the custom to this day is to keep a blessed candle burning during the last hours; while sometimes the Angel of the Annunciation is made to bear a palm. Hans Schaufflein also treated this subject. His picture is in the Munich gallery.

The Byzantine and early Italian artists treated the death of the Blessed Virgin as a sleep, it being an old thought that she did not die, but only slept until the Assumption; this has, however, been forbidden as false. She was not exempt from paying the debt of nature. In later Greek art, the scene is always one of mystical and solemn simplicity, as, for instance, in the Kensington Palace. The couch is in the centre foreground, and Mary lies upon it, wrapped in a veil, with closed eyes, and hands crossed on her bosom. Angels hover about, bearing lighted tapers, and the grieving Apostles are there. Our Saviour stands behind His Mother, holding in His arms her soul. A seraph in glowing carmine spreads his wings over the Saviour's head. On either side stand Dionysius the Areopagite and Timothy, bishop of Ephesus. In front the archangel Michael bends forward to cut off the hands of the high-priest Adonijah, who had attempted to profane the bier. Giotto gives us a lovely picture, in which two angels stand at the head, and two at the feet, holding up the pall upon which the Mother lies; again, Angelico has not neglected this subject—his work is in the Florence gallery. Albrect Durer has given us several variations of this touching theme, but I will only mention one as particularly interesting from its historical association. The picture is in the Fries gallery at Vienna, and in it not one of the legendary or supernatural adjuncts have been omitted. The face of the dying Mother is that of the young duchess Mary of Burgundy, the first wife of Maximilian, for whom the painting was made. On the right her son Philip, the husband of Joanna the Mad and father of Charles V., stands as St. John the Beloved, and presents the taper; the other Apostles are there, and St. Peter, in bishop's vestments, reads from an open book. The bishop of Vienna, George à Zlatkonia, the friend and councillor of Maximilian, is portayed in the Prince of the Apostles. Behind him, as one of the Apostles, stands Maximilian himself, with head bowed down. Three ecclesiastics are entering with the cross, the censer, and holy water. Over the bed floats the figure of the Saviour, with the soul of His Mother in His arms in the likeness of a babe, with hands clasped ; and above all, in an open glory, her reception and coronation in Heaven. Upon a scroll over her head, and upon other scrolls in the hands of angels, are sentences from the Canticles. The picture bears date 1518. In those pictures in which the Mother is only preparing for her translation, if she kneels, she is supported by St. John, and if she reads, the book is held by St. Peter. Cola della Matrice introduces the three great Dominican Saints as witnesses to the event. In the centre is St. Dominic, on the left St. Catherine of Siena, and on the right St. Thomas Aquinas. St. Peter in cope of scarlet reads, and St. John, weeping bitterly, holds the palm. Ludovico Caracci, Domenichino, and Carlo Maratti have each treated the subject.

Angelico has given us an entombment which is very beautiful. The Blessed Virgin lies on a white pall held reverently by the mourners, beside a marble sarcophagus. St. John, who bears the jewelled palm, is dressed in a doctor's cap and gown, the figure being intended for Dionysius the Areopagite. Above, in the sky, the Mother's soul is seen supported by angels and received into Heaven.

And being dead, having paid nature's debt, the pure, sinless flesh of the Mother must not see corruption. She rises like the morning, uplifted by angel hands from all chance of the decay of the tomb, and is carried out of human vision to those sublime spheres where dwell the heavenly hosts, where reigns the Trinity.

Here the artistic sense has revelled, as it did in the Immaculate Conception and the hidden life. Guenta Pisano, Andrea Orcagna. Taddeo Bartoli, to mention a few. The latter artist represents the moment when the soul and body are reunited. Mary is robed in white, her garment powdered with stars; she appears in the attitude of one rising from repose, the action expressed by the support of many-colored wings of angels, and the attraction of her love for her Divine Son, who bends above her, and gathers her clasped hands into His. This is one of the most exquisite conceptions of the thought. The ecstasy of love and joy in her face, and the spiritual tenderness in that of her Son, have seldom been equalled. Domenico di Bartolo's altar-piece in the Berlin gallery is a noble picture—the Mother is majestic. One of Raphael's is peculiar: the Blessed Virgin is seated within the horns of a crescent moon, with joined hands. On each side an angel stands, bearing a flaming torch; the empty tomb and the eleven Apostles are below. In his great painting Titian rejects the customary white, star-spangled robe, and clothes the Mother in her usual blue and crimson garments. We are all familiar with the picture. Palma Vecchio paints the Mother looking down, not up, and in the act of loosening her girdle to drop it to St. Thomas, who stands below. Several other painters have chronicled the legend of the girdle.

The Coronation of the Blessed One follows at once upon her Assumption, and some artists have included the two in one picture. It is somewhat difficult to distinguish the Coronation of the Blessed Virgin from those pictures of her which are called the *Incoronata*, in which the figure, veiled and crowned, represents the Church, apart from all real human association. In the Coronation we have the triumph of the human Mother, the meek, simple woman raised to the highest immortality. The open grave below, with the grim faces of the Apostles beside it, show that she has attained this glory through the dark portal of Death.

It is the last scene in the life of the Blessed One, and as Queen of Apostles, Martyrs, Confessors, Virgins, All Saints—all the Saints of Heaven gather about her. In all the paintings our Saviour, sometimes alone, sometimes assisted by the Father (represented as an old man), places the gleaming diadem upon her head, while the Dove is seen either between the Father and the Son, or hovering over the head of His Immaculate Spouse. Angels, too, are there, for she is Queen of Heaven and its Angelic cohorts as well as of mortals.

Thus, from the girlish days in the Temple, through the marvel of the Angelic Visitation, the ecstasy of Bethlehem, the anguish of Calvary, to the stupendous glory of the Assumption and Coronation, has human love and human genius in immortal coloring recorded the story of her who was foretold from the beginning as the human factor in the great act of man's redemption—of Mary, the Immaculate Virgin Mother of the Son of God.

SKETCHES OF VENEZUELA.

REV. BERTRAND COTHONAY, O. P.

I.

OR a long time I had earnestly, anxiously, desired to visit Venezuela, one of those South American Republics which succeeded in securing its emancipation from Spanish rule at the beginning of the present century.

It is said that the early Europeans who gained these shores, chancing to meet with a village built upon a lagoon by means of huge piles, were reminded of the city of Venice; hence the origin of the name of Venezuela, or little Venice.

The whole extent of Venezuela lies within the torrid zone. Its area, including a portion of territory which is a matter of contest between the Republic and the British Crown, is 1,110,059 square kilometres, that is, twice the size of the entire area of France; it is about equally divided into pasturage, tillage, and forest land.

According to the last census, made in 1891, the whole Republic is said to contain 2,323,527 inhabitants. A large number of Indians, descendants of the aborigines, are to be met with in Venezuela. Some savage tribes wander on the banks of the Orinoco and in the forests of the Andes. Many of the families that are of European descent have preserved the integrity of their race; nevertheless the greater part of the Venezuelan population has a mixed progeny of Indian, African, and European blood in various proportions, as also in a variety of shades.

The country is ruled by a President, elected for two years. The election of the President, as well as the transmission of the power, has frequently given rise to most violent revolutions in consequence of the antagonism of the political parties and the great number of claimants for the Presidency.

The Republic of Venezuela consists of nine States, one Federal District, four Territories, and two Colonies,—a plan of division similar to that adopted by the United States of North America

THE CHURCH OF THE DIVINE SHEPHERDESS, CARACAS.

Caracas is the capital of the Federal District, as well as of the entire Republic. It is a city of nearly 72,000 inhabitants; but so great is the influx of foreigners that before the end of the century the number of its inhabitants will probably reach 100,000. The town is built at the foot of the mountain of Avila, and is only a few kilometres distant from the port of La Guayra. Caracas thus stands at an altitude of only 3,000 feet, and communicates with La Guayra by so circuitous a route that the railway is thirty-one kilometres in length. Caracas, so-called from the name of an Indian tribe settled in the valley which it occupies, was founded, in 1567, by Diego de Losada. This metropolis has suffered much from violent earthquakes. That of 1812 almost completely destroyed the city, and brought death to more than 10,000 persons.

The climate of this city is very mild, the mean temperature being but 20 degrees centigrade. But the decrease or increase of heat is felt in proportion as we ascend or descend the valley of the Guayre. In Venezuela one is at liberty to choose the temperature he prefers, from the chilly regions of the Andes where the thermometer marks several degrees below the freezing point, down to the burning plains of the sea-coast where it frequently registers thirty-five or forty degrees in the shade.

The Venezuelan metropolis contains fifteen churches or chapels, and eight parishes. Most of these churches are built after the Roman style of architecture; they are adorned with pictures and gildings of the Spanish taste of the seventeenth century. A few of the churches, however, are of recent construction, and very neatly kept. That of La Pastora deserves special mention. It is a large and beautiful edifice with three aisles, built at the north of the capital by the Rev. Father Olegario, whose respectable age of four score years has not bereft him of all his youthful vigor. This venerable Capuchin Father belongs to the ancient missions of the sons of St. Francis, who have accomplished so much by spreading the Gospel in Venezuela. The church just mentioned is dedicated to our Lady, and called by the name of La Divina Pastora, "the Divine Shepherdess," a Catalonian devotion dear to all Spaniards.

The church of Our Lady of Mercy, which is not, however, a parish church, is also very fine. All its statues, as well as those of

La Pastora, are in exquisite taste, and very valuable.   In the choir
of Our Lady of Mercy there is an inscription, sacred to the memory of Mgr. Hyacinthe Madeleine, Apostolic Prothonotary, and a
native of France, but, says the inscription, " A son of Venezuela
by adoption as well as by his priestly functions and the imperish-

A VENERATED IMAGE IN THE CHAPEL OF THE DIVINE
SHEPHERDESS, CARACAS.

able legacy of his works.'   This same beneficent prelate had
raised, upon a heap of ruins, a temple, which, according to the
inscription we have been quoting, "proclaims the heroism of his
extraordinary piety "   " El levanto de la nada este templo que

proclama al espectador el heroismo de su piedad.—Agosto 28 de 1856."

The Cathedral is large, and contains five aisles. It was completely restored in 1867. The sanctuary is skilfully painted, and has a charming effect. Unfortunately the roof of this great church is too low, and many of the paintings and statues are works of but moderate skill.

Amongst the remaining churches we may mention that of Saint Theresa, of Saint Joseph, the Holy Chapel where perpetual adoration of the Most Blessed Sacrament is kept, and lastly, the new chapel of the Sacred Heart.

Among the views we secured is one of the small chapel of Calvary. On the left is to be seen a hill, which groves of trees, gardens, and walks transform into a veritable pleasure resort. From here we command a fine view of the whole city. Upon an eminence we observe the reservoirs which supply the town with water. On all sides we meet with fountains that greatly help in keeping the locality in a state of delightsome coolness. This is a spot much frequented and cherished by the inhabitants of Caracas. Beyond the chapel of Calvary, the hills in view give an approximate idea of the vicinity of the capital.

Caracas was formerly a city renowned for its piety. In the last century it gloried in the title of " the City of Mary "—" Caracas Mariana Civitas." It boasted also of being called a great convent. Indeed, each of its streets bore the name of a saint or of some mystery of the life of our Blessed Lord. At every street corner a lamp was kept lighted in honor of the patron saint of that street. Moreover, on the inner door of each house hung an image of the tutelary protector of the dwelling. The confraternities and religious associations were very numerous, and the celebration of festivals, novenas, and processions was the principal occupation of these devout people. The harmonious prayer of the Holy Rosary preached by the Dominican Fathers was the chief delight of the pious families of Caracas. This devotion has, in fact, the uncommon excellence of being a summary of the Gospel, and the faithful whilst reciting its inspired words are interiorly elevated by the representation of the mysteries of our Holy Redeemer. Bishop Diez Madronero, who held his see from 1757 to

1769, warmly seconded the Friars Preachers in the extension of
the beloved devotion.   A Venezuelan writer says that "not a
week passed during his episcopal career without witnessing the
public recital of Mary's Psalter; nor was there a home in Caracas
or its vicinity where the family omitted the recitation of the
chaplet between the hours of three and seven in the afternoon."

But, alas! revolutions and wars, and with them religious indifference and impiety, passed over this city of Mary, and have dis-

CHURCH AND CONVENT OF ST. HYACINTH, CARACAS, DESTROYED
BY GUZMAN BLANCO.

figured it.   The bright lamp at the street corner is no longer seen
because the Patron's image has disappeared; nowadays it has
become the exception to meet with a zaguan from which the image
of the Patron Saint has not been removed.[1]   Many of the shrines
much resorted to by celebrated confraternities have been de-

[1] The houses in Venezuela are furnished with a double door; the space enclosed between them, resembling a small gallery, is called "zaguguon."

stroyed, and in consequence the confraternities themselves and other religious associations no longer exist.

Among the celebrated churches razed by the sacrilegious hand of Guzman Blanco, that of San Jacinto, or of Saint Hyacinth, belonging to the Dominican Fathers, is, I believe, the one which the inhabitants have most regretted. Even to-day, twenty years after its destruction, older ones among the people still speak of it with admiration. This church was formerly one of the finest and richest in the city. The inhabitants called it " Roma chiquita," or little Rome, on account of its valuable relics and the precious indulgences which the faithful could gain within its precincts. When on the point of being destroyed, a venerable ecclesiastic had it photographed, in order to preserve at least a remembrance of the beloved monument. I would add that this priest has had the kindness to present to me the sole remaining photograph of a church which he knew was dear to me.

Caracas formerly contained splendid convents for both sexes. The buildings have been ruthlessly destroyed by the same sectary who for twenty years has been at the head of the Republic; the Religious themselves have been expelled from the homes they had founded and sanctified, and have retired to some unknown spot, there to die in misery and poverty, yet praying for their persecutors. The very spot on which formerly stood the Convent of the Dominican Fathers is now occupied by a market; that of the Nerist[1] Fathers has made room for Washington Place; that of the Franciscans now forms the University, National Library, Museum, etc. Not long ago a magnificent front has been added to this last building, at the public expense, and whenever a stranger visits the metropolis these words are wont to catch his ears: " See the matchless buildings of our city!"

The convent of the Carmelite Nuns is a Government office called " Hacienda." That of the Dominican Nuns is transformed into a House of Refuge for women insane, charged with crime, or in helpless old age. The splendid Church of St. Paul has been converted into a theatre, etc.

---

[1] The Oratorian Fathers, founded by Saint Philip Neri, have been thus named in Venezuela.

FAÇADE OF THE UNIVERSITY, CARACAS, FORMERLY THE CONVENT
OF THE FRANCISCANS.

In front of the University stand the capitol buildings. The sessions of the Chamber of Deputies and of the Senate, as also several Government agencies, take place here.

This was formerly a convent belonging to the Nuns of the Immaculate Conception, who are said to have numbered one hundred and twenty, when they were compelled to withdraw.

The streets of Caracas are perfectly straight, and intersect at right angles; nevertheless, it must be said that they are rather dirty, and badly kept. There is no system of drainage.

The town is traversed by three small rivers, and this has caused the construction of several bridges. Some of these attain to a remarkable height, and attest the great quantity of work and money spent in building them. The town also contains several large public squares, which are well provided with shade trees. We find erected in many of these squares the statue of one of the great men of the land—"Los heroes de las guerras de la Independencia."

The most remarkable of these squares bears the name of Bolivar. It is situated in front of the Cathedral and the ancient Seminary; the latter building, sharing the fate of the convents, was confiscated by the Government. In the same square there is a magnificent equestrian statue of Bolivar, who, from his gallant steed, salutes his countrymen.

Bolivar is the great man of the Republic; he is the Liberator or "Libertador," the Father of his native land, the Founder of five Republics, as Venezuelans are wont to say. They omit to say, however, that this great man was exiled by his own countrymen, and that he died in exile, regretting the whole work of independence which he had brought about. Some time before his death, Simon Bolivar is said to have exclaimed: "I have driven a plough across the ocean"—"He arado en el mar." Venezuelan patriots have repaired all injuries, as far as may be, in bringing back to the bosom of the Republic the ashes of its hero. They have been placed in a magnificent marble tomb, which may be seen in the National Pantheon.

Venezuelans make a boast of their Pantheon, where the great men of the country are laid to rest. It is, in point of fact, the most artistic building of Caracas. Its style is Gothic, and it pre-

THE CAPITOL, CARACAS.

sents a magnificent appearance with its lofty steeples and towers. Scarcely twenty years ago this very building was called Trinity Church, and the Sacrifice of the Mass was daily offered to God. But Venezuela needed a *Pantheon*, and now possesses one!

For the Venezuelan of to-day, Bolivar is not only a great man, but also a demi-god. One can hardly understand the nature of the veneration paid to his memory. Everything in his regard has been exaggerated: his qualities, his deeds, the importance of his political influence. A stranger would create an unfavorable impression by holding a contrary opinion concerning this hero. No doubt he possessed real military and administrative ability, and gave evident proof of uncommon tenacity and perseverance in all his enterprises; nevertheless, he brought dishonor on his reputation by such acts as historical impartiality does not fail to stigmatize as disreputable. He was accompanied for years by an Englishman's wife, to whom posterity has attached the name of "Libertadora del Libertador," because, as they say, she saved his life. Bolivar displayed considerable exertion to bring about the separation of Venezuela from Spain. This is what is called Independence; but apart from the lawfulness and morality of this act of rebellion, has Bolivar exercised the influence attributed to him? History seems to deny it. General Miranda made greater efforts than he to prepare and to carry out the Revolution; Bolivar did no more than to appear at the critical moment, when, taking advantage of Miranda's achievement, he became conspicuous, and won the title of "Libertador." It is likewise an historical fact that Bolivar was less successful in the war than many of his generals whose glory has all been attributed to himself.

During the wars of Independence, the Revolutionists believed, right or wrong, that the clergy were hostile to them. This persuasion enables us to account for the persecutions which the Church suffered at that time by the banishment of the bishops and of hundreds of priests, as also by the many atrocities committed against harmless missionaries. Many of them were shot, others drowned, and a large stone is still shown in Venezuelan Guiana, where some unfortunate Capuchin Fathers perished by a slow fire when they had left parents and country to evangelize the savage tribes along the banks of the Orinoco.

Here is an anecdote which I have gathered from other sources than from the annals of the country. Bolivar being once in the town of Angostura, called after his name, Cindad-Bolivar, cried out one night to one of his aides-de-camp: " You'll lay hands, to-night, on the eight Capuchins that I have got here in prison, and

GENERAL BOLIVAR.

send them over to glory." The officer, accustomed to Bolivar's hints, understood the right meaning of this speech, and laid hands upon the Capuchins that very night; and after leading them on board a vessel anchored in the Orinoco, beheaded them and threw their bodies into the water. There are those who would excul-pate Bolivar from this horrible assassination. They pretend that he was out of his mind, and that the officer had misunderstood him,—that his intention was simply to order that the victims be brought over that same night to a place beyond the river by the name of "the glory," or "la gloria," and this the unfortunate aide-de-camp had interpreted as "the glory of Heaven."

One can scarcely restrain a smile of disdain on reading the connection which Venezuelan authors pretend to find between Bolivar, their famous Libertador, and the mystery of the Most Blessed Trinity. First of all, they say that the devotion of this incomprehensible mystery was hereditary in Bolivar's family. His Christian name was Simon José Antonio de la Santisima Trinidad. He was born in 1783, the very year in which took place the dedication of the beautiful church which has become the Pantheon, and where his remains, brought back from the land of exile, await the day of the Last Judgment. Eight days after his birth, he was brought before the high altar of the same church to be consecrated to the Most Blessed Trinity. During his lifetime he never omitted the annual solemnization of this great day.

One Sunday in June, 1827, the Liberator and his family assisted at the festival of the Most Blessed Trinity, in the Cathedral Church of Caracas. Doctor Alejandro Echezuria ascended the pulpit to preach to a select congregation. His Grace, Archbishop Mendez, pontificated. After speaking on the great mystery which Holy Church commemorates on that day, the orator thought it good to dedicate a few words to the Liberator, and to the members of the family present. He said: "This solemn day, on which I have the honor of addressing this select assembly, has been rendered more illustrious by the presence of the Liberator himself. The devotion of the mystery of the Most Blessed Trinity is the priceless jewel and the precious legacy bequeathed to this man of renown by his ancestors. Thus it is that through the course of ages domestic virtues are handed down, passing from father to child till the end of time. Does it cause you any astonishment, gentlemen, to hear one speak of Bolivar on the festival day of the Adorable Trinity? Is there not in this great man a perfect representation of this mystery? Is not Bolivar the

Father of the land, the Son of glory, and the Spirit of liberty?"

The speaker would have continued had not the Archbishop vehemently rung the signal bell and put immediate close to the
discourse.   Towards evening, that same day, the news was spread
that Dr. Echezuria was placed under an ecclesiastical suspense for

TOMB OF BOLIVAR, IN THE PANTHEON, CARACAS.

the space of two months.   Not long after Archbishop Mendez suffered banishment for having done his duty.

Not to seem unfair towards Bolivar, we must note two circumstances in his favor: the first is that he died poor, and the second

is that he died in sentiments of reconciliation with the Catholic Church. He had the means, it seems, of acquiring great wealth, and could even put on a king's crown, as one of his generals prompted him to do. Bolivar looked with scorn upon riches as well as upon all dangerous renown.

The last days of his life were passed in a state bordering on misery. It is said that after his death, his physician gave one of his own shirts to bury him in, for he said within himself: " I would not that history impute to us the fault of burying the Liberator of South America in such a wretched state."

Before going before the judgment-seat of the One in whose presence he was to account for the tremendous responsibility he had assumed, he called for His representative upon earth. At the feet of the priest of God, in the confessional, he acknowledged with deep contrition the guilt of his whole life, and asked the forgiveness which the Church of Christ is never known to refuse, even to the greatest sinners.

The neighborhood of Caracas is very pleasant, and well cultivated. The hills about the city are barren, and give to the surrounding country a certain appearance of sadness: but a glimpse on Avila's vast protuberance changes the scenery into one of majesty and grandeur. An irresistible impulse made me attempt the ascent of this very mountain which Humboldt had ascended at the beginning of the century, January 2d, 1800. The 23d of November, about noon, I stood upon an elevation more than 6,000 feet above the level of the sea. My first thought was to enjoy the view of the ocean from this remarkable height, but a thick cloud frustrated my intention. In exchange I mused upon the landscape which looks towards the valley of Caracas. I admired, at leisure, the double range of mountains which lowers by degrees till it overtakes those hills along whose base flows the Guayre in a serpentine course, resembling a great silvery thread. The landscape was bathed by the sun in a flood of dazzling light. Some fleecy clouds, tinted with the most delicate shades, floated lightly hither and thither. In a word, the metropolis seated in the plain below, with its regular streets, its church steeples, and its myriads of red house-tops, was a delightful scene from the distance.

The most important town of Venezuela, next to Caracas, is Valencia, chief town of the state Carabobo. Its foundation dates from the 16th century. Its position is in the vicinity of the lovely lake of Tacarigua, at an altitude of 472 metres above the level of the sea. The temperature here is much hotter than at Caracas. The population of the town numbers about 50,000 inhabitants. A railway line affords communication with Puerto-Cabello and the ocean. Another line will soon join it to Caracas.

A small town of twelve to fourteen thousand inhabitants is Cura, and the capital of the state of Miranda. It stands upon an elevation, 509 metres above the sea, and contains a hospital, known as St. Dominic's.

The capital of the state of Bermudez, Barcelona, with a population of 12,758, at a late census, lies on the banks of the Neveri River; its altitude is no more than 16 metres above the level of the sea.

A GARLAND OF ROSES.

JOSEPH W. S. NORRIS.

ILENCE and splendor of a garden where
    The Flower of flowers is lovingly enshrined;
    Where hearts devoted secret sweets divined,
And dwelt enamoured of the fragrant air!
Fresh blossoms all, yea, roses all most rare,
    Gold-hearted, velvet-petaled, such in kind,
    Agnes, Agatha, Cæcilia's noble mind,
Lucia's white soul, Dorothea, heavenly fair.

And just as dear and near the Master's Heart,
    While centuries of change have shaken bare
        The purple throne, and tyrant emperor hurled
To deeps unknown, the garland twined with art,
    Erin's Bride, Spain's Teresa, dear Saint Clare,
        And Lima's Rose, Flower of the Western World.

DOMINICAN ABBEY OF OUR LADY OF THANKS, YOUGHAL.

LAURA GREY.

HE sun was tinting with an amber glow the waves breaking on Youghal strand, when my friend and I strolled down the main street of the old town.

.That morning we had sailed up the Blackwater from Mount Melleray Abbey, and our day had been spent rambling through quaint alleys and rows of gabled houses.

We had visited St. Mary's ancient church, Sir Walter Raleigh's mansion, the site of the Franciscan abbey, and our tourist's catalogue was nearly exhausted. One item still remained, and that was the ruins of the Dominican Priory. The inhabitants of Youghal seemed unconscious of its existence, yet in old histories of the County Cork, I had read of its strong tower and fortified walls. Conflicting guides pursued us on all sides; some pointed one way—their opponents the other. Thrown on our own resources, we resolved to discard their services, and pilot our own footsteps.

On the northern outskirts of the town we discovered a crowded burial ground, with a clump of trees standing sentinel amongst the graves.

Here and there, through the foliage, peeped out a fragment of masonry, and stepping across the green mounds we found ourselves underneath the Western window of the Priory of "Our Lady of Thanks." [1]

All that remains of this once famous Dominican abbey are sundry broken columns, a shattered arch, and a window, yellow with lichen. One graceful cluster of pillars riveted our gaze. Twined round the capitals were lilies carved in stone, white and waxen, as if they had but left the artist's studio.

---

[1] Strictly speaking, "*Priory*" is the correct term applied to the abode of Dominican Communities. The word *Abbey* is generally used in reference to *all religious houses of men.*

This group formed the entrance to the shrine of " Our Lady of Thanks," from which the abbey derived its title.

It was Thomas Fitzmaurice Fitzgerald, Lord Offaley, who invited the Dominicans to Youghal, and built this Priory for their reception. Hither the brethren came on August 5th, 1268, and here they flourished until the year 1581, when Elizabeth of England levelled their home to the ground, and sent them adrift.

In 1296 the founder, Lord Offaley, died, and was buried at the right-hand side of the altar. Seven years later, the abbey doors were flung open to receive the mortal remains of its munificent benefactor, Robert de Perceval.

In the year 1351, a funeral cortège might be seen wending its slow course along the avenue of yew trees, fronting the massive portals. On the bier lay the lifeless form of Maurice Fitzgibbon (" the White Knight,") and the second founder of Kilmallock Abbey, County Limerick. He was advanced in years when he took the habit of St. Dominic in his own Abbey of Kilmallock, but later on joined the Community at Youghal. On his dying bed he craved to be buried with his consort in the tomb he had erected for both in Kilmallock, and his request was granted.

Time wore on, and the once thin band of Dominicans had grown into an opulent Brotherhood. Repelling the inroads of avarice amongst men vowed to lead a life of evangelical poverty, we find the Master-General of the Order, Bartholomew de Comatio, on Irish soil, making a visitation of Youghal Abbey. In 1493 he reformed its inmates.

*   *   *   *   *

In the days when the Dominican Abbey at Youghal was at its zenith, there stood at the gates an Italian youth—a sculptor, seeking admittance amongst the brethren. No dowry he possessed, save his chisel and a block of Carrara marble. These he placed at the disposal of the Community, and was accepted by them as a novice, taking the name of Carthage.

A year after he had assumed the white habit, St. Brendan's feast came round.[1]

---

[1] St. Brendan, an Irishman, known in history as " the traveller," on account of his voyages. He is credited with being the first discoverer of America. He founded the School of Clonfert, in the fifth century.

4

The name of Ireland's "traveller" saint was borne by the Prior, and the brethren were vying with each other in preparing divers simple offerings to present to their spiritual Father. Brother Carthage was selected to carve a statue of the Blessed Virgin, with the Infant Christ standing on her knee. The block of marble, which had been the novice's dower, had been hewn into a stately column, and nought remained for his chisel to fashion. But one day, strolling by the seashore, a piece of bone floated in on the tide, and he carried it home in triumph, resolved to frame a statue, and paint it in glowing colors. How his design was accomplished we shall read.

"Summon hither Brother Carthage, that my unworthy blessing may rest on the soul that conceived, and the hands that modelled, yonder miracle in carving," spoke the Prior to his religious children on St. Brendan's feast. But nowhere was the artist Brother to be found. Morning ripened into day, and heavy grew the Prior's heart at the absence of the novice. The bell sounded for the mid-day repast. The brethren were all seated, when slowly up the refectory moved Brother Carthage, his back bare, and bleeding from strokes of the discipline. Advancing towards Father Brendan's chair, he knelt, with downcast eyes.

"Rise, son," was the reassuring greeting. "Nought but smiles should wreathe thy brows to-day." But the prostrate friar still wept on.

"In the virtue of holy obedience, I command thee to unloose the fountains of thy grief," continued the Prior, rising.

But Brother Carthage waved him back, and pointing to the statue, said: "Into yonder piece of bone thou thinkest truly, I have breathed a soul. I shall not gainsay thy words. God be praised for having guided my chisel aright! Since I crossed this sainted threshold one sombre winter ago, I have not wilfully transgressed the rules of the brethren. Last midnight, when all had sunk to rest, a temptation fell upon me, crushing in its force. I rose to sate my vanity with a view of my handicraft—the Mother and the Son carved in bone, for thy festal day. The pale moonbeams lit up the chapter room. Hard by lay my brush and colors. I seized them. Divers last strokes were wanting, and I painted them.

A voice whispered: 'Work on,' and I obeyed. A ray of starlight played on the figures whilst I flushed with nature's tints the sullen bone. Not until the Matin chime stole upon the breath of morning did I falter. Ah me! I have bartered the heritage of Blessed Dominic's trammels for a mess of pottage. Kind Father, forgive an erring son."

The Prior rose, and, casting his mantle over the kneeling novice, said: "Brother Carthage, thy humble confession has unsealed the well-springs of God's compassion towards thee. In His Most Holy Name, and in the Name of His Virgin Mother, I absolve thee from thy fault. Arise; be comforted."

The Brother stood erect, and his brethren crowded round to imprint the kiss of peace.

A year later, a costly shrine was erected to receive the image of the Blessed Virgin. In course of time the statue was deemed miraculous, and the title of "Our Lady of Thanks" was bestowed on it by the pious pilgrims who thronged the abbey. Jewels, gemmed lamps, and diamond-hilted swords hung from the walls, and flashed in the blaze of a hundred lights. But dark days were near, when the spoiler's hand would quench the flame, and wrest the votive offerings from the shrine.

Father Carthage had grown into an aged man when the sacrilegious tocsin of Elizabeth of England rang throughout Ireland. Yesterday, the Franciscan Abbey at Youghal had fallen, and the oaken magnificence of its roof was reduced to smouldering embers; to-day, the "requiem" of the Dominicans would be chanted!

The Community had entoned Vespers for the last time, when the tramp of soldiery was heard in the hush of evening.

In that wild hour Father Carthage thought of the statue he had carved. How he longed for the elasticity of youth to scale the walls and bear it away to a place of safety! In his distress he commissioned a younger Brother to execute the task. Seizing the relic, the novice wrapped it in his scapular, and retreated to a knot of trees. Perceiving one hollow yew standing apart, he dropped the statue down into the centre of the trunk, and fled. His life paid the penalty of his devotion. A mailed hand was laid upon his shoulder, and he was slain under the green leaves where he stood. Father Carthage meantime was ignorant of the Brother's death, and of the fate of the statue.

The shrine of " Our Lady of Thanks " had become a shapeless ruin, and the tower of the abbey from which the sweet chimes once pealed, now reeled under the roar of artillery. The trees were cut down and shipped to England. The brethren were dispersed, hiding amongst the crags, and wandering by the margin of the Blackwater; the devoted peasantry supplied them with the necessaries of life, craving in exchange, a Mass in some dark sea cave.

Father Carthage was one of those who survived the wreck of Youghal Abbey. Even the hirelings of Elizabeth respected his silver hairs and noble bearing. A benefactor once presented him with a gift of firewood. Amongst the brushwood was found an ancient yew tree, covered with lichen, and scarred with years. All day long the brethren strove to separate the trunk from the branches. The limbs of the aged Fathers were numb from exposure, and fuel was needed to kindle a fire. Axe and saw were alike employed in vain. Some one whispered, " Call Father Carthage to our aid. In the springtime of his youth he was wont to carve the solid rock; in the fall of his years he can surely pierce the porous rind of the yew tree."

At their summons the hoary Dominican appeared, leaning on his staff. " This log of timber hath long lain in brine," quoth the old man, separating the fibres of the bark with his hands.

" Yea, Father," answered one of his companions. " The donor hath even now told us that it was swept in yester morn by the tide."

" Give me the saw, my son," said the priest.

He pressed the sharp teeth into the sides of the tree.

With a crash the hollow trunk sprang open, and lying within, wrapt in a roll of white serge, lay the long-lost statue of " Our Lady of Thanks."

A layer of young wood had grown across the upper end of the aperture, sealing the trunk against the inroads of wind and rain.

The sight of the statue proved too great a joy for Father Carthage. Clasping it passionately to his breast, he leaned against one of the brethren for support, murmuring the " *Nunc Dimittis.*" They were his last words on earth. He died of an overflow of delight.   The aged heart was unable to bear the pressure of that unexpected meeting.

The Geraldines seem to have been the tutelary angels of this monastery.   There are those who ascribe the safety of the miraculous statue, so dear to the faithful, to a daughter of this family, who is said to have watched her opportunity and carried it off during the days of carnage.   However, we have here given the beautiful and touching legend of "Our Lady of Thanks."

We have not been able to trace the relic further through the vicissitudes of that troublous era.   Its voyage across the sea to Youghal must always remain a mystery.   No doubt, it had never quitted the hollow trunk in which the Dominican novice had placed it the night the abbey was stormed.   The new growth of wood was clearly a miracle wrought by the Mother of God to shield her image from harm, and to gladden Father Carthage's eyes before he sank to rest.

In the year 1644, we find the statue mentioned in a General Chapter of the Order held in Rome.   At the present time the Dominican community in Cork preserve the statue under the title of " Our Lady of Youghal."

There, in these later days, a solemn Triduum was celebrated on the occasion of the consecration of two new altars, and installation of the miraculous statue.   One of the altars is dedicated to the Holy Rosary, and the other to St. Dominic: both are of polished marble.[1]   The ceremony of consecration attracted great numbers of the faithful.   The prelates who officiated were, the Most Rev. Dr. Browne, Bishop of Cloyne, and the Most Rev. Dr. O'Callaghan, O. P., Bishop of Cork.   The Pope, at the request of Dr. O'Callaghan, granted a Plenary Indulgence to all who, after Confession and Communion, should visit the Rosary altar and pray for the intentions of his Holiness.   The faithful availed themselves of this great favor granted by the Holy Father, and during the three days of the Triduum the altar rails were crowded with communicants at all the Masses.

On the last day of the Triduum, the ceremony of installation of the miraculous statue took place.   It was borne in the procession

---

[1] The altars are the gift of Miss Susan Murphy, a devoted friend of the community.

by the Bishop, and placed in a silver shrine on the altar of the Rosary. The procession was composed of the Fathers of the community, and other distinguished ecclesiastics, the Altar-boy's Sodality, the Sodality of St. Thomas of Aquinas, consisting of about 300 young men, and the members of the Confraternity of the Holy Rosary.

The statue is enclosed in a silver gilt shrine, presented by Lady Honor Fitzgerald, of the Geraldine family. It is elaborately ornamented, and bears the following inscription, in Latin:

" Pray for the soul of Honor, daughter of James Fitzgerald, who caused this to be made A. D. 1617."

Many miracles are said to have been worked through the intercession of our Lady of Youghal, and the statue itself bears evident traces of the ardent devotion of the faithful. Parts of it are very much worn, owing, no doubt, to the kisses of devout pilgrims, who came, in a past century, from every part of Ireland, to visit the miraculous shrine, in the old Dominican convent of Youghal. The convent gave many martyrs to the Church, and conferred many glories on the Order.

PITY THE FALLEN.

William Sheran.

Pity the fallen round about thee flung,
　　Self-wronged and trampled 'neath an iron world,
　　Prone on the thorny way, they find few hearts
Throbbing in sympathy, few tears that flow,
Few helping hands—the passing pilgrim scorns,
Or draws perchance within the narrow shell
Of selfishness, when but a little aid—
A kindly word or deed—would vanquish vice,
And raise a hapless brother from the dust.
Too oft the Christian tramples with the crowd;
His eyes to Heaven turned, he brushes by,
The while poor bleeding hearts in anguish break,
And shadows steal o'er all the ways of life,
And the pale star of hope in darkness dies.
Not thus the Master; He made pause, and spake
The word of comfort e'en to Magdalen;
Ay, more,—the heavy stone He heaved away
That crushed for ages long our hapless kind.
Learn of His love, exhaustless as the deep:
Pity the fallen—God hath pitied thee.

CARDINAL ZIGLIARA, O. P.

Rev. Reginald Walsh, O. P.

I.

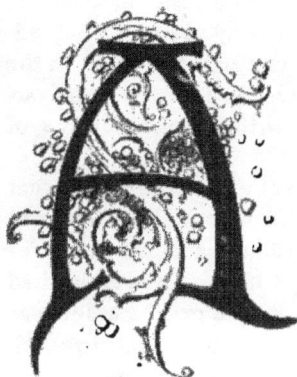

MONG the many distinguished Cardinals that have adorned the Church in the course of the present century, a high place will ever be assigned to him, a short description of whose career is now laid before the readers of THE ROSARY MAGAZINE.

Born in 1833 at Bonifacio, an important seaport town of Corsica, Francesco Zigliara had many splendid gifts in common with his celebrated countryman, Napoleon. In both the germs of future greatness were visible from their tender years. But how different were their after lives, when each on his respective path reached the zenith of renown! The victories of the one were appalling scenes of carnage; those of the other were visions of peace. The one recked not of the woes which his own insatiable ambition and greed of gain inflicted on nations; the other, in his humility and charity, thought he never did enough to make his brethren happy and blessed by the possession of the truth. Fresh streams of blood were for years ruthlessly poured out to swell that gory torrent which it was fondly imagined would carry Napoleon on to the ocean of his boundless desires; Zigliara's peaceful path in life was marked by countless deeds of love, and strewn with tokens of gratitude from all that ever knew him. Napoleon coveted the fleeting splendors of worldly fame, and certainly obtained it, for on history's roll, among all the names of conquerors, scarcely one other shines with such dazzling lustre as his own; while Zigliara despised earthly reputation, and the everyday world has seldom or never heard of him, because his life was hidden with Christ in God. The one, in the hour of military success, blinded by his own glory, turned his victorious arms against the Pope; the other acknowledged throughout the learned world as the supreme authority on the doctrine of St. Thomas, consecrated his genius to the defence of truth, and was the Church's most devoted servant. Napoleon in Saint Helena, when his feverish dreams were over, repented of the past, and returned with all the ardor of his mighty soul to the lessons of boyhood's happy years in Ajaccio; Zigliara not only remained faithful to his early training, but advanced continually in virtue, and at the end of a life spent in the sunshine of God's friendship, could, when his last moments arrived, look back on every bygone hour without one shadow of disappointment or regret.

In Bonifacio, his first classical teacher was a Jesuit, Father Aloysius Piras, for whom he entertained throughout life the warmest affection. When he was created Cardinal he at once sent for his old professor, and made him live with him. The Jesuits had been turned out of their house in Rome, so the good Father was doubly glad to accept the not merely pressing, but irresistible invitation of his illustrious pupil. It was touching to see their mutual veneration. Some one has said that the best sign of a man is love and respect for his former teacher; if this be so,—and who can doubt it?—what a noble nature was that of Cardinal Zigliara!

But we must not anticipate. Under his excellent master Francesco progressed so rapidly that when he was eighteen he was qualified to enter the Order. At his reception he took the name of Thomas Mary. The choice was a happy one, and a true presage of the young novice's future. For he was destined to apply the magnificent teaching of St. Thomas to the varied requirements of our times, to express it in a manner agreeable to modern tastes, and to give a new impetus to its study outside the Dominican Order. Of course, in the Dominican schools, in some universities and seminaries, the genuine exposition of the Thomistic system had been handed down from generation to generation, but it was reserved for Zigliara, under the present Pope, to be the chief instrument of propagating the true philosophy throughout the entire Church. While thus pre-eminent in learning, he was to be equally distinguished for piety, especially towards the Blessed Virgin. He loved to honor her, to speak of her in

school, and to dedicate his books to her. The prayer written by
him as a novice shows the fervor of his youthful devotion, which
increased as time went on:

PRAYER TO THE VIRGIN MARY, MOTHER OF GOD.

O holy Mother of God! O refuge of all the sinful and afflicted! Knowing
that my salvation depends on you, I commence to desire it more ardently. It
is true that your Son is my Redeemer, but He is also my Judge. His goodness inspires me with confidence, but His justice fills me with dread. As I
know that I am a sinner, I dare not present myself before Him. But in you, my
Mother, I find no cause of fear. You are the Mother of Mercy, not the Mother
of justice. You consented to be a Mother only to give me a Saviour. Would
you be Mother of God, if there were no sinners? In a certain sense you
owe to them the sublime dignity to which you have been exalted and therefore
you love them, you watch over them with tender solicitude, and grant them
favor.

Great though my sins may be, I cannot despair of my salvation. What have
I to fear, if I firmly purpose to amend, seeing that I have an all-powerful Advocate with the Father, and so powerful an advocate with the Son! I wish to
be your servant in order to be of the number of the predestined.

He wrote this prayer in the Little Office Book of the Blessed
Virgin which he was accustomed to use, and from that book it
has been copied by the present writer.

Zigliara's career as a student was, as might be anticipated, one
series of brilliant triumphs. His philosophical studies were made
in Rome, his theological ones in Perugia, where, on May 17th, 1856,
he was ordained by the Archbishop of the diocese, Joachim Cardinal Pecci. The two were often to meet again.

The young priest began soon afterwards to teach philosophy
in Rome, and then at Corbara, in his native Corsica. He was
subsequently appointed to the same chair in the diocesan seminary of Viterbo, while at the same time he was Master of novices
in the famous convent of Gradi, which lies just outside the city
walls. His holiness and the sweetness of his disposition made
him beloved by all. Thus for some years he lived in peace, and
laid the foundations of his future greatness. Then came troubled
times for the Church and for the Order. Garibaldi, Cavour, and
the other Freemasons who have undermined the prosperity of
their country, and built " United Italy " on its ruins, were then at
work. The Piedmontese government had its secret emissaries
everywhere, in order to create dissensions, and to spread irreligious and revolutionary doctrines. At length, when all was ready,
when all was done that treachery and perjury could do, war was
declared. Here iniquity was once more successful. The Papal

army was gradually driven back by the immeasurably more numerous one of Victor Emmanuel, and, in September, 1866, after the defeat at Bagnorea, which is only a few miles from Viterbo, the hospitals in the latter city were crowded with wounded soldiers.   Many
of these noble fellows were French Zouaves.   Zigliara at once devoted himself with the greatest zeal to alleviate their pains and
to minister to them in their spiritual needs.   This was not done
without considerable danger, for, sad to say, the Carbonari and
other secret societies had already become powerful in Viterbo.
At last the Garibaldians gained possession of the historic town,
and the Dominicans were driven out of their ancient home and
from the sanctuary where the miraculous image of the Blessed
Virgin had been venerated for centuries.

Of course, he who had signalized himself by his devoted care
of the soldiers of Pio Nono was the object of special hatred.
But Zigliara was not the man to be frightened by Freemasons,
nor to be daunted by difficulties; with one companion he remained
within the city walls, and, thanks to his persevering efforts, the
convent of the Quercia was, after a short time, restored to the
Order.

The origin of this celebrated sanctuary may be told here in
few words.   Centuries ago, in the forest near Viterbo, a woodman
who was engaged in felling an oak (Italian *Quercia*) found, to
his astonishment, in the middle of it, a picture around which (if
it was not inserted there by supernatural agency), in the course
of ages, the wood had grown.   The picture represented the Blessed Virgin, so it was called the Madonna della Quercia.   When
the news of the discovery spread, people came in crowds to pray;
then miracles were vouchsafed in rapid succession, and the citizens
vowed to build a magnificent basilica on the spot where the oak
tree had stood.   When it was finished they resolved to entrust
the church to the care of a Religious Order.   But which?   On
the council day, with that spirit of childlike trust and love which
made the Middle Ages so beautiful, the decision was gracefully
left to the Blessed Virgin.   The Order, a member of which would,
on the following morning, be the first to enter the city by the
Porta Romana, should be regarded as the heavenly-appointed
guardians of the shrine.   A Dominican came, probably one be-

longing to the great convent of Gradi, which is about twenty minutes' walk from Viterbo. Ever since that memorable day the
Quercia has been one of the most cherished sanctuaries in the
keeping of Mary's white-robed sons. The Rosary is said there
continually, and every evening after Complin the community,
in fulfilment of an ancient vow, sings the Litany before the miraculous picture. It is over the high altar of that church, which is
one of the grandest monuments of Bramante's genius. The edi-

MIRACULOUS PICTURE OF OUR LADY OF THE OAK.

fice is rich in exquisite ornaments by Lucca della Robbia, and in
the adjoining convent is the glorious cloister designed by Vignola;
but we prefer to linger for a moment in the other one, the cloister next the church, which is regarded as another of Bramante's
masterpieces. It reveals the same unerring perception of the
most delicate lines of beauty, and the faultless sense of harmonious proportion, joined to that inimitable power of combining gran-

deur and grace which the world admires in the great artist's other works: The Church Over the Holy House in Loretto; in Rome, the Cancelleria with San Lorenzo, the Vatican Palace, etc., etc.

But incomparably dearer than all the works of genius that adorn the Quercia are the memories of that hallowed spot. Here generations of sainted Dominicans have dwelt—in this century, for instance, Jandel and Lacordaire. Here countless pilgrims have knelt in prayer before Heaven's Queen, and here she has showered down innumerable graces on her children. No wonder then, that Zigliara, with his Napoleonic fearlessness and tenacity of purpose, determined that the shrine of the Virgin of the Rosary should not be profaned.[1]

When his work in Viterbo was finished, his superiors summoned him to Rome. He was again appointed Master of Novices, and, after a short time, Regent of the Minerva (a title given to the head professor in Dominican colleges of theology and philosophy). In 1873 this community was driven out by the Italian government, and the great convent of the Minerva, the largest in Rome, became the office of the Minister of the Interior, etc., etc. Zigliara, with the other professors and the students, then found refuge under the hospitable roof of the Fathers of the Congregation of the Holy Ghost, who had charge of the French College. Here the lectures were held until a house near the Minerva was obtained. This house, we may observe, continued to be Zigliara's home until his death; in it his greatest works for the Church of God were to be accomplished.

Meanwhile his fame as a theologian had rapidly spread throughout Rome. Pius IX. had the greatest esteem for the learned and holy Dominican, as the following anecdote will be sufficient to show. The writer heard it from the young French priest, the genial Abbé D——, to whom the episode had occurred. He was an officer in the Zouaves up to 1870, and when he could no longer serve the Pope, an officer in the Chasseurs d'Afrique. At length he heard the call to quit all lesser things for the love of Christ, and to become an ecclesiastic. He immediately returned to Rome, and as he was well-known to the Pope, his first visit was to the

---

[1] One of his best sermons was that preached 27th Oct., 1872, on the occasion of a great pilgrimage to the Quercia. (8vo. Sperandio Pompei, Viterbo, 1872.)

Vatican. Pius IX. was extremely pleased to hear of his resolve,
and conversed a long time with him about his vocation. During
the audience the ex-captain, who was evidently a great favorite of
Pio Nono's, asked direction about many things, one of his questions being: " Under what professor does your Holiness wish me to
learn theology?" The Pope's face at once lighted up with the
well-known smile as he answered: "Quite right! I wish you to
study under the best professor in Rome; attend the lectures of
Father Zigliara."

And how much those lectures were prized! Every one was
an intellectual treat, a fresh exhibition of profound learning, and
of consummate mastery of the most difficult subjects. He had
thoroughly grasped the meaning of St. Thomas. The whole Summa, as well as the mutual relation of its every part, lay clearly
visible before him in the sunlight of his own intellect; he was
perfectly sure of his ground, never more so, indeed, than when he
led us into what were to many the dark depths of some metaphys-
ical problem. The result of this clear, comprehensive knowledge
was that he could elucidate, develop, amplify, at will. Where an
ordinary mind or an imperfectly educated one would report only
of chaos and darkness, his splendid intellect brought everything
into a focus of order and light; and the whole man was speaking. Zigliara always became enthusiastic over his subject. H.s
was not a dry, formal lecture, but an eloquent, impassioned defen:e
of truth. He warmed in the opening sentences of his address, and
then the professor was transformed into the sacred orator speaking
on the things of God to those whose vocation it was to go forth
and teach all nations. He not only enlightened the minds of his
hearers with the knowledge of the truth, he inflamed their hearts
with the love of it.

The present writer has no intention of attempting an analysis
of the matter of those learned discourses. But as regards their
style and the manner in which they were delivered, suffice it
to say that he was often reminded by them of the sermons of the
great Irish Dominican, Father Burke. Not, indeed, that Zigliara
was his equal in eloquence, or that a theological lecture could be
a sermon, but that both Dominicans knew St. Thomas' works to
their very depths, the one devoting himself to their scientific exposi-

tion, the other using them as only he could for the highest and most sacred ends. In this way the comparison of their respective methods was most interesting. Father Burke had the Summa at his fingers' ends, and from it he learned that surpassing knowledge of the dogmas of our holy faith, and acquired that marvellous power of setting them forth in all the splendor of truth, so that a child could understand him and a theologian might learn from him. Zigliara's great gifts were of a different order. Though, whenever he occupied the pulpit of the Minerva, his fervent sermon went straight to the hearts of his hearers, and though his confessional was the means of reconciliation to many an erring one, yet his sphere was the lecture hall. Here he was supreme. Here he showed to the full that rare faculty of clear exposition, and with it the gift of being able to rivet the attention of his hearers, until whatever he wanted to teach went home, and was too firmly fastened to their souls ever to be forgotten. The power of vivid delineation in which he excelled, and the oratorical finish of his discourses, were the secret of this. He brought out in crystal language all the beauties of the Queen of sciences, and made the study of theology most attractive and fascinating. The Summa is in its literary form the most exquisite work of art that the mind of man ever conceived. Apart from its intrinsic beauties, which are those of Heaven itself—never to be seen more clearly until they are beheld in the light of glory—the expression of them so far transcends the highest effort of any other human genius as to merit for its author the title of the "Angel of the Schools." Seldom has the Summa been in worthier hands than those of Zigliara. When listening to him one felt instinctively that he breathed the atmosphere of heavenly knowledge and love, that every word was spoken for the greater honor and glory of God. The Regent of the Minerva could well say, with his Master and Model: "Mihi quidem studere est orare." How, then, could he fail to achieve the most brilliant success? Zigliara was a man of fervent piety, who continually implored light from Him who is its only source, and a man of such conscientious industry that although he had gone through the whole course of lectures on the Summa *three* times over, besides teaching philosophy for years, and had before him the lectures written and continually improved, yet from the day he commenced, up to the very last, he always spent five or six hours in preparation for his next lecture. No wonder that his hearers hung on his words with spellbound attention!

There were students there from many lands, almost every nation in Europe being represented. Some belonged to the various religious Orders, others to the secular clergy. Quite a large number had taken University degrees, several were Doctors in Divinity, and some five or six had already taught in their respective seminaries. Yet all these were proud to be his disciples, and glad to find that their previous studies enabled them to derive still greater fruit from his lectures. The lucid exposition which made everything intelligible to the youngest student was in itself a model lesson for these professors. This, combined with the exhaustive treatment of any question proposed for solution, made those discourses simply invaluable. Many years have passed since then, yet there is no more pleasing memory than that of those mornings in the Minerva. Some Sulpicians now in France say the same. Indeed, wherever Zigliara's students are met—in America, Australia, or Europe,—a unanimous expression of unbounded admiration and affection may be heard to the present day at the very mention of his name.

His exposition of theology was as clearly defined, as brilliant, and as enduring as one of Girolamo's gem engravings. It more than justified the wisdom of the French, Italian, German, and English bishops who put some of their best and most promising students, and even young professors, under his tuition, in order that on their return home they might be fully qualified to explain the doctrine of the " Prince of Theologians," contained in his immortal Summa. Many of them have since become distinguished professors: for instance, Mgr. d'Hulst and the younger Vigouroux, in Paris; the Abbé Thomas, in Toulouse University; F. Thomas Esser, O. P., of Fribourg University; Dr. O'Mahony, All Hallows, Dublin; Dr. Commer, Breslau University; the editor of the *Thomist Jahrbuch*, etc., etc.

Besides the students going through their course preparatory to taking their degree, there were also the "auditors," who came for the pleasure of hearing the great theologian. Many were dignitaries, and not unfrequently a Bishop would appear in the audience. But as we look back on those days, the recollection of one stands out clearer than that of all others, and though he was never *seen* during the lectures, his name must not be omitted from these pages—Joachim, Cardinal Pecci, Archbishop of Perugia. He was the most enthusiastic admirer and intimate friend of the Regent of the Minerva. In all his multifarious employments, in the midst of his great labors for his diocese and for the Church, the Cardinal was always a deep student of St. Thomas. Whenever he came to Rome one of his greatest pleasures was to discuss with Father Zigliara some interesting point of theology that had occupied his mind since his last visit. He never missed a lecture. He used to spend hours in the Regent's room, which was next the lecture hall, and whenever the door between them was left slightly ajar by the Regent as he came out to class, we knew that behind it sat that most attentive of listeners—Joachim Cardinal Pecci.

When he was created Pope in 1878, it was commonly said that the Regent of the Minerva would certainly be raised to the purple, yet perhaps few were prepared to see it done in the very first Consistory. It took Rome by surprise, but no one more so than the humble religious himself; it overwhelmed him with amazement and fear. The lectures were immediately stopped, the Cardinal designate was inconsolable; for about a week, only his most intimate friends were admitted to see him, and they found him in the deepest desolation. Then he reappeared in school, tried to speak, to say a few words of adieu, but in vain; he broke down utterly, and his thoughts found expression only in tears. It was evident to all that the obedience demanded of him was contrary to every feeling of his soul, that it was a heartrending sacrifice.[1] We saw that in our midst stood a man of God, one possessed of consummate humility. Great as was his learning, it was not so great as his virtue. This was well known outside, and, of course, most of all places, in the Vatican. The report in Rome at the time was that the new Pope said to the assembled Cardinals when he

---

[1] Leo XIII. commanded him strictly to obey. He had already declined to be Prior of the Minerva, and refused a Bishopric.

A few days afterwards his students presented him with an address and a jewelled mitre in token of their unchangeable veneration and gratitude.

announced the name till then reserved *in petto:* " In creating Thomas M. Zigliara Cardinal, I do not so much honor him as honor your Sacred College of which he will be the ornament."

He was, indeed, in every sense a worthy companion of Pitra, Bartolini, Manning, Franzelin, Gonzalez, and others whose learn-

ing and virtues have shed new lustre on the Roman purple, and especially of Newman and Hergenrœther, who were created with him. The occasion to which we have just alluded was not the first one on which the Minerva students perceived the Regent's profound contempt of self. He had always, as far as he could, kept in the background, and studiously avoided the notice of men. Nothing could have inflicted keener pain on him than to know that he himself was the object of universal admiration. Happily, he was quite unconscious of it. He had ever present to his mind the saving truth that his talents and knowledge were the gifts of God, to whom alone all the glory belonged. At the time of his elevation to the Cardinalate he had reached the pinnacle of his fame as a theological lecturer, and who could be meeker and humbler than he! The following incident deserves to be recorded not only as an example of his solid virtue, but also because it was in fact the immediate cause of his getting the red hat.

For a number of years the doctrine of St. Thomas had been attacked by certain professors, who spoke flippantly about it as a system that had seen its day, but which now, in this age of progress, this glorious nineteenth century of ours, was shown to be erroneous, utterly incompatible with the discoveries of modern physical science, and so forth. On one point, namely, on the nature of the union between soul and body, the saint's doctrine and the traditional exposition of it was especially singled out for censure. Either it was to be silently put away as a mediæval fancy, or the Thomist school, with its headquarters in the Minerva, was to confess that it did not understand the teaching of its founder. Zigliara, as being in Rome the chief official expounder of Thomism, was severely spoken of, and sometimes severely spoken to, in school by visitors that had been students of the professors in question. The Regent's meekness was admirable,—as admirable as his knowledge of the truth. On the two occasions when contradiction of St. Thomas's system was attempted, he listened with smiling patience, even assisted his opponents to formulate their objection, and to give it the finishing touches, and when it was complete—then came down on it like a sledge-hammer, and pulverized it. Those who were present can never forget the scene. For those who were not, the best thing to do is to read his philosophy, where they will see with what invariable kindness he speaks of his adversaries, and with what crushing might of irresistible logic he disposes of their objections.

One could not but be reminded of an anecdote in the life of St. Thomas. When he was at Paris, lecturing in the University, a

young man, confident of his own opinion, asserted in public what
was known to be contrary to the teaching of the Dominican professor.   That professor would have been the last in the world to
force his own convictions on others, or to interfere in any way
with their freedom of thought.   He would indeed be glad to receive more truth, or to impart what he knew to others, but he was
averse to controversy.   So far as he was personally concerned,
that juvenile philosopher might have gone on rejoicing in his new
and original views to his heart's content.   However, the latter
could not be satisfied with this; he should broach his theory, and
defend it, too, in the very presence of Thomas of Aquin, just to
see if the scholastic professor would be able to give any reply.
He made the attempt one fine day.   The Angelical listened sweetly and gently, then with one word annihilated the theory.   It was
never heard of more.

Such, too, in a measure, was the virtue and the learning of one
of the greatest, if not the. very greatest Thomist of the present
century.   Unalterable in mildness, he was invincible in theological
science.   The Regent of the Minerva was more than a match for
all his adversaries combined.   The true explanation of the union
of soul and body, the fundamental truth of psychology, was to
them incomprehensible, self-contradictory, etc., etc.; to him it was
plain and perfect in the cohesion of its every part.

More than five hundred years ago, a false theory on this very
subject was put forward by a certain Peter John de Oliva.   There
was during the discussion we are speaking of a doubt on the part
of some people as to the precise nature of Oliva's error.   No one
for generations had seen his work, which was condemned in the
Council of Vienne, A. D. 1355.   At last, in 1878, when it was again
brought to light, those people found that the doctrine of St.
Thomas maintained all along by Zigliara was the doctrine of the
Ecumenical Council, and that the tenets for which Oliva had been
condemned were the very objections of Zigliara's adversaries.

Long before that distinguished critic, the late Father Fidelis à
Fanna, O. S. F., (who was engaged in searching for manuscripts,
and collating them for the new edition of St. Bonaventure's
works) discovered an Oliva manuscript hidden away in a dark
corner of the Borghese library, Zigliara had repeatedly declared

his conviction that the long-lost works, if they were ever recovered
(and for months the search seemed almost hopeless), would show
.that Oliva contradicted a dogma of faith which was the foundation
of what was taught by St. Thomas, and that he was condemned
for his contradiction. And so the facts turned out to be.*

Zigliara's opponents were, to say the least, all quite disconcert-
ed, and they beat a hasty retreat. He was not in the least surprised, nor in the least elated. All that the present writer ever
knew him to say on the matter was whispered to the future bishop
of C——, the morning after the discovery of the manuscript, as he
passed along the rows of expectant students up to his chair: *Vicit
schola nostra,* " our school was right." The immediate results of
the philosophical controversy which thus terminated were that the
two professors who had been foremost in the opposition to St.
Thomas' doctrine were removed from their chairs in Rome, and
that its defender was made a prince of the Church.

THE FIFTH GLORIOUS MYSTERY.

MARY IRWIN.

Be glad, O earth! thy saints of every land,
  They who have passed through tribulation, they
  Who have retained the Faith, are crowned to-day:
The patriarchs holy and the prophets grand;
The martyrs crimson clothed; the virgin band
  In white; and parents in soul-gemmed array—
  Earth's sorrows past, and earth's tears wiped away,
Receive their great reward at Jesus' hand.

All, all are crowned. The ceremony o'er,
  They rise with all the bliss of Heaven thrilled,
  With its deep peace in fullest measure filled,
And glorifying God forevermore.
  Strike sweet their golden harps and tuneful lyres,
  And sing His praise with all the heavenly choirs.

* NOTE.—A similar fact is recorded of Cardinal Newman. In a note to his translation of St. Athanasius, he expressed his opinion regarding the heretical tendencies of the teachings of Hippolytus. When the Philosophoumena was afterwards discovered, and the nature of the controversy between Hippolytus and
Callistus was made evident, scholars saw that the editor of St. Athanasius had divined the truth. Call it an intuition of pure genius, if you will; or if not, the almost infallible perception which is acquired by accurate scientific training, but
the fact remains that Newman was right.

COLUMBUS AMONG LIARS.

JOHN A. MOONEY.

N the October number of "Self Culture," a "Magazine of Knowledge," published at Chicago, in the
interest of the "Home University League," some
unnamed person prints an article entitled: "Columbus—An Historical Estimate." Having read
the article, I have no hesitation in saying that the
writer is one of the most dangerous of the Western manipulators of "self-culture." Solemnly do
I warn all the members of the "Home University
League" against him; cautioning them, that, if they do not guard
their magazine of knowledge, by day and by night, he will blow
it sky-high. And let me suggest that all the Home guards be
men liberally educated.

Though he is alarmingly self-cultured, I can see that the writer of the "Historical Estimate" studied English under a Master;
and this master was either Justin Winsor, to whose unique talent I
have tried to do justice; [1] or else the master was an honor-man of
the Winsorian school of Style.

From the first sentence to the last, we note the pleasing, eu-
phonious, nonsensical, and illiterate language of the Master. We
read of one: " supplying an effective correction " ; of " Columbian
views of history "; of " the public at large in connection with the
World's Fair "; of " the proper celebration of four-hundred years
of America "; of " statements that were alarmingly off the mark
of truth or even of actual recital." I know of but one school in
the United States where a pupil may learn to write thus, barbar-
ously; it is the " alarmingly off " school of Justin Winsor.

In order to do full justice to the modest pupil of *the* Master, I
shall detach a gem or two from the bejewelled pages of " Self
Culture." Here is a literary diamond of the first water:

" He (Columbus) contrived to cut a great figure, but he is found, when the
facts are properly considered, to have been a great man in no real and true
sense, and to have been a good man only after the fashion of professions which

---

[1] American Cath. Quarterly Review, Oct. 1892.

were no restraint upon a full measure of the worst passions of the human animal."

In this glowing *parure*, I discover only one flaw; and it is only a tiny little flaw. Remove the gem on which are inscribed the words: "a full measure "; insert another gem with the words: "a half peck,"—and you have a thing of beauty; one that will everlastingly "contrive to cut a great figure." You cannot make sense out of the stuff! My dear and misfortunate Sir, the Winsorites do not print sense; they polish diamonds of illiteracy, and jewel unintelligent thoughts that are "alarmingly off."

One other precious gemlet of the Self-Culturer invites inspection:

"It seems, therefore, not amiss to get carefully into shape for student-readers the evidence on *which what* may be called the CASE AGAINST COLUMBUS rests, and will forever rest."

The dear, dainty thing it is! "Not amiss to get carefully into shape "; how nice! "The evidence on which what.". O Master Winsor! thy pupil hath almost excelled thee; and, like thee, he shall "contrive to cut a great figure " in the "Whichwhat " literature, of which thou art the student-founder!

From these few specimens of "Whichwhat " English, my readers can form an estimate of the culture and capacity of the writer of the article on "Columbus," in the Magazine of Knowledge. Nor would the article deserve closer examination, were it not for the intelligent interest we have in the "Home University League." Only a heartless student could be silent, seeing the risk the Leaguers run of becoming "Whichwhaters " in history, as well as in literature.

To aid the "League " in forming an estimate of the Discoverer of America, the artificer of the article on "Columbus," quotes a certain Dr. Charles Parkhurst, "who has achieved distinction by his unflinching pulpit work." This gentleman, it is said, used the following language about Columbus:

"I think him the most consummate liar that I have ever found in the history of the country. He made lying a fine art, and practised it all his life. I do not say this because he was a Roman Catholic, but because he professed to be so profoundly religious, when, as a matter of fact he was very far from a saint. You can study his whole life, and you will find that it was one of fabrication and greed for gold. He not only *lied himself,* (the Doctor is a whichwhater!) to Ferdinand and Isabella, but he compelled his crew to lie also. Lying was not his worst trait either, for he was the first to establish slavery in America, which cursed the new country for centuries. He was not a benefactor, for all that he did was for gold. He would not sail on his voyage until he was made an admiral by the king and received a promise of fabulous remuneration."

After the self-cultured Dr. Charles F. Parkhurst, the historian of "Self Culture," appeals to "Hon. Charles Francis Adams, whose views occasioned the Boston *Transcript* to say that Mr. Adams said:

"Columbus brought with him the Inquisition, persecution and that greed for gold that brought with it so many misfortunes. Columbus was a bigot. Columbus was visionary.... America would have been better to have delayed that discovery one hundred years."

As if the "Columbian views" of these two speechmakers were not all-sufficient, the Chicago word-artist informs us that:

"Dr. Poole, the eminent scholar-librarian of Chicago, in two or three important articles, made clear that learning cannot accord Columbus the praise of either remarkable greatness, or what would now be considered respectable goodness."

With a peculiar delicacy, the name of Mr. Justin Winsor is introduced at the end of the "Whichwhater's" list of historical authorities. The pupil's opinion of the Master may be gathered from the following quotations:

"Mr. Winsor's admirable "Life of Columbus" left but one thing to be desired—a more exact sentence upon the criminal on trial in his honest and learned pages....The truth is that Mr. Winsor notably spares Columbus, and puts into the picture touches which concede to the popular conception somewhat more than the severest regard for truth permits....It is more than just to recognize Columbus as "the conspicuous developer of a great world movement," and "the embodiment of the ripened aspirations of his time." This honor belongs elsewhere. Columbus embodied only a corrupt and degraded form of the aspirations which were the glory of the age of discovery, and the world-movement was conspicuously marred, damaged and demoralized by the hand which he put upon it.".... "Columbus... was a curse to America rather than a benefactor, and a miserable fraud, a wretched failure as a discoverer." ... "Of genius for any high task, Columbus had none. The most sadly definable thing in him was the air not of authority, but of pretension, which savored more of the crank than the scientist, and for great parts of his conduct and utterances suggests a mind almost or quite off its balance. The movement in hand when he "paced his decks" would have ended far better if he had gone down with his "crazy little ships," and his crazy scheme of westward greed, which was a seed of sin and shame without a parallel, through more than three centuries of Spanish lust for gain from the new world."

I shall never tell any one, but deep down in my soul, I believe Justin Winsor is the confectioner of every word I have quoted, and

indeed of every word of the article in "Self Culture." But if I
am in error, Heaven help our dear mother-tongue! a second conspicuous "marrer," damager and demoralizer, has put his hand
upon that tongue, and he will wring, twist, wrench and maul it,
unfeelingly and interminably, unless the "world-movement"
should, considerately, throw him "almost or quite off the world-
balance,"—a consummation devoutly to be wished for!

Were I to omit the closing paragraph of the unknown, photo-
graphic "developer" of the Magazine of Knowledge, my grateful duty would not be fulfilled. Here it is:

"Columbus, in fact, took on a citizenship which was the worst in Europe, and
accepted the most evil fates under the banner of Spain. He did this in a kinship of his own spirit to the Spanish spirit. Of fairly large natural intelligence
and quick perception, he yet had emotion rather than intellect, imagination
rather than judgment and knowledge, and enthusiasms, flaming and wandering, rather than convictions well based and principles firmly held. A confident and determined visionary, indefinitely incapable of self-deception and delusion, of pious fraud and pious falsehood, he found his place with Spain at her
worst, and achieved a mission, perhaps the worst for failure in success and
shame amid glory, in all human history."

The "student-reader's" humor has been satisfied by these quotations. Therefore we may now seriously consider the historical
estimate of Columbus, presented to the Home University League
by the leaders of the "Whichwhat" school.

To form a thorough, and an independent estimate of the Discover of America, one must read studiously all the letters of Columbus, the diaries of his voyages, the grants conceded him by
Isabella and Ferdinand, the grants conceded by the Papacy, the
letters of the Sovereigns to him and to their agents, and the testimony adduced at the several trials in which his heirs were involved. These documents are the first in importance. After
them, as contemporary sources, one must become familiar with
the works of Andres Bernaldez, Peter Martyr, Oviedo, Las
Casas, and the *Historic* referred to Fernando the son of Columbus.
No complete and authentic English translation of these documents or works has been published. They must be consulted in
the original Spanish, Italian or Latin.

Basing their conclusions on these documents and books, many
learned men have discussed the character, the acquirements and
the deeds of Columbus; and no conscientious student would pre-

sume to write about The Discoverer, without first perusing the volumes of Herrera, Muñoz, Navarrete, Von Humboldt, Irving, Major, De Lorgues, and Harrisse.   The labor such a course of reading compels, must preclude even Home University Leaguers from forming a grounded, independent judgment on Columbus; and consequently the majority of men must be dependent on some writer who has fairly and thoroughly controlled all the sources, and all the critical studies of the sources; or on some writer, or talker, who has unfairly, unintelligently, uncritically, ignorantly scribbled or gabbled, when silence was most becoming.

In a list of educated, critical, intelligent and fair-minded students of Columbus, no self-respecting writer would place the name of Parkhurst, Adams, or Winsor.   Do we mean to imply that they are not educated, fair-minded, intelligent or critical?   Would we place them among the ignorant scribblers and gabblers?   To these not improper questions, we prefer that our readers should answer, when they have estimated the testimony we shall here present, and the standing of our witnesses.

Mr. Prescott, though not a Roman Catholic, has been recognized as a historian of merit, who was sometimes truthful, and seldom visionary.   From Vol. III., p. 244, of the "History of Ferdinand and Isabella," I quote Mr. Prescott's "historical estimate" of Columbus:

"Whatever were the defects of his mental constitution, the finger of the historian will find it difficult to point to a single blemish in his moral character.   His correspondence breathes the sentiment of devoted loyalty to his sovereigns.   His conduct habitually displayed the utmost solicitude for the interests of his followers.   He expended his last maravedi in restoring his unfortunate crew to their native land.   His dealings were regulated by the nicest principles of honor and justice.   His last communication to the sovereigns from the Indies remonstrates against the use of violent measures in order to extract gold from the natives, as a thing equally scandalous and impolitic.   The grand object to which he dedicated himself seemed to expand his whole soul, and raised it above the petty shifts and artifices, by which great ends are sometimes sought to be compassed.   There are some men, in whom rare virtues have been closely allied, if not to pos-

itive vice, to degrading weakness. Columbus's character presented no such humiliating incongruity. Whether we contemplate
it in its public or private relations, in all its features it wears the
same noble aspect. It was in perfect harmony with the grandeur
of his plans, and their results more stupendous than those which.
Heaven has permitted any other mortal to achieve."[1]

Alexander von Humboldt was one of the most cultured men
of this century. He had genius rather than talent. A sceptic
and an infidel, if not an atheist, he had no love for the Catholic
religion. His pursuits, as a naturalist and a geologist, interested
him in The Discoverer of the New World. Not only did Von
Humboldt familiarize himself with the documentary history of
Columbus, but he sailed over the great Italian's course, and also
trod in his footsteps. Thrice he published the results of his studies on the life and achievements of the Discoverer: in the " *Essai
politique sur l'isle de Cuba* " (Paris, 1826), in the " *Examen critique
de l'histoire de la Géographie du Nouveau Continent* " (Paris, 1836);
and in " Cosmos " (London, 1848).

" Columbus is distinguished for his deep and earnest sentiment
of religion," says Von Humboldt.[2] He was " endowed with a high
intelligence, and with an invincible courage in adversity." He
was eloquent, poetical; and the extent of his reading is astonishing. " What characterizes Columbus is the penetration and the
extreme delicacy with which he seizes the phenomena of the exterior world. He is just as remarkable an observer of nature, as
he is remarkable as an intrepid mariner."[3].... " Columbus does
not confine himself to gathering isolated facts; he combines them,
he seeks their mutual relations, sometimes he rises boldly to the
discovery of the general rules that govern the physical world.
This tendency to generalize facts and observations is all the more
worthy of attention, because, before the end of the 15th century,
I might almost say, before Father Acosta, we see no other attempt
at it."[4] Navigators, astronomers, geologists, geographers, com-

---

[1] History of the reign of Ferdinand and Isabella, Boston, 1838; Vol. III., pp.
244–245.
[2] Cosmos, Vol. II., p. 420.   [3] Examen critique, Vol. III., p. 9.
[4] Examen critique, Vol. III., p. 29.

merce, "all the physical sciences," and philology, are indebted to Columbus, Von Humboldt says and proves [1] by references to the writings and the doings of the Discoverer of the New World. Columbus "dominates his century," the learned German scientist declares: "The majesty of the great memories seems to be concentrated on the name of Christopher Columbus. It is the originality of his vast conception, the breadth and fecundity of his genius, the courage opposed to long misfortunes which have raised the Admiral above all his contemporaries." [2]

What Columbus did for human science, Von Humboldt knew, and told. "He discovered *a magnetic line without variation*, and this discovery marks a memorable epoch in nautical astronomy.' .... The actual *equatorial current*, the movement of waters between the tropics, was first described by Columbus.' .... But not only had the Admiral the merit of finding the *line without variation* in the Atlantic, he remarked thereon ingeniously that the magnetic variation could be used, within certain limits, to determine the longitude of the vessel.' .... He discovered also the influence of longitude on the distribution of heat, following the same parallel.' .... Columbus served the human race by offering it at the one time so many objects for reflection; he enlarged the mass of ideas; through him human thought progressed." [7]

Mr. Clements R. Markham, like Von Humboldt, an educated, studious, observing traveller, and a writer of merit, holds, as he deserves to hold, a high place among living scientific men; and to-day, Mr. Markham honors the honorable office of President of the "Royal Geographical Society." He has written a short "Life of Christopher Columbus," which is, without exception, the fairest and the most instructive "Life" of the Discoverer, published in the English language.' What estimate has Mr. Markham formed of the character and the achievements of the man who is described, by the "Whichwhater" of the "Self-Culturist," as a "criminal"?

"Columbus," Mr. Markham writes, "had a very active and imaginative brain, the bright thoughts following each other in

[1] Examen critique, p. 155.   [3] Examen critique, Vol. V., p. 177.
[2] Cosmos, Vol. II., p. 657.   [4] Cosmos, Vol. II., p. 662.
[5] Examen critique, Vol. III., p. 38.   [6] Examen critique, Vol. III., p. 99.
[7] Examen critique, Vol. III., p. 153.   [8] London, George Philip & Son, 1892.

rapid succession, and his enthusiastic and impressionable nature produced visions and day-dreams which often impressed him with all the force of reality. Like Joan of Arc, and other gifted beings who have been the instruments to work out great events, Columbus heard voices, which had the practical effect of rousing him from despondency and bracing him to his work. He has recorded two occasions on which this happened, but probably "the voices" made themselves heard at other critical turning points of his life. Yet there was no danger of his becoming a mere visionary. His clear, penetrating intellect saved him from that; and it was this unrivalled power, combined with a brilliant imagination, which constituted his genius. He prepared himself for his great work by long study, by the acquisition of vast experience, and by a minute knowledge of every detail of his profession. But this would not have sufficed. He added to these qualifications a master mind endowed with reasoning powers of a high order; and an ingenious, almost subtle, way of seizing upon and utilizing every point which had a relation to the subject he was considering. His forecasts amount to prevision. Assuredly the discovery of the New World was no accident. "His genius and lofty enthusiasm, his ardent and justified previsions, mark the Admiral as one of the lights of the human race." [1]

"It was, however, as a navigator that the genius of Columbus found the most suitable field for its display. He was a consummate seaman, and without any equal in that age as a pilot and a navigator; while his sense of duty and responsibility gave rise to a watchfulness which was unceasing and untiring. His knowledge of cosmography, of all needful calculations, and of the manipulation of every known instrument was profound: but he showed even greater force in his forecasts of weather, in his reasoning on the effects of winds and currents, and in the marvellous accuracy of his landfalls, even when approaching an unknown coast....His genius was a gift which is only produced once in an age. But his reasoning power, carefully trained and cultivated, his diligence as a student, his habits of observation, and

---

[1] Life of Columbus, by Clements R. Markham. C. B., pp. 296, 297. The sentence quoted by Mr. Markham, at the close, is a sentence he takes from Col. Yule's admirable work on : " Marco Polo."

the regularity of his work, especially in writing up a journal and taking observations, are qualities which every seaman might usefully study and imitate. He has been accused of carelessness and inaccuracy in his statements: *but every instance that has been put forward can be shown to be consistent with accuracy. The blunders were not those of the Admiral, but of his critics. Considering the circumstances under which many of his letters were written, his careful accuracy of statement is remarkable. It is another proof of a mind long trained to orderly and methodical habits....* He was amiable and of a most affectionate disposition, and made many and lasting friendships in all ranks of life. . . We reverence and admire his genius, we applaud his large-hearted magnanimity, we urge the study of his life on all seamen as a useful example, but his friendships and the warmth of his affections are the qualities which appeal most to our regard. Columbus was a man to reverence, but he was still more a man to love."

" The work of few men in the world's history has had such a lasting influence on the welfare of the human race as that of Columbus. It created a complete revolution in the thoughts and ideas of the age. It was a landmark and a beacon. It divided. the old and the new order of things, and it threw a bright light over the future. In ten years he discovered the way across the Atlantic, he explored the Gulf stream and the regions of the trades, of the westerlies and the calms; he discovered the Bahamas and the West Indies; he inspired the work of Cabot and Cortereal; and he or his pupils discovered the coasts of the new continent from 8° South of the equator to the Gulf of Honduras. But the greatest achievement was the first voyage across the ocean. It broke the spell and opened a new era. All else he did, and all that was done after his death for the next fifty years, followed as a natural consequence. The originator and supreme leader of all, was Christopher Columbus." [1]

To these "estimates" collected from American, German and English authorities, I shall add a few sentences written by Prof. John Fiske in the second volume of his work on: *The Discovery of America.*[2] " The Discovery of America may be regarded in one

---

[1] Life of Columbus, C. R. Markham. pp. 299, 300, 301.   [2] Page 553.

sense as a unique event, but it must likewise be regarded as a long and multifarious process. The unique event was the crossing of the sea of Darkness in 1492. It established a true and permanent contact between the eastern and western halves of our planet, and brought together the two streams of human life that had flowed in separate channels ever since the Glacial period. *No ingenuity of argument can take from Columbus the glory of an achievement which has, and can have, no parallel in the whole career of mankind.*"

Before again addressing the "Home University League," it may be well to state that I do not know what religion Mr. Markham professes, though I am certain he is not a Catholic. As for the good-humored Mr. Fiske, I fear that, for a second, but no longer, he would be angry with any one who charged him with having a "denominational" religion. He is a "Fiskian" philosopher. Any educated gentleman can be truthful, if he will ; and there is no reason why the most predestinated and self-cultured Calvinist should not be a liar.

Comparing the standing of the competent scholars whom I have called as witnesses to the character, ability, and deeds of Columbus, with the want of standing of Messrs. Parkhurst, Adams, Winsor, and the anonymous composer of the vile and ignorant article in "Self Culture," I know that the intelligent and honest Home Leaguers will thank me for warning them to guard their magazine against the conscienceless "historical dynamiter" who has secreted himself in the League's "midst." The man or men, who, to-day, in the face of the scholarship of five centuries, would seek to mislead any portion of American youth, by representing Columbus as a life-long and practised liar, greedy for gold, a bigot, a visionary, a criminal, a curse to America, a miserable fraud, a crank, deficient in intellect, judgment, and knowledge, a pious fraud, the worst failure and the greatest shame in all human history,—such man or men, because of consummate ignorance, or phenomenal malice, deserve the reprobation of every lover of truth, of learning, of grand ideals and grand actions. More than wife-beaters, they are worthy of the whipping-post. They poison the springs of truth ; they destroy honorable reputations ; they sow the seed of falsehood, thus endangering the very life of society. Hated of God, the knowing falsifier should be pursued and punished by men. The ignorant falsifier, if less guilty, is no less dangerous, and should be promptly exposed.

The managers of " Self Culture " are evidently committed to the " Whichwhat " school of defamation; for, besides the article I have discussed, they print, in the Magazine of Knowledge, " Readings in American History," whose purport is further to mislead the members of the Home University League concerning Columbus, and at the same time to advertise the " Encyclopædia Britannica; " a work in which, apparently, the publishers of " Self Culture " are not unselfishly interested. Woe! Woe! to the University whose corner-stone is an encyclopædia, and whose dome is topped by the illuminated statue of Justin Winsor enlightening Chicago.

Certain false charges made in the Winsoresque estimate of Columbus, I shall repel in a second article. They refer to his relations with Doña Beatriz, and to his dealings with the Indians. Again and again and again these charges have been answered, and therefore I can say nothing new; but, lest the members of the H. U. L. may not find an answer in the E. B., I may serve them by repeating an old story. Loving truth and my mother-tongue as ardently as the "self-culturedest" self-culturer, I shall spare no effort to preserve the Magazine of Knowledge from the incendiary " Whichwhaters."

Beautiful Mother of hope and of love,
Waiting for us in our glad home above,
When wilt thou call us? and when shall we be
Ready, sweet Mother, to fly unto thee?

Often we sigh at the lengthening way,
Often for patience and courage we pray ;
Oh, can it be that we ever shall hear,
Mother, thy call, and yet linger through fear?

Often we think of thy fifteen long years
Spent in this valley of exile and tears,
Ere thou wert called the full glory to share,
Which thou hadst helped thine own Son to prepare.

Prophets and patriarchs passed to their rest,
Took their bright seats in the ranks of the blessed,
Martyrs and magi and virgins, before
Mary, who still was of mercy the door.

Patience then, Mary, though weary, we ask ;
Patience for trial, and grace for each task ;
Then, at thy mild, whispered call may we be
Ready, sweet Mother, to fly unto thee !

—*Eliza Allen Starr.*

STORY OF A BRIDAL VEIL.

L. M. POWER.

CHAPTER I.

"SISTER Agnes, I can scarcely believe that to-morrow I shall leave school for ever, and begin that enchanting life I have so often longed for! Is it possible that you never wish to return to the bright world beyond the convent walls?"

Ethel Carlton paused, and glanced for reply at the tall figure by her side, wearing the white habit of the Dominican Order.

Turning her dark eyes on her companion, Sister Agnes answered slowly, "Ethel dear, God grant your rosy day-dreams may not be rudely dispelled, but somehow I feel sad, very sad at the thought of losing you to-morrow; but I shall pray daily that God may keep you in His hands, and direct your future as He sees best."

"Ethel, my child," the nun continued with increased earnestness, "I entreat of you not to turn a deaf ear to His voice, for when we despise His call a fearful silence follows, and desolate indeed is the fate of those who walk without His light. Think of the worthless bauble you are choosing in preference to a great destiny."

"But, Sister, you are making sure that I am called to the religious state, while I am quite uncertain that such is my vocation. In fact, I think it was presumption on my part ever to imagine such a thing, and I am now convinced that God intends me to remain in the world."

The nun sighed, and looked intently at Ethel's flushed face, which just then wore an expression of mingled sorrow and determination, as though her heart reluctantly consented to the wilful resolve of her mind.

Taking her hand, Sister Agnes said gently, " Come with me to the chapel, dear, and let us say the rosary together before St. Dominic's altar.   You remember Cardinal Newman's beautiful lines, ' Lead Kindly Light.'   Ethel, let us too say earnestly, ' Lead Thou me on,' and then be sure that however dark the night, or however rough the way, that God will guide our steps aright."

The girl allowed herself to be led to the cloisters, through which they passed into the chapel, where both knelt before the sculptured marble shrine over which was placed an exquisite window of stained glass, representing St. Dominic receiving the Rosary from the hands of our Lady.

In after times that scene came vividly to Ethel Carlton's mind, and often she recalled every incident of her last evening at the convent where she had spent so many days of innocent happiness, and where her life had glided by, free from the cares and sorrows that inevitably accompany our later years.

Sister Agnes and her companion made as pleasing a study as ever was pictured on an artist's imagination, as the shaded light from the colored glass overhead streamed down on the bowed figures before the altar, lighting up the perfect proportions of the building—the choir with its carved oak stalls, the children's transept to the left, and the fine old doorway leading to the terrace beyond, while the softened rays of the August sun rested lovingly on the white-robed nun and the young girl by her side.

Their devotions ended, Sister Agnes rose, and Ethel followed her through the cloisters to the peaceful cemetery, where the last resting-place of each Religious was marked by a small wooden cross, on which her name and the date of her death were inscribed in black letters.

The girl paused as she gazed on the line of quiet graves, and a wistful expression stole over her face as she remarked: " A short time ago I fancied that when I died I should be buried here, but now I think differently."

" It matters little what *we* think, Ethel, or how our fickle minds may change.   It is God's will that is to be our rule, and that alone should determine our choice of a vocation.   Listen to me, my child, for the last time," the nun went on, " for I shall not mention the subject again.   You know, dear, as well as it can be

known, that God has called you to the religious state, and I am
disappointed and deeply grieved to find, that while He honors
you so singularly, you refuse to listen to His voice, and deliberate-
ly frustrate His designs by returning to the world. Ethel, I implore of you to think well before taking such a step, and ask our
Lord to give you strength to obey His inspirations.

" Remember, each soul is appointed a special task in a special
sphere, and if we refuse to walk in the path marked out by Providence, blindly pursuing our own way without reference to His will,
how can we hope for the grace of salvation, living thus a life of open
defiance and rebellion?   When death comes, how bitterly we shall
repent of our wasted years, and how can we dare to meet Him
with empty hands?"

The girl stood silent, and tears came to her eyes as she heard
the fervent pleading of the nun.

Clasping her hands together, she looked on the graves around,
and remembered, how differently a short while ago she had resolved
to shape her life—how after a few years of labor and devotion to
God and His poor she had hoped to be laid to rest in this peaceful spot, a veritable God's Acre, where He had sown on fruitful
soil, and a rich harvest awaited His coming on that Great Day,
when He would gather to His arms this little band of chosen
souls.

But this was now a dream of the past, a castle-in-the-air, Ethel
mentally decided; yet it was not without a pang of remorse that
she realized how changed were her aspirations, and how different
her visions of the future.

At last she exclaimed passionately, " O Sister, I do feel so
pained at the thought of leaving this dear old place to-morrow!
How sorry I am that I ever went away last winter! If I had only
known then how serious would be the consequences of my visit
home!"

"You can prevent what you call the consequences, Ethel,"
the nun interrupted. "You told me only last month that Father
Vincent still insisted that you had a religious vocation, and implored of you to enter the novitiate after the mid-summer holidays.   But why should I hope to move your will when you refuse
obedience to such a wise, holy director? The fact is, during

those four months of home-life, you acquired a taste for the amusements and vanities of the world, and your young eyes were dazzled by the deceitful glitter that leads so many souls astray. Believe me, Ethel, you cannot find peace away from God, and I feel certain that one day you will return to His feet, sorrow-stricken and disappointed, saying with St. Augustine, ' Thou hast made us for Thyself, O Lord, and our hearts can never rest till they rest in Thee.' Now, farewell, my own dear child. I hear the Vesper-bell ringing, and I must go to the chapel. I shall see you again at six o'clock. Wait for me on the Oak avenue, and we shall have another talk together before I give you back to your mother, and alas! to the world. Of course you have written to her, mentioning by what train you will travel to-morrow?"

At these words, the girl burst into tears.

" O Sister, I do so dread the parting now that it has really come to pass, and leaving against your wish makes it so much harder, but yet—," she paused for an instant, and then went on— " but yet, I could not endure to enter religion, at least for the present. I know it would kill me, and I don't want to die quite yet."

The nun smiled sadly, and putting her arm around her old pupil, kissed her fondly, then turned away and disappeared into the choir, leaving Ethel alone.

CHAPTER II.

As the Convent bells rang out the Angelus, Sister Agnes rose from her knees, and hastened to rejoin her companion, whom she found sitting under the shade of a giant oak, lost in thought, and wearing an expression of deep dejection. As the nun approached, Ethel ran to meet her with a bright smile.

"You are very good to come back so quickly, Sister. You can't think how miserably lonely I feel at the idea of leaving you to-morrow."

" That is a trial you can easily avert, dear," the nun answered. " You know how I should welcome you if you wished to remain here forever, but you are choosing the road that I, by God's grace, left many years ago."

After a short silence the girl exclaimed suddenly, "Won't you come to the cemetery, Sister? You know that is my favorite walk, and it may be a long time before I see it again."

At the farthest end, a rustic seat was placed under the thick foliage of a splendid copper beech, and near it stood a large stone statue of the Madonna and Child, which had been placed there nearly a century before by the foundress of the Convent.

As the two figures paced the neatly-kept walk, they suddenly paused at a grave, which, like the others, was marked by a plain wooden cross, close to which a tall lily reared its waxen blossoms.

" Poor Aunt Lily! " Ethel murmured, reading the inscription. " How young she died!—only twenty-two. I was quite a little child when she came here, but I remember how bitterly I cried when she kissed me, and said good-bye, and grandmother was never the same after she went away. But why is the lily planted there, Sister?"

" Sit down here, Ethel, under the shade of the beech tree, while I tell you the story of your Aunt Lily, who sleeps so quietly in these holy cloisters.

" She and I were school-fellows for several years in this very Convent, and we then formed an attachment that was never broken. I loved her deeply, and in all my experience I never met so perfect a character,—so loving, so gentle, yet strong and heroic.

" Six months after leaving class, I returned here, and entered the novitiate. The following year Lily Neville wrote, announcing that she was engaged to be married. Her letter was indeed a happy one, full of bright dreams of the future, and idealizing her future husband in her own rapturous way.

" His name was Ernest Leslie, an officer in a cavalry regiment, a young man gifted with the natural qualities and the worldly position that rendered him a desirable suitor for your aunt. She enclosed his photograph, and certainly his appearance pleased me immensely, and made me confident that my darling's future could be safely trusted to his care.

" He was not only handsome, but there was a manly, intellectual expression in his dark eyes, combined with an air of firmness and gentleness, that made his countenance singularly pleasing.

" ' I wish you could see my hero,' Lily wrote. ' He is everything that I pictured my ideal lover should be—brave and noble, tender and true. When we are married, I must bring Ernest to see you, and I shall never forgive you if you don't admire him. Unfortunately, his regiment has been ordered to India, and we must embark a few weeks after our marriage. It is so hard to leave mother and the dear home circle, but still Ernest will console me for all; he assures me, too, the separation will only last for three years.'

" I wrote at once, Ethel, congratulating your aunt on her happiness; and a few days later a letter came, announcing the day of her marriage, and enumerating the costly gifts received from Major Leslie, and from her many friends.

"'Ernest has given me such an exquisite wedding veil,' Lily wrote. 'It is made of the finest Mechlin lace, richly embroidered with sprays of orange blossom and lily-of-the-valley. The latter flower decided his choice, as suiting my name, and indeed it is a gem of its kind, such as would please any bride; but, as I tell Ernest, if my wedding veil was of coarse serge, instead of delicate lace, it would not lessen in the least degree the delight of being his wife.'

" On the date fixed for the marriage I got a hurried note from your grandmother, telling me that Lily had been laid low with typhoid fever, and begging the prayers of the Community for her precious life. I felt stunned at this intelligence, and fervently I implored our Lady to restore my poor Lily to her distracted mother. For weeks life hung in the balance, and at last I received a joyful letter from Mrs. Neville, saying that the crisis was past, her daughter was saved, and progressing rapidly towards convalescence.

" Later on the invalid herself wrote, but how sadly it contrasted with her previous letter! The first couple of sentences showed me that a great change had occurred, and that her vocation would be differently chosen. The letter was short, but full of the spirit of self-sacrifice that made her character so grand and enduring. In a few words she told me all; told how, in those sleepless, restless hours of fever, she had resolved to do battle with her affections, and abandon all idea of marrying a Protestant. She had not mentioned before that her lover belonged to a different religion,

and I felt thankful that she had saved herself from the consequences of a mixed marriage. She intended meeting Major Leslie in a few days, and declaring her resolution to forfeit his love
rather than consent to marry him unless he embraced the Catholic faith.

"I could see by the tone of the letter that your aunt had little
hopes of being able to influence him on this point, and I
could also surmise what her future would be in case he refused
her conditions. Poor Lily! how I prayed for her during those
days, that her courage might not falter, and that God would specially direct her vocation in return for the generosity of her sacrifice.

"Knowing your aunt so intimately, I could well imagine her
sufferings in the coming ordeal, and how her strong love would
plead in favor of the man whom she idolized with all the
fervor of her earnest nature. I waited impatiently for further
news, and at last a heart-broken letter came from Lily herself.
The poor child related the result of the interview with the young
officer. He positively refused to change his religion, and boldly
declared that, much as he loved her, he never could be induced to
abandon the Creator for the creature. In vain he argued that
they could both adhere to their own belief, and pledged his word
never to interfere with her in such matters ; that they could reach
Heaven by different paths, and that it was narrow-minded bigotry
to believe that he and all others outside the Catholic Church had
less hope of salvation than those within it.

"But the hardest trial was still to come, when Lily had to listen
to the reproaches of her lover, as he accused her of heartlessness
and inconstancy, and that at the bidding of some deluded priest
she was ready to cast him away forever, wrecking the happiness
of two lives.

"Was she willing to say a final good-bye, and part from him and
all those bright dreams they had woven together, as they sat hand
in hand, and spoke of the golden future and all it was to realize?
Lily's tears fell fast, as she heard his passionate pleadings, and
again and again she assured him that her love had suffered no
change, but her religious principles being at stake, she was prepared to relinquish his affection rather than act against her con-

science.   Ernest Leslie was a staunch Protestant, and asserted
that he, too, was equally determined to lose his betrothed sooner
than be false to the creed of his baptism.

"Then Lily Neville's pride was touched.   Brushing away her
tears, she stood before her lover, and in a few brave words told him
that then and forever she would be true to the faith of her ancestors,
which had been their proud heritage through centuries of persecution, and that, in obedience to the Catholic Church, she was
resolved to forego all she most prized rather than act without its
sanction.

"'Then am I to understand that our engagement is at an end?'
Major Leslie asked, as he gazed earnestly at the slight figure
standing before him.

"The answer came slowly.   'Yes, Ernest, it must be so.   I cannot marry you.   You will never understand what I suffer, and what
I shall always suffer, deprived of your love; but it is God's will.'

"'Good-bye, then, forever, my sweet Lily.   May God bless you,
and keep your life in His own care.   I shall never forget you, my
darling.   Pray for me sometimes, and may we meet in a happier
world.'   He kissed her fondly, and so they parted.

"All this, Ethel, and much more your aunt told me in that
first distracted letter, written after the departure of Major Leslie,
and God alone knew the misery she endured, and the awful blank
that was left in her life now that she had renounced her idol.
But our Lord in His mercy decreed that He Himself should replace the love she had dethroned for His sake, and gradually the
storm of grief was calmed, and a serenity born of sacrifice reigned
in the lonely heart.

"After a few months I was one day summoned to the parlor,
and what were my surprise and joy to see my old companion
standing before me.   But how changed!

"The once radiant face was now pale and sorrowful, the color
had faded from her cheeks, and the laughing eyes showed traces
of constant tears.

"Surely she bore the marks of the 'furnace of tribulation'
through which she had passed, and her whole expression was
chastened by suffering.

(*To be continued.*)

The Children of the Rosary.

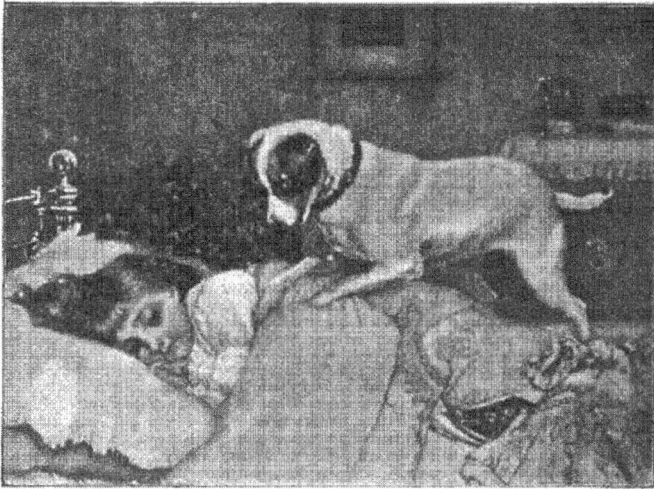

The Morning Call.

"He's coming to tell me ' Good Morning,'
   Dear Carlo !—He thinks I'm asleep;
I'll just make my eyes stay half open,
   Just open enough for a peep.
And I'll lie here quiet, and watch him,
   And see how long quiet he'll keep."
But Carlo knew better, wise doggie!
   Beside her was he with a leap!
And he barked such a happy "Good Morning!"
   It banished the make-believe sleep!

THE PEARL ROSARY.

MARY HANCOCK ALLEN.

CHAPTER II.

"GEORGIE."

s soon as breakfast was over the next morning, Agnes darted out of the house, prepared to station herself with her dolls on the porch, as on the day before, and watch the movements of her new neighbors.

She was surprised to see the spectator of yesterday's incident ahead of her, sitting on the gate-post, and complacently dangling her feet. She was evidently taking in the view about her. When Agnes made her appearance, she turned her head, and stared at her unconcernedly, as if to take her in the view with the rest.

Agnes grew very uncomfortable under this steady gaze. She colored guiltily as she thought of the disastrous ending of her tea-party and the wholesale pummelling of her brother; and she was tempted to run back into the house, but a friendly " halloo " made her change her mind.

" Halloo!" she replied cautiously.

" Lived here long? " was the next remark.

" About two years."

" Like it here? "

" Y-yes."

" I don't," said the girl on the post, emphatically, shaking her head until her short, bushy hair seemed to be hopelessly entangled.

Agnes looked curiously at the small figure, with its saucy turn-up nose, firm mouth, and reckless air. Here was a girl with decided opinions, she thought.

" Why don't you like it here? " she asked, wondering what would come next.

The dangling feet which had been beating a steady tattoo upon the gate-post, gained in speed as their owner replied: " Because —there are too many flats here."

Agnes opened her eyes with surprise, and then burst out laughing. " Why, how funny! " she exclaimed. " What's the matter with flats? Look out, you will fall down," she added, becoming alarmed at the girl's activity.

" Oh, no, I shan't," she laughed; but she grew a little more moderate in her motions.

"What's the matter with flats?" repeated Agnes.

" Oh, they are so big and high, and take up so much room; and most of them are not a bit pretty, do you think so? "

" I? no; I don't think so," replied Agnes with uncertainty, having, in fact, given the matter very little thought.

" And there's not much room in them, though they look so large, because there are so many families in each building, you know; and there are no yards, either. Now look at that one across the street; there isn't a speck of a yard to it, and all the children have to stay in, or play out in the street."

Agnes looked at the tall building over the way, and acknowledged the truth of her companion's remark. The building was new, occupied a wide piece of land, and was built close to the sidewalk. As Agnes' mother said, you might as well live in the street as in one of those flats.

"When there *are* pretty flats, I think they might not have put the ugly ones on our street," Agnes' new neighbor said. "I didn't want to come here, but my aunts did. They like the city, and I don't. I like the country best, don't you? "

Agnes shook her head. " I wouldn't like to live in the country," she said. " I love to visit my grandmother, who lives in the country; but I wouldn't like to live there."

" Oh, my! I wish I could stay in the country always. I had such good times. I used to run around and do everything I wanted to, and I had so many pets. Papa gave me everything I asked for; but now since papa is dead, I have to live with my aunts, and everything is changed. I have to be so prim and proper." Georgie straightened herself, and assumed a very stiff and comical attitude, which made Agnes laugh.

" Don't tell anyone," she said, speaking in a confidential tone, "but I am in disgrace now. Aunt Isabelle sent me out here early this morning, because she said she couldn't stand me in the house. You see, I couldn't stay in bed after the sun was up, so I got up and romped about the house with Tib. It was so much fun when everything was upset, you know; but we knocked over so many things, and made so much noise, that Aunt Isabelle sent me out. Tib sneaked out, and is hiding somewhere in the back yard. If it weren't for him, I don't know what I should do. He's the only one that's left me."

"Is your mother dead, too?" queried Agnes, growing interested in the girl's history.

"Yes; she died when I was very little."

"How lonely you must be! Don't you like your aunts?"

Georgie shrugged her shoulders. "I don't like Aunt Isabelle very much, because she is so strict; and I know she dislikes me, because she says I am a tom-boy. I like Aunt Lillian pretty well. She is good to me when Aunt Isabelle is away. She is afraid of Aunt Isabelle."

"Dear me," said Agnes, rather shocked at this state of affairs.

The greatest harmony prevailed in the Barnett family, and Agnes dutifully loved all her relatives, and was a stranger to strife and discord.

"Oh! I want to find Tib!" exclaimed Georgie, anxious to change the subject, now that the conversation was becoming so personal; and jumping down from her lofty position. "I wonder where he is? Come on and let's find him."

Agnes hesitated.

"Come on," returned Georgie, impatiently, starting to run. "Your mother wont mind, will she?"

"Oh no," replied Agnes, following her new acquaintance reluctantly.

They went through the yard, and came to the wood-shed at the back of the house, Georgie calling the dog's name.

"Here he comes," exclaimed Georgie, as a silky skye-terrier came running out of the shed, and gambolled around his mistress. "Isn't he a beauty?"

"Yes, indeed," answered Agnes, with a fruitless attempt to embrace him.

" Papa gave him to me only a short time before he died, and I love him, don't I, Tib? " and she bent down, and rubbed her face against the dog's soft hair.

" Did you have him with you last night? " queried Agnes. " I didn't see—"

She stopped in confusion, for Georgie looked up quickly with laughing eyes, just as Agnes had seen them peering through the gate the night before.

" Yes; I had him in my arms. Say, was that your brother that you—, that you—" here Georgie paused and laughed, "that was on the porch with you? " she concluded.

" Yes," replied Agnes, her face growing scarlet.

" What times you must have together! He seemed to be getting the worst of it. Does he always get the worst of it? " Georgie was enjoying Agnes' confusion hugely.

Agnes did not answer.

" What were you doing, anyway? Playing? " continued Georgie unmercifully.

" I wont tell you," returned Agnes angrily, unable to restrain herself any longer. The tears started to her eyes, as she turned quickly away, and walked in the direction of the front gate. Georgie stopped in surprise. She had no idea that her careless words would produce such an effect. She started to call her by name, but suddenly she discovered that she did not know her name.

" Oh say," she called, running, and reaching Agnes before she came to the gate. " Say, I didn't mean it, you know. Wont you come back and be friends? "

Agnes, by this time, had nearly recovered her composure, and could not resist the girl's penitent advances. She smiled, and said, taking her hand from the gate: " I cannot stay long. Mamma does not know where I am."

" She will not have very far to look for you." laughed Georgie. " Its funny, but I don't know your name. What is it?"

" Agnes Barnett. Yours is Georgie, isn't it? "

Georgie nodded her head.

" Wasn't it funny? " said Agnes, " I thought you were a boy at first! "

" Did you? " and Georgie looked very much surprised.

" Yes; I saw your name on your trunk, and it's a boy's name, you know; and I saw a little gun, too."

Georgie laughed.

" Yes, that's my gun. You see, I am named after papa. He used to call me his boy. I wish I were a boy; I do so love boys' games. I went several times with papa on his hunting expeditions, and we had such good times. I went nearly everywhere he went. He took me to Europe with him. We stayed a long time in Paris. I hated to leave; it is so pretty and clean there. Then we went to Rome."

"Oh, did you? " exclaimed Agnes, eagerly. She thought that if she could go to Rome, and see the Pope, she would be happy. " Did you see the Pope? "

" Yes, papa had an audience with him. He was so nice and kind; he patted me on the head, and said something in French to me about my 'bright eyes.' He is quite old now, you know, and feeble."

" My! I wish I could have been with you," said Agnes, breathlessly.

" Yes, wouldn't it have been fine! " replied Georgie, rather wondering at Agnes' excitement, not thinking so much as Agnes did of the advantages she had had.

" You went to St. Peter's, then? "

" O yes, often. I used to love to go there; it was so quiet and solemn, and so large. We went to so many places; and papa told me all about the ruins and historical places. I bought this necklace in Rome," and Georgie pulled out from her dress a necklace of green beads strung with silver wire.

" Isn't it pretty! " exclaimed Agnes.

" I bought it of an old Italian who had lots of pretty curiosities to sell. He said these were Malachite beads, I think. Papa thought it funny I should take a fancy to it. He wanted me to get something else, but I wanted this."

" Why, it's a rosary," said Agnes, who had been looking at the necklace closely.

" A rosary? What is a rosary? Oh, I know. The beads the old women use in church. I didn't know this was a rosary."

"Yes it is; but other people beside old women use them. But aren't you a Catholic?"

"Oh, no," replied Georgie, "I am not a Catholic; are you?"

"Yes."

"Are you, really? I'm so glad." Lowering her voice, she said, "But don't let my aunts know it."

"Why?" questioned Agnes.

"Because they don't like Catholics. None of my father's family do; but I do," and Georgie gave one of her emphatic nods of her head. "When I was in Rome, I used to go to church with Amina, a good old Italian woman, who took care of our apartments. First, papa said I mustn't go; but as I couldn't always be with him, and could never go out by myself, I got lonely, so he gave me permission; but he made me promise to say nothing about it when I got home. I am telling you all about it now, you know, because you are a Catholic, and the first I have been able to talk with since I came home. I wish my aunts didn't dislike Catholics so much. I don't see why they do. *They* don't go to church, and Catholics do. Oh, may I go to church with you some day?" she added, eagerly.

"Yes; but— no, your aunts wont let you."

"Yes they will," replied Georgie, stamping her foot angrily. "I wish papa was alive, then I could do as I wanted to."

It is plain to be seen that Georgie was a wilful child.

"Well," said Agnes, sagely, "when you are older you can."

"But what am I going to do until then?"

Agnes laughed. "Obey your aunts, I suppose."

"But what if they are wrong?"

This was a question that puzzled Agnes.

"Oh, don't ask me about it," she said. "I don't know. I must go."

"Don't go yet. I have so many things to talk with you about. Oh, say, I have some white pearl beads in my jewelry box, that I believe is a rosary. Do you suppose it is?"

"Is it strung like this?"

"Yes, I think so."

"I guess it is then. Did you get that too in Rome?"

"No, papa gave it to me before he left home, just before he

died. You know he died away from home; no one was with him
but a friend. I felt so badly because I wasn't with him. He
wouldn't let me go with him that time. The last time we were
together, he put the necklace, as he called it, into my hand, and
told me to keep it; that it belonged to mamma. I asked him if I
could wear it. He said no, that I must keep it with my mother's
picture in the little locked jewel-box that he had given me. I
asked him why. He only said that his family did not like my
mamma very well. I asked him why, again. He wouldn't tell me,
but said I should know when I grew older. He did not say much
more; but he kissed me several times, and said that he hoped
that I would be as good as mamma, and I saw tears in his eyes."
Georgie's bright face had grown grave during her recital.

Agnes listened with great sympathy. " I think your mother
must have been a Catholic," she said, when Georgie finished.

"What!" Georgie awoke from her revery. " Do you really
think so? What makes you think so? Oh, on account of the
rosary? Dear! I wish I had it here to show it to you. I wonder if
mamma really was a Catholic? " she added meditatively.

" If she was, then you ought to be one."

" Ought I?"

"Yes; if your mother was a Catholic, you were probably baptized in the Catholic Church."

" Well, I just wish I knew about it. I can't talk with my aunts
about it. I don't know what to do. If I ought to be a Catholic, I wonder why I am not one. Oh, dear, it is all so strange, and
I don't understand it at all! " and Georgie looked very much perplexed.

" Don't bother about it," said Agnes, conscious that she had
caused the disturbance in her companion's mind. " Perhaps I am
wrong, you know."

" I don't know. It seems as if you were right. I will get my
jewel box as soon as I can."

" Then bring it over," added Agnes.

" All right," replied Georgie, I will.

" Now I must go. Good-bye. Don't forget to come over," and
Agnes went home, her mind filled with Georgie's sad and strange
history.

(*To be continued.*)

AN ANGEL TEACHER.

FIRST SORROWFUL MYSTERY.

With locks dishevelled, sweating blood,
  He kneels, the Eternal One,
And 'mid His anguish murmurs, " Not
  My will, but Thine be done."
                —Mary A. Mannix.

HE child who turned to the Angel, invisible, but so truly at her side, for lessons in the prayer of meditation, lifted eyes so full of pain that her Angel could see that already the young soul had thought deeply of the sorrows and the suffering of the Blessed Lord. There was no question asked by the lips of the little one; her uplifted eyes spoke, and the Angel gave his sad lesson on the Agony in the Garden—the First Sorrowful Mystery:

Dear Little Child:—You have heard of the five Joyful Mysteries. Now we come to the second part of the Rosary, counting the five Sorrowful Mysteries. The first of these Mysteries is the Prayer and Agony of our Lord in the Garden.

This mystery tells us of our good and Blessed Lord going into the Garden, after He had given to His disciples the Last Supper and the Blessed Sacrament, so that He might there spend the night in prayer. And while He prayed, the disciples fell asleep and left Him alone. Then the terrible thought came of the wickedness of men, and of the many sins that had been committed for which our Lord would have to suffer. So dreadful was this to Him that He cried out in agony, and said He was so sad that He could die. And His soul was so full of sorrow that the precious Blood came out in big, red drops, as of perspiration, and ran down to the ground.

Dear little child, do you not feel sorry because your good Master suffered so much? And it was all because of sin, because people have been wicked, because they break God's commandments. You will not offend your dear, good Lord? No; you will be sorry for sin, you will keep God's commandments. You will pray, because your dear Lord teaches you how to pray ; and your Blessed Mother will watch over you.

Think of these things while you say the first sorrowful decade, and may God put His true love and true sorrow for sin into your young heart, never to leave it.

A Cross Mamma-Cat.

Mamma-cat and kitties three
Just as still as still can be.
Mamma-cat has scolded well—
And for what?—Ah, who can tell?
Kitties were just having fun
Round their mamma-cat—cross one!
Mamma-cats forget, you know,
They were kittens long ago.

THANKSGIVING AT SISTER RAYMUNDA'S.

AQUINAS.

LL was joyous anticipation in the school. The long-promised sight-seeing trip was but a day off. On the afternoon of Thanksgiving the class was to meet at 2.30 sharp, in the library, and with Sister Raymunda and Sister Lucy to guide and guard, was to visit the exhibition of wax works in a neighboring town seventeen miles away.

"Nothing so beautiful has ever been seen." Such was the verdict of fathers and mothers, brothers and sisters, and all friends and relatives who, during the two preceding days, had flocked to the scene. And who, able at all to travel, had not been there? The excursion tickets and admission price were placed at a figure within reach of all.

The merry Thanksgiving dinner in the children's homes was set at the sensible dining hour of noon, not so much, perhaps, from motives of sense, as because it accommodated the children.

It was half-past two, at last, and the children were gathered in the convent library, the roll called, a response given to every name. A moment of silence, then Sister Raymunda said,—not the happy "Come children, take partners, come," as anticipated by the young folks, but the following heart-depressing words:

"Girls, I have a painful duty to perform. I can only call upon your highest sense of the duty of obedience. A few hours ago I received from Mother Superior a telegram which I feel will inflict a keen disappointment upon you all. But she is a loving Mother, and her will is best.

"'Do not go to the exhibition to-day. Letter on the way.'

"Such, children, is Reverend Mother's message. The mail which holds her letter, I presume one of explanation, arrives at three.

"My children, this is a sore disappointment to you all, I feel sure, and I need not tell you that it is a pain to me to thus take from you, at the last moment, the long anticipated pleasure."

Sister's pause was met by exclamations of sore disappointment from many, of resentment from not a few.

"O Sister! it's the last day, and I could have gone with mamma yesterday!" Clare Blakeman's words expressed the feelings of many a young heart.

Sister Raymunda glanced over the young faces before her; in not one, not even Lucy Colton's—and from Lucy she seemed always to look for good example to come—not even in Lucy's did she see an expression of loyal submission to an unexpected and unexplained withdrawal of a permission given weeks before.

Somehow, for the first time, Sister Raymunda found herself at a loss for words with her pupils. She longed to talk to them of the merit of blind obedience, of prompt sacrifice—but she was not a woman to cast seed in unyielding soil; and as a sudden late frost hardens the ground that before its fall was ready for the seed, so she felt had the chill of this disappointment made repellant, for the time being, the fruitful soil of these young hearts.

The three o'clock mail brought the promised letter. After a quiet perusal, Sister said:

"Girls, with my letter there is one for you all. Mother bids me read it to you:

'MY DEAR CHILDREN:—Weeks ago I promised you a merry excursion for Thanksgiving Day. How can I explain the withdrawal of such a pleasure? Not at all to your satisfaction if you do not trust the Mother who loves you—to whom God has confided you. A strange fear is in my heart; a voice seems to say to me over and over—*do not let the children go.* I have driven it away for days, but at last I listen to it, and, as it grows clearer I obey, and I risk my children's displeasure sooner than risk despising what may be an angel's warning. So unworthy does your fond old Mother feel herself to be of protecting and guiding you all, that she daily asks the help of the Guardian Angels of every one of you whose precious young souls God has confided to her keeping.

'If I write more I shall miss the mail. I have told Sister Raymunda to give you as pleasant a day as possible, and to give you, too, the love of your devoted Mother,

SISTER ANTONINUS.'

The faces of the children, as Sister Raymunda looked upon them after the reading of this letter, were a study indeed. But if we except Lucy Colton, not one of them seemed to have read anything in the letter but a reasonless withdrawing of a permission. To them the letter did not make things clearer than the telegram had done. Angel warnings were something beyond their comprehension, and if of this disappointing nature, certainly beyond their appreciation.

And Sister Raymunda? Was the going or staying a matter of total indifference to her?

Only one who had known her girlhood's talent of wax modelling, a talent buried by her own will beneath that higher talent of moulding to God's design the pliant minds and souls of His children, could measure the sacrifice the withholding of the promised sight-seeing was to her. There was a beautiful *Ecce Homo* in a side chapel of the parish church near the country home of her girlhood, that gave evidence of her genuine, though untaught, undeveloped talent in those days. Nun though she was, with more, perhaps, than her pupils' ardor, she had yearned to feast eyes and soul upon the exquisite representations of sacred subjects outlined in the catalogue of the exhibition. But Sister Raymunda " offered it up." She had a happy fashion, in her intercourse with her class, of leading them to " lift up" their youthful sorrows,—she seldom tried to dissipate them by mere amusement. And to-day, taking for a text, as it were, the Reverend Mother's tender reference to the Angels' power to help, she related touching examples scripture and biography afford of the visible or invisible help of these blessed spirits. And so time sped, if not merrily, at least not drearily on.

Suddenly there was a lusty shout on the street. Another,—still another! Sister Raymunda caught the opening word " *Extra!* " the rest was unintelligible, as newsboys' cries usually are; but she thought—or was it merely imagination?—that she caught the word *accident.* A strange thought seized her, born of her knowledge of Reverend Mother's devotion to, and trust in, the Holy Angels, and their many answers to her simple faith. Can it be—! But she resolutely crushed the thought, and went on with her talk to the children.

This time it was the tale of the first New England Thanksgiving Day,—when the trusting faith of the Puritans was rewarded by the welcome vessel of supplies. And then, to the great delight of the girls, she showed them a copy of Washington's proclamation—the first prescribing a national festival of Thanksgiving. The old-time spelling they enjoyed and commented on.

There was a frantic ring at the convent gate; in a few minutes there was a tap at the door of the library. Sister Raymunda went out; when she returned her face was serious beyond anything the girls had ever known; when she spoke, her voice was tremulous, and told of suppressed emotion.

"Children," she said, at once, "come with me; come to the chapel! The *Extra* we heard called has just been brought me by the mother of one of you who came with aching heart to inquire for her daughter. Come to the chapel, and let us there sing a *Te Deum* of thanksgiving. *You are safe, all safe*—the excursion train we would have been on, but for Reverend Mother's telegram, was wrecked a mile from the town!"

When the distracted parents learned of the accident they came in haste to the convent to hear sad tidings, so they feared, of their children. Truly was it for all a Thanksgiving Day when they found the young voices blending exultingly in the *Holy God, we praise Thy Name!* and with emotions of deepest gratitude did they utter the responses, when, at close of the hymn, Sister Raymunda said earnestly:

"Now, children, let us say the beads for the dead and dying of the wreck from which God has so mercifully preserved us; and as it is the month of the Holy Souls, let us pray, too, for all the faithful departed."

Guardian angels hovering, unseen, about the kneeling group, bore heavenward from their repentant young hearts many a fervent act of sorrow for the rebellion with which each had met the disappointment which proved to be so great a "blessing in disguise."

Crown her Queen of Angels,
  Queen of Patriarchs, too;
Crown her Queen of Prophets,
  And Apostles true.

Crown her Queen of Martyrs,
  Of Confessors strong;
Crown her Queen of Virgins,
  Staid and beauteous throng.

Of All-Saints we crown her
  Ever gracious Queen,
Aiding mortal struggles
  With her prayers serene.

Crown her, with sweet anthems,
  Queen of Heavenly love;
Sweeter songs surround her
  In the courts above.
                —*Eliza Allen Starr.*

Puzzles.

ANSWERS TO PUZZLES IN SEPTEMBER.

CATHOLIC AUTHORS.

MOONEY, STARR, EGAN, ANGELOE, COYLE, BRUNOWE.

All the authors were found by Casimer Herold, Anna Donohue, Alice Mannix, and J. H. Flattery.

The following found all but STARR: Catherine Drury, Etta C. McDonough, A. Hurley, Minnie C. Humphrey.

The following found all but EGAN: May Maxcy, Thomas H. Curran, Rose Cahill.

PUZZLES FOR NOVEMBER.

PRODUCING FRUITS.

Prefix two letters to an animal and produce a fruit;
Prefix four letters to a bed and produce another fruit;
Prefix one letter to a part of the body and produce another;
Prefix four letters to an insect and produce still another;
Prefix one letter to a household implement and produce another;
Add two letters to a vegetable and produce one more.

A NUMERICAL THAT IS FULL OF TROUBLE.

Don't fall into a 2, 5, 6, 3, or you'll be in trouble.
Don't spill 10, 11, 6, 1, or you may get into trouble.
Don't too loudly 13, 3, 6, 6, or you'll cause trouble.
Don't meddle with 4, 3, 11, 1, or you'll feel in trouble.
Don't stub your 1, 9, 3, 10, or again you'll feel in trouble.
Always feel 10, 9, 12, 8, 7, when you are the cause of trouble.
Repeat 1, 2, 3, 4, 5, 6, 7, 8, 9, 10, 11, 12, 13, often, and you'll be often kept out of trouble.

—J. H. F.

ELEVEN.

Sister Mary Alphonsus, O. P.

Eleven o'clock ! the number calls
  With warning voice to me,
Who came in the " Eleventh hour,"
  An idler, Lord, to Thee.

But, still, the kindly parable
  Doth my slow soul invite,
Since I have come, the last of all,
  To work with all my might,

And strive with right good-will to pay
  The long arrears I owe,
But working for no hire, save what
  Thou deignest to bestow.

CONDITIONS FOR BECOMING SOLDIERS IN THE ANGELIC WARFARE.

1. Send your full names to be enrolled.

2. Wear around the waist under the clothing, the little white linen girdle that must be blessed by a Dominican priest, or by a priest who has permission from the Dominicans.

3. Strive in every way to be pure in soul and body.

4. If you cannot buy the girdles in your neighborhood AQUINAS will buy them for you. When you write enclose ten cents to cover the expense of the girdle, leaflet, and postage. You may send stamps. But let no child hold back from becoming a Soldier in the Angelic Warfare on account of poverty. To those who cannot pay we shall send all free.

5. Address your letters to AQUINAS, ROSARY OFFICE, 871 LEXINGTON AVENUE, NEW YORK CITY.

THE CORONATION.

Words by Marcella A. Fitzgerald. Music by Louisa Morrison.

1ST SOP.

2D SOP.

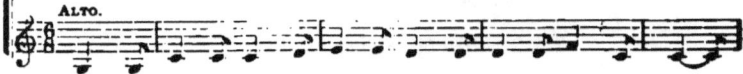

1. An - gel hosts, in hom-age bend-ing, Fill the air with glad ac - claim;
2. In the pres-ence of the Fa - ther She re-ceives her blessed re - ward;
3. Spot-less Vir-gin, ten-der Moth-er, Queen to faith-ful hearts so dear,

ALTO.

Loy - al love and hon - or yield-ing To our La - dy's glorious name.
Je - sus gives a crown and king-dom To the Hand-maid of the Lord.
Pray for us, thy err - ing chil-dren, Teach us how to per - se - vere.

Chorus.

List-en, O Moth-er, while we pray, We show thee all our cares and needs,

pray,... needs,

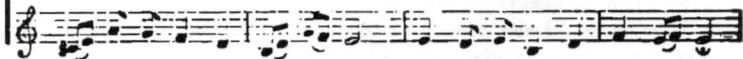

As plead-ing for thy aid we say The A-ves on thy bless-ed beads;

As plead-ing for thy aid we say The A-ves on thy bless-ed beads.

EDITORIAL

The month of November is gloriously ushered in by the triumphant celebration on earth and in Heaven, in honor of God's elect, the angels and the saints who hail as Queen the Blessed Mother of our Lord. The mystery of the Beads commemorating this glad day is the crown of all that has preceded, in lowly and unknown ways, in the bitterness of sorrow and the Cross, for our Redeemer, for our Lady, for the saints who have walked in the conquering path after them. For Rosarians, therefore, the Feast of All Saints is not only a day of jubilation because of those who have fought and won and now see God face to face, but it is a time of encouragement, of cheer, of hope. The lessons that have been learned in the meditation of the mysteries of joy and sorrow tell us of life's hidden paths, and of the burdens we must bear along them, in the following of our Master. Were this all, the stoutest heart would fail, and the bravest would succumb. But God's gracious mercy has otherwise ordained. Be our lot never so humble, the light of Heaven is its divine sunshine. Be our cross never so heavy, the beckoning of loved ones beyond the bar so urges us on that its weight is forgotten in the swiftness of our eager running to our Father's Home. Thus the cheer and the gladness to the weary pilgrim, that come of the vision of God's saints and the glory of our Blessed Queen. The melody of Heaven we catch on earth, and the music of our loving and oft-repeated Hail Marys mingles in sweetest harmony with the songs of the angels whose Queen our gracious Lady is again proclaimed to-day. In height of bliss and glory, next to her Divine Son, Mary our Mother receives the homage of angels and saints and loving souls on earth. Assuredly, Rosarians should lead in this greeting to her who is so exalted, and from whose dignity and splendor, as St. Bernard says, the heavenly country illumined by her glorious rays, shines with a greater brilliancy. Power-

ful because of her divine influence, the Queen of the Angels and Saints, the beloved Daughter of the Father, the chosen Mother of the Son, the immaculate Spouse of the Holy Ghost, the honored Tabernacle of the Holy Trinity, will give special ear, on this great day, to the prayer of her children, on her own dear Beads.

Catholic piety dedicates the month of November to the relief of the souls in Purgatory. The charity of Christ, through which we ought to be bound, in loving sympathy, to those suffering souls, urges us to their help. Justice and piety may also have claims, but we insist only on the broad motive of charity. And to our Rosarians we earnestly commend the powerful means of the Beads. The wealth of Rosary indulgences is applicable to the faithful departed, for whose benefit we may labor most advantageously. The interests of our Blessed Mother may be involved in the presence of some of her clients, for whose release we should especially pray. And most fitting will it be that we use that comforting prayer which was their delight when on earth— the Rosary of our Lady. By its indulgences, which we may gain and apply to them, abundant refreshment may be brought to the "prisoners of the King." In devout and prayerful memory, dear Rosarians, hold God's faithful departed, especially during November.

Our readers have already had an apportunity of studying the recent encyclical of our Holy Father, the Pope, on the Rosary, as the full text has been published by some of the Catholic weeklies. We regret that its announcement was too late for notice in our October number. In subsequent issues of THE ROSARY MAGAZINE we shall lay before our readers some of the special features of this important declaration. In the meantime, we commend to all our Rosarians the Holy Father's earnest desires for prayers in behalf of Christian union. To our Lady he looks for powerful help, and on our devoted offerings and pleadings in the Rosary, he confidently counts.

During a recent visit to the Pacific coast where we had the privilege of meeting many of the old-time Catholics of the extreme West, as well as many of the present generation, we were deeply impressed by the general and generous devotion to our Lady of the Rosary that we found among all classes. On great Rosary Sunday, October 6, we had the pleasure of taking part in the ceremonies in St. Dominic's Church, attached to the Convent of the Dominican Fathers in San Francisco. From all parts of the city devout Rosarians came. While a constant stream of people had visited the church from the hour of first Vespers on Saturday, October 5, it was reserved for the grand celebration on Sunday to draw a congregation exceeding the capacity of the vast church. The beautiful cere-mony of blessing the roses, at which the Very Reverend Provincial, Father Murphy, O. P., officiated, began at 10 o'clock. Thousands of roses were then distributed to the waiting multitude, who pressed forward eagerly and piously for the precious flowers. After the solemn Mass and sermon, the procession took place. It was a soul-stirring spectacle. Marshalled in groups, headed by their respective banners, with the Rosary bannerets appropriately disposed, the various confraternities, including the Third Order of St. Dominic, the Holy Name Society, the Angelic Warfare, the Christian Doctrine Association, the St. Vincent de Paul Society, the Children of Mary, and the large concourse of Rosarians from various other parts, marched solemnly from the church. The statue of our Lady, surrounded by flowers and lights, was borne by four men. The officiating clergy, preceded by the Fathers and Brothers of the Convent, closed the line. Making a complete passage of the square, chanting the Rosary and singing hymns in honor of our Lady, the procession wound its way through Bush and Pine and Steiner and Pierce Streets, returning to the church for the close. Hundreds of spectators crowded the streets, watching the moving host of young and old. The scene was one of mingled beauty and solemnity. Rich vestments, gaily attired acolytes, children in white, the sober dress of the Tertiaries and the picturesque habits of the Dominicans, with the Rosary colors everywhere conspicuous, made an admirable blending that judicious arrangement and a multitude of flowers and lights set to most striking advantage. The following day all the San Francisco papers devoted considerable space to a description of the festival. We take pleasure in recording these edifying facts, not only in memory of our many California subscribers, but as an encouragement that others may go and do likewise.

Among the special days in honor of our Blessed Mother, during November, are the feasts of the Patronage and the Presentation. The former should remind us of Mary's power in defence of her children. "Visible enemies," says St. Bonaventure, " fear less the mightiest armies than the powers of darkness fear the name and protection of Mary." Let us, therefore, fly to the protection of the Mother of God, the glorious and ever-blessed Virgin, who will not despise our prayers in our necessities, but will deliver us from all dangers.

In the Presentation of our Lady, we celebrate, according to a venerable tradition, the offering by Joachim and Anna, of their holy child, when she was only three years old, that she might receive the special care and training of the priests of the Temple. Ratified, as this offering was, by our Blessed Lady in her vow of virginity to God, the sacrifice was most acceptable to God. In memory of her most beautiful offering, dear Rosarians, present to your gracious Queen, your hearts and souls, and beg her to keep them, as in the Temple, pure and unspotted of the world, for her Divine Son.

The celebration of Thanksgiving Day by the people of the United States is an annual reminder to all, of the duty of gratitude to God, the bountiful Giver of all good things. "Let us give thanks to the Lord our God, for it is meet and just." This is the spirit of the Mass, it is the teaching of the Scriptures, it is the lesson of the Church, it is the prompting of our hearts. The story told of St. Antoninus, O. P., Archbishop of Florence, is edifying and instructive. On one occasion, a peasant brought to him a basket of choice apples. The saint acknowledged the gift by saying devoutly: "Thanks be to God." But the poor man, who had expected some other recognition, showed both dis appointment and bad temper. Seeing this, St. Antoninus sent for a pair of scales. He wrote on a little piece of paper the words " Deo gratias," Thanks be to God, and placing the slip in one side of the scales, and the basket of apples in the other, he proceeded to weigh them. The side bearing the tiny paper went down, while the apples were carried upwards. The peasant saw the meaning, and from the miracle, learned the value of gratitude to God. So, Rosarians, be ever mindful of the claims of our loving Lord, on our heart's devoted thanksgiving. Use your Beads in praise to His Holy Name, and never allow yourselves to wander away with the nine ungrateful lepers.

The thoughtful observer who has watched the course of events during the past twenty years, is prepared to give testimony touching that remarkable outgrowth of American enterprise, the great newspapers of our large cities. The character of this testimony will depend largely on that accommodating quantity known as the point of view. A sensational manager, an unscrupulous reporter, an avaricious publisher or reckless editor will hardly stand on the same ground with a conscientious teacher, an honorable writer, a watchful parent, or a zealous clergyman. There is, however, a meeting place, agreeable to the honest men of all ranks and classes, where practical unanimity of opinion may be found. And this opinion finds strong expression in condemnation and protest and warning. Clean-handed men, of upright soul, among editors and publishers, as well as among teachers and parents and the clergy, are agreed in viewing as a dangerous tendency the steadily increasing growth, in size and scope, of the modern newspaper. The legitimate functions of the daily press have been gradually widened and extended during the past quarter of a century, till at the present time there seem to be no more worlds that enterprising manager or ubiquitous reporter may conquer. The events of the world as they enter into the great public life of nations, having their varying effects on the progress of human affairs, furnish ample material for the newsgatherer's industry and the careful editor's skill. To both of these the expectant reader looks, not only for " news," but for reliable news, valuable news, public news. With this, the intelligent reader will be satisfied; for it he will be grateful. But too often he is grievously disappointed. The enormous output of many of the modern daily papers is bewildering, and the tendency is to give more. Petty events,

the insignificant actions of insignificant men, a calendar of vulgar crimes and scandals, detailed reports of court trials, revelations of private lives that in no manner concern the public, interviews on all conceivable subjects and with all sorts of people, opinions, especially on politics, that mean nothing, and that only illustrate the capacity of the American " legislator," " office holder," " party leader," " prominent politician," and dodging candidate, to say as much as possible without saying anything at all— such is the material that occupies much space in our newspapers. And who can say it is unto profit? Mingled with these and with advertisements of every description, frequently of doubtful morality and often openly shameful, we find repeated attempts, especially in the Sunday editions, to make the newspaper a substitute for magazine and book and pulpit. Where will it end? This is the question for thoughtful men, for parents. The deplorable condition, intellectually, into which many Americans have fallen, because of their mania for mere newspaper reading, should be a warning to all who do not wish to become newspaper fiends, newspaper dyspeptics. The true love of reading is suffering because of the indiscriminate newspaper " bolting " in which so many indulge. All taste for solid and profitable study dies with the man whose chief purpose, in reading, is to " keep up with the times." Literature, in its best sense, ceases to be an attraction or a help. And so far as morality is concerned, we seriously doubt the purity of mind, the piety of soul, the kindliness of speech, the breadth of charity, the tenderness of true pity for human infirmity, in the case of those who are merely inveterate, indiscriminate newspaper readers. Coarseness, vulgarity, the narrowness of a well-worn rut are the most sharply marked characteristics of such people. The interests of the home are often sacrificed by the neglect of all precautions in behalf of children. Indifferent parents allow the young to read the questionable newspapers, with a painful result of which the clergy are well aware, while their firesides know not the cheer or blessing of a Catholic publication. We urge upon our friends the great duty of guarding the purity of the home, and the innocence of the young. Earnestly we say: Beware of indiscriminate newspaper reading; be cautious as to your journal, and over the best, waste not valuable time.

BOOKS.

Studies in the New Testament is the name of a handsome volume of 170 pages, issued by the Rosary Publication Co. The author is the Rev. James H. O'Donnell, rector of St. John's parish, Watertown, Conn. The book is appropriately dedicated to his parishioners. We cannot speak too highly of Father O'Donnell's book, nor recommend it too strongly to the readers of the ROSARY MAGAZINE.

Studies in the New Testament bears unquestionable evidence of great and painstaking research. The writings of the best and latest authorities in biblical literature have been judiciously consulted, and the author has arrayed his facts in so discriminating, and, at the same time, so simple a manner, as to impress them vividly upon the mind of the student. Father O'Donnell's book occupies a unique place in New Testament literature. He has the field to himself. As he states in the Preface to his book, the plan adopted in the presentation of his facts is original, and we know of no Catholic firm that has published any book written on similar lines. For opening up this new field, the author deserves the thanks and practical encouragement of every student of Holy Writ.

We congratulate Father O'Donnell on the production of a book that is destined, we believe, to increase our love for the sacred volume, and to stimulate to deeper research than has hitherto been given to Sacred Scripture by the laity.

That the merit of the book may be better understood and appreciated, we present a brief summary of its contents.

The Introduction is from the pen of Very Rev. John A. Mulcahy, Vicar-General of the diocese of Hartford, and is a clear, well-written paper. There are five parts or sections in the book. Part First is devoted to chapters on Inspiration, the Canon, the Scriptures as a rule of faith, and the reading of the Scriptures. An interesting chapter is entitled "Ancient Manuscripts of the New Testament." Part Second lucidly treats of the Authenticity, Integrity, and Veracity of the New Testament, the four gospels in order, and the Acts of the Apostles, besides treating of other matters of interest pertaining to the New Testament in general. Part Third comprises clear and scholarly chapters on the fourteen Epistles of St. Paul, the seven Catholic Epistles, and the Apocalypse. In treating of the different books of the New Testament, Father O'Donnell gives the date and place of composition, the scope of each book, and the circumstances that led to its writing. Following each chapter is a comprehensive synopsis of each book. Part Fourth is biographical, and contains thirty-three sketches of New Testament characters. Parth Fifth is of a miscellaneous character, and comprises the miracles, parables, and discourses of our Lord, so tabulated as to render it easy for the student to find them. In an admirable manner are grouped also many interesting facts concerning the New Testament, which are found scattered here and there in separate volumes, but never before brought together, as far as we know, in one book. An exhaustive appendix, giving the order of events in the life of Christ, closes this truly admirable little book.

Studies in the New Testament is arranged in the form of question and answer, and is therefore adapted to advanced classes in our Parochial and Sunday Schools, as well as for students in our Colleges and Seminaries.

In devoting so much space to Father O'Donnell's book, we believe we are rendering a service to the grand cause our Holy Father Leo XIII. has so much at heart, namely, the diffusion of accurate knowledge of the Scriptures among the people.

Studies in the New Testament is attractively and substantially bound, and the press-work is faultless, reflecting great credit upon the printing department of the Catholic Protectory, West Chester, N. Y. Orders may be sent to the author, to the ROSARY PUBLICATION Co., and to booksellers in general. The price is only $1.00.

MAGAZINES.

The New England Magazine for September contains a detailed and very interesting account of that admirable work, the Pratt Institute of Brooklyn. "License and No-License in Cambridge" tells the record and result of five years' license and nine years' no-license in that city. The writer quotes strong words of approval from Fathers Scully, Flatley, and O'Brien, three of the leading pastors of the Diocese of Boston, whose churches are in the city of Cambridge. The candid reader will admit, that although no-license has not ushered in the millenium or put an end to drunkenness, or abolished the liquor traffic, it has made the streets safer, quieter, cleaner; it has removed allurements from the young, and pitfalls from the path of the weak and tempted; it has made it, for many, much easier to do right and much harder to do wrong—and who will not be grateful for such blessings? "The New Northeast" gives a pleasant glimpse of Maine, especially in the Aroostook county, showing the fine opportunities of development in colonization afforded in those parts. Another paper deserving special mention is, "Pioneer of China Painting in America," a beautifully illustrated sketch.

The Scottish Review (July–October) contains a very agreeable variety of matter. "A Scottish Free-Lance" is the romantic story of a soldier of fortune in the days of the Stuarts, Sir Andrew Melville; "Fragments of Caithness Folk-Lore" teems with the canny and the weird; "The Canadian Dominion and Australian Commonwealth" is a valuable political discussion by the clerk of the Dominion House of Parliament, a very capable man. The most interesting contribution, however, in our view, is "The Vision of Tundale," an account of that remarkable work of an Irishman which deservedly ranks as a forerunner of the "Divina Commedia."

The latest issue (April-June, 1895) of *The American Journal of Archæology* is a fine number. A valuable paper is that on Byzantine art and culture in Italy, and especially in Rome. The subject will be continued by the author, A. L. Frothingham, Jr. Another article of much interest is, "Some Early Italian Pictures in the Jarves Collection of the Yale School of Fine Arts at New Haven." The notes and archæological news are timely and instructive. Several beautiful plates representing the works of various early Italian painters enrich this number of the *Journal.*

In *The Forum* for September, Frederic Harrison gives his estimate of "George Eliot's Place in Literature." The unbiassed student of Marian Evans' works will be disposed to agree largely with Mr. Harrison. The paper on "Criminal Anthropology; Its Origin and Application,"

by Professor C. Lombroso, is a cunning, unfair plea for the extension to other countries of the immunity from capital punishment enjoyed by Italian criminals, his countrymen. The fallacy and contradiction underlying his "school of treatment" consists in the assumption that a criminal may be such by birth. This we deny.

Among other articles in the September *Forum* are Theodore Roosevelt's defence of his excise law enforcement policy touching Sunday closing; "Unsanitary Schools and Public Indifference," and "The Civil Service As a Career."

Thirteen of the leading English reviews are represented in *The Eclectic Magazine* for September. Among the most interesting articles, we mention, "Night Scenes in Chinatown, San Francisco"; "Old Italian Gardens"; "Roadside Singers and Covert Warblers," a refreshing view of the nightingale, the fuzwren, and the cricket-bird.

The Peterson Magazine for September publishes an illustrated account of "The Carnegie Library of Pittsburgh"; "The Making of a Modern Newspaper," with thirteen portraits of New York editors; "Women Play-Makers of To-day," with five portraits; and an enthusiastic account of "The World's Woman's Christian Temperance Union," with fourteen portraits of women distinguished in this cause.

The Cosmopolitan for September contains one of Conan Doyle's good stories, "Tempted by the Devil," a bit of Napoleonic literature; "Brigham Young and Modern Utah;" "A Famous Crime," the story of the Webster-Parkman murder in Boston nearly fifty years ago; "The Ancient Capital of Cuba," a passing view of Santiago; "A House Party at Abbottsford," pleasant reading for lovers or admirers of Sir Walter Scott, and "In the Realm of the Wonderful," a beautifully illustrated and very interesting paper on some of the oddest forms of sea life.

Persons interested in mountain climbing will find congenial reading in *The Contemporary Review* for August, and in *McClure's* for September. The former publishes a highly dramatic account of the ascent of the Matterhorn of the New Zealand Alps, by E. A. Fitzgerald. The latter gives the story of an amateur's

·climb to the summit of the Swiss Matterhorn.

Other papers in *McClure's* follow this magazine's special line, and include a dashing account of Garfield's ride at Chickamauga, and some of the Pinkerton reminiscences.

The following poem by J. A. Middleton, entitled "Fidelity," appeared in *The Pall Mall Magazine* for September :

> I do not want you when your feet
> With buoyant footsteps tread on air,
> And you can smile on all you meet,
> And banish care ;
> But when the road is long and cold,
> And cruel seem the ways of men,
> And you are weary, sad, and old—
> Come then.
>
> I do not want you when your name
> From lip to lip is proudly rolled ;
> I do not want you when your fame
> Has brought you gold ;
> But when you fight and strive and press,
> And no one reads the songs you pen,
> And life is full by loneliness—
> Come then.

The sentiment is worthy of the title. Fidelity, like honor, is a precious thing that the world knows not too well, and for which naught else can be a substitute, for whose want no forms of religion can supply, and in whose full development there is much that tells of religion's very essence.

Grant Allen continues his papers on "Evolution in Early Italian Art," with copious illustrations, and Judge O'Connor Morris concludes his vivid sketch of "The Campaign of Trafalgar," to which the maps and diagrams add special value in clearness.

The Seminary for September contains Mr. John A. Mooney's fourth paper on Emile Zola. It is sufficient to say that the work is done after Mr. Mooney's best style.

We also remind our readers of an article in the October number of *The Seminary* by the same capable and zealous writer on the recent Italian celebration and the breach of Porta Pia. It makes reading that one must appreciate, for it is truly Catholic as well as truly scholarly.

Frank Leslie's Popular Monthly for October contains a fine array of illustrated articles, several of which are of special interest to Catholics. "Souvenirs of Siena" and "Monte Oliveto" are pleasant reminders of Blessed Bernard, the Founder of the Olivetans, with descriptions of his famous monastery and its beautiful frescoes.

"The Town and Cloth Halls of Fland-

ers," an instructive and interesting paper, with many pictures; "Alpine Soldiers," an account of the frontier armies of France, Italy, and Austria; "The Last Days of Torquato Tasso," by Marie Walsh, and "Light-Givers," a sketch of the rise of various illuminants, are all good articles.

"American Posters, Past and Present," is the title of a fancifully illustrated paper by H. C. Brunner in the October number of *Scribner's Magazine*. Robert Grant continues his series on "The Art of Living," the present article being a judicious discussion of "The Case of Woman." "A History of the Last Quarter Century in the United States" is brought down to the days of Kearney, the "sand-lot orator," of San Francisco, whose memorable cry, "The Chinese Must Go," is still remembered on the Pacific coast, chiefly because the Chinese have not gone. But the most interesting article in this number of *Scribner's* is the beautifully illustrated "Domesticated Birds," an instructive but popular treatise on barn-yard fowls, turkeys, pigeons, etc.

The Fortnightly Review for September contains, among other papers, interesting contributions on "Stambalouff's Fall," "The Awakening of China," "Coleridge and His Critics," and "Denominational Science," by St. George Mivart.

In connection with *The Fortnightly* article on China, a paper in the September *Nineteenth Century* that will be found of interest is Sir Alfred Lyall's able discussion of the question of "Permanent Dominion in Asia" by the Caucasian race.

In the same number of *The Nineteenth Century* Prince Kropotkin lays bare "The Present Condition of Russia" in a manner that must shock civilized men who read this story of "the indescribable misery of the peasant" subjects of the Czar. "Lion Hunting Beyond the Hand" is full of adventure and daring. "The Romance of Leonardo da Vinci" is rather vaguely told, leaving the reader unsatisfied, and with the feeling that the writer aimed more to make suggestive sentences than to establish the truth.

The Contemporary Review for September publishes a fine article on "Macedonia and the Macedonians." The writer is familiar with his subject, and while he is unsparing in his denunciation of the Turks, he proves that the practical outcome of the Treaty of Berlin, as it is understood by the Turks, and apparently approved by the Christian Powers, is to leave the helpless people of Macedon a at the mercy (?) of "bloodthirsty brigands whose profession of Mohammedanism not only entitles them to Heaven in the next life, but allows them to condemn honest Christians to something like hell in this." This writer adds that "there is probably no district within the Turkish Empire in which life is less secure, and violent death more certain, than in this romantic country." "The universal cry of horror at crimes which from their very wantonness seem to proceed from inborn malignity rather than mere crass egotism" has been too long unheeded by Christian nations. Despite the specious plea of Mr. Justice Ameer Ali in his article "Islam and Its Critics," which appears in the September *Nineteenth Century*, and in which he tries to present to us a mild-mannered, gentle Turk, to which history gives the lie, it is proved, by bloody facts, that "European cattle are better treated than the Macedonians, for these are at least well fed,before being slaughtered, and enjoy immunity from that moral anguish which sears the soul and almost shakes the foundations of man's belief in good and God." Strong words, but they tell of a condition that assuredly cries to Heaven for vengeance. Of old it was said: "Carthage must be blotted out." The Christian world should blot Turkey as a ruling nation from the face of the earth.

In the same number of *The Contemporary*, William T. Stead attempts to answer Senator Lodge and other staunch Americans who are determined to prevent England from stealing any more of the American Continent. Mr Stead's article is either stupid or insincere—"babyish" might be a suitable term; but at all events, it will make no impression on intelligent men who know how ready John Bull is to arbitrate—when he is not able to fight or to "bully."

The Ave Maria, October 5, publishes as its leading article the beautiful paper by Mother Augusta Theodosia Drane, O. P., entitled "Thoughts on the Rosary," which originally appeared in THE ROSARY MAGAZINE for November, 1894, by special arrangement with the Dominican Sisters of Stone, England. As *The Ave Maria* states, in a footnote, that the paper is now published for the first time, the worthy editor must have been misinformed.

The Cosmopolitan for October publishes, in "The Land of Epicure," a very interesting account of the delicacies abounding in Chesapeake Bay and along its shores. "Famous Miniatures" is a sketch of some of the celebrated painters of "paintings in little," by Nancy Huston Hanks, who also contributes to *The Ladies' Home Journal* for October, a brief notice of the distinguished miniature painter, Amalia Küssner. In her *Cosmopolitan* article this writer indulges in the following stupid thought: "What longings for the world may not have found expression in the vivid colors of these capitals and borders?" This may not have been intended as a little bit of bigotry, but it looks like a fling at the monks whose art was lovingly, and not regretfully, dedicated to God and to religion.

L. W. Reilly contributes to the September number of *The American Ecclesiastical Review*, an estimate of the priestly character and virtues of Father Burke, O. P., that will serve to dispel some of the prevailing notions fostered by that wretched biography issued by Fitzpatrick.

In the October number of the same *Review*, Mr. Reilly begins a biographical sketch of Father Gabriel Richard, the only priest who ever held a seat in the United States House of Representatives.

The October *Forum*, under the heading, "Significance of the English Elections," gives a symposium of three articles, the best of which is Justin McCarthy's "Why, Whence, and Whither." Ex-Senator E. G. Ross contributes another of his interesting reminiscences, being brief but vivid sketches of the "Political Leaders of the Reconstruction Era." "The Actor, the Manager, and the Public" is the title of a thoughtful article on the decadence of the American stage. The writer, John Malone, formerly a member of Booth's company, discusses the question in a broad and intelligent way. He resents the usurpations of the manager; he regrets the multiplication of "stars" and the disbanding of the stock company; and he attributes to greed and a sensational press a goodly share of responsibility for the degradation of the stage: "An occasional editorial appears, in which the lamentable condition of the public theatre is deplored, but the columns set apart for notices of the drama continue to be stuffed out with the sawdust of box-office literature. So long as the managerial promoter of inane or erotic suggestions is permitted to furnish for publication, in daily and influential journals, his own estimate of the monstrosities of impudence and vice with which he degrades the stage, reform in the theatre can have little encouragement." Again: "It is the privilege" (and we add, the *right*) "of the American people to have a clean stage, and some day they will sweep the rubbish from it." So we hope, for "every succeeding season develops a new weakness in the decaying edifice which shelters the usurping pretenders of the drama." When the day of relief comes, "the public will turn with delight to the refreshing influence of the honest, world-old, heart-touching play wherein virtue is applauded and vice condemned in good set terms."

In the same number of *The Forum* other readable articles are, "Higher Pay and a Better Training for Teachers," in which we suggest the transposition of these heads; "Well-meant but Futile Endowments: the Remedy;" and "Demand and Supply Under Socialism," by W. H. Mallock. "The Resuscitation of Blue Laws" is a plea for greater personal liberty in regard to the Sunday sale and use of liquors. The writer says, "the perverted minds of exalted ascetics would fain turn a day which had been chiefly intended for rest and pleasure into one of fasting and prayer." This is extremely inaccurate. Had the author written, "narrow fanatics" for "exalted ascetics," he would have shown a better knowledge of terms. He would also be more in harmony with the Scriptures which he likes to quote, had he remembered that the chief end of the "Sabbath" is to afford to man greater leisure for the worship of God, while giving just recognition to innocent enjoyment and recreation.

The Century for October brings Sloane's life of Napoleon down to the murder of the Duc d'Enghien, the details of which are vividly given. The recent centenary of John Keats has called forth various tributes to the memory of the young poet. *The Century* contains several interesting articles, with pictures and fac-simile specimens of Keats' writing. The second instalment of "Life in the Tuileries Under the Second Empire" sustains the promise of the first. "The Marriage Rate of College Women" is an article full of figures and suggestions; but Josiah Flynt's "How Men Become Tramps" is a paper of far greater value for the student and the thoughtful citizen.

The author is capable, and his work is thorough.

The North American Review for October presents, as the opening paper, "The Atlanta Exposition," by the Governor of Georgia. Several articles are devoted to the "liquor question." Doctor H. S. Williams contributes an excellent study of "Politics and the Insane," in which he shows the abuses begotten of the "spoils system." Hiram S. Maxim, on "Birds in Flight and the Flying Machine," is, as usual with him, instructive and interesting. The personal history of the second Napoleonic empire reaches the causes of the Mexican War. The symposium, "A Study of Wives," omits the American wife, and other wives quite as important as the Scandinavian, the German, the English, and the French wives who are discussed.

McClure's for October is a very interesting number. Stories by Stanley J. Weyman, Anthony Hope, and Ian Maclaren; Fables by Robert Louis Stevenson; James Creelman's stirring history of the London *Times;* "The Real John Keats," by J. G. Speed; "Grant and Lincoln in Bronze," an illustrated account of the works of William R. O'Donovan and Thomas Eakins; and "The New York Tribune in the Draft Riots," make a varied compilation.

In the October number of *The Ladies' Home Journal* the editor writes agreeably of "Where American Life Really Exists," making his article, with good show of fact and argument, an earnest plea to young men not to rush to the large cities, but rather to seek the advantages of the smaller cities and towns. The tendency to herd in large cities is one that often robs many people of some of the most pleasant things in life, including leisure, the society of a limited number of chosen friends, and the blessings of home life and family intercourse.

Lippincott's for October contains a little sketch of the King of Rome, Napoleon II., better known by his Austrian title of Duke of Reichstadt. It is a contribution to the Napoleonic literature of the day. In the same number, "French Roads," and "The Highways of the World," are brief but instructive papers. "Inside New Guinea" is a glimpse of that strange land which is known by comparatively few.

(After a Painting.)

Dark is the world in its grief and sin;
    The bleak winds blow,
And out in the night there is such pain
    And endless woe.

But the Christ who felt so free from care
    On His mother's breast,
Doth bid me come to His arms to-night,
    And there find rest.

The Rosary

| VOL. VII. | DECEMBER, 1895. | No. 6. |

ON MARY'S BREAST.

CHARLES HANSON TOWNE.

Dark was the night when the Christ-Child came
    And humbly lay
'Mid the breath of kine in the manger stall,
    'Mid the scent of hay.

Oh, cold was the air and bleak the wind,
    Yet safe at rest
The Christ-Child slept in His peace and joy
    On Mary's breast.

And He felt secure and free from harm
    As He nestled there,
For He knew the touch of His mother's hand,
    And her loving care.

Dark is the world in its grief and sin ;
    The bleak winds blow,
And out in the night there is such pain
    And endless woe.

But the Christ who felt so free from care
    On His mother's breast,
Doth bid me come to His arms to-night,
    And there find rest.

Letter of Her Most Serene Highness, the Dowager Crown-Princess of Austria, Archduchess Stephanie, authorizing the publication of " Lacroma " in THE ROSARY MAGAZINE.

(*Translation.*)

ABBAZIA, VILLA ANGIOLINA,

7 Feb., 1895.

By these lines I permit the publication of my " Lacroma " in the Catholic magazine, THE ROSARY, greatly rejoicing if my readers in America will give their attention to my unpretentious description, solely devoted, as it is, to a charitable object.

STEPHANIE.

LACROMA.

ITUATE under the same happy strip of sky as Naples, and lavishly ornate with the enchantments of an almost tropical vegetation, a charming island rises out of the still, soft floods of the blue Adriatic, opposite the venerable old city of Ragusa. It is called Lacroma, and a description of it is the purpose of these unpretending pages.

With its rare site, Lacroma is like an evergreen fairy-isle, and it fully merits its popular name of the " Pearl of the Adriatic." Wherever the eye is directed, it is met by charmingly picturesque spots and scenes of varied beauty. To the south, the boundless ocean stretches afar in serenest blue, and

"The wavelets of the slumbering sea,"

with the graceful lines of their white edges, shimmer and glisten like silver, while deep peace reigns over the broad expanse of waters.

A splendid contrast presents itself in the snow-capt giants of the Cernogara, here forming the rugged, austere masses of the Montenigro mountains. Their precipitous, wildly jagged cliffs merge below into terrace and tillage on the friendly green shores of Benno bay, to rise again, beyond Ragusa, more rugged and bleak, indeed, but beautiful with a refinement of color and grace of outline peculiarly their own.

These lofty, barren rocks, now crowned with forts, were once clad with forests of oak. Unhappily nothing of their former woodland wealth remains at the present day. In the Middle Ages, their huge oaken boles must have furnished the material for many a proud ship that swept the seas under the flag of the Ragusan republic. They, too, must have given the city its present Slavic name, for *Dubrovna* means an oak forest.

A city picturesquely reposing at the foot of these Karstenite mountains, within a girdle of fortifications grown grey with age, and washed by a surge of sapphire blue, vaulted by a clear and cloudless sky, and breathed upon by the pure, mild breath of the

South—such is Ragusa, the old patrician town. One glimpse of it cannot but afterwards be treasured, a pleasant picture in the memory—an extent of palaces all aglow in the richness of gold, glimpses of domes and pinnacles shining in the sun, houses of dazzling whiteness, solitary palms beckoning from the midst of stately towers and walls that can boast long, historic years of existence, and finally, a romantic harbor in beautiful prospect, where countless fisherboats are rocked on the waves.

ARCHDUCHESS STEPHANIE.

The scene northwards, no less attractive, likewise engages the attention. Far out on the horizon, fisherboats gracefully rise and fall, flashing their sails of luminous white, or sometimes of red or yellow. But for them, there were no token of life to break the solemn quietude. They steer past chains of islets scattered about in picturesque disorder and half shrouded in a sweet smelling haze of blue, past the *Pettine*, comb-like reefs, the terror of seamen, boldly and grotesquely rising out of the water, and overtopped only by the neighboring lighthouse—ever onward they hold their course and away from us, abroad on the high seas.

As we turn landwards again, the scene that meets our eyes resembles the shores of Greece by a certain pride of form and outline, and by the deep, cavernous ravines, whose rocky walls precipitate themselves into the sea's reflection of their varied and lively hues. Another point brings up vivid recollections of Italian coast scenery which finds a rival in this delightful strand. Bright rural homes lie scattered along the ridge, or with their leaf-covered roofs, they thrust themselves forward down to the Riva, and stand out of the verdured framework that encloses them. A solitary little church, almost hidden in the shade of laurel and olive trees, is occasionally an added charm to the rich landscape or, again, a lonely dwelling only partly visible under melancholy cypresses or broad-stemmed chestnut or spreading plane trees, lends its romantic picturesqueness to the prospect.

In the midst of this region so richly blessed, and so profuse of nature's rarest loveliness, lies the little gem to which we shall now devote our attention.

The island of Lacroma, with an area of less than 200 acres, falls naturally into two parts. Its northern side rises into a considerable mountain, which is covered with olive trees and brushwood. Old dismantled Fort Royal crowns its summit. The southern portion of the island, less of altitude, contains a pine forest, a fine large park, and the famous old Abbey of Lacroma, whose geographical position is described as 42° 37′ 5″ North latitude, and 18° 7′ 55″ longitude, east of Greenwich.

There is a charm here in all the year's seasons except Summer, which becomes insufferable with heat next to tropical in its intensity. The spring, as elsewhere, comes in with the rich blessing of an abundance of flowers, prodigal of varied tint and rarest beauty, and laden with an almost overpowering fragrance. A southern autumn, however, does not bear any resemblance to the melancholy season of death and decay. It brings in its train a magic of vivid color and luminousness that eludes the subtlest efficacy of artist's brush—gradations of light and tone from clearest ochre to darkest red, imparting a softness and warmth of life such as an Alpine glow will rarely call into being in our dolomitic regions. The winters are mild and beautiful. I myself experienced days there both sunny and warm, as only the South can exhibit them, recurring regularly for months, a joy to the chilled hearts and minds that come from elsewhere to seek them.

A narrow channel, scarcely a league wide, separates Lacroma from the Dalmatian coast. Still, when the sea works high, it costs hard labor to reach the island. At times the passage is not without danger, and when *Bora* and *Sirocco* meet in conflict, even impossible. It once happened that the islanders were obliged to submit to Neptune's watery sway for five days, feeling themselves cut off from the world during all this time, notwithstanding that the Dalmatian coast was apparently less than a stone's throw distant.

In fine weather, the ride to Lacroma is to be described as delightful, when the deep blue sky overarches us, and the sunbeams

VIEW OF RAGUSA AND OF THE ISLAND OF LACROMA.

quiver on the curling eddies like thousands of flashing diamonds. As the brawny oarsman speeds our boat onwards across the glistening surface of the channel, we rapidly approach our destination. The nearer we approach, the more plainly we catch the melodic plash of the waves pouring themselves into countless bays and inlets, and breaking against the rocks that skirt the entire island.

Denser and richer to the eye is the fair island's vegetation as we gradually draw near, spicier and more aromatic the fragrance

A CLOISTER GARDEN.

of the atmosphere that is wafted around us. One's heart begins to throb in the presence of nature so grand, and thus, with up-lifted spirit, we land at the miniature mole which here, in a deeply indented bay, serves us the purpose of a pier.

On a stone embankment above, an iron pillar provided with a lantern is the nightly Pharos for the smaller craft of these parts, to which alone, indeed, the harbor is accessible. A simple dwell-ing rises to view on the right, the residence of the overseer and gardener.

Hastening up a few steps, the visitor finds himself in the midst of a wonderful garden, adorned with an overflowing abundance of all the floral charms of the tropics. The paths are carefully strewn with gravel blossomy white. In the shade of palms and exotic plants, of oleanders and laurel trees, between evergreen shrubbery, myrtles, pistachios, and high-stemmed ericas, we pass through the ivy-clad ruins of the old abbey, venerable yet in the desolate fragments of its former greatness, and enter the castle, whose walls hint at a history of many hundreds of years.

In the year 1023, as a destructive fire was raging in Ragusa, un-controllable in the high storm blowing at the time, and threaten-ing to devour the city, the inhabitants, in their extremity, sent up fervent prayers to St. Benedict, whose feast occurred on that day. They promised to build a church in his honor, if, by his interces-sion, the impending calamity was averted. Their prayers were heard. The flames became extinct, and the city was saved from the ruin that had seemed inevitable.

The senate and citizens then consulted the Benedictines of the island of Trimiti, with the result that these chose Lacroma as the site of the promised church, thereby manifesting their keen sense of the beautiful, to which the island owes the origin of its abbey.

The monks soon found themselves at home in their peaceful retreat, and it was not long before Lacroma had attained fame and importance. The devout brethren knew, too, how to pro-mote the good repute of both church and abbey, so that they be-came known abroad in distant lands. The south Slavic princes, kings of Servia and Bosnia, afford us proof of this fact; for they were wont to make pilgrimages to the holy place, always leav-ing rich gifts for the monastery at their departure.

One who contributed much to the enrichment of the monastic community was King Bodinus of Bosnia. The chronicles relate that " when this ruler, at the instances of his blood-thirsty consort, Jaquinta, caused the prisoners he had taken at Scutari to be executed in a most inhuman manner, Archbishop Pietro of Ragusa besought the highly influential abbot of Lacroma, Adalbert, to betake himself to Bodinus' camp at Trebinje in order to exhort the king to do penance for his cruel deeds. Abbot Adalbert so well succeeded in softening the disposition of the cruel prince that he not only became repentant, but he also gave the monks the entire Granchetta valley, in which the Ombla rises, as a gift of propitiation.

By this and other important donations on the part of the wealthy patricians of Ragusa, such as the Gondolas, whose sons the monks were educating, the possessions of the monastery became greatly extended, and the abbey rose to increased influence and power when Innocent III. bestowed the episcopal dignity and insignia upon its reigning abbot.

Even Richard Lionheart plays a part in the history of Lacroma. This king, in the year 1190, was engaged in the third crusade. According to the narrative of the " *Memorie storiche sull'- Isola di Lacroma,*" as he was returning from Palestine, he was overtaken by a fearful storm on the Adriatic, and stood in imminent danger of shipwreck. In obedience to the devout practice of those times, Richard in the extremity of his peril, vowed to have a church built on the spot where he should first set foot on dry land. It was on the island of Lacroma that the distinguished crusader found safety, and there, too, he received the homage of the senate and *rettore* of the Ragusan republic.

Since Lacroma was already provided with a church, Richard was besought to undertake the construction of a house of worship at Ragusa, and the Lionheart yielded to the entreaty on condition of the Papal approbation, which indeed under the circumstances, was obtained without difficulty. Such is the origin of the Cathedral of Ragusa, which remains to this day, an interesting memorial of its kingly founder.

The fortunes of Lacroma, true to life, were subject to many vicissitudes. The quiet, peaceful, flourishing home of the Benedictines was not to endure.   It was the scene of darkest calamities in 1570, when some Turkish pirates, defying the then ineffectual and dispersed naval forces of Ragusa, landed on the island, plundered the monastery and church, and wasted the fruits of years of patient toil by fire and sore devastation.   Other troubles then arose, enhancing the former havoc, and adding to the number of the trials of the impoverished community.   On April 6th, 1667, an earthquake, the unhappy effects of which are still recounted in the traditions of the neighborhood, caused great destruction in Ragusa and the surrounding country.   Lacroma was not spared.   A portion of the old abbey was seriously impaired, and the church was demolished.   Nothing but its picturesque ruins remain to-day to tell the story of its ancient splendor. Its old-time greatness was now become a thing of the past.   Inner decay and strife with the outer world made it impossible for the old abbey to recover from the shocks and misfortunes which it had been its ill-fortune so often to meet.   Its only hold and support, the Benedictine Order, perished there after many centuries of power and vigorous existence.

The story of the abbey's ultimate decline stands in remarkable connection, as may be seen in the chronicles of Apendius, with the history of a painting.

The Senate of Ragusa, deeply concerned in the renown of the famous old abbey, ascribed the fault of its decay to the Abbot Lorenzo, and went so far as to charge him with neglect of his duties.   The action of the Senate led to a careful examination of the affairs of the church and monastery, and the search resulted in the discovery of the loss of a picture which was ascribed to Rafael Urbino.   After protracted investigations, it was found that the abbot had sent the painting to Italy to be restored.   Further inquiries proved that it had there been sold, and had passed into other hands.   Eneas di Vechi, an official of the Tuscan embassy at Rome, had disposed of it to an unknown French nobleman.   The republic bestirred itself to recover the lost treasure.   So vigorous a search was instituted that the noblemen, Gradi and Diorda Bosdani, who had travelled to Italy for the express purpose, had the good fortune to regain its possession.

The Senate then determined, instead of delivering it back to the

church of Lacroma, to place it in the keeping of the Cathedral
church of Ragusa, where it is still to be seen.   Although the authenticity of the picture, as a genuine Rafaelite production, is
questioned, it is nevertheless a masterpiece of high art.

This conflict naturally created a great deal of dissatisfaction in
the ranks of the
monastic breth-
ren, for it was
decidedly pred-
judicial to their
r e p u t a t i o n.
Hence it is that
towards the end
o f t h e seven-
teenth century,
we find that the
Benedictines
dis a p p e a r e d
from the pages
of the history
of Ragusa.

At the end of
the eighteenth
century, a few
monks still re-
mained u p o n
t h e island o f
Lacroma; b u t
they led a pre-
carious e x i s t-

HIS MAJESTY, THE PRESENT EMPEROR OF AUSTRIA.

ence, tolerated at one time, at another proscribed.   Even among
themselves, enthusiasm for the concerns of the Order became
slackened, and, wandering staff in hand, they gradually separated,
and betook themselves elsewhere.

Such was the melancholy fate of this beneficent institution, which
after eight centuries of life, of labor, of budding promise and ripened power, was abandoned to decay, seemingly to live on only in
the memory of its past greatness.

The fate of the abbey was then placed in the hands of the Ragusan Senate. After some deliberations, they sold the island, not however, without having first obtained the papal permission required for the dissolution of the old convent. Wealthier citizens of Ragusa then utilized the island, devoting its excellent soil to the culture of olives and of the vine.

But it was still reserved to Lacroma, in the designs of Providence, to be reintegrated in its ancient honor. Better times were in store for the forsaken island. A melancholy accident drew the attention of a distinguished personage thither.

It was on a beautiful evening in the month of May, 1859. Deep and peaceful tranquillity reigned in the harbor of Ragusa. Out upon the high sea, the ships of the French fleet were cruising about, while, at the *Rhede*, in the Ragusan channel, the Austrian war brig, " Triton," lay at anchor guarding the harbor. A sudden flash, a stunning detonation that shook the ground, broke the stillness that lay upon the sea. The brig " Triton" was no more. An explosion in the powder magazine, the cause of which is likely never to be known, brought about this terrible catastrophe. From among the floating fragments of the ill-fated vessel, there was a pitiable moaning to be heard for a few moments, and the agonizing plaints of the wounded, who afterwards found their grave opposite Lacroma.

The Archduke Ferdinand Max, then commander-in-chief of the navy, was immediately informed of the fearful disaster, and in a few days, notwithstanding the blockade of the Adriatic by the French fleet, the noble prince appeared on board the yacht " Fantasie," to inspect the scene of the calamity, to give consolation and encouragement to the wounded, and to pay the last honors to the many dead. It is well known how deeply he was ever concerned for the welfare of the navy which he prized so highly, and which was so near and dear to him.

Just opposite the spot where the brig disappeared under the cold waters, Archduke Ferdinand caused the Triton Cross to be erected to the memory of the brave officers and seamen who met their death there, and its shaft perpetuates their honored names.

This was the occasion that led to the first visit to Lacroma, of the Archduke Ferdinand Maximilian, afterwards the unfortunate

Emperor of Mexico. To him the island had previously been un-known. The Archduke's impressionable heart and his keenly in-telligent sense of the beautiful, found unending enjoyment in the lovely island, then in the flower of its spring-tide beauty, and he acquired possession of it for his consort.

THE TRITON CROSS.

With delicate understanding and judicious taste, with the same rapidity that this noble friend of nature knew how, as if by magic, to bring the fairy gardens of Miramare into being on the scoglias of Punta Grignana, he transformed the rocky reefs of Lacroma in-to a paradise of plants and flowers, and out of its old ruins he created himself an enchanting home, an undisturbed place of ref-uge, a real " buen retiro," which, despite the fiercest storms, could yet afford him pleasure, peace, and enjoyment.

It is not surprising, therefore, that we find the Archduke on his various visits there, extolling the merits of his treasured " gem," Lacroma, in verses of deep sensibility, often revealing keen appre-ciation of the higher beauties of nature.

After the tragic demise of the ill-fated sovereign, the island passed into the possession of Sanitary Chief-Lieutenant Duum-vitch, and from him, in turn, to a lawyer who thought of estab-lishing a climatic sanitorium there, but who could not, however, realize his plans.

Taken, in like manner, with the rare beauty of its position,

CLOISTER OF THE DOMINICAN CONVENT, RAGUSA,
MOTHER-HOUSE OF THE DALMATIAN PROVINCE TO WHICH LACROMA BELONGS.

Crown-Prince Rudolf [1] then purchased the island, enlarged the castle by an additional structure, though without making any not-able changes in the interior of the whole.

Now, thanks to the generosity of His majesty, our worthy em-peror, the island belongs to the Dominicans.[2] This bestowal, on the part of the Austrian monarch, ends the present history of La-croma, which, after so many centuries of varied existence, thus reverts to its original condition.

(Conclusion next month.)

---

[1] Princess Stephanie, of Belgium, author of this sketch, was married to Crown Prince Rudolf, of Austria, on May 10, 1881.—*Translator's note.*
[2] Of the Dalmatian Province.

UNCLE SETH'S INVENTION.

MARY I. HOFFMAN.

CHAPTER I.

INCE mother's death, five years before, I had presided over my father's home. Our family consisted of father, hale and hearty, aged about fifty-six or seven; Millie—that is, myself—a tall, lank girl of twenty; Beth, a plump little dumpling of seventeen; Charley, a petted, lively boy of fifteen, and Uncle Seth Hart, our mother's youngest brother. He was thirty, but he seemed to us nearer sixty. I suppose our idea of his advanced age arose from his gravity and indifference to youthful amusements. We lived on a farm of seventy-five acres, which afforded us a comfortable living. Uncle Seth was not a farmer; he occasionally helped father when his work was driving, but the most of his time was spent in making window-blinds, cornices, picture-frames, and various knick-knacks, which found ready sale in the neighborhood and surrounding villages. Since his coming to us, three years before, he had devoted every leisure moment to the perfecting of some invention, of what nature, or for what purpose, we did not know. Father had been duly informed all about it; but the only answer our numerous questions received from Uncle, was, " time will tell; till then you must wait;" from Father, "you wouldn't understand if told, and besides, it's of no consequence to you to know." This mysterious affair was in an inner room of Uncle's workshop, the door of which was always kept locked, and the window shaded by a thick muslin curtain. Poor Charley got more than one shaking from Uncle, and once had his jacket well dusted by Father for prying round, and yet never caught a glimpse of the " hateful old thing," as he in his wrath contemptuously termed it. But still there were two or three points we did learn. First, that Uncle had suffered failure after failure in trying to make it work, but was still hopeful of ultimate success; secondly; that Father for the first year or two was as hope-

2

ful as Uncle, but when the third year dawned on its unfinished
state, its unfulfilled prophecies, his hope began to flag; third,
that from looking on Uncle as one whose genius the world would
yet acknowledge and admire, he now considered him one to be
pitied for his foolish infatuation.   Uncle Seth was slight, frail,
and in his quiet ways and the gentle tones of his voice reminded
Father of our sainted mother.   However much he might grumble
behind his back, and lament the cormorant that was swallowing
all he earned, the vampire that was sucking away his life and
vitality, before his face he was kinder than ever.   A tender compassion marked his bearing towards him.   I am sure poor Uncle,
with his sensitive nature, felt the change from hearty encouragement to soothing, pitying gentleness, but without a word or a sign
he pursued his way.   His step grew firmer; his eyes had a clearer,
deeper light.

It was about this time that Beth and I received a shock that
fully roused us from our summer languor.   For a year or more we
had been corresponding with our cousin, Blanche Newell.   Her
mother was Father's sister.   When Mother died, Aunt and Uncle
Newell attended the funeral, and staid with us a week after it.
Aunt was kind and loving, and showed great sympathy for us in
our sorrow.   On leaving, she begged us to visit them, assuring us
of the warmest welcome.   But Uncle Newell did not favorably
impress us.   He was a successful merchant, had amassed wealth,
lived in elegant style, and had a proud, pompous bearing.   To do
him justice, I believe he tried to be kind, but his kindness had in
it something so scornful and overbearing that we could not be
grateful for it.   He left, feeling hurt, and taking no pains to hide
it, at our coldness and want of appreciation; and we, on our part,
remained crushed and humiliated by his pride and insolence.
The consequence was, we never went to them, and they never
again came to us.   Great, therefore, was our astonishment on receiving Blanche's first letter.   It was kind and affectionate in
tone.   We answered it; others came, till we learned to look for
her letters, and loved her, though we had never seen her.   But as
much as we loved her we shrank from the thought of meeting
her.

Had we been dainty specimens of humanity, and our home an

ideal spot of loveliness, more than glad would we have been to
have a wealthy cousin from a grand city home come to visit us.
As it was, consternation seized us when we got her letter early in
June, telling us that she would be with us by the end of the month.

Everybody in the family was called upon to render aid in beau-
tifying our humble home as much as possible. Uncle Seth was
fidelity itself throughout the siege of preparation for the expected onslaught of wealth, youth, and beauty. There was one comforting thought,—she would appreciate the merits of golden butter,
freshly-made, of rich milk and cream, newly-laid eggs, to say
nothing of the luscious fruits preserved so perfectly that they
rivalled those fresh from the vine.

Late in June we received a dainty little note, telling us that she
would arrive on the twenty-fifth, at five P. M.—that very afternoon!
Would we meet her at Middleton, the nearest station, seven miles
away?

How every one flew around, making the final preparations of
welcome! Beth and I filled several glasses with flowers and put
them in the parlor, and the room back of it which we had prepared
for her. Six, seven o'clock came, and Father had not yet returned with Blanche. She had probably come on a later train,
Uncle Seth said, so we did not worry. The chores done, the
table set, making, with its snowy cloth, napkins, silver, glasses,
cakes, tarts, preserves, cold ham, etc., etc., with especially the lighted lamp above it, a grand display, we could not bear to disturb it.
Still feeling the need of a meal, we marched, a quartette of hungry
mortals, into the buttery, and regaled ourselves on bread and
milk till the supper could not, by any possibility, be more than a
mere form. We were laughing and talking when Uncle, sharply
turning his ear to the window, said: " Whist! isn't there the sound
of wheels? " It was too dark to see. Yes, Father had returned.
Uncle Seth and Charley took the lanterns, ready lighted, and
hurried out. Beth instantly gathered the bowls and spoons into
an empty pan, whisked up the crumbs, and hastened with me to
the front hall. Father must have been introducing her to Uncle
Seth, for we heard a sweet voice say:

"This must be the Uncle Seth Cousins Millie and Beth have
written to me about."

"The same, Miss Newell," was Uncle's answer.

He lifted her from the wagon, and assisted her up the walk to the door.

Her picture had given us the impression of a rather large, handsome woman with fine features, and there she stood before us, a perfect fairy-like little beauty, looking, with her short curls, diminutive size, large, innocent, pleading eyes, more like a child of twelve than the young lady of eighteen we knew her to be. She flew to me, threw her arms around my neck, drew my head down, and gave me a resounding kiss. Releasing her hold, she turned and saluted Beth in the same way.

"There, Cousins," she said, "be glad to see me. Don't let the gladness be all on my side."

Charley was in by this time. He had made short work of giving the horses their oats. He walked right up to her, took both her hands, and gallantly kissed her.

"I am more than glad to see you. If my sisters are not, it's because they are afraid of you."

"Afraid of me!" she repeated; "of me?" She laughed; we all laughed, and catching her in our arms, Beth and I hugged her and kissed her till she must have found her welcome almost too warm. With deft fingers Beth removed her hat and light scarf, and touched up the curls that clustered round her lovely face. Assuring her she needed no freshening, and after her long ride must be faint, we at once led the way to the dining-room. Father and Uncle Seth brought in her trunk, and carried it to her room, after which we sat down to supper. Blanche and Beth were seated on one side, Uncle Seth and Charley opposite, Father at the head, and I at the foot. To judge from the way he disposed of the viands, Father enjoyed the meal. As to Cousin Blanche, she only tasted and pointed at them as we were doing. Charley watched her dainty movements awhile, then demurely asked:

"Did you, too, Cousin, have a bowl of bread and milk?"

"Why!" exclaimed Father, looking round; "it seems you've all had bread and milk or something, and so can't eat anything."

Charley rose, darted into the buttery, and brought in the empty pan and bowls. I could have boxed his ears for betraying little family secrets; there never was a worse boy.

"See, Father," he said, "the mysterious cause of our lack of appetite. You were so late we couldn't wait."

"And now," rejoined Blanche in great glee, "if you only had my empty lunch-basket, the mystery would be wholly unravelled."

"You, too, were most starved?"

"Yes, Charley."

"And you had fortunately a lunch with you?"

"I had."

"It was your duty to dispose of it, and like the good little body you are, you performed your duty."

"It is enough to say," she laughingly answered, "when I reached Middleton my basket was empty."

"Let us shake hands again," he said, laying down the pan and bowls; "I too," he gravely added, "am faithful in discharging my duties, and am glad to meet one like me in this respect."

"Faithful," I exclaimed—the inclination to box his ears still strong within me—"when the duty is nothing more than the disposal of favorite dishes! When it is anything else, he generally contrives to shirk it."

Blanche again held out her hand. "Charley," she said, "we *must* be friends. With so many points of resemblance between us, it would be a shame if we were not."

"Then you, too, shirk disagreeable duties?" Father laughingly remarked.

"Sister Floy and Brother Will accuse me of it; but I do not, and will not admit it. In this non-admission, I believe there is still further resemblance between Charley and me."

"Indeed there is," Charley in high spirits rejoined. Father through his meal, they all but me repaired to the parlor. I staid to wash the dishes and reset the table. The breakfast was already prepared. It was not long before I joined them, and a delightful evening we had. Father told stories of his boyhood, in which her mother largely figured, and Blanche repeated several of her mother's of the same period in which Father shone as the principal character. Uncle Seth, whose hilarity had never before exceeded a grave smile, laughed more than once; and a pleasant, musical, no-way-rusty laugh it was. Our sweet Blanche enjoyed all this; but the family recitation of the Rosary, never

omitted in our humble home, we could see touched her deeply.
Her exquisite voice arose with ours in the glad carol of thanksgiving: *Holy God, we praise Thy Name*, which Uncle Seth entoned,
and we all sang in our untuned way, in gratitude for the many
mercies of the day.

From the first, Blanche was perfectly at home with us. Our
old house, with all its dilapidation, delighted her, it was so picturesque; our plainness did not distress her in the least,—we were
" free from shame, and therefore charming." What could be
more real than Beth's rose-leaf complexion and wealth of golden
hair! Charley called the latter carroty in hue, and Blanche boxed
his ears for his disrespect—and what would she not give if she
had Cousin Millie's lofty stature! As to Charley, though she had
now and then to chastise him, he was the dearest boy in the
world—so good natured, and so delightfully provoking. She did
not give her opinion of Uncle Seth. He seemed to puzzle her.
She asked about his workshop, and evidently did not know what
to make of our answers. He was engaged in some invention he
was trying to perfect. What invention, we did not know, therefore could not tell her. After this she appeared to stand in awe
of him. If he came in while we were laughing and talking, she
suddenly became silent; if in his quiet way he smiled or addressed any remark to her, she blushed, and stammered out some
little monosyllabic reply. Uncle was more absorbed in his mysterious labor than ever. From the window of my room I could
see his shop, and many a time on awaking in the small hours, and
glancing out, I saw its light still shining.

From the first Blanche had insisted on sharing our labors so
we could get through sooner, and be with her in her rambles
through field, orchard, and wood. In one of Beth's substantial
ginghams, with a bibbed apron before her, and sleeves rolled up,
she looked as dainty and winsome as in her summer silks and
muslins. And what a childish joy she showed when the pie or
pudding she made came out all right!

Thus the weeks passed. What a sunbeam she was in our old
home! How we loved the dear, cheery little cousin whose coming we had so much dreaded! At length a letter came, telling
her she must leave. How grief-stricken we all were! But

strange to say, none took it so bitterly as Uncle Seth. He had been looking very joyous of late; but the brightness faded from his face,—a wild sadness spread over it.

"Going home!" he hoarsely exclaimed. "Oh, it can't be! Just now, above all times."

Beth and I were surprised to see Blanche, who had seemed in such awe of him, step up and lay her little hand in his open palm.

"Mr. Hart," she tremulously said, "did you think I came here to stay always?"

"No," he answered, "I did not. I knew you only came to gladden us for awhile, and would then flit away, leaving only the memory of a glorious vision behind."

"Then you will remember me when I am gone?" she said, her beautiful eyes filling.

"Could I forget you if I would?" he answered. He opened his lips as if to say more, but without another word, turned and walked slowly, stiffly, out of the room.

I did not see him again till evening. I was in the kitchen preparing the breakfast. Father had gone to see one of the neighbors. Beth, Blanche, and Charley were in the parlor. We could hear Beth and Charley singing. Blanche's voice did not, as usual, blend with theirs. Uncle Seth did not join them; he preferred solitude. He sat silently watching my movements. I spoke, but he did not answer. At length, pausing in my work, I went up to him and laid my hand on his shoulder.

"Uncle," I said, "what has come over you? Father told me to-day you have got your machine at last all right, and that it will be a grand success. Why are you so cast down? I should think your heart would be full of joy and gratitude."

He started like one awakened from a troubled dream.

"I have been a fool!" he sententiously replied.

"No, a wise man," I rejoined; "one who has long and patiently labored with difficulties, and at last, with God's help, risen above them."

"Don't, Millie," he entreated; "don't mock me; I am a fool! a miserable fool!"

The singing in the parlor had ceased. Charley at this moment

burst out in a boisterous laugh. The windows and doors were
open. As the laugh died away, we heard him say:

"Uncle Seth a hero! Why he is only a dull, plodding soul,
without a thought or hope beyond that beloved machine he's
been pottering over for the last half dozen years. And to think
you should call him a hero, old, dull, and prosy as he is!" and again
his laugh rang out. Silence again restored, plainly Blanche's reply
reached us.

"Old, dull, and prosy!" she contemptuously repeated; "is that
what your highness considers him?"   :

"To be sure it is," he gaily answered.

"Then let me tell you you are a conceited monkey. He is
neither old, dull, nor prosy. You will yourself be old before him,
and you will never be so wise."

"Why, my precious little cousin?"

"Because," came the clear, incisive reply, "you are not so persevering, so industrious, so conscientious in using the powers
given you. You are only a rattle-headed boy now, and if you
don't mend, a few years hence will make a rattle-headed man,
incapable of appreciating true worth."

Uncle's pale cheek flushed. "This will not do," he remarked,
rising; "it seems like evesdropping to be listening when they do
not know it." He lighted his lamp, but before leaving, said:
"To-morrow, Millie, I am going away for a while. I take a heavy
heart with me. Your father is jubilant about my future."

"And you, Uncle, why are you not jubilant too?"

"Because, Millie, my hope is by no means clear. One moment
it flits before me a dazzling light; the next it is dark, extinguished,
and a despairing blackness enfolds me."

Was it Uncle Seth's invention that was thus affecting him? My
heart told me it was not. But his secret was safe with me. I
wanted to ask him where he was going, but his sad, pleading eyes
so plainly said "Don't" that I could not; I only told him I
would pray for him more fervently than ever.

"Do!" he exclaimed; "never before did I stand in such need of
heavenly aid." The door closed; he was gone; gone with his
hope and despair. I fell on my knees and wept passionately.
What had the future in store for him?

The next morning Uncle came down to breakfast ready dressed for his journey. He was to leave immediately after the meal. Beth and I could hardly restrain our tears; Blanche tried to be cheerful, but I noticed she hardly tasted a morsel. The meal over, Uncle's trunk was carried to the wagon standing at the gate; then he hurried back to the house to bid us good-bye. Blanche held out her hands. He took them, tenderly stroked them, and bending, left a warm kiss on each. Her lips trembled, tears filled her eyes; she attempted to speak, but her words ended in a sob. With one of her bird-like movements she flitted from the room.

Uncle had been gone an hour or more when she again made her appearance. Beth was in the kitchen, I in the cool dairy. She came to me. I was through packing the butter, and about to leave the dairy, but she piteously begged me to stay.

"I can't hear them here," she said.

"Hear what?" I asked.

"The clocks," she answered; "the house is so still I can hear them in my room, in the parlor, dining-room, and kitchen. They keep saying, gone, gone, gone, till I am fairly distracted."

"You miss Charley?" I innocently rejoined. He had insisted on going with Father and Uncle to the station.

"No, I don't," she indignantly retorted; "I am glad he is gone."

"You don't like him as much as you did at first," I remarked.

"Yes I do," she said, burying her face in her hands, and uttering a painful sigh, and after a brief pause:

"You have known your Uncle Seth a long time, Millie?"

"Yes, ever since I can remember. When I was a little girl he used to come and stay with us a week or two at a time. He was then a puny boy, undersized for his age, and still and quiet as he is now."

"Was he much given to reading?"

"No; his chief delight was whittling any stick or piece of board he could get hold of. I remember some slats Father had got for hen-coops that he whittled into arrows for some bows he had made. As arrows they were good for nothing. Father would have shaken him well for his whittling propensities, but Mother begged him off."

"Was he fond of play?" she asked, listening with evident pleasure to anything relating to him.

"No; he was too busy cutting and hacking things up to have time to play. Once he spoiled Father's best axe, cutting up a knotty board, and another time gave the death-blow to a saw Father greatly prized."

"Did Uncle punish him for it?"

"No; Father didn't find it out till he was gone, and by the time he came again his wrath had cooled."

"But he was great company to you, and you loved him dearly?"

"I don't know about that. I would have liked him better if he had been fond of romping plays. As it was, with his quiet ways he seemed more like a grandfather to me than a companion. Still, if I did not love him, I by no means hated him."

"No one could do that," she quickly rejoined.

The sun was now shining in through the dairy window. I closed the blind, and asked her if she thought she could stand again the ticking of the clocks. She blushed, laughed, and said she was ready to try. Accordingly we left the dairy. Beth had the dinner so well under way that I went at once to my room and wrote to Aunt Newell, asking her to leave Blanche with us a little longer. In the afternoon we would walk to the post-office, two miles away, and mail the letter.

Father and Charley were back in time for dinner. They were in high spirits, but reported Uncle as being unusually silent during the ride, and having hardly a word to say at the parting.

"I don't see what it means," said Father, making a vigorous onslaught on the dishes; "he was all hope when he couldn't make it work right, and now that it's a sure thing, and one likely to pay well, he goes moping about as if he hadn't a friend in the world. "I declare!" he exclaimed, viciously biting a pickle, "I could have shaken him for his glum looks when he bid us good-bye! I don't know what has come over him." The pickle went down, and, instead of increasing his asperity, it seemed to soften it.

"Poor boy!" he tenderly added; "maybe he is dazed at the success that has at last been vouchsafed him."

"Poor boy!" Blanche repeated; "then he does not seem old to you, Uncle?"

" No, Miss Blanche; and he isn't old."

" He is over thirty! " exclaimed Charley.

" Do you call that old, my boy? "

" Yes; old for Uncle Seth. But then he never was young. When he was a creeper he was old, old as the hills, and years and cares weighed him down."

" I suppose," Blanche remarked, " you saw him at that interesting period of his life."

" If I didn't," he gravely returned, " I can tell you just how he looked. He was toothless, bald-headed, and tottered when he tried to walk. If he wasn't deaf himself, he made every one around him deaf with his melodious howls."

Father listened in amazement. " I declare! " he exclaimed, " to hear that young imp one would think he had been apprenticed to Baron Vanchausen in his babyhood."

Charley laughed as if a compliment had been paid him. " Oh, dear me! " he said, moving back from the table, and settling himself comfortably in his chair, " I wonder if ever a bright, handsome little fairy will be ready to fight for me, as some one I could name but won't, is ready to fight for poor old Uncle Seth with all his prosy dulness." His eyes twinkled with mischief.

A crimson wave swept over Blanche's face, but mastering her emotions, she turned to Beth and gaily said:

" I can't reach Charley, but you are near him; will you do me the favor to give him a good screw pinch, as a mark of my especial regard for him? "

Beth, with the heartiest will, instantly complied. A roar from Charley followed.

" That is worthy of an encore! " cried Blanche, clapping her hands. Another pinch, another roar, and Charley beat a hasty retreat.

" If that is your regard for a fellow," he growled, leaving the dining-room, " I want no more of it, and I pity "—rubbing his arm—"any one who has it."

Father, on finishing his meal, had drawn a newspaper from his pocket, and, ensconced behind it, had neither seen nor heard anything for the last few moments. Now raising his eyes and seeing Charley go out, he peremptorily called him back.

"I suppose," said Charley, reluctantly obeying, "it's a pleasure to you to see me stung to death by these hornets."

"Hornets!" said Father, looking mystified, and glancing round; "I see none."

"I see them," petulantly returned Charley; "three full-sized and as vicious yellow-jackets as I ever met."

"That comes," said Father, in an irritated tone, "from your not minding me. I told you when you found that nest in the south barn the other day to destroy it instead of bringing it to the house."

"I did destroy it, I did not bring it to the house, and yet there are hornets here—spiteful, venomous ones, too."

With our merriment and Charley's distress Father was still mystified.

"I don't see, girls," he severely said, "if your brother has been stung, what you can find laughable in it."

"But he's not been stung," said Beth, trying in vain to say it gravely; "he's only been pinched, as he well deserved to be. Millie, Blanche, and I are the hornets he means." With a satisfied "eh! eh!" Father, forgetting to tell why he called Charley back, was again fathoms deep in his paper.

"And a nice brother and cousin he is to call us that," said Blanche, trying to draw an injured look to her mirthful face. "If he would only come within reach of my fingers, I assure him, with the kindest interest in his future welfare, that he would be stung right royally. Come, Charley," she entreated, holding out her fingers, ready for the stinging business; "come and be stung again. That's a good boy, come."

"If I did come," he answered without stirring, "maybe you would find I could sting, too." Then as if it was a subject he had trifled with long enough, he turned to Father, and in a business tone remarked: "I believe you wanted me to take the horses to the blacksmith's this afternoon?"

"Yes," said Father, from behind his paper, "and tell Brown to see that the shoes are right. Roan's feet are tender, and I believe it's because the shoes hurt her."

With an air of pity for our childish levity, Charley went to the stable.

A few days brought Aunt's answer, graciously permitting Blanche to prolong her visit.

As the weeks passed, and we heard nothing from Uncle Seth, we wondered what the silence meant. A thousand fears beset us. Was his invention something no one cared for? Were all the hopes founded on it to prove mocking illusions? Why didn't he write? Why leave us in such cruel suspense? Our afternoon rambles in the fields and woods were given up. In our anxiety we could no longer enjoy them. Blanche began to droop; when we expressed a fear that she was getting home-sick she stoutly denied it. She had never been so happy as since she came to us, and, leaving us, would never be happy again. I knew why, but dared not hint it to her. Dear little cousin had lost her heart; it was in Uncle Seth's possession. Did she know she had his in return? I doubted it. She might now and then have a faint suspicion of the fact, but it was a suspicion,—no certainty. I wondered how her proud, pompous father would look on the attachment. Not very favorably, I feared. 'Tis true, with his invention perfected, Uncle Seth might be considered a rising man; but he had not yet risen, and never might. Able to invent, he might lack the business tact to push his invention forward. The more I pondered the matter, the less hope I had for the success of his suit, and the after happiness of Blanche. With her warm, generous impulses, she would probably be offered up a sacrifice to mammon, the modern Moloch.

Aunt Newell's letters had at first been long and frank: though still kind, they were now short and reserved. I asked Blanche what was the burden of her letters to her mother.

" How bad we all feel for your Uncle Seth's silence and prolonged absence," was her guileless reply.

That brevity and reserve had then for me a sinister meaning.

The shortened days of October, with their mournful winds, fitful showers, and scudding clouds, had come. Blanche, Beth, and I were in the dining-room, which, since the chill of autumn, was also our sitting-room, sewing and trying to make talk, when we heard the rumbling of wheels. We glanced out, and saw a carriage drive up the broad path, and stop before the front door. The next instant Uncle Seth, with a buoyant step, alighted; then came Aunt and Uncle Newell. We rushed out, and what joy, what confusion there was! Uncle Seth kissed Beth and me, and folded Blanche to his heart. We shook hands over and over again with Aunt and Uncle Newell, while Blanche hugged them and danced round them like one demented. I don't know how we got into the house again, but I know we were there when Father and Charley came in from the fields, and there was again a joyous clatter and confusion of tongues.

. That evening, seated round a cosy fire in the parlor, the breath of winter already in the air made a fire necessary to enjoyment, we heard the history of Uncle Seth's success. His invention was not as we had supposed, a labor-saving farm machine, but something relating to the working and managing of cars. The patent secured, with a letter of introduction from Father—to think of Father keeping from us the writing of that letter!—he called on Uncle Newell; Uncle Newell, at once seeing the importance of his invention, made it his business to consult the right parties about it. Some "circumlocution office" aggravations followed, but in the end its merit was acknowledged, and Uncle Seth put in the way of making what Uncle Newell termed a good job of it. , This happily accomplished, Uncle Seth was encouraged to lay another matter before him. With the fine fortune looming up before him, and the social position said fortune would give him, it was favorably considered. Result : Uncle Seth and Cousin Blanche were the happiest of mortals. They all remained with us a week. At leaving, Uncle Seth put a sealed packet in Father's hand; on opening it, an hour or so after their departure, he found the mortgage on our farm had been lifted. We couldn't keep back the tears at this mark of his thoughtful kindness. And, oh, how lonely we felt when they were gone; how sad and silent the old house! Some six weeks later—no " circumlocution office " ways here— we were bidden to one of the most aristocratic weddings in New York. Beth and I, in splendid robes of Aunt's providing, were among the bridesmaids, and Charley, beardless boy that he was, in elegant suit, one of the groomsmen.

We liked our cousins, Florence and Will, but they could never take the place of dear, loving, winsome Blanche in our affections.

, Before she and Uncle Seth visited us again we had the old

house thoroughly repaired, and refurnished throughout. If this made no difference to them, it was a great satisfaction to Beth and me.

It was close work, but everything was ready for Christmas, and the holy season was indeed a merry one, for we had the two dear ones with us. Success had taken years from Uncle Seth, and he did not seem at all too old for our darling girl, Blanche.

There is a matter that troubles Charley a great deal. It is this: While Uncle Seth and Cousin Blanche were no way related, the former on our mother's, the latter on our father's side, were respectively uncle and cousin to us; now, by their marriage, has Uncle Seth become our cousin, or Cousin Blanche our aunt? I hope some one will be able to settle the matter for him before his brain is irrecoverably injured.

TOWER OF IVORY.

EUGENE DAVIS.

SAINTLY Tower, fairer by far than aught
   Born of the mind, wrought by the hand of man:
Through the unnumbered ages' circling span—
Through endless space mortals had vainly sought,
Peering with hope, for one sweet glimpse of thee ;
   For thee the prophets pined, the sages yearned,
   And eyes grew dim with tears, and bosoms burned,
And suppliant hands were raised from sea to sea.

Till on Judea's plains one blessed day
   Thy dazzling beauty, wonderful to see,
Void of the taint of this, our mortal clay,
   Carved by God's skill, made sin's poor bondsmen free!
May thy pure light shine on us here alway,
   Lamp of the soul! loved Tow'r of Ivory!

SKETCHES OF VENEZUELA.

Rev. Bertrand Cothonay, O. P.

II.

IUDAD-BOLIVAR, or Bolivar's city, is the capital of the state of Bolivar. This town was founded in 1764, by Joachim Moreno de Mendoza, and was called at that time by the name of Saint Thomas of Guiana. It is situated on the slope of a rugged hill on the right bank of the Orinoco. It stands at the moderate height of 57 metres above the level of the ocean; its mean temperature is 25 degrees centigrade. Its population is about 12,000. Previous to 1846, this town was called Saint Thomas of Angostura, on account of the relative narrowness of the river at this place. In fact, the Orinoco, which has a mean width of 3 to 4 kilometres, is but 734 metres wide in front of Ciudad-Bolivar, owing to the confinement of the river between the rocky hills, whence it rushes down as a torrent.

The Orinoco is one of the most majestic rivers of the world. The province of Guiana, through which it passes, is of remarkable fertility, is covered with forests of valuable wood, and contains gold mines of immense value. The future prosperity of Venezuela depends mainly on this part of the country. But the very fact of the wealth of this region has made it a bone of contention between England and Venezuela. The title to that vast tract of land, extending between the Orinoco and British Guiana, and inhabited but by an insignificant number of people, is claimed by the rival Governments. Venezuela seems likely to claim its rights, but England has the upper hand. If it be true that Venezuela has gained the succession to the rights of Spain in these quarters, this shall convince us the more of the legitimacy of Venezuela's claims, it being a known fact that Spain possessed these lands, and had established flourishing missions upon them. But it may be asked, why has Venezuela brought about the ruin of these missions,

POTOSI, REGION OF THE MINES, LA GUYANA, VENEZUELA.

massacred the missionaries, and driven the native Indians to different parts? Here we presume to note an additional proof of the historical fact, that war against God and against His Church has never brought prosperity to any nation. After all, the English have done no more than to take possession of abandoned and unproductive grounds. They came forward to protect some British companies legally settled in these quarters, and, besides, they have declared rights of ancient date. Who can prevent them from laying hold of this gold-producing portion of Guiana? Who even could prevent them from numbering the whole of Venezuela among their colonial possessions?

Ciudad-Bolivar is a bishopric first erected in 1790, and most creditably administered at present by Bishop Duran, consecrated at Caracas on the 6th of December, 1891. The immediate predecessor of this prelate was the late Bishop Rodriguez, who died prematurely after an Episcopal career of only two years.

Guanare, capital of the state of Zamora, is a town of some eleven or twelve thousand inhabitants. Its foundation dates from 1593. It lies upon the slope of a hill, and is surrounded by a plain which is 143 metres above the level of the sea. Its climate is salubrious, although hot. The mean temperature is 28 degrees centigrade.

Barquisimeto, founded in 1552, and first called New-Segovia, is the chief town in the state of Lara. It stands on an elevation 522 metres above the level of the sea, in a vast plain at the junction of the Carabobo and Zamora high-roads. This town is likewise one of the five bishoprics of the Republic. The first Bishop appointed to this diocese was Mgr. Victor José Diez, who died recently at an advanced age.

Barquisimeto has 32,000 inhabitants; its climate is healthful, and the highest degree of temperature ever observed is known to be 29 degrees centigrade. Towards the lower part of the town there are some very fine estates, situated in a luxuriant valley, watered by the river which flows to the south of the city. A railway line unites this capital with the port of Tucacas.

Capatarida, although small and unimportant, is the capital of the state of Falcon. This petty capital stands at the inconsiderable height of 11 metres above the level of the sea, and at about 2 kilometres' distance from the mouth of the river whose name it bears. The population is 3,600. This town, it seems, has deserved the title of capital chiefly on account of its favorable position; it stands almost at an equal distance from Coro and Maracaïbo.

Coro, the first of these last-named towns, was founded by Juan de Ampies, in 1527. This was the second settlement of the Spaniards on the mainland. This town remained, till 1578, the capital of Venezuela. It was also, during that period, the only bishopric of the country. The fifth bishop of this diocese, Rt. Rev. Juan Martinez Manzanillo, of the Order of the Friars-Preachers, after the plundering of the town by the English in 1577, had the Bishopric transferred to Caracas, where the government of the Colony had already fixed its residence.

Maracaïbo, situated on the bank of the large and beautiful lake of the same name, is a town of 35,000 inhabitants. At the time of its foundation by Alonzo Pacheco, in 1571, it was known by the name of New-Zamora. It stands at a height of nine metres above the level of the sea, and its mean temperature is 27 degrees and 50 minutes centigrade. The appearance presented by this town is very pleasing. A profusion of palm and cocoanut trees envelops it as in a mantle of verdure.

Merida, the capital of the state of the Andes, was founded in 1558, and then called "Santiago de los Caballeros de Merida." This town stands at an altitude of 1660 metres, and its climate is cold and moist. Merida is encircled by a majestic chain of mountains covered with perpetual snow. The highest peak of the Andes in this section is " El Toro," 4,950 metres above the ocean. The town is said to have 13,000 inhabitants. It is a bishopric, erected, in 1778, by Pius VI. Since the year 1880 the diocese is governed by Bishop Roman Lovera, one of the most distinguished prelates of the Republic.[1]

There are several other towns of some importance besides those already named. The following are worthy of mention: Saint Lucia, which, during the present year, will secure communication with Caracas by means of a railway under the control of a Brit-

---

[1] This distinguished prelate died recently.

ish company; Victoria and Calabozo, in the state of Miranda—
Calabozo is a bishop's See, erected in 1847. Bishop Felipe N. Send-
rea is at present in charge of this diocese. Cumana, Carupano,
and Maturin are situated in the state of Bermudez; San Fernando,
San Felipe, Carora, and Tocuyo in that of Lara; Trujillo and San
Cristobal in that of the Andes, etc.

As far as religion is concerned, there is still much to be done
in Venezuela. Since the wars of Independence, the persecution
waged against the clergy has greatly diminished the influence of
religion upon the people. Since that time, irreligious books,
brought over from Europe, have been disseminated throughout
the country in such prodigality as to engender a lawless and immoral press. On many occasions the Catholics have tried, not
however, without timidity and excessive moderation, to assume
their rights in the liberty of the press, which their enemies had
been greatly abusing. It must be said that the modest exertions
displayed by these Catholic papers were of no long duration.

Within the last two years a creditable daily paper has been edited at Caracas, under more able management, and it continues to
exert a beneficial influence. This paper is known by the name of
" La Religión." It bears, as heading, the engraving of St. Peter's
church of Rome, with the words " Diario Católico," and a little
lower down are to be read these other words of dedication: " Under the patronage of the Sacred Heart of Jesus." Its editors deserve the title of Confessors of the Faith, inasmuch as they have
suffered imprisonment and banishment for God's holy cause; besides, they are men of learning and piety, the standard-bearers of
religion, who, whilst showing to Catholics the way of salvation,
fearlessly chide their adversaries for their adherence to ignorance,
unreasonableness, and insincerity. This journal has a wide circulation, and has given evident proofs of being a benefit to the country. It is furthermore destined, with God's help, as we confidently
hope, to bring about the regeneration of the whole of Venezuela.

On account of the revolutions and persecutions which have dispersed religious communities, molested the clergy, and suppressed the seminaries, the number of priests left is by far too
small to meet the wants of the people, and to withstand the flow
of evil which threatens to do away with faith and morals.

THE VILLAGE OF NEW PROVIDENCE, IN THE REGION OF THE MINES, LA GUYANA, VENEZUELA.

Hence, the people are for the most part uninstructed, especially in the country districts. Their faith still survives, but there is much to be done as regards their Christian duties. Attendance at Mass and the reception of the sacraments are greatly neglected. However, the old Spanish faith is not completely dead; Venezuelans have preserved all the exterior rites of religious worship; for instance: they take special delight in processions and in their patron saints' festivals, which they celebrate with mirth amid grand display of music and fireworks. The people pay great reverence to the crucifix and all sacred images; they also retain the good old practice of asking the priest's blessing, whenever they can do so, even in the streets, etc.

The faith of this Spanish race has taken such deep root, that it reproves heresy almost by instinct. Protestant preachers have endeavored on divers occasions to introduce their religion into Venezuela, but without success. Some fifteen years ago, Rev. Rawle, the Anglican bishop of Trinidad, made a last attempt at Caracas, on the instigation of Guzman Blanco. The honorable clergyman had even brought over his wife with him, which circumstance was somewhat attended with bad luck. The youth of Caracas mocked them, and pursued them with taunting jests. The couple could not be seen in the streets without being hooted at, and even assaulted with projectiles, most improper in themselves, if not very dangerous. Some young vagabonds even presumed to ask a blessing from the Rev. gentleman's lady, a circumstance to which she was not accustomed. In consequence of these vexatious circumstances, and such an inhospitable reception, Bishop Rawle thought it more prudent to retire, and he never came back.

It is not very easy to express any opinion upon the characteristic habits of a people, or of a country, without having led, for months, or even years, the life of the people of whom we speak. This being so, I am the first to own that the remarks I have made in these excursion notes can scarcely be perfectly exact.

Venezuelans have preserved, to a certain extent, the pride and courage of the Spanish race. In the annals of the wars of the country, feats of true heroism and of magnanimity are not wanting. Moreover, the Venezuelan is generally sweet-tempered, affording the most cordial hospitality to strangers, although at first sight he may seem to be distrustful.

The general aspect of a Venezuelan town is of a somewhat suspicious and mysterious character. A double door leads to the entrance of every dwelling. After passing the second door, the visitor has not yet entered the house, properly speaking. The place in which he stands is the yard, always necessarily enclosed, in every Venezuelan dwelling, with shrubs and plants to protect the interior of the house and its inmates from the indiscreet looks of passers-by. Hence it is impossible to cast a glance into the apartments of the house while passing through the streets. Nor can thieves effect an entrance, for the windows, situated a foot above the pavement, are made fast with iron bars, behind which hangs a thick curtain. If this way of constructing windows be inconvenient to the passers-by, it fosters to a great extent the curiosity of the inmates of the house. In the evening especially, one cannot take a step in the streets without perceiving, behind the iron bars and lattice-work, the faces of Venezuelan women, framed in, as it were, by the muslin and lace of the curtains, and gazing on all who chance to pass in the street. It is surprising to think of the amount of time which the women of Caracas lose in vain curiosity from their lattice windows.

The families of high extraction have preserved the polite manners of the great families of Spain; these refined manners frequently degenerate into affectation. These distinguished personages are likewise said to be arrogant and disdainful; the influential as well as the rich, when sprung from an inferior lineage, are not easily admitted to any family relations with them. This high class of Venezuelans have raised to its highest degree the scruple of relationship by marriage. No wonder that we find among them some individuals of rare beauty.

The middle class, to which belong most of the politicians, commercial men, etc., is largely made up of strangers, adventurers, and self-made men whose prosperity is frequently the result of ill-gotten gains. It is in this manner that the richest of the land have made their way. Persons of mixed descent are not uncommon in this social class. Irreligion is most prevalent among them; the women especially, have but a scanty appearance of even outward faith.

COVINA, A PASSAGE OPENED IN THE FOREST, IN THE REGION OF THE MINES, LA GUYANA, VENEZUELA.

The common people, which includes by far the greatest portion of the population, is made up of the descendants of the Indians variegated with African and Spanish blood in a great diversity of proportions. They were converted to the true faith by missionaries. Here, as elsewhere, and more perhaps than elsewhere, the lower class is speculated upon. Slavery is abolished in principle, but in point of fact, judging from daily occurrences, it may be said that the people are subject to an intolerable bondage.

In Europe, dwellings of the country people are palaces compared with those of the Venezuelan peasantry. As regards clothing and food, our European peasants are kings when confronted with the Venezuelan rustic, whose scanty habit is all in tatters. Here the ordinary food consists of " arepa," a sort of bread made out of Indian corn. On feast days the treat consists of some fried bananas, and from time to time is added the delicious dish of "caraotas negras," or black peas. I succeeded in gaining admission to some of these huts, and invariably found them very dirty, and in the greatest disorder. A pig-sty occasionally occupies an entire half of the house, whilst in the other part some half-naked children are to be seen crawling about. The household utensils are laid down, pell-mell, with soiled clothes, a broken bench and a mat, which is stretched out at night for the family to sleep upon.

As a rule, the peasant does not even own the portion of ground occupied by his hut; his work is for the benefit of a rich man, who gives him in return such scanty pay as scarcely suffices for the purchase of the most necessary and indispensable articles. All such articles of commerce as are really requisite for his clothing, his dwelling, or his food, are out of his reach.

This race does not at all resemble our strong French peasants; their very mien excites pity.

I once asked a porter, who groaned whilst carrying my small valise, if he were not strong. "Oh!" he made answer, "you are all strong men, because you have much wheat-bread to eat."

In truth, wheat-bread is a luxury little known to these wretched people.

They are generally good and peaceable, but extremely ignorant. One of them, a strapping fellow of twenty-five or thirty years,

made his confession to me, some moments before receiving the
sacrament of Confirmation. He was unable to name the Persons
of the Blessed Trinity. Another named St. Joseph as forming
part of the Blessed Trinity. A third owned that he had never heard
of such a thing as the Blessed Trinity. Alas! it is not the fault
of the poor people. They have among them but a small number
of priests, and the Government has not been doing much, up to
this time, for their instruction and moral training.

There are certain things, however, which seem to be luxurious
in themselves, and which even the poorest of the land cannot do
without. For instance, the use of coffee, chocolate, and tobacco
is much more extensive than in our country. This last-named
article especially, is of such common usage that rarely one finds
a person not addicted to smoking. Women, as well as men, smoke
anywhere, and almost continually. By the grated window or near
the gateway, the country woman may be seen with her lighted
cigar ; the nurse goes about the walks, tending the children,
with a tobacco pipe in her mouth ; the village woman mounted
on her donkey and making for the market to sell her vegetables,
seems to prevent the fatigue of the road by indulging in an agreeable smoke.

The malady of the Athenians, who were said to spend the live-
long day in gossiping, is quite prevalent in Venezuela. The most
minute events occurring in Caracas, especially in the way of
politics, is commented upon, exaggerated, and known in no time
to almost everybody.

" News," as Perez, a humorous author, says, " is the incentive
which keeps up the enthusiasm of the people. No wonder that
town conspirators, who are as numerous as those who are without
employment, invent a hundred wild events each day! Strange to
say, the inventor of such news finds it so much changed and dis-
figured the next day, that it seems to be an entirely different occurrence, and as such he gives it credence."

" I have known persons," writes the same author, " who count
the day as lost which does not bring to their ears the recital of
some scandalous occurrence."

As may be seen, Perez does not flatter his countrymen.

I was invited to take part in the patronal feast of a parish. I sincerely hailed the occasion, for it afforded me a pleasant walk, besides, it enabled me to study at leisure the habits of the people, and also it gave me the opportunity of performing an act of devotion.   It was the festival of Saint Lucia.

Accordingly I set out for the small city which is called by the name of the virgin of Syracuse.   This small city stands on the banks of the Guayré river, and is situated in the same valley as the city of Caracas, but fifteen leagues distant.

An English company has undertaken to establish railway communication between these cities, but the work, which is only half completed, is suspended for the present.   The train crosses a fertile plain, covered with luxuriant coffee estates, until it reaches the small town of Petare.   Here the valley becomes narrow, and is changed into a dreadful wilderness.   The train descends a steep declivity, passes over viaducts of extreme length and bold structure, and winds around so many curves as to make the passengers sea-sick.   For a distance of ten kilometres along the mountain-side, not a hut is to be met with in this savage gorge. On either side of the valley huge masses of rock are seen suspended, sometimes perpendicularly overhead.   In a certain passage by the name of " el encantado," where formerly there was a cascade, the mountain has given way into the torrent, and so the Guayré flows as best it can beneath immense masses of rock, half-covered with an exuberant vegetation.

After two hours of travel amid such frightful scenes, the train puts down the passengers in a desert and lonely tract of land, called " Los Mangos" from the couple of wretched mango trees which are to be found there.   For the time being this is the railway terminus.   I succeeded in obtaining an animal with which to perform the remainder of my journey to Saint Lucia.   The entire distance left to be traversed was some 19 kilometres, which afforded me a ride of two hours and a half.   After an hour's ride in the same savage pass, the valley became wider, and at length I found myself in the midst of an extensive plain.   Shortly before reaching the town I came to an elevation, whence I enjoyed a most delightful view.   I gazed down below upon the river, grumbling slowly along, winding across a great many small, green valleys which rise, in a crown of graceful and luxuriant hills, to the plain in the middle of which I stood, and also to all the country around at a considerable distance.

Saint Lucia I found to be a small town containing some four or five thousand inhabitants, and the parish some ten or twelve thousand scattered about over an extent of fifteen square leagues. Some years past this region was under better cultivation, and its population larger, by at least five thousand inhabitants. For the last ten years the plague of locusts has greatly reduced the prosperity of this place, and lessened the number of its inhabitants. Nevertheless, the " junta directiva," or committee in charge of the festival, had collected about 3,000 francs to be spent for the decoration of the church, for fireworks and feasts, to remunerate the three panegyrists of the patroness of the parish, as also to meet the expenses of three Masses accompanied with the orchestra, and for a series of amusements, such as bull-fights, balls, etc. It must be observed that the people have no scruple in combining the sacred with the profane!

The festival was to take place on December 13, but already on the 12th, at five o'clock in the morning, there was High Mass, with orchestra, in due form. I, then, said Mass, and was astonished to find the church filled with people at such an early hour, although the parish priest had told me that on ordinary Sundays the attendance rarely exceeded forty persons.

That same day, the eve of the festival, Archbishop Crispulo Uzcátegui arrived, accompanied by several priests, and some distinguished gentlemen who had gone to meet him. His Grace would add all possible lustre to the religious festivity celebrated in honor of Saint Lucy; he also intended to utilize the opportunity in making the pastoral visit of the parish. The Archbishop of Caracas was solemnly received. Upon entering the town he put on the pontifical vestments. Wearing the mitre, and carrying the pastoral staff and a heavy reliquary, he walked a quarter of a mile beneath a tropical sun with the temperature at 38 degrees centigrade. A number of young girls threw flowers upon the way as he passed, whilst the vast congregation hailed him with cheers, amidst the singing of the clergy and the display of fireworks in his honor.

At the close of the ceremonies performed inside the church,

the civil manager entertained the Archbishop and his suite in the vestry, where he greeted His Grace's welcome arrival in a long, elaborate speech, carefully learned by heart. The orator's first words were: "May it please your Grace:—As the morning dew imparts beauty, vigor, and life to the half-open buds on which it falls, so does your Grace...."

The benevolent prelate replied at length, after which he was invited to take breakfast. It was four o'clock in the afternoon.

The grand display of sky-rockets and fireworks took place on Saturday, December 12, immediately after the church service, at which the young parish priest of Ocumare preached. The square in front of the church was brilliantly illuminated with Venetian lanterns. For the space of two whole hours there was a deafening uproar; crowds of people obstructed the paths, the band played, the bells rang, tremendous discharges of petards resounded in the air, and the multitude, dazzled at the sight of balloons which rushed far on high, broke out into exclamations of joy that announced to the ethereal regions the jubilee of Saint Lucy's parish. It was impossible to think of sleep before midnight; moreover, the following night would witness a repetition of the scene.

At four o'clock, on the morning of the 13th, the joyous bells announced to all the country round, the expected dawn of the festival day. The discharge of petards and fireworks carried the general enthusiasm to its highest pitch. At seven, His Grace, the Archbishop, said Mass, which was accompanied by music. At ten o'clock, after the hour of Tierce, a solemn High Mass took place, with an increase of the orchestra, and of all sorts of musical instruments. The Rev. Aimenes, parish priest of Saint Theresa's, delivered the sermon. All was over at noon. In the evening the sacraments of Baptism and Confirmation were administered.

Nothing in our land bears less resemblance to the administration of the sacrament of Confirmation than the performance of this same ceremony in Venezuela, where doubtless on account of the scarcity of visits, the Bishops are in the habit of administering this sacrament to all those who are brought before them, from the infant of thirty days, to the decrepit old man of eighty years who has not yet received the strengthening ointment of the life-giving Spirit.   But by far the greater number of those confirmed are mere infants of some months, or children only a few years old.   Last Sunday, in the Church of Saint Lucy's parish, there were about two hundred of these who screamed together, whilst the prelate made the round in bestowing upon each one of them the grace of the Holy Ghost.   This is a scene worth witnessing at least once during a life-time.

On Sunday night, December 13, the procession of the statue of Saint Lucy took place, mounted upon a magnificent throne, decorated with flowers and lights.   Fifteen men served as bearers, and walked under the ornamental hangings of the throne in such measured pace that we spent two hours to make but a short cut around the market-place.   The square was again brilliantly illuminated; the night was calm and beautiful.   An enthusiastic crowd followed the statue, which towered above their heads, and seemed to smile upon them.   The gay chime of bells, the unavoidable rockets, the harmonious strains of the orchestra, afforded to the nocturnal procession in which several thousands of people assisted, a character " sui generis "—the peculiar character of the locality.   Whilst the procession was passing, the exclamation " Que bonito " (how fine it is!) was heard on all sides.

A sermon was delivered at the close of this long ceremony, and about midnight, when all was over, the people withdrew, and then only could one think of sleep.

According to the programme, Monday, Tuesday, and Wednesday were considered as holidays, during which were to take place the bull races, as well as the procession on the river side, the bathing of the statue, balls, etc.   But as regards myself, I had enough of it, and accordingly at six o'clock on Monday morning, December 14, I mounted on horseback, and made for Los Mangos, situated at 19 kilometers' distance.   I arrived in time to take the train for Caracas.

At last Thou art come, little Saviour !
  And Thine angels fill midnight with song ;
Thou art come to us, gentle Creator !
  Whom Thy creatures have sighed for so long.

Thou art come to Thy beautiful Mother ;
  She hath looked on Thy marvellous face ;
Thou art come to us, Maker of Mary !
  And she was Thy channel of grace.

Hail, Mary's Little One,
Hail, God's Eternal Son,
Sweet Babe of Bethlehem !—*Father Faber.*

A CHRISTMAS MORNING SONG.

IN A DOMINICAN CONVENT REFECTORY.

ANNIE CHAMBERS-KETCHUM.

OOD will and peace!
We sing the sweetest song of all,
First sung in Bethlehem's stable stall;
We sing of Him who filled it first,
The Christmas cup for all who thirst—
Good will and peace!

Good health to thee,
Our Mother, Lady Bountiful,
Beneath whose wise and gentle rule
Each heart to-day set free
From care and pain, exults and sings
Until we almost look to see
Some raptured Sister speed her wings
And soar away
To keep the eternal Christmas Day!

Good health to you,
Dear Sisters of the holy choir!
Child Jesus, set our hearts on fire!
Inflame the mind, instruct the tongue
That psalm and hymn be rightly sung;
So we, with reverence true,
May chant the glories of the Godhead Trine
In presence of the Majesty Divine.

Good health, we pray,
To you, lay-Sisters kind, who spread
This earthly feast to-day!
(For earthly saints must still be fed

Along the earthly way.)
O ye so near our Lord!
Ye household saints, without whose care
Our work would fail in praise or prayer,
 Beseech Him to accord
Each one of us some measure of your grace,
That, toiling on in our appointed place,
 To us it may be given
Labor and pain with equal mind to bear,
Until with you we may be called to share
 The Christmas feast in Heaven.

 Good health to long-eared Mick,
Who jogs, albeit we must confess,
With rather too leisurely gait for express.
 Though his pace may never be double-quick,
  May his shadow never grow less!
And Sukey and Brindle, whose butter and milk
 Have set off this table with right good cheer,
May their new coats come out as fine as silk
 In the sweet Pasque-time of the year.
O all ye beasts and cattle! say
Your Christmas Benedicite!

 Good will and peace!
Child Jesus, begotten before all time,
 Child Jesus, born to-day,
Bless all our nonsense of joke and rhyme,
And antic and prattle and trick and mime
 This merry Christmas Day!
Let each deed, whether of work or play,
Be a step in that ladder by which we climb
  To the heights of peace,
  To the skies of joy,
To the Stronghold no foe shall ever assail,
To the Table whose viands shall never fail,
 To the Christmas Cup without alloy,
  To the Rest that shall never cease.

OUR LADY'S ROSARY.

VERY REV. THOMAS ESSER, O. P.

OUTER FORM (MECHANISM) OF THE HOLY ROSARY. VINDICATION OF THE SAME.

> " Invan sono in più secoli, ed ínvano
> Sonerà ancor di cieche menti il riso,
> Che il bel culto a Maria chiamano insano."
> —*Silvio Pellico.*

To the exposition of what the Rosary is in itself, there yet remains to be added, for the sake of completeness, a more detailed examination of its outer form, or what may be called its mechanism. We have here to do with the mode and method in which we outwardly tell off the prayers of the Rosary. Two things, then, must be taken into account. the frequent repetition of the Hail Mary, and the computation on the beads. Since the attacks of unbelief and unreason have all along been directed against just these points, we cannot but stand upon the defensive in our treatment of them. And as our vindication of the Rosary has chiefly a practical end in view, we may almost entirely pass over the objections brought forward on the part of heretics.

1. From its origin, the Marian Psalter has been the target against which infidels and heretics and scoffers, and all, indeed, that have broken with the Church, have aimed their poisonous missiles. For what is the recitation of the Rosary but a thorough *Credo* of right faith, and the beads we carry about with us, but an open profession of our Catholicism?

Protestantism, rising up against the honor paid by Catholics to the Mother of God, naturally had to take a foremost position in the ranks against this most beautiful of Marian devotions, the Holy Rosary. "At the Reformation," thus speaks a Protestant, "this devotion (of the Rosary) wholly strange to antiquity, was

4

most vigorously denounced, as may be seen in Luther's writings, in the Augsburg Confession, and in the Schmalkaldic Articles." [1] To adduce but one of the wonted sententious passages of the " dear man of God," Martin Luther: " All, indeed," he says, " curse her (Mary's) fruit, who curse and persecute Christ's word, the Gospel and the Faith, as now do the Jews and Papists. It follows then that no one now so almost curses this mother and her fruit as those who bless her with many rosaries, and who always have the Hail Mary in their mouth; for it is they who most curse the word and faith of Christ." [2]

And yet the Rosary itself is the most telling refutation of the reasons that Protestants oppose to Catholic worship of Mary. For the honor we pay to the Mother of God is not otherwise, is not less nor yet greater than that which was paid to her by the Archangel Gabriel at the injunction of the Most Blessed Trinity. Let, then, those who reproach us with praying to Mary first cast their reproach, if they have the heart to do it, on God's messenger, whose words we have but learned to repeat.

That we do not expect to be saved by Mary as by an efficient cause is most apparent in the Rosary itself. For in it we only call upon Mary to be the mediatrix between us and her Divine Son, while, in its mysteries, Christ's work of the Redemption is made the special, exclusive subject of our meditations. It was Jesus who bore the heavy Cross for us. It was Jesus who was crucified for us; but as He was the blessed Fruit of her womb, we turn to her with the words, " Mother of God, pray for us." Nor even that before we have addressed the Lord's Prayer to our Father who is in Heaven, and to His Son, who is one essence with Him. But that we address Mary ten times, and God but once, in each decade of this prayer, is surely sufficiently explained when we say that the Rosary is, above all, a devotion in her honor. Moreover, even when we show her special honor, we do not separate her from her Divine Son, nor even think of her as separated from Him. In the Rosary mysteries we consider Mary's life only in so far as it begins with, bears upon, and is coincident

---

[1] Augusti. Denkwürdigkeiten aus der christlichen Archæologie. Leipzig, 1817-31, v. 133.

[2] Luther's Samtliche Werke. Erlangen, 1828, xv., 298.

with, the life of our Blessed Redeemer Himself.   Therefore it is,
too, that we preface our greetings to her with the Our Father.
"Yet people sometimes thoughtlessly speak as if devotion to the
Mother was a little trifle allowably cut off from devotion to the
Son; that it was something surrendered by Jesus to Mary; that
Jesus was one thing and Mary was another, and that devotion to
the two was to be divided between them, proportionately to
their respective dignities,—say a pound to Him and an ounce to
her.   If such persons really saw what they mean, which they do
not, they would perceive that they were talking impiety."[1]   The
famous convert, Frederick Von Hurter, makes mention of a sermon by the renowned pulpit orator, Father Ventura, which he
heard before his conversion, the last night of the May devotions
in 1844, in the Theatine Church at Rome.   "At the close," thus
does he describe his impression, "he (the preacher) touched
upon the Rosary, and clearly showed that it is impossible to practice this devotion without at the same time being forcibly reminded of the highest mysteries that are associated with the person of the Redeemer.   Consequently the reproach is vain, that
by making so much of the Mother, the Son is quite forgotten."[2]
Beautifully says the Protestant poet, Lavater :

> "When the Ave Marys ring,
> Is it not to Thee they sing ?"—i. e., to Jesus.[3]

We will therefore pass over a further detailed consideration of
the objections advanced by heretical opponents of the Rosary, in
order to turn to those directed against our devotion from another
standpoint : from that, namely, of the movement known under
the name of illuminism.

2. There was a time, not long past, that boasted this movement. Its supporters, looking with disfavor upon what they
chose to call the antiquated lumber of Catholic worship, that was
no longer in touch with the times, undertook to do away with it,

---

[1] Faber. All for Jesus. 4 ed. London, 1854, p. 154.

[2] Hurter. Geburt und Wiedergeburt. Erinnerungen, etc. Schaffhausen.
(3). 1849, ii., 471.

[3] "Wenn die Ave Maria schallen,
Bist Du's nicht dem sie wiederhallen?"
—Gedichte. Winterthur, 1785, p. 61.

and seriously set about to bring the Church, and above all, the forms of her cult, into harmony with modern requirements. In proposals to compile a new Catholic catechism, not even the Hail Mary, the chief component part of the Rosary, was spared. " The Hail Mary," it was unblushingly said, "being a private prayer, and not having any connection with our religion, as the Lord's Prayer, must silently be dropped in all Christian catechetical instructions." [1]

By these reformatory efforts, the Rosary, of course, could not hope to remain unaffected. In the so-called "contributions to the betterment of the exterior worship of the Catholic Church," [2] it was openly stated : "We wish to see the Rosary totally proscribed. Devotion cannot possibly hold out so long. The telling of the beads is a merely mechanical process, at which the heart certainly remains quite empty."

Even a journal that was called the " Church-Newspaper," [3] scoffed at and rejected the Rosary, and testified its great pleasure when the Elector of Treves, in his "excellent pastoral letter of the 1st Wintermonth, 1783," inveighed against " rosaries, blessings, amulets, and other Church trumpery." [4]

It will be further light upon these attacks against the Rosary

---

[1] (Werkmeister). Neber den neuen Kathol. Katechismus. Frankfurt, A. M., 1789, p. 109.

[2] Published anonymously by Blau and Dorsch. Frankfurt, A. M., 1789, p. 182.

[3] This journal was the " Wienerische Kirchenzeitung," published by Provost Wittola. In one of its issues in the fourth year of its publication, 1787, the Rosary is decried as an utterly objectionable devotion. " If we are to petition Him—our Heavenly Father, for any good, to what purpose those rosaries and the endless greetings of the Blessed Virgin?" And one Bishop is made to bear the stigma of " informing himself, on his visitations, of nothing more momentous than whether the Rosary is recited in Church: so that often the most experienced (!) pastor, with a highly intelligent (?) congregation under his charge, and with good hymns and prayers, cannot so much as take it upon himself to permit the Rosary to be omitted at early Mass." Forcibly to do away with the Rosary, however, does not appear to the writer to be advisable. " I can well conceive that nothing should be torn down unless something better is built to replace it. Deprive the people of their Rosary, and they will no longer know how to pray, and will certainly fancy they are to be turned into Lutherans. But could not the Rosary, without being especially cast aside, be quietly brought into oblivion ? " (Column 519, and foll.) In the same year, it was said, " to the honor of Bohemia, that the Scapular, Portiuncula, and Rosary feasts had already been banished from the calendar, which put the Vienna calendar to shame, it having still, in the present year, retained those feasts in all their splendor." (Column 383.)

[4] I. Jahrg, 1784, col. 219, etc.

to add that the Davidic Psalter came off no less menaced.   For it was the design of those illuminates to clear the breviary of its "legends and all superstitious matter," and, as they expressed themselves, " to introduce, instead of the sorry old medley, a new breviary in the vernacular." [1]

3. To what extent this movement gained the sympathy of even well-meaning persons, or rather quite carried them away, the following examples, out of hundreds, will suffice to show.   Herenæus Haid, in other respects a worthy man, wrote a treatise on a proposed "Metamorphosis" of the Rosary according to the spirit of the Catholic Church, or on the Rosary devotion : 1st, as it has hitherto been practised ; 2d, but how it can and ought to be practised according to the spirit of the Catholic Church. [2]

Like all books of its kind at that time, not yet bent on simply rooting out the Rosary, Haid's work opens with an apology for treating of a prayer " which every enlightened man denounces with the utmost zeal, in which priests, on clear principle, most reluctantly take a leading part with the faithful, which they see to be wholly fruitless, and which they despise as an exceedingly mechanical form of devotion."   He goes on with the avowal to his readers : "You would justly reprehend me as a promoter of false devotion, as an instrument of the ruinous mechanism, if I wished to stand up for the Rosary as hitherto practised, and to further it in its usual form."   But he relieves their apprehensions by adding : "I further, at least I seek to further, a new birth, a metamorphosis (*i.e.*, a transformation) of the Rosary."   Now what about the name ?   I would have the name Rosary and Rosary prayer become extinct, and be dropped, inasmuch as the designation, compared with the object in its old and new form, is wholly without meaning.   I would give up the name for a trifle, I would abandon it spontaneously ; only for the sake of the people, however, I yet seek to retain it."

But to come to a more serious part of the treatise: " In the ordinary practice of the Rosary," says Haid, "Christians manifestly sin against our Lord's ordinance, so full of meaning.   (Matt.

---

[1] Beiträge zur Verbesserung des aüssern Kathol. Gottesdienstes," p. 311.

[2] "Abhandlung (als Ankündigung) über die Metamorphose des Rosenkranzes nach dem Geiste der kath. kirche, etc."   Landshut, 1809.

vi. 7.) 'When you are praying, speak not much as the heathens,
for they think that in their much-speaking they may be heard.'"
In a note on the etymological derivation of the original of the
word much-speaking, the writer endeavors to strengthen the co-
gency of the expression. [1]

"The Rosary as practised hitherto" is, therefore, according to
Haid, nothing but "pure battology, idle babbling, antiquated
mechanism worthy of being thrown aside."

The Breviary lessons on the origin of the Rosary—they were
only some decennaries anterior to Haid himself—he thought
should be "stripped of such ways of thinking as were current in
St. Dominic's time, and of that diction in which the legends of
those days were wont to be written." The residue he would retain is, in substance, that "the saint, in order to stay the progress
of heresy, encouraged the faithful devoutly to meditate on the
mysteries of our redemption. These should be brought before the
minds of the people by means of terse, pithy expressions, proof
that he desired only, as it were, slight, suggestive hints to be
given. For example, 'whom thou didst conceive by the Holy
Ghost,' etc., etc." [2] The people could easily grasp and retain certain leading points of Faith, hence the brevity of these expressions,
which should fix the mind on the life, passion, and death of our
Redeemer, and on their concomitant circumstances. Meditation
should be substituted for whatever is over and above this. Behold, here, then, under the uncouth outer deformity, the lovely
hidden spirit; under the rubbish, the pearl."

Thus speaks the critic, Haid. To him, the Lord's prayer and

---

[1] It is a pity that Haid did not see fit to learn the meaning of this word from
St. Gregory of Nyssa,—De Oratione Dominica. (Orat. I.) St. Augustine says, in
reference to the passage cited : "Neque enim, ut nonnulli putant, hoc est
orare in multiloquio, si diutius oretur. Aliud est sermo multus, aliud diuturnus
affectus. Nam et de ipso Domino scriptum est, quod pernoctaverit in orando,
(Luc. 6. 12.) et quod prolixius oraverit. (Luc. 22. 43.).... Absit ab oratione
multa locutio, sed non desit multa precatio, si fervens perseverat intentio.
Nam multum loqui, est in orando rem necessarium superfluis agere verbis; multum autem precari, est ad eum, quem precamur, diuturna et pia cordis excita-
tione pulsare." Epist. 130 ad Probam (al 121) cap. 10.

[2] The critic is unfortunate in his strictures. This mode of suggestion and
hint, by inserting, for example, after the Holy Name of Jesus in each Hail
Mary, the words, "whom thou didst conceive by the Holy Ghost," etc., is of
much later origin than the Rosary itself, is practised chiefly in Germany, and
is by no means a necessary appendage to our devotion. It is, therefore, least
of all to be traced back to St. Dominic.

the angelical salutation are but " rubbish " and " uncouth deformity." But let us see in what his reform of the Rosary consists,
the transformation that is to take the pearl out of its surrounding
rubbish and uncleanliness.

Speaking of the " Rosary in its common form and as hitherto
practised," Haid himself expressly admits that the " Mysteries
of the Redemption as contained in it, may be adapted to the various seasons of the ecclesiastical year." But this is not enough for
him, and of oral prayer, there is a great deal too much. His first
care, therefore, is to reduce the number of Hail Marys in each
mystery to five, and in regard to the mysteries themselves, he is
of the opinion that " although some of them excellently set forth
the chief elements and the real mysteries, still not all were
equally well chosen. They could be increased or diminished in
number, and several could undergo change. I see this very clearly.
However, we must set about our work softly, and make changes
unobserved, until gradually the new form shall stand faultless in
all its beauty and superior utility." In order to put meditation
in a way to get full justice, Haid would preface each mystery
with a short exposition of its contents, or point out its bearing
on or application to the occurring feast, or he would even introduce
it with a strophe of some hymn, or conclude the whole with
a prayer, " wherein the faithful shall pray that God may grant
them constantly to look upon what is high and holy in the mystery, perfectly to understand the same, and to accomplish that to
which its spirit directs and impels them. To facilitate the practical working of this plan, Haid composed six formularies which
" any clergyman can develop with meditations of his own, and
form and change according to his own views and judgment." [1]

---

[1] These formulas were published in a book bearing the title, " The Rosary according to the intention of the Holy Catholic Church, for public and private
(family) use. A book of prayer and devotion, etc. Landshut, 1811." This, his
reform of the Rosary devotion, was approved by several episcopal ordinaries
(Freising, Ratisbonne, Constance, Salzburg, and Passau), and Haid appeals
to their words, both in the title of his work and in the preface. The approbation from Constance of this "clever book of devotion" was signed by the
Vicar-General, J. H. Fr. von Wessenberg, to whom the second part is also
inscribed.

Long before Haid's time, however, there was no lack of similar formulas to facilitate and promote the Rosary meditations.[1]

But by reason of the complete departure of his contemporaries from the old traditions, perhaps nine of them were known to him, or at any rate, taken into account. For they were written less in conformity with what he would call "reason," but more in accordance with "faith."

In what, then, briefly, does Haid's reform consist? Haid took up arms against a mere phantom, against an abuse that was a mere creation of his fancy, and then reduced the number of Hail Marys in each mystery by one-half!

But is it really true that in the Rosary there is an insufficiency or a total want of meditation? and, if so, is a merely oral, but nevertheless devout prayer, not a good prayer?

In a former article it was clearly shown that meditation on the mysteries of the Rosary constitutes one of its essential parts, and is just as necessary to it as its oral prayers. If Pope Benedict XIII., by way of favor in the case of simple and unlettered persons unable to meditate and not given to reflection, saw fit not to insist on such meditation as a condition of gaining the Rosary indulgences, he nevertheless added the remark: "It is our wish, however, that even such persons should, by all means, be gradually instructed (by the directors of the confraternity) to meditate on the holy mysteries of our redemption according to the spirit and object of the Rosary."[2]

It was just this spirit and object of the Rosary that Haid did not rightly understand, and hence he sought, most unskilfully indeed, to metamorphose or transform it, to alter it from what it so excellently was and had been from the very time of its origin.[3]

Only such a mistaken notion of the nature of the Rosary can

---

[1] More than two hundred years earlier, St. Francis of Sales had already urged his "Philothea to get one of the many books that are guides to a right recitation of the Rosary."

[2] Benedictus XIII., Constit. "Pretiosus," etc., as cited in first article.... (month, page, etc.)

[3] Other priests, too, some of whom were the foremost men of their time—Jais, Weber, Reiter, and others—gave themselves no little pains to effect a reform, a "transformation" of the Rosary, by means of meditations and readings which were to be incorporated with its other prayers.

account for the utterance of another worthy priest of that time, Rev. Mr. Gehrig, in a sermon on this devotion: " It is even a fault in one to have recourse to the Rosary when he is able to employ some other devotion." And as late as the year 1830, William Smets, widely and not unfavorably known as a poet, spoke, in an address in vindication of the Rosary devotion, of "various superstitions and abuses" that prevailed in it, notwithstanding its excellence in other respects.'

4. If such, then, were the views of the best intentioned men of that unhappy period, what must have been those of the great number of really evil-affected " illuminates "? We fear we should wound Catholic sensibility by here adducing their utterances on the question. Let one man, however, tell us what he really thought about the Rosary.

A clerical privy-counsellor and chief school inspector[2] says briefly and plainly that " the Rosary was an invention of the centuries in which the people could not read, in which they were only capable of mechanically counting off a certain number of *Aves* on a string of beads; add to this the degrading and unintelligible manner and method of alternate recitation, and the Rosary is too often but a meaningless bawl of the self-same words, whereby the soul is far from being lifted up in devotion, and in the whole, nothing but a bad impression can be left upon a rationally devout mind."[3]

This is the same judgment that enlightened ignorance and elegant poverty of thought form of the Rosary even to this day. Men rail at what they do not understand; for understanding is his alone who has faith.

[1] Köln, 1830, p. 24.
[2] G. L. C. Kopp, Die Kathol. Kirche im 19 Jahrhundert, und die Zeitgemässe Umgestaltung ihrer äussern Verfassung, etc.: Mainz, 1830.
[3] The reader will here the more readily appreciate what the late Bishop Martin of Paderborn said in the preface of his " Schönheiten des Rosenkranzes " (Mainz, 1876): " Some fifty years ago a treatise on the Rosary could have made its appearance, even before the great Catholic public, only in fear and trembling. The Rosary carries its positive Christian character too plainly stamped on its front to have found favor with the image-storming illuminism of that time. Truly, one could then speak of good fortune when he did not see the Rosary publicly censured, even by priests, in their sermons and instructions, and ridiculed, degraded, thrown away like old iron."

THE ROSARY OF FLOWERS.

A LEGEND.

HARRIET M. SKIDMORE.

THE little lay-Sister's work is done,
  For the West is rich with the sunset ray,
And the busy hands of the meek-souled nun
Are resting now, in their wonted way.
On the kitchen table those hands had made
  As fair, in its spotless loveliness,
As her own white robe, they are gently laid·
  But the toil-worn fingers fondly press
The beads of a Rosary-chaplet old
  That had hung at her girdle many a year.
(Ah! priceless pearls, and a chain of gold
  Could never be to her heart so dear!)
But she gazeth now through a tearful mist
  On the Cross that figures the Man-God's pain,
Till the nail-rent feet·she hath often kiss'd
  Are wet with the flow of that ceaseless rain,
And sadly she murmurs: "My Lord! My Love
  Who hast giv'n so freely Thy life for me,
What gift do *I* send to Thy Throne above?
  What meet reward have I proffer'd Thee?
My Sisters waft, from their missals fair,
  Full many a tender and pray'rful thought,
And they offer Thee broideries, rich and rare,
  And delicate lace, by their deft hands wrought;
But I, unlettered, unskilled—no gift
  Is mine, that even Thy saints may see;
And these ill-said prayers! Can I dare to lift
  Such worthless offerings up to *Thee?*
Wilt Thou bear to look, with Thy gracious eyes
  On *my* 'Gloria Patris?'" Ah! wondrous sight!
As the words she breathes, on the table lies
  A knot of violets, purple, and white!

Then, startled, knowing scarce *what* she said,
  She tremblingly uttered her Lord's own prayer—
And a radiant lily, from leaves outspread
  Its sweet balm poured on the grateful air!
"Ave Maria!" the Heaven-blest nun
  Went on, in her rapturous ecstasy,—
And the brightest of roses, one after one,
  Made haste in a circle entwined to be!
So, decade by decade, in murmurs glad
  She said, till a Rosary bloomed like these:
Snow-white for the Joyful, and red for the Sad,
  And gold for the Glorious Mysteries!
That marvellous wreath! it is fashioned well—
  But a bright flush dyeth her faded cheeks,
For a voice as soft as the acolyte's bell,
  When the Host is lifted, above her speaks:
"O follower blest of the Better Part!
  Arise, and see, at thy Spouse's Feet
Thy Rosaries, kept with celestial art,
  For the wreaths are finished! the chain's complete!"

*   *   *   .   *   *   *

The little lay-Sister, prompt before,
  Came not to the chapel on that strange night;
So the good nuns sought her the Convent o'er,
  And found her—dead! 'mid the garlands bright!
But lo! on the table, in lines of gold,
  These words with a flame-like lustre burned:
"The prayers of a pure heart here behold,
  By Love to a blooming Rosary turned!"

MAKE for me, if you will, a new road to go to Jesus, and pave it with all the merits of the Blessed, adorn it with all their heroic virtues, illuminate and embellish it with all the lights and beauties of the angels, and let all the angels and saints be there themselves to escort, defend, and sustain those who are ready to walk there ; and yet in truth, in simple truth, I say boldly, and I repeat that I say truly, I would prefer to this new perfect path the immaculate way of Mary,—*Posui immaculatam viam meam.* It is the way without any stain or spot, without original or actual sin, without shadow or darkness.
  —*Blessed Louis Mary Grignon de Montfort, O. P.*

CARDINAL ZIGLIARA, O. P.

CARDINAL ZIGLIARA, O. P.

Rev. Reginald Walsh, O. P.

II.

THE great share which Cardinal Zigliara had in the triumph and the propagation of Thomistic philosophy should never be allowed to fall into oblivion. Neither should it be forgotten that his elevation to the Cardinalate was an emphatic declaration (if such was needed) that his school of the Minerva was the school of Saint Thomas. In a pamphlet, published about 1878, a learned and well-informed Jesuit, Pére Botalla, quoted with approval a statement to this effect, that the Minerva was the only college in Rome in which a certain doctrine regarding the union of the human soul and body was held. To-day that doctrine is taught in all schools of philosophy throughout the length and breadth of the Catholic Church:[1]

It is found in every text-book of Catholic philosophy published since (even in those which appeared before the condemnation

---

[1] Dans une lettre publiée par un theologien connu et très autorisé de l'Univers du 2 Decembre, 1877, sur l'enseignment de notre doctrine à Rome nous lisons les paroles suivantes: "Voici quel est cet enseignment sur le point particulier de la composition du corps. Dans *une seule* des ecoles Romaines, celle des RR. PP. Dominicains de la Minerve on sontient sur cette question la vieille doctrine des scolastiques Thomistes. Partout ailleurs on est persuadé que cette doctrine est inconciliable avec les dècouvertes modernes des sciences physiques et chimiques: nous en jugeons par le choix des auteurs classiques qu' on fait dans ces ètablissements. Au seminaire romain de l'Appolinaire et a l'école dite del la Pace l'auteur du cours est Bonelli, au seminaire de la Propagande la philosophie du Pére Tongiorgi: au seminaire Pio Vaticano fondé au Vatican même par Pie IX. et confié pour la direction spirituelle et disciplinaire aux fils de S. Dominique l'auteur adopté pour le cours est le recent ouvrage du R. P. Palmieri, Nous ne parlons pas de l'université grègorienne des RR. PP. Jèsuites, qui depuis longtemps comme personne l'ignore, se sont affranchis sur le point en litige des doctrines Thomistes.

La lettre de Mgr. Czacki et le Thomisme, reponse, etc.

Par le P. Paul Bottalla, C. de Jesus, Professeur à la faculté de thèologie de Poitiers.

of Rosmini's 22d and 24th propositions). No Catholic would now dream of denying it. It matters little that Zigliara's '*Philosophia*' or his '*De Mente Concilii Viennensis*' is not always referred to as the source of the knowledge of the correct interpretation of various passages in the works of Saint Thomas, etc., or on the other hand, that the views of his quondam opponents are no longer heard of except, perhaps, as curiosities of philosophical literature. Leo XIII. and Cardinal Zigliara never sought for the applause of men; they had at heart only the diffusion of true philosophy, and desired nothing but that the Church should continue to enjoy the inestimable advantages which in all ages she has derived from it. The great Pope and the great Cardinal saw one of the most serious evils of the present day, and they applied a specific remedy to it. A pressing need of educated society appealed to them, and they supplied it.

The present century will indeed ever be a memorable one in the annals of Catholic philosophy. Two distinct stages of development may be perceived in it, and they are made by the Church's action. In this science there has not been any advance from within, no great intellectual conquests have been achieved, no problems hitherto insoluble have yielded to original thought. Philosophers of our times have made no appreciable advance on their predecessors. But the Church has had to speak to the philosophers, first, to tell them what was not true philosophy, and then to tell them what was true.

Some sixty years ago the pernicious system of Hermes was formally condemned. About forty years ago those of Bautain, Bonnetty, and Günther were added to the list. Then, about thirty years since, that of Froschammer. Rosmini, too, belongs to this era, though his propositions were not censured till quite recently. These mistaken men, all of them Catholics possessed of unquestionable ability and industry, despised the patristic and scholastic philosophy, and set themselves respectively to form one which each in turn considered to be true. Their various doctrines were disseminated widely in Germany, France, Belgium, and Italy. Some of them labored more or less to supply their Catholic brethren with what they considered an effectual weapon against the errors of the day. Some of them in their

blindness, or as it is called, intellectual pride, wanted to teach the
Church philosophy.   All alike fell into error, and their great tal-
ents only made their fall greater.   "*Non hos elegit Dominus.*"
So ended the first period.

To it succeeded one in which the truth about the nature of the
union between body and soul was declared.[1]   The philosophical
doctrine of St. Thomas was praised.[2]   The true interpretation of
the Brief[3] was given by the famous letter of Mgr. Czachi, June 5,
1877, in which, moreover, the substantial unity of human nature as
a theological truth was declared to have been previously taught
by the Church.   This second period at length culminated in the
encyclicals in which, so to speak, the philosophy of Saint Thomas
was made the philosophy of the Catholic Church.   Thus what was
begun by Gregory XVI., was continued by Pius IX., and completed by Leo XIII.   The first period is characterized by the authoritative refutation of error; the second by the authoritative revival of
scholasticism.   The one period is destructive of error, the other
is constructive of truth.   It is clear that the Letter, "Tuas libenter,"
of Pius IX. to the Archbishop of Munich, December 21, 1863,
expressed approval of the scholastic method in theology, and
that the approval is implicitly repeated by the condemnation of
the opposite or contradictory proposition.   "The method and principles which the old scholastic Doctors employed in theology are
by no means suitable to the requirements of our times and to the
progress of science."   No. 13 in the second section of the Sylla-
bus, viz., " Rationalismus moderatus," that in which the errors of
Froschammer and Günther are proscribed, shows that the two
periods are logically, rather than historically, distinct.   A hard and
fast line cannot be drawn between them by means of an almanac,

---

[1] Letter against Baltzer's theory, addressed by Pius IX. to the Bishop of
Warsaw, April 30, 1860.

[2] Brief addressed to the president of the Academia Philosophico-Medica,
July 23, 1877.

[3] There is, of course, as every theologian knows, a long series of Briefs issued
century after century in commendation of St. Thomas' theology.   In some of
these his philosophy receives encomiums, too; and the fact that his system is
one throughout, in human and divine knowledge, is sufficient to show that his
philosophy has repeatedly received implicit approval in the others.   Of all the
Doctors of the Church, St. Thomas and St. Augustine have been most honored
in this way by the Popes.

though, as in the course of all such developments, the difference between the stages is quite evident.

It might seem to those who have never devoted much thought to the present subject, and who do not know philosophy, that, after all, decisions regarding it are not of such great importance. Certain though it is that the decisions in question are true, they will say, yet after all, where is their practical utility? No Catholic worthy of the name would talk thus. Whatever the Pope does is right, and the fact that he speaks shows there was need of speaking. But people who do not understand what they are saying, who have not the 'sensus Ecclesiæ,' or whose pet notions have been disturbed by a Papal utterance, can never see why the Pope was right in speaking. We may be allowed under correction to say a word in the hope of setting such people right.

The sixteenth century bears upon it a distinctive mark, the fundamental principle underlying all heresy; the falsehood implicitly contained in every revolt against the teaching authority, was then openly proclaimed and professed as a creed. As Protestantism is the very essence of religious error, so is Rationalism that of philosophical. As the sixteenth was by excellence the century of heresy, so is the nineteenth that of false philosophy. In our day heresy is fast succumbing to Rationalism—the parent is being strangled by its worthy offspring. Rationalism is preying on the very vitals of that system of private judgment which gave it birth. It is the hydra which it is at present the Church's mission to slay. Millions of souls have already been ruined by it. Three hundred years ago, under the pretext of ' the Bible and the Bible only,' and the other shibboleths of pure religion, only such truths were to be deemed divine as commended themselves to private judgment; in this nineteenth century, in the name of pure reason, not only all revealed, but even human truths, those evident to the mind of man, are denied.

Hence the need, as regards the world, of the reprobation of Rationalism; hence the need as regards Catholics of being told what is true philosophy. If we can read the signs of the otherwise changing times, or those of the past as they cross the stage of history, and those of the century in which we ourselves live, we

see that even in error, as well as in truth, the law of continuity
holds good.   Luther detested the scholastics, and mocked them;
so do his progeny.   The scholastics as a body were conspicuous for
holiness of life and the true perception of the dependence of reason on faith, hence their successors to-day find themselves in harmony with the Pope.

So much for philosophy considered in itself.   Theologians
know, moreover, that even the correct apprehension of many
terms in theology—for example, in the all-important treatises of
the Incarnation and the Eucharist—is impossible to him who has
not learned philosophy.   On the other hand, a thorough knowledge of it is of untold worth to the future divine.   This is particularly true of scholastic philosophy, and pre-eminently true of the
Thomistic, for as Cardinal Newman rightly observes, the Dominicans have given its form to the theology of the Catholic Church.
Their philosophy is, we may add, theological, and their theology,
philosophical.   In the Thomist school there is perfect unity of
system all through the student's course.   The philosophy he
learns is that of the master-mind of antiquity—Aristotle, corrected
and developed by the master-mind of Christianity—Thomas of
Aquin.   He is shown how all philosophy is tested by theology,
how its value or worthlessness is proved by its usefulness or its
uselessness in theology; and he is trained to think scientifically,
to apply the true philosophy he has learned, and to help himself
by means of it in his study of divine truth, in other words to understand the Summa in spirit and in truth.

Still more significant than the continual employment of philosophical language, still more important than the scientific form
of theology, is this subordination of human to divine knowledge,
ever insisted on by the Prince of Scholastics.   Philosophy cannot be divorced from the theology, nor taken out of the sphere
of ecclesiastical supervision.   The 'magisterium' extends to it,
removes the errors incident to it in the mind of man, and raises
it to the highest possible dignity by making it theology's hand-
maid.

Every theologian knows that Oliva's heretical tenets ran coun-
ter to the Church's teaching on the mystery of the Incarnation and
on the nature of man, and many theologians know that they have

5

been moreover the prolific source of objections against Saint Thomas' doctrine regarding the Blessed Eucharist. That scholastic doctrine indeed is not a part of the Catholic faith, but it is in wonderful harmony with it, and to the present writer's mind the very fact that Oliva's tenets are opposed to it is a *prima facie* confirmation of its truth. Those two great mysteries of salvation, the Incarnation and the Real Presence, or rather the central mystery and its perpetuation, have shed a flood of light on questions that lie indeed within the domain of human reason, yet which without such revelation might never have been solved. How clearly has the bright ray from Heaven, coming through the crystal medium of a definition, shown in one mystery, not only the distinction between nature and person, but also the nature of the union between soul and body, and in the other how much has it enlightened us about the nature of corporeal substance! The dim, flickering gleam of fallen reason would probably never have sufficed to discern these things. But he to whom his Creator gave an intellect almost superhuman in its range and power, he whom we venerate as the Angelical, has penetrated into these depths farther than any other child of Adam. In him surpassing philosophical genius and a supreme gift of faith were combined. God gave one Saint Thomas Aquinas to His Church, and in him the Church honors her greatest theologian and philosopher. His whole system of physical and psychological science consists of conclusions inferred from self-evident principles, and tested and approved of wherever possible by their being in accordance with the supreme rule of all truth—the Catholic faith. He continually turns to this; it is his pole star. For instance, the teaching contained in Scripture and Tradition, that man is one substance, and that in man the soul is the one specifying and vivifying principle, is a corner-stone of St. Thomas' philosophy. The place which it holds in common with cognate truths cannot be better described than in the following words: " *Ego autem sic reputavi, sic sentio. Thomistici systematis, pro scientia universali et dogmate perscrutando, duo hæc esse potissimum fundamenta et criteria: unum illud de substantiali corporum constitutione et reliquum de nominum analogia.*" They are from the pen of him who was professor in Cardinal Pecci's own seminary in

Perugia, who was brought by Leo XIII. to Rome, and made Professor in Propaganda, and who is now his Apostolic Delegate in Washington, the learned Mgr. Satolli.

Every Catholic knows what the Pope has done for the prayer of the Rosary, but every Catholic does not know what Leo XIII. has accomplished for the study of philosophy.[1] Yet the two courses of action are in some respects precisely similar; as he defends the Church by Mary's prayer, so does he defend Catholic schools by her Son's truth. For one purpose he makes use of what was revealed to Saint Dominic; for the other of what was more or less revealed to Saint Thomas. The Pope has written several Encyclicals on these two subjects which are so dear to him. Besides those in which the Angelical Doctor was declared Universal Patron of studies in the Catholic Church, his philosophy was inculcated, and the Leonine edition of all his works decreed; the present illustrious occupant of Peter's chair rendered no more signal service to the cause of philosophical truth, than by conferring the Cardinal's hat on him who had so well defended it in the very front of the conflict.

Theologians will realize the full significance of the act. It bore precisely the same relation to the Encyclicals that a decree about a dogmatic fact bears to an abstract definition. Not only did the Council of Ephesus proclaim the truth about the Incarnation, it also declared that the truth was contained in the twelve propositions of Saint Cyril. The first without the second would not have been sufficiently effectual against Nestorius, the victory of truth would not have been complete. So, too, in the present instance. Not only did Leo XIII. in one Encyclical express a desire that the Thomist philosophy should be held by all, and in another mention Zigliara as pre-eminently well versed in it, but by bestowing on him previously the greatest honor possible, the Pope showed in the most unmistakable way the meaning of his own words, and put the crown on his own work. The significance of the act was perfectly understood in Rome at the time.

After his elevation Zigliara's virtues shone even more brightly

---

[1] The well-known philosophical writer, whose pseudonym "Ausonio Franchi" may now be laid aside for his real name, says that he was led back to the Church by Leo XIII.'s pronouncements on philosophy.

than before.   He ever remained one among his brethren, and in
spirit the least of them all.   Not only did he continue to wear the
habit of his Order and to recite his Office according to its rite, but
his greatest joy was to have the novices in his sitting-room during recreation.   He worked with redoubled ardor for the glory of
God and the welfare of His Church.   What he accomplished was
simply marvellous.   It may be said in passing, that of the many
Congregations of which he was a member, not one possessed a
greater attraction for him than that of the Propaganda.   He did
his utmost to help the work of the Church in missionary countries, and visitors from the States and from Great Britain were
often surprised to find what an intimate knowledge he possessed
of their local circumstances.[1]

Soon after his creation as Cardinal he was entrusted with the
superintendence of the Leonine edition of all Saint Thomas'
works.   This was occupation after his own heart.   It recalled
old times.   The first volume contains Zigliara's own commentary,
a copious explanation of some of the most abstruse treatises of
Saint Thomas, and, needless to say, one of the best of the kind
ever produced.   It is, moreover, unless the present writer is mistaken, the only commentary ever written on the treatises in question.   Yet this was only a portion of his daily task.   In addition
to this, and to elucidating any other matters, to discharging with
the greatest fidelity the multifarious duties of his high office, he
found time to publish his *Propedeutica ad Sacram Theologiam*, and
to write a large work on the Sacraments.   The part on Baptism
and Confirmation was the only one that had received its final re-
vision at the time of the author's death; but whenever the whole
is published, it will be found worthy of his great reputation.

The most important of all his other works, his '*Philosophia*,' enjoys already a world-wide circulation.   Years ago the Pope expressed his wish that all schools of philosophy should adopt as
their text-book either Zigliara's or Sanseverino's '*Philosophia*.'
The preference, almost universally given to the former, is the best
proof of its superiority.   Its perusal, it is said, has always been one

---

[1] He was a member of no fewer than seven Congregations, besides being
Prefect of the Congregation of Studies, and Co-President of the Academia of
St. Thomas Aquinas.

of the present Pope's greatest pleasures.   In the first year of his
Pontificate his blessing was asked for a priest who had fallen into delicate health, and in consequence was obliged to give up his
mission, and devote his time to study.   "What is he doing? "
asked Leo XIII.   "Translating Zigliara's philosophy into French,
Holy Father."   "He could not be better employed," was the reply,
"for that is the book where the truth is."   This has been recognized
even outside the Church.   Some years ago, in accordance with the
suggestion of the President of the Queen's College, Belfast, Ireland, the work was made the text-book for the Philosophical
Examination in the Royal University, Ireland.   Testimony such
as this needs no comment; it is the highest homage that could be
paid to intellectual supremacy, and to the unrivalled possession
of the truth.   Few things, moreover, could give the Pope greater
pleasure than to hear that even outsiders were coming towards
the centre and source of the noblest of all human sciences.   His
own Encyclicals are proposed as models of Latinity in the University of Oxford, where students are bid to imitate his style, in
order to acquire, as far as may be possible, something of the Pope's
classic purity and elegance.   But something higher than literary
excellence, namely, the truth on the sublimest objects of man's intelligence, has met recognition in the University of Ireland.   It
is a sign of the times, an avowal on the part of scholars that only in
the Catholic Church is true philosophy to be found.   Nothing like
it has occurred in the history of Great Britain since the days when
King James and King Charles commanded young students in divinity to begin with Lombard and Thomas.[1]

These glorious results were some of the fruits of tenderest piety
and intense devotion to the truth.   Every moment of the Cardinal's life was spent in prayer or in study.   His ceaseless application however, gradually undermined his strength, and for some
years it was evident to all that he was in failing health.   Nevertheless he continued to work up to the last, as much as his weak condition would permit.   To those who endeavored to persuade him
to desist, he used to answer with a smile, "I was not made Cardinal to become idle."   He was particularly indefatigable in working for some eight or ten causes of Beatification, including that of

[1] English State Papers, Charles I., June 14, 1631.

the Venerable Olier, of which he was the protector, or, as it is technically called, Ponens, and of the Venerable de la Salle. But none of the causes with the promotion of which he was entrusted was dearer to his heart than that of the five lately beatified Chinese martyrs, whom he used to call " our brothers."   He often said to those around him that he looked on his own endeavors to expedite the glorification of these Dominicans as his last work on earth.   The anticipation was verified.   He was not destined to witness the final triumph.   When it was being celebrated in St. Peter's, he to whom the success of that protracted investigation was in great measure due, was at rest.

In January, 1893, he was preconized Bishop of Frascati, one of the seven suburban sees.   But his sickness prevented him from receiving episcopal consecration.   Thomas M. Zigliara was never to rise from his bed again.   As the end drew visibly near, his hopefulness and joy increased.   Though often racked with pain, he never uttered a word of complaint.   In fact, he used to remark that his Heavenly Father, knowing his weakness, laid a very light cross upon him.   His cheerfulness and conformity to God's holy will edified every one, so much so that the General of his Order often said that he had never seen the like.   The Cardinal spent those months of pain in dictating a little work in honor of the Blessed Virgin.   It was his final effort, the crowning act of love. He was fully convinced for a long time that he would die in her month, and the thought filled him with consolation.   He frequently said to those who came to see him: " In the month of May I left my home and received the habit of the Order, in the month of May I was ordained priest and subsequently made Cardinal, and in the month of May I shall give up my soul to the hands of my Creator."   The day of deliverance came as he had expected (May 11th), and we may confidently hope that the Blessed Mother of God, whose devoted client he had ever been, obtained for him a speedy entrance into the joys of Heaven.

*   *   *   *   *   *   *   *

He has left behind him a name that will be held in the highest veneration as long as virtue and knowledge are honored by men. " Many shall praise his wisdom, and it shall never be forgotten." Cardinal Zigliara's works have been the chief means by which

Thomistic philosophy has been rendered accessible to men imbued exclusively with the modes, and familiar only with the expressions of modern thought. It is hardly necessary to say that to them the Summa was a sealed book. But from Rome the truth has radiated unto the furthest limits of the Catholic world. Schools of theology and philosophy that twenty years ago could not understand, much less appreciate, Saint Thomas, have now been taught to see his meaning, and to regard him as the supreme thinker of the Church in all ages—her approved teacher of philosophy as long as time shall last.

He whose profound knowledge and whose intimate intercourse with the then future Pope led in God's good time to all this, is now gone to his reward. But his work lives after him, and blest by the voice of Peter, it will last forevermore. The highest aspiration of that noble heart, which now lies still in the cemetery of San Lorenzo, has been realized. The great Dominican, whose fondest wish it was to do all in his power for the Church, has succeeded in his glorious task.

It sometimes happens that a few words spontaneously uttered show the whole character of the speaker. In that moment the inmost secrets of his heart are revealed and the guiding principle of his whole life is expressed, for the voice of nature itself is heard coming forth from the very depths of the soul. When we hear its unmistakable accents, we know the man as we never knew him before. A presentiment that we always had about him has been fulfilled, our estimate of him is confirmed by the most unerring, the most reliable of all testimonies, his unconscious self. No photograph nor phonograph was ever truer. From that day on, the mental image we retain of him bears upon it as its legend or motto, the indelible impression of his own words.

So is it with the expression of the great Regent of the Minerva previously quoted. What was then a passing observation on his part has remained imperishable; it epitomized the history of his whole life; it expressed, as nothing else could, his self-effacement and princely devotion to the cause of truth. Whenever a statue is raised to his memory, the most fitting inscription for its pedestal will be:—VICIT SCHOLA NOSTRA—"Our school was right."

These are some of the treasured recollections of the springtime of a priest's life, of those golden days when it was his privilege to enjoy very intimate relations with the great Cardinal.
Slight though this tribute to his memory be, yet it is dedicated
by a grateful heart; small though the offering be, yet it has been
a work of love to him who was one of his students.

THE IMMACULATE CONCEPTION.

D. J. DONAHOE.

CHOSEN out of David's line,
　　The Virgin Queen of David's Lord,
　　The Mother chaste of grace divine,
　And Vessel of prophetic word;
No taint is on thy deathless bloom,
　No soil of earth or air or sea:
Where, in our wanderings, shall we come,
　Immaculate! but unto thee?

Behold the world, how full of guile,—
　A reeking fen, a stagnant pool,—
The tempter's false and treacherous smile,
　And the vain wisdom of the fool!
Behold the hives of wretchedness,
　Of want and crime and blind despair,
Where virtues struggle in distress
　Like flowers in foul and murky air!

And lo, the gilded palaces
　Of wealth, the world's unrighteous king,
Built on the woes and miseries
　Of manhood wronged and suffering;
In darkness of despair we grope;
　We need thy prayers, pure, luminous,
That love may fill our hearts with hope,—
　Immaculate! shine thou on us!

THE STORY OF A BRIDAL VEIL.

L. M. POWER.

CHAPTER III.

"FOR some moments after our warm greeting, neither of us spoke, but Lily wept piteously as she met my glance of silent sympathy.

"Then she grew calmer, and related to me the history of her brief romance. Often I strove to comfort her, Ethel, but without success. She could think of nothing, speak of nothing, but her lost lover, and as yet she had tasted only the bitterness of the cross.

"'I wonder will existence ever again be the same to me?' Lily asked wistfully. 'I fear not,' she went on, presently, 'for since I parted from Ernest everything seems so changed, so dark and dreary, without his presence. When I look forward, the future appears a cheerless waste.'

"As I listened, Ethel, a sudden light broke on my mind, and taking her hand, I said, 'Lily dear, I feel certain that God will reward your generosity by Himself replacing the loss you have suffered, and will fill the void in your soul by raising it to a higher and a holier love. Would not that be a blessed exchange?' I asked. 'What do you say, dear?'

"'I say,' she rejoined, 'that such a thing appears quite impossible. I feel utterly listless and unworthy of such a grace. But,' and her lovely face brightened, 'if God would deign to call me to the religious state, I should count the sacrifice of my earthly idol as nothing in comparison to the happiness of such a vocation. I have felt the passion and pain of human love, and what has it brought me but a weary struggle, an anguished separation, and a joyless heart!'

"Just then she rose to leave, but somehow I felt the worst was over, and that Lily would waste no more time in useless regrets. She kissed me when going away, whispering: 'Thanks again and again for all your sympathy and prayers. I feel ever so much better since I came to this dear old convent. I will follow your advice, too, and try to bear my loneliness bravely, and to banish the thought of my poor Ernest. It has been such a comfort to pour out all my grief to my best friend, and your words have cheered me wonderfully.'

" She kissed me again, and Sister Julia, having announced that the carriage was waiting, Lily ran lightly down the steps, and was driven away.

   *   *   *   *   *   *   *

" After six months, Ethel, I received a letter from your aunt, containing the glad tidings that, under the advice of her director, she had resolved to enter religion, and that in three or four weeks I might expect to see her at St. Dominic's.

" ' I feel so contented ' the letter went on; 'and the peace you foretold has been given me in abundance. God has mercifully heard your prayers, and I am no longer sad and hopeless as when last you saw me. I have taken up my life with renewed earnestness, and I trust it may be devoted to His service forevermore.'

" She then told me that a letter had reached her a few days previously from Major Leslie, telling of his immediate departure for India, and begging her to reconsider her resolution, and not to send him out on the world, lonely and disappointed.

" ' Only write one line, my darling, and say " come back," and all will be well. I am yours now and forever.'

" This was the young officer's last appeal. You know Aunt Lily's answer. She did not say ' come back,' and three weeks later Ernest Leslie embarked for Madras, and his betrothed wife entered the noviceship.

" With the ardent enthusiasm of her nature, she began her new duties of labor and prayer, and grew not only resigned, but bright and cheerful, while the freshness of youth quickly returned to the pensive face.

" She became the favorite of her companions as well as their edification, and among the novices she attracted affection as readily as when a school-girl in the old times. The day of her reception arrived, after six months of probation, and Aunt Lily was to be given the white veil on the 22d of June, the eve of Corpus Christi. No wonder her mother wept as she gazed on that touching scene! Never had the girl looked lovelier than on that sunny morning when she glided up the choir, clad in purest white, and knelt before the altar with downcast eyes.   Truly she was a bride too fair for an earthly lover, and her physical beauty was enhanced by that spiritual expression one sees in pictures of St. Agnes.   She was dressed in a robe of soft, glistening satin, and her rich hair was concealed beneath a veil of costly lace that fell to her feet in graceful folds.

"It was her wedding veil, embroidered with orange blossoms and lily-of-the-valley, and chosen by Major Leslie as a gift to his betrothed.   Yes, Lily had worn it on her nuptial day, but her heart had been given to another Bridegroom.

"The following day was the feast of Corpus Christi, and the new novice was one of those deputed to arrange the altar for exposition of the Blessed Sacrament.   The fairest offerings from garden and field were grouped by loving hands round the golden niche where the monstrance was to stand.

"As the work progressed, one of the nuns suggested that the background of colored marble would be relieved by a drapery of lace, behind the gorgeous bloom of the flowers.   'If we only had Sister Catherine's veil,' she whispered, 'it would suit exactly.'   'Yes, the very thing it wants,' her companion assented; 'your taste, dear Sister, is always perfect.'

"Lily heard the consultation, and, leaving the chapel, she went straight to the Novice Mistress, and asked to have her veil used as Sister Martha had proposed.

"Mother Theresa listened to the girl's eager request, remembering the while the different purpose for which it had been intended by the donor, and willingly she answered: 'Of course, my child; do as you please, and let Sister Martha arrange the lace as she thinks best; but don't forget the veil is to be returned to your mother afterwards.   She asked as a special favor that she might keep it as a souvenir of the great day of your espousals. I know she will be pleased that it was used to-day in such a holy cause.'

"Sister Catherine tripped away with the required permission, and soon the novice's skilful fingers had draped the snowy folds behind the brilliant glow of scarlet geraniums, water-lilies, and roses of crimson and yellow.   The effect was exquisite, and Lily rejoiced to think that Ernest Leslie's gift had helped to beautify the Eucharistic throne of God Himself. Her life, too, with all its glorious promise, would henceforth be laid at His feet, as a perpetual incense of gratitude and love.

"The rest, Ethel, you know; how, after two years of fidelity to our rule, Sister Catherine made her final vows, and was professed a Religious of St. Dominic's Order.

"But soon I noticed a change in her appearance, and a great fear fell on my heart as I began to realize that she was fading, slowly but surely, and that her time on earth was short. Her health failed rapidly, and one year later her blessed soul was called to its reward.

"I remember well the silent anguish of her mother as she gazed lovingly on the calm, still face of her child, resting so sweetly in the sleep of death.

"Her remains, clothed in the white habit, were placed in choir during the Requiem Mass, and then carried to our little churchyard, to await the reward promised to those who have left all things to follow Christ.

"You asked me, Ethel, why that lily was planted on her grave. Three months after her death, Major, now Colonel Leslie, returned from India, and hastened to make inquiries respecting the girl to whom his affections still clung. Deep was his sorrow on learning the truth, and his tears fell fast as he listened to your grandmother's account of the last moments of his first and only love. Again and again he murmured, 'My poor Lily! my lost darling! God grant I may yet meet her in Heaven!' He then took leave of Mrs. Neville, and a few days later she received from him a letter and a small packet, bearing the Southampton postmark.

"The letter told her that he was leaving England forever, and intended starting for Bombay; that, having abandoned all idea of marriage, he wished to separate from his old surroundings, and devote himself to military service. As a last favor he begged that the tiny lily the parcel contained might be planted on Sister Catherine's grave as a memento of his fidelity.

"'I shall not see England again,' he wrote. 'In it I found the best joy and the deepest sorrow of my life; but I shall never cease to think of you with kindness, because you were so good to me, and because you are Lily's mother.'

" Your grandmother brought the flower here, and asked Reverend Mother's permission to have it grown on yonder spot, telling her of Colonel Leslie's parting request. Accordingly it was planted there by her hands, and has since flourished round the cross, a fit emblem of that pure, holy soul God had drawn to Himself by the thorny path of suffering."

As the nun ceased speaking, she glanced at her companion, who had listened with much interest to the history of that gentle life. The girl was weeping, while her eyes were fixed on the green mound, beneath which Aunt Lily was calmly sleeping, expecting the recompense of her early sacrifice. Sister Agnes rose, saying, " Now, dear, it is time for you to join your class before they go to the refectory for tea. I have kept you out too long already; but now, before we go away, let us say a little prayer together, that, like Sister Catherine, we may in all things fulfil God's will."

Reverently Ethel obeyed, and, in the hush of that sweet summer evening, the nun and her companion knelt for the last time in the old convent cemetery, while the shadows deepened round the graves of the blessed dead.

CHAPTER IV.

The morrow brought many tearful farewells at the ivy-clad gate of the convent, for the first day of vacation is often a sad one to the nuns and their pupils.

The latter regarded it with various sentiments. Most of those leaving St. Dominic's forever, felt the parting intensely, and gratefully remembered the peaceful days of school life, and the loving devotedness of their teachers. Others, who had strongly rebelled against the monotony of study and discipline, now that the hour of release was come, felt supremely happy, and the first taste of liberty was very sweet. But the most thoughtless spirits grew serious as the hour of departure drew near, as they embraced the nuns for the last time, whispering words of thanks, and petitions for prayers; looked for the last time on the fair landscape surrounding the gray walls of the home that had sheltered their innocent youth; kissed for the last time the companions who had shared the duties and the little ups and downs of their class days; shaken hands for the last time with old Kitty the lodge-keeper; passed for the last time through the ancient doorway, and realized for the first time, that childhood was over, and beyond the threshold, life awaited them.

Even those who had longed most eagerly for emancipation from dull routine, felt doubtful now whether the bright world beyond would fulfil their golden hopes, or bring that perfect contentment that once appeared so secure if only they could get outside the convent walls.

A final parting somewhat resembles the separation caused by death. In both cases our petty grievances, and even our aversions, disappear, and are replaced by thoughts of forgiveness and self-reproach.

When we stand face to face with the dead, or look for the last time on one who has wronged us, but who never again shall cross our path, then too late, we find that we have exaggerated their misdeeds, and our better nature tells us that many of their faults existed only in our imagination, or were the result of our own injustice.

So in like manner we quarrel with our present circumstances, finding them hard and unbearable, rising in senseless mutiny against our fate. With Rasselas in the Enchanted Valley, we think what joy it would be to escape the bounds of our narrow horizon, and begin a new career beyond the hills, with new surroundings, with new interests.

But at last there comes a crisis, when a chapter of our life is written and closed forever, and we are called upon to walk in a different path, with other companions and other duties. Then often and often we look back with sad, regretful eyes, to the old road and the old friends from whom we have drifted away.

Thus felt some of the so-called " scamps " of the school, who had been conspicuous for idleness and discontent; yet now when vacation set them free, they began to " hug their chains."

" O Sister! " sobbed Kate O'Connell, the ringleader of the rebels, " I am broken-hearted at the idea of leaving you and this dear old convent to-day. After all, it *is* a dear old place, and I ought to have been very happy here."

The nun smiled as she heard the incorrigible Kate, the head and font of all mischief, thus retracting her errors amid showers of tears.

" Do forgive me, dear Sister, for all the trouble I have given you in the last seven years.   I am awfully sorry for being such a hasty, ungrateful child."

" You were never hasty, Kate,--only a little reckless sometimes; but then I always made allowances for you as being the ' wild Irish girl ' of my class.   Now, good-bye, dear; don't miss your train, and don't meet your father with that woe-begone face."

Another outburst of sobs, another embrace of her kind teacher, and Kate O'Connell, with flushed cheeks and streaming eyes, was lost to sight.

Sister Agnes turned to look for Ethel, and saw her standing listlessly against a rustic niche, in which was placed a statue of St. Thomas Aquinas, finely cast in bronze.

" Come, my child, your luggage has been brought out, and you must not be late," the nun began as she hurried towards her.   But the girl only sighed, as she answered wearily: " Though I have such a bright home to return to, I feel very unhappy at leaving St. Dominic's, because I fear I am doing wrong."

" If you really think so, Ethel, you can rectify your mistake by coming back to us after the mid-summer vacation, but at present it is certainly your duty to go to your mother, as you have promised. Now be brave, dear.   May God guide you forever, and give you courage to do His will."

" Good-bye, dear, dear Sister !   I never can thank you enough for all your devoted care and patience."

The girl was crying bitterly, but the nun drew her firmly to the gate, where the cabman was noisily cracking his whip.   A last kiss, and Ethel entered the waiting vehicle, looking back to catch another glimpse of her old mistress, who stood in the doorway, waving adieu to her departing pupil.

Ethel Carlton was a prey to sad thoughts as she travelled towards her destination in Hampshire, but after a few hours her cheerfulness was gradually restored, and her eyes sparkled as she recognized each landmark of the familiar country adjoining Norwood Park.   Her face beamed with pleasure as the train steamed into the station at Hurley, and looking out she saw a stylish little pony-carriage drawn up beyond the platform.

Springing out, she ran eagerly towards a tall youth, who was evidently expecting her arrival.

"O Herbert!" she exclaimed, "here I am! How delighted I am to see you, and to know that I have come home forever!"

The meeting between brother and sister was a very affectionate one, and the young man smiled pleasantly as he kissed Ethel, and listened to her enquiries about her mother, and each of the home circle.

Herbert Carlton was Ethel's senior only by two years. From the first they had been close companions, and now, as in their childhood, the old love was strong, and a perfect sympathy existed between them. Merrily they talked and laughed, as they passed along the country roads, and the girl was radiant with health and spirits, as they reached the entrance gate, where the lodge-keeper smiled and courtesied a welcome to "Miss Ethel," who was a prime favorite with her and her rosy-faced children.

"Home, sweet home" never looked fairer to her eyes than on that sultry August afternoon, as she drove under the drooping lime trees that bordered the wide avenue, and came in sight of the stately old mansion that had belonged to her family for many centuries, and was all the dearer for its associations with the past. Lovingly she gazed on the verdant lawn, with its neatly-kept flower-beds, the extensive park, studded with ancient oaks and beeches, elms and golden walnut trees, while in the distance the river flowed like a silver ribbon, completing the beauty of the landscape.

"I never, never could leave all this," thought Ethel. "Never could bring myself to say good-bye to mother and Herbert, and this lovely place, and live forever in the convent, teaching, working, and praying. No, God could not expect so much, for He wishes us to be happy, and I cannot be happy away from Norwood. Father Vincent was right when he said that if I once came home I never would have courage to leave it. My only chance was to enter the novitiate direct from class, for now I never can go back. But I have still time to change my mind, and at present I need do nothing definite.   Later on I may have strength for the sacrifice.

So she argued, as most or us argue when we want to defer the evil day, and Hood says truly:

> " The mind flies back with a glad recoil
> From the debts not due till to-morrow."

The family circle, to which Ethel's return brought fresh brightness, was a pleasant one in every sense, combining as it did affection and wealth, and all the surroundings that tend to make existence easy, and to soften the daily trials that cannot be excluded even from an earthly paradise.

Mrs. Carlton was still hale and vigorous, and looking at her youthful face and active bearing, one could scarcely believe that she had been married twenty-two years, and that her eldest son would come of age in a few months.   But so it was, for Ethel's mother had become a bride at seventeen, and retained yet much of the girlish beauty that once made Dorothy Neville so widely known in the gay world of fashion.

Her husband's death, after twelve years of wedded life, was the one permanent grief of what otherwise had been a sunny life, but when that trial came, and left her a widow of twenty-nine with five helpless children, the blow fell with cruel swiftness, and for the first time she found herself face to face with a great sorrow.   After the loss of her husband, Mrs. Carlton devoted herself entirely to her children, and as they grew up, and became more companionable, her wild regrets were subdued, and she realized that her vocation, with its many duties and interests, still lay before her.

Herbert, the eldest, was only two years older than Ethel; then came Robert, and next the " babies," Daisy and Jack, aged respectively ten and twelve.

Ethel's home-coming brought new gladness to her mother, and it was small wonder, for her character was peculiarly lovable. Sister Agnes, who perhaps knew her most intimately, often acknowledged to herself that a striking similarity existed between Aunt Lily and her niece, the former being her ideal of all perfection.

(*To be continued.*)

(After Carlo Dolci.)

We the sleeping Babe can see
The Redeeming One to be.

CHRISTMAS.

MARGARET E. JORDAN.

Softly Christmas chimes are falling
　On the wintry air,
Hearts throughout the wide world calling
　To adoring prayer,
Where a Mother vigil keeps
O'er a Babe who calmly sleeps.

Christmas bells are loudly ringing
　Praise to Jesus' Name;
Angel choirs from Heaven bringing
　Tidings glad, proclaim,
That to-day the waiting earth
Welcomes the Redeemer's birth.

Christmas notes are sweetly waking
　Joy in human hearts;
Christmas light is on us breaking—
　In its rosy darts,
We the sleeping Babe can see
The Redeeming One to be.

On our chaplet beads we're telling
　This sweet mystery o'er,
By their wondrous power, indwelling,
　We, sweet Babe, implore:
To the Holy Souls be given
Christmas joy to-day—in Heaven.

The Children of the Rosary.

(After Minthrop.)

From His beauteous home in Heaven,
Jesus comes our joy to be.

CHRISTMAS HYMN.

MIXED VOICES.

Moderato. (♩ = 88.)

Music by Father Ossenmacher, S. J.

1. Bright - ly shines the star o'er 'Bethle - hem,
2. From His beau - teous home in Heav - en,
3. Let us take our Moth - er's chap - let,

Where the lit - tle Christ-Child sleeps, While His Moth - er with St.
He hath come our joy to be; Let us hast - en to the
Tell - ing this sweet mys - t'ry o'er, And the bless - ing of the

dim.   mf

Jo - seph O'er Him ten - der vig - il keeps,
man - ger, Christ the New - born King to see!
Christ - Child Ev - er lov - ing - ly Im - plore,

pp   , mf   , dim.   p

O'er Him ten - der vig - il keeps.
Christ the New - born King to see!
Ev - er lov - ing - ly im - plore.

CARL'S CHRISTMAS.

A. San Jose.

I.

HRISTMAS eve. The snow came fluttering down, and robed the earth in a shining garment of spotless white. It added a new beauty to the tastefully-adorned housetops of the rich, and hid the unsightly black roofs of the great weather-beaten tenements. At an attic-window in one of these latter stood a little boy watching the falling snow. His face was pinched and thin, and want and ill-treatment had written their names across his delicate features. The room was fireless and desolate. The one tiny window had neither blind nor curtain. The plaster had fallen from the walls, leaving the laths bare in many places. Furniture there was none, and the only other occupant of the room, a man, lay on the dirty floor, without even a mat beneath his head.

The boy stood gazing eagerly at the soft, downy shower as it hid the black, dingy shingles of the roofs stretching into the distance as far as the eye could reach. At last nothing could be seen but hills and hollows of the purest white, and the grey sky arching over all. And then, as he watched the flakes grow larger and larger, he thought that they must be angels hurrying on to the Crib at Bethlehem to worship the new-born Saviour, for was this not Christmas eve? And he remembered that long, long ago, a sweet voice had whispered into his ear that the Babe of Bethlehem was born on each Christmas eve in the hearts of those who loved him, as He had been born in that midnight cave so many hundred years before. He was a very little fellow to think of something that had been told him *long ago.* It would make one smile to hear such a tiny child use the words, but when one counts time by the number of blows one gets in a day, and by the sharp knocks of pain and hunger at the door of one's being, and the unkind words and rough, angry threats that pierce a poor little human heart so deeply, then to think of the happy past as *long ago* is not so ludicrous at all. Counting by years, it was four Christmases ago that he had heard the sweet story for the last time, from the lips of his mother. And as he saw again the sweet face, and the bright, loving eyes looking into his, he seemed to hear her say: "Offer the Infant Jesus something for His birthday, my pet," and he stretched out his arms, but they touched only the bare walls, and the vision faded. He thrust his little hand within the breast of his ragged coat, and pulled out a small object carefully wrapped in a rough covering, and attached to a cord which was fastened about his neck. He glanced furtively at the sleeping figure on the floor, but it neither spoke nor stirred. The boy carefully removed the soiled wrappings, and revealed a golden locket, on one side a ruby heart encircled with thorns, and on the other the single word "mother." Opening it, he gazed long and lovingly at the two faces it contained. One was the same bright, beautiful countenance he had seen in his day-dream, and the eyes gazed into his with the same loving light that he remembered in that *long ago* which was to him now but a blissful memory. The other was an older face, and one more gentle and serene, and the resemblance between them told its own tale. Any one would have known they were mother and daughter.

Kissing the bright and beautiful face of the younger lady, and pressing the ruby Heart also to his lips, Carl restored the locket to its hiding-place. It was getting dark. Far in the distance the electric lamps began to glimmer. The little fellow turned away from the window, and looked fixedly at the figure on the floor. What was there about his posture that seemed so strange? He went a few steps nearer, very quietly, for if he disturbed him, he knew that the angry man would shower blows upon him. But this time, little Carl, there is no fear. The hour has come when the father to whose care God entrusted you has given an account of your soul and his own. Nearer and nearer the little fellow crept, and at last laid his tiny hand timidly on his father's face. It was cold, and with a cry of terror the child fled from the room where the shadows had deepened into night, and where the still darker and more sombre shadow of death had fallen in its most awful form.

John Temple was a man who would seem to merit a better fate.
Good-natured. large-hearted, and gay, he was a favorite with all
the young people in his native town, but the old folks shook
their heads, and said: "Ah! poor John! his passion for gambling
will bring him to no good end;" and when pretty Hilda Morgan, the
old Squire's only daughter, told her father that she had given this
gay spendthrift her heart, and promised to follow it by the donation of her hand, the old Squire waxed angry, and declared that
his curse was the only wedding-gift she need expect from him.
But threats and coaxing alike proved useless, and Hilda left her
home and her kind parents to follow the fortunes of John Temple. Her married life was a happy one, the only drawback being
the displeasure of her parents. All attempts at communication
with them were immediately repulsed by the Squire, who threw
at once into the fire, unopened, all letters bearing the hand-writing of his discarded daughter. When little Carl was five years
old, Hilda died, and then the heart-broken man relapsed into his
former habit, until he fell to the depths of degradation and
misery which we have just witnessed, and which the poor little
boy, the idol of Hilda's loving heart, was obliged to share, his sorrows being augmented by the cruel treatment he received from
the man who now lay cold and dead in the deserted attic.

Poor Carl wandered about the streets tired and foot-sore. He
had eaten nothing that day, and he felt weak and famished. He
thought of the dreary attic, and shivered. He could never go
back there. That cold, dead figure filled him with horror. What
should he do? Where should he go? For hours he wandered
about. One by one the lights in the houses went out. Even the
great shops were closed. He must keep clear of the police. If
they saw him alone in the street at that hour of the night he
would be taken to the lockup. At last he curled himself up
under a bench in the park, and sleep came with her gentle wings,
and rocked him in her soft embrace. At length he awoke. It
was still dark, and the electric lamps lit up the lonely streets.
But just opposite him was a blaze of light. It came from a great
building, and as he gazed, the doors opened, and he heard strains
of heavenly music. He advanced nearer, and saw that among the
crowds coming out were some boys no larger than himself, and

many of them dressed no better than he. He went in the door, and inside the lights were so bright that they were fairly dazzling. Two boys with their black cassocks and white surplices (angels, Carl thought they were) were extinguishing the lights on the main altar, but to the left a brilliant glare attracted him. He went up the broad aisle, seeing but one object. Could it be possible! He must be in Heaven. There lay the Infant Jesus on straw, His little arms outstretched, and such a sweet smile on His face that Carl smiled back into the gentle eyes that seemed to fix themselves on his. Other worshippers came and went, but Carl noticed them not. His eyes and thoughts were with the Divine Babe. If this was Heaven, where was his mother? Perhaps the Infant Jesus did not know him, and so did not take him to her at once. With the thought of her came again the words: " Offer the Infant Jesus something for His birthday, my pet." What could he offer? And then he noticed that other visitors had come to the Crib, and that each one dropped something into the box that stood near, with an opening in the top. That must be why the Infant Jesus had not taken him to his mamma. He had not given Him any offering. What could he do? A sudden thought seized him. His tiny hand sought the cord that hung about his neck. His precious locket! Could he give that? It was the only thing to remind him of the happy past. Never to see that sweet pictured face that once had smiled upon him! He looked again at the Divine Babe, and with a sudden resolution he took the soiled and faded coverings off of his treasure, kissed the face within, then pressing the ruby heart to his lips, advanced with his offering. The opening was too narrow to admit the locket, but, turning once more to look at the countenance of the Holy Infant, he laid his treasure on the top of the box, and knelt once more before the Crib.

(Conclusion next month.)

HAIL, Queen of the Heavens !
  Hail, Mistress of earth !
Hail, Virgin most pure,
  Of immaculate birth !
Clear Star of the morning
  In beauty enshrined !
(Lady, make haste
  To the help of mankind !

Thee God in the depth
  Of eternity chose,
And framed thee all fair
  As His glorious Spouse ;
And called thee His Word's
  Own Mother to be,
By whom He created
  The earth, sky, and sea.

—*From the Office of the Immaculate Conception.*

TWELVE.

Sister Mary Alphonsus, C. C.

The clock strikes Twelve !—Twelve fishers rude,
　　Of humble speech and birth,
Did Christ send forth to preach His word,
　　And plant His Church on earth;

For God works not by human ways,
　　Nor bends to human doubt,
And rarely do His means seem fit
　　To bring His ends about:

But simple heart and ceaseless prayer,
　　With will prepared to do,
May bring us yet to serve His Church
　　As saints and martyrs, too.

------ ——

Puzzles.

A SEASONABLE PUZZLE.

My first comes in two seasons of the year;
In only one my second doth appear;
In three my third I'm very sure you'll find;
In two look for my fourth, if you don't mind;
To get my fifth in three you'll look in vain;
In none at all my sixth can you obtain;
In none my seventh; but my eighth you'll see
In one; while 'tis in two my ninth will be;
In two you'll find my tenth.　Now, who can tell
What friend of children these few letters spell?

THE PEARL ROSARY.

Mary Hancock Allen.

Chapter III.

THE TREASURED BEADS.

"I WENT over to see the girl next door," said Agnes, as she, Tom, and her mother sat down to luncheon.

"Girl?" said Tom, scornfully. "I thought you said it was a boy."

"Well, I thought it was a boy; but it isn't. Its name is Georgie, though."

"'Georgie' would be highly flattered to know that she was being referred to as 'it,' I am sure," said Mrs. Barnett, smiling.

"Well, Tom called her 'it' first," said Agnes, laughing.

"But you called her 'it' three times, and I only called her 'it' once," said Tom, triumphantly.

Agnes made a face at Tom, and Tom grinned maliciously.

"How do you like her, Agnes?" asked Mrs. Barnett, anxious to keep peace in the family.

"Oh, very much," she replied; and she related her interesting visit. "She's funny," she said in conclusion. "I thought I shouldn't like her at first, but after talking with her, I changed my mind. I feel so sorry for her, because she has no father nor mother. You will like her, Tom; she likes boys and boys' games."

"Pooh!" returned Tom, majestically. "Girls don't know anything."

"Don't they?" retorted his sister, her eyes flashing. "Well, I guess they know more than boys, anyway."

This struck Tom as being so funny, that he laughed and choked over his glass of water, and was accordingly sent away from the table.

During the afternoon, Agnes cast many glances over at the newly-tenanted house, but Georgie was nowhere to be seen. Notwithstanding Tom's bold declaration that girls did not know any-

thing, he engaged his sister in a lively game of ball, and enjoyed
it hugely. He was obliged to confess that Agnes threw a ball
very well for a girl. The supper-bell ended their sport, and Tom
ran into the house, ravenously hungry. Agnes followed, more
leisurely. As she reached the door, she looked up and beheld a
flushed, tear-stained face at a second-story window of the house
next door. It was Georgie's.

"Why didn't you come over this afternoon?" she said, going
to the window.

"I couldn't," said Georgie, in a low tone. "I am locked up.
Don't talk loud, or you'll be heard. I will tell you all about it
to-morrow. I hear my aunt coming. Good-bye."

The head disappeared, and Agnes went into the house, wondering what Georgie meant.

She found out the next morning, when Georgie went over and
sat on the steps with her. The jewel-box was in her hand.

"I got it," she said; "but I had so much trouble about it. You
have no idea."

"Why, what was the matter?"

"Well, you see, after you left yesterday, I unpacked my trunk,
and took out the box, which was in the bottom. I unlocked it,
and was looking at the pearl beads, when my aunt Isabelle came
in. I thought she was down-stairs, and didn't hear her until she
was at my elbow, when she said, 'Why Georgie, what have you
there? I never saw those before.' I was awfully startled, and
tried to hide the beads, but it was too late. Then she saw the
little picture of my mother, that I had laid upon my bureau.
'Why, who is this?' she asked. I told her, and I noticed her
manner changed, and she said coldly, 'Yes, to be sure. Where
did you get it?' 'From my father,' I said. Then she took the
beads from my lap, and looked at them with a heavy frown upon
her face. 'I suppose your father gave you this too,' she said.
'I do not think you want it now. I will keep it for you.' And
she started to go out of the room. I ran after her and tried to
get it out of her hand, and said, 'No, it is mine. Papa gave it to
me, and you can't have it.' She stopped and smiled at me, but
did not give me the necklace. I got so mad then, that I just
fought for the beads in a perfect rage. She soon gave them to

me, saying, 'There is no necessity to get into such a passion, Georgianna. See what you have done,' and she showed me her hand, which was bleeding where I had dug my nails. Of course I didn't mean to do that, and I had to ask her pardon. But she made me stay in my room all the afternoon to punish me. She left me my beads, though." Georgie laughed triumphantly, opened her box, and took from it a little pearl case, which she unfastened, and displayed the pearls.

"Now, this is a rosary, isn't it?"

"Why yes," replied Agnes. "And what a beautiful one it is!'

"And you think mamma was a Catholic?"

"Yes, I do."

Georgie's face grew thoughtful. "Yes, I believe mamma must have been a Catholic, and that was the reason papa's family did not like her. Lots of people don't like Catholics. I wonder why? I think it is a very nice religion. When I was in Rome, I often thought I should like to be a Catholic. Oh, dear! I wish I was back in Rome with papa and Amina. I hate it here," she added, her dark eyes flashing. "I believe I'll run away."

"Oh, no, you mustn't," said Agnes, much horrified, evidently fearing that Georgie anticipated immediate flight.

"Well, I must do something. I can't stand it any longer."

"You will feel differently to-morrow."

"No, I shan't," returned Georgie, warmly. After a moment, she broke into a laugh. "I wonder what my aunts would do if I should become a Catholic? My! I don't know what they wouldn't do. I have a good mind to go to church with you next Sunday, May I?"

"Ye-es," said Agnes hesitatingly. "But what will you tell your aunts?" she asked, her conscience not quite clear upon this point.

"Oh—why, that I am going to church with you—a new friend. They wont think anything about it. That will be all right. If you wont let me go to church with you, I will go by myself," she added, noticing the doubt on Agnes' face.

"Well, all right," said Agnes, seeing how determined Georgie was. "I'll take you."

(*To be continued.*)

CHRISTMAS EVE.

How often I've wondered how Santa,
　　That darling old Santa Claus, looks!
　　　I'm sure, oh, quite sure, I would know him,
　　I've seen him so often in books.

He's old and he's fat, and all covered
　　With toys from his head to his foot,—
How does he get down through the chimney
　　Without spoiling the toys with the soot?

I wish I could keep my eyes open,
　　And banish that horrid old sleep
Till Santa Claus comes with my presents,—
　　Oh, wouldn't I steal a good peep!

CHRISTMAS MORNING.

I couldn't keep my eyes wide open,
　　On a watch for Santa Claus;
But I'll tell you a fine secret,—
　　I saw him, all the same, because .

Santa tumbled over something—
　　'Twasn't in the chimney, though,
'Cause he came in through that doorway,—
　　When I saw him, don't I know?

And he woke me with the racket,—
　　'Course it scared away the sleep,—
And the moon came in so brightly
　　That I got the loveliest peep!

Why, that dear old darling Santa
　　Isn't old, nor doesn't look
One wee bit like any picture
　　That I've seen in any book.

Santa looks like my own papa
　　When he wears his dressing gown;
And I guess we're the last children
　　That he came to in this town,

'Cause he put in our four stockings
　　All the presents that he had,
Dear me! Isn't he like papa!
　　Darling Santa! I'm so glad!

Notes for the Children.

Christmas greetings, fervent little Rosarians, brave young soldiers! May the dear feast come to you with all its rich blessings. Take the beads in your hands often in December, and pray that your young hearts may be free from sin, and bright with virtue for the coming of the dear Christ-Child. And when Christmas will have come, and you kneel around the little crib in your parish church, or convent chapel,—or perhaps in your own happy homes you may have the dear Christ-Child's crib—you will be able, knowingly and lovingly, to meditate on the third joyful mystery of the Rosary. Your dear little Lord will not be a stranger to you. And, children, do not forget to help the poor souls in Purgatory! Pray for them very often. How grateful they will be to you if you help them to reach the joy of Heaven on Christmas Day!

But on the great, beautiful feast do not spend all the prayer-time *asking* for favors. Kneel sometimes at our dear Lord's crib, and let your minds go back over the years of your young lives; let them think of all the good things you can remember that God has given you, think of them gratefully, and tell the dear Christ-Child how thankful you are.

From an earnest pleader for God's poor little ones comes a timely and practical suggestion, which we gladly pass on to our young people. Christmas will soon be here, and with it comes the collection for the orphans. Times being hard, it is to be feared that the collection will suffer. Suppose that now, at the opening of December, the boys and girls place in their homes, on mantle or table, where everybody may see it, a box marked FOR THE ORPHANS' CHRISTMAS GIFT. We are sure that fathers and mothers, big brothers and sisters, and friendly visitors, too, will drop in dimes and nickels and pennies for Christ's poor little ones. And we know the boys and girls themselves will not spend any money foolishly,—they will be too anxious to set a good example to the grown people. Little sacrifices thus made will help us to be generous on Christmas morning to the poor for the Christ-Child's sake, and the sake of His Blessed Mother. If we bring joy to the little orphans, we shall surely give " Glory to God in the highest," and shall win for ourselves the promised " peace on earth to men of good will."

How many young folks will make God's poor unfortunate ones in prison the gift of THE ROSARY MAGAZINE for a year ? How many cards will be filled for these New Year's gifts ?

With the January issue we shall begin the eighth volume of the Magazine of our Lady's Beads, and we hope that earnest work in aid of souls who need the help of good reading will draw that dear Mother's blessing on our magazine. We have prepared some beautiful pictures as a reward for the filling of ROSARY CARDS for the poor. One little soldier, aged seven, has already filled four cards, and is thus sending the magazine to four prisons. She is at work now on her fifth card.

Who in each state will be the first to fill a ROSARY CARD for some prison in that state? We shall watch for letters from every part of the country.

Many ask if they are too old to become members of the Angelic Warfare. No one is too old. And during the coming year, we trust that many will seek to be enrolled in the beautiful confraternity. For conditions of membership, see page 551 of November issue.

As the lessons on the Holy Rosary, taught in the Angel Teacher's words, have reached the sorrowful mysteries, we shall hold them till the Christmas season, so specially a joyful one, has passed.

When you are planning Christmas presents for relatives and friends, *do not forget books*. And Aquinas would remind you that there is a Christmas present that will be new the whole year round—THE ROSARY MAGAZINE every month will come bright and new into the homes of your friends as it does now into your own. A subscription to the Magazine of our Lady's Beads would be a good choice, we are certain.

Applications for leaflets and girdles of the Angelic Warfare, and for ROSARY CARDS, and answers to puzzles, should be addressed to AQUINAS, office of THE ROSARY MAGAZINE, 871 Lexington Ave., New York.

AROUND CHRISTMAS TIME IN BAVARIA.

ALGUIEN.

NE of the prettiest old customs that Catholic Bavaria still keeps up, and which dates from time immemorial, is the visit of St. Nicholas (or Nicholaus, as they say) to the little ones on the day of his feast, the 6th of December.

Children in Catholic countries are brought upon such a familiar footing with saints and angels, are taught to regard them as personal friends and companions, and are so familiar with their lives and miracles, and know so well what particular saint or angel is to be called on in each particular trouble or necessity, that their lives are, as it were, interwoven with those of their celestial friends, and a constant intercourse is kept up between them.

In no way is this more demonstrated than in the Bavarian children's unquestioning faith in the reality of the visit of St. Nicholas, in flesh and blood, on the day of his feast. They do not doubt for a moment that the holy bishop of Myra, their own particular patron, who so loved little children that his whole life was full of miracles in their favor, steps down from Heaven on that day, and trudges through the snow, from house to house, in order to visit and admonish them, and prepare them for the visit of the " *Liebes Christkind'l*" in a few weeks' time.

His arrival is expected in fear and trembling, for the good saint, represented for the nonce by some grown-up member of the family—an elder sister, brother, mother, governess or nurse, as the case may be—comes in the twofold character of judge and benefactor. The naughty ones know they will be punished and shamed by having their sins and iniquities read out publicly, and the good or middling good ones, though they hope to be rewarded with apples and nuts and other little presents, out of St. Nicholas' sack, yet fear that their shortcomings may also be made public, so that the saint's visit is not all unalloyed pleasure. As a rule, by the time the dreaded visitor appears, which is usually when it begins to get dusk—for the obvious reason of making it less easy to recognize him,—the naughtiest and most unmanageable child has become a very lamb of meekness and docility, reciting acts of sorrow and amendment, which generally have the desired effect of softening the saint's heart into forgiving the repentant sinner; so that after he has still more excited their contrition by a good scolding and a sermon, he relaxes from his sternness into geniality, and no child is left empty-handed. Smiles take the place of tears, and the saint takes his departure amidst a chorus of small voices shouting: "*Aufwiedersehen Nicholaus!*"—"Good-bye till next year," etc.

St. Nicholas is usually dressed like the pictures of old Father Christmas, with a long mantle which covers him to his feet, on his head a hood or cowl, and in his hand a long staff. He always has a flowing white beard, and carries over his shoulder a large sack filled with apples and nuts and other little presents. He also has with him a formidable looking bundle of rods (*rute*), which he always leaves with the father, mother, or other responsible person, whom he desires to hang it over the door, where the children can always see it, and be constantly reminded of his visit and their good resolutions.

Sometimes, as is the case in convent schools and other large establishments, where there are a great many young people to see and admonish, St. Nicholas comes dressed in his episcopal robes, with mitre, crozier, etc.; but in this case he is always accompanied by an attendant, the *Knecht Rupprecht,* as he is called, who carries the sack, it being naturally out of place for a bishop in full canonicals to carry a sack.

Once the visit of St. Nicholas is over, the children can breathe freely, and begin to prepare with unalloyed pleasure and anticipation for Christmas and the visit of the *Christkind'l*— (Child Christ). They write Him letters, beginning with: "*Liebes Christkind'l,*" and send Him long lists of the various presents they would like Him to bring them at Christmas. When they are finished and duly addressed to " The dear little Child Christ in Heaven," they leave them out on the window-sill when they are going to bed at night, and in the morning, when they find them gone, they feel quite happy in their minds, for do they not know that the *Christkind'l* has taken them up to Heaven, and will be sure to bring them something they wish for, even if He does not give them all they asked?

It is not alone the children who look forward to Christmas here. In no country in the world is it so universally kept as a high holiday, and so enjoyed by all classes and ages, as in Bavaria.

The Christmas-tree plays the principal role in the festivities, and is not confined to the little ones, or the rich and well-to-do, as with us; young and old, poor and rich, all equally participate, according to their means, in the simple pleasures of the Christmas-tree, without which Christmas would not be Christmas. The old English plum-pudding is not a more indispensable appendage of an English Christmas, than the tree is of a Bavarian one.

There is not a family here, from the royal ones of the land to the very poorest, that has not a Christmas-tree of some kind or other. The former have high, towering firs, blazing with lights and loaded down with ornaments and glistening gee-gaws, and on the top an angel with radiant wings; the less favored by fortune have smaller trees, according to their means, and the very poorest have tiny little firlings, often not two feet high, with a few little tapers and a small wax angel, or Child Christ, on the top. But be they large or small, gorgeous or humble, innocent enjoyment and childlike gayety are to be found in the groups gathered round the Christmas-tree in every Bavarian homestead, that does not happen to be shut out from all wish of mirth or enjoyment by some misfortune or grief, such as an illness or death of some of its members. Even the old men and women in the hospitals and asylums have their tree, and the soldiers in their barracks. Each regiment has its tree, generally given, as well as money for beer and *Wurst* (sausage), by their captain and chief officers.

For weeks before the feast the shop windows are decked out in all their gayest and most tempting wares, and the streets become very forests of green trees of all sizes, ages, and prices, on sale there.

EDITORIAL

In the glad and blessed spirit of the third joyful mystery of the Rosary, we send, with this issue of our magazine, cordial greetings for the Christmas time, to all our readers and friends. May the Christ Child come into their hearts and fill them with the holy joy of the first Christmas night. May the Blessed Mother plead for them with her beloved Son, our Infant Lord. May St. Joseph reveal to all our Rosarians some of the beauties of his divine Charge. And may the angels enable us to sing in our hearts, with heavenly music, the glory of our dearest Lord, become a little Child for us, in poverty, in suffering, in the lowliness of the manger-crib.

Touching are the lessons of the third joyful mystery of the Beads, and fittingly do they apply to our daily lives. Day by day the opportunities come, and willingly should we embrace them. of living a life hidden with Christ in God, through humility, poverty of spirit, and mortification—the first lessons taught to us by our Blessed Master. As a very watchword they are proclaimed from the Crib, and all who would follow Jesus Christ must know that His infant banner bore no other device.

We regret the necessity of holding, till our next number, the concluding paper by Mr. John A. Mooney on "Columbus Among Liars." The first installment appeared in November, and the second part was prepared by the gifted author for this present issue. But pressure of other matter obliges us to defer its publication till January. The article will not suffer from delay, for its excellence gives it a standing value.

The month of December offers feasts of special devotion in favor of our Lady's clients. Pre-eminent is the day of her Immaculate Conception in which we honor that most precious privilege of our dearest Mother, on which all her other glor-ies rest. On the tenth we are reminded of the Incarnation, in the commemoration of the Holy House at Loreto, and on the eighteenth we hail her in the joy of her blessed expectation. To our readers we commend these feasts as days of special, loving honor to our Lady. Rosarians should be first among those who celebrate, with glad hearts, the festivals of our Blessed Mother.

In the present condition of political affairs in Venezuela, special interest attaches to our series of articles by Father Cothonay.

In our November number we warned our readers against the dangers of indiscriminate newspaper reading. Our observation leads us to add a few words touching magazines. The multitude of periodical publications is bewildering. No man familiar with their variety and number would entertain the notion of becoming familiar with their contents. He recognizes the practical impossibility of knowing even their names. He prudently decides, therefore, to confine his magazine reading to certain standard publications. We realize that judgments will differ as to "standard"; but we feel at the same time, that intelligent men will agree in determining what is "not standard." And we give our opinion that the magazine market is so rapidly becoming overstocked, that much of this material is the most wretched stuff, utterly unworthy of the name of literature. Subjects that only sensational newspapers follow, are the theme of some of these so-called magazines. With poor writing and "catchy" illustrations that have little bearing on the text, one cannot resist the thought that these cheap magazines are put together chiefly as a scheme for securing advertising. That they succeed in this way, and that they run into the hundreds of thousands in the way of circulation, are only painful evidences of degenerate public taste. To the readers of these sensational compilations on popular actors, cheap singers, poor artists, prominent sporting characters, genuine literature has little value, and a solid and meritorious magazine will find small favor in their eyes. When the merest froth, thinly disguising sensationalism and viciousness, enlists the labors and energies of so-called publishers whose zeal (?) is constantly spurred on by "success," which means money gain, it is timely for honest men to protest. And with many who think more seriously than the average newspaper or magazine would have us think, we warn our friends against the deteriorating tendencies of much that to-day is supposed to be literature in a popular, periodical form. It used to be said that the "almighty dollar" was the American's god. Viewing the course of events, we would say that many have added another idol to the temple of their false worship—and his name is the "newspaper-magazine."

In his latest Encyclical on the Rosary, our Holy Father praises the active zeal and ingenuity of the Dominican Order in spreading this beautiful devotion. Our magazine is an earnest effort to present to American Catholics the literature of the Beads. In this blessed light, devotion will flourish. Therefore do we urge upon our friends the excellent and meritorious work of extending the field of our labors. Let each reader of THE ROSARY MAGAZINE speak of this publication to a friend or acquaintance. Every new subscriber, every new reader secured, will be a distinct gain for the cause of our Blessed Mother's honor. Good Rosarian, now reading these words, what have you done? What will you do on this line?

The article on Lacroma by the Archduchess Stephanie, the concluding part of which will appear in our January number, has been translated and adapted by Father Raymond Volz, O. P. The illustrations are from original photographs sent from Vienna. The autograph letter of the Archduchess, which we have reproduced, will give additional interest to the publication.

Good reader, what think you of Christmas presents? What think you of a year's subscription for THE ROSARY MAGAZINE in favor of a friend? Not a passing trifle or a bauble for a day, but a delight the year through, and a constant and refined reminder of your friendship. Will you act on the suggestion?

MAGAZINES.

St. Luke's Magazine for October concludes a very interesting sketch of the famous Monte Cassino Monastery, which had been running through several preceding numbers. "The Story of the English Benedictines" continues its course. "Job: the Handbook of Nature," is the title of a series of valuable articles, the October installment dealing with light and darkness and atmospheric phenomena. A short biography of Dom Gasquet, O. S. B., gives an insight into the life of this distinguished historian whose works, "Henry the Eighth and the English Monasteries," and "The Last Abbot of Glastonbury and His Companions," have been warmly commended by *The Quarterly Review* for July, in a remarkable article entitled, "The Passing of the Monk." Tardy justice is there done to the memory the maligned and outraged victims of Henry's persecuting greed. The paper in *The Quarterly* abounds in passages that we would gladly quote did space permit. Most earnestly do we advise our friends to read it. In the same number of *The Quarterly* other notable articles will be found, including a history of roses, a discussion of the life and teaching of Mohammed, and an account of "the evil eye."

Harper's Magazine for October contains one of Captain Mahan's able articles on sea power, "The Future in Relation to American Naval Power;" the fourth part of Poultney Bigelow's "The German Struggle for Liberty;" "Queen Victoria's Highland Home;" a study of "Hindoo and Moslem;" and Monsignor Bernard O'Reilly's "Ronzano," a reminiscent sketch of the famous Villa di Ronzano, formerly a Dominican convent, situated on a spur of the Apennines, near Bologna. The story goes back to the days of St. Dominic and Blessed Diana, one of his earliest religious children, who was the sister of Loderingo, one of the two founders of the White Knights of St. Mary. Dante also revisits the scene, for the owners of the villa at the time of

Monsignor O'Reilly's visit were the Count Giovánni Gozzadini and his wife, the Countess Maria Teresa di Serego-Alighieri, both descendants of the immortal poet.

The Review of Reviews for November contains a sketch of the late Professor Louis Pasteur.

The Independent for November 7, with its usual enterprise, published a symposium on the Sunday observance question. Nineteen distinguished writers contributed papers, among them Cardinal Gibbons, the Reverend Dr. Rooker, of the Apostolic Delegation, and Father Doyle, C. S. P.

Among the excellent matter of the October number of *The Catholic University Bulletin*, we mention "The Teaching of English," by Maurice Francis Egan; "The Progress in Gaelic;" "The Study of Greek," by the editor and Father Quinn; "The Ambrosian Library at Milan," by Dr. Bouquillon; and "St. Patrick and Palladius," by Father Schaefer.

The Pall Mall Magazine for October continues the series of articles on evolution in early Italian art, the present theme being the adoration of the Magi. "On Bell Tones" is a contribution that will be of special attraction to musicians. It deals with the subject in a thorough manner.

The Contemporary Review for October contains a thoughtful paper on "The Japanese Constitutional Crisis and the War," written by a resident of Japan familiar with the situation. The Countess Martinengo Cesaresco touches, in very agreeable fashion, on the country homes of the old Romans. The Reverend W. Bonner scores the English for their treatment of the natives of East India, in an article that bristles with ugly facts against his own countrymen. With great pleasure we quote one paragraph from this earnest paper: "I cannot refrain from bearing testimony to the noble example set by the Marquis of Ripon while he was Governor-General (of India). By his affability and unfailing courtesy to natives of all ranks, and by his manifest sympathy with them in their higher aspirations, he so won the hearts of the people, that when he came to lay down his high office and return to England, he received an ovation such as no viceroy had ever dreamt of. * * * * I remember

about that time asking a native friend of mine—a very near relative of one of the princes of India, and whom the Government has more than once selected for special diplomatic service—what he thought of the Marquis of Ripon. Pausing for a few moments, he replied, ' Well, my candid opinion is that if the Queen of England were to send a succession of such viceroys to India, she might withdraw every red-coated soldier from the country, as there would be no need for them.' " As the Marquis of Ripon is a devoted Catholic, the testimony of this English Protestant clergyman, coupled with the Indian nobleman's warm words, is truly gratifying.

Under the heading, "Norse and Irish Literature," William Larminie begins a series of papers that give promise of interest and worth. The Reverend Doctor Lindsay contributes an article on "The Unity of the Church in Apostolic Times." It bears evidence of scholarship, earnestness, and honesty; but the lameness and halting are also in evidence that tell of the struggles and divisions now rending the Church of England. There is, therefore, a certain fitness, probably not intended by the Editor of *The Contemporary*, in another article in the same number, entitled, "The New Clergy," by the Reverend H. R. Haweis. The character of this contribution and the condition of affairs revealed by it will be best understood by a few selections in the author's own words: "As leaders of thought or originators of policy, they (the bishops of the Church of England) are not over-helpful. No one expects any considerable bill to be brought in or even supported by the bishops in the Lords; * * * * nor can I point to any book by any bishop in the last fifty years (barring Colenso's) which has had any considerable effect upon the thought or theology of the age." The fact of the social and intellectual decline of the Episcopal clergy Mr. Haweis considers incontestable; and quotes a bishop to the effect that "it's worse every year." Speaking of the Broad Church, our author says, "the only quarrel the laity seem to have with the Broad Church clergy, *of every shade*, is that they are dishonest—that they have no business to teach and believe as they do, or as they don't, within the Church." Assuredly a terrible indictment against a body of men claiming to speak in the name of Divine Truth! Of the rulers of the English Church Mr. Haweis writes : " They have been smitten with a mighty apathy about heresy; many of them are heretics themselves; they cannot, it seems, be goaded into showing fight." This simply means that the English bishops dare not teach as they pretend to believe, dare not direct the clergy who are supposed to be under their guidance and restraint. How sad is this! And yet it may mean the dawning of the light that will bring England back to Catholic unity. Commenting on the growth of the Non-Conformists, Mr. Haweis says: "The blight of Anglican deterioration extends to the Continent, and the Episcopal chaplains abroad are almost by-words (with shining exceptions no doubt); whilst in the Colonies the Church can hardly hold her own. The same decline is noticeable (with again a few bright exceptions, looked askance at by their clerical brethren) on the Pacific coast, and the same is true, more or less, throughout the United States, barring a few lights in New York, Chicago, and Philadelphia. In influence and up-to-dateness there is no comparison at present between the Episcopal and non-conforming bodies. The non-conformist preachers lead in the big cities, whilst the Roman Catholic Church throughout the States and Canada *more than holds its own, against all the sects put together,* by its single-heartedness, power of adaptation, instinctive recognition of popular thought-currents, its personal devotion and sagacity." Words worth weighing, and full of suggestion, above all things, for prayer in the spirit in which our Holy Father pleads for unity. Consider the following passage from Mr. Haweis' article: "The inaudible mumbler, the sporting "Dodo" curate, the lifeless drone, the weakling parasites who take orders, some for social positions, others to fill family livings, and many because they could not get 6*d* per day in any other profession, these, of course, must be put aside at once, as malignant if not incurable sores; no doubt they all help greatly to reduce the tone of the Established Church, but they are no new social evils. The real crux is rather to be found in the sort of thing the clergy are trained, or even expected, to preach, and the sort of thing the people decline any longer to listen to.

The man in the pew thinks he has a right to remonstrate with the man in the pulpit who denounces him as an unbeliever. He may fairly say to his clergyman: "You complain of me for not believing what you call Church doctrines; how much do you believe yourself?"

Such a condition must grieve the heart of every man who loves his fellow-men. From the exposure of this unhappy state of affairs, let us hope and pray that the coming of the remedy may be hastened. We again appeal to our author: "I was talking the other day to a very orthodox bishop" (we wonder what he means by *very* orthodox),—" not in his sanctum, but at his dinner table, which makes all the difference—about the doctrine of eternal torments. 'Well,' he said, 'we may not be able to accept literally the fire and the worm and their everlasting duration, but we may infer from these symbols that the fate of those who have sinned against light, and rejected all offers of atonement and pardon here, will be something very terrible hereafter, so disastrous that it may be impossible for us now to estimate realistically at all the serious and far-reaching consequences of our actions; therefore, it may be safe for us to resort to such awful figures of speech as we find in the New Testament." And Mr. Haweis commends, in a manner, this duplicity, this evasion and shuffling. May God help the flock committed to the tender mercies of such shepherds as this vacillating bishop! And is it uncharitable to ask, what of those who close their eyes to the light, and continue to stumble in darkness, because the darkness means place, power, worldly ease and enjoyment? Need we feel surprise, therefore, when Mr. Haweis, after praising the fitness and zeal of the Catholic Priesthood, to which he joins the non-conformist ministry, writes the following: "The Established Clergy need not be able to preach at all, or even to speak audibly. They are not authoritative like the Roman Catholic, nor eloquent like the non-conformist; they are endlessly apologetic and habitually dull. Their sermons are stuffed with arguments which prove nothing, and apologies which require to be apologized for. The Anglican Church is orthodoxy without unction, and ritual without life." We shall not dispute Mr. Haweis' statement on orthodoxy, since he has already told us that many of the rulers are heretics. And as their tendency is to keep things as they are, Mr. Haweis expects little from the Anglican pulpit lights whose brightness he likens to the poor glimmer of a glow-worm. "Protestantism," he continues, "as I have elsewhere observed, is more true to life (we presume he means the natural life) than Romanism; it throws in the sop of a married clergy, and gives other liberal fees to a secular life ; but it is only more liberal because less logical than the Mother of Churches." Aye, there's the rub ; and when we recall our Lord's injunction about a man hating his life in this world that he may keep it for the next, we admit, and with deep regret, that Protestantism has thrown many a sop to that which Mr. Haweis pleasantly calls "the secular life," but which the Scriptures mention with greater clearness and vigor. The chief difficulty that our author presents is that of the Divinity of Jesus Christ. He tells us that the Church of England is split into two opposing factions on this vital doctrine of Christianity. The revival among Anglican clergymen, of some of the old heresies that attacked the Divinity of Jesus Christ and the prerogatives of the Blessed Virgin, His Mother, is a matter of greater sadness than surprise. By the Catholic mind the relationship between our Lord and His Blessed Mother is so intelligently and so tenderly appreciated, that we are not slow to detect a certain consequence almost of necessity and of punishment, in the abandonment of faith in the Divinity of Christ, by those who have previously assailed the honor of Mary. The history of the disintegration and decay of Protestantism points the painful lesson that many of those who most loudly asserted their veneration for our Lord, by heaping insults on His Mother, have eventually drifted into denial of the Divinity of her Son. Whether the sin of the angels was their refusal to acknowledge the fore-ordained Mother of the Divine Son whose Incarnation had been determined as one of glory and not of pain, we do not say. Rather with St. Thomas and against the theologians who so teach, we claim the Incarnation for us men and women sinners, and for our salvation, and for this alone. But we note the suggestiveness of the thought, and we make the application that is not distorted, when we maintain that a great original sin of Protestantism was the denial of Mary's honor, which has brought an almost logical penalty in the denial of Christ's Divinity. The unhappy condition of the Church of England, rent asunder ot this foundation belief of Christianity, would seem, therefore, to be the result of its abjuring its ancient and glorious treasure of true devotion to our Blessed Lady. It is not without significance, then, that the Holy Father calls on his devoted children to beseech the Mother of tender mercy and fair love and holy hope, that England, once her own dower, may yet return to the peace and unity of the Catholic Fold.

The November number of *The Century* is a silver jubilee issue. As an exponent of high-class periodical literature, *The Century* stands out in conspicuous contrast to the cheap and trashy pamphlets whose chief aim seems to be the publication of advertisements. These compilations, under the name of magazines, seem to run the gauntlet successfully, but they will scarcely endure. Their growth, however, like that of the sensational newspaper, is a sad commentary on cheapness of the people's taste as well as cheapness of the stuff with which these so-called magazines are filled. The career of *The Century* is honorable, despite the occasional "breaks" that have marred its course. From time to time we have commented on these incidents in the same impartial spirit in which we have commended the good things of *The Century*. On this line we observe in the November number an improbable tale of a nun running away from a convent, stealing a child, to whom she had become unduly attached, and taking refuge among the Good Shepherds. "On Account of Emmanuel," reads as the work of a Catholic, or of one intimate with conventual life. We confess that we know not Bride Neill Taylor, the author, nor is the name much of a guide. Rather, it may be a disguise. But the tale, though told with some skill, is beyond the border line of probability.

In the same number Mr. Sloane's fine "Life of Napoleon" introduces his coronation as Emperor of the French, and later as King of Italy, and brings the reader to the third coalition formed against France. "Mural Decoration in America" is the first of a series of papers by Royal Cortissoz; "Kaiserwerth and its Founder" is an interesting account of the life-work of Theodore Fliedner, the German philanthropist. The author blunders somewhat in speaking of the conventual life and deaconesses in the early Church; but her description of Fliedner's deaconesses, imitations, in a manner, of our Catholic sisterhoods, is very agreeable.

The November 'number of *The Irish Ecclesiastical Record* publishes an instructive account of Monte Cassino and its peculiar privileges and prerogatives. In the same number, Father Michael O'Kane, O. P., tells the story of the distinguished Spanish Dominican, Cardinal Gonzalez. Of this eminent prelate we intend to give, in due season, a biographical sketch in THE ROSARY MAGAZINE.

The most interesting papers in *The Nineteenth Century* for October are, W. S. Lilly's " The New Spirit in History," in the course of which he pays merited tribute to Lord Acton, the Catholic nobleman who was appointed to the chair of modern history in Cambridge by Earl Rosebery; a very entertaining sketch of "The Land of Frankincense and Myrrh"; "The Closing of the Indian Mints " by Lord Brassey, an instructive lesson on the silver question; "The Need for an Antarctic Expedition," by the President of the Royal Geographical Society, Mr. Clements R. Markham; "The Religion of the Undergraduate," by the Reverend A. C. Deane, who makes and proves the serious charge that in the English universities, the prevailing attitude of the young men towards religion is one of agnosticism, which is regarded as a hall-mark of intellectuality and a sign of 'culture' best expressed by ridicule and cheap jests at Christianity; and a most agreeable bit of reading on " Ruskin as Master of Prose," by Frederic Harrison. We quote one paragraph from this last named article, which not only gives the keynote to the whole, but is furthermore full of suggestion valuable to aspiring writers:

"It cannot be denied that Ruskin, especially in his earlier works, is too often obtrusively luscious, that his images are often lyrical, set in too profuse and gorgeous a mosaic. Be it so. But he is always perfectly, transparently clear, absolutely free from affected euphuism, never laboriously ' precious,' never grotesque, never eccentric. His besetting sins as a master of speech may be summed up in his passion for profuse imagery, and delight in an almost audible melody of words. But how different is this from the laborious affectation of what is justly condemned as the ' poetic prose ' of a writer who tries to be fine, seeking to perform feats of composition, who flogs himself into a bastard sort of poetry, not because he enjoys it, but to impose upon an ignorant reader! This Ruskin never does. When he bursts the bounds of fine taste, and pelts us with perfumed flowers till we almost faint under their odor and their blaze of color, it is because he himself is intoxicated with the joy of his blossoming

thoughts, and would force some of his divine afflatus into our souls. The priestess of the Delphic god never spoke without inspiration, and then did not use the flat speech of daily life. Would that none ever spoke in books until they felt the god working in their heart ! "

The Fortnightly Review for October contains a very bilious and bitter article on " Ireland " by a writer who conceals his identity under the pen name of "A Disenchanted Nationalist." The true things he writes are not new, and the new things are without further value than that of invective. More cheerful and offsetting papers on the Irish situation can be found in the October *Westminster*, by two Irishmen who are not afraid or ashamed to give their names: "Wanted: A New Liberal Programme," by Thomas Scanlon, and "The Prospects of Home Rule," by M. Dalton.

In the October *Fortnightly* Dean Farrar makes a poor attempt to discount the growth of Catholicity in England. The chief notes of his article are the offensive and ill-bred use of the words ' Romish ' and ' Romanists,' blundering on dates, juggling of figures and quotations, and the following gratuitous and venomously false innuendo: " We fear that to bring back the old power of the priests would be very soon to bring back the horrors of intellectual bondage, if not of the Spanish Inquisition." And this because of " the ferocity " which he charges against certain Catholic writers who have asserted that the Archbishop of Canterbury is a mere layman. Dean Farrar is a dangerous champion—to the cause he espouses.

In the same number of *The Fortnightly* there is a delightful " Roman Reverie " by Alfred Austin, with reminiscences of the unhappy Charles James Hemans. Other notable papers are " Expressiveness of Speech "; " Islam and its Critics," a crushing rejoinder to a recent defender of the infamous Mohammedans; and a fine estimate of the character of Ferdinand Brunetiere, the distinguished French critic who has so thoroughly dissected Zola.

In the November *Cosmopolitan* we find "Joseph the Dreamer," a smart piece of Zangwillism. Whenever we read Mr. Zangwill's stories we are reminded of a two horse power, electric action Orchestrion, rolling off a rattling, concert pitch, mechanical *morceau.*

When Mr. Z. changes a "barrel," we miss nothing. There is no *vox humana* in his instrument, but there is a pleasing rattle and bang. In "Joseph the Dreamer," though, we think Mr. Zangwill has played a trick on his audience, and one that is hardly pardonable. At least he should have tagged a note to the end of the story, and worded it somewhat like this: "My readers have divined that the scene of this story is a mad-house. It is a lunatic who tells the story to a group of fellow-lunatics. A sane keeper is present. His version of what he has heard, I pretend to repeat here." With an explanation of this sort, the readers of *The Cosmopolitan* would not have a just cause for resentment at the joke played upon them. Joseph the Dreamer is an insane Jew. In one of his mad fits, he determines that he will become a Christian. A lunatic pagan nobleman and his lunatic pagan daughter have induced the lunatic Joseph to love Christianity. The scene of the story is laid in Rome; and there, at the time, everybody is insane: the Pope is insane; all the clergy are insane; the monks, and the Dominicans especially, are insane. It is not clear whether all the Jews are insane, or not; but probably Mr. Zangwill meant to leave this matter in doubt. Of course the mad priest baptized the mad Joseph without instructing him even in a mad way; and then Joseph, naturally, joined the very mad Dominicans; and they, like proper lunatics, not only permitted Joseph to act after the craziest of crazy fashions, but they egged him on. A half crazy Jewish girl had fallen in love with him before his mad conversion, and the pagan mad girl became madly in love with him as soon as he grew crazy enough to join the crazy Church she madly detested. The poor fellow, in a paroxysm of lunacy, strips off most of his clothes, and runs a Jew foot-race during carnival time. As one would suppose, he carried a Crucifix with him, and used it as none but a crazy man would use that holy emblem. He wins the race, and then loses his senses, wholly. All the other insane people in the city retain their chronic madness; and one may well imagine the consequences. Joseph, insisting that he is the only sane Jew and the only true Christian, is jailed forthwith; and, having been tried nowhere by nobody, is crazily burned in "oily tow" and then drawn and quartered. Some crazy fellow hastily shoveled Joseph's bones nowhere. Then Mr. Zangwill's Jews, who have cursed Joseph, as

only lunatics could, during his lifetime, gather in his father's house to rejoice over Joseph's slaughter, with "great rejoicings," feasting and dancing. Meantime, the half-crazy Jewish girl and the whole-crazy pagan girl walk out to the "heap of stones thrown by pious Jewish hands" on the "renegade's" grave, and kiss each other. *Finis.* Our wonder is that the pegs on this "barrel" held out while Mr. Zangwill turned the crank; they are so fine and delicate, nay, so tender. We beg to suggest to the Editor of *The Cosmopolitan,* that the truthful history of a sane Jewish convert to Catholicity might serve *The Cosmopolitan's* readers more than the crazy story of "Joseph the Dreamer." We offer the names of the brothers Ratisbonne, and of the Abbé Lehmann for the Editor's consideration; and hereafter we hope that Mr. Zangwill will inform his cultured audience, when he assumes again the rôle of a reciter of: "Tales told by a Jewish mad-man in a Jewish mad-house."

Among other good material pleasantly presented in *The Chautauquan* for November, we read with special satisfaction, a well-written account of the wild pigeon of North America, the Indians' "o-me-me-wog." The article is from the pen of Chief Pokagon, the last Pottawattamie chief of the Pokagon band. Known as the "Red-skin poet, bard, and Longfellow of his race," Chief Pokagon is assuredly a figure of unique interest in the history of Indian tribes.

The most agreeable paper of the November *North American Review* is "The Girlhood of an Actress," a delightful autobiography of Mary Anderson, whose beautiful Catholic life has shed a peculiar glory on her dramatic success.

Other papers of the *Review* are, "Quick Transit Between New York and London," by Austin Corbin, a competent authority; "True Source of American Wealth," by the President of the Farmers' National Congress; "Jingoes and Silverites," by Edward Atkinson; and "Improvement in the Civil Service," by U. S. Civil Service Commissioner Rice.

Students of political economy will find a serviceable article on the subject of income taxation, in *The Westminster Review* for October, under the heading, "Graduated Taxation in the Canton de Vaud," Switzerland. "The Incidence of Rates" is another contribution on the tax question. " British Constitution *vs.* Evolution " will also be found helpful to those interested in the study of parliamentary development.

The October number of *The American Catholic Quarterly* has a good table of contents. St. George Mivart leads on "The Evolution of Evolution." B. J. Clinche, a capable man, discusses "The Outlook for Ireland." Professor Herbermann contributes a long article on "Education in Ancient Greece." "Rome and Its Ancient Ruins"; "Leo XIII. and Historical Research"; "Joseph de Maistre," a sketch of his life and work; "The School Question in Manitoba"; and Father Freeman's scientific chronicle, continuing the story of precious stones, make the balance of the number.

"Recent Recrudescence of Superstition " is the title of a two-part paper, which appears in *The Popular Science Monthly* for October and November. It was written by a professor named Evans. We confess that this great man was previously unknown to us; but his present performance clearly reveals him as excelling in rudeness and crudeness rather than scientific attainments on which he plumes himself. His purpose seems to be to sneer, and without any argument in support of his claims, rather in defiance of well-sustained proofs, he inveighs against the sacred relics of our Lord's coats, at Treves and Argenteuil. He snarls at miracles, and raves over cases of diabolical possession. He quotes laboriously and, at times, erroneously, from liturgical works, showing that his scantiness of real knowledge is more than counterbalanced by his excess of bigotry. Without offering any authorities or acceptable references for many of the incidents he alleges, he pours out his ridicule in a manner equally offensive to Catholic instinct, to good taste, and to genuine criticism.

In the October number, among other articles that are of value, may be mentioned, "War as a Factor in Civilization"; "Trout Culture"; "Hunting with Birds of Prey"; and "Pleasures of the Telescope," viewing Pisces, Aries, Taurus, and the northern stars.
The November number contains several articles of interest: "The Past and Future of Gold"; "Principles of Taxation," the opening of a series by David A. Wells; "Evolution in Folklore"; and Professor Sully's "Studies of Childhood."

But we desire to call special attention to a curious article in the October number of *The Popular Science Monthly*, by Andrew White, LL. D., Ph. D., entitled, "From the Divine Oracles to the Higher Criticism." The very name of this contribution is singularly presumptuous. But for those who have been accustomed to the scientific study of the Bible, the paper contains many interesting revelations.
The author intends to give us a summary of the progress accomplished by critical science in its interpretation of the Holy Scriptures. His intention is truly good and laudable. Exegesis has made some progress in this country, and Catholics are the first to acknowledge it, and to take advantage of modern discoveries to explain and vindicate the sacred text. But Dr. White does not speak of this kind of progress. For him progress is nothing else than the annihilation of creeds, and before all others, that of the Roman Catholic Church.
Dr. White assumes that "even the most devoted apologists have become discreetly silent" before the conclusions of Higher Criticism. Dr. White is not well acquainted with biblical literature. We would only refer him to the recent commentary on Genesis by Hummelauer.
Dr. White draws many conclusions that do not follow from his premises. We find in Assyrian monuments, the same (!) stories as in Genesis. Therefore, he concludes, the stories of the Bible are false, mere myths. It seems to us that more logically we may conclude: Therefore, the stories of the Bible refer to a primitive tradition that was common to Assyria, because it is a true tradition.
At times Dr. White is as enthusiastic as Don Quixote before the windmills. For instance, what victory has the scientific method gained over biblical chronology? What says the Bible about the date of creation? Nothing at all. On this point Higher Criticism is without an opponent.
Dr. White gives as decided the difficult problem of the synoptics and the non-authenticity of the fourth gospel. Here again Dr. White forgets many books and many articles that treat of these important questions.
Further, he gives ridiculous praise to the Revised Version, because it has rejected one verse from I. John, and omitted the word "God" in I. Tim. iii. 16. If they had used the Vulgate, they would have been spared the trouble of this correction.

Moreover, the Revised Version has admitted "His father" instead of "Joseph" Luke ii. 33. That was already in the Vulgate. It has also rejected twelve verses from St. Mark. Nothing more! What victories for Science! What a beautiful thing this Higher Criticism!

Dr. White is so simple as to suppose that "comparative mythology and folklore, comparative religion and literature" will give the solutions to "these great problems which dogmatic theology has long labored in vain to solve."

He is no less simple when he dares affirm that the discoveries of Higher Criticism have been met by the traditional interpretation of the Bible in a spirit of "hatred, malice, uncharitableness, feticism, subtlety, pomp, tyranny, bloodshed, and solemnly constituted imposture." These extracts are sufficient to give an idea of the method of Dr. White, a method that the famous impostor Renan tried with some success in his "Life of Jesus" and in his "History of Israel." Occasionally we are indebted to the school of Rationalists for works of some merit on the Bible, but in Dr. White's paper, we can find only an occasion to laugh at his pretensions, or to be indignant at his unscientific methods.

Regarding his calumniation of the Catholic Church, in relation to Buddhism and Buddha, we would direct Dr. White's attention to a good book on the subject, by Oldenberg, the famous Orientalist, who cannot be suspected of partiality. "We cannot," he says, "think of an influence of the Buddhist tradition on the Christian tradition."

As for the imposture of the canonization of Sakya Muni under the name of S. Josaphat, we leave it to the conscience of Dr. White. Sakya Muni and S. Josaphat are the same "*mutatis mutandis,*" says the Encyclopædia Britannica. By a like method we could prove that Mohammed is the same as Jesus of Nazareth. Oh, the honesty of magazine history as illustrated by some scribes, and we were about to add, pharisees!

Students of political economics will find some instructive articles in recent numbers of *The Social Economist.*

Among other papers of merit contained in *The American Magazine of Civics* for November, we mention an article in reply to the Convention of Irish Americans recently held in Chicago. The writer, Thomas B. Grant, takes just exception to the violent and unnecessarily bloodthirsty denunciations emanating from such gatherings.

Littell's Living Age (November 23) has a special interest for Catholics, because of a tribute to the memory of Louis Pasteur, and a most appreciative sketch, from a non-Catholic writer, of the life and character of St. Bruno, the Founder of the Carthusians.

The latest addition to the list of Catholic magazines in this country is *The Hibernian Monthly,* published at Seneca Falls, N. Y. This periodical announces its scope as one of special interest to the Ancient Order of Hibernians, the Catholic Knights of America, the Catholic Foresters, and the Father Matthew Societies. The editor modestly proclaims the purpose to make the new magazine a channel of instruction and entertainment to the Irish in America. We greet *The Hibernian Monthly* in friendly spirit, and wish it Godspeed on its course.

Twelve of the English reviews are represented, with variety of matter, in *The Eclectic Magazine* for November. This periodical affords an easy means of securing much good material at a low price.

The thirteenth issue of Benziger Brothers' *Catholic Home Annual,* for 1896, contains a variety of pleasant reading. Maurice F. Egan, Eugene Davis, Mary Catherine Crowley, and other well-known Catholic writers, are among the contributors.

"It is meet to extol daily with more splendid eulogy and to invoke with more ardent confidence the Virgin Mother of God, the powerful and gentle Help of Christians. The motives for confidence and praise are, in fact, increased by the varied fulness of benefits which through her is daily spread far and near more profusely for the common good. Indications surely are not wanting of the most eager desire on the part of Catholics to discharge the duties of gratitude imposed by so much benevolence; since, now more than ever, in these times so bitter for religion, we see love for, and devotion to, the most Blessed Virgin revived and inflamed in every grade of society. * * * * And it is a remarkable fact, and one which is agreeable for Us to recall, that among the many forms of this same devotion, the MARIAN ROSARY, a form of prayer so excellent, has now grown to be held more and more in esteem, and to be practised more and more widely. This, We say, is very agreeable to Us, for if We have taken considerable pains to promote the devotion of the Rosary, We see clearly how the kind Queen of Heaven has been moved by prayer to grant Our wishes; and so We trust that she will be near Us to lighten the cares and soothe the sorrows which the coming days shall bring. But above all, We look to the power of the Rosary to secure for Us more efficient aids in spreading the kingdom of Christ."—*From the Encyclical of Leo XIII.,* Sept. 5, 1895.

INDEX OF VOLUME VII.

CHILDREN OF THE ROSARY.

POETRY.

MUSIC.

www.ingramcontent.com/pod-product-compliance
Lightning Source LLC
Chambersburg PA
CBHW022122020426

42334CB00015B/721